THE CAMBRIDGE HISTORY
OF THE NATIVE PEOPLES OF
THE AMERICAS

VOLUME II

Mesoamerica

THE CAMBRIDGE HISTORY
OF THE NATIVE PEOPLES OF
THE AMERICAS

VOLUME I: NORTH AMERICA
Edited by Bruce G. Trigger and Wilcomb E. Washburn

VOLUME II: MESOAMERICA
Edited by Richard E. W. Adams and Murdo J. MacLeod

VOLUME III: SOUTH AMERICA
Edited by Frank Salomon and Stuart B. Schwartz

THE CAMBRIDGE HISTORY OF THE NATIVE PEOPLES OF THE AMERICAS

VOLUME II

MESOAMERICA

PART 2

Edited by

Richard E.W. Adams
*University of Texas
at San Antonio*

Murdo J. MacLeod
University of Florida

CAMBRIDGE
UNIVERSITY PRESS

PUBLISHED BY THE PRESS SYNDICATE OF THE UNIVERSITY OF CAMBRIDGE
The Pitt Building, Trumpington Street, Cambridge, United Kingdom

CAMBRIDGE UNIVERSITY PRESS
The Edinburgh Building, Cambridge CB2 2RU, UK   http://www.cup.cam.ac.uk
40 West 20th Street, New York, NY 10011-4211, USA   http://www.cup.org
10 Stamford Road, Oakleigh, Melbourne 3166, Australia
Ruiz de Alarcón 13, 28014 Madrid, Spain

First published 2000

Printed in the United States of America

Typeface Adobe Garamond 11/13 pt.   *System* DeskTopPro$_{/UX}$® [BV]

A catalog record for this book is available from the British Library.

Library of Congress Cataloging in Publication Data
Mesoamerica / edited by Richard E. W. Adams, Murdo J. Macleod
p. cm. – (Cambridge history of the Native peoples of the Americas)
Includes bibliographical references and index.
ISBN 0 521 65204 9
1. Indians of Mesoamerica–History.
I. Adams, Richard E. W.   II. Macleod, Murdo J.   III. Series.
E77.N62   2000
970.004'97–dc20   95-46096
                                                          CIP

Volume I: North America ISBN 0-521-34440-9   hardback complete set
   Volume I: North America, Part 1   ISBN 0-521-57392-0
   Volume I: North America, Part 2   ISBN 0-521-57393-9
Volume II: Mesoamerica ISBN 0-521-65205-7   hardback complete set
   Volume II: Mesoamerica, Part 1   ISBN 0-521-35165-0
   Volume II: Mesoamerica, Part 2   ISBN 0-521-65204-9
Volume III: South America ISBN 0-521-33393-8   hardback complete set
   Volume III: South America, Part 1   ISBN 0-521-63075-4
   Volume III: South America, Part 2   ISBN 0-521-63076-2

CONTENTS

v

ILLUSTRATIONS

FIGURES TO PART 1

TABLES TO PART I

MAPS TO PART 2

TABLES TO PART 2

12

MESOAMERICA SINCE THE SPANISH INVASION: AN OVERVIEW

MURDO J. MACLEOD

The nine chapters in this volume, all by mid-career or younger scholars, are a collective attempt to survey what is known of the history of Native American peoples in Mesoamerica since the Spanish invasion. Obviously, what we know about the various nations, groups, and regions varies widely. Nomadic peoples and those who leave behind little of their material cultures are generally less studied and less understood. The same can be said for peoples who did not write, either before or after the invasions, or about whom others wrote less.

Geographical definitions have been kept deliberately fluid. Meso-american frontiers, as classically defined, were extended, especially over what today would be called the Mexican north. Many of these areas, after all, interacted with, or felt influences from, the sedentary centers. Nor did the editor try to impose geographical boundaries – which would have been arbitrary anyway in many cases – among the various essayists. Probably, as independent and idiosyncratic scholars, most would have ignored these admonitions anyway. So there are some overlapping discussions, and some areas that, falling between two stools somewhat, no doubt do not receive their deserved attention. Nor did the editor try to impose thematic unity, which would have been another thankless task, simply asking that certain basic informational themes be covered. Thus each chapter has individual emphases and interpretations, something that should surely be considered not a fault but, rather, a window through which variety and debate can be illuminated.

The nine contributors, to the best of the editor's knowledge, include four natives of the United States, two Canadians, two Europeans, and one Mexican. (Attempts to recruit more scholars from the Mesoamerican area were frustrated by one death and three refusals because of previous commitments.) That there are no Native Americans among the contrib-

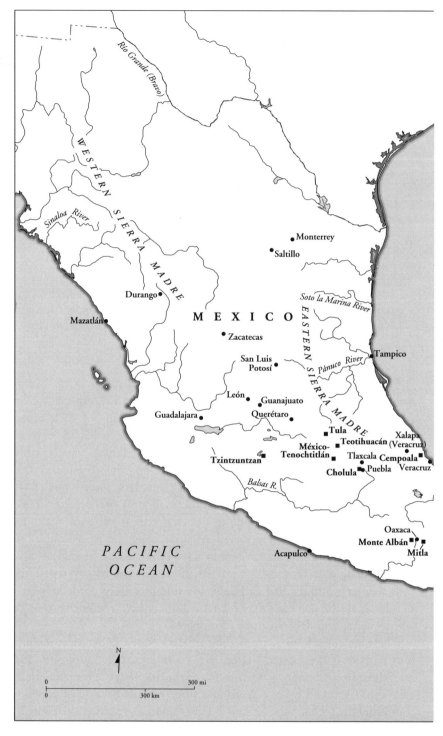

Map 12.1

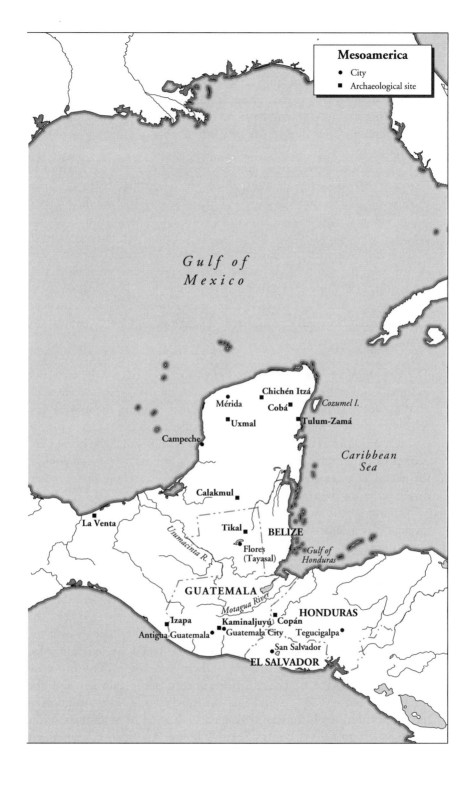

Mesoamerica
● City
■ Archaeological site

Gulf of Mexico

Chichén Itzá
Mérida ● Cobá ■
Uxmal ■ *Cozumel I.*
Campeche ● Tulum-Zamá ■

Caribbean Sea

Calakmul ■

La Venta ■

Usumacinta R. Tikal ■ BELIZE
Flores *Gulf of*
(Tayasal) *Honduras*

GUATEMALA
Motagua River

Izapa ■ Kaminaljuyú ■ Copán ■ HONDURAS
Antigua Guatemala ● Guatemala City ● Tegucigalpa ●
San Salvador ●
EL SALVADOR

utors may well say something about the way educational systems have failed to train native peoples. Other factors, such as the relative youth of some historians, or the emphasis on oral history among many of the people who are encouraging the new ethnic consciousness, may also be of importance.

This introductory chapter, greatly compressed, is less an attempt to introduce the following chapters, all of which can more than speak for themselves, than to provide a general introduction to some three centuries of colonial, and about 175 years of national, history. In the national period, the emphasis is on the areas constituting the nation states of Mexico and Guatemala, although other Central American states are mentioned from time to time. What has become ever more apparent during the writing is the extent to which native peoples have been written about by others and how little we have from native peoples about themselves. This situation, fortunately, is already changing, and offers radical and startling prospects for a more equitable history.

The very word *Indian* is representative of the problem for the collective imagination, for the classificatory impulse, which the Europeans' invasion of the Americas created. In post-Renaissance Europe there were few relativists of the genius of Michel de Montaigne. So the problem for the invaders was how to fit all these "discovered" peoples into the Europeans' preconceived notions of the world, including the nature of humankind, the relationship between humans and the supernatural, and the supposed divine order for the structure of the world and beyond.

Naming all the varied peoples of the Americas "Indians," then, was the first classificatory imposition, as imprecise a category as "Asians," so reductionist that it would have been an irrelevant and unimaginable collective label to peoples living in the American continents before Europeans first came ashore in the Antilles.

Once all the native peoples had been lumped together, and the true geographical nature of the so-called New World had emerged (i.e., the Caribbean islands were not Asian outliers), then the real debate over the true nature of this one people, the Indians, could begin. Some, for philosophical or expedient reasons – there was for a short historical moment an alliance of convenience between some thinkers and the conquerors and settlers – found that the quickest and tidiest solution to the classificatory problem was to assign a subhuman or nonhuman status to the American natives, a sort of earthly limbo. As evidence, proponents adduced whatever customs and criteria seemed most alien or appropriate in a given region – cannibalism, nomadism, lack of discernable codes of law, polytheism, and so on. The party that argued against the humanity of the American native peoples had a momentary advantage too. To the extent that European monarchs and their court thinkers felt obliged to justify their invasions and conquests – and only the Castillians made much of a fuss over this early on – to that extent the inhumanity of the natives was a temporary convenience.

"All Mankind is One," proclaimed the great "Protector of the Indians," Fray Bartolomé de Las Casas, and he prevailed, at least among the thinkers and writers of the time, if not often among the exploiters of native labor. While humanists such as Las Casas were, to an extent, ahead of their times, they were also a convenience of another kind to those in power. This *one* people, the Indians, could now be fitted comfortably into previous understandings, especially religious and political ones, of humankind.

Now, then, all natives of the Americas were one, Indians, and part of the human race. Humankind, however, created by God, had left the Garden of Eden in original sin and had been redeemed by the sacrifice of Jesus Christ. Could the Indians, seemingly cut off from other humankind, have been left out? Were they an unrecorded "lost tribe" or one of the famous lost tribes of Israel? A search for remnants of a previous Christianity continued sporadically. Had Saint Thomas or other disciples visited America? After all, he had converted the Nestorians of Southern India, Saint James had reached Spain, or at least his bones had, and Saint Francis Xavier had reached Japan. (Even today some major religions believe Christ himself preached to the pre-conquest native peoples.)

Spaniards, or at least the minority among them interested in such matters, thus concluded that the Indians were relapsed early Christians or, somewhat differently, theological children once lost and now found, and thus appropriate to be assigned as "free" – i.e., not enslaved – but lowly vassals of the Crown, to be protected by Crown and Church.

Tidy enough, but there were lots of loose ends. Indians had created large and intricate polities, with kings, courtiers, warrior castes, priests, tribute-paying serfs, and slaves. The peoples of central Mexico and elsewhere built cities, wrote law codes and tales of genealogies and great deeds, that is, created histories, all criteria of *vida política,* of civilization, according to some of the derivations of natural law as understood by Catholic Europe. If the hierarchies involved had emerged according to the divine order of things, then Spanish legal minds, reaching for a legitimacy that would satisfy them and their regal patrons, had to accord Native American nobilities a place within that order – thus the *señores naturales* or natural lords, incorporated, with various degrees of enthusiasm, into Mesoamerican elites.

Spaniards on the ground, however, more practical regarding their aims and the need for a rapid subordination of the conquered peoples, took care to kill all the overarching or imperial nobilities that could reunite multiple regions or cities in revolt. In areas of city-states such as Yucatan, some higher ranks were allowed to continue, but in general the Indian colonial nobility that remained was mostly local, or strategically intermarried with the conquerors.

In spite of these legal fictions and realities, law books, royal histories, and creation myths, among other written matter, presented a problem. The most common solution was to pronounce them to be unchristian, the work of the devil, and to destroy them. Bishop Diego de Landa of Yucatan, also a student of his Native American flock, was the most notorious book burner.

Fortunately, three circumstances helped to preserve some native manuscripts. One was the recalcitrance and local pride of some native elites, who early discerned the imperial aims of the invaders and simply hid away these manuscripts, some of which were then rediscovered by more eclectic future generations. A few of these native leaders became writers, and incorporated pre-conquest documents, in whole or in part, within their compositions. The third circumstance, paradoxically, was the Spanish fondness for souvenirs or trophies. Such astonishing and marvelous artifacts as the Dresden Codex and the headdress of Mochtezuma II (or Montezuma) had three important and related roles once in Spanish hands. First, they were of use to impress upon the monarch the importance of the conquered area whence the artifacts came. Next, they were evidence of the heroic nature of the deeds of individual conquerors or groups of conquerors, a kind of unwritten and symbolic proof of "merits and services." And in some cases they were used to "buy" *ex post facto* approval from the Crown of acts and campaigns of dubious legality. Hernán Cortés, perhaps our main example, was essentially bribing Carlos V to approve his "illegal" conquest of central Mexico from Cuba when he sent him parts of Mochtezuma's treasure. For these and other reasons, then, native writings were preserved, and some ended up in European and other museums and archives.

Native American manuscripts are not the only source for trying to reach some general knowledge of the societies of Mesoamerica at the moment of contact with the other continents. There are at least six other categories, each of which presents problems.

Archaeology is the leading origin of data on these peoples but suffers from various deficiencies. The Mesoamerican frontiers, such as present-day El Salvador and Pacific Nicaragua, and especially the northwestern and northeastern regions of Mesoamerica, have drawn relatively few archaeologists and sustained excavation projects. Moreover, contemporary interests have emphasized the great Classic civilizations, and what might be called the very late Postclassic, or the century or so before contact, has been all but ignored. So, too, have the areas where the great Classic era and its building projects never reached, again mainly peripheral regions. Everywhere they work archaeologists are limited by what they find, which means that in general such features as monumentalism, elite artifacts, perdurable materials (stone rather than wood), dry cold climates, and urban concentrations, leave more evidence. Apart from some interesting work on housemound counts and analysis, and on coring for ground cover and pollen count analysis, we have little information, for example, on the peasant agriculturalist of the humid tropical coasts of Caribbean and Gulf Mesoamerica. The native manuscripts just discussed could have told us much, had more survived, but they were also elite in origin and limited to certain topics.

Of equal interest to moderns investigating these societies at or before the Spanish invasion have been the categories of writing that arose in the decades after the Conquest. Indian nobilities, or mestizos descended from nobility and conquerors, taught by friars to write either Spanish or their native language in Roman script, composed accounts of the world they or their parents had just lost, and sometimes their views of the strange new world that was just emerging.

Trapped in an ambivalent status, these authors, few in number but of considerable significance, wished to restore through eyewitness descriptions and commentaries the glories of their ancestors, the magnificence and elaborate nature of their empires, arts, and customs. Yet they were confined by their more or less enthusiastic conversion to the new religion – a religious adherence they could ignore only at their peril, witness the burning at the stake of the *cacique* of Texcoco and perhaps even the execution of the Tarascan Cazonci – and by their having to proclaim that the coming of the divinely supported Spanish monarchy had brought not only the true religion and an end to"superstition and idola-try" but also general peace, civilized life, and an end to numerous "barbarous customs." Given that such limits produced contorted and ambivalent writings – not to speak of the torments the authors them-selves must have suffered – they nevertheless remain one of the best sources of evidence as we try to draw a baseline for later study. Such writers as Chimalpahin, Fernando de Alva Ixtlilxochitl, Diego Muñoz Camargo, and Hernando Alvarado Tezozomoc, and the known or anon-ymous native authors of texts such as the Códice Pérez, the Books of Chilam Balam, and the Annals of the Cakchiquels, have attracted the attention of modern authors, although none to the extent of the Peruvian Guamán Poma de Ayala, about whom modern scholars have created a veritable industry.

It is a truism that the writings of the winners survive, and that their version prevails. Yet not all the winners saw the Indian world alike. Several observers have noted the almost peculiarly European indifference to newly discovered flora, fauna, and landscapes – or was it, once again, European refusal of relativism and a subconscious determination to fit everything into preexistent and tidy schemes? But Europeans were inter-ested in people, especially the attributes they could understand. Span-iards, especially, with that peculiar sixteenth-century alliance between pragmatists and philosophers, trained their eyes on Native Americans, as a workforce, as providers of wealth and information, and as potential souls for Christ.

In the person of one great scholar these concerns combined with Renaissance humanism and scholasticism to produce a pioneer ethnolo-gist. Fray Bernardino de Sahagún shared the utilitarian urges of his contemporaries. To know the native peoples of central Mexico, to turn them into good Christians and loyal vassals, one had to understand them and where they had been. Even more, however, and perhaps subcon-sciously, he was possessed by a genuine spirit of inquiry, interested in the life and culture of these new subjects of the crown in a very modern ethnographic way. To describe Sahagún as democratic would be anach-ronistic, but in his instinctively egalitarian need to understand that which might be swept away, he interviewed and recorded everyone he could, and wrote down his findings in both Nahuatl and Spanish so that they would be available to all, including some of his informants.

Sahagún stands alone, but many other Spaniards wrote extensively about the first generation of peoples they met in the New World. Toribio de Benavente (also known as Motolinía), Diego de Landa, and many others in the sixteenth century; Andrés Pérez de Rivas and Ignaz Pfefferkorn during the much later conquests in the north of New Spain, recorded the ceremonies, rites, and daily doings of those they met, even if, as in the case of Pérez de Rivas, what they recorded has to be seen through a screen because they considered that they were describing "the Most Barbarous and Fierce Peoples of the New World." Where texts were available, many of the sixteenth-century writers, such as Fray Diego Durán, Fray Juan de Torquemada, and the aforementioned Motolinía, depended heavily on native texts.

Even the conquerors can tell us much, some of it inadvertently, as they recount their deeds in a self-justificatory fashion. Such men as Hernán Cortés, Pedro de Alvarado, the "Unknown Conqueror," and Bernal Díaz del Castillo were concerned with native peoples mainly as opponents and then subjects, but their letters reveal details about states and state structures, native alliances and wars, settlement patterns, and many political and diplomatic matters.

The early chroniclers, too, such as Juan Herrera de Tordesillas and Gonzalo Fernández de Oviedo y Valdés, relying as they often did on early conquest accounts, are full of information, some of it interstitial, about native society during or just after the conquest wars. Official recorders such as Juan López de Velasco, writing in the 1570s, used earlier material, such as tribute lists, and can be of help with conquest-era demography.

The Crown and its officials, as soon as they had wrested control of the invaded parts of Mesoamerica from the conquistadors and imposed some order, wanted to know what they possessed, not only in general but with a view to assessing native taxes (the tribute), local products and production possibilities, and potential natural resources. To these ends they counted and requested surveys. Tribute counts, *cuentas de tributos*, or general assessments of population size, began early, and some relied, more or less, on previous native assessments of regional specializations in produce and manufacture. From then on village counts (*padrones*) were made periodically, yielding, in many cases, serial demographic information.

In the 1570s the Crown sent out a standardized questionnaire to local officials demanding qualitative and quantitative answers, which some officials answered incompletely, idiosyncratically, or not at all. Nevertheless, many of these so-called *relaciones geográficas* relied on earlier accounts

and knowledge, and contain a variety of information on the years immediately before and after the arrival of the first Spaniards. Later *relaciones geográficas* continued to be of value as sources of information on
native society throughout the colonial period.

Native American town leaders themselves, in the half century and
beyond after the Conquest, described the "times of their gentility" in
numerous appeals and petitions directed to higher authorities, even the
Crown. As the genre would indicate, these letters to the government had
a political motive – what writing does not? Much of their writing was in
Nahuatl, which became the indigenous *lingua franca* of large parts of
colonial Mesoamerica. Much of it was also in Spanish, and a little of it
was in other native languages. It usually had to do with intrusive Spanish
or neighbors' local violations of what the writers claimed were ancient
rights, or claims to lands that had, they said, been in their legal possession
"since times beyond memory." Sometimes these petitions were accompanied by confirmatory evidence, such as land title documents, some
authentic and some clearly forgeries.

So much for the establishment of a baseline, a sort of general knowledge of Mesoamerican society around 1500 in the areas of high culture
and structured politics, and at the moment of the later conquests in the
northern and southern peripheries. Is this knowledge of these many and
varied societies immediately before and at the moment of invasion sufficient to study complex social change during the early colonial period and
later? The quantity of information varies by region and native nation or
linguistic entity. On the great centers of the Aztec tributary confederacy,
on the Tarascan state, on the petty states of highland Guatemala, and on
the so-called city-states of Yucatan, to mention some leading examples,
information is relatively plentiful. On the huge Mesoamerican peripheries, especially those invaded and subdued late, knowledge of the preexisting situations can be minimal or less. On this varied and to some fragile
base, at any rate, some impressive and elaborate scholarly structures have
been built.

All these materials, and many other local writings and reports to Spain,
provided fuel for the great debate that followed chronologically upon the
one about the true nature of Native American peoples. Were the invading
Spaniards, the first generation of conquistadors and settlers, as Fray
Bartolomé de Las Casas proclaimed, the cause of the "destruction of the
Indies"? From the moment of Spanish arrival native populations declined

catastrophically. In the major islands of the Caribbean and in many of the humid tropical coasts of Mesoamerica, native peoples virtually disappeared. On the Mesoamerican highlands and plateaus populations may have fallen by 90 percent or even more.

According to those at the time who denounced the scandal, and to many others in subsequent centuries, the catastrophe was the result of Spanish cruelty and depravity, the so-called Black Legend, which led to wanton killing, brutal enslavement that the Crown was able to modify and abolish only slowly, and overwork. Las Casas's fulminations were seized upon by Spain's imperial rivals, especially the English and the Dutch, whose treatment of colonial peoples was similar to that of Spain, as propaganda material for use against Spain. The opposite argument, dubbed the "White Legend," defended Spanish colonialism and pronounced that native populations in the Americas had never been large, and that Spanish government and culture had brought many benefits, including Christianity, a *pax hispanica* that ended internecine warfare, and an end to such barbarous customs as human sacrifice and cannibalism, among others.

The debate has continued to this day under numerous guises and new emphases. Using "upstreaming" from early tribute counts, modern knowledge of the laws of epidemiology and immunology, and a variety of other methods, most scholars of the question now agree that preinvasion American populations, and specifically those of Mesoamerica, were very large. One of the side issues now, which becomes in some hands quarrels over methodology and which is probably impossible to resolve, is just how large. By the middle of the seventeenth century – earlier in the core areas and much later in the far peripheries and in "unconquered" areas – native populations had fallen to a remnant. That much appears to be established, and the debate moves on. What caused this catastrophe? Was it the evils of Spanish colonialism as the Black Legend asserts? Then how does one explain the slow demographic recovery in the middle and late colonial period? Conquest warfare and the vaguer notion called culture shock seem insufficient given the technologies of warfare of the time, and the slowness, at least in much of Mesoamerica, of Spanish cultural conquest. For the moment, with many caveats, pandemics are the villains, brought on by the introduction of Eurasian and African diseases to a population that had no acquired immunities to them.

The disease history of Mesoamerica, indeed of the Americas before

Spanish intrusion, is far from clear, and there is new research from the Gulf Coast of Mexico into the presence of fevers and other similar calamities there long before Cortés and his men landed. There is also suggestive evidence that intermittent demographic crises of a Malthusian nature had long afflicted some regions, bringing with them illnesses and failures to thrive associated with nutritional shortages. In spite of advanced technologies as far as such matters as irrigation, fertilizing, and crop rotation and fallowing were concerned, communication systems and food distribution were primitive, and it was difficult and market inefficient to convey large quantities of basic commodities such as maize, beans, or tubers from areas of plenty to ones of dearth. Nevertheless, and very tentatively, an epidemiological disaster similar to those that occurred in isolated invaded regions such as Hawaii and Australia, seems to be the main explanation for the population collapse.

The arguments provoked by the basic facts of the demographic decline continue to grow. What were the effects of such a loss on Indian society, and on relations between the Indians and other sectors of society? Growth in the non-Indian populations caused by Spanish immigration, importations of African slaves, some as a replacement labor force for disappeared natives, and miscegenation, obviously led to a different proportionate ethnic distribution, and thus to readjustments in such inter-ethnic matters as labor relations and systems, methods of conversion to Spanish Catholicism, intrusions upon village government and customs, and land tenure and use structures, to name but a few. The extent to which these relationships changed, if at all, has been the subject of several long and recent historical debates.

Some parts of Mesoamerica remained outside Spanish control until late in the colonial era; the highlands of Nayarit, the Sierra Gorda, and the Petén come quickly to mind. For most of Mesoamerica, however, the first two centuries after the Spanish invasion have set the scene for a series of related debates about change in native Mesoamerican societies. A few caveats are in order. There was, all agree, immense regional variation within Mesoamerica, and the degree to which we know the histories of some areas, eras, events, and classes also differs widely. Nor has there been any commonality, any agreement, among historians and ethnohistorians as to method, and so scholars have approached change as a set of institutional, agricultural, economic, cultural, linguistic, or even psychological problems (although acculturation is no longer a concept with wide acceptance), thus coming to different results and to disagreements over rates and types of change. The debate over the first two centuries of native societies in colonial Mesoamerica has been, then, over the nature, periodization, pace, and regional and temporal variations of change, without much agreement over what change or the lack of it means.

A definite trend in recent years, however, has been to attempt to see change, or stasis, from the native point of view. This new history "from the inside out" has taken several forms. One small tendency has been to examine differences in Indian cultures and social structure comparatively, comparing villages, cultural groups, or even regions to see if difference disposed some collectivities to be more or less receptive to pressure or advantageous innovation. Two apparent problems with this approach, hard to overcome, are the difficulties in obtaining similar baselines and qualities of data between the two (or more) entities to be studied, and the equal difficulty of demonstrating that innovative forces or pressures were more or less equally presented to the entities being compared. Still, the importance of this comparative approach to change is that it begins with the possibilities and variations within native society, and thus breaks with the earlier model that discussed mainly the forms of oppression imposed on a mostly supine or passive mass.

A much larger school, basing itself on the study of the heartland of central Mexico, has also emphasized a history from the Native American viewpoint. This school, of whom Sarah Cline (Chap. 16, this volume) is a leading representative, concentrates much of its research on writings in Nahuatl, the metropolitan language of the region when the Spaniards arrived, and one fostered by them. Native leadership learned to write Nahuatl in western European script and kept many of its local records in that language. These historians tend to use such local materials as town council minutes and records, native land transactions and petitions, *títulos* (historical records, some partly or wholly fictional, outlining the histories of contemporary land ownership), wills, and similar materials. Such writers have emphasized continuity and the slowness of change in central Mexican communities, at least in the first colonial century or so. They point out that there were as yet few Spaniards present, either laymen or clergy, and that in a tribute and forced-labor economy the new lords of the land were obliged to rely on the administrative, recruiting, and social control abilities of the native elite. Spanish, as a language, penetrated very slowly and so then did Spanish culture. Natives eagerly adopted Spanish tools, crops, and some domesticated animals but clung to former administrative units (*altepetl*), smaller subdivisions (*calpulli* or *tlaxilacalli*), and nobilities (*tlatoque* and *pipiltin*), all under new Spanish guises such as *cabildo, cabecera,* and *sujeto, encomienda,* and *gobernador.* Even as far as the new religion was concerned change was slow. There were few clergy for many years, and in spite of mass baptisms, many ordinary people remained unbaptized and uncatechized for decades after 1520. Certainly the large central Mexican populations of the early colonial years had few opportunities to hear, far less read, detailed explanations of the intricacies of the new Christianity. Even confession, which a few scholars have presented as a clerical means of indoctrination, took place for many only once a year, or not at all. So, while formal and outward Christianity took root, folk and local beliefs continued, either as a new range of beliefs via integration of the old and the new (synchretism), or, in a few spectacular cases, as outright opposition to the imposed beliefs.

This Nahuatl school tends to regard the population collapse, the imposition of new tributes and Spanish officials, and phenomena such as *congregación* and Indian slave migrations, as important but secondary factors, compared to the persistence of preconquest ways of life. Others would argue, no doubt, that the disappearance of 90 percent of a population would have a considerable impact – the emptying of the countryside in an essentially agrarian society, and the disruption of normal promotions in the leadership process, to mention only two. It may also be a truism that local administrative records produce histories of continuities, that village records everywhere seem to pass quickly over plague, death, and revolution. Above all, there is a philosophical problem involved in links among form, practice, and conviction. *Cabildo* records in western alphabet Nahuatl were themselves a dramatic imposition, but the deeper question, according to Blaise Pascal, is how to separate form, practice, and belief. How much do formal actions, even those forced on people, become practice, and how quickly, if ever, does constant repetition become part, at least, of structures of belief? How soon does a scribe, surrounded by *cabildo* members, become part of the imposed formulas and the kind of thinking behind these formulas, and how soon do they become part of his world? How quickly do new tools and days of work and workplaces change the attitudes of a person toward work and the greater world? Perhaps the most important contributions of what may be called, in shorthand, the Nahuatl school, is to bring a native perspective and voice to native history, and to show that colonialism and oppression, while taking many forms, were often in their early stages ineffective and inefficient, thus enabling strong local cultures to assert great amounts of continuities and initiatives.

Away from the Nahuatl center the debate has taken somewhat different forms and sources, depending far less, for example, on texts in native languages. In Yucatan, some scholars have ascribed the relative cohesion and continuities of the early and mid-colonial Maya not only to the ingenuity and doggedness of their cultural leaders, especially the local political elites, but also to the relative neglect of the area by the invaders, who found no silver mines or plantation agriculture possibilities – until the henequen boom of the nineteenth century – to draw their attention and numbers.

Other scholars believe in a more nuanced and more economic interpretation. Although somewhat of a backwater, Yucatan, they would argue, was very much part of an extractive world economy. It was the kind of economic roles assigned to and adapted to by the local native peoples that slowed the cultural rate of change, allowing them to remain somewhat outside Spanish conformist pressures. To put it another way, the onset of capitalism in its colonial modes included, perhaps at its extremities more than at the center, anachronistic or even somewhat hostile cultural forms of production – tributary labor and capitation tax combinations being the most common – until the full impetus of the mature capitalist system unfolded.

Oaxaca and surrounding areas, as María de los Angeles Romero Frizzi so well describes them (Chap. 19, this volume), were somewhat similar. Native peoples retained their lands and languages far more than elsewhere, in part because Spaniards were relatively few in number. More important, however, was that the sought-after local products, silk and, especially later, cochineal, were luxuries requiring intricate processes and specialized manual labor, not tasks to which elites were likely to flock. The solution local peoples found generally acceptable, if not pushed beyond unwritten mutually agreed levels of "moral economy," was an indigenous production system with surpluses extracted by petty merchants and, above all, government officials, especially the *alcaldes mayores*. Both merchants and *alcaldes mayores* themselves were merely the local agents of, and debtors to, larger interests in Mexico City, Veracruz, and Spain. Once again, a combination of local indigenous cultural strength and the inconsistencies of early capitalist production at the periphery provided the dynamic for considerable cultural autonomy and continuity, at least in the first two colonial centuries.

Those who have studied the Mesoamerican part of Central America –
Chiapas, Guatemala, present-day El Salvador, and Pacific portions of
Honduras and Nicaragua – have found that the north and northwest of
that region resemble Yucatan and Oaxaca, only more so. There, in most
of Chiapas and the Cuchumatanes especially, as George Lovell points out
(Chap. 21, this volume), comparatively large numbers of native peoples,
few Spaniards, and a lack of a much desired export product, made native
production systems and native labor the only real sources of wealth. So,
again *alcaldes mayores* and other officials became the agents that extracted
tributary surpluses from a basically indigenous economy and society.

The difference there was that the indigenous north and west was,
especially during several economic cycles, adjacent to a complementary
Creole–ladino production zone, the areas south and east of Antigua and
Guatemala City, plus much of the Pacific Coast, including Soconusco
and El Salvador, where migrant labor was required. The indigenous areas
experienced heavy seasonal migrations, some forced and others at least
somewhat voluntary, to these intensive zones, with disruptive and destructive effects but surprisingly little impact on local cultures. Again,
anachronistic forms of production, plus seasonal migrations and strong
indigenous cohesiveness, slowed certain kinds of change and fostered
others.

The indigenous north that Susan Deeds and David Frye describe
(Chaps. 13 and 14, this volume) was very different from the center and
south of Mesoamerica. Conquests were later, the spaces more vast and
often desert. Above all, many of the native peoples in these regions
presented the Spanish invaders with cultures that they could not understand and, consequently, did not know how to manipulate or control, at
least for some time. Few in number and scattered compared to central
Mesoamerica, and often seasonally or permanently nomadic, the numerous tribes and nations of the north, accustomed to a warfare economy,
could not even be defeated piecemeal as in Yucatan and Guatemala.
Murderous, brutal wars of attrition were usually the result, with native
groups almost always the losers as they faced new diseases and Spanish
willingness to use scorched-earth and search-and-destroy tactics.

In fact, one has to reorder one's factors in order to understand the
processes of change in the north. Inhospitable from the environmental
point of view, and with a population that could be transformed into a
servile or semi-servile labor force only with great difficulty, these vast
deserts seemed to hold few attractions. The great lure, especially in the

northwest, was silver. A lure for the clergy, especially the Jesuits and Franciscans, was the harvest of souls. Thus the setting-up of missions to which local people came with varying degrees of willingness, and the brutal conditions in mines and on their subsidiary haciendas, where dislocation, *encomienda*, draft labor, and introduced Tlaxcalans and others from the south created an unsatisfactory labor force. Periods of raiding and enslavement on both sides alternated with uneasy truces and acceptance bought by bribery and resignation. Seemingly pacified areas erupted frequently into revolt, and the Spanish general tactic that worked best became extermination and demographic obliteration by weight of numbers.

Two problems intrigue students of these indigenous peoples. One is the paucity of information. Obviously such factors as Eurasian diseases and cimarron cattle and horses arrived before the invaders, and at any event, the native peoples had no written records and few common traditions. Few monumental buildings or even habitation sites of any permanence have been found. The result is that little is known of these cultures before contact, and Spanish failure to understand them makes their descriptions even more ethnocentric and disparaging than usual.

The other mystery is how to explain the stubborn survivals, a problem that, in the case of the Tarahumaras, Tepehuanes, and peoples of Sonora, Susan Deeds makes a valiant attempt to elucidate. The Yaquis, for example, seemed uniquely capable of turning to their advantage cultural traits, or the migrations forced upon them. Another factor, to which we now turn, is the ability to flee or migrate to more inhospitable areas, of use to some Native Americans in the struggle to accommodate, resist, and survive as identifiable groups.

Grant Jones discussing the lowland Maya (Chap. 20, this volume) and in his other writings has used the open frontier as an explanatory factor when discussing indigenous change. It was, at its simplest, an escape valve from pressure from the Spaniards or from an oppressive village or *cacique*, as Tarahumaras and later Apaches in the north also knew. Open frontiers on unconquered deserts, mountains, or jungles were also porous. People moved there to escape pressures or find new fields, and often returned when conditions improved. In these large and somewhat amorphous areas refugees from various villages and nations mingled and reformulated their ways. Renegade Spaniards, a few idealistic friars, or the occasional wandering, sometimes lost, Spanish *entrada*, would bring these areas into touch with the "pacified" side of the frontier. At times a

Spanish expedition would seize parts of such an area, only to withdraw later. At any event these "zones of refuge" helped to reduce pressure on subjugated peoples, and thus increased their resistance to cultural and other impositions. Who knows, the very existence of a nearby porous frontier may have made neighborhood Spaniards more cautious about imposing onerous labor systems or exorbitant taxes.

The transformations brought by the introduction of Christianity have themselves been the subject of considerable debate, with the extent and nature of the "spiritual conquest" and the degree or even existence of "conversion" giving rise to some of the most polemical and overheated writing. At the extremes, some have argued that conversion took place sooner or later, and apart from some local superstitions most Indian peoples became essentially Catholics. Others, at their most extreme the "idols behind altars" school, would claim that Catholicism was overtly or passively resisted, and that conversion was a sham or subterfuge. Others, more moderate in their views, hold that there was a Nahuatl or Maya, or Zapotec, and so on, worldview, or conception of the cosmos, which endured in spite of various changes in ritual and observance.

More nuanced views have come to the fore. Some scholars would now rather dissect these phenomena regionally and piecemeal. What to make, for example, of the *cofradía,* or religious confraternity, more or less autonomous and financially secure depending on region, politics, and era, accused of superstitions and revival of "heathen" ways by some clergy, and of being used for teaching of orthodoxy and personal enrichment by others?

In fact, as one scholar has noted, there was the creation of many Catholicisms at the level of ordinary people, probably rather like early medieval Europe after Christian conversion. There was no new synchretism or fusion of old and new religions but, rather, ad hoc mixtures of belief and even, to a lesser extent, of ritual, with outright, always spectacular idolatry and defiance being the noticeable – and thus written about – exception rather than the rule. In the Mayan area, for example, there seem to have been various hierarchies of belief, from the saints and guardian spirits and prayers of the hearth and household, to the tutelary semi-official protectors of the village and community, to the orthodoxy preached on Sunday in the parish church or by a bishop on *visita*. Most priests accepted minor idiosyncrasies, folkways, or local superstitions, as indeed local Catholic clergy have done in many converted parts of the world. In fact, one scholar has noted that, at least by the eighteenth century in central and western Mexico, there was less friction over belief, ritual, and practice between priests and their flocks than we had previously been led to accept. This, of course, varied by region, era, and indigenous group. On the peripheries of Mesoamerica there was more outright resistance after the first conquests, and a more hesitant or reluctant mixture of old and new, so that peoples such as the Tarahumara or some Talamancans appear decidedly unchristian even today.

Another boom industry in the last two decades has been research on colonial Indian resistance and rebellion. Sympathy for the underdog, the desire to write the history of ordinary people "from below," and the general mood of dislike for the various forms of colonialism and imperialism, have combined to give impetus to research of this kind. Another factor has been the availability of documentation. Violence and dissent worried, even at times panicked, the Spanish authorities, who then investigated and reported at length, perhaps, in the heat of the moment, overestimating the importance of these crises.

Some of the resultant research has consisted of a rather naive search for any form of native violence, which is then dubbed as resistance, so that anything from fisticuffs among a handful of villagers, through a town riot against the local *corregidor* or his assistants – with stonings, burnings of buildings, or even the deaths of some Spanish officials – to full-scale pan-regional rebellions, which were exceedingly rare except on the Mesoamerican frontiers, is classified as a revolt against the colonial power. Other scholars, noting that there were, indeed, few colonial uprisings, few fortifications around inland cities, and only some disorganized local militias until the reforms of the eighteenth century, have decided that whatever the imperfections of Spanish colonialism in Mesoamerica, it did bring a *pax hispanica* to many fractious peoples.

Researchers in between, impelled by the new interest in native peoples as actors, as creators of their own history, and in part inspired by James Scott's ideas of "everyday resistance," Edward Thompson's writings on "moral economy," and the "subaltern" school of Ranajit Guha and others, have found that the search for accommodation and resistance must be widened to include the many forms, passive and active, through which native peoples, as political actors and cultural agents, expressed their autonomy and their desire to reformulate the daily conditions of colonialism and a violent society.

There are at least three major problems in this new and refreshing tendency. One is to fail to note that resistance – and especially the revolts, which almost always failed until just before independence – seldom brought more than temporary improvements in conditions, and often selective executions or other punishments. Another is to forget who won, the basic facts of Spanish colonialism, and the findings of the "old school" that stressed the oppressive impositions made upon Indians. Yet another is to ignore the fact that the struggles of a peasantry or people living in more or less subsistence agrarian economies is one of survival against many hostile factors – sources of credit, soils, yields, plagues, animal and human, and the vagaries of climate among them – so that the exigencies of colonialism are only one of many daily problems. Here again, however, this new group of writers is revealing a history from below, a history of Native Americans from their point of view.

About the middle of the eighteenth century, after two centuries of Spanish colonialism, much of Mesoamerica underwent a series of significant changes to which Eric Van Young, in Chapter 15 of this volume and in numerous other works, has devoted considerable attention. These changes, more in some parts of the region, less in others, brought new and in some places different pressures on Native American populations. Native demographic growth found little available land in parts of western Mexico and the Bajío because village lands had been rented out or lost to the increasingly commercial and expansionist haciendas. Malthusian pressures were the result. Haciendas became especially market-oriented near some of the larger cities, and their need for land and labor caused increased migration from native townships and some loss of ethnic identity. Notable growth in plantation industries such as sugar and indigo also attracted labor. In the north migration of non-Indians took up scarce cultivatable lands, at last in the northeast, and nomadics and seminomadics had to retreat further into barrancas and *sierras*.

On top of all these gradual changes came one old and one new enemy of Native Americans. The great epidemics returned in several great outbursts. The *matlazáhuatl* (probably typhus) of 1737–38 caused some native villages to disappear completely, and in its differential impact may have been a major factor in turning some parts of the center west into definitively mestizo areas. The still more infamous *año de hambre* epidemic of 1786 probably killed fewer but was long remembered, as the name suggests, for the great dearth and hunger that accompanied it. Eighteenth-century prices for maize and other staples fluctuated wildly, not only seasonally but during the recurrent subsistence crises, when hoarding, the urban preferences shown by the poorly organized city *alhóndigas* and *pósitos*, left parts of the native countryside near starvation. The last twenty years or so before independence saw a great increase in the price of maize in Mexico, especially between 1808 and 1811, and the livelihood of the poor deteriorated correspondingly.

The new scourge, or, rather, an old scourge in new and more vigorous guise, was government intervention. The Bourbon regime, via its representatives in cities such as Mexico, Guadalajara, Puebla, and Guatemala, in spite of many half starts and failures, was much more interventionist and ambitious than the Habsburgs had been. Taxes seem to have been collected more efficiently, including the tribute. Government sought to lessen the power of the clergy, seen by some Indians as their protectors. The *cofradía,* that Indian refuge and cultural redoubt in some regions, was heavily attacked in the late eighteenth century, and lost many of its sources of funds. So also did some *cajas de comunidad* or community chests. Concessions to the native population, such as the abolition of the tribute in 1812, came too late.

In some regions, then, renewed pressures and diseases wiped out remnants of native populations in the second half of the eighteenth century. In others, commercialization, migrations to new workplaces, rising prices for basics, and pressure on Indian lands from population growth and encroaching haciendas meant a disappearance of ethnic distinctiveness and increasing proletarianization, hunger, and unrest. In the predominantly indigenous south, in provinces such as Oaxaca, Yucatan, Chiapas, and Guatemala, native populations grew but their levels of living and coherence of community organizations probably declined. New calls for labor and forced labor drafts, intervillage disputes over increasingly scarce lands, epidemics, and government attacks on *cofradías,* the parish clergy, and tribute delays, meant increasing discontent and a failure to participate in the eighteenth-century boom.

Research and writing on Native American roles in the dramatic events of the first third of the nineteenth century are still meager and, of course, vary by region and ethnic group. The best-known area, naturally enough, is the one where the first great insurgencies broke out, the ones more or less led by Fathers Miguel Hidalgo in the Bajío and the Guadalajara region, and José Morelos farther south, especially in the modern states of Morelos and Guerrero.

As Van Young's chapter indicates, the nineteenth century saw the disappearance of large groups speaking native languages in the center west, and the emergence of a rural proletariat with wretched levels of living and a resentful, conservative, anti-Spanish and messianic set of beliefs, if not quite an ideology. Many of these people supported some or all of the stages of the Hidalgo revolt and the other insurgencies in that region, and to the extent that distinguishable Native American communities remained, they rose in support also.

The Morelos revolt, and the insurgencies that continued after the priest's execution, took place in regions more to the south, ones that had remained more clearly indigenous, and so perceptible indigenous participation is more obvious. Just why these peoples would join movements such as the one led by Morelos is far from clear. Perhaps some of their motives and general beliefs were similar to the ones farther north.

In the north there is little information on the era of independence. A common sentiment seems to be that, in general, there was little enthusiasm for or against the insurgency. We know even less about the participation, or lack of it, by the isolated indigenous groups such as the Tarahumaras or Yaquis.

To the south, in Guatemala specifically, there is a notable increase in Indian village unrest in the half century or so before Central American independence. At first sight, many of these Indian town riots appear to be based on familiar local grievances such as overcollection of taxes or abuses by regional ladino or Spanish officials, but the frequency of such upheavals, compared to the preceding period, may be of significance, and some students have seen this as an increase in antigovernment and ethnic anti-Spanish expressions.

In Guatemala itself, writing on putative indigenous participation in the struggle for independence – if there really was much of a struggle in that region – has become somewhat anachronistically ideological, and at least some of the writing argues from that basis rather than from deep research in the documents or local folk history of the time.

A further impediment has been that Central America's approach to independence was fragmented, in places hesitant, and above all regional, so that in spite of the efforts of major scholars it continues to be confusing. What to make of San Salvador, for example, where in any case few Indians remained: that some leaders briefly sought union with the United States; that the province was, in fact, occupied by Mexican imperial troops, united with the other Central American provinces, then broke away, via several local and regional wars, to full independence?

Although challenged by a few, the received knowledge has been that the great assault on Native American society, and especially its communal lands, was not during the colonial period, although intrusions and invasions were certainly common and often pervasive, but during the Liberal Reforma in Mexico. The focal villain has usually been the Ley Lerdo of 1856, which prohibited corporate-owned lands and broke up or alienated those then in existence. (The law took the name of Miguel Lerdo de Tejada, finance minister under President Ignacio Comonfort.) Several chapters in this volume (chaps. 13, 19, and 15, by Deeds, Romero Frizzi, and Van Young, for example) demonstrate that these attacks on village lands, in a number of the new states of the Mexican nation, began earlier. Loss of land was worse in the west, especially Jalisco, and minor in the center.

There seem to have been two general reasons for this new wave of intrusions and confiscations, at first sight paradoxical in that they took place just after wars waged for the proclaimed purpose of freeing society from the shackles of colonialism. The first reason was that Spanish paternalism, and the best among Spanish administrators, conceived of native society as a thing apart, a caste, composed of free but lowly vassals in need of protection. To a variable and limited extent this paternalism did provide some shelter, and native peoples, especially their local leadership, learned quickly and fairly effectively how to use it. A commonplace of the colonial period was the litigious nature of the indigenous village, especially over its lands, boundaries, and local government.

Several Spanish institutions, adopted eagerly by Mesoamerican peoples, attracted local patrons and guardians from outside Indian society. The religious confraternity (*cofradía*) was often protected, and sometimes taken over, by the higher clergy and especially by the local parish priests, who frequently had a financial interest in it. The *caja de comunidad* (community chest), tied to the collection of government and local taxes, was at times protected by local officials, who hoped to get various payments from it. *Cofradías*, especially, were often exploited by outsiders, but in some places and at some times they were also barrier and broker institutions that could be used to preserve some degree of cultural identity.

Many such protections were swept away after the wars. The *cofradía*, severely weakened anyway by the late colonial reforms and changes, came under renewed attack after independence and began to lose its lands. In fact, the local ambitious elites took over regional government and began to structure it for their own profit. One benefit they sought was access to more land. Even social protest against the situation of the native peoples showed a peculiar indifference. Ignacio Rodríguez Galván, a leading poet, defended the Indian against the evils of former Spanish colonialism.

Paradoxically, however, the Liberals, in both Mexico and Guatemala, also had positive ideological reasons for their programs. Rejecting the corporate structure of the colonial period, and convinced that a society of free individuals under the law was the only path to economic growth and a modern state, they also rejected protectionist legislation, corporate courts and laws, and corporate ownership. All of which, when worked out on the ground, adversely affected the communal village with its rights as a corporate entity and its common lands. And, in fact, in many places state laws breaking up such landholdings led not to a redistribution among the previous occupants or among the landless – although there were major exceptions – but, rather to their purchase by the powerful, and thus concentration of such lands in fewer hands. The Liberals, then, claimed to seek equality in an era of deep-rooted inequalities.

In Guatemala, too, attacks on peasant and village communal land began early. Under the presidency of Mariano Gálvez (1831–38) a new head tax on peasants of two pesos accompanied many confiscations.

Native Americans resisted in a variety of ways. Some resorted to legal proceedings and were successful enough to resist alienation of their lands throughout the Reforma. Others switched to smallholdings, especially in areas unattractive to others, and were able to obtain grants of the lands they had once owned collectively. There were many revolts by rural people, some of them indigenous. A revolt in the Sierra Gorda dragged on for years.

Perhaps the most famous was the so-called Caste War in Yucatan. There, embittered by their loss of land to henequen plantations, Maya peoples revolted in 1847 and tried to drive all others from the land. Years of warfare reduced the population by perhaps half, and an autonomous regime was constituted, mostly in the area that is today the state of Quintana Roo, with its own reconstructed form of government and religion. This independence lasted until 1901, or even beyond in isolated areas, and several expeditions by the Mexican army were needed to defeat it. Curiously enough, the Yucatan elites, which had become independent of Mexico to all intents and purposes after a revolt in 1839, now had to call in national troops or lose the entire peninsula. Thus the Caste War, paradoxically, brought Yucatan definitively into the Mexican state while affording local Maya a long period of autonomy.

In Guatemala, resistance took many of the forms already mentioned, but above all, native peoples and peasants urged on by some of the rural clergy rallied to the cause of a *caudillo* who promised to reverse the Liberal program. Rafael Carrera, who governed directly or indirectly from 1837 until his death in 1865, probably did little to improve indigenous levels of living but did halt land confiscations and even reversed some of them. His armies had large Mayan village and rural components.

The Ley Lerdo of 1856 had exempted *ejidos*, or village communal lands, from confiscation, although some were lost, as were *cofradía* lands. The Liberal constitution of the following year, however, incorporated the Ley Lerdo without mentioning *ejidos* and was thus more drastic. Wealthy rural people bought former church lands and became supporters of the government.

The War of the Reform (1858–60) and the French intervention and Maximilian's empire (1862–67) were periods of such upheaval and destruction that indigenous participation is hard to determine. Conservative *caudillos* such as Tomás Mejía of Querétaro opposed the Ley Lerdo and *ejido* alienations, and threw their support to the opponents of President Benito Juárez. Others fought for their fellow Indian, Juárez. Nor has the French intervention been studied from the indigenous point of view. Maximilian's government was surprisingly liberal, at least in its proclaimed intentions, and put an end to debt peonage in 1865, something the Liberal regimes had not done. The imperial government also reversed some of the clauses of the 1857 constitution, restoring to Indian villages the right to corporate ownership of land and granting *ejidos* to many landless villages. Doubtless such policies attracted some native people and brought them to Maximilian's armies, at least sporadically. Most, however, seem to have responded to Juárez's call for patriotism and a national crusade against foreign intervention.

With the restored republic of President Juárez and his successor Sebastián Lerdo de Tejada, native opposition to the Liberals' land polices and anticlericalism continued. Apart from the Caste War in Yucatan, the most notable rebels were the followers of Manuel Lozada of Tepic, the so-called Tiger of Alica, who set up a somewhat autonomous republic in Nayarit, returning confiscated lands to villages. Juárez made little attempt to control him, no doubt preoccupied elsewhere. President Lerdo attacked with federal troops, captured Lozada, had him shot, and returned much of the Indian village lands to haciendas.

Revolts continued during the first term of Porfirio Díaz (1876–80), some protesting seizures of Indian village lands. Especially after his first term President Díaz proved to be a greater enemy of Indian landholdings than any of his predecessors. Much Indian community land remained at the end of the Reforma, but in 1875, 1883, and 1894 the Díaz government extended an earlier decree of 1863, insisting on clear titles to land – which often led to their sale – and permitting large numbers of colonization projects. It has been estimated that under these new attacks some 96 million acres of *baldíos,* or vacant state lands, were turned over to private ownership.

The 1883 law especially encouraged land companies to survey public lands for "subdivision and settlement." For these surveying services some companies, among them ones of doubtful repute, obtained up to one-third of the land in question and permission to buy the rest at bargain price. If owners or *ejidos* could not produce clear titles, their land became public *baldíos* and subject to survey and reallocation. If, on the other hand, villages could show clear titles, but these were *ejido* titles, then these lands were threatened under the terms of the Reforma Constitution of 1857. Sugar interests in the small state of Morelos fared especially well in the first decade of the twentieth century, and Indian communities, later to rally to the cause of Emiliano Zapata, were stripped of most of their landholdings. In the nation in general, land companies held one-fifth of the total land mass of Mexico by the first years of the new century, and most villages had lost all or part of their ejidos. By 1900, peons, including hacienda workers, were living in poorer conditions than they had been in the final years of the colonial period.

Corruption and greed were certainly part of the Porfiriato, especially during its later decadent period, but its land policies were part of an overall view of society expounded by some of Díaz's advisors, the so-called Científicos. Some of these economists and social planners had become believers in the mixture of modernization theories and Social Darwinism called "positivism," and firmly believed in the leadership, in fact dictatorship, of progressive elites. Accordingly, to the extent that the Científicos were interested in the Mexican Indian it was in ways to bring the Indian into the modern world. European culture was best, the *criollo* or westernized class was next, and the Indian was a drag on national development: thus the mixture of paternalism and oppression under which native peoples suffered thoroughout the nineteenth century, and especially under the Porfiriato.

Indian groups that stubbornly remained outside the Porfirian development projects or, worse still, resisted in defense of their lands or rights, suffered most. The government used them as a forced-labor force in frontier agricultural projects, many of them foreign-owned or -financed. The Yaquis of Sonora, that peculiarly persecuted yet fiercely autonomous nation, suffered a series of deportations, mostly between 1900 and 1910, to Yucatan's henequen plantations and elsewhere. Estimates of the numbers ejected from tribal lands and enslaved ranged as high as 15,000, although many authorities agree that perhaps slightly more than half as many were deported. Other Yaquis, perhaps a thousand or more, fled across the border, many of them to southern Arizona, where their descendants live today.

Equally notorious was the treatment of the highland Tzeltals and Tzotzils of Chiapas, whose sufferings and deportations to the lowlands of Tabasco were recorded in B. Traven's novels. Trapped into various kinds of forced labor by advances of money and goods, or simply forced to sign contracts with Tabasco companies, many died on the foreign-owned rubber plantations and lumbering projects of the lowlands.

Such treatment, the many wars and revolts, a wretched level of living, epidemics, and loss of land were obvious factors in the demographic trajectory undergone by native peoples in nineteenth-century Mexico. Much of this demographic history is still unknown, but it is obvious from what we do know that Indian peoples suffered a considerable relative decline between independence and the overthrow of the Porfiriato.

None of the figures we have can be considered more than impressionistic. Modern censuses are notoriously unreliable – witness the furor in the United States in 1998 over the methods to be used to capture the millions of uncounted – and the ones of the nineteenth century were probably even less accurate. Above all there was the problem of classification. Who was Indian? Was it a linguistic category or one related to "culture" or lifestyle? Obviously, little could be made of biology or phenotype, although many nineteenth-century people seemed to believe that such nebulous categories could be used to distinguish people from one another. There was considerable confusion, then and in the twentieth century – see Van Young, Chapter 15 – between the two categories of peasant and Indian. Above all, classifications varied over time and place, depending on local politics, interethnic relations and perceptions, and, of course, the categories and ethnicities assigned to and by the local census taker or enumerator.

As long as specific burdens such as the head tax or labor drafts were assigned on the basis of being Indian, there was considerable incentive to escape from that category. Such matters as dress, diet, language, urban residence, and occupation also led to people being reassigned to new ethnic classifications. According to at least one author, the opposite could also be true, especially in the second half of the twentieth century. Census officials and other authorities found it expedient, if not politically necessary, to paternalistically assign an Indian category to people because of local cultural and political circumstances.

Such confusion, and many others still to be explored, make any statements about the size or demographic movements of Indian populations very dubious. Nevertheless, especially in Mexico, the student has a general impression of relative decline in the nineteenth century.

The population of Mexico around the time of independence was probably slightly over 6 million. Perhaps about half were classified as native or indigenous. By the time of the Reforma the total population had risen to about 7,800,000, but the indigenous population seems to have fallen to about one-third of that total. It may be that processes of rural proletarianization and changes in methods of classification rather than mortality rates account for this fall. Thereafter, although the Mexican population continued to grow – 8,750,000 in 1874, and just over 15,000,000 in 1910 – the native component grew very slowly or not at all, and remained under 3 million.

Central America's population at independence may have been about a million and a quarter, of whom perhaps 40 percent or so lived in Guatemala. There Indian peoples were a clear majority, especially in the rural areas, the north, and the highland west. In fact, if one were to omit cities and towns such as Guatemala City and Quezaltenango as well as some sixteen villages with large ladino populations, out of several hundred rural settlements, then indigenous inhabitants were an overwhelming majority. On some coasts, however, and in El Salvador, Honduras, and Nicaragua, native populations were a small remnant by 1825.

The general patterns observed in Mexico in the nineteenth century also prevailed in Guatemala, generally at a slower pace but with great regional variation. In the "zones of refuge," the *tierra fría* of the Cuchumatanes, and in Alta Verapaz, native populations held their own; in other areas, especially in Guatemala City, population growth was limited to the non-native populations, and many Indians probably passed into the categories of landless peasants and urban proletariats.

The Liberal Revolution of 1871 ended the rule of President Vicente Cerna (1865–71), who had continued the policies of Rafael Carrera. President Justo Rufino Barrios led this revolution and was president of Guatemala from 1873 to 1885. He increased the power of the state and set up a neoliberal and positivist regime that, under various guises, lasted until 1944. Barrios believed in export-led development and favored large-scale commercial agriculture, especially coffee. To these ends he permitted encroachment on Indian lands and various forms of long-term rentals, and initiated measures that made Indian labor, voluntary and forced, more available to others. The Reglamento de Jornaleros of 1877 was especially significant, and reconfirmed *mandamientos,* the forced-labor drafts that had existed since the colonial era. Uncoordinated Indian village resistance took many forms, including a few riots and the murder or expulsion of land surveyors. Work on haciendas as peons, or flight, were also used to avoid these impositions.

The impact of the coffee boom and Liberal economic policies were even more drastic among the remaining Indians and peasants of El Salvador. There, in the 1880s, President Rafael Zaldívar (1876–85) deprived them of communal lands, forcing them to become resident peons on haciendas or seasonal coffee workers.

Manuel Estrada Cabrera, who was dictator and president of Guatemala from 1898 to 1920, the longest rule in that nation's history, continued Barrios's policies, favoring coffee, exports, and the army and militias. The telegraph and telephone, combined with rapidly deployed militias in ladino towns, gave greater social control to the central government than ever before. *Mandamientos* were no longer respectable, especially on the international scene, and so were officially restricted or abolished from time to time, but in fact persisted in various forms until the end of the Estrada Cabrera regime, and probably well beyond. Labor recruiters (*habilitadores*) swarmed in the highlands in the first decades of the twentieth century, recruiting workers for lowland plantations via advances. Local ladinos, such as store owners, local officials, or teachers, often bought and sold labor contracts. Indian village authorities played a difficult and sometimes paradoxical role as brokers, suppliers of labor, petitioners and protectors of their own people, often at the same time. Their choices among these functions varied widely over place and time. In general, although Indian communities lost many lands, their legal struggles and resistance to the Liberals' attempts to establish a land tenure regime of private ownership were more successful than in El Salvador or Nicaragua, and in some regions much land remained under village control. One student of the land question even doubts if the coffee boom significantly lessened the quantity of land available to *milpa* agriculture. What it did was to block the expansion of subsistence agriculture at a time of rapidly growing urban and rural populations.

The role of indigenous Mexicans in the series of events and policies that came to be known as the Mexican Revolution (1910–29 and later) is hard to analyze. In the first place, there has been considerable disagreement over the meaning and accomplishments – if any, according to some – of the Revolution. Moreover, the emphasis, indeed the theories and policies, of revolutionary leaders and presidents changed drastically over time. Some claim, for example, that the neoliberalism and land policies of Presidents Carlos Salinas de Gortari (1988–94) and Ernesto Zedillo (1994–) are a return to the Porfiriato, as if the Revolution has now gone full cycle. Once again, moreover, the role of native people as actors rather than as a group acted upon, for better or worse, has been relatively neglected until the last decade or so.

In general, the leaders of the Mexican Revolution have been benevolently authoritarian and have believed in incorporation of native peoples into the modern state. Thus even the most pro-Indian of them, such as Lázaro Cárdenas (1934–38) and Adolfo López Mateos (1958–64), promoted assimilationist policies including education in Spanish. The various organizations provided to foment development among Indian peoples, such as the Instituto Nacional Indigenista of the Secretariat of Public Education, have also been accused of paternalism and assimilationism. The work of the Instituto Nacional de Antropología e Historia, founded in 1939, has once again been about Indians rather than by Indians until very recently.

One of the proclaimed aims of the revolutionary leaders, with varying degrees of enthusiasm, was the reversal of the agrarian policies of the Reforma and Porfiriato. In the early stages of the fighting there were notable differences between the leaders of the north, many of them Sonorans, and those of the more indigenous center and south. Northern *caudillos*, later presidents, including Francisco Madero (1911–13) and Venustiano Carranza (1917–20), showed little interest in agrarian reform or

the fate of indigenous peoples. Emiliano Zapata, the famous peasant leader from Morelos, distrusted these northerners, especially Carranza, a hacienda owner with ties to Porfirian policies, and fought for the return of village lands alienated during the previous half century, and the expropriation for peasant common lands, or *ejidos*, of one-third of all hacienda lands.

Zapata's mistrust was justified by Carranza's agrarian policies. He distributed little land, and even ordered the return to previous owners of haciendas seized during the Revolution, including those assigned by the counterrevolutionary Victoriano Huerta (president 1913–14), whose land distributions had included the granting of seventy-eight *ejidos* to the Yaquis and Mayos.

With some reluctance, however, Carranza accepted the revolutionary Constitution of Querétaro of 1917, which, in its famous Article 27, decreed that all lands seized illegally during the Porfirian regime be returned to the previous owners. Lands, the document stated, could be seized by the state for the public good. Lands could now be held in common, a reversal of the Ley Lerdo, and this soon led to an emphasis on the *ejido*, or village communal lands. The redistribution of land, especially to village *ejidos*, speeded up under Carranza's two successors, Alvaro Obregón (1920–24), and Plutarco Elías Calles (1924–28). Some 11 million acres were reassigned, and the beginnings of a system of agrarian credit were established. Of equal significance, perhaps, was the new emphasis on rural education. José Vasconcelos, Obregón's minister of education, put into effect a rural school-building program in which over one thousand schools were constructed between 1920 and 1924, more than all those built in the previous half century. It is important to note, however, that, especially during the Calles regime, there was no segregation of Indian education, and all instruction was supposed to be in Spanish. Again, assimilation rather than cultural autonomy or reinforcement was the goal.

The regime of Lázaro Cárdenas (president 1934–38) brought the stated goals of the Revolution to the countryside at last. It is estimated that some 26 million acres of agricultural lands had been redistributed by all the revolutionary regimes before Cárdenas, and then 49 million acres by Cárdenas's government in just four years. Some twelve thousand villages benefited. By 1940 one-third of Mexicans had received land under the agrarian reform, most of the nation's arable land, and much of it had been granted in the form of *ejidos*.

Land use and credit were and are matters of debate. The creation of the Banco de Crédito Ejidal was supposed to solve the problem of the credit needed for agricultural development, but critics assert that in some instances it became as much of a tyrant as the worst of the *hacendados*, imposing conditions on peasant agriculturalists and villages that may not have been in their best interests. Officially organized Peasant Leagues became part of the governing apparatus of the ruling party, and also ignored *ejido* interests in many cases. At any event, the general opinion of those who studied such matters, until the most recent one or two decades, was that the agrarian reform, and especially the *ejido* program, had been an economic failure in most places, but a social and political success. Long after the death of their hero Zapata, for example, the peasantry of Morelos gained collective title to many of the sugar lands they had sought.

Individual Native American groups had varied experiences with the Mexican Revolution. The Yaquis, for example, who supported Obregón, felt betrayed by him and by President Calles, and continued to lose tribal lands. Cárdenas restored some of these, but conflict with non-Indian neighbors continues to this day.

The revolutionary political movements of the early decades of the twentieth century were the parents of widespread intellectual movements that came to be called *indigenismo*. In Mexico it was very much part of the Revolution, and, in various forms, it became government policy under Cárdenas. *Indigenistas* such as José Vasconcelos, miníster of education under Obregón, were put in charge of important programs, and Vasconcelos's book *Indología* (1927) argued vigorously in favor of ways in which Indians could be assimilated into national life via education, changes in the law, and economic development. Since the time of Cárdenas, pro-Indian policies have been part of government programs and rhetoric, although many critics claim that these have been paternalistic, ineffective, and above all hypocritical.

Most students believe the cultural by-products of the political movement to be of more importance. Archaeologists and anthropologists began to delve into the pre-Spanish past and to restore its monuments. A brilliant series of muralists and painters, such as Dr. Atl (1875–1964), Diego Rivera (1886–1957), and José Clemente Orozco (1883–1949) depicted Indian life, past and present, attacked clerical, upper-class, military, and North American exploiters of the native peoples, and pushed the revolution to greater aims. All were internationally famous. Similar movements appeared in architecture, philosophy, and, above all, literature, where novels of protest such as Mariano Azuela's *Los de abajo* (definitive edition, 1920) or Gregorio López y Fuentes's *El Indio* (1935) try to represent types and classes rather than individuals.

Mexican *indigenismo* spread to other countries with large Native American populations, although once again its cultural results were more impressive than the political ones. In Guatemala a series of folklorists and novelists made the world aware of the Indians' plight. Miguel Angel Asturias (1899–1974) won the Nobel prize for literature, and among his novels *Hombres de maíz* (1949) is one of the most Indianist.

By the 1960s *indigenismo* had suffered internal divisions and outside attack. Critics debated such questions as incorporation versus autonomy. The partisans of economic development and assimilation were accused of paternalism or even genocide, and they replied by claiming that their opponents were romantic and racist. *Indigenismo* was condemned for lack of results, even on its own terms. Government programs, art, and fiction were criticized for being, with a few exceptions, from outside Indian society. Little success could be expected, these critics said, until Indians took charge of their own political, economic, and cultural futures.

After Cárdenas's presidency, land reform lost much of its impetus. The last spurt of redistribution took place during the presidency of Adolfo López Mateos (1958–64), whose regime gave titles to about 30 million acres, more than any presidency since Cárdenas's. Once again, however, it should be noted that the López Mateos regime, while popular, brooked little dissent from below, even though López Mateos himself was a former labor minister. The reinforcement of the nation state on the capitalist model, with fully integrated citizens, was still one of the main goals.

After 1940, in fact, the peasantry and most of Mexico's native peoples began to lose ground, and their relative share of income, health facilities, education, and much else, declined. Land redistribution almost ceased, and large commercial agro-businesses found new favor, especially with the government of President Miguel Alemán (1946–52). Starved of credit, most *ejidos* failed to generate sufficient funds for their members, many of whom left for agricultural enterprises, the big cities, or the United States. By the 1970s and 1980s, living conditions in the most indigenous states of Mexico, such as Oaxaca, Yucatan, and Chiapas, had begun to fall noticeably. Population pressure and land hunger combined with the failure of policies. The poorest became poorer, according to the government's own statistics, and malnutrition and high infant mortality became obvious and urgent problems. Production of staple foods declined, and imports of maize grew, in spite of government subsidies for basic commodities. A growing middle class and an ephemeral oil export boom in the 1970s, which ended abruptly in 1981, helped to disguise these worsening inequities.

In the late 1980s and 1990s, neoliberal "free market" economists, many of them trained in the United States, became the dominant voices in Mexican government, especially during the presidency of Carlos Salinas de Gortari (1988–94). Their beliefs, when applied to the worsening situation of the Mexican rural poor, led them to conclude that the *ejido*, and even price supports to some extent, had failed, and that privatization in industry and a free market in land would begin to solve endemic problems. Not all price supports were withdrawn, but the cost of many staples rose steeply. Article 27 of the constitution was altered, and the *ejido* system based on Article 27 ended. Individual landowners could now rent, mortgage, or sell their shares as they saw fit. Salinas's support of the North American Free Trade Agreement (NAFTA) led to an uprising in Chiapas (January 1994), under the aegis of the Ejército Zapatista de Liberación Nacional (EZLN). Most people within the movement appear to be Chiapas peasants of indigenous background. Negotiations with the central government have continued intermittently ever since. Within the governing party (Partido Revolucionario Institucional, or PRI) debates over neoliberal solutions to national problems have intensified.

In Guatemala the last of the Liberal presidents and dictators, Jorge Ubico (1931–44) built a powerful regime allied to banana and coffee export industries. His vagrancy laws (1934), which resembled earlier labor drafts, helped supply inexpensive Indian labor to these industries.

His overthrow in the Guatemalan Revolution of 1944 seemed to promise some improvement in native conditions. Decree 900 (1952), proclaimed by President Jacobo Arbenz (1951–54) made a small beginning as far as redistribution of land was concerned, but quickly brought opposition from the United Fruit Company (UFCO) and from the U.S. government. Arbenz was overthrown by a U.S.-sponsored invasion from Honduras, and the reforms of the revolution were canceled. With brief intermissions, the military have ruled Guatemala ever since. Civil wars have devastated the countryside and poisoned national political life. Rising poverty and terror in the countryside increased greatly during the regime of General Romeo Lucas García (1978–82), killing thousands, emptying villages, and sending refugees to Mexico and the United States (see George Lovell, Chap. 21, this volume). Massacres of entire Indian communities made the military governments notorious in the world press in the 1980s and 1990s. Some possibility of a peace pact, brokered by the Catholic Church, led some refugees to return after 1996, but the depleted Indian community, publicized by Nobel Peace prize winner Rigoberta Menchú, although remarkably resilient, remained wary.

In both Mexico and Guatemala, Indian leaders have struggled to create more autonomous and vigorous entities. Faced by privatization, NAFTA, the demise of the *ejido*, army massacres, and, above all, by a great disillusionment with government programs and what they perceived to be the paternalism of *indigenismo*, such organizations as the Frente Independiente de Pueblos Indios (FIPI) in Mexico, and the Consejo de Organizaciones Mayas de Guatemala (COMG) have sponsored many programs. Texts and school programs in native languages, group participation in politics, and pan-Indian meetings and exchanges, may lead to some improvement in the desperate situation in which Mesoamerican native peoples now find themselves.

BIBLIOGRAPHICAL ESSAY

Those looking for a place to begin studies of the native peoples of Mesoamerica since the Spanish invasion are fortunate to have two very considerable sources: *The Handbook of Middle American Indians* (Austin, TX, 1964–76), under the general editorship of Robert Wauchope, 16 vols., was augmented by another six volumes, *Supplement to the Handbook of Middle American Indians* (Austin, TX, 1981–92), Victoria R. Bricker, general editor. Even more up-to-date is the fine series, still under way, of Mexican Indian regional and topical histories, the many volumes of *Historia de los pueblos indígenas de México*, ed. Teresa Rojas Rabiela and Mario Humberto Ruz (Mexico, 1994–). Several of these studies are mentioned later in this essay.

Equally valuable are the various journals published in Mexico, Guatemala, and elsewhere, which devote themselves to the study of Mesoamerican native peoples. Good examples of this type have been *Estudios de cultura maya*, *Estudios de cultura náhuatl*, *Guatemala indígena*, and *Tlalócan*. Several other categories of journals contain appropriate materials. Those dedicated to the study of Native Americans in general, such as *América Indígena* and *The American Indian Quarterly*, have published many essays and research notes about native Mesoamericans. Also worth careful review are the various journals on Mexican or Central American history, such as *Anales de la Sociedad de Geografía e Historia* (Guatemala), *Historia Mexicana,* and *Historias* (Mexico). Mexican regional journals such as *Estudios Jaliscenses* and *La Palabra y el Hombre* (Veracruz), to name but two of many, are also of use and have published many essays about regional native peoples.

From time to time, researchers have attempted to review the state of long periods of Mesoamerican Indian historiography. A good example is Francisco G. Hermosillo, "Indios en cabildo: historia de una historiografía sobre la Nueva España," *Historias* 26 (1991): 25–63, which covers the colonial period.

The arguments in Spain itself over the nature of Native American peoples continued in the colony. What was the nature of, for example, Aztec religion, and what respect was it due? Were the larger Indian languages civilized, or the babblings of savages? Essays such as Georges Baudot, "Fray Toribio Motolinía denunciado ante la Inquisición por Fray Bernardino de Sahagún en 1572," *Estudios de cultura náhuatl* 21 (1991): 127–32, or Ignacio Guzmán Betancourt, " 'Policía' y 'Barbarie' de las lenguas indígenas de México, según la opinión de gramáticos e historiadores novohispanos," *Estudios de cultura nahuatl* 21 (1991): 179–218, attest to the seriousness and intensity of these debates. Supposed Indian sexual vices, their cannibalism, human sacrifices, and other traits, caused scandal, condemnation, and some moderate discussion. For the European views on native sexuality, see Pierre Ragon, *Les Amours Indiennes ou l'Imaginaire du Conquistador* (Paris, 1992).

Had the Indians encountered Christianity in some remote past, or were they, in fact, wandering Jews from Eurasia? Typical of these discussions is Chap. 23, "That the opinion of many who say that the Indians are of Jewish descent is false," in José de Acosta, S.J., *Historia natural y moral de las Indias,* ed. Edmundo O'Gorman, (Mexico, 1962). Louis-André Vigneras sums up these beliefs and debates in "Saint Thomas, Apostle of America," *Hispanic American Historical Review* 57 (1977): 82–90.

The archaeology of Mesoamerica is thoroughly discussed in Part 1 of this volume, and in at least six volumes of the *Handbook of Middle American Indians* and its *Supplements.* So, too, are most of the extant codices.

For the great age of native and mestizo chroniclers, see, for example, Domingo Francisco de San Antón Muñón Chimalpahin Cuauhtlehuanitzin, *Codex Chimalpahin*, 2 vol., Susan Schroeder, general editor (Norman, OK, 1997); Fernando de Alva Ixtlilxochitl, *Historia de la nación chichimeca*, ed. Germán Vázquez, (Madrid, 1985); Diego Muñoz Camargo, *Historia de Tlaxcala*, ed. Germán Vásquez, (Madrid, 1986); Fernando Alvarado Tezozomoc, *Crónica mexicana*, 2nd ed., ed. Manuel Orozco y Berra, (Mexico, 1975); and *Memorial de Sololá, Anales de los cakchiqueles. Título de los señores de Totonicapán*, 2nd ed. (Guatemala, 1991).

For Sahagún, see Bernardino de Sahagún, *General history of the things of New Spain: Florentine codex*. 13 vols. in 12, ed. and trans. Arthur J. O. Anderson and Charles E. Dibble, (Santa Fe, NM, and Salt Lake City, 1950–82), and the many other writings by Anderson and Dibble on Sahagún and related topics. Sahagún studies continue to flourish, e.g., Pilar Máynez, "Sahagún y Durán: Intérpretes de la cosmovisión indígena," *Estudios de cultura náhuatl* 26 (1996): 163–72.

Hans Lenz describes how these native codices were produced in "Breves comentarios sobre algunas cosas relacionadas con el papel indígena," *Historias* 31 (October–March, 1994): 147–59. The aims and accomplishments of the native historiographical tradition, ending more or less with Alvarado Tezozomoc, are discussed in Hanns J. Prem, "Historias. Una tipología y las consecuencias para sus interpretaciones," *Historias* 32 (April–September 1994): 21–43; and the uses that moderns can make of these writings can be seen in such as Herbert R. Harvey, "Household and Family Structure in Early Colonial Tepetlaoztoc. An Analysis of the Códice Santa María Asunción," *Estudios de cultura náhuatl* 12 (January–April 1994): 275–94.

Some of the major editions of the other chroniclers are: Diego Durán, *Historia de las Indias de Nueva España e islas de la Tierra Firme*, ed. Angel Garibay, (Mexico, 1967); Gonzalo Fernández de Oviedo y Valdés, *Historia general y natural de las Indias*, 5 vols., ed. Juan Pérez de Tudela Bueso (Madrid, 1959); Antonio Herrera de Tordesillas, *Historia general de los hechos de los castellanos en las Islas y Tierra firme del Mar Océano, o Décadas*, 4 vols. ed. Mariano Cuesta Domingo (Madrid, 1991); Diego de Landa, *Relación de las cosas de Yucatán*, ed. María del Carmen León Cázares (Mexico, 1994); Juan López de Velasco, *Geografía y descripción universal de las Indias*, ed. Marcos Jiménez de la Espada, (Madrid, 1971); Motolinía (Toribio de Benavente), *Historia de los indios de la Nueva*

España, 2nd ed., ed. Edmundo O'Gorman, (Mexico, 1973); Andrés Pérez de Ribas, My Life Among the Savage Nations of New Spain, ed. and trans. Tomás Antonio Robertson (Los Angeles, 1968); Ignaz Pfefferkorn, *Sonora: a description of the province*, ed. and trans. Theodore E. Treutlein, (Tucson, 1989); Antonio de Remesal, *Historia general de las Indias Occidentales, y particular de la gobernación de Chiapa y Guatemala*, 2nd ed., 2 vols. (Guatemala, 1932); and Juan de Torquemada, *Monarquía indiana*, 3rd ed., 7 vols. (Mexico, 1975–85).

On the tribute, see José Miranda, *El tributo indígena en la Nueva España durante el siglo XVI* (Mexico, 1952), and Francisco González de Cossío, *El libro de las tasaciones de pueblos de la Nueva España* (Mexico, 1952). René Acuña took on the enormous task of publishing the transcribed and edited *Relaciones Geográficas*. See *Relaciones Geográficas del Siglo XVI: México* 10 vols. (Mexico, 1982–87). For discussion, consult the essays by Howard Cline and Robert West in vol. 12 of the aforementioned *Handbook of Middle American Indians*.

The literature on the Black Legend and the indigenous population collapse is vast. The following collection tries to establish a baseline: William M. Denevan, ed., *The Native Population of the Americas in 1492*, rev. ed. (Madison, WI, 1992). Sherburne F. Cook and Woodrow Borah, *Essays on Population History: Mexico and the Caribbean*, 3 vols. (Berkeley, CA, 1971) is typical of the work of these pioneers. See also the various views in Elsa Malvido and Miguel Angel Cuenya, comps., *Demografía histórica de México, siglos XVI–XIX* (Mexico, 1993). For Central America, the appropriate bibliography is to be found in W. George Lovell and Christopher H. Lutz, eds., *Demography and Empire: A Guide to the Population History of Spanish Central America, 1500–1821* (Boulder, CO, 1995). For epidemics in colonial Spanish America in general, a recent source is Noble David Cook and W. George Lovell, eds., *Secret Judgments of God: Old World Disease in Colonial Spanish America* (Norman, OK, 1992). Enrique Florescano's classic work, *Precios del maíz y crisis agrícolas en México (1708–1810)* (Mexico, 1969), deals with agrarian conditions in the eighteenth century but has appropriate information and analysis, as does Enrique Florescano and Elsa Malvido, comps., *Ensayos sobre la historia de las epidemias en México*, 2 vols. (Mexico, 1982).

Attempts to differentiate between Spanish-imposed rates of change according to differences within indigenous social structures can be found in, for instance, Miguel Alberto Bartolomé, "La identidad residencial en Mesoamérica: fronteras étnicas y fronteras coloniales," *América Indígena*

52 (January–June 1992): 251–73, and above all in Judith F. Zeitlin, "Ranchers and Indians on the Southern Isthmus of Tehuantepec; Economic Change and Indigenous Survival in Colonial Mexico," *Hispanic American Historical Review* 69 (February 1989): 23–60.

James Lockhart is the leading U.S. scholar of the group that has emphasized documents in Nahuatl. See his comprehensive book, *The Nahuas After the Conquest: A Social and Cultural History of the Indians of Central Mexico, Sixteenth Through Eighteenth Centuries* (Stanford, CA, 1992). A comparison with Charles Gibson's classic, *The Aztecs Under Spanish Rule: A History of the Indians of the Valley of Mexico, 1519–1810* (Stanford, CA, 1964), will show how the emphasis has changed in studies of approximately the same place and time. Several of Lockhart's students have followed his lead. Good examples are Sarah L. Cline, *Colonial Culhuacán 1580–1600, A Social History of an Aztec Town* (Albuquerque, NM, 1986), and Robert S. Haskett, *Indigenous Rulers, An Ethnohistory of Town Government in Colonial Cuernavaca* (Albuquerque, NM, 1981). Nahuatl studies of historical processes in Mexico are, of course, much older and still continue, although many of them have followed different interests. One of the great pioneers is Miguel León-Portilla, whose many contributions, on both precolumbian Mesoamerica and the centuries after contact, are too numerous to list here. His *The Broken Spears: The Aztec Account of the Conquest of Mexico* (Boston, 1986) has gone through several editions and has been their first introduction to the native Mesoamerican for many students in the United States. Other notable works of a similar tradition are: Pedro Carrasco Pizano and Jesús Monjarrás-Ruiz, eds., *Colección de documentos sobre Coyoacán*, 2 vols. (Mexico, 1976–78), which contains much analysis; Bernardo García Martínez, *Los pueblos de la sierra: El poder y el espacio entre los indios del norte de Puebla hasta 1700* (Mexico, 1987); and Constanza Vega Sosa, *Códice Azoyú 1, el reino de Tlachinollan* (Mexico, 1991).

For Yucatan, see the contrasting view of Indian survival and connection to the outside world in Nancy M. Farriss, *Maya Society Under Spanish Colonial Rule: The Collective Enterprise of Survival* (Princeton, NJ, 1984), and Robert Patch, *Mayas and Spaniards in Yucatan, 1648–1812* (Stanford, CA, 1993.) See also Pedro Bracamonte y Sosa, *La memoria enclaustrada; historia indígena de Yucatán, 1750–1915* (Mexico, 1994).

The Indian–ladino dichotomy, in both settlement and culture, is well covered in Lovell's Chapter 21 and its bibliography, this volume. Local studies, especially in eastern Guatemala, may prove some of the argument to be too large a generalization. Grant Jones in Chapter 20, this volume, stresses the relationship of native peoples to porous frontiers. The idea of zones of refuge was first thoroughly explored by Gonzalo Aguirre Beltrán in his *Regiones de refugio* (Mexico, 1967; English translation, 1979).

In the same fashion Deeds and Frye, in Chapters 13 and 14, this volume, discuss the situation in the north of our area. The latest word on that unique nation, the Yaquis, is Evelyn Hu-Dehart's *Adaptación y resistencia en el Yaquimi: Lost yaquis durante la colonia* (Mexico, 1995).

The old classic on Indian conversion is Robert Ricard, *La "conquête spirituelle" du Mexique* (Paris, 1933). All the debates mentioned here and the appropriate bibliography can be found in William B. Taylor's very important work, *Magistrates of the Sacred: Priests and Parishioners in Eighteenth-Century Mexico* (Stanford, CA, 1996). See also Christian Duverger, *La conversión de los indios de Nueva España* (Mexico, 1993), which contains more Sahagún documents.

The literature on native accommodation, resistance, and revolt is so vast and scattered that only a few examples can be mentioned here. Some of them are: Alicia M. Barabas, *Utopías indias. Movimientos socioreligiosos en México* (Mexico, 1989); María del Carmen León, Mario Humberto Ruz, and José Alejos García, *Del katun al siglo: Tiempos de colonialismo y resistencia entre los mayas* (Mexico, 1992); John Tutino, *From Insurrection to Revolution in Mexico: Social Bases of Agrarian Violence, 1750–1940* (Princeton, NJ, 1986); and, for the nineteenth century, Leticia Reina, *Las rebeliones campesinas en México (1819–1906)* (Mexico, 1980). An especially good case of Indian assertiveness is Irma Guadalupe Cruz Soto, "Querellas de cabildos en la 'Garganta del Reyno': indios y españoles en Orizaba al final de la Colonia," *La Palabra y el Hombre* 99 (July–September, 1996): 37–71.

For the great changes in late-eighteenth-century Mexico, see Van Young's Chapter 15, this volume, and his *La crisis del orden colonial: Estructura agraria y rebeliones populares de la Nueva España, 1750–1821* (Mexico, 1992). For prices, see the aforementioned work by Florescano, *Precios del maíz*. The beginnings of the creation of a rural proletariat can be seen, for western Morelos, in Brígida Von Mentz, *Pueblos de indios, mulatos y mestizos, 1770–1870. Los campesinos y las transformaciones protoindustriales en el poniente de Morelos* (Mexico, 1988).

The works already cited by Eric Van Young and William Taylor discuss popular participation in the struggles for independence. So, too, did somewhat earlier work, such as Brian Hamnett, *Roots of Insurgency:*

Mexican Regions, 1750–1824 (Cambridge, 1980). Perusal of documentary collections about the wars yields some glimpses of Indian and popular participation. See, for example, Juan E. Hernández y Dávalos, comp., *Colección de documentos para la historia de la guerra de independencia de México de 1808 a 1821*, 2nd ed., 6 vols. (Liechtenstein, 1968); and Juan López, ed., *Insurgencia de la Nueva Galicia en algunos documentos*, 2 vols. (Guadalajara, 1984).

The full story of Central American independence is far from clear in spite of a large monographical literature. Nor is it clear to what extent the increase in Indian rebelliousness in the half century or so before independence was related, if at all, to a desire for the overthrow of Spanish colonialism. For the moment, compare Robert M. Carmack, *Rebels of Highland Guatemala: The Quiche-Mayas of Momostenango* (Norman, OK, 1995), and Severo Martínez Peláez, *Motines de indios: La violencia colonial en Centroamérica y Chiapas* (Puebla, 1996).

The assault on Indian lands during the nineteenth century, beginning regionally long before the Ley Lerdo (1856), has produced an enormous literature. In some places resistance was fairly successful, e.g., Frank Schenk, "La desamortización de las tierras comunales en el estado de México (1856–1911). El caso del distrito de Sultepec," *Historia Mexicana* 45 (July–September 1995): 3–37, and Robert J. Knowlton, "La división de las tierras de los pueblos durante el siglo XIX: el caso de Michoacán," *Historia Mexicana* 40 (July–September, 1990): 3–25. In other regions the concentration of land in few hands was startling, e.g., Francisco Javier Castellón Fonseca, "Reparto agrario en Nayarit (1934–1938)," *Estudios Jaliscenses* 4 (May 1991): 38–51. For a general survey, see Miguel Mejía Fernández, *Política agraria en México en el siglo XIX* (Mexico, 1979). The Guatemalan situation, then and later, is skillfully analyzed in David McCreery, *Rural Guatemala, 1760–1940* (Stanford, CA, 1994).

The Caste War has produced some recent literature and two older classics: Nelson Reed, *The Caste War of Yucatan* (Stanford, CA, 1964) and Moisés González Navarro, *Raza y tierra: La guerra de castas y el henequén* (Mexico, 1970). It also produced its share of atrocities, such as the deportations described in Javier Rodríguez Piña, *La guerra de castas. La venta de indios mayas a Cuba, 1848–1861* (Mexico, 1990).

For the life and times of Manuel Lozada of Tepic, see Jean Meyer, *La tierra de Manuel Lozada* (Mexico, 1989), and the older Silvano Barba González, *La lucha por la tierra: Manuel Lozada* (Mexico, 1956).

For Porfirian land policies, consult R. H. Holden, *Mexico and the*

Survey of Public Lands: The Management of Modernization, 1876–1911 (DeKalb, IL, 1993). Positivism has also produced a considerable literature, then and now, such as Gabino Barreda, *La educación positivista en México* (Mexico, 1978); Abelardo Villegas, *Positivismo y porfirismo* (Mexico, 1972); and W. Dirk Raat, "Los intelectuales, el positivismo y la cuestión indígena," *Historia Mexicana* 20 (1971): 412–27.

For Yaqui deportations, see Evelyn Hu-Dehart, *Yaqui Resistance and Survival: The Struggle for Land and Autonomy, 1821–1910* (Madison, WI, 1982), and Claudio Dabdoub, *Historia de El Valle del Yaqui* (Mexico, 1964). There are five novels in B. Traven's (Chiapas) "Jungle Cycle." Typical is *March to the Montería* (New York, 1971).

For Mexico's nineteenth-century population, see Viviane Brachet de Márquez, *La Población de los Estados de México en el siglo XIX* (Mexico, 1976), and several of the essays in Consejo Nacional de Población, ed., *El poblamiento de México: Una visión histórico-demográfica* (Mexico, 1993). For Guatemala, see the aforementioned book by McCreery, *Rural Guatemala.*

A fine general survey of rural unrest over land is Tutino, *From Insurrection to Revolution.* For agrarian policies and land reform, consult Dana Markiewicz, *The Mexican Revolution and the Limits of Agrarian Reform* (Boulder, CO, 1993), and Jesús Silva Herzog, *El agrarismo mexicano y la reforma agraria: exposición y crítica,* 2nd ed. (Mexico, 1964). Contrasting views of Lázaro Cárdenas and his achievements emerge from Heather Fowler Salamini, *Agrarian Radicalism in Veracruz, 1920–38* (Lincoln, NE, 1978), and Marjorie Becker, *Setting the Virgin on Fire. Lázaro Cárdenas, Michoacán Peasants, and the Redemption of the Mexican Revolution* (Berkeley, CA, 1995). See also Adolfo Gilly, *El cardenismo, una utopía mexicana* (Mexico, 1994).

For *indigenismo* at the time of the revolution, a useful collection is Alfonso Caso et al., *La Política indigenista en México: métodos y resultados,* 2nd ed., 2 vols. (Mexico, 1973). Also indicative of thinking at that time is Gonzalo Aguirre Beltrán's *El proceso de aculturación* (Mexico, 1981).

Modern critiques of the government's Indian policies and of *indigenismo,* and attempts to redefine the situation with Indians' own concerns in mind, have created a large body of work. Typical critiques of neoliberalism are Gilberto López y Rivas, *Nación y pueblos indios en el neoliberalismo,* 2nd ed. (Mexico, 1996), and the same author's "México en la encrucijada: reformas constitucionales y autonomía indígena," *La Palabra y el Hombre* 103 (July–September 1997): 79–88. Doubts about educational aims appear in Cheng Hurtado, "El dilema de la educación indígena: Desindianizar o fortalecer la etnicidad, *América Indígena* 40 (July–September 1995): 35–64. Critiques about past revolutionary policies in education are in Engracia Loyo, "La empresa redentora. La casa del estudiante indígena," *Historia Mexicana* 46 (July–September 1996): 99–131, which discusses the Calles regime. Similar questions about the utility of agricultural modernization for Indian peoples can be found in essays such as Alvaro González R., "Agricultura indígena y modernización ¿un matrimonio desastroso?" *América Indígena* 50 (April–September, 1990): 309–41, mostly about Oaxaca.

Two essays emphasizing the drive toward autonomous Indian organizations and action are Miguel Alberto Bartolomé, "Movimientos etnopolíticos y autonomías indígenas en México," *América Indígena* 40 (January–June 1995) (an issue largely devoted to both Chiapas and the EZLN), and Rodolfo Stavenhagen, "Las organizaciones indígenas: actos emergentes en América Latina," *La Palabra y el Hombre* 97 (January–March, 1996): 59–78.

13

LEGACIES OF RESISTANCE, ADAPTATION, AND TENACITY: HISTORY OF THE NATIVE PEOPLES OF NORTHWEST MEXICO

SUSAN M. DEEDS

INTRODUCTION: GEOGRAPHY AND ETHNOLOGY

"Listen, son," said an old man to his grandson, "you will be the one who strengthens the world. You will pass on all the things I have ever told you. If you don't tell others, they will be lost.

"We are the Rarámuris. We are the ones who hold up the world. We are its pillar. We must to remember what our forefathers told us because that is how we become more Rarámuri.

"We needn't be sad if others make us suffer. We must be strong even if they make us suffer."

That boy told others everything he had heard, but he couldn't do it everywhere. That is why in some places these truths are being lost.[1]

Although historians and anthropologists may understand the indigenous history of northwestern Mexico as multiple processes of cultural change in which discrete and composite groups continuously fashioned and refashioned their identities in the context of attempts by outsiders to dominate them, very different convictions shape indigenous views of the past. As the text quoted above indicates, the Rarámuri or Tarahumara rendering of history emphasizes the importance of memory in preserving an incorruptible worldview as well as the polarization that distinguishes "the people" from outsiders. The reproduction of knowledge is a culturally embedded social process for this particular northwestern Indian group – just as it is for non-Rarámuris (known to natives as *chabochis*, or children of the devil).[2]

---

[1] Translation of a text written by Dolores Batista from the municipio of Bocoyna in Chihuahua and reproduced in Carlos Montemayor, "La voz de los tarahumaras," *La Jornada Semanal*, July 9, 1995, 4.

[2] William L. Merrill, *Rarámuri Souls: Knowledge and Social Process in Northern Mexico* (Washington, DC, 1988).

The recounting that follows, although told with deep regard for indigenous cultures, is one that will be most intelligible to outsiders. It will be told as a history, not of a simple tension between survival and incorporation but of complex processes of resistance, obfuscation, accommodation, appropriation, subversion, revival, and invention. Nor is it a history in which critical symbols of cultural identity such as language, religion, land, and purity of blood can be neatly isolated to account for ethnogenesis. Moreover, in the northwest the interaction of native peoples with European intruders bore the peculiar stamp of a frontier volatility that lasted beyond the colonial period. Incorporation of the region by Spain and Mexico took place erratically over more than three centuries as expansionist states competed in North America, transforming interaction and migration patterns among groups less sedentary than Indian peoples to the south.

Contributing to the complexity of cultural change is the variety of indigenous groups encountered in the region at the time of contact. The geographic focus of this chapter is the most northwestern extension of Mesoamerica that today falls within the boundaries of Mexico. Anthropologists and historians customarily include it as a part of the even more amorphous Greater Southwest, whose connections to Mesoamerica are still being debated. The area considered here is synonymous with all but the eastern edge of Nueva Vizcaya into the eighteenth century and with the present states of Baja California Sur, Baja California Norte, Sinaloa, Sonora, Chihuahua, and Durango (Map 13.1).

Although physiographically diverse, the area shares a semi-arid to arid climate, with higher elevations receiving the most rainfall. The eastern part of the region is dominated by the Sierra Madre Occidental with its canyons and vast plateau crossed by rivers. The largest river system is the Conchos, which eventually empties into the Rio Grande. To the east of the rolling uplands and valleys at the foot of the mountains is the desert of the Bolsón de Mapimí. The western side of the Sierra Madre, with its canyons of 2,000 to 3,000 feet, drops precipitously down to the coastal plains that stretch along the Gulf of California in Sinaloa and Sonora. Rivers flow down through the plains to the Pacific. As one moves north, the hot, humid valleys of southern Sinaloa gradually give way to a dry desert climate. The entire northwestern region contains a wide variety of habitats and vegetation including high mountains with pine and oak forests, upland plateaus, deep canyons, lowland valleys, deserts, and seacoast.

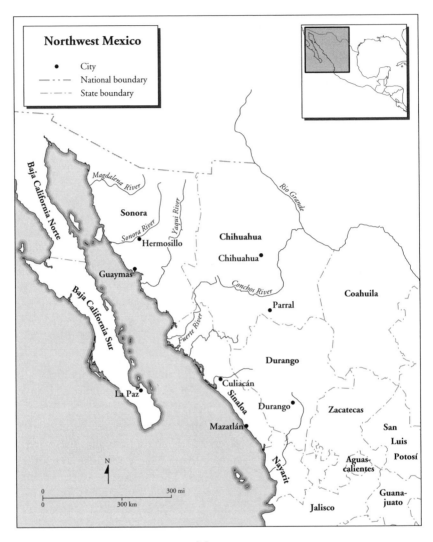

Map 13.1

Indian groups living in the northwest when the Spaniards arrived in the sixteenth century were far more numerous than they are today. Their exact numbers and distribution are impossible to determine for several reasons. Among them is the rapidity with which many groups lost their separate cultural identity because of either biological extinction or absorption by other groups. Another problem is that some of the peoples identified early by Spaniards may have been subgroups of larger units. The following is a conservative listing of peoples that most probably had a distinct identity or language (although with the exception of the Yuman and Athapaskan linguistic groups, most belonged to the Uto-Aztecan linguistic family). On the Lower California peninsula lived the Pericú, Guaycura, and Cochimí Indians. Across the gulf starting from northern Sinaloa were the Sinaloas, Zuaques, Tehuecos, Tahues, Tepahues, Mocoritos, Guasaves, Mayos, and Yaquis. Seris, Pimas, Opatas, and Eudeves occupied northern Sonora. Along with the Opatas, Eudeves, and Jovas who extended into the western foothills of the Sierra Madre were the Guarijíos, Guazapares, Chínipas, Témoris, and Tubares who lived at even higher elevations along the mountain divide. The present-day border between Sinaloa and Durango was the home of barranca-dwelling Acaxees and Xiximes. The Rarámuri occupied some of the eastern side of the Sierra Madre, but most lived in the lower plateaus and valleys to the east, as did the Tepehuanes and the Conchos. The area straddling the present border between Chihuahua and Coahuila contained countless band groups, among them Laguneros, Tobosos, and Cocoyames. After European contact, Apaches moved into northern Sonora and Chihuahua areas occupied by Pimas, Opatas, Janos, Jocomes, Sumas, and Jumanos.

Of the more than thirty groups at the time of contact, only a handful are recognized in the region today as exhibiting some linguistic and cultural characteristics that clearly differentiate them from the dominant society. The 1980 census counted approximately 150,000 native speakers over five years of age. Notable among these are Mayos, Yaquis, Seris, Pimas, Guarijíos, Rarámuri, and Tepehuanes. In the middle of the twentieth century, the work of anthropologist Edward H. Spicer persuasively encouraged reconstructing the history of some of these groups, which he designated as "enduring peoples." The fate of all of the northwestern groups is the story of this chapter, although for many of them the historical record and even the archaeological evidence so far unearthed have left scant traces. The colonial history of these oral societies is overwhelmingly a record created by outsiders, one that historians must read with critical and skeptical imagination. Even on those rare occasions when Indians were given voice in Spanish civil and criminal proceedings, we cannot forget that those voices were muted, edited, and transposed by alien authorities and legal structures. What follows is an attempt to analyze processes of change over more than four centuries in northwestern Mexico. The story begins with the eve of European contact in the

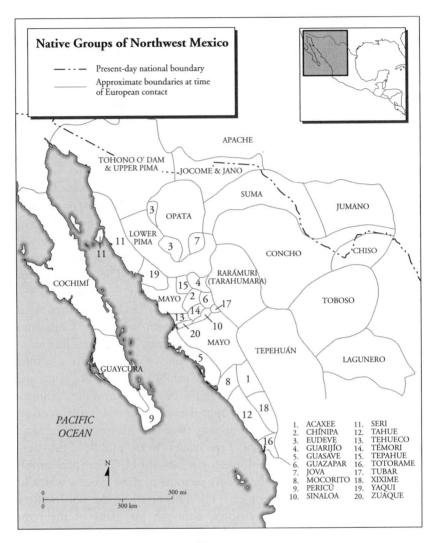

Native Groups of Northwest Mexico

— ·· — Present-day national boundary

——— Approximate boundaries at time
of European contact

APACHE

TOHONO O' DAM
& UPPER PIMA · · · JOCOME & JANO

SUMA

JUMANO

3 OPATA

LOWER
11 PIMA   3   7

11

CONCHO   'CHISO

19

RARÁMURI
(TARAHUMARA)

COCHIMÍ   15 4

MAYO   2 6   17

14   TOBOSO

13   10

20

MAYO

TEPEHUÁN

LAGUNERO

5

GUAYCURA

8   1

18

PACIFIC
OCEAN   9   12

16

1. ACAXEE	11. SERI
2. CHÍNIPA	12. TAHUE
3. EUDEVE	13. TEHUECO
4. GUARIJÍO	14. TÉMORI
5. GUASAVE	15. TEPAHUE
6. GUAZAPAR	16. TOTORAME
7. JOVA	17. TUBAR
8. MOCORITO	18. XIXIME
9. PERICÚ	19. YAQUI
10. SINALOA	20. ZUAQUE

N

0 — 300 mi
0 — 300 km

Map 13.2

region – with that "pristine" moment that should be seen not as static but as the point at which ever-changing cultures are first captured and described in written records. Although the evolutionary process was to be uniquely altered by the moment of contact, we must not forget that change, in some form or another, would have occurred inexorably without it.

THE MESOAMERICAN CONNECTION

Scholars disagree about the Greater Southwest's contacts with Meso-america in the late prehistoric period. The Mexican northwest, in partic-ular, has not undergone the extensive archaeological examination that would help us to understand what was happening in the fourteenth and fifteenth centuries, before Europeans arrived. The evidence we do have reveals the existence of many large towns with adobe architecture, sed-entary agriculture accompanied by canal irrigation, and interregional trade from the twelfth to the fourteenth centuries, not only among the Hohokam and Anasazi and their descendants in Arizona and New Mex-ico, but also in northwestern Mexico. The latest, largest site was in northwest Chihuahua at Paquimé in the Casas Grandes Valley. At its height in the fourteenth century, Paquimé housed more than 2,000 people in multistoried apartment blocks. Its features included an exten-sive irrigation system, a ceremonial complex, and large amounts of trade goods suggesting its role as a Mesoamerican trading outpost.

Many scholars therefore assert the existence of long-distance trade or of a series of connected smaller trade routes between the Southwest and Mesoamerica during certain times of the prehistoric period in such items as copper, turquoise, shells, salt, pottery, and obsidian. The trade routes and timing of contact are not as well established. Some argue that a Pacific Coast trading route through west-central Mexico was prominent in the Postclassic period. Within the settlement system of the Greater Southwest (where interregional ties may have transcended simple trade relations), some groups had hierarchical sociopolitical structures and well-differentiated administrative and trading elites. Most archaeologists have agreed that in the fifteenth century, the larger settlements of the Greater Southwest collapsed as a result of an unknown combination of several factors: climatic and demographic shifts, related environmental deterio-ration, warfare, and social and political upheavals. Following this line of interpretation, when the Spanish arrived in the sixteenth century, they found the aftermath of the collapse of the previous century: relatively small communities that did not reveal clearly differentiated socioeco-nomic strata and were neither economically nor politically interdepend-ent. In many groups, the notion of local community was less geographi-cally constrained than the European conception of a town.

For other scholars, however, this reversal resulted later and from different factors. They argue that, in spite of discrepant dendrochronological and ceramic evidence, the region had evolved into several statelets by the fifteenth century, and that although certain factors weakened those societies before contact, the death knell did not come until Old World diseases were carried up existing routes from Mesoamerica even before Europeans actually arrived in northern Mexico. According to this view, historians and anthropologists have exaggerated the differences between groups of the Greater Southwest and underestimated their interdependence and level of political organization. The spotty historical record of the sixteenth-century expeditions is not very helpful in resolving the dilemma, and we are forced to rely on the reports of seventeenth-century Spaniards as the main descriptive source for native societies on the eve of concerted Spanish attempts to incorporate them. The controversy, so far unresolved, is important, not least because its debaters posit different demographic and cultural realities that conditioned the outcome of encounter.

If precipitous demographic decline coincided with Spanish arrival in central Mexico, Spaniards moving northward may have encountered native societies at varying stages of disorienting socioeconomic transformations. Attempts by demographers to estimate contact populations have proven more difficult than identifying what groups inhabited which areas. One-half million is a conservative estimate for the region; others posit twice that number or more. When compared to central Mexico, even the higher counts point to scantier populations, as one would expect given the societal, cultural, climatic, and soil conditions. Population densities seem to have been greater in Sinaloa and southern Sonora than in the rest of the region.

ETHNOGRAPHIC CHARACTERISTICS OF CONTACT POPULATIONS

The geographic, ecological, and demographic peculiarities that defined the physical landscape of the Mexican northwest in the early sixteenth century would figure decisively in the subsequent patterns of interaction between natives and outsiders. Equally important, of course, were the traits that characterized the human panorama – in terms of political, economic, social, and religious organization. Once again, the latter cannot be easily summarized for so many diverse groups; even though the following synthesis conveys a false homogeneity, it is useful for identifying the elements that would figure in ensuing cultural encounter and conflict. With the exception of some riverine towns, by the late sixteenth century most northwestern Indians lived in dispersed settlements, or *rancherías*, where they cultivated maize, beans, and squash with digging sticks along water sources. They supplemented agriculture with hunting and gathering, sometimes changing *ranchería* locations in accordance with seasonal cycles and climatic conditions. These clusters could comprise from one or two dwellings to a hundred; in highland areas, *rancherías* tended to be smaller and more scattered. Perhaps a few of the more densely populated nuclei among various groups (for example, some of the Sinaloa Indians, the Xiximes, the Tepehuanes, and the Opatas) resembled towns with fortifications, more permanent adobe edifices, and irrigation ditches. It is even possible that these groups may have been attempting to establish some type of hegemony over neighboring groups. At the other end of the continuum, a scattering of groups (Seris as well as peoples of the California peninsula and the eastern deserts) depended solely on hunting and gathering, traveling in bands.

Political organization for all these groups was decentralized, with a headman or elders (*principales*) guiding the affairs of each band or *ranchería*. The degree of their political control ranged from more coercive among war chiefs to less authoritative among *ranchería* elders, who exercised moral suasion with oratorical skill in endeavoring to promote the well-being of the community. During the frequent periods of intertribal warfare that characterized the region and whose objectives included the acquisition of captives and goods, the influence of chief warriors extended over a larger territory within linguistic groups. War leaders earned their positions through demonstrations of bravery, and combat provided avenues for social mobility. There was trading between groups, although it is not clear to what extent these exchanges resembled earlier patterns of long-distance trade. Although the political hierarchy did not appear very complex to Spanish observers, some differentiation was noted. *Principales* tended to have more wives and goods. Ritual specialists with magical powers to cure and predict (called *hechiceros*, or sorcerers, by the Spaniards) also commanded community respect.

Ritual practices linked to material survival through agriculture and warfare incorporated the use of intoxicants (usually fermented maize or cactus) as well as dancing and chanting. Dreams were a source of knowledge and power, as were certain sacred spaces of the natural world. Supernatural powers were associated with sun, moon, and rain; dual supernaturals controlled wet and dry seasons. Idols symbolizing these and other forces, such as fertility and sickness, were common to most groups. Warfare was accompanied by ritual cannibalism or purification ceremonies with enemy scalps. The dead were feared and thought to pressure the living to join them.

Most of these groups had bilateral forms of kinship organization, and extended families cooperated in economic activities (through their productivity, additional wives and children added to a male's wealth and prestige). Among *ranchería* groups, households or family units had individual use-rights on communal croplands. Uncultivated areas were sources of wild animals and plants that were efficiently utilized, given the paltry productivity of much of the region. Agricultural and gathering tasks were performed by both men and women, whereas hunting with bow and arrow was men's work. Women, who were also weavers, potters, and basketmakers, for the most part seem to have occupied subordinate roles politically if not economically.

COLONIAL INTRUSIONS

Spaniards, therefore, encountered a rather disparate array of peoples whose disaggregation apparently increased during the sixteenth century after the first ephemeral contacts by Alvar Núñez Cabeza de Vaca and Francisco Vázquez de Coronado in the 1530s and 1540s, and the more pernicious *entradas* of slavers like Diego de Guzmán, who raided from Nueva Galicia into Sinaloa in the 1530s. Southern Sinaloa groups were quickly decimated by warfare and disease as Spaniards established more permanent settlements. The lure of silver drew non-Indians increasingly to the mining camps of Topia and Durango after the midcentury *entrada* of Francisco de Ibarra. Depopulation by disease was most precipitous in the areas of densest native settlement: the various Sinaloa groups below the Mayo River, the Acaxees and the Xiximes almost totally vanished within a century. In these areas, Indians were first enslaved, then made to pay tribute (Sinaloa) or to provide labor in *encomienda* or *repartimiento*. Where the early higher rates of population decline owing to virginsoil epidemics were accompanied or immediately followed by a significant Spanish coercive presence and unrelenting demands on native labor, the Indian population was less able to recover over time.

Although variant patterns of demographic decline manifested themselves, it must be noted that within a century after sustained European contact, all of the northwestern Indian groups experienced rates of population decline which have been estimated as ranging from 70 to 95 percent. The first appearance of an epidemic disease, such as smallpox or measles, had the potential to eradicate very high numbers of people in all age groups in a given locality, and elevated population loss from recurrent cycles of disease continued during the next two generations. Later disease episodes perpetuated the downward trend with high mortality rates among infants, children and pregnant women. The ability to reverse patterns of low birth rates and high death rates or to rebound from these epidemics, which tended to occur at intervals of five to eight years, depended upon many factors. These included degree of isolation, density of population settlements, time elapsed between epidemics, state of subsistence and nutrition, living conditions, potency of endemic diseases like syphilis and respiratory or enteric disorders, degree of ethnic intermixing, and extent of exposure to mistreatment and warfare. Among the groups like the Yaquis and Rarámuri that did recover, the demographic shift began in the mid-eighteenth century; this pattern resembles that of central Mexico, with contact and nadir taking place a century later in most of the northwest. Mortality induced by epidemic disease, then, was a constant during the colonial period; how it produced culture change was as multifaceted as were Spanish tactics of subordination and indigenous strategies for coping.

The colonial methods for subordinating indigenous groups varied in northwest Mexico according to the density and complexity of native populations, their proximity to mining areas, the numbers and types of invaders, and the degree of force that Spanish miners, *hacendados,* soldiers, and missionaries could exert. In addition, Spanish penetration was chronologically broken in the region, occurring at intervals that spanned more than a century. Native reactions were conditioned by even more complex combinations of variables. Among them were the rate of indigenous demographic recovery; the intensity of Spanish attempts to extract resources; timing, that is, the coincidence or interaction of the first two variables; ecological-geographic factors; native sociopolitical organization and mobility; and the indigenous capacity to manipulate ostensibly oppressive colonial features to maintain socioreligious cohesion. To make some sense, briefly, of chronological and cultural diversity, this chapter outlines several patterns of Spanish infiltration and indigenous responses. One must keep in mind that such a typology is arbitrary and cannot account for the instances where there is leakage from one category to another, and where there are not only differences between groups but also within them.

Although the initial Indian tendency was to flee or offer a friendly reception, after the devastation of the southern Sinaloa groups became known, their northern and eastern neighbors tended to react with hostility to intruders. Nonetheless, a combination of Spanish military force and disease usually served to overcome any armed resistance within a short time. Missionaries were then brought in to resettle Indians in villages, at first under Franciscan and then, after 1590, Jesuit tutelage. By the seventeenth century, Franciscan missions in Nueva Vizcaya were limited to the eastern and northeastern fringes. Missions organized agriculture with new patterns of cultivation and irrigation and imposed an alien hierarchy of officials (*gobernadores, tenientes, capitanes, alcaldes, fiscales*, and others), plus the ideals of town life and monogamy. To reinforce these ideals, civil and religious authorities brought Tlaxcalan and Tarascan settlers from central Mexico to provide the proper example of indigenous conformity. This practice was more common in the Mexican northeast, but Tlaxcalan barrios were founded in Durango and Chihuahua, and Nahuatl became a *lingua franca* in some areas. Later, more acculturated local Indians would serve this edificatory function. Notwithstanding the multifaceted attempt at suasion, where Jesuit missions were established in areas that had already attracted the economic interest of miners and landowners, they invariably met with rebellion within a generation or two.

FIRST-GENERATION REBELLIONS

First-generation rebellions dominated the early seventeenth century in the mining regions of Topia and Durango, where *encomenderos* had forced Acaxees, Xiximes, Conchos, and Tepehuanes to provide labor service in mining and agricultural activities. These groups had been increasingly pressed into service when slaves, either black or Indian (captured by Spanish slave raiders in the New Mexican and Sonoran frontier areas), could not fill the demand for labor. Although these disruptions along with smallpox and measles epidemics might have made the Jesuits attractive at first as shamans, organizers, and buffers, it was not long before Indians saw the disadvantages of mission life. The policy of congregating Indians in larger, more dense population nuclei eventually made them even more vulnerable to labor requirements, increasingly in the form of *repartimiento*, or forced rotational labor, and to epidemics.

When the labor demands and the disease episodes did not abate, rebellions erupted with the intent of removing all outsiders, religious and civilians alike. This goal must have appeared more feasible in the early stages of Spanish colonization, and varying numbers of non-Indians lost their lives in each case. Uprisings were led by Acaxees in 1601, Xiximes in 1610, Tepehuanes in 1616, Conchos, Rarámuri, and other eastern Nueva Vizcayan groups at midcentury, and Rarámuri and Pimas in the 1690s. Their basic common characteristic was that they occurred within a generation or two of the first effective penetration of Spaniards in mining areas and were responses to the cataclysmic labor demands, population decline, *congregación* in villages, and psychological pressures that accompanied the violent disruption of social networks and ritual activities for sustaining life. These rebellions were led by former war leaders and shamans, who invoked a vision of the past that was clearly autochtonous (often without rejecting all Spanish material introductions and the more abstract concepts of political hegemony embodied in kings and bishops) and inspired followers with millenarian promises of redemption and utopian paradises on earth. In first-wave rebellions, the imposed hierarchy of officials, the insistence on monogamous relationships and *congregación* in permanent villages, as well as the prohibition of rituals and warfare associated with subsistence, combined to deprive entire communities of former assurances and benefits. Although gift-giving by missionaries initially produced a compensatory interlude, this practice declined even as labor obligations increased and death from epidemic disease became more identified with Christian baptism and its administrators.

In spite of high mortality, in first-generation revolts, precontact extended kinship and ceremonial ties were still intact enough to promote solidarity and facilitate communication across sizable territories. Where rebels were best able to inspire intergroup loyalty and attract neighboring groups, as in the case of the Tepehuanes, they were more successful in disrupting Spanish activities. The Tepehuan rebellion was extinguished only after several years as well as the deaths of more than a thousand rebels and several hundred non-Indians (making it the most destructive of all of Nueva Vizcaya's first-generation revolts). Inevitably, in the end all of the revolts failed. They could not sustain indigenous solidarity as Spaniards recruited Indian allies from within their own groups as well as from traditional enemies, nor could they stockpile enough resources to outlast Spanish militias. Spanish governors imposed exemplary punishments on rebel leaders – executions with heads displayed on pikes and forced servitude – to deter future uprisings.

For most of these groups, the first-generation revolt was the sole armed resistance to Spanish rule. Some Acaxees and Xiximes participated in the Tepehuan uprising of 1616, but after 1620 they remained congregated in a handful of villages in the mountainous Jesuit mission provinces of Topia and San Andrés. With these groups, high mortality in virgin-soil epidemics, warfare, labor exploitation, and continuing cycles of disease combined to prevent demographic recovery. By the end of the seventeenth century, their villages looked largely mestizo, and a century later there were virtually no biologically pure Indians. There, much of the non-Indian population had become impoverished after the mines played out; a mixed population lived at subsistence level, cultivating corn and raising stock on smallholdings.

For the Tepehuanes, mixed results followed the failure of their rebellion. Some of them retreated into the mountains and barrancas of southwestern Chihuahua and along the Nayarit–Durango border, where others of their group had eluded missionization; today's several thousand surviving Tepehuanes stem from these nuclei, which had limited interaction with Europeans until the late nineteenth century. But the large majority of Tepehuanes succumbed to the renewed *congregación* that followed the uprising. Because their missions were closest to Spanish *reales* and haciendas in the Nueva Vizcayan heartland between Durango and Chihuahua cities, they were subject to escalating demands for seasonal agricultural labor through *repartimiento* in the seventeenth century, and their lands were increasingly encroached upon in the eighteenth by Spanish *hacendados*, whose markets for agricultural produce grew along with an expanding mining economy.

The several Rarámuri rebellions at midcentury did deter further penetration of their northwestern territory for nearly a quarter of a century, but those Rarámuri living in the eastern foothills and valleys of southern Chihuahua followed the pattern just described for the majority of Tepehuanes. From their mission base, they traded corn and other foodstuffs to Spanish towns for cloth and livestock, and sometimes sold their labor in the silver mines.

Although a significant number of Conchos served the Spaniards as military auxiliaries, another cohort – including some who lived in Franciscan missions and others who had eluded them – took part in the warfare waged by their more nomadic neighbors to the east and north (Tobosos, Salineros, Chisos, Cabezas, etc.) at mid-seventeenth century. Particularly among less sedentary groups, intertribal wars continued parallel to skirmishes with Spaniards. Although the latter had some of the characteristics of first-generation revolts, they also conformed to the actions of frontier raiders for whom intruding settlers offered a source for extracting surplus goods. The extremely arid Bolsón de Mapimí was a base of operations for many nomadic groups until the nineteenth century, and their raiding activities, which escalated in the dry season, tended to be most vexing to Spaniards, who found them more difficult to stem than rebellion. Raiding parties tended to increase in size over time as interband alliances became more common, and they ranged over wider areas as horses provided greater mobility. Salinero and Toboso Indians who were captured and resettled by Spaniards on haciendas or missions often joined the raiders or provided intelligence to them.

Because Spanish penetration of the northwest proceeded erratically in response to changing economic and political imperatives, some first-generation revolts occurred relatively late in the colonial period. After missions and mines finally penetrated the upper Tarahumara area in the 1670s and 1680s, rebellion erupted twice in the 1690s, with Rarámuri joined by northern Conchos, eastern Pimas, and other groups along the Sierra Madre divide between present-day Chihuahua and Sonora. Harsh repression followed the second revolt, and some Rarámuri accepted affiliation with the missions (rebuilt by Jesuits perhaps more willing to overlook Indian lapses in obedience and fugitivism). Not all chose this path, opting instead to isolate themselves farther west in extremely inhospitable mountain canyons.

One of the last instances of first-wave rebellion occurred in southern Baja California when Pericúes and Guaycuras revolted in 1734. In this case, the Indians were not responding to secular Spanish pressures since the Jesuits (who had arrived at the turn of the eighteenth century) had been very successful in keeping Europeans (except for a small contingent of soldiers) out of the peninsula. Rather, they were reacting to the catastrophic changes wrought by sedentarism in an ecological environment for which mission *reducciones* were ill-suited. Even food subsidies from mainland missions could not mitigate the effects of epidemic disease and starvation induced by disruptions in the delicate hunting-and-gathering subsistence system worked out by Indians in this mostly barren desert region. Attempts to enforce monogamous relationships further crippled the possibility of population recovery and wrecked subsistence strategies. The revolt was subdued by troops from Sonora after two Jesuits had been killed. "Civilization" proved especially calamitous for Baja California groups, which boasted few survivors by the early nineteenth century.

LATER REVOLTS, RAIDING, AND FLIGHT

Another pattern of indigenous response can be discerned in Sonora, where silver strikes occurred later and in mines that produced less copiously than in Parral and Chihuahua. There, resettlement proceeded with less direct interference from the civil society, and *ranchería* groups (Mayos, Yaquis, Opatas, and Pimas) were less hostile to many of the changes imposed by the mission regime, in part because they had more latitude to manipulate the process. Even in this scenario, however, rebellion could and did occur after many generations of colonial rule, when the relatively autonomous social and psychological spaces Indians had negotiated within the colonial milieu had been violated either by Jesuit inflexibility or by the growing demands of Spanish secular society.

After repelling earlier Spanish *entradas*, Yaquis accepted Jesuits; by 1623, Yaquis from about eighty *rancherías* had been resettled in eight mission villages. For a hundred years, Yaquis and Jesuits coexisted with limited interference from Spanish secular society. Yaquis maintained ceremonial sodalities within new structures, not only contributing to the production of mission surpluses in the fertile lands along the Yaqui River, but also selling their labor in mines as far away as Parral. Jesuit failure to block Spanish settlement became manifest when the province of Sinaloa and Sonora was detached from Nueva Vizcaya in 1733. Their monopoly over much of the region's productive labor and land was challenged by the alliance of the governor with growing numbers of Spanish miners and landowners. The competition for labor and the civilian challenge to the Jesuits fanned the flames of Yaqui grievances. Over time, the Jesuits had become more arbitrary in appropriating mission surpluses (which mostly went to support their poorer Baja California missions) and in appointing outsiders to village office. Meanwhile, the Yaquis became more astute about taking advantage of Spanish legal mechanisms to assert their rights, no longer perceiving the Jesuits as the best or only insurance for survival within the colonial order.

Rebellion broke out in 1740 after poor harvests and flooding. Yaquis were joined by some Mayos and Pimas, although rebel military actions were never coordinated. Nor did all Yaqui villages participate. Rather than a concerted attempt to obliterate the entire Spanish presence, this revolt was an effort to secure adjustments within the colonial situation. Having more successfully negotiated the early transformation to a more sedentary existence, Yaquis now faced an intensification of the extractive system. The 1751 rebellion of their northern neighbors, the Pimas, also resulted from the grievances of subordinates who found their few perquisites threatened; the expropriation of lands around the mission of Pópulo for the presidio of Horcasitas added fuel to the fire.

Armed protest in the form of rebellion, either first-generation or later, failed to expel the intruders, but continuous resistance and raiding served band groups like Apaches and Seris in avoiding settlement in permanent agricultural villages, at least during the colonial period. A relatively small number of Seris managed to survive the extermination campaigns waged against them (and condoned by the Jesuits, who despaired of further missionary efforts) during the eighteenth century. Apaches, with the advantage of larger numbers and horses, were more successful. Having been pushed southwestwardly by migrations of Comanche and other Plains Indians, these Athapaskans had moved into northeastern Sonora and northwestern Chihuahua in the seventeenth century among other groups ranging from nomadic to semisedentary (Sumas, Mansos, Jumanos, Chinarras, Jocomes, Janos, and Conchos). By the early eighteenth century the Apaches dominated the area, the other groups having moved out or been absorbed. As skilled horsemen, Apaches increasingly raided into Chihuahua and Sonora, as far south as Durango and Zacatecas, and to the southeast across Coahuila and into Nuevo León. At different times, their activities were matched or joined by other groups such as Janos and Jocomes and, later, Tarahumaras in the Sierra Madres, and by Comanches in the eastern areas. By the late 1780s Spanish authorities were buying Apache acquiescence with material goods. For some non-sedentary groups, then, greater mobility and hunting-and-gathering skills facilitated resistance. But the refusal to submit made the Apaches more vulnerable to virtual enslavement when they were captured. Many a Spanish household had Apache servants acquired or "ransomed" when they were children.

Versatility in subsistence patterns also served those Indians for whom flight to remote areas was an option. This was the case of sierra groups on the divide between Chihuahua and Sonora. There, some Rarámuri, Tepehuanes, Guarijíos, Jovas, and others lived in isolated *rancherías* in deep canyons or on high mesas, supplementing a meager corn and bean production with wild plants and animals. European-introduced livestock, especially sheep and goats, accompanied them to places that had little attraction for non-Indians, at least until the twentieth century.

MIXED STRATEGIES AND DIVERGENT OUTCOMES IN THE COLONIAL PERIOD

Where Indians could not sustain raiding or flight, varying combinations of accommodation and resistance in missions produced different outcomes by the end of the colonial period. We have already noted that some groups who resisted aggressively and then were forced to adapt became biologically extinct in a relatively short time. This was the case of smaller band-groups in the California peninsula and in Nueva Vizcaya's eastern deserts, whose biological reproduction was most severely threatened by *congregación*. But it also occurred among more densely settled Sinaloa and eastern Durango groups, where Spanish attempts to extract resources were especially exploitative and unrestrained during the period of highest population decline in virgin-soil epidemics.

What of the other groups that had to adjust to the Spanish presence and accommodate to the mission regime? Incipient demographic recuperation in itself was not enough to guarantee the perpetuation of a separate ethnicity – especially in areas where the non-Indian population multiplied at higher rates. Preservation of a cultural identity distinct from the dominant society had less correlation with the degree of accommodation than with the nature of that accommodation and the extent to which it promoted intergroup solidarity. Two general patterns can be discerned: in one, acculturation to a peasant economy more attuned to market forces took place with or without racial *mestizaje*; in the other, greater cultural separateness was maintained along with a greater degree of ethnic distinctiveness.

The first scenario was the long-term outcome for most Indians who had survived into the eighteenth century, although the timing of this process varied, culminating in virtually complete absorption at different points ranging from the late eighteenth into the twentieth century. The Jesuit mission regime was similar for all groups, and certain accommodations to it were universal. Some of the adaptations can be explained by the use of coercion; corporal punishment and incarceration were frequently imposed by both missionaries and civil authorities for transgressions. But force was not the only explanation. Missions could provide sanctuary from traditional Indian enemies who continued to raid. Material benefits in the form of nutritional supplements (grains, fruits, vegetables, and meat protein), the by-products of animals used for clothing and fertilizers, and outright gifts from the missionaries (iron tools, cloth, shoes, tobacco, and chocolate) were readily accepted. The degree to which Indians had control of the resources of their mission communities is not clear. *Cofradías*, or confraternities dedicated to the cult of a saint and used to support communal fiestas and activities, were not the rule, and we have virtually no records of their transactions or those of communal *cajas* (civil treasuries). Although mission lands were communal, family units enjoyed the products of the individual plots they worked. Other lands were dedicated to the support of the missionary and the church; Indians worked these without monetary compensation despite attempts of royal officials to make the Jesuits pay. Whether or not the communal ownership with private usufruct had roots in precontact society, Indians conceived of the mission lands as belonging to them communally. Missions fostered corporate ideals, precolumbian or not. In the more productive areas, surpluses were sold locally, linking missions to Spanish administrative and mining centers, or shipped to Baja California. Certain new technologies were adopted, especially in the creation of diversion weirs for irrigation; and some Indians learned smithing and building trades.

There was substantial participation in religious dramas, processions, dances, and fiestas, which had material benefits and facilitated the perpetuation or reinvention of socioeconomic solidarity forged through reciprocal exchanges. Holy Week, Christmas, and saints' days offered occasions for congregating and feasting. At these times, religious sodalities (which more closely resembled precontact ceremonial organization than Spanish-introduced *cofradías*) performed music and dances that combined Christian themes with elements of earlier practices associated with reverence for the natural world. Fiestas were especially popular when they coincided with precontact rituals performed at significant times in the agricultural cycle. Over time, as Catholic priests outlasted shamans, these syncretic practices lost much of their precontact significance. Even the resistance to doctrinal conformity through the sacraments diminished. Baptism tended to be accepted early, whereas evasion of marriage-enforced monogamy persisted. The latter concept was particularly injurious to economic support strategies. The benefits of communion and confession were even less readily discerned, and the problems of translation posed an obstacle to understanding their conceptual bases. As more Indians became bilingual, these difficulties waned, but the sacraments were not eagerly embraced by all, especially by women.

The limitations of the documentary record have discouraged anything other than general speculation about the extent to which gender analysis could shed light on the colonial experience of northwestern Indians. Agricultural tasks came to be shared in new ways, with women assuming more of these in groups for whom hunting and gathering remained important, albeit less in sedentary societies. In band societies before conquest, women tended to perform more demanding tasks than their counterparts in more agrarian societies; it is not clear whether this pattern suggests greater subservience or a more equal sharing of complementary tasks. During the colonial period, women were increasingly confined to household tasks such as food processing, weaving, and pottery making. Although some evidence suggests that select women had more important ceremonial roles before contact, there are other signs that they were largely subordinate and especially vulnerable to raiding in most northwestern cultures before contact. Although intertribal warfare decreased, colonial rule introduced new perils for Indian women. Certainly Catholicism with its support for Spanish domination and the patriarchal family did nothing to empower women, and as kinship networks were eroded, Spanish insistence on monogamy tended to isolate women from support systems that mitigated abuse. The female avoidance of confession so often noted by missionaries suggests not only their greater adherence to traditional beliefs and native languages but also that for women the perceived benefits of the colonial system were few indeed.

Evasion of or minimal compliance with new obligations often enabled Indians to thwart mission goals of producing agricultural surpluses that exceeded the social and ceremonial needs of the community. The persistence of the drinking parties around planting and harvesting, so condemned by missionaries as debauches, indicates that older rituals continued to be associated with the agricultural cycle. When Indians did have extra produce to market, some circumvented the missionary and sold or bartered it to trade brokers. Pilfering of livestock and other mission produce became a way for some Indians to compensate for the reduction of gift-giving by authorities. When missions failed to provide sustenance because of drought, flooding, disease, neglect of lands (while Indians were away in labor drafts), and collusion of missionaries with the local elites, many Indians left the missions periodically to forage. (In the reverse, some groups that continued to subsist primarily by hunting and gathering used the missions for their convenience during bad seasons or years.) The villages in areas of greater settlement learned to appeal to civil authorities, sometimes benefiting from Spanish legal mechanisms. Some Indians deliberately left the missions to acquire more permanent work on haciendas, and others actively sought more acculturated marriage partners. Marriage records reveal a high incidence of intervillage migration.

To a large extent, the dialectic of adaptation and resistance was accompanied by growing immigration of non-Indians to the north, ethnic mixing, and the formation of a mestizo population; in some cases, full-blooded Indians elected to "pass" as mestizos. The peasant communities that emerged in the late eighteenth and early nineteenth centuries displayed differing cultural and class features: some peasant economies looked less Indian in their tendencies to acquire private property and livestock; some, more, in their continued reliance on gathering to supplement a meager agriculture.

Among the former were Tepehuanes, southeastern Rarámuri, Opatas, and Mayos. In the mission areas of northern Durango and southern Chihuahua, the mining and agricultural heartland of Nueva Vizcaya, the non-Indian population was three times that of the Indian population by mid-eighteenth century. Increasing numbers of non-Indians took up residence in the Tepehuan and Baja Tarahumara missions, and fluid migration patterns in the region expedited racial mixing. Once exclusively Indian, these villages began to resemble acculturated peasant communities. Recognizing this demographic transformation as well as the penury wrought by labor exodus and land attrition at the hands of *hacendados* expanding their wheat and cattle holdings, the Jesuits volunteered to secularize the Topia, Tepehuan, and lower Tarahumara missions in the 1740s, turning them over to diocesan control and hastening their incorporation into the regional economy. This transition did not occur without protest from the mission residents themselves, who were losing their tax exempt status. As parishioners, they would now pay tithes and fees for sacraments.

To the west in northern Sinaloa and Sonora, a similar trajectory occurred at somewhat later intervals as outsiders were attracted to the middle Yaqui and Sonora river valleys and the silver mining towns in Ostimuri as well as the fertile valleys (especially along the Yaqui River) in the coastal region, where the missions had monopolized agricultural production. The effectiveness of the Jesuits in limiting Spanish settlement in the latter area began to be challenged in the second quarter of the eighteenth century and was one of the reasons for the Yaqui rebellion of 1740. In the Opata, Eudeve, and highland Pima areas, by the mid-eighteenth century, outsiders had already taken over much of the mission land not worked individually. Not only was migration out of villages in *repartimiento* and in search of salaried labor common by then, but Opatas, in particular, had assumed the role of military auxiliaries in the growing confrontations of all settlers with Apache raiders. While these collaborators were rewarded with entitlements, they also became more enmeshed in the colonial order that was trying to reduce their corporate strength.

COMMUNAL STRUCTURES UNDER SIEGE: BOURBONS AND
MEXICANS

Indian movement out of villages was accompanied by the inflow of Spaniards and mixed groups. Even when recurrent epidemics, endemic diseases, and subsistence crises did not prevent a modest rise in the Indian birthrate, Indian communities could be swamped by a proportionally larger number of non-Indians. A significant number of Indians opted for exogamous marriages as a way to reconstitute their communities, which had gradually disintegrated from pressures on labor and land. In many areas new crops, more intensive irrigation, the proliferation of livestock, and deforestation around mining areas had radically altered fragile eco-systems. Soil erosion, shifting alluvial deposits, and changing rainfall patterns threatened agricultural output, and as deforestation advanced with overall population growth, subsistence strategies – which relied upon wilderness areas – could not be employed effectively by most groups. The exceptions occurred in selected areas of the Sierra Madre divide and the Sonoran desert, isolated from more promising stock-raising or agricultural lands and mines, where Pimas, Jovas, Guarijíos, Tepehuanes, Rarámuri, and others combined a meager agricultural production with hunting and gathering and seasonal migrations to villages and haciendas to trade and provide labor for harvests.

The shifting patterns in the northwest were characteristic of communities coping with a growing market economy. These changes occurred relatively later than in central Mexico and coincided with imperial policy shifts implemented by Bourbon reformers. In line with other policies designed to strengthen Spain's position militarily and economically vis-à-vis its European rivals, the creation of the Provincias Internas for northern Mexico was envisioned as a means of making the region secure by subduing recalcitrant Indians and defending it against foreign incursions. French and British trading activities east of the Mississippi River and the widespread adoption of the horse by Plains and southwestern Indian groups had resulted in increasingly threatening Comanche and Apache pressures on the northern frontier of present-day Mexico. The post-1780 policy of purchasing peace by subsidy reduced Apache raiding for a few decades, furthered Spanish settlement in northern Sonora and Chihuahua, and boosted the tendency of sedentary groups to assimilate. This was true of the Opatas, for example, who probably had experienced precontact links with the regional system of Paquimé and who subsequently collaborated militarily with their Spanish rulers.

An even greater assimilative inducement had occurred earlier: the expulsion of the Jesuits in 1767. Imperial policymakers saw the Jesuits as obstacles to royal control of economic resources. Their missions were also seen to retard Spanish entrepreneurial activities that could be taxed and to delay the more complete integration of Indians in the labor market. The clergy who replaced the Jesuits, mostly Franciscans and secular priests, never achieved the same degree of economic and political control. This was nowhere more evident than in Baja California, where the few surviving Indians now under Dominican supervision quickly declined in numbers as the peninsula became a staging ground for the occupation of Alta California. In all areas, Spanish demands for Indian labor and encroachments on mission lands escalated, proliferating even more as the non-Indian population grew, tripling in size between 1776 and 1821. Seris, Pimas, Opatas, Eudeves, Jovas, Mayos, Yaquis, Guarijíos, Tepehuanes, Rarámuri, and Apaches could still be identified separately at independence, but for many of them progression toward cultural and biological *mestizaje* could not easily be reversed. The non-Indians who surrounded each of these groups now outnumbered them on average by two or three to one.

The new Mexican government conferred citizenship on Indians, reversing the colonial policy of separate or transitional judicial status. Although the special protections accorded by colonial legislation were often abused, they had been moderately effective in safeguarding communal lands. Even before independence, Bourbon recommendations, like those expressed in the 1750 report of Sonoran visitor José Rodríguez Gallardo and the policies of José de Gálvez, had battered away at the concept of communal ownership, encouraging subdivision of the *común* into individual plots and threatening local mechanisms for exchanging goods and services. Officers and soldiers attached to the new northern presidios of the late eighteenth century became the recipients of land formerly held in common by mission pueblos or *rancherías*. The reinvigorated Bourbon onslaught helps explain why some Indian communities at the close of the eighteenth century were attracted to the occasional preaching of itinerant messiahs urging the ouster of venal *Spaniards* and offering millennial deliverance. In the nineteenth century, the trend toward accumulation of land by privileged elites, even Indian elites, escalated, and the capacity and will of Indian communities to withstand it was a key determinant in maintaining cultural separateness.

During the 1820s and 1830s, the various state governments of the northwest promulgated legislation regarding municipal government and land ownership that had the effect of making newly designated citizens more vulnerable to manipulation by elites and to appropriation of their lands by legal and extralegal means. The laws broadened the definition of *terrenos baldíos* (vacant lands) to include communal lands that were used either in crop rotation or for traditional purposes other than agriculture, making them subject to auction. The corporate governing traditions of the former missions were also assailed in legislation that not only facilitated the appropriation of communal revenues by municipal governments dominated by non-Indians, but also refused to recognize the more informal regulation of community affairs by elders. Throughout the nineteenth century, the concept of private ownership of land became increasingly sacrosanct to those in power; the intent of the state legislation of the early national period was reinforced by the Juárez liberals in the 1850s and 1860s and extensively applied during the Porfirian era of the late nineteenth and early twentieth centuries.

All of these measures contributed to the formation of a class structure in which most Indians became peasants, increasingly indistinguishable from their mestizo counterparts in a lifestyle that, although traditional and syncretic, had few features that were uniquely indigenous. Thus, by the mid-twentieth century there were very few Opata and lowland Pima speakers in Mexico. These groups, along with most of the Tepehuanes, had gradually lost the fight for their lands, becoming smallholders or laborers in various service arrangements on the expanding cattle, wheat, and cotton haciendas of the northwest. Some Indians deliberately chose the path of incorporation, trying to benefit as best they could from an economy increasingly linked to distant markets. Others did not accede to these changes without a fight. Even many traditionally cooperative Opatas joined Yaquis, Mayos, Pimas, and others in the 1828 insurrection against the Sonoran state led by Yaqui leader Juan Banderas. Rebelling against the measures of the new government in pursuit of autonomous rule and collective control of the lands of the Yaqui River, Banderas called on the other groups to join the Yaquis in a pan-Indian movement.

This revolt was suppressed in 1833, but Yaquis continued to resist actively the onslaught against corporate autonomy, making them one of the few northwestern groups to endure with a separate identity. It should be noted that substantial numbers of Mayo-speakers, some mountain Pimas, and very few northern Baja California Yuman-speakers from tiny groups still appear in the national censuses, but virtually all are bilingual and their communities are not easily distinguished from mestizo culture. Although Seris, Rarámuri, Tepehuanes and even smaller groups in the Sierra Madre (such as Guarijíos) can be distinguished more easily from the dominant mestizo society in terms of ethnicity and culture, only Yaquis managed this outcome in an area so assiduously coveted by outsiders for its natural resources.

A brief examination of the national period history of each of these groups will help to elucidate the variant patterns. Overall, it is well to keep in mind that the national trends in Indian policy and economic development that increased their vulnerability to loss of lands in the nineteenth century were not much altered in the twentieth. The Mexican Revolution of 1910 decelerated the disintegrative forces that were ravaging Indian communities, but even though the Constitution of 1917 laid the basis for restoration of some native lands, the awarding of *ejidal* or indigenous community grants did not ensure economic viability for autonomous communities. And in spite of official recognition of indigenous contributions to Mexico's past and the creation of institutions like the National Indian Institute, twentieth-century governments have generally fostered attempts to assimilate or integrate Indian peoples into the national economy.

NOMADS AND BOUNDARIES

The less sedentary and primarily nonagricultural groups that occupied territory that now falls on both sides of the Mexico–United States border present somewhat of an anomaly. After the Gadsden purchase in 1855, many surviving upper Pimas of the Sonoran desert migrated northward to the Tohono o'dam (Papago) villages in Arizona, but a substantial number ignored the artificial boundary line by engaging in seasonal migrations to traditional sources of wild foods. Reservation status in the United States did not favor assimilation. In northern Baja California, the few remaining Cochimís and other Yuman-speakers like the Kumiaí also coped with a political solution that ignored their traditional subsistence patterns. Apaches, whose southern bands constituted the largest group of border nomads, were eventually confined to the United States.

In the late eighteenth century, Spanish officials had partially resolved the problem of Apache raids (deep into Mexico and sometimes abetted by other groups, including the Rarámuri) by furnishing supplies to them in peace establishments like the ones set up at the presidios of Janos and Fronteras. This solution was jeopardized after Mexican independence around 1830 when these subsidies were discontinued. Southern Apache bands (predominantly Chiricahuas) renewed their raiding, discouraging further Spanish settlement in northern Sonora and Chihuahua and wreaking havoc farther south. The growing U.S. occupation of the Southwest after 1848 provided increased opportunities for Apaches to market stolen goods on both sides of the border. For most of the rest of the century Apache–white relations were in turmoil as U.S. authorities increasingly applied force to coerce the Indians onto reservations. In spite of Mexican policies to subdue Apaches by offering bounties for Apache scalps and providing land to colonists in return for military service, the less fortified Sonora–Chihuahua border area intermittently provided refuge and sustenance. Only in the 1880s, when Porfirian federal troops were employed in pacification efforts and the United States and Mexico coordinated relentless pursuit, did whites succeed in bringing Apaches under their control. The twentieth century found Apaches resettled on U.S. reservations, but it had taken the conquerors two centuries to impose sedentarism on a people who adroitly adopted aspects of European technology and material culture (especially guns and horses) to maintain independence.

SERIS

This hunting-and-gathering society has also persisted in Mexico to the present day. Seris who had survived the deportation and extermination campaigns of the colonial period, sometimes aided by desert Pimas, numbered only a few hundred by the nineteenth century. They skillfully manipulated their limited environment, combining fishing and gathering with raids on western Sonora haciendas and highway banditry. Tiburón Island provided a refuge for Seris despite periodic military expeditions dispatched there to round them up and concentrate them near Hermosillo. The "civilizing" efforts by government, preachers, or philanthropists, whether harsh or benign, produced little change before the 1920s, when government officials convinced them to apply their marine skills to help supply a growing market for fish. In the next few decades, Seris clustered around Kino Bay and Desemboque experimented marginally as commercial fishermen; attempts by the National Indian Institute in the 1950s to foment a modern fishing cooperative failed. Seris continued to resist alien educational and religious institutions; they endured at barely subsistence levels, supplementing traditional activities with ironwood carvings and baskets introduced into artisan cooperatives in the 1960s and 1970s. During the latter decade, in granting a coastal *ejido* and Tiburón Island (also designated as a wildlife preserve), the Mexican government paid niggardly and belated tribute to Seri tenacity. Their ability to subsist in a desert environment that has little commercial attraction for others is a key factor in explaining this persistence. While peaceful coexistence in the twentieth century fostered some marital exogamy and modest population growth, the approximately 500 Seris counted in 1980 retained autochtonous worldviews and rituals still not well understood by outsiders.

PEOPLES OF THE SIERRA MADRE OCCIDENTAL:
TEPEHUANES, GUARIJÍOS, PIMAS

A slightly less barren landscape than the Sonoran coastal desert, the Sierra Madre Occidental also sheltered several indigenous groups that remain today in varying numbers, speaking Indian languages and perpetuating social networks through fiestas and rituals that have some precontact antecedents. Farthest south are the Tepehuanes, who inhabit mountain canyons and uplands extending from southern Chihuahua, through Durango, into Nayarit. Their number is difficult to determine because of the growing mestizo population in the region, but the southern Tepehuanes acculturated more rapidly than the more isolated northern Tepehuanes, who live in *rancherías* in the most southwestern corner of Chihuahua, where they grow corn, beans and squash. Responding to appropriation of their lands in the nineteenth and twentieth centuries, some southern Tepehuanes joined other peasants in armed resistance during the Mexican Revolution and the Cristero rebellion. Since the 1960s, increased contact with outsiders in lumbering and ranching activities around Guadalupe y Calvo has resulted in the waning of traditional customs pertaining to material culture and rituals, such as the fiestas in which dancing and the drinking of *tesgüino* (maize beer) ensure good crops, promote health, and honor the dead. The number of Tepehuan-speakers has also declined. The several thousand remaining Tepehuanes have increasingly been forced to supplement agricultural subsistence production with salaried work on ranches and in sawmills.

To the northwest, perhaps a thousand people who identify themselves as Guarijíos inhabit mountain canyons northwest of Chínipas and into Sonora along the Mayo River. During the colonial period, Guarijíos mostly avoided the missions set up among their neighbors – Chínipas, Témoris, and Guazapares who were wiped out or absorbed by other groups – and continued to subsist by cultivating corn and gathering wild plants, even as the mestizo population grew around them. Occasionally migrating to work on ranches, they escaped much notice from outside until the 1970s, when Chihuahua state officials charged them with harboring a guerrilla band linked to antigovernment kidnappings and terrorist acts. Subsequently, the National Indian Institute initiated schools and *ejidos* in the area and introduced new cultigens such as sesame. Still farther northwest, along the Sonora–Chihuahua border around Maicoba, a few communities of mountain Pimas have been trying to balance tradition with modern intrusions for much longer. The last of the lower Pimas coexist with a mostly mestizo population. The men frequently migrate from their meager *ejidal* lands to work in mines, sawmills, and ranches while women handcraft straw items. In all of the sierra locations, the disproportionate number of mestizos (many of whom also subsist poorly) and the continuing expansion of forest industries increase the likelihood that their indigenous inhabitants will be integrated into the larger society and culture.

THE RARÁMURI

For the Rarámuri, that outcome is also possible but less probable, at least in the immediate future. With a population of 60,000 they are the largest group, not only of the Sierra Madre but of all the northwest. Except for the inhabitants of the Jesuits' lower Tarahumara missions in the plains east of the foothills who were early engulfed by Spanish settlement, the Rarámuri have maintained rigid proscriptions against intercourse with non-Indian outsiders. After their rebellions at the turn of the eighteenth century failed to expel the Spaniards, many Rarámuri remained in the upper Tarahumara missions of central western Chihuahua. Others migrated to the south and west, continuing a pattern of flight to upland and canyon areas of less interest to the intruders and intermixing with other sierra groups. Even the Rarámuri attached to missions tended to opt for an itinerant lifestyle. They lived away from the mission towns in *rancherías*, changing locations seasonally for subsistence reasons and sometimes raiding Spanish haciendas on their own or with Apaches. Rarámuri raiding may have increased after the Jesuits were expelled in 1767 and mission livestock and grains were appropriated by royal authorities. In the late eighteenth and early nineteenth centuries, Franciscans reestablished some of the missions, but many Rarámuri communities were left alone for long periods. Some of the Rarámuri never came under Catholic influence.

Varying patterns of syncretism evolved throughout Tarahumara country in the nineteenth century. Mexican independence went unnoticed in the Sierra Madre, and for a time, with silver mining in decline and authorities preoccupied with Apaches, the Rarámuri enjoyed a de facto autonomy. Yet even outside the Franciscan mission enterprise, aspects of material culture and religion introduced by missionaries persisted. Domestic animals, new cultigens, and metal tools could be found among the least acculturated, and Christian concepts mingled with native cosmology in the elders' public sermons on the requisites for ensuring the well-being of the community. Ceremonial life was crucial to placating supernatural forces – syncretic blends of God, devil, sun, moon, Jesus, Mary – in rituals that corresponded to the Christian calendar and the agricultural cycle. Sodalities enacted Christian dramas and sponsored fiestas where the consumption of *tesgüino* was a central element in consolidating social networks that linked dispersed *rancherías*. The hierarchy of native officials introduced by the missions persisted in pueblos. Worldviews continued to evolve and change, often with regional variations, but commonly with a propensity to stress reciprocal obligations for ensuring harmony (by restoring balance between a non-Christian god and devil) and with a concept of soul very different from the Christian idea but key to understanding Rarámuri cosmology and behavior.

In the half century after independence, as encroachments in their territory increased and demonstrated that others were incapable of appreciating their community values, Rarámuri beliefs developed a heightened antipathy to outsiders. Chihuahua's colonization law in 1825 was the first in a series of legislative acts, state and national, that opened up eastern Tarahumara crop and grasslands to non-Indian farmers and ranchers. Many Rarámuri retreated deeper into the foothills and mountains; renewed mining activities after midcentury pushed them even farther. During the Porfiriato, U.S. mining interests proliferated in Chihuahua, moving deep into the Tarahumara, especially around Batopilas. They were soon followed by the forestry industry and railroads from Chihuahua City. By 1890, more than 2 million acres of southwestern Chihuahua came to be controlled by the Batopilas Mining Company along with Cargill and Hearst lumber interests. By this time most of the former eastern Rarámuri villages as well as those to the north in the upper Papigochi Valley were predominantly mestizo. At the end of the century, very few Rarámuri made common cause with mestizos who reacted to the intrusions of foreign capital, loss of land, and labor exploitation with localized revolts like that of Tomóchic in 1891. Most, however, tried to survive off isolated, meager lands, often migrating to take temporary jobs in the new capitalist enterprises but generally seeking to avoid permanent peonage in mines and sawmills. Attempts were made by the state government and the Jesuits (allowed by the federal government to return in 1900) to continue their "civilizing" efforts in various parts of the Sierra Tarahumara.

Rarámuri seem to have participated in only limited fashion in the Mexican Revolution of 1910. In opting for withdrawal rather than violent resistance, they expressed their pervasive distrust in alliances with outsiders, even those who promised help to restore Rarámuri lands. In the end, the agrarian goals of the revolution brought little benefit to the Indians, for although much of western Chihuahua's forested mountain area was eventually assigned in *ejidos*, it was the mestizo beneficiaries whose population expanded much more rapidly and who tended to control local political affairs. In the twentieth century, the Rarámuri have continued to be displaced by non-Indians, most seriously since the large-scale resumption of lumbering in the 1950s and 1960s. Subsistence agriculture on marginal lands and recurrent droughts force growing numbers of Indians to seek work as laborers. Even in sawmills owned by their own *ejidos*, Rarámuri often toil in the most subordinate jobs. The *ejidos* have not provided the basis for communal autonomy.

Since the Revolution, efforts of the Mexican state and the Catholic Church (predominantly Jesuits) have continued in the direction of paternalism and acculturation, through the cultural missions of the 1920s and 1930s, the organizing efforts of the National Indian Institute, and religious proselytization. Although less dogmatic and racist than the colonial power structure, the twentieth-century agents of change have been largely intolerant of obstacles to modernization. Governments have grudgingly sponsored some bilingual education efforts and allowed communities to police themselves, for example; health-care providers have made an attempt to understand traditional curing practices; and Jesuits, once the staunchest defenders of Tridentine orthodoxy, have allowed a more flexible Catholicism to be practiced, one that draws on a historical tendency of the Church to incorporate folk practices and beliefs.

Passive resistance and withdrawal are still the main weapons for evading acculturation as elders continue to advocate the avoidance of interpersonal ties with non-Indians, who are stigmatized as malevolent, decadent, unprincipled, and shameless. Whether these moral boundaries will be effective against growing penetration by a capitalist society remains to be seen. Recent trends do not augur well for this outcome: growing tourism in the Barranca de Cobre (Copper Canyon) and the increased cultivation of marijuana by unscrupulous outsiders. Rarámuri runners, famed for their fleetness in rugged terrain, have taken to competing in U.S. races in order to raise money for famine relief.

YAQUIS AND MAYOS

For the Yaquis of southern Sonora, neither isolation nor passivity held the key to the pursuit of cultural and political autonomy from the late colonial period to the mid-twentieth century. The Yaquis are the most widely studied of all the northwestern Indian groups during the modern period because of their high visibility as resisters and their presence in the documentary record. But there is considerable disagreement among anthropologists and historians about how to explain their unremitting defiance and cohesion, a remarkable feat for a people whose choice lands have long been the target of commercial agricultural entrepreneurs and who have spent long periods outside of their Yaqui River homeland.

During the late colonial era, acquisition of land by Spaniards on the circumference of their eight pueblos intensified. At the same time, civil and religious personnel did not interfere heavily in the Yaqui villages, which retained much of the former economic organization and governing apparatus set in place by the Jesuits. They produced cattle and grains for internal and external consumption and some migrated periodically to sell their labor in mines and haciendas in other parts of Sonora and Chihuahua. While the traditional hierarchy of governors and elders remained in place, there were some new adaptations. The new leadership that evolved had a stronger military component and more importance was given to the office of captain-general, which had authority over all of the pueblos. Within the traditional hierarchical organization of the villages themselves, a new power structure began to evolve, which would eventually distinguish between five spheres of authority that regulated civil and military affairs, and divided religious activities into general church matters, the patron saint fiesta, and Lenten/Holy Week ceremonials. The religious blending that had begun earlier progressed undeterred by the wariness of priests. What resulted was ostensibly Christian, with some peculiar elements. Yaqui religion placed strong importance on the interdependence among Christian teachings and the natural world, positing a dual division between the cosmological significance of towns and their natural surroundings, imparting a sacred relevance to their collective lands. As pressures from the outside increased in the nineteenth century, ceremonial mechanisms (also with dualistic features) for strengthening community solidarity intensified, often in reinvented form that drew on an evolving and changing historical memory, even as significant numbers of Yaquis worked outside the pueblos.

The reinforcement of solidarity and growing militarization coalesced when Sonoran laws limiting the political autonomy of Yaquis and inviting colonization of their lands were enacted and resulted in the Banderas rebellion of 1828. Charismatic leadership by this captain-general and millenarian promises attracted other Sonoran groups to the resistance movement, which was extinguished with the leader's execution in 1833. Pan-Indian cooperation deteriorated from this point on, and the other groups became less resistant to incorporation. Opatas were fully hooked into the assimilative process by the 1850s, and Mayos, the Yaquis' Cahitan neighbors and traditional allies to the south, were not able to present unified, concerted resistance to the loss of autonomy after the 1880s.

Yaquis continued to resist through shifting military alliances with state political leaders and armed uprisings against encroachments on their lands, especially around Cócorit in the north. The military strategy, juxtaposed with continuing temporary migrations to mines and haciendas in other parts of the state, was relatively successful until Sonoran Liberals launched a new assault on Yaqui land and political control at midcentury. Ineffectual piecemeal resistance was transformed in the 1870s by José María Leyva, better known by the Spanish rendering of his Yaqui name – Cajeme – who had served in the Liberal army. Under his leadership many Yaquis returned to their villages and concentrated on producing agricultural surpluses that could be marketed to the outside and used to subsidize military strength against state militias. He also fostered cere-monial incentives for solidarity. This Yaqui "republic," which recalled elements of the Jesuit regime, would prove an obstacle to the moderniz-ing Porfirians who took over the state in the 1880s.

The Porfirian elite in Sonora vigorously promoted railroads, mining, and commercial activities. Landowners in Sonora and Sinaloa expanded their holdings, with particular interest in acquiring the irrigable land along the Yaqui and Mayo rivers. For the Mayos by this time, resistance was fragmented and inchoate; it was expressed primarily in their adher-ence to the millenarian movement inspired in 1891–92 by Teresa Urrea (La Santa de Cabora), the illegitimate daughter of a Mayo mother and a non-Indian rancher, and held to be a saint because of her curing powers. A substantial number of Mayos, Yaquis, and poor mestizos of the Tara-humara region came to believe that the better, more egalitarian and harmonious world Teresa predicted offered salvation from rapacious Por-firian policies. Except for an insurrection in Tomóchic (Chihuahua), most of Santa Teresa's followers channeled their devotion through tradi-tional Cahitan-Christian ceremonies (*pahkom*), which projected the idea of a great purifying flood. Porfirian police forces responded harshly to these threatening manifestations, deporting adherents to work in Baja California. Most Mayos continued to accommodate and ultimately to closely resemble mestizo society. Nonetheless, the Mayo language and a ceremonial tradition that was revitalized after the Revolution have per-sisted, as has the phenomenon of Mayo prophets or saints.

Yaquis did not succumb to Porfirian economic infringements, or to the brutal military campaigns that subdued Cajeme in 1887, without a protracted fight. Mexican officials and U.S. investors vigorously pursued the idea of converting the Yaqui Valley into an agricultural export center. The railroad between Nogales and Guaymas was completed in 1883, followed by intense land surveying and speculation. Yaquis refused to accept the scheme for parceling out individual plots to them and offering the remaining land for sale. Nonetheless, fortified by the federal army, officials proceeded with their plans, alienating hundreds of thousands of valley acres to a succession of land and irrigation companies, culminating in 1903 with the Richardson Construction Company. Many Yaquis were forced to withdraw to haciendas. A smaller number took refuge in the Sierra de Bacatete and from there launched guerrilla strikes against the intruders. When military responses did not produce a durable peace, the Díaz regime resorted to the deportation of several thousand Yaquis to work on the henequen plantations of Yucatan. Because officials sought to deprive rebels of any possible sanctuary or support, the deportations did not discriminate between guerrilla fighters and noncombatants. Hundreds of Yaquis sought refuge in Arizona and formed pueblos that still exist today. By 1908, Yaquis appeared to be headed for cultural extinction in Mexico.

Although the Mexican Revolution reversed the Yaqui diaspora, its benefits were long elusive and probably transitory. Many Yaquis returned to Sonora after Díaz was deposed and took up arms among various revolutionary factions between 1910 and 1915, interpreting the promises of revolutionary leaders as the means to regain the lands of the traditional eight pueblos and communal autonomy. Not even serving the Sonoran dynasty that came to lead the revolutionary regime after 1920 produced this outcome, however, for communal landowning was not compatible with the export agriculture envisioned by Presidents Alvaro Obregón and Plutarco Elías Calles. Determined not to let Yaquis stand in the way of their acquisition of Richardson Construction Company lands and irrigation canals, Obregón provoked a confrontation in 1926 that allowed federal troops to occupy the Yaqui Valley once again. Unable to defy the revolutionary state, Yaquis in the reestablished villages saw non-Indian colonists increasingly divert Yaqui river water and expand their landholdings especially on the left bank.

In 1937, President Lázaro Cárdenas responded to growing Yaqui marginalization by recognizing the governing authority of the traditional Yaqui towns and creating a *zona indígena* encompassing the agricultural lands on the right (north) bank of the Yaqui River, the Sierra de Bacatete, and the coastline. Also included was a small area on the south that did not encompass the flourishing agricultural export zone around Ciudad Obregón (formerly Cajeme). The benefits from the land grant were short-lived as by the 1950s the Angostura and Obregón dams had deprived the Yaqui communities of any control over the floodwaters. Over time, government policies, which have steadily favored the expansion of modern, mechanized agriculture, have not only affected Yaquis' subsistence by forcing them to buy water and plant cash crops to obtain credit, but have also reduced the number of unskilled jobs that Yaquis have performed for centuries. Although some alternative sources of income have evolved through such activities as cattle raising and shrimping, the green revolution has made Yaquis highly dependent on government or private financing for agricultural production and distribution of wheat and vegetable oils. This has happened even as Yaqui corporate strength has increased through revitalization of cumulative traditions, collective symbols, and rituals that reinforce their separate cultural identity. Paradoxically, this is a flexible identity that does not prescribe specific ethnic markers, prohibit marital exogamy, or demand the participation of all Yaquis. The interplay of cultural autonomy, economic marginalization, and social stratification will continue to influence the destiny of perhaps 15,000 Yaquis.

CONCLUSION

As the cases of the Tarahumaras and the Yaquis attest, no one set of assumptions or patterns provides a convenient umbrella for assessing the total historical experience of northwestern Indians. Social scientists studying surviving groups have applied a variety of heuristic approaches to explain culture change in the region: among them, theories of acculturation, integration, isolation, regions of refuge, directed and nondirected contact, enclavement, demography, modes of production, and world systems. Historians (still overwhelmingly cultural outsiders) trying to reconstruct the past of these groups since contact have increasingly turned to such models to aid in interpreting the patchy archival record. The primary and secondary sources drawn upon for this chapter are just as varied in their analysis as are the characteristics of the Indian peoples of the largely arid northwestern Mexican region. Much smaller in total numbers than Mesoamericans to the south, they nonetheless comprised many different groups. Attempting to order this diversity has the potential for reductive explanations that obscure the indigenous legacies of the region as they are expressed not only in the material culture and religion of identifiably Indian groups, but also in the mestizo culture that dominates.

What we can say with certainty is that no single batch of ingredients constituted a formula for indigenous survival in the northwest. This chapter has attempted to elucidate the impact of many factors conditioning cross-cultural contact in the region: demographic shifts, the availability and accessibility of labor and natural resources valuable to the dominant society, the intensity of extractive pressures and assaults on communal autonomy, ecological-geographic factors, native sociopolitical organization and mobility, and the ability of indigenous peoples to mold aspects of the colonial regime to serve their ends. Demographic factors are certainly among the key variables in explaining early cultural collapse, but alone they do not account for the persistence of groups as diverse in numbers as the Seris and the Tarahumaras. Isolation from areas of interest to the dominant culture and its coercive power sheds light on the experience of those two groups, but it has little explanatory power in the case of Yaquis. Nor does the degree of preconquest sociopolitical complexity provide the full answer since the enduring peoples encompass a range from nomads like Seris and Apaches through Tarahumaras to the even more sedentary Yaquis. Recurrent militant resistance could result in disaster as with the Baja California groups, and endurance in the Seri example. And how were some groups able to use partial accommodation with the conquerors to strengthen their separate cultural identity (for example, the Yaquis' sale of their labor and Tarahumaras' adoption of livestock), while other patterns of conformity resulted in total absorption by mestizo society, as in the case of the Opatas?

The "right mix" of variables has been different for each of the surviving groups in responding to assorted sets of intrusive, destabilizing elements that, except for the effects of epidemic disease, have intensified over time – especially in the modern onslaughts on communal autonomy and land. What is universal is the fact of vigorous Indian responses to coercive pressures and structural, material changes, whether in the form of flight, aggressive resistance, or selective accommodation. This dynamic of action has been heavily influenced by a shared, but historically evolving and changing, set of cultural memories and religious values. The degree to which these memories and beliefs, often transmitted through mothers and elders, have reinforced social cohesion within each group and have imprinted communal solidarity upon a structurally inegalitarian reality is a crucial factor. Such resilience, although undeniably poignant, is also salutary in its explicit and implicit critique of the conquerors' "superiority and progress." The interpenetration of cultures, ecosystems, and microbes after contact transformed subsistence and fashioned a complex mosaic of life in which the indigenous elements, although often submerged, are vital counterpoints to perpetual and frequently destructive capitalist modernization and development in the Mexican northwest.

BIBLIOGRAPHICAL ESSAY

The ethnohistorical examination of northwestern Mexico has until recently been dominated by anthropologists and geographers. Still the most comprehensive approaches to the indigenous history of the region are Edward H. Spicer, *Cycles of Conquest: The Impact of Spain, Mexico and the United States on the Indians of the Southwest, 1533–1960* (Tucson, 1962), which examines acculturation, and Peter Gerhard, *The North Frontier of New Spain* (Princeton, NJ, 1982), which compiles detailed geographic and demographic information for the colonial period. An outstanding example of regional ethnohistory that also incorporates environmental and gender studies is Cynthia Radding, *Wandering Peoples: Colonialism, Ethnic Spaces, and Ecological Frontiers in Northwestern Mexico, 1700–1850* (Durham, NC, 1997). Daniel T. Reff, *Disease, Depopulation and Culture Change in Northwestern New Spain, 1518–1764* (Salt Lake City, 1991), attributes monumental importance to the early impact of disease on Indian demography and culture. For a sampling of the many demographic analyses undertaken by Robert H. Jackson, see his *Indian Demographic Collapse in the Mission Communities of Northwestern New Spain* (Albuquerque, 1994). The influence of Spicer and Gonzalo Aguirre Beltrán on approaches to assessing ethnogenesis in the region are evident in N. Ross Crumrine and Phil C. Weigand, eds., *Ejidos and Regions of Refuge in Northwestern Mexico* (Tucson, 1987). Useful syntheses are also found in the *Historia general de Sonora*, 5 vols. (Hermosillo, 1985), especially the essays by Sergio Ortega, Ignacio del Río, Cynthia Radding de Murrieta, and Ernesto Camou Healy; Thomas E. Sheridan, "The Limits of Power: The Political Ecology of the Spanish Empire in the Greater Southwest," *Antiquity* 66 (1992): 153–71; and Sheridan and Nancy J. Parezo, *Paths of Life: American Indians of the Southwest and Northern Mexico* (Tucson, 1996). The *Handbook of North American Indians*, vol.

10 (Washington, DC, 1983), includes historical sketches of Pimas, Seris, Yaquis, Mayos, Tarahumaras, and Tepehuanes.

For more recent contributions that review much of the extensive literature dating from the 1940s on the connections of the Greater Southwest to Mesoamerica, see Carroll L. Riley, *The Frontier People: The Greater Southwest in the Protohistoric Period* (Albuquerque, 1987); Riley and Basil C. Hedrick, *Across the Chichimec Sea: Papers in Honor of J. Charles Kelley* (Carbondale, IL, 1978); F. Joan Mathien and Randall H. McGuire, eds., *Ripples in the Chichimec Sea: New Considerations of Southwestern–Mesoamerican Interactions* (Carbondale, IL, 1986); Michael S. Foster and Phil C. Weigand, eds. *The Archaeology of Western and Northwestern Mesoamerica* (Boulder, CO, 1985); and David H. Thomas, ed., *Columbian Consequences,* vol. 1: *Archaeological and Historical Perspectives on the Spanish Borderlands West* (Washington, DC, 1989).

The first attempts of modern social scientists to identify the native groups at contact, to place them spatially and to count them, are presented in Ralph Beals, *The Comparative Ethnology of Northern Mexico Before 1750* (Berkeley, CA, 1932); and Carl O. Sauer, *The Distribution of Aboriginal Tribes and Languages in Northwestern Mexico* (Berkeley, CA, 1934) and *The Aboriginal Population of Northwestern Mexico* (Berkeley, CA, 1935). Historians did not follow their lead.

The intent of Herbert E. Bolton to downplay the Black Legend mightily influenced the evolution of "mission" history, for decades the vehicle for illuminating the Spanish past of the region and not much concerned with ethnohistory. Bolton led the way with "The Mission as a Frontier Institution in the Spanish-American Colonies," *American Historical Review* 23 (1917): 42–61, and *Rim of Christendom: A Biography of Eusebio Francisco Kino, Pacific Coast Pioneer* (New York, 1936). Not surprisingly, many of his students were Jesuits who adhered to tradition in writing the history of their order's apostolic work, following in the footsteps of Francisco Xavier de Alegre, S.J., whose eighteenth-century *Historia de la Provincia de la Compañía de Jesús de Nueva España* used previous manuscripts, published and unpublished, to illuminate the Jesuits' labors of conversion (4 vols., Ernest J. Burrus, S.J., and Félix Zubillaga, S.J., eds. [Rome, 1956–60]). Latter-day Jesuits took up the challenge: Peter Masten Dunne, S.J., *Pioneer Black Robes on the West Coast* (Berkeley, CA, 1940), *Pioneer Jesuits in Northern Mexico* (Berkeley, CA, 1944), and *Early Jesuit Missions in Tarahumara* (Berkeley, CA, 1948); John F. Bannon, *The Mission Frontier in Sonora, 1620–1689* (New York,

1955); Gerard Decorme, S.J., *La obra de los jesuitas mexicanos durante la época colonial, 1572–1767*, 2 vols. (Mexico City, 1941); and John A. Donohue, S.J., *After Kino: Jesuit Missions in Northwestern New Spain, 1711–1767* (St. Louis, 1969). A useful survey of Bannon's legacy is found in David J. Weber, "John Francis Bannon and the Historiography of the Spanish Borderlands: Retrospect and Prospect," *Journal of the Southwest* 29 (1987): 331–63.

Because it contains valuable ethnographic information, the best contemporary account of the early missions written by a Jesuit observer and first published in 1645 is Andrés Pérez de Ribas, *Historia de los triunfos de Nuestra Santa Fé entre gentes las más bárbaras y fieras del nuevo orbe* (Mexico City, 1944); the 1645 edition has been translated and annotated by Daniel T. Reff, Maureen Ahern, and Richard K. Danforth, *History of the Triumphs of Our Holy Faith Amongst the Most Barbarous and Fierce People of the New World* (Tucson, 1999). Hundreds of Jesuit mission reports have been published in documentary collections far too numerous to mention in their entirety. Among those covering more than a single region are: *Documentos para la historia de México* (Mexico City, 1853–57); Ernest J. Burrus, ed., *Misiones norteñas mexicanas de la Compañía de Jesús, 1751–57* (Mexico City, 1963); Ernest J. Burrus and Félix Zubillaga, eds., *El noroeste de México: Documentos sobre las misiones jesuíticas, 1600–1769* (Mexico City, 1986); Charles W. Polzer, S.J., *Rules and Precepts of the Jesuit Missions of Northwestern New Spain* (Tucson, 1976). Collections reproducing ecclesiastical and civil reports include: Charles W. Hackett, ed., *Historical Documents relating to New Mexico, Nueva Vizcaya and Approaches thereto, to 1773*, 3 vols. (Washington, DC., 1923–37); Fernando de Ocaranza, ed., *Crónica y relaciones del occidente de México* (Mexico City, 1939); *The Presidio and Militia on the Northern Frontier of New Spain: A Documentary History*, vol. 1: *1570–1700*, ed. Thomas H. Naylor and Charles W. Polzer (Tucson, 1986), and vol. 2, part 1: *The Californias and Sinaloa–Sonora, 1700–1765*, ed. Charles W. Polzer and Thomas E. Sheridan (Tucson, 1997).

Published chronicles and *visita* reports include: Baltasar de Obregón, *Historia de los descubrimientos antiguos y modernos de la Nueva España [1584]* (Chihuahua, 1986; English version: George P. Hammond and Agapito Rey, eds., *Obregón's History of 16th Century Explorations in Western America* [Los Angeles, 1928]); Alonso de la Mota y Escobar, *Descripción geográfica de los reinos de Nueva Galicia, Nueva Vizcaya y Nuevo León* (Mexico City, 1940); Thomas H. Naylor and Charles W. Polzer, eds.,

*Pedro de Rivera and the Military Regulations for Northern New Spain,
1724–1729* (Tucson, 1988); José Rafael Rodríguez Gallardo, *Informe sobre
Sinaloa y Sonora, año de 1750,* ed. Germán Viveros (Mexico City, 1975);
Pedro Tamarón y Romeral, *Demostración del vastíssimo obispado de la
Nueva Vizcaya, 1765,* ed. Vito Alessio Robles (Mexico City, 1937); Eliza-
beth A. H. John, ed., *Views from the Apache Frontier: Report on the
Northern Provinces of New Spain by José Cortés [1799]* (Norman, 1989).

Several publications deal with colonial Indian rebellions across the
region: María Elena Galaviz de Capdevielle, *Rebeliones indígenas en el
norte del reino de la Nueva España (siglos XVI y XVII)* (Mexico City,
1967); María Teresa Huerta Preciado, *Rebeliones indígenas en el Noroeste
de México en la época colonial* (Mexico City, 1966); José Luis Mirafuentes
Galván, *Movimientos de resistencia y rebeliones indígenas en el norte de
México, 1680–1821* (Mexico City, 1975); Roberto M. Salmón, *Indian Re-
volts in Northern New Spain: A Synthesis of Resistance, 1680–1786* (Lanham,
MD, 1991); and Susan M. Deeds, "Indigenous Rebellions on the
Northern Mexican Mission Frontier: From First-Generation to Later
Colonial Responses," in Donna J. Guy and Thomas E. Sheridan, eds.,
*Contested Ground: Comparative Frontiers on the Northern and Southern
Edges of the Spanish Empire* (Tucson, 1998), 32–51.

The following consider Indian history in limited fashion as part of the
colonial milieu: Luis Aboites, *Breve historia de Chihuahua* (Mexico City,
1994); Francisco Almada, *Resumen de historia del estado de Chihuahua*
(Chihuahua, 1955); John Francis Bannon, S.J., *The Spanish Borderlands
Frontier, 1513–1821* (Albuquerque, 1974); Mario Hernández Sánchez
Barba, *La última expansión española en América* (Madrid, 1957); Chantal
Cramaussel, *Primera página de historia colonial: La provincia de Santa
Bárbara en Nueva Vizcaya, 1563–1631* (Ciudad Juárez, 1990); Charles R.
Cutter, *The Legal Culture of Northern New Spain, 1700–1810* (Albuquer-
que, NM, 1995); José Ignacio Gallegos, *Durango colonial, 1563–1821* (Mex-
ico City, 1960); Oakah L. Jones, Jr., *Nueva Vizcaya: Heartland of the
Spanish Frontier* (Albuquerque, 1988); Cheryl E. Martin, *Governance and
Society in Colonial Mexico: Chihuahua in the Eighteenth Century* (Stan-
ford, CA, 1996); J. Lloyd Mecham, *Francisco de Ibarra and Nueva Vizcaya*
(Durham, NC, 1927); Michael C. Meyer, *Water in the Hispanic South-
west: A Social and Legal History, 1550–1850* (Tucson, 1984); Luis Navarro
García, *Don José de Gálvez y la Comandancia General de las Provincias
Internas del Norte de Nueva España* (Seville, 1964), and *Sonora y Sinaloa*

en el siglo XVII (Seville, 1967); Guillermo Porras Muñoz, *La frontera con los indios de Nueva Vizcaya en el siglo XVII* (Mexico City, 1980), and *Iglesia y estado en Nueva Vizcaya, 1562–1821* (Pamplona, 1966); Pastor Rouaix, Gerard Decorme, and Atanasio G. Saravia, *Manual de historia de Durango* (Durango, 1952); Michael Swann, *"Tierra Adentro": Settlement and Society in Colonial Durango* (Boulder, CO, 1982) and *Migrants in the Mexican North: Mobility, Economy and Society in a Colonial World* (Boulder, CO, 1989); María del Carmen Velázquez, *Establecimiento y pérdida del septentrión de México* (Mexcio City, 1974); and Robert C. West, *The Mining Community in Northern New Spain: The Parral Mining District* (Berkeley, CA, 1949). Although it deals primarily with the U.S. Southwest, David J. Weber's *The Mexican Frontier, 1821–1846: The American Southwest Under Mexico* (Albuquerque, 1982) provides context for changes in the northwest after Mexican independence.

For specific regions and groups, there exists an extensive bibliography, once again preponderantly anthropological. The following represents a selection of works that contain significant ethnohistorical content:

Baja California

Among the secondary sources are Ignacio del Río, *Conquista y aculturación en la California jesuítica, 1697–1768* (Mexico City, 1984), and *A la diestra mano de las Indias: Descubrimiento y ocupación colonial de la Baja California* (Mexico City, 1990); W. Michael Mathes, *Las misiones de Baja California* (La Paz, 1977); Harry Crosby, *Antigua California: Mission and Colony on the Peninsular Frontier* (Albuquerque, 1994); Robert H. Jackson, *The Spanish Missions of Baja California* (New York, 1991); and Homer Aschmann, *The Central Desert of Baja California: Demography and Ecology* (Berkeley, CA, 1959). The many published accounts by Jesuits include: Francisco Javier Clavigero, S.J., *The History of Lower California* (Palo Alto, CA, 1937); Sigismundo Taraval, *The Indian Uprising in Lower California*, ed. Marguerite E. Williams (Los Angeles, 1937); Miguel del Barco, *Historia natural y crónica de la Antigua California*, ed. Miguel León Portilla (Mexico City, 1973); *The Letters of Jacob Baegert, 1749–68: Jesuit Missionary in Baja California* (Los Angeles, 1982). On the Dominican period, see *"Edificar en desiertos": Los informes de Fray Vicente de Mora sobre Baja California en 1777*, ed. Salvador Bernabéu Albert (Mexico City, 1992).

Sinaloa

The early demise of Sinaloan groups and a dearth of documentation have inhibited study in this region. Exceptions are Ernesto Gámez García, *Historia antigua de Sinaloa del Mocorito al Zuaque* (Culiacán, 1965); Salvador Alvarez, "Chiametla: Una provincia olvidada del siglo XVI," *Trace* 22 (1992): 5–23; and José Luis Mirafuentes Galván, "Identidad india, legitimidad y emancipación política en el noroeste de México (Copala, 1771)," in *Patterns of Contention in Mexican History*, ed. Jaime E. Rodríguez O. (Wilmington, DE, 1992), 49–67. Some Jesuit *visita* reports have been published in *Father Baltasar Visits the Sinaloa Missions, 1744–45*, trans. Jerry Patterson (n.p., 1959).

Seris, Apaches, and Other Nonsedentary Groups

On the Seri, see A. L. Kroeber, *The Seri* (Los Angeles, 1931); William B. Griffen, *Notes on Seri Indian Culture, Sonora, Mexico* (Gainesville, FL, 1959); Charles DiPeso and Daniel S. Matson, eds., "The Seri Indians in 1692 as Described by Adamo Gilg, S. J.," *Arizona and the West* 7 (1965): 33–56; Thomas E Sheridan, "Cross or Arrow? The Breakdown of Spanish–Seri Relations, 1729–1750," *Arizona and the West* 21 (1979): 317–34; Richard Felger and May Beck Moser, *People of the Desert and Sea: Ethnobotany of the Seri Indians* (Tucson, 1985); and José Luis Mirafuentes Galván, "Colonial Expansion and Indian Resistance in Sonora: The Seri Uprisings in 1748 and 1750," in *Violence and Resistance in the Americas*, ed. William B. Taylor and Franklin Pease (Washington, DC, 1994), 101–23. Apaches, Conchos, and other less sedentary groups have been studied extensively by William B. Griffen: *Culture Change and Shifting Population of Central Northern Mexico* (Tucson, 1969); *Indian Assimilation in the Franciscan Area of Nueva Vizcaya* (Tucson, 1979); *Apaches at War and Peace: The Janos Presidio, 1750–1858* (Albuquerque, 1988); and *Utmost Good Faith: Patterns of Apache–Mexican Hostilities in Northern Chihuahua Border Warfare, 1821–1848* (Albuquerque, 1988). See also Arturo Guevara Sánchez, *Los conchos: Apuntes para su monografía* (Chihuahua, 1985); Carlos Enríquez, *Namiquipa: Misión-presidio* (Chihuahua, 1989); and Víctor Orozco, *Las guerras indias en la historia de Chihuahua: Primeras fases* (Mexico City, 1992).

The Sierra Madre Occidental: Tepehuanes, Tarahumaras,
and Others

On the Tepehuanes, see Campbell W. Pennington, *The Tepehuan of Chihuahua: Their Material Culture* (Salt Lake City, 1969), and José Guadalupe Sánchez Olmedo, *Etnografía de la Sierra Madre Occidental: Tepehuanes y mexicaneros* (Mexico City, 1980).

For the Rarámuri, the several collections and studies edited by Luis González Rodríguez are particularly useful: *Révoltes des indiens tarahumars, 1626–1724,* by Joseph Neumann (Paris, 1969; Spanish translation: *Historia de las rebeliones en la Sierra Tarahumara, 1626–1724* [Chihuahua, 1991]); *Tarahumara: La sierra y el hombre* (Mexico City, 1982); *Crónicas de la Sierra Tarahumara* (Mexico City, 1987); and *El noroeste novohispano en la época colonial* (Mexico City, 1992). Also outstanding is the work of William L. Merrill, which includes *Rarámuri Souls: Knowledge and Social Process in Northern Mexico* (Washington, DC, 1987); "Conversion and Colonialism in Northern Mexico: The Tarahumara Response to the Jesuit Mission Program, 1601–1767," in *Conversion to Christianity: Historical and Anthropological Perspectives on a Great Transformation,* ed. Robert Hefner (Berkeley, CA, 1993); and "Cultural Creativity and Raiding Bands in Eighteenth-Century Northern New Spain," in *Violence and Resistance in the Americas,* 124–152. Valuable ethnohistorical documents are reproduced in Thomas E. Sheridan and Thomas H. Naylor, eds., *Rarámuri: A Tarahumara Colonial Chronicle* (Flagstaff, AZ, 1979). Other ethnohistories and ethnographies include Ricardo León García, *Misiones jesuitas en la Tarahumara: Siglo XVIII* (Ciudad Juárez, 1992); Manuel Ocampo, S.J., *Historia de la misión de la Tarahumara, 1900–65* (Mexico City, 1966); Pedro de Velasco Rivero, S.J., *Danzar o morir: Religión y resistencia a la dominación en la cultura tarahumara* (Mexico City, 1983); Carl Lumholtz, *Unknown Mexico,* 2 vols. (New York, 1902); Wendell C. Bennett and Robert M. Zingg, *The Tarahumara: An Indian Tribe of Northern Mexico* (Chicago, 1935); Campbell W. Pennington, *The Tarahumar of Mexico: Their Environment and Material Culture* (Salt Lake City, 1963); John G. Kennedy, *Tarahumara of the Sierra Madre: Beer, Ecology and Social Organization* (Arlington Heights, IL, 1978); and François Lartigue, *Indios y bosques: Políticas forestales y comunales en la Sierra Tarahumara* (Mexico City, 1983). See also W. Dirk Raat and George Janecek, *Mexico's Sierra Tarahumara: A Photohistory of the People of the*

Edge (Norman, OK, 1996); and Eugeni Porras Carrillo, "Los Waryó de Chihuahua: Una etnografía mínima," *Cuadernos de Trabajo* (Universidad Autónoma de Ciudad Juárez) 34 (1997): 1–25.

Studies examining the colonial effects of contact on Nueva Vizcayan groups (including Acaxees, Xiximes, Tepehuanes, Rarámuri, and Conchos) can be found in several anthologies published by the Universidad Autónoma de Ciudad Juárez. In *Actas del Primer Congreso de Historia Regional Comparada* (1989), see Chantal Cramaussel, "Encomiendas, repartimientos y conquista en Nueva Vizcaya," 139–60; in *Actas del Segundo Congreso de Historia Regional Comparada* (1990): Cramaussel, "Evolución de las formas de dominio en el espacio colonial: Las haciendas de la región de Parral," 115–40; and Salvador Alvarez, "Tendencies regionales de la propiedad territorial en el norte de la Nueva España, siglos XVII y XVIII," 141–79. In *El contacto entre los españoles e indígenas en el norte de la Nueva España*, vol. 4 of *Colección conmemorativa quinto centenario del encuentro de dos mundos* (1992), see William B. Griffen, "Aspectos de las relaciones entre indios y europeos en el norte de México," 41–74; and Susan M. Deeds, "Las rebeliones de los tepehuanes y tarahumaras durante el siglo XVII en la Nueva Vizcaya," 9–40. See also Deeds, "Rural Work in Nueva Vizcaya: Forms of Labor Coercion on the Periphery," *Hispanic American Historical Review* 69 (1989): 425–49; "Mission Villages and Agrarian Patterns in a Nueva Vizcayan Heartland, 1600–1750," *Journal of the Southwest* 33 (1991): 345–65; "Indigenous Responses to Mission Settlement in Nueva Vizcaya," in Erick Langer and Robert H. Jackson, eds., *The New Latin American Mission History* (Lincoln, NE, 1995); "Double Jeopardy: Indian Women in Jesuit Missions of Nueva Vizcaya," in Robert Haskett et al., eds., *Indian Women of Early Mexico* (Norman, OK, 1997), 252–72; "First-Generation Rebellions in Seventeenth-Century Nueva Vizcaya," in Susan Schroeder, ed., *The Pax Colonial and Native Resistance in New Spain* (Lincoln, NE, 1998), 1–29; and "Colonial Chihuahua: Peoples and Frontiers in Flux," in Robert H. Jackson, ed., *New Views of Borderlands History* (Albuquerque, NM, 1998), 21–40.

Yaquis and Mayos

The pioneer anthropologist was Ralph Beals with *The Aboriginal Culture of the Cáhita Indians* (Berkeley, CA, 1943) and *The Contemporary Culture of the Cáhita Indians* (Washington, DC, 1945). Mayos have been studied by N. Ross Crumrine in *The Mayo Indians of Sonora: A People Who*

Refuse to Die (Tucson, 1977). On the Yaquis, see Edward H. Spicer, *Potam: A Yaqui Village in Sonora* (Menasha, WI, 1954), and *The Yaquis: A Cultural History* (Tucson, 1980); Jane Holden Kelley, *Yaqui Women: Contemporary Life Histories* (Lincoln, NE, 1978). Evelyn Hu-Dehart, *Missionaries, Miners and Indians: Spanish Contact with the Yaqui Nation of Northwestern New Spain, 1533–1880* (Tucson, 1981), and *Yaqui Resistance and Survival: The Struggle for Land and Autonomy, 1821–1910* (Madison, WI, 1984); Luis Navarro García, *La sublevación yaqui de 1740* (Seville, 1966); Claudio Dabdoub, *Historia del Valle del Yaqui* (Mexico City, 1964); Thomas R. McGuire, *Politics and Ethnicity on the Río Yaqui: Potam Revisited* (Tucson, 1986); Thomas E. Sheridan, "How to Tell the Story of a People Without History: Narrative versus Ethnohistorical Approaches to the Study of the Yaqui Indians Through Time," *Journal of the Southwest* 30 (1988): 168–89; and María Eugenia Olavarria, *Análisis estructural de la mitología yaqui* (Mexico City, 1989), and *Símbolos del desierto* (Mexico City, 1992). For Yaqui and other Sonoran Indian group reaction to the expanding Mexican society and economy, see Stuart F. Voss, *On the Periphery of Nineteenth-Century Mexico: Sonora and Sinaloa, 1810–1877* (Tucson, 1982). Paul Vanderwood's *The Power of God Against the Guns of Government: Religious Upheaval in Mexico at the Turn of the Nineteenth Century* (Stanford, CA, 1998) examines Mayo and Yaqui attraction to Santa Teresa de Cabora.

Opatas, Pimas, and Other Sonoran Groups

Published contemporary accounts by Jesuits include: Juan Nentvig, *Descripción geográfica, natural y curiosa de la Provincia de Sonora*, ed. Germán Viveros (Mexico City, 1971; English version: *Rudo Ensayo: A Description of Sonora and Arizona in 1764*, ed. Albert Pradeau and Robert Rasmussen [Tucson, 1976]); Joseph Och, *Missionary in Sonora: The Travel and Reports of Joseph Och, S.J., 1755 and 1767*, ed. Theodore Treutlein (San Francisco, 1965); Ignaz Pfefferkorn, *Sonora: A Description of the Province*, ed. Treutlein (Tucson, 1989); and Luis González Rodríguez, ed., *Etnología y misión en la Pimería Alta, 1715–40* (Mexico City, 1977). For works by anthropologists, see Thomas E. Sheridan, *Where the Dove Calls: The Political Ecology of a Peasant Corporate Community in Northwestern Mexico* (Tucson, 1988); David L. Shaul, *Language, Music and Dance in the Pimería Alta During the 1700's* (Tumacacori National Historical Park, AZ, 1993); Thomas B. Hinton, *A Survey of Indian Assimilation in Eastern*

Sonora (Tucson, 1959); and Jean B. Johnson, *The Opata: An Inland Tribe of Sonora* (Albuquerque, 1950). Recent studies include: Cynthia Radding, *Entre el desierto y la sierra: Las naciones O'odham y teguima de Sonora, 1530–1840* (Mexico City, 1995); Robert C. West, *Sonora: Its Geographical Personality* (Austin, TX, 1993); Saúl Gerónimo Romero, *La privatización de la tenencia de la tierra en Sonora, 1740–1860* (master's thesis, Universidad Nacional Autónoma de México, 1991); Cynthia Radding and Juan José Gracida Romo, *Sonora: Una historia compartida* (Mexico City, 1989). See also Radding: *Las estructuras socioeconómicas de las misiones de la Pimería Alta, 1768–1850* (Hermosillo, 1979); "Peasant Resistance on the Yaqui Delta: An Historical Inquiry into the Meaning of Ethnicity," *Journal of the Southwest* 31 (1989): 330–61; "Población, tierra y la persistencia de comunidad en la zona serrana de Sonora, siglo XVIII," *Historia Mexicana* 41 (1992): 551–78; and "Crosses, Caves, and *Matachinis*: Divergent Appropriations of Catholic Discourse in Northwestern New Spain," *The Americas* 56 (1998): 177–203. Among works by José Luis Mirafuentes Galván, see "El 'enemigo de las casas de adobe,' Luis de Sáric y la rebelión de los pimas altos en 1751," in Felipe Castro et al., eds., *Organización y liderazgo en los movimientos populares novohispanos* (Mexico City, 1992), 147–75; and "Estructuras de poder político, fuerzas sociales y rebeliones indígenas en Sonora (siglo XVIII)," *Estudios de Historia Novohispana* 14 (1993): 117–43.

14

THE NATIVE PEOPLES OF NORTHEASTERN MEXICO

DAVID FRYE

Around the year 1623 two Spaniards accompanied by their Mexicano servant set out to establish a sugar plantation in the new kingdom of Nuevo León, which for a generation had formed the northeastern frontier of New Spain. The place to which Pereyra and Pérez, the Spaniards, laid claim as their own happened to be occupied at the time by the *ranchería* of an Indian named Nacastlagua. Nacastlagua had his people help Pérez and Pereyra dig their irrigation ditches, prepare their fields, and plant their cane, as was expected of him and of them; yet, unexpectedly, Nacastlagua also assumed the right of sitting down first at the table every day when dinner was served. Pérez and Pereyra suffered from being so mocked by the shameless Nacastlagua, who seemed oblivious to his proper place in the Spanish scheme of things. Worse, they could think of no way to put him in that place.

But the overseer they hired for the new plantation, Antonio Durán, a bold man with no doubt some small experience in these frontier Indian affairs, soon decided to settle the matter. The day after Durán arrived, he stood waiting when dinner was served, fingering a club cut especially for the occasion. As soon as Nacastlagua sat down as was his custom, Durán set about beating the surprised and confused Indian to a pulp. The next day Antonio Durán, suspecting the denouement, packed up his household and left for the provincial capital of Monterrey. The end came a few nights later, when Pereyra woke up to the sound of loud cries from one of the Indians' shacks. Going out to investigate, he was mortally wounded and the shack set ablaze. Pérez, getting the message, snuck out through the back fields and escaped unhurt. The Mexicano servant also tried to escape, protecting himself as he ran with a *chimal*, but was hit by an arrow and died a few days later in Monterrey. As for Pereyra, it is said that he was barbecued and eaten by the rebellious Indians, and the plantation was left deserted. A generation later, a village of Tlaxcalans were settled in its place.

This anecdote was told in 1649 by the Mexican-born Captain Alonso de León, in the first written history of Nuevo León.[1] Setting it down under the rubric "Of some murders which occurred in this Kingdom, of Spaniards, and how they were punished," de León offered the story as a parable of the settling of his adopted homeland, of the fierceness of the native Indians, of the rough ingenuity of and the hardships suffered by his fellow Spaniards. That the anecdote cannot be taken as a straightforwardly true history should be clear enough; the alleged cannibalizing of the unfortunate Pereyra, for example, which took place after all the witnesses had left the scene, is pure border lore.

We can take this story as a parable as well, for it presents in condensed form the key elements in the history of the native peoples in northeastern Mexico since the Europeans began invading the region around the year 1545. Before that time, the northeast lay beyond the vague line that separated the settled, agriculturalist civilizations of Mesoamerica from the bewildering variety of indomitable hunting-and-gathering peoples known collectively to central Mexicans as Chichimecs). The key elements in this history of conquest include the introduction of new technologies for exploiting the land; ethnocide, the fate by and large of the indigenous people of the region; the mass migrations, planned and unplanned, that brought in Purépechas, Otomís, Mexicanos, and Tlaxcalans from the heavily populated center of Middle America to acculturate or replace the local "barbarians"; and the development of a colonial ideology of race that defined both the indigenous peoples of the region and the newcomers from central Mexico as "Indians." Perhaps a final distinctive feature of the northeast, arguably important in the development of its subregional cultures, is that each subregion and most of the major towns there were first settled as *fronteras*, or border zones. As the Spaniards and their workers and allies entered the Bajío, Zacatecas, San Luis Potosí, Monterrey, Coahuila, and Tamaulipas, each area served in its turn as the boundary between an already tamed center and an unsubdued wilderness (Map 14.1).

---

[1] Alonso de León, "Relación y discursos del descubrimiento, población y pacificación de este Nuevo Reino de León; temperamento y calidad de la tierra," in Genaro García, ed., *Documentos inéditos o muy raros para la historia de México* (Mexico, 1909): XXV, 112–14.

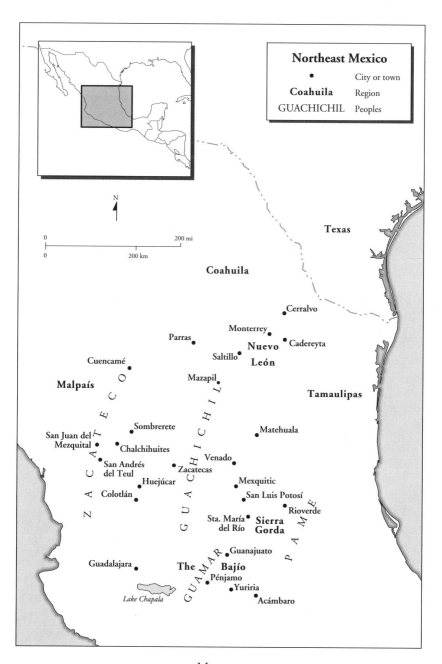

Map 14.1

The anecdote of Nacastlagua's Revenge begins with the imposition of a sugar plantation, a novel means of producing wealth, as defined by the Spanish, upon a landscape they perceived as barren, unexploited, and essentially uninhabited. A defining feature of the Spanish colonization of the northeast of New Spain – and what distinguishes it from most earlier Spanish conquests in the Americas – is that it was set in motion by this transformation of the mode of production. Here, colonization was characterized from the beginning by an interest in land, not people. The invading Europeans and their allies and entourages set about, in the first place, to control "unused" local land and resources by discovering and mining silver and gold, by promoting the spread of cattle and sheep ranching, and by introducing European agriculture to sustain the growing regional economy. Securing the labor needed to exploit those resources was, in comparison, only a secondary consideration – except to the degree that the indigenous peoples of the northeast were themselves considered a kind of exportable raw material and were rounded up and sold as slaves, especially in the early years of warfare and conquest. The colonizers never passed through, or even considered, a stage of relying on tribute from the resident hunting-and-gathering population.

This emphasis on transforming the landscape (both geographic and social), on making "vacant lands" produce, was the fundamental historical process in the region, and it ultimately determined the fates of the indigenous peoples and societies of the northeast. The new means of production imported by the colonizers required labor or, rather, it invented labor as a commodity needed to make the imposed systems function. Wherever the hunting-and-gathering societies lived, and for as long as they survived, the colonizers satisfied their need for labor by conscripting them as miners, as domestic servants, or, in the case of Nacastlagua's people, as field hands.

But the need to secure a supply of labor does not entirely explain the behavior of the Spaniards in northeast Mexico, or in the anecdote. This is true only in part because the colonizers had alternative sources of labor, stemming from the introduction into the northeast of two streams of native population and culture from central Mexico. One stream, represented in the anecdote by the Spaniards' Mexicano servant, brought north indigenous people, mestizos, and blacks, enslaved, indentured, and free, to labor for (and sometimes alongside) the Spanish, and formed the basis of the mestizo culture of the northeast into which most of the native peoples of the area were ultimately absorbed. The other, smaller but still important, stream – represented here by the Tlaxcalan village that in the end replaced both the plantation and the earlier *ranchería* – was organized by colonial officials and brought central Mexicans (mainly Tlaxcalans, but also Otomí and some Purépecha) north to reproduce the settled agricultural villages of the center, perennial labor reserves and usually sources of political stability.

Neither of these migration streams, foreshadowed here, plays a large role in the anecdote, for the two Spaniards easily received the labor they needed to run their plantation from Nacastlagua's people. What drives the narrative is the colonizers' need to impose hierarchy and subjugate the indigenous social order, not in order to keep their sugar plantation in production but to ratify their notions of who they were and of who the barbaric others were. Like the owners and enforcers of the Putumayo rubber company described by Michael Taussig, though at a lower (and much more typical) level of violence, the Spaniards in this border tale lost sight of market forces and put sugar production out of their minds as they anguished over the shameless impudence and barbarity of Nacastlagua, until one of them took a cudgel in hand to put an end to it. Given the long-standing representation of the nomadic peoples of the north as not only without fixed homes and agriculture but without religion, law, or human feelings, it is no surprise that the narrative passes easily from the opening accusation of "shamelessness" against Nacastlagua to the final mention, as if in passing, of his people's cannibalism.

Accusations of inhuman cruelty, and especially of cannibalism, were routinely used in the early years of Spanish colonization of the northeast (roughly 1545 to 1590 in the southern part of the region, and lasting into the seventeenth century in Coahuila and Nuevo León) as pretexts for variously deporting, enslaving, or massacring entire populations. The precise fate of Nacastlagua and his people was not spelled out in de León's history (had they fled to avoid punishment? been massacred, or enslaved en masse, in retaliation? died from disease in the interim?). The silence of the text on this point precisely mirrors the silence of all sources on the disappearance of indigenous peoples throughout the region – just as the laconic note that the Spaniards' sugar plantation remained deserted after the incident reflects the ultimate depopulation of the entire native landscape of the northeast – which had been proceeding apace since the inception of the so-called Chichimeca War a century before.

SURVIVING THE CHICHIMECA WAR

According to a story told by another early chronicler, Gonzalo de Las Casas, it was a group of Indians enslaved for their part in the Mixtón War (1541–42) who discovered the silver mines of Zacatecas, and who thus inadvertently began the European invasion of northeastern Mexico. These captives had managed to escape from the distant mines of Taxco and had returned north to hide out among the Zacateco people, in the land known to the Spanish as "La Gran Chichimeca." But in Taxco they had become experienced in mining and recognizing metals, and when they found silver "so near their own land," they purposely pointed out the lode to the Spaniards so that their people would no longer be taken to slave far away in the mines of central Mexico.[2]

The great, arid land of hunting-and-gathering peoples that spreads north of Mesoamerica had not seen a large settled population since the end of the Toltec period some three centuries earlier. The Purépechas and especially the Otomí who lived along the nervous Chichimeca frontier pushed into the southernmost corner of this region soon after they themselves had been invaded by the Europeans, taking advantage of the military protection offered by the conquerors with whom they now styled themselves allies. Purépecha outposts at Yuriria and Acámbaro seem to have consolidated their control over the Guamares and Pames in what is now southeastern Guanajuato state by 1528. In 1531 an Otomí force under Don Fernando de Tapia, formerly known as Conín, conquered and dispersed the southern Pame, founded the town of Querétaro, and in effect annexed the area to Mesoamerica. After this minor northward advance the Spaniards, like the Aztecs before them, continued to avoid the vast nomadic region until the silver strike at Zacatecas. The development of the mines of Zacatecas from 1548 led to the rapid incursion of hundreds of miners, with their thousands of workers and dependents, and to a lively traffic in silver and goods between Zacatecas, Guadalajara, and Mexico City. A road system was developed to support this commerce, presidios and settlements were established to safeguard the roads, and cattle ranches grew up to supply the settlements and the mines. Near one of these ranches the silver mines of Guanajuato were discovered in

---

[2] Report from about 1572 by Gonzalo de Las Casas, "Noticia de los chichimecos y justicia de guerra que se les ha hecho por los españoles," in H. Trimborn, ed., *Quellen zur Kulturgeschichte des präkolumbischen Amerika* (Stuttgart, 1936), 168.

1552, redoubling the traffic through the area. All of this commerce crossed directly through the heartland of peoples completely unknown to the Spanish – and indeed to their central Mexican allies and subjects – and whose way of life was utterly foreign to their thought.

The word Chichimeca (Nahuatl *chichimecatl*) is of uncertain origin, but a frequently repeated folk etymology incorrectly derives it from Nahuatl *chichi* (dog) and *mecatl* (rope) to mean "of the dog lineage" or, as some would have it, "dirty sons of dogs," pointing to the pejorative connotations the word had and still has when referring to the nomads of the north. At the same time, many of the ruling Nahua lineages of central Mexico insisted on their own descent from ancient Chichimecs, and the title Chichimecateuctli (Chichimeca Lord) was proudly borne by the military leader in several of their states. The mixture of dread and fascination implied by these ambivalent usages appears to be the common response of sedentary peoples everywhere when they have confronted nomadic peoples across their borders, from the British in Australia to the Inkas facing the "Aucas" of the eastern rainforests in Peru. Everywhere human understanding and even observation fall by the wayside as the sedentaries fall back upon a limited set of stereotyped images of fierceness, wildness, and lawlessness to explain these inexplicable others.

The Chichimecs went naked, a fact that particularly struck the Spanish from whose writings this description is drawn, without the cloaks or breechcloths of central Mexico, and instead decorated their bodies with paint and scarification. They had no permanent houses or property, moved about constantly in search of food, and were in an equally constant state of warfare with each other. Married men followed their women's groups, and women were free to divorce. Women did most of what the chroniclers described as work, gathering and cooking foods, nursing their children, and carrying the few material possessions whenever a group moved on. This last fact impressed writers such as Gonzalo de Las Casas, who, taking patriarchy for granted and considering work undignified, ascribed it to the power of Chichmeca over their women, whom they treated "as their personal slaves," and saw in it yet another sign of the nomads' lack of human civility. It should be clear, though, that his judgment was not necessarily shared by Chichimeca women, who certainly were not restrained from voicing their opinions before the group, when they would urge their men on to greater acts of war. The women of a group also would shoot arrows from a distance into a cactus leaf before their men went to war, as a form of divination. Many of the foods that they gathered and cooked were unfamiliar to even the peoples of central Mexico: mesquite seeds that they made into hard cakes, prickly pears, wild tubers, roasted maguey leaves, and fermented drinks made from prickly pears or mesquite seeds and brewed in tightly woven baskets, for they reportedly had no pottery. The Spanish attributed the ferocity of the Chichimecas to their wild diet.

Men and boys were prohibited from doing anything the Spanish regarded as work, and spent their days at hunting deer, hares, birds, and small animals, playing the Mesoamerican ball game (again, according to Las Casas), at gambling for arrows or hides at the north Mexican game of beans and sticks – or at making war. The two principal male activities reinforced each other, for both in hunting and war men relied on their skill with their long bows and narrow, fire-hardened, leather-piercing arrows. Boys practiced this skill from the time they were able to walk, hunting mice and lizards with toy bows, and were not weaned until they had hunted a hare or rabbit at the age of five or six. The men of the various groups spent a great deal of their time and energy planning and making war on each other. Guachichil and Zacateco groups in particular were reputed to be great enemies, constantly at war with one another before they acquired a common target in the European invaders. Chichimeca warriors fought nude, in full body paint, a practice that horrified the Europeans almost as much as their sacrifice of war captives. The latter were reportedly placed at the center of a nighttime, firelit circle dance by their victorious enemies, who danced around them, arms linked, without music, for hours, shooting arrows into them at random intervals. The chroniclers' emphasis on the Chichimecas' fierce, warlike nature can be attributed in part to their aim of supporting the war against the nomads, but both comparison with other nomadic peoples and the fact that the Guachichiles were able to maintain a state of war with the Spanish for more than four decades lend some credence to the accounts.

A few Chichimecas living in places blessed with somewhat more abundant rainfall, such as the Pames in the southeast and reportedly the Zacatecos of the Malpaís region, practiced limited agriculture and lived in semipermanent villages, though there, too, "at times they went out to the *despoblados* to enjoy the fruit season," according to the Spanish captain Pedro de Ahumada.[3] Groups in the northern Laguna district also

---

[3] "Relación de Pedro de Ahumada," in R. H. Barlow and George T. Smisor, eds., *Nombre de Dios, Durango: Two Documents in Nahuatl Concerning Its Foundation* (Sacramento, CA, 1943), 58.

lived in semipermanent villages, sustained by the fish, ducks, and edible water plants of the marshy lakes. But from the Spanish point of view, all of the Chichimecas were simply living fortuitously from what they found growing in the wild, not occupying or using the land itself. As a result, Las Casas tells us, "the Spaniards, seeing the land unoccupied and apt for ranchland – since they neither sow nor cultivate – began to settle it with cattle ranches." By the time Las Casas wrote, around 1572, these ranches must have covered most of the modern state of Guanajuato, and were tithing totals of up to 14,000 calves a year, suggesting that as many as a million head of cattle already occupied the Bajío.

The relative peace that at first held between Spanish and Chichimeca did not last long. In 1550 a group of Zacatecos attacked, robbed, and killed some Purépechas on the road to the mines, thus beginning the four-decade-long series of assaults, ambushes, and skirmishes that came to be known as the Chichimeca War. The changes wrought in every aspect of Chichimeca life by Spanish expansion must have been drastic, even decades before the eventual "pacification" of the region. The new ways of exploiting the land introduced by the Spaniards – the mining economy, long-distance trade, and especially cattle ranching – altered the local ecology, the means of subsistence, the population patterns, and the politics of warfare of the Chichimecas. The means by which the Spaniards prosecuted the war wrought equally drastic social changes. Yet our knowledge of how the indigenous peoples of the region were affected is limited by that fact that it was only in the context of the war that the Spaniards and their allies came to know, or to write about, the groups known collectively as Chichimecas.

We can only speculate, from the few meager accounts produced by the veterans of the Chichimeca War, on the immediate social consequences of this prolonged military encounter with the Spanish empire. As elsewhere in the Americas, the Spaniards distinguished various "nations" among the natives of the region, including the Zacatecos in the northwest, the Guachichiles in a long band running from the east of Lake Chapala to modern Saltillo, the Guamares in present-day Guanajuato, and the Pamíes or Samues (Pames) in the east. These "nations" were said to be composed of people who spoke the same or closely related languages. What these languages might have been, however, or how they may have been related, is unknown and probably unknowable with the lone exception of Pame (related to Otomí), still spoken by the only surviving indigenous group in the area. Few of the chroniclers of the northeast, from the days of the Chichimeca War to the colonization two centuries later of Texas and Tamaulipas, ever saw fit to learn any of the local languages, and none left any record of them apart from a handful of proper names. It is equally difficult to determine whether there were any actual social, political, or military bonds that held the "nations" together as societies, while the cultural differences that distinguished them are, like their languages, lost, probably forever.

Within each nation the Spaniards distinguished a varying number of *parcialidades*, presented as the basic political-military groups of the Chichimecas, each under the leadership of an eponymous "captain," such as Macolia, leader of the Macolias. The *parcialidades* were divided in turn into *rancherías*, small, usually temporary settlements of about a hundred people who camped and foraged together. It is, again, unclear whether the hierarchical arrangement of nation, *parcialidad*, and *ranchería* corresponded to any social reality. Similarly, the so-called captains, always male, who negotiated with (and sometimes were hanged by) the Spanish, were not necessarily locally recognized leaders who had arisen from the warring traditions of the Chichimeca peoples. The position of captain may have come into existence only with the advent of long-term war against the Spanish, as a result of the Europeans' insistence on dealing with the "leaders" of the various groups when making peace and war.[4]

The sixteenth-century chroniclers generally presented nations as cohesive military threats, and even raised the specter of "leagues" and "confederations" of nations. After the early seventeenth century, with the Chichimeca War over, there is no more mention of leagues. In the chronicles of Nuevo León and Coahuila, colonized after the end of the war, the mention even of nations and *parcialidades* drops off, leaving the *rancherías* as the only recognized social units of indigenous life – though these reduced entities are frequently granted the title of "nation." The shift from nations and leagues to *parcialidades* and *rancherías* in these early sources may indicate a difference in social organization between the southern peoples of the region, who lived in contact with Mesoamerica, and the more isolated northern bands; or it may reflect the changing biases, agendas, and local knowledge of the chroniclers. The earliest authors wrote with the express agenda of calling for assistance to their fellow soldiers and of glorifying their own exploits, whereas later

---

[4] Powell's report of a powerful tribute-demanding leader of the Mazapil Guachichiles whose influence reached far to the south in the mid-1500s, tentatively repeated by Gerhard, is based on a misreading of several dubious passages in the "Relación" of Pedro de Ahumada.

chroniclers of Nuevo León relied on the diminutive Indian "nations" they periodically corralled from the unsubdued countryside to provide them and their fellow colonists with agricultural labor, and they had no desire to draw the attention of a viceregal authority that might enforce the long-standing ban on Indian slavery. The sources may also point to real social changes caused by the war and the peace that followed. The possibility of gaining the quantities of food and booty represented by the Spanish caravans and ranches may indeed have led during the era of the Chichimeca War to alliances among the various native groups, many of whom had previously been at war with each other. In addition, the rapid spread of cattle ranches across the war region lends some credence to the report that even people "from very far inland" were being attracted to the war "by the fame of the cows, which they call large deer."[5] It is conceivable that the population of the Gran Chichimeca actually grew during the second half of the sixteenth century as the result of such immigration, even given the casualties resulting from the war itself. Later, when the peace of the colonizers was imposed and warfare and nomadic raiding were suppressed, the Spanish were wary of any signs of alliances among their new subjects, who were, moreover, already devastated by depopulation. Both the usefulness of large grouping and the ability to form them were sharply curtailed in the era of the Spanish colonization of Nuevo León; it is not surprising, then, to find a multiplicity of scattered *rancherías* and *parcialidades* there. The evidence on these matters, then, is tantalizing but diffuse.

The first military conquests of the northeast, like those of central Mexico, were accompanied by parallel spiritual conquests. The latter were sometimes presented, especially by religious chroniclers, as preceding the inroads of soldiers and presidios, but we may suppose that in most instances they instead followed, just as the soldiers of the Chichimeca War followed the trade roads already opened by miners and ranchers. The hagiographic chronicles of the Franciscans, in their histories of the region in the sixteenth century, depict the customary scenes of devout and self-denying friars, intent only on the saving of souls and the greater glory of God, spending long years tracking through the wilderness of the borderlands in search of yet uncontacted tribes to convert. Unfortunately for future historians and anthropologists, none of these early friars seem to

---

[5] "Relación de Pedro de Ahumada," 60.

have paused from their works to write so much as a note about the lives, customs, or languages of the native peoples whose souls they saved. Unfortunately for the natives themselves, the mission congregations that the friars engineered, for the most part in the years of peace after 1590, were breeding grounds for fatal contagions.

As for the rituals and beliefs from which the Chichimecas were to be weaned, the chroniclers tell us remarkably little, and in fact generally agree with Las Casas that they have no "religion, I mean idolatry," at all. By this they meant that none of the indigenous peoples of the northeast participated in any of the organized, ceremonial, or architectural forms that made cultural activities recognizable to them as religion. Just as the Chichimecas lacked agriculture, permanent settled villages, and clothing, so they lacked the Mesoamerican religious complex of temples, altars, sacrifice, prayer, fasting, and bloodletting, "for all this was used by all the nations of New Spain," as Las Casas noted. All they did in the way of religion, Las Casas continued, was to make "certain exclamations to the sky, looking at certain stars," and to dance around their victims before killing them, "which the Spaniards have understood is their manner of sacrifice." The dead were buried (according to some chroniclers) or burned (according to others), and surviving relatives painted themselves black in mourning. The antlered heads of deer were saved after the rest of the hunted animal was consumed, to be used in obscure and diabolic rites. Beyond this, the world of Chichimeca beliefs and religious practices is a blank.

That the religious practices of the Chichimecas, like so many other aspects of their life, were defined in Spanish writings by their absence, is due in part to the chroniclers' rhetorical representations of their opponents as savages, in a state of nature (or worse). It also results from the enormous cultural gulf that separated the Europeans, and indeed the central Mexicans, from these nomadic peoples. Las Casas found such "rites and customs" as he did describe worthy of note chiefly because they were "so remote from the customs and common life of all men, that it does not cease to cause great wonder how they should live and maintain themselves and raise their children with such a way of life." The shamanic practices that probably did constitute the core of religion for most Chichimeca peoples thus went predictably unnoticed by many of even the most observant Spanish writers, and were dismissed as superstition or witchcraft by the rest.

An indication of what some of these practices may have been for one of the largest Chichimeca nations, the Guachichiles of San Luis Potosi, comes from a criminal case dating a decade after the end of the war.[6] In 1599 an old Guachichil woman, who like a minority of her compatriots was still unbaptized, and who had attempted to evade the Spanish program of accommodation and acculturation by moving for some years to the still unconquered east, began to call upon all Guachichiles of the area to rise up, destroy the Spanish churches, and kill the invading Spaniards. The Spanish magistrate who caught, tried, and hanged her all in one day, accused her of the political crime of insurrection, while her Spanish counsel ineffectually defended her as a harmless, drunken old woman. Her actions appear, instead, to be those of a shamanic prophetess and leader, and suggest as well that the chroniclers who identified all indigenous leaders as male warriors may, with their emphasis on the masculine arena of war, have ignored other realms of political power in Guachichil society.

Although the accused witch denied that she used peyote – that small hallucinogenic cactus grows wild throughout the area, and undoubtedly formed a part of shamanic practice there – she admitted to her power to transform people into animal forms, and she spoke at length of her visions. She had seen, she said, two deer figures (deer are key religious symbols in other northern Mexican communities), one of them riding a horse and the other bridling it (symbolizing, perhaps, the subjugation of the invading Spanish); these figures had healed her illnesses, removed cataracts from her eyes, and made her young again. And when she entered the church of the Tlaxcalans in San Luis, she had seen her dead daughter, who unlike her had received baptism, rise from her grave in the church floor, but then hide from her behind the altar. This symbolic turning of her daughter from her and toward the colonizers' religion provoked the old woman to begin her religious war by destroying the Christian crosses and images there and in the nearby church of the Purépechas. Finally, to the bewilderment of both defense and prosecutor, she admitted that she had resurrected the dead Indians of the area, and resettled them in a village she was forming near her house. According to other witnesses, she had made this last claim vociferously to all the Guachichiles of the area, with added warnings that any Indian who did not join with her to kill the Spaniards would not share in her immortal

---

[6] This account is drawn from Ruth Behar, "The visions of a Guachichil witch in 1599: A window on the subjugation of Mexico's hunter-gatherers," *Ethnohistory* 34 (1987): 115–38.

life and youth, but would be swallowed by the earth. This threat was
what convinced the magistrate, a veteran of the Chichimeca War himself,
to put the woman to death; ironically, with its millenarian overtones, it
is also a clear indication of the impact of the invading ideology even on
a strong believer in the old ways.

No other religious or millenarian movements have been reported
among the colonized native peoples of the northeast. Past the beginning
of the seventeenth century the early evangelists and martyrs disappear
from the record as well. The chronicles bear no more notice of rugged
friars struggling to convince a wayward *ranchería* to leave their damp and
isolated cave and join a mission settlement. This was in part because the
position of friar had become routinized in the northeast with the establishment of parishes and the delineation of provincial borders, and in
part because with the passing of time there were fewer and fewer uncontacted bands surviving there. A later wave of missionization brought
Franciscans north into Coahuila in 1674 to convert and settle indigenous
bands long subject to slaving raids from Saltillo. From 1742 to 1748
Franciscans followed in the wake of José de Escandón's military expedition, which led to the "reduction" of the Sierra Gorda, for 150 years a
refuge for the Pames south of Rioverde, and to the conquest of Tamaulipas, the last area of the northeast to come under Spanish control (Map
14.2).

The environmental changes caused by the Spanish invasion were as
profound as the social disruptions, and somewhat easier to document.
Las Casas, after discussing the traditional diet of the native peoples of the
northeast, implied that hunting the enormous herds of cattle that roamed
the Bajío in the 1570s had replaced foraging for traditional foods when
he condemned the Chichimecas as "robbers of cattle" who "maintain
themselves" on the stolen cows. By 1582, as the herds moved north into
the Tunal Grande, a group of ranchers complained that the local Guachichiles had taken to riding horses and driving the cattle "by the thousands
. . . to barter and sell to the rancherías for women and munitions."[7]

We must allow for a good deal of exaggeration in this claim, but that
the petitioners could seriously suggest that Guachichiles had taken to

---

[7] "Petición ante el Virrey de los criadores de ganados vecinos y moradores de la frontera Chichimeca," in Philip Wayne Powell, *War and Peace on the North Mexican Frontier: A Documentary
Record* (Madrid, 1971), 223.

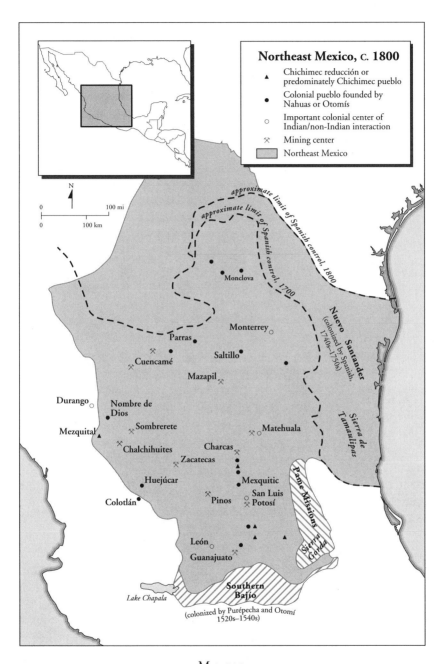

Northeast Mexico, C. 1800

▲ Chichimec reducción or predominately Chichimec pueblo

● Colonial pueblo founded by Nahuas or Otomís

○ Important colonial center of Indian/non-Indian interaction

✕ Mining center

▨ Northeast Mexico

N

0 ——— 100 mi

0 ——— 100 km

approximate limit of Spanish control, 1800

approximate limit of Spanish control, 1700

Monclova

Parras

Cuencamé

Monterrey

Saltillo

Mazapil

Nuevo Santander *(colonized by Spanish, 1740s–1750s)*

Durango

Nombre de Dios

Mezquital

Sombrerete

Matehuala

Sierra de Tamaulipas

Chalchihuites

Charcas

Zacatecas

Huejúcar

Mexquitic

Colotlán

Pinos

San Luis Potosí

Pame Missions

León

Sierra Gorda

Guanajuato

Southern Bajío

Lake Chapala

(colonized by Purépecha and Otomí 1520s–1540s)

Map 14.2

riding horses and rounding up large numbers of cattle – in an area where twenty years earlier Ahumada claimed "one could not fight on horseback" because of the thickness of the nopal cactus – suggests important changes in the local landscape as well as in the Guachichil way of life. If the spread of Spanish cattle ranches in the sixteenth century began a process of semi-desertification such as has been documented for the neighboring Mezquital Valley, it was several decades yet before that process reached its climax with the spread of sheep ranching, which peaked in the San Luis Potosí area around 1630 and somewhat later further north in Nuevo León and Coahuila, and after 1750 to the east of the Sierra Madre Oriental in Tamaulipas. The simultaneous expansion of mining enterprises in San Luis Potosi and Zacatecas, with their constant demands for large amounts of timber, hay, firewood, and charcoal, put additional strains on the environment. The Zacatecos were named by Nahuatl speakers after the tall grasslands (*zacatlan*, "place of grass") they inhabited; after centuries of overgrazing by European cattle, central Zacatecas is today a semi-desert with little hint of prairie. Early reports of pine forests in the Gran Chichimeca and later reports of flocks of sheep numbering in the tens of thousands now read like fiction. In this arid environment of denuded hills and plateaus, only goats can graze.

The means the Spanish used to wage the Chichimeca War wrought another set of changes in the indigenous societies of the northeast. In spite of the importance of securing the roads north to the mines, the Spanish Crown in the second half of the sixteenth century was in no financial position to underwrite the costly enterprise of a full-scale war against the Chichimecas. As a result, the Spanish fought the Chichimeca War largely through private initiative, with Spanish captains recruiting and arming their own men and providing horses at their own expense. Since the great attraction of the northern frontier for the Spanish and mestizo adventurers of central Mexico was the fortunes being made there, few soldiers would have been content with the annual wages offered by the Crown, which were limited to 350 pesos for the highest-paid soldiers. In some other war of conquest, booty confiscated from the vanquished might have made up the difference. Here, where the enemy owned no property, a system was quickly established of confiscating the very bodies of those taken in war; of selling captives as slaves.

The justice of enslaving prisoners in the Chichimeca War was debated, as indeed was the justice of the war itself, yet in the absence of any other source of revenue, the practice continued, lightly regulated. In theory, captives had to be tried and convicted of complicity in robbery and murder before they could be sentenced to slavery for a period of eight to twenty years; children could not be enslaved; and the new owners of the Chichimecas were charged with converting and catechizing their slaves. These regulations, however, did not stop frequently reported abuses of the system. Gonzalo de Las Casas recounted at length the types of deception used to lure peaceful Chichimecas into slavery, such as calling them to mass or asking them to help in fighting other Chichimecas, and then capturing all who came. It was standard Spanish practice to avenge Chichimeca robberies or massacres by moving against entire *rancherías* without stopping to ascertain matters of guilt or innocence. Typically, the Chichimeca "captains" were executed on the spot as the alleged ringleaders of the attacks, and all the other men and women were sentenced to slavery as participants. Chichimeca slaves sold by the soldiers brought about 80 to 100 pesos at the auction block, about a third of the price of enslaved Africans at the time. For the average soldier, capturing and enslaving Chichimecas represented a much more realistic chance of making a small fortune than did the rather more remote odds of discovering a rich mine.

The violence and cruelty of the campaign against the Chichimecas were rhetorically disguised in chronicles that heavily emphasized the cruelty and wildness of the nomads themselves. They were described as "wildmen," *alárabes*, a word that literally means "Arabs" and that reminds us of the roots of Spanish colonialism in the conquest of Andalusia. On the subject of the cruelty of the Chichimecas, all commentators waxed eloquent: the tortures, the scalpings, the brutal dances ending in the killing of a captive, the corpses that the Spaniards would find hanging from trees with arms, heads, and genitals cut off. The prominence of these acts in the Spaniards' accounts of the Chichimecas reflects, more than their civilized shock or disgust, the specific purpose of their writing, which was to justify the war they themselves were waging. Accounts of cannibalism among the Chichimecas are especially likely to have been distorted, inflated, or invented. In 1562, for example, Ahumada related that only the Guachichiles of Mazapil "ate human flesh"; he got this information not from eyewitnesses but from the neighboring Zacatecos, who at the time were at war with the alleged cannibals. The same Pedro de Ahumada, in his role as captain of the Spanish forces in the north, was himself capable of exacting cruel vengeance, according to a witness in a suit calling for the escalation of the war. One day, the witness recalled, Captain Ahumada found the body of a friar "filled with arrows" and soon afterward captured the supposed assailants of the friar, "and since the crime was so great, he took them alive and cut off the hands and feet of more than three hundred Indians."[8] Such cruelties, exacted by the Spanish or their allies upon the Chichimecas, were omitted from their chronicles, or presented as stern justice.

Ironically, though not atypically, the life among civilized Europeans that was forced upon enslaved captives was often seen as only corrupting those wildmen. The most insistent denunciations of the practice of enslaving Chichimecas were not based on its injustice or dubious legality, but on the fact that, because so many escaped from captivity, the system did not help to end the war. Worse, as Las Casas and others had warned, "from the communication which they have had with Spaniards" the escaped captives "become *ladinos* and cunning, . . . and being such, as soon as they return to their lands they are made caudillos and captains, and these are the ones who have done most of the damage and the raids, since they are astute and sly."[9] Some witnesses swore to have seen "ladino Indians among the raiding Indians, who speak Castilian."[10] Such statements testify to European beliefs both in their own innate superiority (of course an Indian who knows Castilian is more cunning that one who can hardly speak) and in the inherently depraved nature of the wildman; nevertheless, it was those same "ladino Indians" who were among the first to negotiate for peace, and to become catechists, captains, and intermediaries with the invading Spanish.

GENOCIDE AND ETHNOCIDE

By the 1580s the economy of the north had been transformed. The Spanish mining colony at Zacatecas was no longer an isolated outpost but was supported by an entire infrastructure of ranches and agriculture, salt mines and logging operations. At the same time, veteran slavehunters from the Chichimeca War had moved beyond the confines of the Gran Chichimeca to found Saltillo and the forerunner of Monterrey, from where they would continue to hunt for slaves to sell in the Zacatecas mines and to work the ranches and plantations they soon established in the north. The war itself had meanwhile changed, and was characterized

---

[8] "Petición ante el Virrey," 256.   [9] Ibid., 221.   [10] Ibid., 249.

less by Chichimeca raids followed by Spanish reprisals than by Spanish slaving raids counterposed by massed Chichimeca attacks on ranches and caravans. The prosecution of the war by private initiative, fueled by the slave trade, was now seen as unnecessarily prolonging the war and damaging the economic interests of the region.

One Spanish rancher, testifying in favor of an expanded Chichimeca War in 1582, devised a practical way to disentangle the slave trade from the war: "It would be well, so the soldiers with the most greed and will could capture and kill the *gandules* [wild Indians], that they should be paid some reasonable amount for each one they kill and capture, as much as His Excellency wishes."[11] This modest proposal for a war of annihilation against the Chichimecas was, for the time, ignored.

In fact, genocide, the deliberate destruction of the indigenous peoples of the northeast, was never adopted as an official program or a long-term solution to the endemic "Indian wars" of the northeastern borderlands. (That was a step not taken until the nineteenth century, by the Anglo pupils of the Spanish colonizers, who carried out the "pacification" of Texas in the 1840s and 1850s with brutal ruthlessness.) Occasional statements by colonial officials and observers that may seem to evoke a policy of extermination are generally expressions, as it were, of wishful thinking. Ethnocide, the destruction of native cultures, was on the contrary not only a specific policy aim but was seen as morally justified, whereas genocide, as policy, could not have been within the Spanish worldview. Moreover, the destruction of native cultures, and especially of native religion, was seen as a positive Christian duty, and even as the justification itself of colonization. As stark as this fact seems to an indigenist sensibility today, it should also make us somewhat skeptical as to whether ethnocide was always as complete, or as planned, as might be supposed. The interests of many colonizers actually ran in other directions, not toward the destruction of native culture but toward its isolation and ghettoization, and toward preserving native peoples as a dependent workforce.

A late example, from the less morality-conscious Bourbon age of colonial politics, might serve to uncover some of the practical considerations behind the policies used to end the Chichimeca War in the 1580s. In his instructions of 1786 to the commander of the Provincias Internas, the viceroy Bernardo de Gálvez admitted that the "complete extermina-

---

[11] Ibid., 232.

tion" of the Apaches would bring "happiness" to the northeastern provinces of Coahuila and Texas, but he viewed this goal as unattainable. The program of immediate tactical goals that Gálvez traced aimed instead at weakening their societies and cultures. The tactics he recommended included spreading warfare between rival "Indian nations," and using force to subjugate the "smaller numbers" who survive, on the divide-and-conquer model; but he placed special emphasis on the systematic use of trade to foster economic and cultural dependency on the Spanish colonists. "In exchange for their furs the Indians may receive horses, mares, mules, cattle, dried meat, sugar loaves, maize, tobacco, brandy, guns, ammunition, knives, clothing, or coarse cloth, vermilion, mirrors, glass beads, and other trifles," he wrote – particularly alcohol and arms. "Supplying the Indians with drink will be a means of gaining their will, discovering their most profound secrets, tranquilizing them many times so that they will think of and carry out fewer hostilities, and of creating for them a new necessity which will strictly oblige them to recognize their dependence upon us." Providing them with long guns, especially ones made with "weak bolts without the best temper, and with superficial adornments pleasing to the sight of the ignorant," would be doubly useful, as the guns would come to replace bows and arrows, which are devastating in short-range combat and which the Indians can manufacture themselves, and would make the Indians dependent on the Spanish for repairs and for gunpowder.[12] This statement is valuable for making explicit the *realpolitik* calculations behind the trade-and-aid policies that had been carried out for the past two centuries on the northeastern borderlands.

In August 1586, Viceroy Villamanrique responded to critiques of the abuses being committed by the slavers of Saltillo and Nuevo León by adopting, in part, the program outlined four years earlier by the northern ranchers. He prohibited the enslavement of Chichimecas, instead offering a bounty of 20 pesos for each Chichimeca warrior captured or killed, but at the same time he reduced the number of soldiers on the northern frontier and thus avoided the scenario of genocidal war. Under these new guidelines, the Spanish captains at last turned their energies toward securing a general peace with the Chichimecas. In 1589, sensing peace was at hand, Villamanrique adopted a policy earlier proposed by Gonzalo

---

[12] Viceroy Bernardo de Gálvez, *Instructions for Governing the Interior Provinces of New Spain, 1786* (Berkeley, CA, 1951), 104–7.

de Las Casas, who had noted that "killing and capturing all these Chichimecas without leaving a single one, which I hold to be impossible, . . . would not be in accord with the law of justice, nor is it good to leave the land barren and depopulated." Rather, they should be "settled on flat ground, indoctrinated in the law of God," provided with food and clothing for at least a year, and people accustomed to agriculture should be settled among them to teach them how to grow their own food.[13]

In the end, both the Chichimeca peoples and their cultures were effectively decimated. The incursion of Spanish ranchers and miners, as well as the decades-long war, had already caused serious disruptions in their way of life. In the course of the war, entire communities were captured and destroyed; surviving captives were enslaved, setting them on a path of assimilation that in the end might have turned out to be more significant than that which the Spanish attempted later to impose on them with the aid of Tlaxcalan exemplar communities.

Several Guachichil captains were already fluent in Spanish by 1590, and were among the strongest supporters of Spanish rule; elsewhere, ladino Chichimecas were employed after the peace settlement as catechists, introducing the religion of the Europeans to their people. By the time Fray Juan de Torquemada wrote his chronicle of Franciscan evangelist activities in Mexico around 1608, the Chichimecas were living in settled communities, their former "captains" now adopting the office of *gobernador* and the title *don*. Where earlier chroniclers had always noted that they lived without houses, using trees or caves for shelter, now they lived "in houses of straw, and many of them in each one; and up to now they are sustained by the King, who gives them meat, that they may eat, and clothes, that they may dress."[14] But the settling of Tlaxcalans and other central Mexicans among the Chichimecas – or, perhaps more accurately, the concentration of hunting-and-gathering *rancherías* into barrios within newly founded Tlaxcalan towns – never led, as some Spanish policymakers seem to have hoped, to intermarriage between the two groups. For many, such as the Guachichiles who remained in central San Luis, this policy did not even have the intended effect of transforming them into agriculturalists. In later years it was more common to find them (and other Chichimecas as well) in the role of servants, a role they had first played during their enslavement in the war – or even, for many years, still in the role of slaves, despite the viceregal prohibitions.

[13] Las Casas, 181 and 184.   [14] *Monarquía Indiana* (Mexico, 1969), I, 669.

Beginning with the first peace talks in this area in 1589, the Spanish captains and friars began a campaign to concentrate the Guachichil *rancherías* into larger, more compact permanent settlements. The same policy of concentration had been carried out all over Mesoamerica, but effects of concentrating the dispersed and mobile *rancherías* of the nomadic peoples who occupied the entire northeast were much more pronounced than the simple gathering in of already settled hamlets and homesteads in the central areas. The gifts of food and clothing, which the Spanish offered in return for peace and an end to raiding, served to help concentrate (*reducir*) the Chichimecas by attracting nomadic communities to the small number of distribution centers. There was a distinct pattern to the location of these centers, which determined the later distribution of Chichimeca communities. The broad areas taken over by Spanish cattle ranches were quickly bereft of their original inhabitants; no distribution centers were founded, and the small amount of labor required by the ranching economy was supplied by Indians and mulattoes from farther south. Mining areas were among the original distribution sites, apparently meant to serve as centers for a local Indian workforce; but at mines that grew rich and attracted people from all over New Spain, Chichimeca settlements were gradually squeezed out and recongregated elsewhere, leaving Chichimeca pueblos only at distant and marginal mining centers such as Cuencamé. Similarly, agriculturally based Chichimeca pueblos were located in marginal areas, with poor resources or on the fringes of Spanish-controlled territory.

Finally, in the regions to the north and east that held little promise of mineral wealth, there was no attempt to bring the land under Spanish control at all. Here, as in the mountainous country of Matehuala and Rioverde, "unreduced" *rancherías* of Guachichiles and other hunter-gatherers continued their nomadic existence until at least the middle of the seventeenth century. Still farther north and east, in the jurisdictions of the new ranching and agricultural colonies at Saltillo and Nuevo León, an entirely different modus vivendi was being developed in the early seventeenth century between Spanish colonists and the *rancherías* whose lands they had invaded. The capture and enslavement of entire *rancherías* that had marked the most intense phase of the Chichimeca War farther south developed, in the far northeast, into a perennial institution. There was little or no attempt to forcibly convert, concentrate, and settle the nomadic hunter-gatherers into "civilizing" agricultural towns. Bands like that of Nacastlagua, described at the beginning of the chapter, were instead allowed and even encouraged to find their own shelter and forage for most of the year for their own food, and were captured and impressed into agricultural service only when the need for labor was highest, at planting and harvesting time, thus saving the landowners the expense of maintaining a large workforce year-round. This system, which clearly contravened royal laws forbidding Indian slavery and repeatedly attracted the attention of viceregal authorities, nevertheless endured into the 1720s, first barely disguised as *encomienda* and later under the institution, peculiar to the region, known as *congrega*. The persistence of Indian slavery here bears tribute to the ability of officials in an isolated borderland to bend regulations in the favor of their own interests.[15]

The Spanish invasion of the northeast led to a drastic population decline of all the peoples known collectively as Chichimecas, and to the eventual disappearance as peoples of all save the Pames of San Luis Potosi and the related Chichimeca-Jonaz of the Sierra Gorda in eastern Guanajuato. The extent of that decline is impossible to measure with any precision, though scattered population counts for later dates make the long-term trend clear. The extremely limited information available on Chichimeca society during the five decades of warfare, and the almost complete absence of information on what may have gone before, makes it unlikely that estimates of pre-conquest population numbers will ever be more than guesses. Peter Gerhard has hazarded a few such guesses for some districts within the region, based on sparse Spanish records of population, troop size, and numbers of *rancherías* or *encomiendas*, and in large measure on his sense of what indigenous population densities must have been like – around one-half to one and a half persons per square kilometer for hunter-gatherers, depending on the local geography. Extrapolations from Gerhard's estimates together with equally plausible estimates based on an assumption of indigenous densities of one-tenth to one-fifth persons per square kilometer (somewhat more for the semi-sedentary Pame) and estimates of the same populations roughly half a century after contact are listed in Table 14.1.

Of the four Chichimeca nations said to be involved in the Chichimeca War, the Guamares appear to have fared the worst. Their original territory, which covered the Bajío and the mountains of Guanajuato, became

[15] See José Cuello, "The Persistence of Indian Slavery and Encomienda in the Northeast of Colonial Mexico, 1577–1723," *Journal of Social History* 21 (1988): 683–700.

Table 14.1. *Some estimates of native population of northeastern Mexico at contact*

	Area (square kilometers)	Estimated population in 1519		Postcontact population[1]
		(high)	(low)	
Guamares	25,000	45,000	10,000	0
Pames	45,000	70,000	40,000	25,000
Zacatecos	60,000	90,000	12,000	1,500
Guachichiles	100,000	125,000	20,000	3,000
Laguneros	40,000	40,000	15,000	1,700
Nuevo León	65,000	100,000	25,000	16,000
Northern Coahuila	50,000	50,000	10,000	1,000
Northern Tamaulipas	65,000	115,000	25,000	2,500
Total	450,000	625,000	142,000	

[1] Dates of postcontact population estimates are approximately 1620–25 for Guamares, Zacatecos, Guachichiles, Laguneros, and Nuevo León (where native population continued to decline to near extinction by the 1720s); 1725 for northern Coahuila; and 1795 for Pames and Tamaulipas (excluding Huasteca in the south), both finally conquered in 1742–48.

Source: Area measures, high estimates, and postcontact populations extrapolated from Peter Gerhard, *A Guide to the Historical Geography of New Spain* (Cambridge, 1972), and *The North Frontier of New Spain* (Princeton, NJ, 1982), except for postcontact Pames (from 1794 Revillagigedo census) and Nuevo León (lowered from Gerhard's estimate of between 30,000 and 50,000).

occupied by cattle ranches and mining towns long before the end of the war. Guamares, Purépechas, and Otomís had cofounded the town of Pénjamo (now in southwestern Guanajuato) in 1549, before the outbreak of the war, but there is no further mention of the Guamares there. After the war, when the surviving Chichimeca groups were "reduced" – induced to settle in permanent villages, usually alongside "civilized" Tlaxcalan settlers – no pueblos of Guamares were formed, and indeed the last reference to the Guamares dates from around 1572.

The Pames, by contrast, fared the best, and indeed are the only "Chichimeca" group who survive today, even though theirs was the first territory invaded by the Spanish or, rather, by their Otomí allies, beginning with the Purépecha settlement of Acámbaro in 1526 and the Otomí conquest of Querétaro in 1531. The Pame-speaking peoples differed from other Chichimeca groups in that some Pame rancherías lived intermingled with Nahua, Otomí, and Purépecha settled villages on the northern frontier of Mesoamerica and apparently were aware of Mesoamerican agricultural techniques. Further, the minor Pame role in the Chichimeca War, limited to small raids on cattle ranches in the Bajío, caused few deaths on either side. The Pame territory in the Bajío of eastern Guanajuato and western Querétaro was taken over early in the 1530s by Otomí settlements and Spanish cattle ranches; the remainder consisted of the rough hills of the Sierra Gorda and the warm country of Rioverde. Cattle ranches began invading the more hospitable areas of Rioverde after 1600, but the Sierra Gorda remained "unreduced" till a belated conquest, by soldiers and Franciscans, in 1742. This therefore was a true "region of refuge" for the Pames and perhaps other Chichimecas as well, and allowed their survival.

The Zacatecos took part in the Mixtón rebellion of 1541 even though they had not yet been conquered, and thus some of the reprisals for that revolt fell on them. The mines of Zacatecas, among others, were within their territory, so that much of the southern part of their lands were effectively occupied by the Spanish by the time of the peace. In 1562, at the height of the war, Ahumada reports leading 300 Zacateco allies from near Sombrerete against more than 2,000 Zacateco archers from Mezquital, some 200 kilometers northwest of Zacatecas, and 500 warriors from the Malpaís near Cuencamé in what is now central Durango; the implication is that already by this time the centers of Zacateco population had moved far north and west of their former territory. A generation later the *relaciones geográficas* of 1585 painted the Zacatecos as uncomfortably adjusted to life and work within an increasingly Spanish environment, alternating between day labor on cattle ranches or in mining camps and raids on silver caravans, in which they were outnumbered by their new allies the Guachichiles. All purportedly spoke Nahuatl, which had become the indigenous *lingua franca* of the border zone. Thirty years after the peace, in 1620, Zacatecos remained in only a handful of settlements. Perhaps seventy families lived in two mining camps near Chalchihuites, and the rest were concentrated in the marginal agricultural village of San Juan del Mezquital (100 families in 1604) and the Cuencamé mining towns. Some had moved farther north among the Indian groups that had not taken part in the war, in the mission town of Parras. Of these various settlements, perhaps the only surviving one was that in San Juan del Mezquital (300 "Indians" in 1746); the Zacatecos in the pueblos farther south apparently assimilated, while the Cuencamé and Parras areas, which remained on the northern frontier of Spanish control to the end of the colonial period, were periodically decimated by disease and by "Apache" raids from the north.

The Guachichiles, thought to be the most numerous of the four nations, once occupied a territory of some 100,000 square kilometers, from Lake Chapala north to modern Saltillo. Pedro de Ahumada wrote in 1562, after a dozen years of warfare, that in the central valley of San Luis Potosi alone "it seemed to us that there were in this Tunal [Grande], according to the signs and the quantity of rancherías, up to 1500 or 2000 people." Ahumada repeats reports of Guachichiles or their allies far to the south around Pénjamo and Ayo near Lake Chapala, and of more than 6,000 archers far to the north in the Mazapil area. These reports, like those for the Zacatecos, would seem to indicate that the Guachichiles had withdrawn their *rancherías* from those parts of their former territory, which had been invaded by Spanish mining towns, roads, and cattle ranches, and had concentrated their forces in a handful of areas from which they launched raids on the silver road.

With the end of the war, the Guachichiles were among the first of the northeastern peoples to be "reduced" to settlements, including the agricultural town of Saltillo and the mining town of Mazapil in the far north, as well as seven agricultural and mining towns of central San Luis Potosi. The Guachichil *rancherías* that had survived in the previously "unpacified" southwestern region around Pénjamo apparently dispersed or were drawn north to settle. Judging from a detailed report of a distribution of clothes to the Guachichil settlements in November, 1593, there were between 2,500 and 3,000 Guachichiles living in pueblos immediately after the war, and an undeterminable number still living in *rancherías* outside of Spanish control around Matehuala and further east.

The next thirty years was a period of continued reduction of the Guachichiles. From 1592 on, the Chichimecas of the Rioverde area were rounded up and settled in the Guachichil barrio at Santa María del Río, where 75 survived in 1622, alongside 112 settlers in the Otomí barrio; some of the Guachichiles, it was noted, "come and go from Rioverde." By 1622 the five Guachichil barrios of the Tunal Grande, all well within the area under Spanish control and far from the independent *rancherías*, had apparently been concentrated in Mexquitic, as their combined population plummeted from over 500 in 1593 to just under 100. The Guachichiles of the Matehuala area were concentrated, sometimes forcibly, in Venado; in later years, this concentration probably included

"Chichimecas" from farther and farther afield, including non-Guachichiles from Nuevo León. By 1622 the Chichimeca population of Venado and the nearby barrio of Agua Hedionda stood at 693, in a region where thirty years earlier there had been nearly a thousand living in settlements, and unknown others in scattered *rancherías*. In the enormous jurisdiction stretching north from Charcas toward Saltillo, there were only 20 Spanish families in 1622, who were served by 100 Indian *naboríos*. The Guachichiles of Mazapil had all but disappeared, and in the northernmost settlement of Saltillo only 116 remained; all told, about 1,000 were in settlements throughout the Spanish-controlled area, which now covered all of the former Guachichil territory.

The Rioverde and Matehuala areas were the only places where independent Guachichil *rancherías* remained after the peace. Over the following decades the occasional energetic friar would convince those *rancherías* to congregate at the Guachichil centers of Santa María del Río and Venado, which were therefore the only settlements to survive, if not thrive, into the eighteenth century. By 1674 only two aged Guachichil women lived in the Tunal Grande at Mexquitic, and one in the north at Saltillo. The twin Guachichil settlements at Venado and Agua Hedionda had declined to 24 families, probably the population nadir; fifty years later, they had rebounded to perhaps 100 families. In Santa María del Río a well-established Guachichil barrio of 28 families had been formed through the concentration of *rancherías* in the area; in 1727, the number of families had grown to 72. This concentration was accomplished through the zeal of such men as a friar from Charcas who traveled far into what is now Nuevo León in search of unconverted *rancherías* before finding a hundred Guachichiles sheltering in a cave, then compelled them to return with him to be baptized and settled. It may be that by constantly congregating the survivors of previous epidemics together with isolated uninfected groups, such zeal led inadvertently to the decimation of the remaining Guachichiles. It was only after the concentrations ended in the 1670s that the Guachichil population began to grow.

The concentration of the Guachichiles ultimately led as well to their assimilation into the societies of the Tlaxcalans and Otomís of Venado and Santa María del Río, or to their disappearance among the general mixed groups of *indios naboríos*, mestizos, and mulattoes who worked the haciendas of the north. Even after they were concentrated, the Chichimecas continued to migrate frequently, moving freely among the pueblos, cities, mines, and unsubdued borderlands of the northeast, although within the area of Spanish control they no longer moved in entire groups or *rancherías*. Many remained within the Tunal Grande, yet outside of the *pueblos de guachichiles*, working as servants – sometimes enslaved – in Spanish houses, mines, and ranches. As servants living outside any established Guachichil community, these migrants would have had little opportunity to maintain a separate Guachichil identity. Living and working with the growing mixed populations of blacks, mestizos, mulattoes, and Indians who were the workforce of northern New Spain, they probably assimilated – not with the Tlaxcalans but with the *castas* (mixed groups). Some evidence that this was in fact what happened comes from the earliest surviving parish registers of San Luis Potosi. In 1651 and 1652, ten "Chichimecas" were baptized here, eight of them adults (indicating that they had recently migrated or been brought to San Luis) and all of them servants or children of servants in the houses of local Spaniards. Significantly, the godparents of seven of them were the black or mulatto slaves of their own employers. In the death records for 1673, the seventeen Chichimecas listed were likewise all servants; the only one whose marital status was mentioned was a woman married to a free mulatto.

To the north and east of the area so broadly affected by the Chichimeca War and its aftermath, the earlier history of the Bajío seemed to be replayed again and again, with the growth of a huge flocks of sheep or cows leading to the development of a Spanish ranching and agricultural economy and a parallel decline of the indigenous hunters and gatherers. Sheep were first introduced in Nuevo León in 1635; by 1685 there were 555,000 sheep in eighteen haciendas near Monterrey alone, and ranches were already spreading east, into what six decades later would become Nuevo Santander or Tamaulipas. Corn and wheat, once imported from Zacatecas, were even being exported from Nuevo León by 1649.[16] At the same time, hundreds of *rancherías* entirely disappeared, after they were captured and enslaved by the new landlords; an early chronicler of the province appended a list of the "nations" – *rancherías* or bands, that is – that had already been "annexed" and "consumed" by 1665 within a dozen leagues of the principal Spanish settlements of Monterrey (47 bands), Cadereyta (44 bands) and Cerralvo (70 bands).[17]

---

[16] León, "Relación," 142–44.
[17] "Historia del Nuevo Reino de León, desde 1650 hasta 1690, por un autor anónimo," in Genaro García, *Documentos inéditos*, 290–93.

Yet there was a crucial difference in the attitudes of the colonizers toward the indigenous peoples of the far northeast from those of the ranchers of the Bajío. Rather than considering these hunting-and-gathering peoples obstacles to "commerce" and "civilization," here, far from the densely populated center of Mexico, the Spanish saw them as a handy workforce and regarded their deaths as a grave misfortune – for the hacienda owners who needed their labor. The chronicler who listed the names of those 161 destroyed bands was not commemorating the peoples who had died but celebrating the feats of the invading Spanish, "so that the reader may see how hard the few Spaniards who lived in this Kingdom have toiled, and with how many turns of fortune." For with the deaths of so many Indians, between 1665 and 1690 the colonizers had been, he wrote, "obliged" to go 40 and 50 leagues afield, covering the length and breadth of Nuevo León and even entering what would become Tamaulipas, Coahuila, and Texas, to round up and capture an additional 89 bands to serve them.

And in the next 20 or 25 years it will be necessary to annex yet more, for these will already have perished, because, as soon as any Indian falls ill, now matter how carefully one treats him, he dies, as they are extremely pusillanimous people and who for their part go to little trouble to recover their health; from which there will come to pass in this Kingdom what Dr. Francisco López de Gómara mentions in the history which he composed of the Indies, that of the million and a half people who lived in Hispaniola, in less than 50 years all had disappeared. We should attribute this to the many sins which they commit and which their ancestors committed, for, although these nations have not followed idolatries, they have held and still hold many superstitions and abuses, for which His Divine Majesty punishes them and is annihilating them; with the result that in the course of time all the Indians of New Spain and Peru will come to an end, as those who live there will see.[18]

By the middle of the eighteenth century, the few surviving indigenous people of Nuevo León, numbering perhaps 500, no longer lived lives alternating between enslavement on Spanish haciendas and an impoverished replication of their former nomadic way of life, but had been concentrated into four mission towns. By the end of the colonial era they had virtually disappeared, absorbed by the growing Tlaxcalan and mestizo barrios founded alongside their missions. To the east, the mountains and coastal plains of Tamaulipas were invaded and conquered in 1748, at

---

[18] Ibid., 293–94.

a time when fewer than 13,000 indigenous inhabitants had survived a century of slaving raids from Nuevo León and introduced disease. By 1821 perhaps one or two thousand remained, scattered among the early mission sites that had, for the most part, become towns of the mixed peoples immigrating from central Mexico; a handful of indigenous people still lived in Tamaulipas as late as 1886. In northern Coahuila, invaded in 1674, fewer than 2,000 "native Indians" survived by the end of the eighteenth century, rapidly becoming a minority among the mestizos, Otomís, and Tlaxcalans who first settled the mission towns into which they were concentrated.

TLAXCALANS, BARRIOS AND PUEBLOS

The only organized, large-scale "settlement" of the nomadic northeast by Indians whom the Spanish recognized as "civilized" (*gente política*) began in July 1591 when a train of a hundred wagons set out from the province of Tlaxcala in central Mexico, carrying four hundred families who would form agricultural villages among the hunters and gatherers. The number of families sent by agreement between the Spanish authorities and Tlaxcalan leaders is significant, for the number 400 simultaneously encompasses Spanish and Tlaxcalan notions of completeness. Four hundred, as 20 times 20, is as effective a way of saying "a great multitude" in Nahuatl as the number 40 was in biblical Hebrew. The colonists were also traveling in four groups, each sent by one of the four "barrios" or constituent *altepetl* into which the province of Tlaxcala was classically divided. Each group was supposed to consist of precisely one hundred families, the European notion of a large basic unit. In reality, these numbers were somewhat fictitious, as we know from a complete list of the future settlers that was drawn up along the route. In order to come up with such a large quantity of families willing to leave their homes and lands in Tlaxcala and journey north into the unknown, so soon after the devastating epidemic of 1587–88, several single men were counted as complete "families," and two or three families were listed twice to make the number come out even. These manipulations perhaps testify to the importance of the number itself to Tlaxcalans and Spaniards alike.

The pueblos founded in the north by the leaders of the caravan continued to respect the quadripartite division of Tlaxcala. Those from the barrio of Tepeticpac settled the adjoining pueblos of Venado, Mexquitic, and Tlaxcala (soon to become San Luis Potosí with the discovery of silver early in 1592). San Esteban de Nueva Tlaxcala was founded, next to the new Spanish town of Saltillo on the northeastern frontier, by people from Tizatlán. The two areas of settlements in the west, Colotlán and Huejúcar among the Cazcanes of the mountains north of Guadalajara, and San Andrés del Teul and Nueva Tlaxcala de Chalchihuites northwest of Zacatecas along the frontier between Huicholes, Tepecanos, and Zacatecos, were apparently settled by people from the other two barrios, Quiahuixtlán and Ocotelulco, respectively. In the northeast, as James Lockhart has noted for central Mexico, "those social patterns not in direct conflict with the operation of Spanish rural structures tended to persist, with Spaniards often ignoring or misunderstanding them. Full-fledged moiety organization, for example, lasted in places until the end of the colonial period."[19]

But the very success of the Tlaxcalan settlers in using their fourfold barrio division to determine the way they divided the north meant the inevitable end of the system. The new pueblos, set in this vast northern space, were so distant from each other that they could not long remain in contact or form any kind of continuing social unit. One of the last real communications among Tlaxcalan pueblos came within a year of their foundation, when the Tlaxcalan governor of Mexquitic and five men of the pueblo journeyed west with two hundred newly "pacified" Guachichiles from central San Luis Potosi to put down a Tepecano uprising that destroyed the Tlaxcalan settlement at San Andrés in early 1592. On the other hand, the Tlaxcalans treated the Spanish designation of their settlements in the north, *pueblo*, as a translation of *altepetl* or ethnic state, and to the end of the colonial period and beyond they acted as if their new pueblos were indeed quasi-autonomous ministates ruled over by descendants of the indigenous nobility, not Spanish-style "towns." We might then identify the divisions that split the heart of each of the new pueblos as an attempt to reduplicate the moiety divisions on a local scale, under the nose of the Spaniards as it were. Typically, the new foundations consisted of a *pueblo de tlaxcaltecas* and a *pueblo de chichimecas*, each with separate, parallel governments, but with the Chichimecas always in a subordinate role. The most elaborate division was that in Venado, which like Tlaxcala itself was divided into four barrios – of Tlaxcalans, Purépechas, Guachichiles, and Chanalas – that lasted at least till the end of the colonial period. These divisions can be attributed

[19] Lockhart, *Cambridge History of Latin America*, II, 281.

to the Tlaxcalans, who were the largest and politically most powerful group and who insisted on maintaining a separation between themselves and other groups, whether Chichimeca or Spanish.

The cultural and political hegemony of the central Mexican settlers over the pacified Chichimecas in the dual settlements of the northern frontier can be glimpsed in the record of a tour of inspection by the *alcalde mayor* of San Luis Potosi in 1674. In Venado, with its four "ethnic" neighborhoods, the *alcalde mayor* attributed the evident decline of the Chichimecas to the explosive growth of the Tlaxcalan community, who he felt were monopolizing the land resources of the pueblo. The Guachichil governor of the pueblo communicated with the *alcalde mayor* in Nahuatl, the language of the Tlaxcalans, rather than in Guachichil, even though interpreters of the latter language were also available at that date. The twelve Guachichil families who composed the nearby *visita* of La Hedionda, in contrast, came out to greet the *alcalde mayor* "with their bodies painted, according to their custom." Perhaps in this, the only apparently pure Guachichil settlement remaining at that date, the "customs" of the Guachichiles survived somewhat longer as they achieved some sort of accommodation with agricultural life without the mediation of Tlaxcalan settlers. During the same provincial *visita* the *alcalde mayor* found the offices of the Otomí governor of Santa María del Río to be "inadequate and indecent" and ordered new ones built, decreeing that the old ones be left to the Guachichil governor.[20]

Land tenure in the Tlaxcalan settlements, as indeed in the Spanish towns and haciendas of the northeast, was based on the legal fiction that the Chichimeca nations, as the "natural lords" of the land, had freely deeded it over to the Spanish monarch when they accepted his sovereignty. The king was thus free to grant it (in royal *mercedes*, or "mercies") to deserving subjects, as he did to the pueblos founded by the four hundred families from Tlaxcala. Following their duty to put the land to productive use – the Tlaxcalans had, after all, been contracted to serve the Chichimecas as examples of loyal subjects, faithful Christians, and, above all, diligent workers – the new settlers immediately began to work the land as they had in their home province. Title to the land, as in central Mexico, was held in common by the *república de indios*, while seeds, tools, and labor, as well as the products of the land, were held by

---

[20] Primo Feliciano Velázquez, *Historia de San Luis Potosí* (San Luis Potosi, 1982), II, 237–58.

individual families. Every year the Tlaxcalan governor would, in theory, indicate to each family the plot of land it would have use-rights over for the next season. In practice, so long as there was enough land to go around in the northern pueblos, for a good 150 years after they were founded, families took whatever parcel they wished and kept it as long as they needed it. It was only toward the end of the colonial era, as populations rose and land became scarce, that families began to guard jealously what they had come to regard as their personal patrimony.

The system of joint land-tenure and family land-use, and the social behavior associated with it of clearing and then abandoning fields at will, coincided and reinforced another system that grew up from the earliest years of the Tlaxcalan settlements. The Chichimeca settlements of the northeast had been formed by concentrating numerous *rancherías* into a center (which then, more often than not, dispersed through flight into areas not yet under Spanish control and through drift away from the centers into haciendas, mines, and towns). The Tlaxcalan pueblos, in contrast, began as single central settlements, yet from this unitary origin a multiplicity of scattered small settlements soon arose. This pattern of dispersal, the system of nucleation and fragmentation by which the pueblo sprouted *ranchos* (outlying households), *ranchos* became communities, and those in turn spawned other *ranchos*, was the main dynamic by which the Tlaxcalans colonized and exploited the land within the territories three leagues in radius typically granted their pueblos. The pronounced tendency of the pueblos to divide, disperse, and form colonies is perhaps also an echo, transformed by time and a new social setting, of the Tlaxcalan notion of the barrio or social division.

For a century and a half the Tlaxcalans of the northeast cleared and settled their new land, land they utilized in a dramatically different and more intensive way than the Chichimecas they eventually dispossessed. Where the Chichimecas gathered mesquite seeds, ground them, and cooked them into hard cakes, the Tlaxcalans ignored the mesquite seeds but cut the wood, which they sold as lumber, firewood, or charcoal to the mining operations that soon surrounded them, signal of the early and enduring market orientation of the pueblos of the northeast. Where the Chichimecas drank the juices of prickly pears and succulent magueys that grew wild across the region, the Tlaxcalans planted desert orchards of domesticated nopal cactuses and pulque maguey plants from central Mexico, processing maguey juice into fermented pulque with the magic of their imported technology, and inventing the sweet cakes of boiled prickly-pear nectar known as *queso de tuna*. And wherever there was water enough, they introduced the central Mexican agricultural complex of corn, beans, chiles, and squash.

During the first century or two of the settlements an ideology developed within them that tightly linked the notions of land tenure, morality, and social justice. Every family within the Tlaxcalan pueblos was thought to have an inherent right to the land it needed to survive, and the governors of the pueblos could only deny that right to someone who had infringed the moral code of the pueblo – for example, through the religiously defined sexual crimes of incest or adultery. The system worked smoothly so long as there was land for all to come and take. But over the same two centuries the population of the Tlaxcalan pueblos grew, as indeed did that of the northeast as a whole, at the remarkable pace of 1 or even 2 percent a year. Thus Mexquitic, founded in 1591 by roughly 100 Tlaxcalans (and 200 Guachichiles), grew to 10,000 Tlaxcalans (and no Guachichiles) by 1800, just over two centuries later. San Esteban, the pueblo adjoining Saltillo founded in 1591 by about 200 Tlaxcalans, had grown to 3,000 by 1767; in addition, Tlaxcalan families from San Esteban had gone out to found at least a half-dozen more pueblos and barrios in Coahuila and Nuevo León, and reportedly as far north as Santa Fe, which, all told, held thousands more people by the end of the eighteenth century. Along with this general population growth came struggles over the use of land, between both the Tlaxcalan pueblos and the pueblos and haciendas that surrounded them, and among Tlaxcalan families within the pueblos themselves. Arguments of morality and social justice were always in the forefront of these struggles; the unresolvable conflict between opposing claims of justice, in a setting of growing land scarcity, would help to fuel the agrarian struggles that erupted in several Tlaxcalan pueblos in the wars of independence and, again, during the Mexican Revolution.

By the eighteenth century the northern Tlaxcalan settlements had in some respects become isolated pockets of central Mexico amid the Spanish-speaking, mestizo culture of the late colonial northeast. In all the settlements, Mexicano or Nahuatl was the common spoken language, spreading even among members of the few surviving Chichimeca neighborhoods, until it was gradually replaced with Spanish by the middle of the nineteenth century. The Tlaxcalan settlers had also brought with them the knowledge of central Mexican ways of life. Some of these, such as the methods of cultivating the pulque maguey and extracting and fermenting its juice, thrived within their settlements without spreading to the surrounding society. The municipality of Mexquitic, site of the principal Tlaxcalan settlement in San Luis Potosi, continues to both produce and consume almost all the pulque in that state.

But the cultural differences between the Tlaxcalan pueblos and the mixed towns, haciendas, and mines of the northeast should not be overstated. The cultural conservatism that was, in essence, official state policy under the colonial regime, as exemplified in repeated appeals to the authority of custom and tradition in colonial court cases, as well as in repeated colonial attempts to segregate peoples (and hence cultures), was responsible for maintaining and occasionally reinforcing "traditional" differences between those defined as Indian and their Spanish, mestizo and mulatto neighbors. Yet even though the Tlaxcalans in the northeast continued to speak Nahuatl until after independence, the great majority of them had been thoroughly bilingual since at least the 1670s, and conducted almost all their official business, whether with the provincial or viceregal authorities or among themselves, in Spanish and without the aid of interpreters. Only the northernmost settlements at Saltillo and Nombre de Dios appear to have produced documents written in Nahuatl during the colonial era.

Moreover, the Tlaxcalan settlements were characterized – perhaps because of the way they were formed – by a slightly more orthodox Christianity than that found in many of the indigenous pueblos of central Mexico, though the orthodoxy of the Tlaxcalan settlement never developed in the direction of the proclericalism shown in the nonindigenous communities of the Bajío and Altos de Jalisco during the Cristero revolt of the 1920s. Hundreds of Tlaxcalans and other central Mexicans uprooted themselves from their homelands to join the organized Tlaxcalan migration or the larger, unorganized migrations of individuals in search of work in the mines, towns, and haciendas of the north. The migrants may have been relatively enthusiastic supporters of the colonial regime, trusting the promises of viceroy and king and conceiving their northward trek in the terms propounded by supporters of the project of serving the king and bringing law and religion to a barbaric land. What is certain is that in this, as in most migrations, most migrants were young and probably had little to lose in their home communities. Consequently, they were less likely than those who remained to feel strongly attached to the increasingly territorialized rituals that made religion in much of central Mexico an amalgam of orthodox Catholicism and prehispanic "pagan" religions.

Religion in the Tlaxcalan pueblos under the colonial regime was in some ways recognizably "Indian," characterized by the full range of religious offices – *tenanches, fiscales,* and so forth – that went into the "civil-religious hierarchies" of central Mexico, as well as by religious celebrations such as elaborate masked dances that had been developed in central Mexico through a collaboration between Spanish evangelism and central Mexican aesthetics. Yet to the degree that religious practice in the Tlaxcalan pueblos was distinctive, the differences were based more on the political implications of pueblo status than on the particular "Indianness" of the people. The colonial "Indian" religious offices collapsed here, along with the fall of Spanish power and the loss of the status of *pueblo de indios,* early in the nineteenth century. The Mesoamerican aesthetics of the dances, songs, and fireworks displays, on the other hand, spread throughout the haciendas and rural pueblos of the northeast, according to class rather than to ethnic status. In the present, the syncretisms that have come to characterize popular Catholicism in the northeast are not those of a conquered, oppressed, and converted nation. They are those of a borderland culture, produced from the mestizo brew of practices and beliefs that have come about over centuries of interactions among people of varied backgrounds and across the varied borders of culture and class and, more recently, of nation-states. Practices have been freely borrowed back and forth, in particular across the borders between the Tlaxcalan pueblos and the surrounding "non-Indian" settlements. Today, no line separates religious culture within the pueblos from that outside them, and there is no indication that such a line was ever clearly drawn.

Perhaps it was only the occasional reinforcement by the colonial regime of the legal differences between the so-called *castas* of Indian, Spanish, African, and mixed blood that kept the system from collapsing before independence. In the San Luis Potosi region the decrees of the Visitor General Don José de Gálvez, laid down in the wake of the tumults of 1767, were specifically intended to reintroduce the *casta* distinctions that had become relaxed over the course of the centuries. Gálvez was particularly concerned about what he regarded as attempts of Indians to dress and act as Spaniards, which he saw both as a symptom of Indian arrogance and in itself a prime cause of the uprisings. In holding this opinion, Gálvez was ignoring not only the social causes of the tumults but also the history of the Tlaxcalans, who had settled the region and who were granted rights denied to the Indians of central Mexico, such as the right to ride horses and bear arms for their own defense. Yet his ignorance was perhaps symptomatic of a general tendency on the part of the Spanish elite to ignore historical differences among various indigenous groups, and to apply a single set of stereotypes to them all – to make, in other words, "Indians," uniformly and stereotypically, of all the indigenous peoples of their colonized world. In his decrees, Gálvez wrote,

I have ordered, among other things, that the justices not permit the Indians to carry any arms, penalty of death, nor wear the clothes of Spaniards which they injustly used, but that they go about with *balcarrota* and *tilma*, according to the usage of such Indians, under penalty of one hundred lashes and one month of prison for whoever disobeys this determination the first time, and of two hundred lashes and perpetual exile from the province for those who repeat their disobedience; . . . and that the said Indians not own or ride horses, under the same penalties.[21]

The *balcarrotas* and *tilma* mentioned here were the distinctive dress – the long strands of hair left uncut at the sides of the head, and the roughly woven poncho – of the Indians of central Mexico. Gálvez evidently wished to see the Indians of San Luis Potosi dress in the same manner so that they could be readily distinguished from the Spaniards and other *castas*. At the same time, the excessive harshness of the penalties he mandated seem to indicate that he realized his decree would be resisted as an affront to the dignity of people long accustomed to dressing and acting as they pleased. Indeed, these very regulations led two brothers living on the border between Mexquitic and San Luis Potosi to discover their true "identity." Declaring that they were "not pure Indians" but the sons of a couple defined by the *sistema de castas* as a mestizo and a *coyota*, they pleaded that they "should not be included in the *balcarrota* since, although we subjected ourselves to it, it was because we were ignorant of our *calidad* and blindly obeyed the precept of the Visitor General Don José de Gálvez."[22]

In view of our own uncertainty as to the meaning that the *casta* terms had for the people to whom they were applied, it is instructive that these brothers apparently accepted an identification with a broad category of "Indian" until an onerous law made them realize the convenience of

[21] Archivo Histórico del Estado de San Luis Potosí (AHESLP), fondo Alcaldía Mayor, year 1767.
[22] AHESLP, AM 1768.

making finer distinctions. But the well-known profusion of *casta* terms in the late colonial period, which these finer distinctions appear to draw on, seems in fact only to have thinly masked a near collapse of the *sistema de castas* itself into two broad categories. A key cultural struggle of that time, which still has strong implications for what we consider the history of native peoples in northeastern Mexico, was whether to frame those two categories as "Spanish" and "non-Spanish," or as "Indian" and "non-Indian"; in other words, whether to stress the "purity" of the Spanish or of the Indian side of the emerging dichotomy.[23]

There was not an inevitable conclusion to this struggle. When the *subdelegado* of Charcas, one of the original Tlaxcalan settlements but much transformed by a small mining boom there, was asked about the schools for Indians in his jurisdiction, he replied that "there is no *pueblo de naturales* in any place under my control, although in Matehuala there subsists a small *congregación* of *castas* which is designated a pueblo . . . whose small population is composed of castas, although they title themselves Indians."[24] The colonial official assumed an exclusive definition and attempted to recategorize those people properly as *castas*, but the people themselves were content with the title of Indians, questions of purity aside, as long as that gave their settlement the somewhat protected legal status of a *pueblo de indios*. The two brothers from San Luis Potosi, on the other hand, by rejecting the category of Indian and the new burdens that it carried, were helping to make the choice eventually taken by Mexican society as a whole – of defining *Indian* exclusively, and eventually of defining all "non-Indians" alike as mestizos.

The leaders of the pueblo of Mexquitic, for their part, displayed no doubt in official correspondence, so long as the colonial regime lasted, about their identity. The word they used was never Indian, but Tlaxcalan. In their incessant lawsuits with neighboring pueblos and haciendas over land, they lay equally incessant claim to their legitimate place of honor as the heirs of the Tlaxcalan allies of the Spanish who settled this rugged country and tamed the wild Guachichiles. Given the history of official racial identities ascribed to the people of the Tlaxcalan settlements, who were constrained by the structure of colonial authority to use an idiom of racial classification created by and for the elite, and who

---

[23] The terms of this cultural struggle also had the effect of completely eliding the contributions of Africans to the peoples and cultures of Mexico.
[24] AHESLP, Poder Ejecutivo, 1796.

were even told what language their children would be allowed to speak, we may see their maintenance of a Tlaxcalan identity for over two hundred years as a successful response, an act of resistance, even a minor triumph. Yet as an act of resistance it was framed entirely within the ideological context of colonial rule. By referring to themselves as the descendants of the Tlaxcalan "conquerors" of the region, they called upon their ancestral service to the Crown to bolster their claims for land, territorial jurisdiction, or whatever "privileges" they could wrest from a grudging provincial elite.

With the collapse of Spanish authority in 1821, the value of being Tlaxcalan (as opposed to being merely Indian) became suddenly worthless in the legal exchanges between the people of these pueblos and the outside world. Under the new republic the civic leaders of the pueblos readily abandoned the use of their Tlaxcalan identity, and suppressed any reference to the pueblo or its government as "Indian" in favor of the new, *casta*-neutral term *citizens*. More recently the people of Mexquitic have retold the story of the foundation of their pueblo as a way of legitimizing their own authority in a new way. In this story, which they readily relate to visitors, they entirely bypass the exploits of the Tlaxcalan settlers and instead trace their ancestry directly to the indigenous "Guachichiles and Chichimecas" of the region. This tale, with its implicit argument that the people of Mexquitic have an autochthonous right to the land of Mexquitic, has taken root at the same time as a revolutionary ideology that lends value to such prehispanic claims to land while devaluing claims that rest on the authority of the Spanish kings.

The Tlaxcalan identity of the people of Mexquitic has meanwhile degenerated into a kind of vestigial ethnic epithet, *teco,* which calls forth the entire gamut of racist stereotypes held about Indians in Mexico. (A woman from Mexquitic confessed ironically to this imposed identity by invoking those stereotypes: "Well sure, we *are* Indians – we don't have money, we don't have anything.") The people of Mexquitic themselves have shed their former identities, perhaps forever, as Indians and as Tlaxcalans, exchanging them for a somewhat vaguer identification as the descendants (physical? spiritual?) of the "barbarous" Guachichiles. The Guachichiles, in the new origin story of Mexquitic, were never conquered, and yielded not to the arms of the Spanish but to the soft words of the friars. Therefore they cannot be painted with the stereotypes that depict Indians as base, servile, and, in a word, defeated. They were also truly indigenous, from this place, with a clear right to the land that the *ejidos* of Mexquitic now occupy. The central theme of this origin story is ultimately that of a close identification with the land. The same theme runs throughout the history of identity in Mexquitic, sweeping away imposed or co-opted notions of Tlaxcalan, Indian, or, indeed, of any ethnic identity.

To speak of a history of the native peoples of northeastern Mexico is to be met with incomprehension by both historians of Mexico and by Native Americanists. The area seems destined to be consigned to a perpetual oblivion: it is too minor, too distant, too dry, and too acculturated; there are too many haciendas, mines, and mestizos, too few natives. The big stories in Native American history, it seems, lie farther south. The big stories of the northeast lie in mines, haciendas, and revolution, and not in Native American history – which today, as in the colonial era, seems only to encompass what fits within the boundaries of a *pueblo de indios*. This view is based on a definition of Native American, and of the people of northeastern Mexico, that ultimately derives from colonial ideologies of race and identity. A broader definition, hinted at many times in the past and the present but always crushed under the oppressive burden laid on the word *Indian*, would encompass many more of the people of the northeast, and would reveal their broad contributions to the history of the society and culture of the region.

BIBLIOGRAPHICAL ESSAY

The historiography of the native peoples of northeastern Mexico is still in its infancy. Works pertinent to the region tend to fall into one of two categories: published primary documents of the synthetic *relación* or chronicle variety, and surveys based on the former and on secondary sources. One recent exception to this rule is Carlos Manuel Valdés's comprehensive ethnohistory of the nomads of Nuevo León, Coahuila, and Chihuahua, *La gente del mezquite: Los nómadas del noreste en la Colonia* (Mexico, 1995), which appeared after the present chapter was written. Valdés, director of the Municipal Archive of Saltillo, draws on recent archeological data and municipal archive documents (a selection is included in an appendix) as well as *relaciones*; his notes and bibliography are very helpful.

Paul Kirchoff was the first to draw a generalized portrait of the "hunting-gathering complex" of the northeast, based on primary sources, in "Los recolectores-cazadores del norte de México," in *El Norte de*

México y el Sur de Estados Unidos (Mexico, 1947), 133–44. Peter Gerhard's *A Guide to the Historical Geography of New Spain* (Norman, OK, 1993) and *The North Frontier of New Spain* (Norman, OK, 1993) are indispensible guides to historical and geographical sources on the region. Isabel Eguilaz de Prado, *Los indios del nordeste de Méjico en el siglo XVIII* (Sevilla, 1965), working within the Spanish historical paradigm of the 1960s, treats the "savages" and their "mentalidad indígena" as objects of antiquarian interest, but includes a somewhat useful bibliography and a servicable estimate of populations and locations, especially for Pames in the era of the Escandón invasion and settlements (1748–56). Martín Salinas, *Indians of the Rio Grande Delta: Their Role in the History of Southern Texas and Northeastern Mexico* (Austin, TX, 1990), compiles a great deal of useful information about the native peoples of northern Nuevo León and Tamaulipas, including what is now South Texas. His bibliography cites numerous primary documents on the area, which are available on microfilm at research centers in Texas. Phillip Wayne Powell wrote extensively about the Chichimeca War and about the peace settlement, especially in *Soldiers, Indians and Silver: The Northward Advance of New Spain, 1550–1600* (Berkeley, CA, 1952), and *Mexico's Miguel Caldera: The Taming of America's First Frontier, 1548–1597* (Tucson, 1977). These are basic texts, indispensible for their rigorously detailed documentation, though strongly colored by Powell's treatment of the Chichimeca War as an epic struggle of "civilization" against "savagery." One of the very few works on the importance of indigenous religion in the conquest of the northeast, and a model for the imaginative use of sparse documentary sources, is Ruth Behar, "The visions of a Guachichil witch in 1599: A window on the subjugation of Mexico's hunter-gatherers," *Ethnohistory* 34 (1987): 115–38. Environmental devastation following the introduction of sheep-raising in the Mezquital Valley, near the southern border of what is here considered northeast Mexico, has been carefully documented by Elinor G. K. Melville, *The Pastoral Economy and Environmental Degradation in Highland Central Mexico, 1530–1600* (Ph.D. diss., University of Michigan, 1983), and *A Plague of Sheep: Environmental Consequences of the Conquest of Mexico* (Cambridge, 1994).

Papers synthesizing the history and prehistory of the Guachichiles and Pames in San Luis Potosi can be found in the mimeographed series *Bulletin de la Mission Archéologique et Ethnologique Française au Mexique*, including Dominique Michelet, "Civilisation et marginalité aux confins nord-est de la Mésoamérique: étude archéologique des poulations sédentaires précolombiennes de la région de Rio Verde" (1980); François Rodriguez, "Quelques apports à l'archéologie des chichimèques: les guachichiles de San Luis Potosí" (1981); and Nicole Percheron, "Contribution à une étude ethnohistorique: Les chichimèques de San Luis Potosí" (1982). See also Percheron, "La pacification des Guachichiles et des Pames de San Luis Potosí," *Cahiers des Amériques latines* 25 (1982): 69–94, and Guy Stresser-Péan, "Les problèmes de frontière de la Huasteca et régions voisines," in *Vingt etudes sur le Mexique et le Guatemala,* ed. Alain Breton, Jean-Pierre Berthe, and Sylvie Lecoin (Toulouse, 1991).

Remarkably little ethnographic work has been carried out with the Pames, the only present-day descendants of the indigenous hunter-gatherers of the northeast, who survive in a handful of communities in central-eastern San Luis Potosi and northern Querétaro. Heidi Bassler de Chemin and Dominique Chemin have lived in the Pame community of Santa María Acapulco for more than twenty years. They have been preparing a Pame dictionary, and have published a few articles on Pame religion: Bassler de Chemin, "Sobrevivencias precortesianas en las creencias de los Pames del Norte, estado de San Luis Potosí, México," *Archivos de historia potosina* 9 (1977): 21–31, and "La fiesta de los muertos entre los pames septentrionales del estado de San Luis Potosí, México," *Archivos de historia potosina* 11 (1979); Chemin, "Rituales relacionados con la venida de la lluvia," *Anales de antropología,* 17 no. 2 (1980): 67–97, and "El chamanismo en la región pame de Santa María Acapulco, S.L.P. y de Tancoyol, Qro.," *Biblioteca de historia potosina* 92 (1988): 1–51.

José Cuello has written incisively about the indigenous history of the Saltillo–Monterrey region in "The Persistence of Indian Slavery and Encomienda in the Northeast of Colonial Mexico, 1577–1723," *Journal of Social History* 21 (1988): 683–700, and *El norte, el noreste y Saltillo en la historia colonial de México* (Mexico, 1990). Leslie Offutt has written about Nahuatl record-keeping in the Tlaxcalan community of Saltillo in "Levels of Acculturation in Northeastern New Spain; San Esteban Testaments of the Seventeenth and Eighteenth Centuries," *Estudios de cultura náhuatl* 22 (1992): 409–43, and in several unpublished papers. The Tlaxcalan colonies are also the subject of David B. Adams's dissertation, *The Tlaxcalan Colonies of Spanish Coahuila and Nuevo León: An Aspect of the Settlement of Northern Mexico* (University of Texas, Austin, 1971), and his "Embattled Borderland: Northern Nuevo León and the Indios Bárbaros, 1686–1870," *Southwestern Historical Quarterly* 95 (1991): 205–20; and more recently of Andrea Martínez Baracs, "Colonizaciones tlaxcaltecas,"

Historia mexicana 43, no. 2 (1993): 195–250. See also Marc Simmons, "Tlaxcalans in the Spanish Borderlands," *New Mexico Historical Review* 39 (1964): 101–10. David Frye's *Indians into Mexicans: History and Identity in a Mexican Town* (Austin, TX, 1995), an ethnographic history of one of the Tlaxcalan pueblos founded in central San Luis Potosi in 1591, treats the history of Indian identity in the region.

The Monterrey-based journal *Humanitas* has published a handful of articles relevant to the indigenous history of the northeast, including Andrés Montemayor Hernández, "La congrega o encomienda en el Nuevo Reino de León," *Humanitas* 11 (1970): 539–75; María Elena Galaviz de Capdevielle, "Crónica del P. Fray Luis de Guzmán de la rebelión de los jonaces en 1703," *Humanitas* 18 (1977): 387–401; and Ignacio del Río, "Aculturación e integración socioeconómica de los chichimecas en el siglo XVI," *Humanitas* 22 (1981): 255–68.

William B. Griffen has written a number of articles and monographs on the history of the Native Americans of northern Mexico during the colonial period, some of which treat an area (Chihuahua and Coahuila) that straddles the regions defined in these chapters as "northeastern" and "northwestern." His *Culture Change and Shifting Populations in Central Northern Mexico* (Tucson: University of Arizona Press, Anthropological Papers of the University of Arizona, no. 13, 1969) presents a good deal of useful information about the "Tobosos" and "Cocoyomes" who lived north of Parras before their destruction and deportation by the Spanish in the 1720s.

The northeast of Mexico has produced its share of well-documented local histories and documentary collections relevant to the indigenous history of the area (with the exception of Zacatecas, where local historians are drawn almost exclusively to the history of mining). The monumental *Historia de San Luis Potosí* by Primo Feliciano Velázquez, 4 vols. (San Luis Potosi, 1982), especially vol. 2, "Bajo el dominio español," contains much useful information culled from documents in local archives, unfortunately unfootnoted for the most part. Velázquez compiled and published many of the most valuable early sources, some of which range far beyond the state of San Luis Potosi, in his (unfootnoted) *Colección de documentos para la historia de San Luis Potosí*, 4 vols. (San Luis Potosi, 1987). Joaquín Meade published a useful *Historia de Valles* (San Luis Potosi, 1970) and a three-volume history of *La Huasteca tamaulipeca* (Ciudad Victoria, 1977–78). Coahuila has received the attention of Vito Alessio Robles in his massive *Coahuila y Texas en la época colonial* (Mex-

ico, 1938) and other works. Pablo M. Cuéllar Valdez focuses on the
Historia de la ciudad de Saltillo (Saltillo, 1975). Gabriel Saldívar wrote *Los
indios de Tamaulipas* (Mexico, 1943) and the useful collection *Archivo de
la historia de Tamaulipas*, 7 vols. (Mexico, 1946). Nuevo León is probably
the most studied state in the region; the most approachable state history,
admirably documented, is Eugenio del Hoyo, *Historia del Nuevo Reino
de León (1577–1723)*, 2 vols. (Monterrey, 1972).

Languages

A sign of the indifference, bordering on hostility, of postinvasion northeastern society to the indigenous nomadic cultures is the extreme paucity
of linguistic information from the area before the eighteenth century, by
which time most indigenous languages here were extinct. The Pame
language was treated in grammars written by Fray Juan Guadalupe Sori-
ano in 1767, *El arte del idioma pame* (reprinted San Luis Potosi, 1990),
and by Fray Francisco Valle in the eighteenth century, *Quaderno de
algunas reglas y apuntes sobre el idioma pame*, the latter published incompletely by Rudolf Schuller (Mexico, Secretaría de Educación Pública,
1925); the original manuscript has apparently been lost. To the far north
of the region, Coahuiltecan languages received a modest amount of
attention in the brief grammar and confessionary by Fray Gabriel de
Vergara, *El cuadernillo de la lengua de los indios pajalates (1732)*, ed.
Eugenio del Hoyo (Monterrey, 1965), written at San Antonio, Texas, for
use with Coahuiltecans congregated there. Between Pame and Coahuiltecan, situated at the extreme south and north of the area considered
here, no other linguistic materials from the colonial era have come to
light. In 1886, A. S. Gatschet collected vocabularies of the languages
dubbed Comecrudo and Cotoname from a handful of aging speakers
who lived near Reinosa, which he published in *The Karankawa Indians,
the Coastal People of Texas* (Cambridge, 1891). Jacques Soustelle, *La Fam-
ille Otomi–Pame du Mexique Central* (Paris, 1937), was the first to demonstrate the unity of the Pame languages and the affinity of Pame and
Otomí, based on his ethnolinguistic research in the area. John R. Swan-
ton, *Linguistic Material from the Tribes of Southern Texas and Northeastern
Mexico* (Washington, DC, 1940), collated all known linguistic materials
from "the so-called Coahuiltecan, Karankawan, Tamaulipecan, and Jan-
ambrian stocks" spoken from Tamaulipas and northern Coahuila into
what is now Texas. Salinas, *Indians of the Rio Grande Delta*, provides a

bibliographic guide to available linguistic materials on northern Tamaulipas and Nuevo León.

Published Sources

Some of the earliest and most useful sources for this area are published in *Nombre de Dios, Durango: Two Documents in Náhuatl Concerning Its Foundation*, ed. R. H. Barlow and George T. Smisor (Sacramento, CA, 1943). These include a fascinating 1563 document written in Nahuatl attesting to the service of the Mexicano founders of Nombre de Dios in subduing the Zacatecos and Guachichiles of the Malpaís between Zacatecas and Durango. An appendix contains the 1562 "Relación de Pedro de Ahumada" (pp. 53–63), which deals mainly with military affairs around Zacatecas but also delineates the territories of the Zacatecos, Guachichiles, and "Chichimecas" (Pames). See also the "Información acerca de la rebelión de los indios zacatecas y guachichiles a pedimento de Pedro de Ahumada Samano. Año 1562," in vol. 1 of *Colección de documentos inéditos para la historia de Ibero-América*, ed. Santiago Montoto. The account ascribed to Gonzalo de Las Casas, written around 1572, "Noticia de los chichimecos y justicia de guerra que se les ha hecho por los españoles," in *Quellen zur Kulturgeschichte des präkolumbischen Amerika*, ed. H. Trimborn (Stuttgart, 1936), 152–85, describes the Guachichiles, Guamares, and Pames in some detail, and goes into an elaborate consideration of the justice of the war itself, particularly regarding the practice of enslaving captured Chichimecas. The documents relating to the Chichimeca War collected and published by Philip Wayne Powell, *War and Peace on the North Mexican Frontier: A Documentary Record*, transcriptions by María L. Powell (Madrid, 1971), contain much information about relations between Chichimecs and Spaniards during the course of the war. Other documents on "The Chichimeca War and Peace, 1576–1606," are published in Spanish with English translations in *The Presidio and Militia on the Northern Frontier of New Spain: A Documentary History*, ed. Thomas H. Naylor and Charles W. Polzer (Tucson, 1986), 1: 33–148. René Acuña, *Relaciones geográficas del siglo XVI: Nueva España* (Mexico, 1982–88), vols. 9 and 10, has transcribed and edited the *relaciones geográficas* of the mining region running northeast from Zacatecas, notably the 1585 relaciones of Fresnillo, Jérez, Sombrerete, and San Martín and the 1608 *relación* of Zacatecas, which contain interesting information on both native peoples and local ecology relatively soon after the Conquest.

The Franciscan Fray Gerónimo de Mendieta, guardian of the monastery at Tlaxcala in 1591 and an opponent of the Tlaxcalan colonization project carried out that year, included some stereotyped observations on the northern "barbarians" in his 1596 *Historia eclesiástica indiana* (Mexico, 1971). Juan de Torquemada, *Monarquía indiana* (Mexico, 1969), written about 1608 and first published 1615, was the first Franciscan chronicler with detailed information on the ongoing missionizing in the northeast. Torquemada was the source for later religious chronicles, such as José Arlegui's rather fanciful *Crónica de la provincia de N.S.P.S. Francisco de Zacatecas* (Mexico, 1851), written in 1737. Padre Andrés Pérez de Ribas chronicled the Jesuit missions among the Laguneros and Zacatecos at Parras and San Pedro and among the Chichimecas (Pames) at San Luis de la Paz in his 1645 *Triunfos de nuestra santa Fe entre gentes las más bárbaras y fieras del Nuevo Orbe* (Mexico, 1944), 245–314. Antonio de Ciudad Real's work of 1584–88 (also attributed to Fray Alonso Ponce), *Tratado curioso y docto de las grandezas de la Nueva España* (Mexico, 1976), has information on the northernmost Tarascan settlements of the late sixteenth century, which formed a frontier with the southernmost edge of the area considered here.

Key sources on the early history of the Spanish invasion of Nuevo León include Alonso de la Mota y Escobar's report of 1605, *Descripción geográfica de los reinos de Nueva Galicia, Nueva Vizcaya y Nuevo León* (Mexico, 1940), one of the earliest sources on the northern section of the northeast, and the lengthy chronicle reprinted in vol. 25 of Genaro García, ed., *Documentos pare la historia de México* (Mexico, 1909), "Alonso de León: Relación y discursos del descubrimiento, población y pacificacion de este Nuevo Reino de León; temperamento y calidad de la tierra (1649); Historia del Nuevo Reino de León, desde 1650 hasta 1690, por un autor anónimo (c. 1690)." The Instituto Tecnológico y de Estudios Superiores de Monterrey has published a very useful series of primary sources on the history of Nuevo León, including Don Josseph Antonio Fernández de Jáuregui Urrutia, *Descripción del Nuevo Reino de León (1735–1740)*, ed. Malcolm D. McLean and Eugenio del Hoyo (Monterrey, 1963), and Fray Juan Agustín de Morfi, *Diario y derrotero (1777–1781)*, also edited by del Hoyo and McLean (Monterrey, 1967). In the same series Israel Cavazos Garza's indispensable *Catálogo y síntesis de los protocolos del Archivo Municipal de Monterrey, 1599–1700* (Monterrey, 1966), with much information on such practices of the era as including Indians in dowries, points to the possibility of a future historiography of the region based on more detailed and local (judicial and notarial) records than have been commonly utilized in the past.

Documents related to the late conquest of Tamaulipas and the Sierra Gorda of northeastern Hidalgo state after 1742 are collected in the Archivo General de la Nación publication *Estado general de las fundaciones hechas por D. José de Escandón en la colonia del Nuevo Santander, Costa del Seno Mexicano* (Mexico, 1930). Around 1790 the Franciscan (and future insurgent) Fray Vicente de Santa María wrote a most interesting report on this area, with some notes on local languages, the *Relación histórica de la colonia del Nuevo Santander*, published with a scholarly introduction by Ernesto de la Torre Villar (Mexico, 1973).

The 1767 rebellions of indigenous pueblos and mining communities in San Luis Potosi and northern Guanajuato were described by the Visitador José de Gálvez, who suppressed them with draconian measures, in *Informe sobre las rebeliones populares de 1767 y otros documentos inéditos*, edited with a useful introduction by Felipe Castro Gutiérrez (Mexico, 1990). Gálvez's nephew, Viceroy Bernardo de Gálvez, left for his successor a set of *Instructions for Governing the Interior Provinces of New Spain, 1786* (Berkeley, CA, 1951; contains Spanish and a defective English translation) in which he spelled out the political rationale behind gifts of food, clothing, and even firearms and horses – by this time, for the pacification of the Apaches of Texas.

15

THE INDIGENOUS PEOPLES OF WESTERN MEXICO FROM THE SPANISH INVASION TO THE PRESENT

ERIC VAN YOUNG

THE CENTER-WEST AS CULTURAL REGION AND NATURAL ENVIRONMENT

Over the past several millennia the physical asperities of western central Mexico – of alpine ranges, lacustrine basins, arid canyon lands, and humid Pacific fringes – have softened and contracted upon each other under the continuing impact of human habitation, and more recently of modern technologies of transport and communication. Even at the end of the twentieth century, however, they still constitute a difficult geography. Nor have progressive integration into a national state or the homogenizing influence of modernity completely eroded the unique characteristics of the several remnant native regional cultures that cohabit in the Center-West. Nonetheless, as in most of what has been called Indo-America the heritage of indigenous culture remains strongest in areas such as the Michoacan highlands, where native population was densest and state-level polities most developed at the advent of the Europeans, or most isolated from contact with the European colonists and subsequent national society, such as the mountains of Nayarit. Those zones less densely settled at the arrival of the Spanish, less culturally advanced, or more quickly and thoroughly depopulated by disease or emigration – such as the hot plains of the Pacific littoral, or the high, cool, semi-arid steppe country of the Altos of Jalisco – more closely resemble the "neo-Europes" the invaders invented for themselves with their material technologies, their cultigens, and their livestock in far-flung corners of the New World, the South Pacific, and Africa (Map 15.1).

In Mexican national mythology the persona of the Center-West has for the most part been that of the classic homeland of the sturdy, independent, smallholding mestizo *ranchero*, rather than an area of a

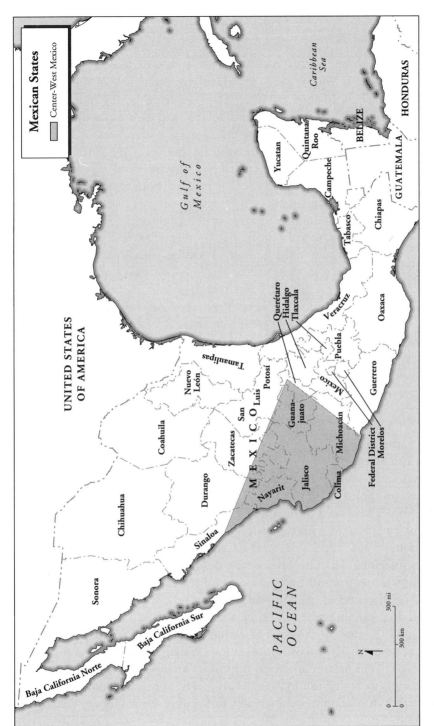

Map 15.1

strong indigenous cultural tradition. The *ranchero* achieved his apotheosis in the Cristero War of 1926–29, which engulfed much of the modern states of Jalisco, Michoacan, Guanajuato, and neighboring zones, during which armies of villagers, rural smallholders, and their social allies fought a tenacious guerrilla war against the national government of President Plutarco Elías Calles in resistance to its Jacobin anticlericalism and agrarian reform policies, while the central government found support among large groups of *agrarista* peasants. The received wisdom tends to obscure the fact that over large parts of this socially complex macroregion large-scale landholdings dominated areas of the countryside for much of its colonial and postcolonial history, finding themselves well into the nineteenth century in an endemic state of tension with identifiably indigenous communities. In these still markedly Indian areas one found something approaching a bi-modal distribution of land resources, comprising villager and estate sectors. The proliferation of *ranchos*, therefore (except in the Altos de Jalisco and proximate zones, where it was already well under way by 1800 or earlier), seems to have been a mid- to late-nineteenth-century phenomenon. The story of this and other agrarian transitions, even if it cannot explain the entire culture history of the Center-West, centrally involved indigenous groups until comparatively recent times, affecting their capacity to reproduce themselves socially and thus claiming our attention as a major theme in any account of the lives of native peoples.

The Center-West is a crazy quilt of cultural traditions and local histories in which many historical processes since the century of conquest have resembled those of other areas in Mesoamerica, but in which the outcomes have been distinctive. On the whole, the history of Mexico has been coterminous with the history of its indigenous peoples, a generalization no less applicable to the Center-West than to other Mexican macroregions. The categories *native*, *indigenous*, and certainly *Indian* are themselves artifacts of European colonial rule, present still in the modern public discourse of the Mexican successor state. However, the extensive and deep-running *mestizaje* of the area has meant that at any time much beyond the close of the colonial period the history of native peoples has been progressively interwoven with (or submerged in) that of non-native groups. Thus certain analytical difficulties arise, for example, when one attempts to distinguish indigenous peoples from peasants more generally, whether in relation to demography, forms of economic life, or collective action.

Geocultural boundaries must often be arbitrary in large measure since the continuities an observer constructs between one cultural space and another lead one continually toward an ever receding horizon. The Mexican Center-West, nonetheless, can be located roughly within a huge pie-shaped macroregion with its apex somewhere in the eastern Bajío and its outer arc stretching south along the Pacific Coast from around Mazatlán to the mouth of the Balsas River, where the states of Michoacan and Guerrero abut. It thus includes all of the modern states of Jalisco, Michoacan, Colima, Nayarit, and Aguascalientes, and parts of Zacatecas and Guanajuato, amounting to about 220,000 square kilometers, or something over a tenth of Mexican national territory.

The varied natural environment has conditioned the culture history of the area in fundamental ways, primarily in terms of barriers to human movement and the possibilities for farming and other sorts of resource utilization. The eastern part of this great macroregion lies within the central Mexican plateau, while the western part fans out and descends to the Pacific through the jumbled ranges and escarpments of the formidable Sierra Madre Occidental. A scant fifty miles from the Pacific, the peak of Colima marks the western terminus of Mexico's transverse volcanic axis, whose violent activity produced the volcano of Paricutín in Michoacan as recently as 1943. The most attractive habitable sites in the Center-West, and therefore generally speaking the areas of densest aboriginal population and long-standing centers of economic and political gravity after the advent of the Europeans, were the fertile and well-watered depressions of ancient lakes – among the most important the Bajío, Morelia, Guadalajara (centered on Lake Chapala), Ameca, Sayula, Tepic, Autlán, and Colima basins, and the Lake Pátzcuaro region. The fertile basins in the western part of the macroregion, separated by volcanic hills and mountain ranges, lie at considerably lower elevations (1,000–1,500 feet) than those in central Mexico, locating them in a milder tropical highland climate. Lying still farther to the west, with a traditionally mixed resource base supporting important aboriginal populations at the arrival of the Spanish conquerors, are a number of deltaic pockets along the Pacific littoral, which widens as it progresses north into Nayarit from Cape Corrientes and the mountainous coastal fringe stretching south all the way to Tehuantepec. Although considerable coniferous forests still survive in some areas (as in the breathtaking alpine elevations of Michoacan, for example), extensive deforestation has occurred since the advent of the Europeans, as also probably dessication and other sorts of environmental degradation associated with the overstocking of Old World ruminants. Much of the western part of the macroregion is drained by the great Santiago–Lerma river system, which originates in the Toluca Valley to the west of Mexco City and debouches into the Pacific after passing through the Bajío and Lake Chapala. The Center-West enjoys all three major types of Mesoamerican climate (*tierra fría, tierra templada,* and *tierra caliente*), sharing central Mexico's May–October pluvial regimen.

INDIGENOUS PEOPLES AT EUROPEAN CONTACT

Ethnologically speaking, at the eruption of the Europeans into the Center-West the macroregion included one great indigenous society of the complex, state-level Mesoamerican cultural type, the Tarascans; a number of more diminutive, city-state–level polities also sharing the core tradition, such as those in the upper Chapala Basin; and less advanced groups of hunter-gatherers and semi-sedentary farmers, mainly to the north and northeast, including those known into the colonial era by the pejorative Nahuatl name of Chichimecas. The cultural transition zone between semi- or nonsedentary and settled farming peoples very roughly bisected the Center-West from southeast to northwest, corresponding respectively to the geographic and climatological division between the formidable mountains of upland Nayarit, arid high steppes of central Zacatecas, and Bajío plains to the north, and the narrow mid-Pacific coastal plain, neovolcanic lacustrine basins, and Michoacán highlands to the south. The culturally more advanced part of the Center-West and the old Mesoamerican core area rubbed together tensely where the Tarascan and Mexica (Aztec) states abutted in the southeast of the macroregion along a militarized political frontier. Like several other states in Meso- and South America, the Tarascans, no less than their Iberian conquerors, were at the advent of the invaders still engaged in a process of military expansion, having only recently consolidated themselves politically. A brief synoptic look at the history and organizational complexity of the Tarascan culture area can give us some idea of the havoc sown by the Spanish Conquest and of the shattered foundations on which colonial society was built.

During the eighty years or so before the Europeans arrived, the Tarascan state had reached its maximum territorial extension, constructing a relatively tight political hegemony over some 75,000 square kilometers between the Río Balsas basin in the south and the Río Lerma basin in the north. The imperial capital Tzintzuntzan embraced a population of 25,000–35,000 people, while the Pátzcuaro Basin, the core of the Tarascan state, counted as many as 200,000 inhabitants and the area corresponding to the modern state of Michoacan nearly 1.5 million, about half its 1980 population. Tarascan political consolidation and territorial expansion were almost exactly coeval with those of the Aztecs to the east, though the Tarascan polity in many ways resembled more the Inka empire than the looser, more ethnically heterogeneous Aztec. The core of the state was more purely Tarascan culturally, while only partially assimilated ethnic enclaves (Otomís, Matlatzincas) existed in certain frontier areas as military buffers against the Aztecs. Until the mid-fifteenth century the natural robust adventurism of a young polity drove Tarascan expansionism, although beyond a certain point Tarascan expansion to the north, south, and west was inhibited more by the state's limited logistical capabilities than by the presence of competing military groups. The Tarascan and Aztec empires were in continual military engagement with each other from about A.D. 1450, the Tarascans giving a good account of themselves in repelling a number of attempted invasions (1480, 1515, 1517–18). As the empire grew, bureaucratization developed concomitantly and the religious belief system adapted to provide an umbrella of political legitimacy; extractive tributary practices bore an increasing weight in supporting the ruling dynasty, aristocracy, and priesthood; and conquered territories were allocated to Tarascan nobles in fieflike arrangements. Most high political positions were apparently hereditary among noble lineages, and the state religious cult, creation myths, and official history all functioned to legitimize the position of the ruling elite, believed linked in the economy of divine power directly to the Tarascan deities. As elsewhere in the New World, official and divine histories were entwined, the Tarascan religious system sharing with others of Mesoamerica many elements of belief and practice. The Tarascan economy rested on a mixed foundation of rain-fed and irrigated agriculture, with considerable evidence, at least in the Pátzcuaro Basin, of fallowing, terracing, horticulture, and other labor-intensive techniques; the Mesoamerican triad of maize, beans, and squash constituted the main nutritional components. Patrimonial farming lands supported the ruling dynasty, royally allotted lands the local lords, state lands the official cult, and commoner lands the mass of the population. An increasing shortfall in food resources for the densely populated core of the empire was met

by tribute extraction from outlying areas. Tributes collected from the
empire's commoners in the form of labor (also supplied by slaves, as
elsewhere in Mesomerica) and goods supported the army, political appointees, and the elaborate royal household. Markets and long-distance
traders certainly played roles in both the mundane and the luxury economies, but how they functioned is not entirely clear.

Outside the Tarascan empire the greatest concentrations of settled
farming peoples in the precolumbian era were on the plateau to the north
of Lake Chapala, and along the Pacific littoral between Banderas Bay and
Culiacán. In terms of the major culture areas of Mesoamerica, the Chapala plateau region lay just on the northern margins of the high cultures,
sharing certain basic characteristics with them but lacking the monumental architecture, developed urbanism, and theocratic sociopolitical structure characteristic of central Mexico or the Tarascan zone. Much less
complex economically than the area to the southeast, the diminutive city-
states of what would later become central Jalisco nonetheless supported
relatively dense populations on the basis of irrigated agriculture. The
dominant cultural influence here was Nahua, but the wider area seems
to have maintained a tenuous political independence through its position
as a buffer zone among the Tarascans, the Chichimecas, and the Aztecs.
Considerable ethnolinguistic variety prevailed within a fairly small geographic area – Tecuexe speech at Tala, for example, and Coca further
east at Poncitlán and neighboring settlements – though the dominant
trunk was Uto-Aztecan. In the post-conquest period native colonization
from central Mexico and Spanish missionary activity combined to introduce Nahuatl as a *lingua franca* all over the Center-West, so that many
of the more geographically circumscribed native languages or dialects
died out. Although the wider area embracing the modern states of Jalisco,
Colima, Nayarit, Aguascalientes, and part of Zacatecas has sometimes
been designated as "Chimalhuacán" or the "Chimalhuacán Confederation," most evidence indicates that in political terms there was no
stronger bond than opportunistic alliance in time of war among a loose
group of independent seigneuries (*señoríos*). Post-conquest sources indicate considerable cultural heterogeneity even among sedentary farmers
within non-Tarascan Chimalhuacán.

Distinct ethnolinguistic groups included Guamare, Guachichil, and
Zacateco speakers to the east and north of the Río Grande de Santiago
and the Tarascan hegemonic zone, and to the west large groups of Cocas,
Tecuexes, Cazcanes, Coras, Huicholes, and Tepehuanes and Tepecanos

(Piman languages), along with pockets of Nahuatl and Otomí speakers. In the so-called Chichimec regions the prevailing social organization was that of hunter-gatherers, and the "pacification" and incremental occupation of these areas were to cost the Spanish colonizers much blood, treasure, and frustration because of the natives' bellicose propensities, rapid adoption of the horse, and flexible social structure. What would later become the modern state of Aguascalientes and the Altos de Jalisco, for example, were occupied by Guachichil-speaking hunter-gatherers, while farther north Zacatecos held sway, and to the east the Bajío was dominated by Pame, Otomí, and Mazahuan speakers (all of the Otomanguean language group) sharing a similar hunter-gatherer social structure. Coastal Nayarit, on the other hand, was occupied by peoples of Totorame speech (related to Cora, of the Aztecoidan family) from around the Tropic of Cancer south to about the latitude of present-day Tepic, while Coras, Tecuales, Huicholes, and Tepehuanes held the uplands. These peoples were part-time farmers living in dispersed settlements, but their populations reached fairly high densities (Map 15.2).

The indigenous culturescape of what Mexicans would come to know as the Center-West, then, was quite heterogeneous. Before the advent of the Europeans it was marked by a degree of internal complementarity constituted in part by the geographical distance of most of the area from the central Mexican core, in part by patterns of exchange and warfare, and in part by the ebb and flow of Tarascan cultural and political influence. The history and character of this complex macroregion were finally formed in large measure by the advent of the Europeans, and by the contingent processes of Spanish conquest and colonization themselves.

THE FIRST CENTURIES OF COLONIAL LIFE

To a greater extent than in some other areas of Mesoamerica, the European conquest of the Center-West was stamped indelibly by the destructive energy of one man, Nuño Beltrán de Guzmán. A well-connected Spanish lawyer and rival of Hernando Cortez (or Hernán Cortés), Guzmán had come to the Indies initially in 1528 as governor of the province of Pánuco on the Gulf Coast of Mexico and was subsequently appointed president of the First Audiencia of New Spain in Mexico City. At the end of 1529, fearing arrest by royal officials after the debacle of his short-lived government, Guzmán fled to the conquest of the Center-West

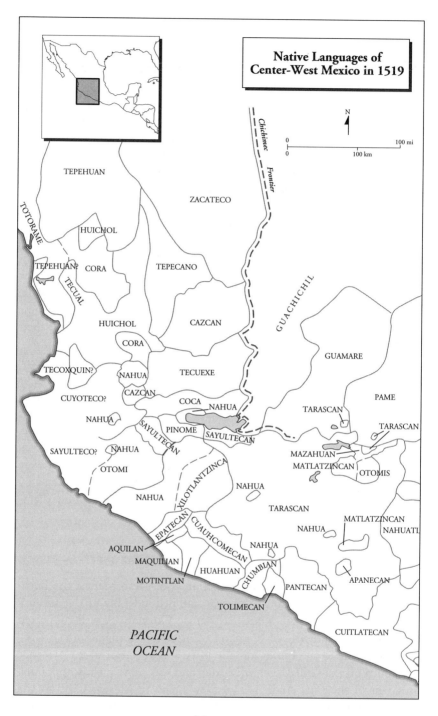

Map 15.2

seeking to strike it rich and carve out for himself a sphere of influence to match that of Cortés. He cut a swath of carnage and enslavement through much of the region, founding along the way such cities as Culiacán and Guadalajara. Guzmán established for himself a virtually independent satrapy in Nueva Galicia over the six or seven years before his disgrace and return to Spain, subjugating a number of native polities in the face of little concerted military resistance, and killing or enslaving thousands of Indians. In the process he and his followers helped build up a mountain of ill will among native peoples in the Center-West. One of Guzmán's most egregious acts was the February 1530 trial and brutal execution of the Cazonci – the Tarascan king Tzintzicha Tangaxoan, known to the Spanish by his Christian name, Don Francisco – whom Guzmán accused of murdering Spaniards, political rebellion, and sodomy.

Guzmán had been preceded into the West by other Spanish expeditions, largely drawn by reports of Tarascan wealth and of gold in the Pacific littoral. The earliest of these probes was that of Cristóbal de Olid in 1522, composed of a small group of Spaniards and several thousand native auxiliaries. Meeting no Tarascan resistance at the eastern border outpost of Taximaroa (where Aztec invaders had been turned back some forty years earlier), Olid's force penetrated as far as the capital of Tzintzuntzan without military opposition. In 1524–25 Hernando Cortez's cousin Francisco established a tentative Spanish presence along the coast between Colima and Tepic, followed by Nuño de Guzmán himself. Silver strikes at Culiacán, Compostela, Bolaños, and other minor sites, along with the major finds at Zacatecas in the 1540s, drew increasing numbers of prospectors and settlers, who gradually subjugated native polities and compressed native economies.

As elsewhere in the New World, the combined effects on indigenous peoples of Spanish aggressiveness, rapacity, and military technology paled beside those of the bacterial phalanx that followed the Europeans into the Center-West. The European diseases to which the Indians had little or no immunological resistance produced overall levels of mortality analogous to those in the Valley of Mexico (also called the Basin of Mexico), amounting to a drop of 90 percent or more between contact and about 1650. The population of the Patzcuaro Basin, for example, estimated at some 100,000 to 200,000 in 1520, had fallen to less than 10,000 natives by 1650. By all accounts, one of the first victims to fall to the shadow invader was Zuangua, the Tarascan monarch (Cazonci), whose death from smallpox in late 1520 anticipated that of the Aztec and Inka rulers, Cuitlahuac and Huayna Capac, from the same cause, and whose son and successor, Tzintzicha Tangaxoan, was later befriended by Hernando Cortez and judicially murdered by Nuño de Guzmán. During the same period, estimates Peter Gerhard, the indigenous population of Nueva Galicia, a Spanish political entity embracing much of the Center-West, declined from some 850,000 to about 70,000. Coastal lowland areas suffered virtually complete depopulation within a very few years, replicating a pattern initiated at first contact in the Caribbean. Into the vacuum, through and beyond the middle of the seventeenth century, were drawn as colonists substantial numbers of Otomís, Tarascans, Tecuexes, and other indigenous groups, as well as black slaves and free persons of mixed blood. Demographic recovery in the Center-West in the late seventeenth and eighteenth centuries generally brought indigenous numbers up to perhaps 30–40 percent of their precontact levels by the close of the colonial period. Within this overall scenario some subregions remained empty of noncolonist native people by 1800 or so, Nueva Galicia's native population reached about 43 percent of the province's total numbers, and the Tarascan area hewed more closely to the higher initial and end points characteristic of the central Mexican situation, with about 60 percent Indians in the overall population.

Not the invasion of Old World diseases alone, but also the imperatives of Spanish military and political control, labor needs, and religious conversion, had profound impacts during the early and middle colonial periods on the indigenous peoples of the center-west. In the first decades after the Conquest, Spanish secular administrative and ecclesiastical policies aimed to encourage through the process of *congregación* the creation of nucleated indigenous villages on the decimated coasts and difficult uplands, and from midcentury in central Nueva Galicia and Nueva Vizcaya to the north, but these efforts (as much other Spanish colonial policy) produced uneven results. Mission villages established in upland zones of Cora and Huichol occupation, for example, throve as long as discipline was maintained by the Spanish friars and soldiers, but the Indians tended to revert to accustomed patterns of dispersed settlement when Spanish surveillance waned. Only after 1590 or so did the native inhabitants of the eastern Nayarit sierra, southwestern Zacatecas, and the *cañones* area of Nueva Galicia (the odd modern projection of northern Jalisco state resembling an extended arm and hand) come under some degree of stable Spanish control with the creation of the special military frontier province of Colotlán, which served as a buffer between the hostile native peoples of Nueva Vizcaya and the more sedentary indigenous areas of Nueva Galicia. Here no *encomiendas* existed, and Tlaxcalteca colonists formed the nuclei of numerous settlements. Despite such efforts, however, some areas of the greater Center-West remained stubbornly unpacified for generations. Only in 1721 did the Cora chieftain journey to meet with the viceroy in Mexico City, and when a peaceful Spanish occupation of the isolated, mountainous zone of Nayarit failed, an expeditionary force subdued the area the following year, provoking repeated Indian uprisings over the next decade or so.

Concurrent with the initial brutal confrontations between Europeans and native peoples in the Center-West, and with the first steps toward pacification and settlement, ran Spanish efforts to institutionalize access to Indian agricultural surpluses through tribute collection, and to Indian labor for mining enterprises, agriculture, urban construction, and other economic activities. As in central Mexico and elsewhere in Indo-America, these extractive relationships were embodied primarily in *encomienda* grants as early as the 1520s. Indian chattel slavery existed alongside the *encomiendas*, particularly in the early mine labor arrangements in the Pacific lowlands. Effective establishment of the *encomienda* in the non-Tarascan areas, however, awaited a more permanent Spanish presence and the advent of Nuño de Guzmán, who started giving them out to his followers about 1530, although he retained many of the choicest assignments for himself (e.g., in Tonalá and Tlajomulco, near Guadalajara, and in the La Barca area on the eastern end of Lake Chapala); many of these grants escheated to the Crown after Guzmán's political disgrace in the 1540s. But indigenous resistance to the imposition of the institution, including the occasional murder of an *encomendero*, was not absent, especially among the less docile, semi-sedentary native peoples to the north and east of the rough cultural boundary already outlined.

The fate and economic importance of the *encomienda* differed between the non-Tarascan and Tarascan zones of the Center-West, as it did elsewhere within Mexico more generally, primarily according to the nature of precontact indigenous society. In the wilder reaches of Nueva Galicia the *encomienda* never really took root owing to the low density of native population and the ease of flight or evasion, and some peoples (the mountain Huicholes, Coras, and Tepecanos) were exempted from *encomienda* or tribute to the Crown by native men's militia service in the frontier province of Colotlán. Before 1600 more than half the Indian communities in Nueva Galicia had escheated to the Crown, though some *encomiendas* survived in areas like Culiacán as sources of Spanish income into the seventeenth century, a situation analogous to that in distant Paraguay and Chile. In the Tarascan zone the institution seems to have been somewhat longer lived, less the object of explicit indigenous resistance, and of greater importance economically. Here Hernando Cortez was the major early player, reserving for himself the densely settled heartland of the Tarascan kingdom, around Tzintzuntzan, although finally this failed to become part of his vast Marquesado del Valle, centered farther to the east and south, and his considerable early influence in Michoacan had almost completely ebbed by 1530 or so. In the end, however, despite (or perhaps because of) the considerable wealth it produced for a few Spaniards, the *encomienda* as a transitional form of social and labor control fell victim to a combination of political pressure from the Crown for its piecemeal abolition, the need for more efficient modes of labor allotment (initially the *repartimiento*, an officially controlled corvée-like arrangement, then increasingly "free" wage labor), and above all to Indian demographic collapse.

Rapidly falling Indian numbers, burgeoning Spanish and mixed-blood population, and the advent of silver mining did much to shape the emergent political economy and settlement pattern of the Center-West, with all too predictable effects upon indigenous populations. The silver strikes of the mid-1540s at Zacatecas spurred a demand for a time for agricultural and livestock products from areas farther to the south, putting concomitant pressure on Indian village economies for land and labor. Later, as fertile Bajío lands were put to the plow to meet the same demand, groups of Christianized Indians were brought from the Valley of Mexico and Tlaxcala areas to colonize the Bajío plains, while nomadic peoples such as the Pames and Jonaces retreated into the rugged mountains of the Sierra Gorda to the northeast, which, like Nayarit, would remain effectively outside Spanish control until the mid-eighteenth century. The silver route to Zacatecas and its northern sister camps was protected by the Crown policy of establishing garrison towns and presidios, planned by Viceroy Antonio de Mendoza and carried out by his successors. Among these settlements were San Miguel el Grande (1555), Lagos (1563), Jérez (1570), Celaya (1575), and Aguascalientes (1576). The silver mining complex at Bolaños, in an area originally inhabited by Tepehuan-, Tepecano-, Huichol-, and Cazcan speakers, sat squarely in the middle of the Colotlán military frontier and was worked by the Spanish beginning in the early 1540s. Driven out by hostile natives within a decade or so, Spanish miners nonetheless returned to make fortunes at Bolaños through the late colonial period. So ill-suited was the area to farming, however, that most food and draft animals had to be imported, which meant that Indian land and labor in more fertile zones had somehow to be expropriated to supply it. The cool, dry plateau lands of areas like Aguascalientes and the Altos de Jalisco were progressively occupied by Spanish cattle estates in the late sixteenth century, displacing northward Guachichiles, Zacatecos, Guamares, and other hunter-gatherers, while the never very densely populated humid coastal lowlands, such as the area around Acaponeta, were also colonized by cattle, Spanish estate-owners, and their African and mixed-blood auxiliaries.

The synergy of Spanish political, economic, and religious advance among New World native peoples along lines suggested by the Iberian *reconquista* has often been noted. Grimly emblematic of this complex relationship is that the Tarascan Cazonci, to be executed by Nuño de Guzmán in 1530, had been sponsored for his 1525 baptism in Mexico City by Hernando Cortez, Guzmán's bitter political rival. Indeed, the Cazonci was baptized by the Franciscans, whose first superior in New Spain, Fray Martín de Valencia (one of the famous first "Twelve" of the Friars Minor to arrive in New Spain in 1524), he subsequently invited to send missionaries into Michoacan. Others of the Tarascan ruling elite were certainly less sanguine about the evangelization project. Purépecha commoners, although they had killed a number of Spaniards in the 1520s and episodically fought the institutionalization of the *encomienda*, also resisted the Franciscan missionaries – so effectively, in fact, that they were twice driven from the Tarascan lands, as Mexican bishop Juan de Zumárraga noted ruefully. Still, Fray Martín de la Coruña (also known as Martin de Jesús) arrived in Tzintzuntzan in 1525, destroyed as many Tarascan temples and religious icons as he could lay hands on, established a Franciscan religious house in 1526, and a few years later tried in vain to defend the Cazonci against Guzmán's murderous intentions. The Pátzcuaro convent was followed in short order by the foundation of Franciscan establishments at Acámbaro, Zinapécuaro, Uruapan, Tarecuato, and other Tarascan towns. Everywhere the friars went they founded nucleated towns to replace the originally more scattered native settlement patterns or to concentrate the survivors of the fearful sixteenth-century plagues, the better to "civilize" and Christianize the survivors. Between 1525 and 1531 the Franciscans penetrated Michoacan rapidly, proving the Tarascan kingdom especially the favorite land of the early apostolate (Map 15.3).

Hard on the heels of the initial heroic period of missionizing in Michoacan, beginning in 1531 the order penetrated into Nueva Galicia and points north and east, with foundations over the next decade or so at Guadalajara, the Lake Chapala area, Etzatlán, Juchipila, Colima, Nayarit, San Miguel el Grande, and other sites; and somewhat later the evangelization of the Colotlán frontier was undertaken by Friars Minor from Zacatecas. The secularization (the handing over of parishes by regular to diocesan clergy) of Franciscan *doctrinas* steadily followed the erection of bishoprics in Michoacan (1536) and Nueva Galicia (1548). In many ways, therefore, the high-water mark of the order's activity in the Center-West was reached with the creation of the Franciscan province of San Pedro y San Pablo de Xalisco in 1565. On the other hand, compared to Michoacan the high plateaus of Nueva Galicia long remained unappealing both to the Friars Minor and to their regular competitors, as well as to secular priests, because of their low population densities, hostility and ethnolinguistic diversity of the natives, scarcity of economic resources, and heat.

The missionary field of the Center-West was overwhelmingly dominated, therefore, by the Franciscans. Two implications of this were, first, that the famously millenarian, apocalyptic, and charismatic theology of the Friars Minor indelibly stamped post-conquest native belief systems, including the Christianity they adopted, forms of cryptopaganism, and even the ideology of native resistance movements; and, second, that other regular orders were effectively precluded from exercising much influence on indigenous groups within the macroregion. By the time the Augustinians arrived in New Spain in 1533, most areas in the Center-West had been preempted by the Friars Minor, though the Augustinians, Dominicans, and others, and later the Jesuits, managed to wedge several missionary establishments into more marginal zones. This essentially amicable if asymmetric competition among the regular orders in the Indian countryside found a noisier analog in the continuing conflicts between the regular and secular Church. In any case, scholars have generally acknowledged that the optimistic, ardently apostolic character of Christian evangelization tended to flag considerably as the first generation of Franciscan and other missionaries died off in the 1560s and 1570s, giving way to a wearier, more businesslike tone in everyday Church practice and a decid-

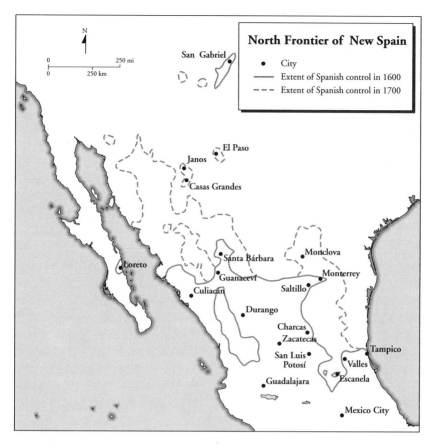

Map 15.3

edly darker view of native cognitive, spiritual, and political potentials, a shift reflected in the pronouncements about the Indians by colony-wide meetings of churchmen between the 1530s and the 1580s.

One of the brighter chapters in the evangelization of the Center-West was the hospital regime established both by the Franciscans and by the diocesan church in native communities in the early evangelical era. In general these establishments were founded for the treatment of the sick and to provide temporary accommodations for travelers for all races. Again, the major impulse came from the Franciscans, many of the hospitals in Michoacan being founded by the peripatetic and indefatigable Fray Juan de San Miguel – consummate Tarascan linguist, architect of native towns (e.g., Uruapan), horticulturist, trainer of native musicians; and the Franciscan foundations in Nueva Galicia (e.g., at Juchipila, Zacoalco, and other important Indian towns) following the epidemic of the early 1540s. Once up and running, the hospitals were often supported by native confraternities dedicated to the Immaculate Conception, attached to the hospital churches specifically for the purpose of their maintenance. But by far the most famous such establishment was the hospital-village of Santa Fé de la Laguna, founded in 1533 on the shores of Lake Pátzcuaro, near the Tarascan capital of Tzintzuntzan, by the secular churchman and future bishop of Michoacan (1537–65) Vasco de Quiroga while he was still an unordained *oidor* (judge) of the Audiencia of Mexico. The elaborate settlement (there was a sister establishment near Mexico City), explicitly inspired by the concept of an ideal Christian community propounded in Thomas More's *Utopia* (1535), included dwellings for hundreds of Indian families, a church, school, storehouses, workshops, medical wards, and garden and agricultural lands. The Indian inmates labored long and hard at their artisan crafts (the area is still famous for pottery styles introduced by Quiroga and his associates) and farming, led austere lives within the strictly disciplined community, and saw the agricultural surpluses distributed to member families on an egalitarian basis.

One of the few forms of unequivocal evidence we have of indigenous responses to the European presence consists in the protracted record of native resistance to the extremely destructive intrusion of Europeans into nearly every aspect of the Indians' economic, social, political, cultural, and spiritual lives. These ranged throughout the Colonial period from sullenness, foot-dragging, and rumormongering, through the clandestine practice of "heathen" religious rituals, coded public performance, and endemic litigation in the colonial courts (at which indigenous individuals and communities became extremely adept), to open movements of riot and rebellion. Religious sensibility and practice were naturally a privileged realm for such manifestations, but what we would think of as political movements were also steeped in religious thinking (e.g., see the discussion of the Independence period later in this chapter). The mid-sixteenth-century *Relación de Michoacán*, for example, in which the Franciscan Jerónimo de Alcalá compiled the testimony of Tarascan elites about the history and culture of the pre-conquest Tarascan people, suggested that under the impact of early Christian conversion efforts native indigenous priests convinced many Purépecha commoners that the Fran-

ciscans killed Indian infants in the baptism process, and that the missionaries were themselves actually dead men whose religious habits were
shrouds and who rejoined their concubines every night in the under-
world. Toward the end of the century yet another Franciscan observer of
indigenous ways, Fray Antonio de Ciudad Real, described (without interpreting it as such) what must be construed as encoded native resistance
to Christian religious thinking in the Epiphany play (a *pastorela*) annually
performed before an enormous audience of Indians and Spaniards at
Tlajomulco, in Nueva Galicia. In this performance the marginalization
of the Holy Family, the prominence of irreverent and clowning shep-
herds (played by Indians), and the portrayal of Herod as a (perhaps)
colonizing tyrant all bespoke an overt counternarrative constructed by
indigenous peoples against the evangelization process.

By all odds one of the most spectacular episodes of large-scale Indian
resistance to European encroachment in the Center-West, the Mixtón
War (1540–41), occurred within scarcely a decade of the establishment of
an effective Spanish presence in the more northerly parts of the vast
region. This formidable military confrontation was to be followed by
many others in the succeeding half century – Guachichiles and Guamares
in the area of Guanajuato and Zacatecas in 1550 and 1607, Zacatecos and
Guachichiles in 1561, the Indians of Guaynamota (Nayarit) in 1584,
uprisings in the Aguascalientes area in 1541, 1575, and 1593, and so forth –
all of which may be seen as related to the larger so-called Chichimeca
War, which racked the near north until nearly 1600. But the Caxcan
uprising of 1540–41 threatened for a time to extinguish Spanish influence
in western Mexico, while its attempted suppression cost the lives and
enslavement of thousands of Indians, as well as the lives of the redoubtable Pedro de Alvarado (Cortez's most famous lieutenant in the conquest
of the Aztecs) and scores of Spanish *encomenderos*, settlers, soldiers, and
missionaries. Occasioned by the substantial draw-down of Spanish military strength in Nueva Galicia attendant on the assembly of Francisco
Vázquez de Coronado's expedition to the north (1540–42) in search of
Gran Quivira and the Seven Cities of Cíbola, indigenous rebellion was
motivated in part by resistance to *encomendero* and missionary demands,
in part by generalized anti-Spanish resentments and festering bitterness
over the activities of Nuño de Guzmán. With the partial military vacuum
in Nueva Galicia, the unpacified tribal peoples north of the Santiago
River, particularly Cazcanes to the northwest of Juchipila, rose in arms
against the Spanish settlers, engaging in numerous raids from fortified

hilltops in the Sierra del Mixtón, wounding or driving out their *encomenderos*, destroying some missionary centers, putting to flight Spanish military forces sent against them, and threatening the precarious existence of Guadalajara. The major Indian leaders were the baptized chieftains don Diego el Zacateco (Tenamaxtle) and don Francisco de Aguilar, *cacique* of Nochistlán. Although not much is known of the movement's ideology, it definitely embraced milennarian elements, including a war of extermination against the Spaniards, the rejection of Christianity, and the return of the old native gods. Failing to forge an alliance with the sedentary indigenous peoples to the south, the uprising was eventually crushed by a Spanish force (aided by large numbers of Indian auxiliaries) under the command of Viceroy Antonio de Mendoza himself. The savage repression included the branding and enslavement of hundreds of captured natives under the Spanish politico/theological doctrine of "just war" so eloquently under attack in these same years from the tongue and pen of Fray Bartolomé de Las Casas.

The seventeenth and early eighteenth centuries essentially witnessed in the Center-West the consolidation of structures of domination and accommodation put in place before 1600. The mixed livestock-farming haciendas so characteristic of this part of Mexico spread, along with their related labor forms, coming to occupy enormous extensions of land where the indigenous population had retreated or died off. With the close of the Chichimeca War after 1600, for example, Spanish occupation of the soil in the direction of Zacatecas proceeded apace, while much the same thing occurred in the coastal zones, where cattle *estancias* were worked by some Indians and black slaves. Smaller, more compact, more valuable Spanish estates, meanwhile, raised wheat, sugar cane, and other European crops, and jostled against rural villages where the Indian population was originally denser and regained its demographic momentum more quickly, as around the major colonial cities of Guadalajara and Valladolid. In the fringe areas of the Center-West macroregion, indigenous population and culture had virtually disappeared or become submerged by the close of the colonial period. Christianity had taken firm root among the native peoples of the Center-West, eventually to produce, under the influence of extensive ethnic mixing, that particularly conservative popular Catholicism that marks much of the area even today, along with forms of indigenous piety – the cult of the saints, *cofradías*, and so forth – typical of Mexico as a whole. An uneven colonial hegemony had solidified (always with certain exceptions, such as the late-

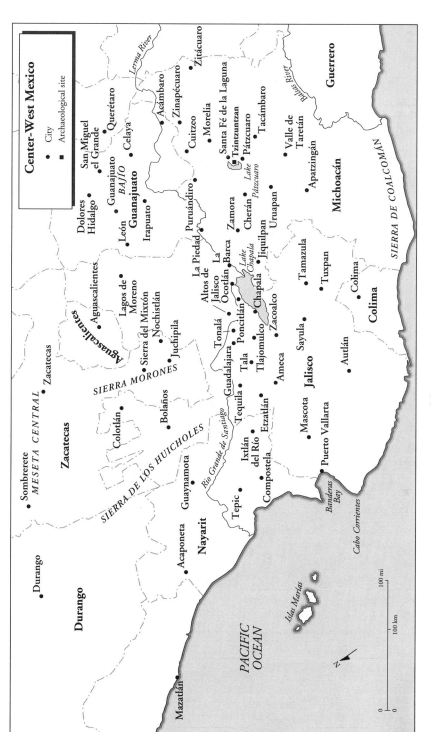

Map 15.4

pacified Nayarit sierra), partly based on the thickening of Spanish colonial institutions on the ground (the multiplication of secular parishes, the extension of government authority, the expansion of market relations), partly on cultural adaptation and concession by indigenous communities (through evangelization and the adoption of Spanish-mandated forms of local government). Over time the locus of specifically Indian rebellion tended to shift north with the cutting edge of Spanish military penetration, mining exploration, land seizure, and settlement, although conflict and contention continued in other forms throughout the Center-West, only to ignite again in the independence wars and burn throughout much of the nineteenth century.

AGRARIAN AND SOCIAL STRUCTURES AT THE CLOSE OF THE COLONIAL ERA

The indigenous landholding villages existing in the Center-West around 1800 or so had arisen from different origins, some dating from precolonial times, some created *ex nihilo* or from the fragments of nearly extinct pueblos by Spanish policies of *congregación* in the sixteenth and seventeenth centuries, and some the result of the demographic cloning of existing settlements in the late colonial period. In addition to their town sites (*fundos legales*) many such communities held large amounts of farming, grazing, and reserve lands owned in common but worked by individual families under the heading of *tierras de reparto* and other legal terms. It was by no means unusual for Indian communities of the late colonial period to hold several thousand acres in this fashion, typically as multiples or fragments of grazing grants for livestock (*sitios de ganado mayor* [cattle/horses] or *menor* [sheep/goats]), introduced all over the New World by the Spanish following the Conquest. In the Center-West no less than elsewhere in Mexico, European legal fictions supporting the commodification of land (e.g., new systems of land measurement, the institution of a free market in land, the making of royal land grants, and the requirement of Spanish-style judicial titles to prove legitimate ownership) were accompanied by the commodification of labor as well, embracing early forms of slavery, tributary (*encomienda*) and corvée (*repartimiento*) labor, and eventually leading to free wage labor (often with an element of compulsion, as in debt peonage). Interspersed over most areas with the indigenous communal holdings institutionalized by Spanish law were large numbers of Indian peasant-owned private parcels whose origins lay in *cacique* holdings officially regularized under Spanish law, piecemeal expropriation of communal lands by individuals, or purchase from non-natives.

Despite the functioning everywhere in the Center-West of the self-equilibrating mechanisms characteristic of Mesoamerican villages (e.g., the *cargo* system of village religious festivals), considerable social differentiation had developed within indigenous communities by the end of the colonial era on the basis of private accumulation of land and other economic resources. While the social reproduction practices of the wealthier Indian peasant group – including marriage, inheritance, and credit arrangements – may have been imperfect and the circulation of wealth frequent, a kulak-like stratum of village notables nonetheless dominated most communities' political and economic life, sometimes in opposition to the interests of powerful outsiders, sometimes in conjunction or outright collusion with them. For example, in the important indigenous town of Tlajomulco, to the southwest of Guadalajara, Indian wealth about 1800 was highly skewed between a propertied group comprising perhaps 5 percent of adult land- and livestock-owners, and the mass of the peasant population. Much the same sort of wealth concentration was to be found in the Tarascan zone. But despite the internal lines of stress generated by this increasing concentration of wealth and power within village society, the vast majority of formal litigation over land occurred not within pueblos, but among them. Indeed, the notorious litigiousness of Indian villages over land titles (the dockets of the royal high courts [*audiencias*] of Nueva Galicia and New Spain were increasingly jammed with land suits during the eighteenth century), whatever the economic and legal reality of such disputes or their real implications for peasant subsistence, may be interpreted in part as a mechanism through which indigenous village elite groups sought to deflect outward the strains of internal social and political differentiation.

Yet as demographic pressure built in the countryside, by the mid-eighteenth century native communities often found themselves inadequately supported by landholdings that had met or exceeded their needs in the seventeenth. Compounding this real tightening of per capita resources was the habit of village indigenous elites frequently to rent out communal property to non-Indians for cash, which they opportunistically appropriated to their own advantage. Some of this money may have stayed within communities in the form of loans to poorer families, investment in land or interstitial economic activities, or public ceremonial expenditure, but there is little evidence indicating that it was directly employed in redistributive social services such as food stocks held in reserve against times of scarcity.

From this perspective the famous decree of Father Miguel Hidalgo y Costilla of 5 December 1810, issued after his insurgent forces had established a rebel government in the city of Guadalajara with considerable military support from the native villagers of Jalisco and Michoacan, should cause little surprise. The order stated that all renters of lands belonging to Indian pueblos within "the district of this capital" were to pay up their back rents and deposit them in a "national treasury," the native communities then to reassume possession of the lands and work them only themselves in future. Even had political circumstances not intervened to block this policy, the effort to restore indigenous lands would have been largely rhetorical, since many communities by this time had few unworked holdings to reclaim in this fashion. At the same time, Hidalgo's measure foreshadowed a precocious and continuing state intervention (in Jalisco, for example) in the structure of rural property, particularly where Indian communal lands were concerned, taking the form after independence of state laws aimed at the parcelization and privatization of village communal lands (and the disamortization of church real property), later enshrined as national policy in the Ley Lerdo of 1856.

The varied manifestations of rural collective resistance – both "everyday" forms and more spectacular episodes of riot, rebellion, and regional insurrection – found their roots not only in agrarian pressures from the Late Colonial period on into the present century (though these were real enough in material and social terms), but also in a still vital if spatially uneven substrate of indigenous ethnicity with deeply etched cultural meanings. Rural society in the less remote areas of the Center-West (especially in central Jalisco and the Bajío, as opposed to highland Michoacan or the mountainous interior of Nayarit, for example) was in some ways more socially porous, more ethnically mixed, less markedly "Indian," it is true, than other regions of Mesoamerica – but even there many areas retained a distinctly ethnic and communitarian character. This showed up, for example, in forms of religiosity and public ritual behavior, high rates of endogamy, and patterns of village political power. Nucleated settlements with strong traditions of communal landholding persisted well into the nineteenth century, when most of them were pulverized by the hammer blows of commercial agriculture, the advent of the railroads, liberal legislation, and internal socioeconomic differentiation, all encapsulated under the rubric of "modernization." In such predominantly indigenous pueblos, the loci of personal identity, group and cultural identity, and livelihood came to be conflated. This meant that conflict over economic resources between Indians and non-Indians, whether in litigation, village riots, or more broadly social upheavals such as the wars of independence, tended to assume at once the character of class and ethnic or "racial" struggle ("caste war"). And because the political legitimacy of native communities was inextricably anchored in the sacral realm through often syncretic foundation myths (the occurrence of religious prodigies, for example, linked to the establishment of communities), public ritual, everyday belief, and the pervasive local influence of the secular clergy, one can readily grasp why cultural conflict and popular protest in the Center-West deployed a religious discourse and were infused with religious meanings from the colonial period through the Cristero rebellion of this century.

THE CUSP OF MODERNITY: INDIAN REBELLION AND THE
INDEPENDENCE WARS

At the beginning of the nineteenth century indigenous people over much of the Center-West – their numbers outstripping the subsistence possibilities of a fixed or even diminishing land-base, their village communities under siege by the forces of economic and cultural change, their ethnic identities increasingly eroding in some regions into a sort of generic Indianness (and with it our ability to trace an exclusively "Indian" history), and thence into a peasantness seldom pure and never simple – gave voice to their frustrations in several episodes of rural collective violence that rocked and eventually helped topple the colonial regime. Differing in scale, duration, and local history, certainly, these movements nonetheless shared certain ideological themes and inner structures, and were to be the harbingers of a troubled century or more in the Center-West (as in much of the rest of Mexico), stretching from 1800 or so into the 1930s. During this extended nineteenth century the concerted forces of liberalism, capitalism, and the sometimes faltering but inevitably lengthening reach of the central state contested local and indigenous lifeways in the name of progress and the construction of a Mexican nation.

The most intriguing and mysterious of these episodes was the abortive indigenous uprising surrounding the (almost certainly) apochryphal native messianic figure and would-be King of the Indies "El Indio Mariano" (*"el de la máscara de oro"*) in the area around Tepic in the years 1800 to 1802. In late December 1800, the civil and military authorities of Nueva Galicia uncovered what they believed to be a widespread Indian conspiracy and rebellious mobilization embracing both coastal and sierra villages in the Tepic area, and also involving such far-flung indigenous groups as Huicholes from the remote Nayarit sierra, Tepehuanes from Durango, and even Yumas and Yaquis from the far northwest. The eponymous Mariano (almost certainly a fabrication of Juan Hilario Rubio, an Indian *principal* of Tepic) claimed to be the son and heir of the deceased indigenous governor of Tlaxcala, a local village settled by native colonists from central Mexico in the early colonial period. The most important cultural and political resonance of this was with the precolumbian city-state of Tlaxcala to the east of the Valley of Mexico, apparently viewed by many indigenous people throughout New Spain as the repository of a residual native political legitimacy and therefore the locus of an anti-Spanish native shadow-state. The Indian pretender Mariano, claiming a mandate obtained in Spain from King Charles IV himself, was to assume sovereignty in January 1801, and in an openly chiliastic gesture specified that he was to be crowned not with gold or silver but with the thorny crown of Jesus the Nazarene (belonging to a local religious effigy), "since he [Mariano/Jesus] came to suffer in order to free his sons." His program consisted of but two elements: the restoration to coastal and sierra Indian communities of land in the possession of non-Indians, and the abatement or elimination of royal tribute payments.

In the end, the conspiracy to crown Mariano Indian king and establish a parallel native state in the central Pacific Coast and sierra came to naught. This failure owed as much to the apparent cultural slippage among the various indigenous groups involved and a resulting lack of coordination in their efforts, as to the vigorous, almost hysterical reaction by the viceregal authorities. But there were in the movement's ideological makeup certain similarities (possibly even a direct political connection, though this has yet to be proved) with other episodes of indigenous messianism, especially that centering on the person of a mentally disturbed Indian pretender named José Bernardo Herrada, which occurred farther to the north, in the Durango area, at almost exactly the same time. These included anti-white and anti-regime overtones within a context of communal autonomism, an actually rather complex naive legitimism focused dually on the Spanish king and a Tlaxcalan Indian monarch, and chiliastic and syncretic religious elements, all of which foreshadowed important aspects of popular ideology – particularly among indigenous villagers – in the ostensibly anticolonial insurgency to follow a decade later.

The Center-West proved fertile ground indeed for the anti-Spanish insurgency initiated by Father Miguel Hidalgo y Costilla in the Bajío in September 1810. This protracted struggle was in part an abortive peasant insurrection (colored with racial overtones) within a political war of national liberation. Many Indian communities were sundered by conflicting political loyalties superimposed on local histories of contention, some falling into the insurgent column and others into the royalist, but active and passive indigenous support for the rebellion ran deep and wide, especially in central Nueva Galicia, areas of adjacent Michoacan, and some zones of highland Nayarit. The Bajío itself, where the movement began and continued stubbornly for a decade, was not by this time heavily indigenous in its ethnic makeup, although some of the neighboring upland areas (the Sierra Gorda, for example) were more notably Indian in character and long proved recalcitrant to royalist pacification efforts. Despite the conventional wisdom that the Creole and mestizo leadership of the highly feudalized insurgency commanded support primarily among other mestizos, a good 50 to 60 percent overall of ordinary insurgents were native villagers. Rebellious Indian peasants saw in the civil unrest of the period an opportunity to expand their farming onto lands they had never legally claimed under the colonial regime, or only noisily coveted, but they also fought stubbornly to preserve a communal way of life as a cultural goal, not only for overtly material ends.

A reflex in part, then, of growing native population densities and a village-based cultural tradition struggling to preserve itself, Indian insurgency flickered and flared throughout the Center-West between 1810 and 1821, while farther east in the Bajío indigenous participation was less marked, and the region embracing Lake Chapala and the capital of Nueva Galicia proved to be an endemic focus of native insurgency. In the remoter parts of the Nayarit sierra "pacified" by Spanish arms only as late as the early eighteenth century, colonial rule had always lain uneasily, and there Cora and Huichol settlements occasionally gave cause for alarm in the form of localized anti-Spanish movements. Meanwhile, in the hot country of the Michoacán coastal lowlands (much of it never brought under royalist military control) a number of diehard insurgent leaders – some non-Indian, such as the mulato Gordiano Guzmán, some native themselves, like the *cabecilla* "El Indio Candelario" – claimed substantial support from indigenous communities, a few surviving the independence wars to carve out regional satrapies (*cacicazgos*) for themselves in the republican period.

THE NINETEENTH CENTURY – LIBERAL REFORM, DISSOLUTION, REBELLION

The careers of Gordiano Guzmán (d. 1854) and Nayarit agrarian insurgent Manuel Lozada (d. 1873), in fact, exemplify in large measure the protracted resistance of some indigenous villagers in the Center-West to forces of change unleashed by Mexican independence. Guzmán became the military strongman (*cacique*) of southern Jalisco, his area of political influence centering on such towns as Tamazula (now Tamazula de Gordiano, actually in northern Michoacan), Sayula, Atoyac, San Gabriel, and Tecalitlán. His obduracy in the face of attempts at economic and social reform after 1821 gained him the enduring support of numerous villages wholly or heavily indigenous, while pitting him against Creole regimes both state and national. One of the earliest such projects was the initiative of the imperial provincial government in Guadalajara in 1822 to divide up Indian corporate landholdings in the name of economic development and individualism, foreshadowing the philosophy and rhetoric of policy efforts in Jalisco, Michoacan, and many other states over much of the next century. Legislative and other official documents in the new states alluded to "those [people] previously referred to as Indians" or "extinguished indigenous communities" to whose inhabitants were extended rights of citizenship theoretically equal to those of whites. Quite understandably some Indian communities resisted the "equalization" with whites because it actually exposed them to legal and economic threats previously obviated in part by protective royal paternalism. Most important among the reforms in the Mexican successor state affecting Indians, because most directly linked to the decline of indigenous ethnic identity, were those seeking to dismantle community land ownership and theoretically redistribute land in a fee simple arrangement to individual households. Indeed, such policies were of transcendental importance for the erosion of indigenous communal identities over the succeeding century and more. On a national level these efforts were closely associated with the Liberals who came to power in the mid-1850s, prominently exemplified politically by Benito Juárez, and philosophically by the Ley

Lerdo of 1856, promulgated by the national government's minister of finance, Miguel Lerdo de Tejada. But the national laws only confirmed what the states of Jalisco and Michoacan had already been doing for some time. By the late 1820s the states of Michoacan (1827–28), Zacatecas (1829), and Guanajuato (1829) had passed repartitional laws, and these disamortization measures were in subsequent years frequently repeated and amplified despite indigenous resistance and evasion, to include ever broader categories of landholdings. In a number of states political pendulum swings over repartitional policies continued until the enactment of the Ley Lerdo (1856) at the national level resolved the inconsistent policies and ambivalences of the preceding decades, but helped plunge the nation into a decade of civil strife, embracing the War of the Reform and the succeeding French intervention (1857–67). This came to pass at least in part from the conflation of Liberal attacks on indigenous community lands with those on Church landholdings, embodied in the anticorporatist policies of the Ley Lerdo and subsequent measures, so that indigenous rural uprisings in defense of community identities after midcentury often coalesced under the banner of "Religión y Tierras!"

The effects of such policies on the cohesion of Indian communities and therefore on indigenous identity in the long term were generally negative, though they varied from one subregion to another. In Jalisco the actual division of lands was well advanced by 1856 (in the Chapala, Sayula, and Zacoalco zones, for example), provoked village disorders and continual litigation in Mascota, Colotlán, Zacoalco, and many other areas toward the end of the century, and went on until the era of massive agrarian reform after the Revolution of 1910. There is no doubt that in Jalisco in the period between independence and the Reform many Indian communities had been effectively (if not legally) extinguished by these means, and racial distinctions expunged on the theory of universal citizenship. Once freed of the constraints of communal ownership, land tended to concentrate ever more in non-Indian hands, while partitioned communal holdings fragmented into *minifundia* and sometimes became economically unviable under the impact of modest but real population gains. As a result, surviving pueblos frequently staged land invasions of neighboring estates, *hacendados* armed their retainers, and rural brigandage strengthened its grip on the central-western countryside. Once the dike was breached, increasing social differentiation within de facto surviving (but actually landless, or now reconfigured) indigenous communities, never egalitarian utopias in the first place, left little alternative to achieve some degree of social peace but further division. In 1866 an elderly sometime Indian official of one of the barrios of Pátzcuaro, in the heavily Tarascan Michoacán highlands, noted bitterly of the effects of continuous partition of community lands:

> Since [18]14 I have served the village carrying out [various] offices and contributing towards all expenses; I am the eldest Indian ("el indígena decano"). I should therefore be more opposed than anyone to the division of lands, but since dissensions within the community have no other cause than enmities arising from interest and power, far from opposing such division, I judge it the only means appropriate [to achieve peace] in our present situation. An indigenous community exists through its harmony, but when all the bonds of fraternity are broken, when caprice and personal interest are the motives of those in power, when the others find themselves under tyrranical oppression, when finally ambition, vengeance, hatred, and falsity are the flag of said officials, it must follow that the community can no longer exist. (Meyer 1986, 209)

While much of Mexico was racked with rural violence during the nineteenth century, the Center-West had more than its share of peasant revolt from the 1840s on, particularly between 1855 and about 1880, with Indian villagers prominently involved and land issues the key grievances. The years 1855–57 saw recurrent risings in the Lake Chapala area, during which some 2,000 or more armed Indians in La Barca and Zacoalco attempted to recover lands lost to neighboring haciendas, a movement eventually suppressed by a combination of harsh government military action, wide pardons, and threats of penal transportation to the Californias. An 1857 rising of Indian campesinos in the Lake Pátzcuaro area failed to extend much beyond northeastern Michoacan and was put down with similar alacrity, but proved symptomatic of deep-seated agrarian problems not so easily resolved. Rural unrest continued in the Tarascan area in 1869–70, 1871, and 1878, the latter episode centered on a "great agricultural community" erected by Tarascan peasants on appropriated hacienda lands in the Valle de Taretán, which provoked a massive federal army attack early in 1879.

Certainly the most highly visible and longest-lived of these uprisings was that headed over nearly two decades by Manuel Lozada, the "Tigre de Alica," in the mountain fastnesses of Nayarit. Lozada's movement was preceded by the shadowy figure of Patricio Guevara, captured and killed at Guaynamota in 1854, who had railed against foreign "monopolists," claimed the powers of black magic and geomancy among his weapons, and advocated the distribution of public lands to his campesino followers.

Himself the mestizo son of poor peasants and hacienda peon, Lozada was already known in the Tepic region as a "bandit" when he began seizing hacienda lands in the early 1850s. These properties he shared out to his largely Indian supporters (among them Cora and Huichol *serranos* [mountain dwellers] who typically migrated down to lowland coastal haciendas to work as wage laborers) partly in response to the Liberal disamortization decrees of 1856, but perhaps due even more to encroachment on indigenous farming lands by non-Indian landowners. Surviving an alliance after 1859 with Conservatives in their war against the Liberals, and subsequently attracted to the French empire by Maximilian's agrarian decrees, Lozada eventually struck an uneasy truce with the restored Juárez regime. He continued his attacks on the important English trading concern of Barron y Forbes, however, and virtually separated off the canton of Tepic from the state of Jalisco. At its high-water mark in the years 1868–73, Lozada's movement embraced nearly all of Nayarit, southernmost Durango and Sinaloa, northwestern Jalisco, and southern Zacatecas, its rapidly spreading influence prompting a war of extermination from the national government of Sebastián Lerdo de Tejada, particularly after the agrarian chieftain made some tentative contacts with regime opponent Porfirio Díaz in 1872–73. Advancing on Guadalajara with an army reputed to number some 11,000 men and including large contingents of independently commanded Cora and Huichol Indians, Lozada met a government counterattack and was captured, tried, and executed in July 1873. After his death, rural unrest continued virtually unabated in the mountains of Nayarit until the early 1890s, pitting substantially (though not exclusively) Indian agrarians against government forces and local landowners. The *lozadista* movement itself revived for a time in 1878 under the leadership of some of Manual Lozada's old commanders and his son Gerónimo, this time with a messianic tinge to its ideology, the martyred chieftain being identified with Jesus Christ and the Huichol culture hero and prankster figure Kauymali. In finally suppressing the *lozadistas* the Díaz government relied on a combination of military action and the deportation of dissidents to the deadly henequen plantations of torrid Yucatan. Brief echoes of the movement in 1884 and 1902 came to little.

Let us now turn to the history of the Huichol, Cora, and Tarascan peoples to bring the story of the indigenous cultures of the Mexican Center-West into the modern period. Small pockets of other Indian groups survived the nineteenth century, it is true, but by the mid-

twentieth century their numbers were so diminished – a few hundred
Indian language speakers in the states of Aguascalientes and Colima, for
example, by 1970 – that our attention is more profitably focused on the
largest groups.

In some ways the postcolonial history of the Coras and Huicholes who
followed Lozada in substantial numbers illustrates, albeit in an extreme
form, the political and economic pressures acting to deethnicize indigenous groups after independence. On the other hand, while many "western Nahuas" in Jalisco and Tarascans in Michoacán became so-called
indios civilizados during the nineteenth century by blending with mestizo
laborers and farmers on haciendas, the degree of Huichol and Cora
ethnic survival (as reflected in language usage, folkways, and artistic
production, for example) has been more marked than for other peoples
in the Center-West.

While the Franciscans missionized the Huicholes, modern Cora culture took definitive shape in the eighteenth century when the Jesuits
concentrated the Indians in their most important population centers.
Many Huichol Indians of the Nayarit sierra at first adhered to the
insurgent cause under the leadership of the redoubtable parish priest José
María Mercado, but switched their loyalties to the loyalist side after 1815
in a complex ploy to pursue local indigenous interests. In the wake of
independence the Franciscan missionaries left the area. By midcentury
many Huichol villages consisted of clusters of huts gathered around half-
abandoned churches, and were held together by simple political structures and subsistence agriculture, tending to remain isolated from Hispanic society except for essential commercial contacts. Ritual life was
dominated by native shamans who claimed the Indian gods "would not
allow foreigners to be enthroned in our lands. The foreigner who tried it
would be made prisoner and brought to the mountains of Ycacapolili,
and would be shot full of arrows and cut up into pieces" (González 1981:
225). Liberal disamortization decrees and *hacendado* encroachments on
their ancestral lands drove Huicholes and Coras in large numbers, as we
have seen, into the ranks of Manuel Lozada's agrarian guerrillas. From
the late 1870s state and national governments renewed their efforts to
enforce liberal land laws, sponsor non-Indian agricultural colonists, build
schools, and reduce Indian political autonomy. As foreign ethnographers

such as Carl Lumholtz (1906) surveyed Huichol culture in the curiosity cabinets of ethnographic texts, government chartered surveying companies took advantage of national legislation (1883, 1894) regarding the measurement and public sale of putatively untitled lands (*terrenos baldíos*) to wrest huge tracts of territory from indigenous communities both in the sierra and around Tepic. In the process, privately owned estates measuring in the hundreds of thousands of hectares were assembled, land concentration reached extreme indices, and by 1925 or so foreigners owned in excess of 50 percent of the rural area of the state of Nayarit (about 35% by value).

The rapid economic changes heralded by the land-surveying companies, increasing commercialization, and estate formation during the Porfirian period were compounded for indigenous peasants by the arrival of railroads in 1928, of agrarian reform aimed at the latifundia beginning in 1932, and the penetration of the national highway network after World War II. Through the decade of revolution (1910–20) and the working out of the postrevolutionary settlement (1920–40), Huicholes and Coras were hardly to remain unaffected. Though many Huicholes had fled active combat, scattering their communities and diluting the number of Huichol speakers, by the end of the armed phase of the Revolution the entire sierra area adhered to the Villista faction led by Rafael Buelna, a young ex-law student from Tepic, while many Coras opted for the faction led by revolutionary chieftain Venustiano Carranza. In the wake of the Revolution some lowland *agrarista* villages seized hacienda lands (e.g., at Tuxpan in 1917) despite the Carranza government's resistance, but by 1930 landholding arrangements, at least in Nayarit, had not changed substantially. By contrast, in neighboring Jalisco, where indigenous ethnicity was progressively fading into mestizo peasantness, strongman-governor Manuel Diéguez distributed land to a number of indigenous communities under the provisions of Carranza's agrarian reform law of 1915, though many such towns (e.g., Tonalá) received much less by way of restitution of communal lands than they had claimed, and many Indian peasants were killed (for example, in Tamazula and Zacoalco) by rural "white guards" as large landowners reacted violently to threats of expropriation. In Nayarit, in the two years before the advent of the Lázaro Cárdenas presidency (1934), however, the carving of *ejidos* from the sprawling haciendas made enormous headway, largely without bloodshed or political violence. The effect of these measures was that by about 1970 nearly 80 percent of rural land in Nayarit was embraced by collective holdings, far above the national average. Hardly had the pervasive violence of the Revolution abated when the Cristero War (1926–29) erupted, bringing with it high levels of indigenous participation all over the Center-West. Many Coras, Tepehuanes, and Huicholes from Durango, Zacatecas, Nayarit, and Jalisco counted themselves *cristero* sympathizers or combatants against the anticlerical Plutarco Elías government of Calles and its *agrarista* supporters. Cora responses were idiosyncratic, some individuals and groups joining or opposing the insurgents, while about two-thirds of Huichol indigenous people could be counted active *cristeros,* though many of the latter scattered as colonists along the lower Lerma River to avoid the hostilities, much as they had done a decade earlier.

In recent times the numbers of Huichol and Cora indigenous people have remained stable or even increased somewhat, although they have rapidly lost ground relative to the growth of the nonindigenous population of the western Mexican states and the country as a whole. In the state of Nayarit, for example, home to most Huicholes, the proportion of Indian language speakers in the total population fell from 7.5 percent in 1910 to less than 2 percent in 1970, while in the decade 1960–70 the number of monolingual indigenous-language speakers declined by some 40 percent. Overall this has been due as much to the process of *mestizaje* and assimilation as to any failure to reproduce, although death rates in heavily indigenous areas long remained inordinately high even as they were falling in the rest of Mexico. Although population figures for these groups are notoriously slippery, the 1990 Mexican national census put the number of Huichol speakers at something under 20,000, many of them living in or near the cities of Tepic, Guadalajara, Durango, and Zacatecas. Of the rural-dwelling population, the Huicholes are today limited to the mountainous areas of northwestern Jalisco and eastern Nayarit, and the Coras to the northwest of them. Both groups favor very dispersed settlement patterns. By the mid-1980s the Huicholes of northern Jalisco were settled in five major nuclei embracing some four hundred lesser *rancherías.* Overwhelmingly still small-scale farmers, the Huicholes hold their lands for the most part communally, still finding themselves in conflict with the "mestizo invaders." In 1986, for example, Mauricio de la Cruz, president of the Huichol Supreme Council, denounced the illegal occupation of 80 hectares of Huichol lands by several mestizo communities, among them Bolaños; *plus ça change . . .*

THE TARASCANS IN MODERN MEXICO

By about the middle of the nineteenth century communities of Tarascan speech were limited quite strictly to the heartland of the old Purépecha empire in northwestern Michoacan, where they made up some 20 percent of the state's population, or about 125,000 people. Colonial era population loss and continuing mesticization accounted for the dying out of Tarascan speech in the peripheral areas of the old pre-conquest empire, while the core of native language use and culture shrank to the shores and islands of Lake Pátzcuaro, the sierra to the west, and the Cañada region, a diminutive valley to the north of the sierra. Reflecting this trend in microcosm was the cultural profile of the former imperial capital at Tzintzuntzan, where Tarascan speakers constituted about 50 percent of the population in 1850 but only about 10 percent a century later. The embattled communal holdings that sustained Tarascan culture were thus concentrated in the districts of Pátzcuaro, Uruapan, Apatzingán, Tacámbaro, Zitácuaro, Zinapécuaro, and Jiquilpan. Already by the mid-nineteenth century the once homogeneous Purépecha communities were increasingly open to other ethnic groups, Spanish was ever more in use, and internal social differentiation was accelerating under the impact of the privatization of communal lands. Involvement in the cash nexus and market connections had made considerable headway, as well as out-migration for wage labor. Many indigenous communities remained neutral in the War of the Reform, or even actively loyal to large landowners who defended the conservative cause, and again neutral or pro-French during the intervention of the 1860s. The last decades of the century saw the continuing disintegration of communal properties, especially from 1869, when state legislation mandated anew the partition of such lands. These pressures were reflected in the state's endemic rural violence in the late nineteenth century, constant complaints by *hacendados* of invasions by "los indígenas de las extinguidas comunidades," and widespread support among various procommunity organizations in the Tarascan zone for the Gran Comité Central Comunero founded in the center of the country by Francisco Zalacosta. The Díaz era (1876–1910) saw certain infrastructural improvements open the area ever more to the forces of modernization and the outside world through the foundation of schools, the penetration of railroads (the Pátzcuaro–Morelia route was opened in 1886), and the development of timber interests in the sierra (partly on the basis of U.S. investment), which put even more pressure on Tarascan economic resources.

The revolutionary period and the ensuing Cristero War proved generally "catastrophic" for the Tarascan people, in the words of one of their modern ethnographers. Growing landlessness (the spread of *minifundismo*) and proletarianization were compounded by the widely destructive effects of two decades of intermittent fighting. The town of Cherán, for example, in the heart of the Sierra Tarasca, was burned twice during the Revolution, and other heavily indigenous communities suffered similar fates; starvation was widespread; and migration to the United States, which had begun as early as 1910 and was to continue (legally) in periodic waves until the mid-1960s, picked up speed after 1916. Parallel to the revolutionary fighting itself, between 1908 and 1913 the districts of Jiquilpan, La Piedad, Zamora, Puruándiro, and Cuitzeo saw a good deal of isolated peasant violence and land invasions, and a concomitantly violent response from the government and large landowners. At the close of the armed phase of the Revolution most indigenous campesinos were no better off than they had been under the Díaz regime. By the early 1920s, it is true, Francisco Múgica – revolutionary general, radical governor (1920–22), and ally of Lázaro Cárdenas – distributed nearly 25,000 hectares of land to indigenous and other peasants with the support of the military agrarian leader Primo Tapia (assassinated 1926), but most claims of the ex-communities still remained unresolved and the *hacendados'* white guards fought militant *agraristas* in the countryside. With the outbreak of the Cristero War in 1926 support for the pro-Church, anti-government cause among Tarascan peasants was virtually universal, fighting against *agrarista* militia widespread, and massacres or expulsions of *agraristas* by *cristeros* (as at Cherán and Charapán, respectively) frequent. These confrontations were bloodiest in the mountain and plateau regions, and many of the episodes seem to have centered on community defense, intercommunity vendettas, and campesino identification with the Church as another persecuted victim of a godless national regime.

The latter part of the 1930s saw an intensive government effort under the presidency of Lázaro Cárdenas, Michoacan's most famous son, to begin to resolve the land problem among indigenous and other campesinos, improve the educational system, and develop the state's infrastructure. Already as governor from 1928, Cárdenas had distributed nearly 150,000 hectares of expropriated hacienda lands to campesinos, nullified by state legislation contracts previously made between communities of the Tarascan *meseta* (highlands) and the lumber companies, and encouraged the formation of forestry cooperatives among indigenous peasants. His efforts first as governor and then as national president (1934–40) to found schools in the countryside, and then instill the benefits of "socialist education," met with a generally hostile response from Tarascan villagers, owing largely to their secularist, anticlerical tone. As the experiment in socialist education cut ever deeper into Tarascan life during the 1930s, in fact, and despite the official end of the Cristero conflict, the tension between allegiance to church and allegiance to school burgeoned along with Tarascan demands for the reopening or reconversion of churches. More successful, and perhaps in the long run more corrosive to "traditional" indigenous lifeways, were the rural electrification and road-building programs initiated by the national government in the late 1930s along with other efforts at directed social change.

Recent decades have seen a recovery in the absolute number of Tarascan speakers in Michoacan, even as their relative weight in the state population declines under the impact of mesticization, their zone of geographic influence continues to shrink somewhat, and the number of monolinguals diminishes. Major indigenous towns of the *meseta* experienced a loss of population during the decades after 1915 or so from a combination of influenza epidemics and mortality in the Revolution and Cristero revolt, but by the close of the 1940s the numbers had rebounded, partly owing to the penetration of modern medical treatment into the area. From a total of nearly 50,000 in 1910, the Tarascan-speech population of Michoacan slipped to 35,000 in 1921, but had rebounded to some 50,000 by 1950, climbed to 63,000 by 1970, and reached as high as 90,000 by the mid-1980s, although by this latter date only about one-third of the inhabitants of the Tarascan *meseta* towns were indigenous-language speakers. Land resources have not kept pace with demographic increase, however, producing significant population pressure and the growth of minifundism. In recent years Tarascan *serrano* towns such as Charapán, Cherán, Nahuatzen Parangaricutiro, Paracho, and Tingambato have experienced considerable political instability arising from conflicts over land, often related to forestry activity. Government development efforts and the natural expansion and integration of the Mexican economy have created some economic growth, but with it a dependent urbanization linked to the continuing dominance of the national capital and foreign markets; urbanization has found further encouragement in industrialization and a tourism industry centering on the Lake Pátzcuaro area. Much of what remains vital in Tarascan culture and folkways, ironically, is represented to the outside world by the artisanal productions so closely associated with individual towns and so widely known and commercialized outside Mexico: lacquerware from the zone as a whole, ceramics from Santa Fé, guitars from Paracho, and so forth. Finally, temporary and permanent out-migration in search of economic opportunities have formed a critical source of income and capital for those returning or remaining behind, and with them has come money for home improvements, funds for trucks and other entrepreneurial capital goods, American clothing, and knowledge of a larger world.

CONCLUSION

According to 1990 statistics, about 90 percent of Mexico's 5.3 million speakers of indigenous languages live in the Center-South of the country, mostly in the states of Oaxaca, Yucatan, Puebla, Veracruz, and Chiapas. From this perspective the Center-West tends hardly at all to figure in discussions of Mexico's indigenous peoples, since such groups constitute less than 5 percent of their respective state populations in the macroregion, and are generally losing ground in terms of relative numbers. Through disease-driven demographic losses in the colonial period, entire zones of the Center-West – the coastal lowlands, for example – were virtually wiped clear of native peoples, and a number of indigenous languages and cultural traditions thus expunged. Yet, as we have seen, there still exists a discernible, even vital, indigenous tradition in the Center-West, its stewards chiefly the Tarascan, Huichol, and Cora peoples.

The history of these cultures since the advent of the Europeans has been one of failed redemptions imposed by other people. In the colonial era the region's native peoples were set upon by European mastiffs and European diseases, suffering on the whole the same 90 percent decline characteristic of other areas in Mexico and Indo-America more generally. When demographic recovery came, it was accompanied by miscegenation, which diluted the Indian cultural tradition in many areas and left indigenous villagers partially submerged in a rising tide of nonindigenous people of color. As the European evangelizing compulsion sought out Indian souls, colonist cupidity devoured Indian lands. In the nineteenth century, indigenous peoples found themselves "saved" yet again, this time by the forces of a burgeoning liberal ideology and an expanding state power that sought to elevate them to effective citizenship and make yeoman farmers out of them. In reality these projects only exposed them more than ever to the forces of the market economy and left them in a political penumbra from which the only effective escape was the spasmodic resort to collective violence. In the twentieth century a more subtle but no less egregious racism found its ironic counterpoint in national-level official *indigenismo*, socialist education, anticlerical campaigns to enlighten the countryside, and developmental projects to modernize it. During this century, internal war, a thickening capitalist regime, and a non-Indian population continuing to grow around them have worn the Indian peoples of the Center-West to a nubbin of their once substantial numbers.

Yet still some native peoples of the Center-West endure, even showing considerable signs of demographic vitality, institutional and economic adaptivity, and cultural self-consciousness. Nor have they remained passive or silent through their long and problematic dialogue with Spanish colonial and Mexican successor states, even if nowadays resort to arms and the revival of messianic or millenarian hopes remain unlikely. We should beware the undoubted temptation to romanticize the efficacy of cultural resistance, however. On the whole, surely, over the long term the forces of cultural dissolution have tended to wear indigenous cultures down in the face of overwhelming numbers of nonindigenous people, the relentless extension of state power, and the strongly homogenizing tendencies of ravenous markets, ineluctable commodification, and steadily advancing technologies. That these peoples still exist, and have bought time for themselves, is as much proof of their own vitality as it is testimony to the view that culture is not a fixed set of values or ideas reached by consensus and preserved like a fly in amber, but, rather, is an artifact of group process and of daily negotiation.

BIBLIOGRAPHICAL ESSAY

On the whole it seems safe to say that insofar as the reconstruction of their past is concerned, the indigenous peoples of central-western Mexico have been better served by anthropologists and archaeologists than by historians and ethnohistorians, and the Tarascans, Huicholes, and Coras best of all. For the post-colonial period, especially, the ethnohistory of these and other groups is often embedded in scholarly works on modern ethnography, demography, politics, economic life, policy prescriptions, and so forth, or must be inferred from silences in those works – that is, in the virtual historiographical absence of indigenous peoples we often need to triangulate on them from data adduced for other ends. Large-scale, general histories of the central-western states often include many data of ethnohistorical interest, although to the degree that they concentrate on the post-1821 political entities these histories need to be culled carefully to yield the information. Particularly useful on the post-independence history of the Tarascans within the context of modern Michoacan is Enrique Florescano et al., *Historia general de Michoacán*, 4 vols. (Morelia, 1989); also worth consulting are José Bravo Ugarte, *Historia sucinta de Michoacán*, 3 vols. (Mexico City, 1964), and for the period of the Mexican Revolution, Jesús Romero Flores, *Historia de la Revolución en Michoacán* (Mexico City, 1964). For Jalisco, the classic (and still in some ways unsurpassed) nineteenth-century *historia patria* is that of Luis Pérez Verdía, *Historia particular del Estado de Jalisco*, 3 vols. (Guadalajara, 1988), complemented by the more modern approaches and interests of José María Muría et al., *Historia de Jalisco*, 4 vols. (Guadalajara, 1981–82), and *Jalisco: Una historia compartida* (Mexico City, 1987), and by Muría's own very useful *Breve historia de Jalisco* (Mexico City, 1988); for the nineteenth and twentieth centuries in Jalisco, there are Mario Aldana Rendón, *Jalisco durante la República restaurada, 1867–77*, 2 vols. (Guadalajara, 1981–83), and Mario Aldana Rendón, general editor, *Jalisco desde la Revolución*, 14 vols. (Guadalajara, 1987–88). José María Muría has also edited a number of extremely useful historical anthologies, among them *Lecturas históricas sobre Jalisco antes de la Independencia* (Guadalajara, 1976), especially useful for the Conquest and early evangelization of native peoples; *Lecturas históricas de Jalisco después de la Independencia*, 2 vols. (Guadalajara, 1981); and *Lecturas históricas del Norte de Jalisco* (Guadalajara, 1991), rich in material on the modern Huicholes. For other general histories of central-western states with information on native peoples, see Everardo Peña Navarro, *Estudio histórico del Estado de Nayarit*, 2 vols. (Tepic, 1946–56); Jesús Gómez Serrano, *Aguascalientes en la historia, 1786–1920)*, 5 vols. (Mexico City, 1988); and a number of volumes in the *historia compartida* series cosponsored by various state governments and Dr. José María Luis Mora of Mexico City's Instituto de Investigaciones, among them Servando Ortoll, ed., *Colima: Una historia compartida*, 3 vols. (Mexico City, 1988), and Rosa Helia Villa de Mebius, *San Luis: Una historia compartida* (Mexico City, 1988). An extremely useful historiographic survey of the central-western states is to be found in Jaime Olveda, ed., *Balance y perspectivas de la historiografía noroccidental* (Mexico City, 1991). Basic to the archaeology, ethnohistory, and ethnology of native peoples, of course, is Robert Wauchope, general editor, *Handbook of Middle American Indians* (hereafter HMAI), 16 vols. (Austin, TX, 1964–76), especially the chapters "Tarascans," by Ralph L. Beals, and "The Huichol and Cora," by Joseph E. Grimes and Thomas B. Hinton, in *HMAI*, vol. 8, part 2, *Ethnology*, Evon Z. Vogt, volume editor, 725–76 and 792–813, respectively. Large-scale works produced within the last decade or so, in which the anthropologist Phil C. Weigand has played a particularly distinguished role, include N. Ross Crumrine and Phil C. Weigand, *Ejidos and Regions of Refuge in Northwestern Mexico* (Tucson, AZ, 1987); Phil C. Weigand and Michael S. Foster, eds., *The Archaeology of West and Northwest Mesoamerica* (Boulder, CO, 1985); and Thomas B. Hinton and Phil C. Weigand, *Themes of Indigenous Acculturation in Northwest Mexico* (Tucson, AZ, 1981). The archaeology, linguistics, ethnography, and history of native peoples of the Center-West from prehispanic to modern times is covered in two recent anthologies edited by Ricardo Avila Palafox: *Transformaciones mayores en el Occidente de México* (Guadalajara, 1994) and *El Occidente de México en el tiempo: Aproximaciones a su definición cultural* (Guadalajara, 1994). For the Tarascans, in particular, over the same grand temporal span, see the excellent anthology edited by Pedro Carrasco et al., *La sociedad indígena en el centro y occidente de México* (Zamora, 1986). Older but still useful for general orientation is Robert C. West and John P. Augelli, *Middle America: Its Lands and Peoples*, 2nd ed. (Englewood Cliffs, NJ, 1976). Studies of linguistic distribution, aside from their inherent interest, often prove to be sources of ethnohistorical data. Among the most useful consulted for this study were María Luisa Horcasitas de Barros and Ana María Crespo, *Hablantes de lengua indígena en México* (Mexico City, 1979); Jorge A. Suárez, *The Mesoamerican Indian Languages* (Cambridge, 1983); Joseph H. Greenberg, *Language in the Americas* (Stanford, CA, 1987); Carl O. Sauer, *The Distribution of Aboriginal Tribes and Languages in Northwestern Mexico* (Berkeley, CA, 1934); and José Ramírez Flores, *Lenguas indígenas de Jalisco* (Guadalajara, 1980). A number of historians and anthropologists have produced interpretive essays on the indigenous cultures of the New World, Mesoamerica, and Center-West, among them Robert McC. Adams, "Late Prehispanic Empires of the New World," in M. T. Larsen, ed., *Power and Propaganda: A Symposium on Ancient Empires* (Copenhagen, 1979), 59–73; Angel Palerm and Eric R. Wolf, "Ecological Potential and Cultural Development in Mesoamerica," *Social Sciences Monographs* 3 (1960): 1–37; N. Ross Crumrine, "Symbolic Structure and Ritual Symbolism in Northwest and West Mexico," in Carl Kendall et al., eds., *Heritage of Conquest: Thirty Years Later* (Albuquerque, NM, 1983), 247–66; and Luis González, "Peculiaridades del oeste mexicano," *Encuentro* 1 (October–December 1983): 5–26.

The culture history of native peoples in the prehispanic period, especially the Tarascan state, is more meaningful when contextualized in large-scale surveys such as William T. Sanders, Jeffrey R. Parsons, and Robert S. Santley, *The Basin of Mexico: Ecological Processes in the Evolution of a Civilization* (New York, 1979); Richard Blanton et al., *Ancient Mesoamerica* (Cambridge, 1981); Walter Krickeberg, *Pre-Columbian American Religions* (New York, 1968); Ross Hassig, *Aztec Warfare: Imperial Expansion and Political Control* (Norman, OK, 1988); Pedro Carrasco and Johanna Broda, eds., *Estratificación social en la Mesoamérica prehispánica* (Mexico City, 1976); and, most recently, the sophisticated textbook treatment of Robert M. Carmack, Janine Gasco, and Gary H. Gossen, *The Legacy of Mesoamerica: History and Culture of a Native American Civilization* (Upper Saddle River, NJ, 1996). Unique among native peoples of the Center-West, the Tarascan civilization has attracted by far the most intense and coherent scholarly attention, the treatment of other indigenous groups being much more superficial and fragmentary, partly owing (in some cases) to their early disappearance. In recent years some of the most outstanding and widely cited ethnohistorical work on the Tarascans has been that of Helen P. Pollard, with its emphasis on ecological and economic questions, including her articles "Agrarian Potential, Population, and the Tarascan State," *Science* 209 (1980): 274–77; "Ecological Variation and Economic Exchange in the Tarascan State," *American Ethnologist* 9 (1982): 250–68; "Ethnicity and Political Control in a Complex Society: The Tarascan State of Prehispanic Mexico," in Elizabeth M. Brumfiel and John W. Fox, eds., *Factional Competition and Political Development in the New World* (Cambridge, 1994), 79–88; and culminating in Shirley Gorenstein and Helen P. Pollard, *The Tarascan Civilization* (Nashville, TN, 1983), and Helen P. Pollard, *Taríacuri's Legacy: The Prehispanic Tarascan State*, with an introduction by Shirley Gorenstein (Norman, OK 1993). Another large-scale ethnohistorical treatment is the unpublished thesis of Ulíses Beltrán, "Tarascan State and Society in Prehispanic Times: An Ethnohistorical Inquiry" (PhD.

diss. University of Chicago, 1982). On Tarascan religious thinking, see José Corona Núñez, *Mitología tarasca* (Mexico City, 1957) and Francisco Hurtado Mendoza, *La religión prehispánica de los Purhépechas: Un testimonio del pueblo tarasco* (Morelia, 1986). The spatial limits of the Tarascan empire and its relations with its Mexica neighbor are dealt with in María del Refugio Cabrera V. and B. Pérez González, *El estado p'urhépecha y sus fronteras en el siglo XVI* (Morelia, 1991); Carlos Herrejón Peredo, "La pugna entre Mexicas y Tarascos," *Cuadernos de Historia* 1 (1978): 11–47; and Alfredo López Austin, *Tarascos y mexicas* (Mexico City, 1981). Useful ethnohistorical studies of other groups include José Ignacio Dávila Garibi, *Los caxcanes* (Mexico City, 1950), and José Guadalupe Sánchez Olmedo, *Etnografía de la Sierra Madre Occidental: Tepehuanes y mexicaneros* (Mexico City, 1982).

Tracing the basic population curves of indigenous peoples from the prehispanic era forward is not a simple matter, though much progress has been made by historical demographers. Perhaps the most important works embracing these questions – essential not only for population figures but also for data on pre- and post-conquest ethnohistory itself, settlement patterns, labor systems, evangelization, and a range of other issues – are the indispensable volumes of Peter Gerhard: *A Guide to the Historical Geography of New Spain* (Cambridge, 1972) and *The North Frontier of New Spain* (Princeton, NJ, 1982). The work of the Berkeley historical demographers is, of course, essential here as well, including (but hardly limited to) Carl O. Sauer, *Aboriginal Population of Northwestern Mexico* (Berkeley, CA, 1935); Woodrow W. Borah and Sherburne F. Cook, *The Population of Central Mexico in 1548* (Berkeley, 1960), and *The Aboriginal Population of Central Mexico on the Eve of the Spanish Conquest* (Berkeley, CA, 1963); and Sherburne F. Cook and Woodrow W. Borah, *Essays in Population History: Mexico and the Caribbean*, 3 vols. (Berkeley, CA, 1971–74). Also useful, though more specialized, are Thomas Calvo and G. López, eds., *Movimientos de población en el occidente de México* (Mexico City, 1988); José Menéndez Valdés, *Descripción y censo general de la Intendencia de Guadalajara, 1789–1793* (Guadalajara, 1980), for the end of the colonial period; Pedro López González, *La población de Tepic, bajo la organización regional (1530–1821)* (Tepic, 1984); Robert McCaa, "The Peopling of Nineteenth-Century Mexico: Critical Scrutiny of a Censured Century," in James W. Wilkie et al., eds., *Statistical Abstract of Latin America*, vol. 30, part 1 (Los Angeles, 1993), 603–33; and for the contemporary period, George Psacharopoulos and Harry Anthony

Patrinos, eds., *Indigenous People and Poverty in Latin America: An Empirical Analysis* (Washington, DC, 1994). The unembarrassed localist historiography that so abounds for Mexico, especially when it has shed its antiquarianism, can be very useful for the ethnohistorian. Among many such works that could be cited, see for Michoacan: Arturo Rodríguez Zetina, *Zamora: Ensayo histórico y repertorio documental* (Mexico City, 1952); Luis González, *Zamora* (Zamora, 1984); Alvaro S. Ochoa, *Jiquilpan* (Morelia, 1978); Francisco Miranda, *Yurécuaro* (Morelia, 1978); Francisco Miranda, *Uruapan* (Morelia, 1979); Pablo Macías, *Pátzcuaro* (Morelia, 1978); Justino Fernández, *Pátzcuaro* (Mexico City, 1936); Esteban Chávez Cisneros, *Quitúpan; Ensayo histórico y estadístico* (Morelia, 1954); Raúl Arreola Cortés, *Tacámbaro, Carácuaro, Nocupétaro, Turicato* (Morelia, 1979); and Jesús Teja Andrade, *Zitácuaro* (Morelia, 1978). For Jalisco, see, among many others, Andrés Antonio Fábregas Puig, *La formación histórica de una región: Los Altos de Jalisco* (Mexico City, 1986); Emilio Guevara, *Historia particular de la Villa de Zapotlanejo* (Zapotlanejo, 1919); and José González Orozco, *Ixtlahuacán de los Membrillos* (Ixtlahuacán de los Membrillos, 1958).

A number of documentary collections (bringing together, for example, the famous *relaciones geográficas* of 1579–80) and general histories of parts of the Center-West exist covering the colonial period. Among the most useful and readily accessible of these are, for Michoacan: Francisco Miranda, ed., *La relación de Michoacán* (Morelia, 1980); Ramón López Lara, ed., *El Obispado de Michoacán en el siglo XVII. Informe inédito de beneficios, pueblos y lugares* (Morelia, 1973); René Acuña, ed., *Relaciones geográficas del siglo XVI: Michoacán* (Mexico City, 1987); Alvaro S. Ochoa and Gerardo Sánchez D., eds., *Relaciones y memorias de la Provincia de Michoacán, 1579–81* (Morelia, 1985); José Corona Núñez, ed., *Relaciones geográficas de la diócesis de Michoacán, 1579–80* (Guadalajara, 1958). Two interesting and innovative attempts by younger scholars to deconstruct some of these early accounts are James Krippner-Martinez, "The Politics of Conquest: An Interpretation of the Relación de Michoacán," *The Americas* 47 (1990): 177–98; and Cynthia Leigh Stone, "Rewriting Indigenous Traditions: The Burial Ceremony of the Cazonci," *Colonial Latin American Review* 3 (1994): 87–114. Later accounts of the colonization and evangelization of Michoacan are Isidro Félix de Espinosa, *Crónica de la provincia franciscana de los apóstoles San Pedro y San Pablo de Michoacán*, ed. José Ignacio Dávila Garibi (Mexico City, 1945 [c. 1752]); and Pablo Beaumont, *Crónica de Michoacán*, 3 vols. (Morelia, 1985 [c. 1777]). For

Nueva Galicia, see Domingo Lázaro de Arregui, *Descripción de la Nueva Galicia*, con estudio preliminar de François Chevalier (Guadalajara, 1980 [1946]); Alonso de la Mota y Escobar, *Descripción geográfica de los Reinos de Nueva Galicia, Nueva Vizcaya y Nuevo León* (Guadalajara, 1966); and Matías de la Mota Padilla, *Historia del Reino de Nueva Galicia en la América Septentrional (1742)* (Guadalajara, 1973). For Nayarit, see Alberto Santoscoy, ed., *Nayarit: Colección de documentos inéditos, históricos y etnográficos de la sierra de ese nombre* (Guadalajara, 1899), including an interesting 1672 report by Antonio Arias y Saavedra on the condition of the sierra (pp. 217–41).

The dramatic and violent decades of the Spanish conquest of the Center-West have often been chronicled. The definitive treatment for the Tarascan area is J. Benedict Warren, *The Conquest of Michoacán: The Spanish Domination of the Tarascan Kingdom in Western Mexico, 1521–1530* (Norman, OK, 1985); and for Nuño de Guzmán's execution of the Cazonci from a modern perspective, see James Krippner-Martinez, "The Vision of the Victors: Power and Colonial Justice," *Colonial Latin American Review* 4 (1995): 3–28. The works of Philip W. Powell are essential for putting the conquest of the Center-West in context and linking it to Spanish entry into the near north and north of the country; see especially his *Soldiers, Indians, and Silver: North America's First Frontier War* (Tempe, AZ, 1975; originally published 1952) and *Mexico's Miguel Caldera: The Taming of America's First Frontier (1548–1597)* (Tucson, AZ, 1977). On the conquest of Nueva Galicia, see Antonio Tello, *Crónica miscelánea en que se trata de la conquista espiritual y temporal de la santa provincia de Xalisco en el nuevo reino de la Galicia y Nueva Vizcaya*, 2 vols. (Guadalajara, 1891); José López Portillo y Weber, *La conquista de la Nueva Galicia* (Mexico City, 1935); and José Luis Razo Zaragoza, *Conquista hispánica de las provincias de los tebles chichimecas de la América septentrional, Nuevo Reino de Galicia* (Guadalajara, 1988), which concentrates mostly on Nuño de Guzmán. The protracted military encounter between Europeans and indigenous groups in the "Gran Nayar" is chronicled in José Ortega, *Maravillosa conquista y reducción de la provincia de San Joseph del Gran Nayar, Nuevo Reino de Toledo* (Mexico City, 1944 [1754]) and *Autos hechos por el capitán don Juan Flores de San Pedro sobre la reducción, conversión, y conquista de los gentiles de la provincia del Nayarit en 1722* (Guadalajara, 1964). Colotlán, the military frontier zone today shared by the states of Jalisco, Zacatecas, and Nayarit was shaped by late military engagement and the need to pacify native resistance in the area; it is treated by María del Carmen Velázquez, *Colotlán: Doble frontera contra los bárbaros* (Mexico City, 1961).

Christian evangelization of native peoples went hand in hand with Spanish military conquest, or hard upon its heels; the classic and still indispensable work on the process is Robert Ricard, *The Spiritual Conquest of Mexico*, trans. Leslie Byrd Simpson (Berkeley, CA, 1982; originally published 1933). Not surprisingly, Vasco de Quiroga's unique sixteenth-century experiment in evangelization and acculturation has generated a huge literature, among which the following works are some of the most helpful: Fintan B. Warren, *Vasco de Quiroga and His Pueblo-Hospitals of Santa Fé* (Washington, DC, 1963); Rafael Aguayo Spenser, *Don Vasco de Quiroga, taumaturgo de la organización social, seguido de un apéndice documental* (Mexico City, 1970), and the same author's *Don Vasco de Quiroga. Documentos* (Mexico City, 1940); A. Gortaire Iturralde, *Santa Fé: Presencia etnológica de un pueblo-hospital* (Mexico City, 1971); Silvio Zavala, *Ideario de Vasco de Quiroga* (Mexico City, 1941); and Francisco Miranda and Gabriela Briseño, eds., *Vasco de Quiroga: Educador de adultos* (Pátzcuaro, 1984), with an extensive bibliography (pp. 181–94) on the theme. On the missions in the Nayarit area, see the documents and commentaries gathered by Jean Meyer, ed., *El Gran Nayar* (Mexico City, 1989), vol. 3 of the invaluable series *Colección de Documentos para la Historia de Nayarit*; and the 1730 report of Urbano Covarrubias, "Algunos triunfos particulares que ha conseguido nuestra santa fé católica de la fatal idolatría en esta provincia de San Joseph del Nayarit, Nuevo Reino de Toledo," in *Boletín del Archivo General de la Nación* 10 (1939): 327–46.

Modern ethnohistorical work bearing on the colonial period is relatively exiguous, or needs to be synthesized from more general histories. Worth looking at are Ralph L. Beals, *The Comparative Ethnology of Northern Mexico Before 1750* (Berkeley, CA, 1932); Donald Brand, *Coalcomán and Motines de Oro: An Ex-District of Michoacán, Mexico* (Austin, 1960); J. Jesús Figueroa Torres, *El remoto pasado del Reino de Colimán* (Mexico City, 1973); Carolyn Baus de Czitrom, *Tecuexes y cocas. Dos grupos de la región Jalisco en el siglo XVI* (Mexico City, 1982); Mari-Areti Hers, "Los coras en la época de la expulsión jesuita," *Historia Mexicana* 27 (1977): 17–48; and Robert Shadow, "Lo 'indio' está en la tierra: Identidad social y lucha agraria entre los indios tepecano del norte de Jalisco," *América Indígena* 45 (1985): 521–78. Altogether better served has been colonial economic and social history, particularly centering on the formation of the Spanish rural estates that had such a profound impact on native farming systems and engendered such deep-running conflict between Indians and non-Indians. For the early *encomienda* and *repartimiento* tribute and labor systems, respectively, see J. Benedict Warren, *La administración de los negocios de un encomendero en Michoacán* (Mexico City, 1984), and Moisés González Navarro, *Repartimiento de indios en Nueva Galicia* (Mexico City, 1977). For the area of Michoacan and its extensions into the more easterly parts of the Center-West, see especially Claude Morin, *Michoacán el la Nueva España del siglo XVIII. Crecimiento y desigualdad en una economía colonial* (Mexico City, 1979); and more specifically on the Tarascan zones, Dan Stanislawski, *The Anatomy of Eleven Towns in Michoacan* (Austin, TX, 1950); Delfina E. López Sarrelangue, *La nobleza indígena de Pátzcuaro en la época virreinal* (Mexico City, 1965); Sergio Navarrete Pellicer, "Las transformaciones de la economía indígena en Michoacán, siglo XVI," in Teresa Rojas Rabiela, ed., *Agricultura indígena: Pasado y presente* (Mexico City, 1994), 109–28; and Elizabeth Barrett, "Encomiendas, Mercedes, and Haciendas in the Tierra Caliente of Michoacán," *Jahrbuch für Geschichte Lateinamerikas* 10 (1973): 71–112, and "Indian Community Lands in the Tierra Caliente of Michoacán," *Jahrbuch für Geschichte Lateinamerikas* 11 (1974): 78–120. For what is now the state of Jalisco, see the classic work of Jesús Amaya Topete on the development of the Spanish hacienda, *Ameca, protofundación mexicana. Historia de la propiedad del Valle de Ameca, Jalisco y circunvecindad* (Mexico City, 1951); Rodolfo Fernández, *Latifundios y grupos dominantes en la historia de la provincia de Avalos* (Guadalajara, 1994); Agueda Jiménez Pelayo, "Los conflictos por tierras de comunidades indígenas: El caso de Teocaltiche, 1691–1794," *Encuentro* 3 (1986): 21–42, and the same author's *Haciendas y comunidades indígenas en el sur de Zacatecas. Sociedad y economía colonial, 1600–1820* (Mexico City, 1989); Heriberto Moreno García, *Haciendas de tierra y agua en la antigua ciénega de Chapala* (Zamora, 1989); Ramón María Serrera Contreras, *Guadalajara ganadera: Estudio regional novohispano, 1760–1805* (Seville, 1977), which includes particularly interesting material on indigenous *cofradías* and livestock holdings; Eric Van Young, *Hacienda and Market in Eighteenth-Century Mexico: The Rural Economy of the Guadalajara Region, 1675–1820* (Berkeley, CA, 1981); and several of the essays in Eric Van Young, *La crisis del orden colonial: Estructura agraria y rebeliones populares de la Nueva España, 1750–1821* (Mexico City, 1992).

Colonial rebellions involving indigenous peoples in the Center-West are still hardly studied, but scholars have made a start. Brief original texts on indigenous resistance movements, particularly in the area to the north and northeast of the Tarascan heartland, have been gathered and glossed in several works, including María Teresa Huerta and Patricia Palacios, eds., *Rebeliones indígenas de la época colonial* (Mexico City, 1976), and María Elena Galaviz de Capdevielle, *Rebeliones indígenas en el norte del Reino de la Nueva España (siglos XVI y XVII)* (Mexico City, 1967). The famous Mixtón War and its aftermath has also been treated in José López Portillo y Weber, *La rebelión de la Nueva Galicia* (Mexico City, 1939), and Pedro Ahumada, *Rebelión de los zacatecos y guachichiles (1562)* (Mexico City, 1952). The Mariano episode has been discussed in passing in a number of works, but still lacks a unified monographic treatment. My account here is based substantially on the brief but thoughtful paper of Felipe Castro Gutiérrez, "La rebelión del Indio Mariano (Nayarit, 1801)," *Estudios de Historia Novohispana* 10 (1991): 347–67, and the still briefer narrative in Christon I. Archer, *El ejército en el México borbónico, 1760–1810* (Mexico City, 1983), 131–35. The movement is treated briefly and contextualized in Eric Van Young, "Millennium on the Northern Marches: The Mad Messiah of Durango and Popular Rebellion in Mexico, 1800–1815," *Comparative Studies in Society and History* 28 (1986): 385–413, and "Religion and Popular Ideology in Mexico, 1810–1821," in Steve Kaplan, ed., *Indigenous and Popular Responses to Western Christianity* (New York, 1995) 144–73; and in Enrique Florescano, *Memoria mexicana. Ensayo sobre la reconstrucción del pasado: época prehispánica – 1821* (Mexico City, 1987). An exhaustive collection of original documents is to be found in Juan López, ed., *La rebelión del indio Mariano. Un movimiento insurgente en la Nueva Galicia, en 1801; y, documentos procesales*, 3 vols. (Guadalajara, 1985). The historiography on the wars of independence in Mexico is, of course, enormous, but the role of indigenous people has not in general been singled out, and still less for the Center-West. A useful starting point is Van Young, *La crisis del orden colonial*.

A burgeoning historical literature exists for indigenous and peasant rebellion (often but not always the same thing) after independence, treated generally – but with much material on the Center-West – in Leticia Reina, *Las rebeliones campesinas en México (1819–1906)* (Mexico City, 1980); and Jean Meyer, *Problemas campesinas y revueltas agrarias, 1821–1910* (Mexico City, 1973). More specifically on the Tarascan zone in the nineteenth century and the period of the Revolution, see Gerardo Sánchez Díaz, "Movimientos campesinos en la tierra caliente de Michoacán, 1869–1900," in *Jornadas de historia de occidente: Movimientos populares en el occidente de México, siglos XIX y XX* (Jiquilpan de Juárez, 1981); Carlos García Mora, "El conflicto agrario-religioso en la sierra tarasca," *América Indígena* 36 (1976): 115–29; and Paul Friedrich, *Agrarian Revolt in a Mexican Village* (Chicago, 1977). The political trajectory of a long-lived independence hero whose career was much affected by political conflict and violence in the Michoacán countryside is detailed in Jaime Olveda, *Gordiano Guzmán: Un cacique del siglo XIX* (Mexico City, 1980). The agrarian rebellion of Manuel Lozada has generated a substantial historiography of its own, including Mario A. Aldana Rendón, *La rebelión agraria de Manuel Lozada, 1873* (Mexico City, 1983) and *Manuel Lozada y las comunidades indígenas* (Guadalajara, 1983); Silvano Barba González, *La lucha por la tierra. Manuel Lozada* (Mexico City, 1956); and a number of eloquent essays by Jean Meyer included in his *Esperando a Lozada* (Zamora, 1984), as well as a documentary anthology edited by Meyer, *La tierra de Manuel Lozada* (Mexico City, 1989), vol. 4 in the *Colección de documentos para la historia de Nayarit*. Jean Meyer has also written widely on the participation of indigenous people in the Cristero War of the 1920s, mainly in his monumental *La cristiada*, 2nd ed., 3 vols., trans. Aurelio Garzón del Camino (Mexico City, 1974), and the shorter English version of the same study, *The Cristero Rebellion: The Mexican People between Church and State, 1926–1929*, trans. Richard Southern (Cambridge, 1976); see also his article, "La segunda cristiada en Michoacán," in Francisco Miranda, ed., *La cultura purhe: II Coloquio de Antropología e Historia Regionales* (Mexico City, 1981), 245–76; and David Bailey, *Viva Cristo Rey! The Cristero Rebellion and the Church–State Conflict in Mexico* (Austin, TX, 1974).

The economic history of surviving indigenous communities is difficult to get at directly for the nineteenth century, since it tends to be subsumed in more general studies, accounts of localities, or sectoral histories. Useful in a general way are Margaret Chowning, "A Mexican Provincial Elite: Michoacan, 1810–1910" (Ph.D. diss., Stanford University, 1984); José Napoleón Guzmán Avila, *Michoacán y la inversión extranjera, 1880–1911* (Morelia, 1982); and Mario A. Aldana Rendón, *Desarrollo económico de Jalisco, 1821–1940*, 2nd ed. (Guadalajara, 1979). Scholars of nineteenth-century politics and economic life have devoted much attention to the effects of the Reforma and of liberalism more generally in transferring land out of indigenous hands and into the non-Indian and commercial farming sectors. For a general orientation on these issues, see Enrique

Semo et al., *Historia de la cuestión agraria mexicana*, 4 vols. (Mexico City, 1988); for general treatments of *desamortización*, Bernardo García Martínez, ed., *Los pueblos de indios y las comunidades: Lecturas de Historia Mexicana*, 2 (Mexico City, 1991), including important articles by Donald L. Fraser and T. C. Powell; the specific situation in Michoacan is treated in Moisés Franco Mendoza, "La desamortización de bienes de comunidades indígenas en Michoacán," in Carrasco et al., *La sociedad indígena*, 169–88. For Jalisco, see the documentary compilation of Ignacio Aguirre, ed., *Colección de acuerdos, órdenes y decretos sobre tierras, casas y solares de los indígenas, bienes de sus comunidades y fundos legales de los pueblos del Estado de Jalisco*, 6 vols. (Guadalajara, 1849–82). Especially illuminating on the *desamortización* are the articles of Mario Aldana Rendón, "El liberalismo y la propiedad indígena en Jalisco, 1855–1858," in Sergio Alcántara Ferrer and Enrique Sánchez Ruiz, eds., *Desarrollo rural en Jalisco: Contradicciones y perspectivas* (Guadalajara, 1985), 19–38; Robert J. Knowlton, "La individualización de la propiedad corporativa civil en el siglo XIX – notas sobre Jalisco," in García Martínez, ed., *Los pueblos de indios*, 181–218; Jean Meyer, "La Ley Lerdo y la desamortización de las comunidades en Jalisco," in Carrasco et al., *La sociedad indídgena*, 189–21, as well as the same author's *Esperando a Lozada*; and for a somewhat later period, Jean Meyer, "Historia del reparto agrario en Nayarit, 1916–1934," *Encuentro* 3 (1986): 43–56.

For the modern era much ethnohistorical material tends to be embedded in ethnographic or other sorts of studies not properly historical, although they may reach backward in time for a considerable period. For the Tarascans, important works from earlier in this century by Mexican scholars include Nicolás León, *Los tarascos: Notas históricas, étnicas y antropológicas* (Mexico City, 1979 [1903]); Lucio Mendieta y Núñez et al., *Los tarascos. Monografía histórica, etnográfica y económica* (Mexico City, 1940); and Pedro Carrasco, *Tarrascan Folk Religion: An Analysis of Economic, Social, and Religious Interactions* (New Orleans, 1952). The better known fieldwork-based studies by American scholars have included Ralph L. Beals, *Cherán: A Sierra Tarascan Village* (New York, 1973), and the same author's extensive chapter embracing modern Tarascan history in *HMAI*, vol. 8; Ralph L. Beals, Pedro Carrasco, and Thomas Mc-Corkle, *Houses and House Use of the Sierra Tarascans* (Washington, DC, 1944); Robert C. West, *Cultural Geography of the Modern Tarascan Area* (Washington, DC, 1948); Donald Brand, *Quiroga, A Mexican Municipio* (Washington, DC, 1951), and the same author's "An Historical Sketch of

Geography and Anthropology in the Tarascan Region: Part I," *New Mexico Anthropologist* 6–7 (1943): 37–108; George M. Foster, *Empire's Children: The People of Tzintzuntzan* (Washington, DC, 1948) and *Tzintzuntzan: Mexican Peasants in a Changing World*, rev. ed. (New York, 1979); Michael Belshaw, *A Village Economy: Land and People of Huecorio* (New York, 1967); Ina R. Dinerman, *Los tarascos. Campesinos y artesanos de Michoacán* (Mexico City, 1974); George P. Castile, *Cherán: La Adaptación de una comunidad tradicional de Michoacán* (Mexico City, 1974); Paul Friedrich, *The Princes of Naranja: An Essay in Anthrohistorical Method* (Austin, TX, 1986); and most recently Marjorie Becker, *Setting the Virgin on Fire: Lázaro Cárdenas, Michoacan Peasants, and the Redemption of the Mexican Revolution* (Berkeley, CA, 1995). More recent scholarship by Mexican anthropologists and others includes Pedro Carrasco, *El catolicismo popular de los tarascos* (Mexico City, 1976); Rudolf A. M. Van Zantwijk, *Servants of the Saints: The Social and Cultural Identity of a Tarascan Community in Mexico* (Assen, 1967); Guillermo de la Peña, ed., *Antropología social de la región Purépecha* (Zamora, 1987); Carlos Herrejón Peredo, ed., *Estudios michoacanos*, 3 vols. (Zamora, 1986); Jane R. Moone, *Desarrollo tarasco: Integración nacional en el occidente de México* (Mexico City, 1973); and Cristina Mapes et al., "La agricultura en una región indígena: La cuenca del lago de Pátzcuaro," in Rojas Rabiela, ed., *Agricultura indígena*, 275–342.

The Huichol and Cora peoples, while they have consistently attracted some anthropological and ethnohistorical interest through the twentieth century, gained Western attention particularly during the last several decades for their artistic traditions and their use of hallucinogens for religious purposes. Useful and representative works along these lines are Robert M. Zingg, *The Huicholes: Primitive Artists* (New York, 1938); Barbara G. Myerhoff, *The Deer-Maize-Peyote Complex Among the Huichol Indians of Mexico* (Ph.D. diss., UCLA, 1968) and *Peyote Hunt: The Sacred Journey of the Huichol Indians* (Ithaca, NY, 1974); Juan Negrín, *El arte contemporáneo de los huicholes* (Guadalajara, 1977); and Kathleen Berrin, ed., *Art of the Huichol Indians* (New York, 1978). The American anthropologist Phil C. Weigand (often in collaboration with his wife, Celia García de Weigand) has emerged as one of the major scholarly figures in the archaeology, ethnology, and ethnohistory of western-central Mexico, not least in relation to the Huicholes. Among many other publications, see: Phil C. Weigand, *Cooperative Labor Groups in Subsistence Activities Among the Huichol Indians* (Carbondale, IL, 1970); "Possible Historical

References to La Quemada in Huichol Mythology," *Ethnohistory* 22 (1975): 15–20; "Contemporary Social and Economic Structure," in Berrin, *Art of the Huichol Indians*; "Role of the Huichol Indians in the Revolutions of Western Mexico," in Lewis A. Tambs, ed., *Revolution in the Americas: Proceedings of the PCCLAS, 22nd Annual Meeting* (Tempe, AZ, 1979), 167–76; "Considerations on the Archaeology and Ethnohistory of the Mexicaneros, Tequales, Coras, Huicholes, and Caxcanes of Nayarit, Jalisco, and Zacatecas," in William J. Folan, Jr., ed., *Contributions to the Archaeology and Ethnohistory of Greater Mesoamerica: Essays in Honor of Carroll L. Riley* (Carbondale, IL, 1985), 126–87; *Ensayos sobre el Gran Nayar: Entre coras, huicholes, y tepehuanos* (Mexico City, 1992); and with Celia García de Weigand, "Contemporary Huichol Textiles: Patterns of Change," in *Ethnographic Textiles of the Western Hemisphere* (Washington, DC, 1976), 293–98.

The famous ethnography-cum-travelogue of Carl Lumholtz – *Unknown Mexico*, 2 vols. (New York, 1902) – still bears a careful reading. Of more recent date in a broad ethnohistorical/ethnological vein are: John McIntosh, "Cosmogonía huichol," *Tlalócan* 3 (1949): 14–21; Evon Z. Vogt, "Some Aspects of Cora–Huichol Acculturation," *América Indígena* 15 (1955): 249–63; Thomas B. Hinton, *The Village Hierarchy as a Factor in Cora Indian Acculturation* (Los Angeles, 1961), and the same author's collaborative chapter on the Huichol and Cora with Joseph E. Grimes in *HMAI*, vol. 8; Wigberto Jiménez Moreno, "Nayarit – Etnohistoria y arqueología," in García Martínez, ed., *Historia y sociedad*; Thomas B. Hinton, et al., *Coras, huicholes, y tepehuanes* (Mexico City, 1972); Gildardo González Ramos, *Los coras* (Mexico City, 1972); Jay Courtney Fikes, "Huichol Indian Identity and Adaptation" (PhD. diss., University of Michigan, 1985); Juan Negrín, *Acercamiento histórico y subjetivo al huichol* (Guadalajara, 1985); Jean Meyer, *Del Cantón de Tepic al Estado de Nayarit, 1810–1940* (Mexico City, 1990), vol. 5 of the series *Colección de documentos para la historia de Nayarit*; and Beatriz Rojas, "Los Huicholes: Episodios nacionales," in Antonio Escobar Ohmstede, ed., *Indio, nación y comunidad en el México del siglo XIX* (Mexico City, 1993), 253–65.

16

NATIVE PEOPLES OF COLONIAL
CENTRAL MEXICO

SARAH L. CLINE

Central Mexico is where the greatest number of both Indians and Spaniards lived during the colonial period, so the region has special importance. This central region of Mexico is a fertile area on a large plateau,
bounded by mountains and containing a number of valleys. Rainfall and
adequate groundwater coupled with productive soil allowed the development of labor-intensive sedentary agriculture and a dense population.
The geographical and cultural boundaries closely coincide. The Valley,
or Basin, of Mexico, ringed by mountains, had a large lake system that
functioned as an inland sea in the prehispanic and colonial periods. On
an island in the center of the lake the city of Tenochtitlan was built. In
the central basin, Nahuas and Otomís were the primary linguistic/ethnic
groups. The Toluca Valley to the west includes Nahuas and Mazahuas;
the Cuernavaca region to the south and the Puebla region to the east
were rich agriculturally and densely populated with Nahuas. The northern bounds of the geographical and cultural region were relatively near
to the center. To the north is desert where nomadic and seminomadic
people lived. They shared some cultural traits with the more settled
southern populations, but are distinct from the groups under consideration here (Map 16.1).

The central Mexican peoples were fairly homogeneous in language
and culture. The two major linguistic groups within the geographical
bounds were Nahuatl speakers and a minority of Otomí speakers. Because of political and economic dominance, Nahuatl was a *lingua franca*
throughout Mesoamerica but was the mother tongue of the majority of
the central Mexican peoples. Although there was considerable linguistic
and cultural homogeneity, even the Nahuas of the region considered
themselves to be of different groups, including the Culhuaque, Acol-
huaque, Xochimilca, Tlahuica, among others. Many of these groups iden-

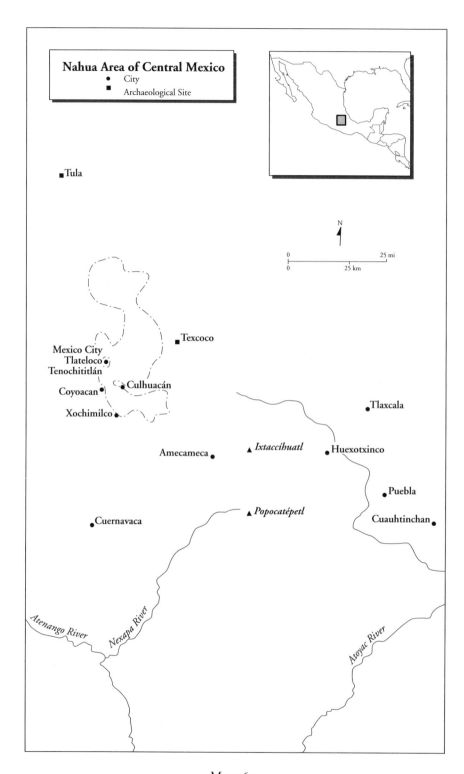

Map 16.1

tified themselves with specific geographical locations and dynastic line-ages. The Otomí were seemingly late arrivals in the region, speaking an unrelated tongue and generally occupying a subordinate position in Nahuatl-speaking communities. Less is known about the Otomí, for there seem to be no extant colonial records in their tongue and few Spanish reports dealing with them separately from the Nahuas. Spaniards referred to all of the native groups of the New World as "Indians," a term either meaningless or repugnant to the indigenous peoples them-selves, but one that has persisted in the literature.

Over centuries in the central region large, sedentary agricultural pop-ulations developed with complex social, economic, and political struc-tures. Agricultural surpluses allowed for the support of political, religious, and military elites as well as artisans. The indigenous peoples built large urban complexes with ceremonial centers, markets, and the residences of a sizable portion of the population. City-states (*altepetl*) imposed taxes, protected their sovereign territory, and made war. Approximately a hun-dred years before the arrival of the Spaniards in 1519, the Mexica (com-monly known as the Aztecs) entered the well-settled central Valley of Mexico. Through warfare and strategic alliance with existing groups, the Mexica achieved hegemony by the beginning of the sixteenth century. Their stronghold of Tenochtitlan, built on an island in the inland lake system in the heart of the region, became the dominant power of the Triple Alliance (Tenochtitlan, Tlacopan, and Texcoco) that controlled a far-flung empire, although one major central-region altepetl, Tlaxcala, remained independent.

In the colonial period, Spaniards settled in great numbers in the center of the Aztec empire. The Aztec capital of Tenochtitlan became Mexico City, the seat of the viceroyalty of New Spain, the northern portion of Castile's New World empire. The changes in the region during the colonial period were the result of many forces, including decimation of populations from epidemic disease, the growth of a major Spanish and racially mixed population within the Hispanic sphere, and the growth of an economy based less on the extraction of tribute from the native peoples and geared more to a large urban Hispanic population. For the indigenous peoples of central Mexico, the Conquest marked the breakup of the superstructure of the Aztec empire, but many of the component polities became bastions of indigenous social, economic, and political life under Spanish Colonial rule. The Spanish capital of Mexico City, built on the site of Tenochtilan, is an important exception.

At contact, the basic unit of political organization was the *altepetl* (a Nahuatl word meaning "water and hill"). These province-size units were essentially city-states with concentrations of populations ruled by dynastic lords called *tlatoque* (sing. *tlatoani*). The altepetl often had a central urban complex with outlying smaller complexes subordinate to it. The empire of the Triple Alliance consisted of many altepetl, brought under control by military conquest or its threat. Conquered altepetl maintained considerable internal cohesion but were required to render tribute to the Triple Alliance and acknowledge their own subordinate status. Thus, while central Mexico under the Triple Alliance had considerable political power when the Spaniards arrived in 1519, there was an inherent instability in the native arrangement because subordinate polities sought political and economic autonomy. Tlaxcala as an independent state under regular attack by the Triple Alliance became a willing ally of the Spaniards, and in the early colonial period reaped some benefits because of it. Its status as a state in modern Mexico is a legacy of its alliance with Hernán Cortés (also known as Hernando Cortéz).

When the Spaniards and the central Mexican peoples encountered each other in 1519, each group had expectations of how the other would act. Native experience with contact and conquest led them to expect that an alliance with a conquering power would bring benefits, but that in any case conquest would not result in complete destruction of existing political, economic, and religious arrangements. For the Spaniards, expectations were shaped by the militant Christianity of late medieval Spain, which had resulted in the final conquest of the Muslims and expulsion of the Jews (both occurring in 1492). This was followed by twenty-five years of dealing with natives in the Caribbean. According to their previous experiences, Spaniards expected to conquer militarily and then rule with the collaboration of existing elites, but even so they assumed that once their rule had been established, Spanish hegemony was irrevocable.

Following standard patterns for conquest developed in the New World, the conqueror Hernán Cortés sought alliances with secondary powers in the region (especially Tlaxcala), which expected better political and economic arrangements than the present ones. The Spaniards' capture of the ruler of the region (Moctezuma, also known as Montezuma) was also standard, as was their vigorous and successful warfare against the Mexica stronghold. To explain the relatively quick defeat of the empire, many factors were at work. European military technology (including steel weapons and armor, cannons and firearms, horses and wardogs, and warships) was superior. Spaniards' strategic alliances with major indigenous groups in the region, especially the Tlaxcalans, but also Texcocans, Xochimilcans, and Huexotzincans, among others, strengthened the Spanish military. An epidemic that ravaged the population of Tenochtitlan while it was under siege by the Spaniards weakened native resistance to the Spaniards' attacks. Nahua prophecies and mythology that questioned Mexica legitimacy to rule may have been at work, although there is some evidence of exaggeration of this element in post-conquest native histories. Finally, the Spaniards' determination to wage war to the death despite all odds was a powerful force in the Conquest. All these factors contributed to bringing about the final defeat of the Aztecs in 1521.

Much is known about the Conquest from the natives' point of view for there are accounts by them written in the early post-conquest period. A unique feature of Mesoamerican culture, as opposed to the Andean (the other New World center of high civilization), is a prehispanic tradition of writing. That tradition facilitated the transfer to the natives of alphabetic writing, and initiated a three-hundred-year tradition of records kept in Nahuatl (and, to a lesser extent, other indigenous languages) by native scribes. For that reason, we know a a great deal about Nahuas through their own written records. The prehispanic records were kept in pictographic form, and there is some evidence for a growing phoneticism of the symbols toward the end of the period. The Spaniards' introduction of alphabetic writing to the natives in the early sixteenth century marked the beginning of the production of native-language documents.

Some of these early documents deal with the Spanish Conquest. Since dynastic and political history were subjects of many prehispanic records, this is not surprising. Several types of written records were kept in the prehispanic period, mainly dealing with functions of the state, historical traditions, and religion. Tribute records indicating size, types, and periodicity of levies, and land records showing boundaries, soil types, ownership, and tribute liability give information about social, economic and political arrangements, both locally and imperially. Records of dynastic lineages and histories of individual polities existed in both oral and written form. The complicated polytheistic religion whose ritual cycle was governed by a complex and accurate native solar calendar was another important type of prehispanic written record. For the conquest of Mexico, we have not only the victorious Spaniards' accounts but also several indigenous versions of the events. Both the defeated Mexica of

Tenochtitlan and some allies of the Spaniards, the Tlaxcalans and the Texcocans, give us a multifaceted and vivid account of this historic clash. However important the Conquest is for the historical imagination, nevertheless the period of colonial rule (1521–1821) constitutes the more important story of culture continuity and change. In this, too, the history can be written with greater confidence because the native written record is substantial for the colonial period. The institutions of colonial rule are documented not only from the Spaniards' point of view but from the indigenous as well. Further insight into daily life in native communities can be gained from native language documenation.

This record has a general chronology that underlies the discussion of different aspects of colonial native life. These are the early colonial, from Conquest until about the 1570s; the middle colonial, from the 1570s to about the 1720s; and the late colonial, which terminates at Mexican independence from Spain in 1821. The rationale behind these divisions reflects the dynamics of both the European and indigenous spheres, separately and in interaction. The early colonial is characterized by dense native populations whose internal structures were left relatively unaffected by Spanish presence and rule. The number of Spaniards was small, and the institutions of Spanish rule, in civil and religious spheres, were generally weak but effective enough to discourage native rebellion, collect revenues, and Christianize a significant proportion of the indigenous population. A series of major epidemics (with a particularly virulent one in the late 1570s) devastated the native population at the same time that the Spanish population was increasing through immigration and natural increase. The middle period is characterized by stronger, more formal hierarchies of Spanish rule, establishment and successful functioning of new political arrangements in native towns, and the growth of a colonial economy that was not based mainly on extracting tribute and labor from the indigenous people. Spaniards were acquiring land and setting up farming and ranching enterprises utilizing paid labor recruited privately. In the late colonial period, the contours of the indigenous population reflect the size and strength of the Spanish population and the importance of natives' interactions with it. The partial recovery in size of the indigenous population meant, almost paradoxically, the greater pressure for change by them, for they had lost land to Spaniards through sale or usurpation. Without access to land and with their population growing, indigenous people were channeled into wage labor on Spanish enterprises or emigration to urban areas. Changes in the Nahuatl language correspond fairly closely to this periodization, and will be discussed below.

POLITICAL ORGANIZATION

The largest unit of organization was the altepetl or city-state. Just as the structure of the Aztec empire had been built on it, so, too, was Spanish colonial rule. In its simplest form, the altepetl was a political unit controlling particular territory, ruled by a single dynastic ruler, the *tlatoani*. Complex altepetl had more complicated structures, with more than one tlatoani, and arrangements for division of rule. Even in the simplest form of the altepetl, with one tlatoani, there were subunits called either *calpulli* or, more commonly, *tlaxilacalli* (often two, four, six, or eight such subdidivisions), each of which had some form of political hierarchy and religious cult unique to it. The structure of these subunits is not well understood, but it is likely that kinship and residence were the key factors in membership. Ethnic minorities in Nahua polities were often clustered residentially.

The political elite of the altepetl was headed by the male dynastic ruler (tlatoani), and under him were hereditary elites, the *pipiltin*, males acting as advisors and high-level functionaries. Some of these noblemen were heads of subunits of the altepetl, with a retinue and special residences of their own (*tecpan*). There are only a few instances of female rulers, but women may have had a role in the hierarchy of the residential wards (tlaxilacalli). Elite women (*cihuapipiltin*) were more often important for linkages between noble families within a given altepetl, or interregionally with elites of other alteptl. At the time of the Spanish Conquest, central alteptl were ruled by noblemen with kin ties throughout the region, and they were key to the functioning of the Spanish colonial system. While these noblemen acted as protectors of their communities and intermediaries with Spaniards, their role also facilitated Spanish rule, indeed was crucial to it. Noblemen who acted in concert with Crown interests were able to maintain their position or advance within the system, while those who did not were summarily removed from office. This relation of dependency on the Spaniards and the necessity to collaborate lessened the rulers' effectiveness as brokers.

The functions of these political rulers were ones basic to any state: to defend the sovereignty and territorial integrity of the unit and to collect taxes. These continued in the colonial era. Households rendered tribute to ward officials who forwarded this to the rulers of the altepetl. Labor duty (*coatequitl*), such as public works projects, cultivation of fields for the maintenance of the ruler or the religious cult, and special levies to deal with emergencies were performed by household members and mobilized by town and ward officials. These labor duties were most prominent in the early colonial period, with tribute continuing almost until independence.

The first institucions of colonial rule with which indigenous peoples interacted were in the economic and religious spheres. In the economic sphere, indigenous institutions greatly facilitated fulfillment of Spaniards' expectations to gain financially from conquest. In the Caribbean, tribute and labor of specific groups of natives were awarded to individual Spaniards in grants called *encomiendas*, and this institution was brought to Mexico. In practice in central Mexico, this meant that the tribute and labor from a given altepetl were directed toward a single *encomendero*, or holder of a grant. The encomienda was also to provide the natives with instruction in Christian doctrine, but this religious aspect was of less importance than the economic. Initially, internal mechanisms for tribute collection and mobilization of labor continued to function after the Spanish Conquest as before. The difference was that the ultimate recipient of the levies was a Spaniard rather than the Aztec Triple Alliance. The encomendero himself seldom if ever had direct contact with his encomienda natives, trusting employees to deal with tribute collection and labor duties, mobilized by the indigenous elites. From the colonial natives' point of view, the altepetl was the highest level of organization dominated by the indigenous themselves. Perhaps even more so than under Aztec rule, early colonial altepetl were able to pursue localism, since Spaniards were not interested in disturbing the structures that produced taxes and mobilized labor.

Indigenous rulers did not passively accept the encomienda. They sought to limit the exactions of the Spaniards and the erosion of indigenous political units, but could only pursue such defenses in a limited way. Too frequent or vigorous protests by the ruler could cause him to be replaced by a ruler more compliant with Spanish interests. For the Spanish encomenderos, the encomienda was key to their own economic success, so extracting as much labor and tribute as they could from the natives was the normal practice but constituted abuse. Encomenderos through their employees (often lower-status Spaniards, blacks, or other marginal social types) mistreated the natives, not just through high labor and tribute requirements but by beatings and other practices – which are enumerated in natives' petitions of protest to the crown, an avenue of redress they increasingly used. Encomenderos sought to expand their own area of jurisdiction and attempted to attach other indigenous units to their existing grants. Sometimes this played on the desires of smaller units within the altepetl for political autonomy. Encomenderos' attempts to rearrange indigenous political and economic units to increase their power were likewise met with native protests to the Crown. As the Crown sought to curb the powers of the encomenderos for its own reasons, it ruled in the natives' favor. Thus, from the 1530s to the end of the colonial period, the indigenous people of Central Mexico actively sought justice from the Crown. Where it suited the Crown's purposes, natives' petitions were granted. For reasons having to do more with the course of Spanish colonialism than the natives' response to colonial rule, the encomienda declined in importance. However, the natives' role in its decline should be taken into account. By 1600, the encomienda ceased to exist as a major institution in central Mexico.

The Spanish Crown supplanted the private institution of encomienda with its own civil institution, the *corregimiento*, and for labor recruitment, the *repartimiento*. Corregimiento divided New Spain into administrative districts, each overseen by a low-level Spanish official, the *corregidor*. Initially there was a period of Spanish private and governmental institutions, both functioning in similar ways, with natives providing goods and services. With the effective decline of the encomienda dating from the 1550s, corregimiento was the prime institution for colonial rule of natives. For conflicts between natives and Spaniards, or among natives alone, the corregidor presided over the court of first instance. The promulgation of Spanish laws and their enforcement were the prime function and formal interaction between natives and the corregidor. Just as the encomenderos had taken advantage of their position to exploit the natives in their charge, so too did the corregidores, for their salaries were low and their tenure in office fairly short. For practical purposes, the natives may not have seen much difference between encomenderos and corregidores. Native petitions of protest against corregidores' abuses are similar to those against encomenderos, but with much less effect.

By the mid-sixteenth century, altepetl were constituted as political units superficially similar to Spanish towns. The main settlement of the altepetl, if any, became the *cabecera* or head town, and subordinate or

outlying units became *sujetos*, subject settlements. Spanish misunderstanding of the traditional political composition of many altepetl, particularly complex altepetl with several component polities each with a
dynastic ruler, meant rearrangement of indigenous rule to fit the new
colonial structures. Spaniards tended to put more emphasis than natives
on the central urban core of the altepetl. Outlying components were seen
by Spaniards to be subordinate, whereas natives may have viewed them
as coequal. Another change was that Spaniards ranked native towns
according to size and importance, just as towns in Spain, as *ciudad, villa,*
or *pueblo.* For native residents, town rankings were either a source of
pride or a sore point, and towns ranked villa and pueblo almost immediately began petitioning the crown to the crown for an upgraded status
and sujetos petitioned for cabecera status. In Nahuatl documents from
towns ranked ciudad, that Spanish term was used by the citizens themselves; in towns ranked pueblo, Nahuatl documents continued to desig-
nate the polity by Nahuatl term of altepetl.

The political towns were headed by a governor (*gobernador*), an office
established by Spaniards sometime in the mid 1540s or early 1550s. Generally in the early period the office was held by the dynastic ruler, the
tlatoani. It is important to note, however, the governor's post was an
office not based on dynastic succession, leaving open the possibility that
Spanish officials could remove recalcitrant gobernadores. In cabeceras,
cabildos or town councils were established and functioning by the late
1550s or early 1560s. These political bodies consisted of officeholders with
the same titles of office as any Spanish town council. *Alcaldes* functioned
as judges; *regidores* were town councilmen; *alguaciles* enforced order;
escribanos were the notaries who kept the towns' records in alphabetic
Nahuatl. In addition to these officials with Hispanic titles, there were
officials with Nahuatl titles, such as *tlalpouhqui* (land measurer), presum-
ably performing functions with prehispanic antecedents. One function
that in the Spanish world was not connected to official town administration – disposition of testamentary bequests – was overseen by native
executors with official status. While the outward form of indigenous
town government was similar to the Spanish model, the workings had a
distinctly native character. There were often more native alcaldes and
regidores than there would be in the Spanish model, with each of the
component political units having representation. In addition, officeholders often rotated according to the rankings of the component units. A

further native practice was a tendency for fewer distinctions to be made between former and current officeholders.

The political process in indigenous towns was shaped by prehispanic precedent and Spanish colonial policy. Elections for office were mandated by Spanish law, but the apportionment of power among component parts of towns seems to have followed native practice. Rotation of offices and officeholders often followed traditional power-sharing arrangements. These are particularly well documented for Tlaxcala, where sixteenth-century municipal records in Nahuatl survive, indicating rotation of office by elites from the four component parts. Almost endemic in indigenous towns were political factions and feuds based on kinship, loyalty to a political subunit, and other factors. These processes can be traced through records in Nahuatl and Spanish of disputed elections, particularly well studied in the Cuernavaca region. Even at the end of the colonial period, town governments were vigorous in pursuing their internal disputes and defending their towns against outside encroachments, whether Spanish or indigenous.

RELIGION

Natives were confronted with conquerors who wanted not just to dominate them politically but also to convert them to Christianity. The first religious personnel most central Mexican peoples encountered were generally the regular clergy, the friars of the Franciscan, Dominican, and Augustinian orders. The "spiritual conquest" tried to transform the native population from their polytheistic, animistic, and fate-determined religion to Christianity. Prehispanic religion was not only polytheistic but constituted an order of belief different from Christianity. The introduction of Christianity, with its emphasis on salvation through Christ, brought changes in native religion, but generally only ones that meshed with their indigenous beliefs. For natives, the Trinity was a difficult concept; there was nothing similar to it in their previous belief system. Much more manageable were Christian saints, intermediaries who could be called on for aid in specific domains (geographical, temporal, and spiritual), and who bore resemblances to native deities. Veneration of saints was a strong feature of Spanish Catholicism, so the native practices (if not their underlying beliefs) were in the mainstream of colonial Christianity.

Prehispanic religion had been a major force for expressing and reinforcing community unity, and Christianity proved a vehicle to continue this. Each town had a Christian patron saint, as did each residential subdivision (tlaxilacalli). The saint's name became part of the name of the town or ward: prehispanic Culhuacan, for instance, became San Juan Evangelista Culhuacan. The saint's day of the town or ward was one of celebration, reinforcing community solidarity as much as religious belief. In general, the sites of the prehispanic cults became the location of the Christian churches and chapels, important for the community. The prehispanic sacred site at Tepeyac became the focus of first a local, then a regional, and finally a national pilgrimage destination for the cult of the Virgin of Guadalupe. In most indigenous towns, the churches built on sacred sites continued to be a focus of native identity through religious expression. The size of a church and the elaborateness of its decorations and furnishings were important to the native community, visible signs of unity and prominence.

In the immediate post-conquest years, central Mexican peoples most often had contact with friars rather than the secular clergy. In order to preach and catechize, the friars of the early to mid-sixteenth century (Franciscans, Dominicans, and Augustinians) were expected to master Nahuatl, the dominant native language and lingua franca of the region. Linguistic minorities were at a further step removed from the Christian message delivered in Nahuatl. Overall, the friars' task was to extirpate native beliefs counter to Christianity. In order to perform their religious duties, the friars with the help of indigenous aides created a rich literature in Nahuatl: confessional manuals, books of sermons, catechisms, as well as dictionaries and grammars. From these texts we can infer how Europeans interpreted Christianity for their indigenous charges so as to reach them.

The indigenous peoples had had prehispanic experiences of conquest, which entailed integrating new gods or new beliefs into their preexisting system. Generally these situations merely brought about elaboration of a pantheon and variations of beliefs. The friars sought a total replacement of native beliefs with Christianity, which meant nothing less than reordering the whole basis of natives' worldview. Something in between these two positions was achieved, perhaps unconsciously by the natives, and more or less consciously by the friars and later the secular clergy.

Some obvious changes occurred under the influence of the Spanish religious. Almost immmediately, natives ceased practicing the most overt and spectacular aspects of their prehispanic religion, such as human sacrifice. And they were fairly quick to take up the rituals of Christianity to build and protect the community, such as the feast day of the patron saint. On the individual level, baptism proceeded at an uneven rate, seemingly correlated to the presence or absence of religious personnel. House-to-house censuses of the 1540s from the Cuernavaca region count many unbaptized people. A substantial proportion of households in some communities were unbaptized and others were a mixture of baptized and unbaptized. Baptism of the polity's tlatoani did not mean all his subjects followed suit, at least not immediately. By the end of the sixteenth century, probably all central Mexican Nahuas were baptized or passing as such. A religious institution many Nahuas adopted enthusiastically was ritual godparenthood (*compadrazgo*), which extended and reinforced family and community ties as much as the Christian religious imperatives. Given the epidemic conditions in the sixteenth century when compadrazgo was introduced, this religious practice offered natives a vehicle for extending bonds of kinship to those not related by blood or marriage, and was one that the church encouraged. Religious confraternities, or *cofradías*, flourished in native towns, some established in the late sixteenth century, but generally becoming prominent in the seventeenth and early eighteenth centuries, providing corporate and individual benefits.

However, Nahuas did not quickly (and some would argue they never did) transform their beliefs to a system where salvation, individual responsibility for actions, and the notion of sin were of overarching importance. Nahuas had nothing precisely analogous to these tenets of Christian theology in their prehispanic beliefs. The outward forms of Christian ritual were practiced, but the Nahuas' understanding of Christian belief is less clear.

In general, there is no evidence of widespread or organized resistance to Christian evangelization in the Nahua region. However, individual communities complained to the crown about ill-treatment by particular friars or priests, with the hope that a new and better religious would be assigned to them. In the central region, the regular clergy maintained a strong hold on their territories, despite pressures to have their parishes turned over to the secular clergy, who in general did not know Nahuatl. Although the first generation of friars was zealous and optimistic about evangelizing the Nahua population, and their congregations demonstrated loyalty to the early regular clergy, by the end of the sixteenth century many friars had lost confidence in the success of their mission. This doubtless affected their treatment of their indigenous congregants, for Nahuatl complaints of neglect and mistreatment enumerated similar abuses committed by friars and the secular priests.

In most Nahua towns of any size or importance, there were resident Spanish religious, initially friars (the regular clergy), later the secular clergy. Smaller settlements were visited at intervals by the religious to perform the sacraments, particularly saying mass and performing baptisms and marriages. Like the Spanish colonial political organization, which was built on existing native patterns, the structure of the Spanish religious structure also was. The altepetl and its outlying settlements became the cabecera and sujeto in the political sphere; in the religious sphere, the altepetl became the seat of religious *doctrinas* and the outlying settlements with nonresident clergy were *visitas*. Doubtless Nahuas living in visitas without resident clergy were less likely to know Christian doctrine, but even in those settlements there was an ongoing religious life.

Natives actively participated in Christian religious life with considerable autonomy, but not on an equal footing with Europeans. Quite early in the post-conquest period, the friars abandoned the notion of training indigenous men for the Christian priesthood, and for a period their ordination was prohibited. In general the sacraments were administered by Europeans, although at the end of the colonial period there were a few indigenous male priests. In the immediate post-conquest period, native aides, often young men, were important for the initial proselytization of Christian teachings; and in middle and late colonial period, elite males assisted priests in their duties, particularly the *fiscal*, the highest-ranking official in the indigenous religious hierarchy. Operating in many indigenous towns were free-lance native healers (*curanderos*) who claimed special contact with the supernatural. But the role of the fully empowered native religious expert of the prehispanic era was not replicated in the colonial period.

In the long term, since Christianity presented the only permissible vehicle of religious life, indigenous men sought leadership roles in performance of Christian rituals and celebrations, and women participated in worship. The churches and chapels of Christian worship were expressions of religious and corporate pride for towns and their wards. In each town a religious hierarchy, composed of indigenous male elites, parallel and equal in prestige to the political hierarchy, was established to organize religious activities of celebration and maintenance of the sacred sites. The creation of this hierarchy was guided by the Spanish religious, as the uniformity in structure and Spanish titles for the officials indicate. But, as with the colonial native political hierarchy, the religious hierarchy functioned according to native patterns. An official, called by the Spanish title fiscal, was the highest-ranking in the native religious hierarchy, closely associated with the resident Spanish cleric. In many ways the fiscal functioned as the presiding native religious specialist, and where there was no resident cleric, the role took on even greater importance.

Religious confraternities, or cofradías, were established in many native communities beginning in the late sixteenth century, growing in importance in the seventeenth century. As with the religious hierarchy, which was established to support town or residential ward churches, the officers of the cofradía were initially elite males. For the cofradía, this changed with time and women also assumed leadership roles. Membership in cofradías, to judge from surviving native records from Xochimilco and Tula, was quite broad. Men, women, and children were members: whole families, married couples, and single women, either unmarried or widowed, though generally not bachelors. Evidence from Tula cofradía records show that native women served as officials by the seventeenth century. A substantial proportion of towns' populations were members of cofradías, and from all residential wards. Large towns generally had several cofradías, smaller towns one or two.

Cofradías functioned as ecclesiastical insurance for their members, a collective savings account to pay for religious rites for the membership. Generally the monies accumulated from membership dues were spent on burial expenses and masses for the living and dead members. Thus, from the Spanish point of view, the cofradías provided a vehicle for native religious practice nominally under the supervision of the resident cleric, with direct benefits to the local cleric, who received income from the cofradias to celebrate masses and provide Christian burial. For natives, cofradías were organizations that provided structural stability after the ravages of sixteenth-century epidemics, and another way in which native collective identity was reinforced. Individual members received benefits of participation in the cofradías. For women, especially, this may have been a major benefit, for some served as cofradía officials. Generally there were virtually no avenues of institutional expression of women's importance, and the cofradía was an exception in some regions. For all members the cofradía provided the assurance that the organization would pay for Christian burial and prayers for their souls.

At the household level, Christian symbols were often given special places within the residence. From the late sixteenth century on, evidence from Nahuatl documents indicates many households had religious objects such as crosses, statues, and painted images of saints. Natives worshiped God through the mediation of saints, a feature of Spanish Catholicism. Such worship formed a strong component of all indigenous corporate life, so it is not surprising that it should also find expression at the household level.

The most difficult aspect of native Christianity to approach is individual belief. Clearly by the late sixteenth century the outward forms of piety were well established. People marked birth, lifelong sexual union, and death with the Christian sacraments of baptism, marriage, and burial. Men and women standardly bequeathed money for masses for themselves and their dear, departed relatives in their testaments made at death. The Spanish effort to indoctrinate the natives was successful to the extent that they conformed to Christian practice, and supported Christian rites and clerics both spiritually and materially. The spiritual conquest sought to go further, transforming not just practice but belief, particularly individual belief.

SOCIAL STRUCTURE

In the colonial period class divisions and family structure changed. Central Mexican native society at the time of the Conquest was divided between elites and commoners, with gradations of status within these two categories. This situation largely continued until the end of the colonial period, but the general poverty of the native population somewhat collapsed the two-tier distinction. Elite men in the colonial period constituted the core of the officeholders, so political and religious hierarchies reflected and reinforced societal divisions. Toward the end of the colonial period non-elite men began to enter the ranks of officeholders, indicating a change in the social system. Men with mixed racial ancestry (mainly mestizos) were often also part of the native elite, but their genealogies became important when rival political factions felt threatened. Elite women were important in the functioning of the social system, for through marriage and kinship they linked elite men.

The family was the basic unit of social and economic organization, but what constituted a family and which relationships were most important shifted during the colonial period. Early-sixteenth-century house-to-house censuses in Nahuatl from the Cuernavaca area indicate a large number of residences with more than one married couple, their children, and other dependents. Unmarried and married children with their spouses lived with their parents; married and unmarried brothers often lived together. Each of these complex households constituted one economic unit with lands worked and tribute owed enumerated in the censuses. There were variations in residence patterns; some settlements showed a higher proportion of nuclear families constituting a single household. Households of rulers' dependents tended to have smaller, less complex family structures. Other detailed records of later sixteenth-century native residence exist for Huejotzinco and some communities in the Texcoco region. In the late eighteenth century the crown ordered house-to-house censuses of many major cities, in order to establish liability for military service; since Indians were excluded from the levy, these detailed censuses do not include information on them. Overall, the sixteenth century is the key period in which to examine changes in residence patterns, for depopulation owing to epidemics and forced resettlement of scattered populations in more concentrated units with the colonial program of *congregación*.

With few exceptions, households were headed by married men. Reports of the prehispanic marital patterns of the rulers of the Aztec empire indicate they had multiple wives and concubines. Early colonial records show wealthy, high status men continued to have more than one wife. But the friars actively worked to eliminate the practice of multiple wives, and were generally successful in doing so, except in isolated areas. A male's status as head of household was generally not affected by the death of his wife nor his own aging. Widowed women did not generally become household heads at the death of their husbands, unless their children were very young. Widows became dependents of their children, generally their sons.

There were some shifts in the importance of particular kin in the colonial period. In the early colonial period, relationships between siblings were important as reflected in a report by Fray Toribio de Benavente (Montolinía) on inheritance customs for the Cuernavaca area that indicate the eldest son inherited the father's property in order to act as his siblings' father, and parcelled it out as they came of age (it is unclear whether females received a share). Testaments from late-sixteenth-century Culhuacan indicate that the sibling tie weakened over time. This shift may be influenced by Spanish inheritance patterns stressing lineal ties (parent to child) rather than lateral (siblings). Nahuatl kinship terminology merged categories, sibling terms used for cousins, for example. This changed during the colonial period, with the introduction of some Spanish kin terms (such as *primo*, or cousin) for relationships were (or became) less close.

Nahuatl testaments show the place of late-sixteenth-century Nahua women more clearly. Women owned property in their own right, which they generally got through inheritance, and they bequeathed it as they saw fit to a variety of kin, emphasizing some relations over others. Men tended to give their property to a broad range of relatives in a less tendentious fashion. Women often specifically excluded kin from receiving property, and stated their reasons for doing so. Perhaps this is because they were expected to follow the pattern seen in men's bequests, but asserted their right to do otherwise. Women seem to have had considerable autonomy within the Nahua family, keeping and bequeathing their own property. Within marriage, they jointly contracted ventures with their husbands, and if not, generally had considerable knowledge of their husbands' dealings.

Personal names are an interesting index of social status and gender difference in indigenous society. Prehispanic names were personal rather than lineage names. The choice of these names for males may have been dictated by the named ritual days of the prehispanic calendar, official titles taken as names, and names of things from the natural world. Female names were very stereotyped, usually birth-order names such as "oldest," "middle child," and "youngest." This is seen especially clearly in early-sixteenth-century Cuernavaca census records, which contain the names of many unbaptized people. By the late sixteenth century everyone had a Christian saint's name as a given name, plus a second name, either Nahuatl or Spanish. Differences emerge between men's and women's names and between high- and low-status names. For males, the range of names in the colonial period, just as in the prehispanic, was much more varied. Women's names continued to be quite stereotyped, Nahuatl birth-order names with only a few Christian saints names as well.

There were some markers for high-status names. Most native men and women of the highest status used the Spanish noble titles of *don* and *doña*. These elites also often took standard Spanish surnames, such as

Hernández or Juárez, as their own. Initially these were not used as lineage names and their children might have another last name entirely, but over the colonial period lineage names for the highborn became more common. In the early colonial period, many elite males used Nahuatl titles, such as *huitznahuatl*, as part of their personal name, but often in combination with a thoroughly Spanish-sounding name. Highborn women were unlikely to have a stereotyped Nahuatl birth-order name, but might have two Spanish given names, usually preceded by the marker *doña*. By the end of the colonial period low-status names for both men and women were two Spanish given names, such as Juan Pedro and Ana María.

As already noted, an innovation in the colonial period was the practice of choosing godparents for children. During the sixteenth century, when waves of epidemics devastated the native population and doubtless strained the fabric of families, godparents were people who could take care of orphaned children and reinforce relationships between people not related through blood or marriage. Testamentary evidence shows that women counted on their children's godfathers a great deal, but that they themselves felt little obligation to their own godchildren. Men, on the other hand, took their role of godfather seriously, often giving property to their godchildren.

LAND TENURE

Nahua life was based on sedentary agriculture, so that understanding the structure of land tenure is crucial. Early sources in Spanish describing prehispanic land tenure delineate a number of different categories of land. Some pertained to the political and religious hierarchies as corporate lands, specifically, land to support the dynastic ruler (*tlatocatlalli*) and the palaces or community houses (*tecpantlalli*); and the gods and temples (*teotlalli*). Commoners had access to land corporately held by the calpolli (*calpollalli*), but worked plots individually. Nobles had lands (*pillalli*) that they held as individuals (but worked by others) and were alienable.

Colonial Nahuatl documents indicate a number of other land categories that doubtless existed in the prehispanic period. These include town lands (altepetlalli), purchased land (*tlalcohualli*), patrimonial land (*huehuetlalli*), inherited land (*tlalnemactli*), "woman land" (*cihuatlalli*), and "Mexica land" (*mexicatlalli*). Natives continued to use prehispanic category names in the late sixteenth century even when the tenure no longer resembled prehispanic practice, apparently because in some residual way its status was affected. The difference between inherited and purchased land seems to have been fundamental in the sixteenth century, and perhaps less important later, since there are fewer references to these distinctions.

The sixteenth century is one of dramatic change in the system of land tenure. The most important was the emergence of a real estate market, but there were also other changes. Land to support the indigenous religious cults disappeared almost immediately after the Conquest, and the category name disappears from use. Land held by the office of the dynastic ruler was separated from the office and passed into the hands of individuals, a process seen in the late sixteenth century, and the distinctive category of noble lands (pillalli) ceased to have importance by the seventeenth century. During this transitional period, rulers attempted to augment their domains and create estates (*cacicazgos*) whose boundaries were confirmed by the Crown, while at the same time nonrulers saw the opportunity to seize land previously under rulers' control.

A major cause for shifts in the land tenure system was the catastrophic drop in native population during the sixteenth century coupled with the increase in Spanish population in central Mexico. Natives simply needed less land for their own use at this point, and Spaniards were acquiring land for their enterprises. Individual native men and women sold large amounts of property to Spaniards for cash. However much the prehispanic system of land tenure emphasized corporate, inalienable landholdings, by the late sixteenth century individual men and women treated land as their private property to do with as they wished. Lands under corporate control came under increasing pressure from Spaniards as the hacienda system developed, and towns attempted to prevent erosion of their holdings, with varying results.

Persistence of prehispanic category names for individual plots indicates natives' cognizance of these categories, but in practice there appear to be fewer distinctions in the way property was treated, particularly regarding its sale. Many indigenous patterns of land tenure persisted throughout the colonial period. Individuals usually held a number of scattered fields, often with different agricultural potentials, and there were common lands held by the community, often for pasturage. For land held by individuals, Nahuatl documents list each of the parcels separately with information about their location by naming specific places, the size in native units, the soil type, and, often, how the owner acquired it, usually by inheritance but sometimes by purchase. Ownership of many dispersed parcels of land is likely due to native bequest patterns. People holding property could receive it from a variety of donors, and they in turn at death bequeathed property to a whole range of heirs. Parcels could be split resulting in further fragmentation. Land could also be purchased.

We have evidence that in the late sixteenth century, women as well as men owned land in their own right and in varying amounts. The best documentation on individual women's holdings is found in a collection of wills from Culhuacan, dated c. 1580. The equality of women's land-holding and their autonomy in bequeathing their property may be an anomaly caused by the abundance of land and the paucity of male heirs during epidemic conditions. Only further research can clarify the situation.

The drop in native population and the growth in the numbers of Spaniards had their effects on land tenure in the later colonial period. Certainly by the late seventeenth century, as native populations recovered their numbers, there was greater pressure on indigenous communities as a whole and families in particular because land had passed from their hands to Spaniards', never to return. The growth of Spanish landed estates in central Mexico began in the late sixteenth century, and increasingly in the colonial period, native communities were in conflict with these enterprises for resources, especially land and water. Some communities were able to buy back land from haciendas to increase their community holdings, but overall the growth of the hacienda meant less land available to indigenous communities and their citizens.

Although there were shifts in land tenure, indigenous communities retained control over substantial holdings, aided by Crown policy. In the seventeenth century, *composición*, a legal process to validate and regularize land titles, was instituted. For a fee to the Crown, towns could put right defective titles and ensure control over land. Although this was a revenue-producing procedure for the Crown (always of interest to royal authorities), composición was part of Crown policy to protect indigenous communities. Other Crown measures for protection of native lands include late-seventeenth-century legislation to increase the amount of land native communities were to hold, with further provisions in the eighteenth century to give native communities access to other types of land, such as pasture. However, in the eighteenth century royal courts generally took a narrow definition of lands reserved for communities, allowing Spanish occupation outside of the standard 600 varas allotted to towns. The situation was, on the one hand, pressure on native landholding by an increasing number of private Spanish enterprises and, on the other, Crown policy that sought protection of the native agricultural base of communities.

Although much native land was alienated to Spaniards in the colonial period, there is one major exception: *chinampas*, artifically built extensions of land into the southern, freshwater portion of the central lake system. They had extremely rich soil, resulting in great productivity, further enhanced because they could be cultivated year-round, independent of rainfall. Chinampa agriculture supplied fresh fruits and vegetables to the markets of Mexico City. Even though this type of land was highly productive, it remained almost exclusively in the hands of natives well into the twentieth century, because of the high labor requirements for cultivation. Spaniards mainly pursued agriculture with relatively low labor requirements, such as wheat as well as cattle and sheep ranching, and did not generally acquire chinampa land. In this way natives retained control of rich agricultural land very close to the Spanish capital. However, even in the chinampa zone, natives usually also owned other types of land with varying soil types and agricultural potentials.

Most native food production continued along traditional lines, maize being the most usual crop. However, with the introduction of various animals to the New World, natives extended their activities to animal husbandry. Sheepherding was the most prominent ranching activity, and natives also were consumers and producers of pork, fowl, and dogs. Although they were enthusiastic beef eaters, they were not generally involved in cattle ranching in the central region.

There is a highly developed vocabulary in Nahuatl to describe different soil types and land forms. The use of these terms persisted in the colonial period, and some passed into Mexican Spanish as loanwords, such as chinampa. Nahuatl soil and land form terms give information on the permeability of water, chemical content, or types of crops able to be cultivated there.

In the colonial period, natives continued to measure land by their own units rather than by Spanish ones. This practice persisted to the end of the colonial period in some areas. Native units included the *maitl* or *matl* (arm or hand), a measure of the outstretched arms, the *yollotli* (heart), the *quahuitl* (rod or stick), and the *mecatl* (cord or rope). There were other terms as well, most of them measurements of body parts. In different places in central Mexico, these units varied in their length. In some areas such measures were equivalent; in others, one was a fraction of another. For small plots of land, the units of measure calculated by measuring stick or body parts sufficed. When natives had to measure a large plot, the mecatl, a cord of standard length, was used. Since land was so important in central Mexico, it is not surprising that natives developed and continued to use a system of relatively precise measures, which might vary from community to community but were fixed within a given town. In Nahuatl documentation, particularly from the sixteenth century, the unit of measure is often not mentioned at all, only the number of units.

Regulation of land tenure was a function of town government. Towns officials were involved in the division of estates left when a native resident died. Many documents in Nahuatl concern land disputes, particularly within families. Disputes over ownership would initially come before town government, and officials called upon witnesses who had knowledge of the status of particular plots of land, indicating a high degree of community knowledge about land use and ownership. Only when local, indigenous adjudication was unsatisfactory to the parties did they resort to Spanish legal mechanisms. Internal regulation of land tenure continued in native towns until the end of the colonial period, but as Spanish population grew and haciendas expanded, many more conflicts needed to be resolved by the Spanish legal system, often to the detriment of native communities.

Although corporate regulation of land tenure was certainly important, individuals treated property as their own, to be bequeathed to their heirs as they saw fit. This was most likely a continuation of prehispanic practices. Increasingly in the colonial period, natives bought, sold, and rented land, with the knowledge of corporate structures and at times with their regulation, but not seemingly in opposition to them.

ECONOMIC ACTIVITY

Some major shifts occurred in the colonial period in economic relations, particularly in economic exchanges. Following the prehispanic precedent of using media of exchange, such as cacao beans and cotton cloaks of fixed value, the introduction of Spanish money was a relatively easy step. Native goods were valued early in the sixteenth century in Spanish currency, although the value for items of small worth was calculated in cacao beans in the sixteenth and early seventeenth centuries. The mixed

system of money and cacao beans is seen as early as the 1540s in a
Nahuatl market inventory from Tlaxcala. Probably to a much greater
extent, natives' land and labor were assigned value in the market economy. As we have seen, the colonial period was characterized by the
alienation of native land for cash. This may well be an acceleration of
the development of a real estate market incipient in the prehispanic era.

The cash nexus for labor became increasingly important in the colonial
period. Rotary labor drafts of the prehispanic era were continued in the
early colonial period with the encomienda. Payment for labor rendered
the Spaniards was the next step, via the repartimiento (or allocation of
workers), a mechanism for making native men available to Spaniards for
labor. The repartimiento proved inefficient and unsatisfactory for both
natives and Spaniards, and more informal means of labor recruitment
were found. Spaniards would hire temporary and permanent native workers for their enterprises in return for cash wages. Tribute obligations of
goods were converted by the Crown to payment in money in the mid-
sixteenth century. This may have forced some natives into the cash
economy, but it is equally possible that natives already participated in
the cash economy to such an extent that tribute in money was not an
additional burden.

Division of labor in native society was by gender. For commoner
natives, the most usual economic activity was agricultural work for men
and the weaving of textiles for women, pursued within the household
structure. Surpluses beyond what was needed for the household could be
saved or sold, but some portion of them were rendered in tribute,
particularly in the early colonial period.

Evidence from that time suggests that in complex households where a
number of adult and adolescent males lived, all of them worked the land
pertaining to all the members of the household, male and female. In
wealthy, high-status families, the maintenance of dependent workers was
a means to have landholdings cultivated. By the late sixteenth century,
however, native men and women sold excess land, probably prompted
by the scarcity of labor because of the drop in population from epidemics, and by the immediate gain of Spanish currency. Land sale records
from the late sixteenth century indicate noblemen and -women selling
land to Spaniards for substantial prices.

Demand for native products was shrinking in the native community,
simply because of the reduced numbers of natives, and Spaniards were
demanding different products. At this point Spaniards began purchasing

land to produce those crops for the Spanish market. These Spanish estates could pay cash wage to natives for permanent or temporary labor. With the recovery of the native population in the late seventeenth century, labor was more available, but native land was not, and the general economic level of the natives declined. To a certain extent, native elites were able to weather these storms with some portion of their holdings intact, but their fortunes also declined as well.

In the prehispanic era there was a vital sector of the population not engaged in agriculture. Artisans of various types existed, such as lapidaries and featherworkers, whose skills became obsolete shortly after the Conquest. Production of baskets, special types of woven goods, pottery, among other craft items, continued in the colonial period, however, although not necessarily by full-time specialists. In the colonial period, native men became skilled artisans in the colonial economy, learning to be tailors, painters, carpenters, and the like, plying their trades for both Spaniards and natives. They used tools and techniques from the Spanish world, and modified them as needed. At times Spaniards attempted to stop the competition of native artisans, but usually without success.

Natives' role in textile production changed in the colonial period from the prehispanic. Prehispanic native women wove the cloth that was an integral part of the systems of tribute and trade. Standard types of cotton cloaks were usually part of every household's tribute payment. These cloaks had fixed values and were used as a medium of exchange. In the early colonial period, native women continued to weave cotton cloth for tribute and for domestic use. Cotton cloaks rendered in tribute to encomenderos were sold by them on the open market. However, major shifts occurred in native weaving. As the encomienda was undermined by the Crown and tribute payments converted to money equivalents, native women wove less cloth, mainly for the household. Simultaneously, native men began to be utilized in textile production outside the household. As urban demand for cheap cloth increased, particularly for wool, Spaniards entered production by setting up small-scale textile workshops (*obrajes*). The main market for the cloth was the growing Hispanic and mixed-blood populations of New Spain's cities.

The growth of obrajes and the type of labor they required indicate the shifts in the colonial situation by the second half of the sixteenth century. Spaniards had introduced sheep to New Spain (and both Spaniards and natives raised them). Spaniards, especially, expected to wear woollen clothes, and because the growing urban population of Spaniards and mixed-bloods represented sufficient demand, obrajes could be profitable. Labor for the obrajes was a problem because the systems of labor procurement through the encomienda and later the repartimiento did not provide the skilled, steady labor that obrajes required. Thus, native male convicts and generally male wage laborers (and a few women) became the mainstay of the obrajes.

In the prehispanic period, an important specialized group included long-distance and local traders who facilitated the exchange of goods in both local and regional markets. Regulated by native government, these markets survived and thrived in the colonial period, continuing into the modern era. Spaniards as well as natives were consumers in these markets, with sale of agricultural products and crafts by both men and women native traders. The Nahuatl word *tianquiztli* (market or marketplace) has passed into Mexican Spanish as the loanword *tianguiz.*

The prehispanic long-distance merchants (pochteca) who dealt in such high-value trade items as gold, exotic feathers, and slaves disappeared as an organized high-status group soon after the Conquest. Important in the colonial period for regional markets were local traders who owned pack animals, such as horses or mules, for hauling goods. Evidence from late-sixteenth-century Nahuatl wills indicates that traders had very little real estate, with most of their capital in their livestock and commercial goods. There is evidence of intermarriage of trading families in the late sixteenth century, and investment by women in pack animals used for transportation of goods. Moneylending also appears to have been part of the traders' commercial activities, with loans to both men and women.

LANGUAGE CHANGE

The importance of shifts within the Nahuatl language in the colonial period have been postulated as indicators of shifts in native culture. This insight has come with the increased study of local-level Nahuatl documentation by a number of scholars. Broadly speaking, the changes in the language can be seen an index of the impact of the Spanish language and culture on the indigenous. Although the correlation is not exact, language changes nevertheless should be taken into account when analyzing colonial changes.

Initially in the immediate post-conquest period and to the midsixteenth century, Nahuas had little contact with Spaniards or Spanish culture. However, there were new phenomena from the point of contact that had to be expressed linguistically. At contact, items from Spanish culture could be described in Nahuatl, often extending a Nahuatl term to something similar enough. An example is the use of the Nahuatl word for deer (mazatl) to denote horses. This is not as laughable as it might first appear, for deer were the only large four-footed animals known to natives. An early stage in the process of language change, then, was the extension of existing terms to denote things from the Spanish world. For natives, this process was informal and not consciously thought out; it was a reasonable and adaptable strategy for naming new things. For Spaniards, particularly the religious, there were areas that should be distinct from their seemingly similar native counterparts. For that reason, certain types of terms from Spanish were consciously introduced by Spaniards into Nahuatl. In the earliest contact period, loanwords from Spanish were largely terms relating to the thought and practice of Christianity. Legal and temporal vocabulary also came into Nahuatl fairly early.

As greater contact between Spaniards and natives occurred, increasing from the mid-sixteenth century, there were more informal interactions between the two groups. The cultural exchange reflected in language was greater. Loanwords of a great variety are the hallmark of this stage; many terms from one language were taken into the other in loanword form. The number of terms from Nahuatl found in Spanish is not as great as the reverse, but Mexican Spanish contains many common words from Nahuatl. Even English has felt the impact of Nahuatl with words such as tomato (*tomatl*), chocolate (*chocolatl*), and avocado (*ahuacatl*). For Nahuas, the second half of the sixteenth century marked a period of widespread borrowing of loanwords from Spanish. At this stage, to use our example, horses are called not mazatl but by the Spanish loanword *cavallo*. Many of the Spanish words that were borrowed named items from Spanish material culture, such as tools, clothing, plants, and animals, all of which indicated Nahuas' familiarity with and often ownership of such items. Not only were Spanish nouns taken into Nahuatl, but also certain Spanish verbs, which were given a typical Nahuatl verb form. This set of changes in Nahuatl closely corresponds to the middle period of colonial history, with the decline in the native population and the rise of the Spanish, greater face-to-face contact with Spaniards, and greater integration of Spanish goods into native material culture.

The last stage of change in Nahuatl is marked by changes in the syntax of Nahuatl, roughly dated to the eighteenth century. With natives' continued contact with the Spaniards, a larger segment of the Nahua population was bilingual. In the early contact period, the Spanish religious learned native languages in order to teach and preach the Christian message. After that, few Spaniards were bilingual in Nahuatl. It became incumbent on natives, functioning in a world increasingly affected by the dominant Spanish culture, to be bilingual. A further step was Nahuas speaking Spanish to one another; this did occur, but to what extent in the colonial period is unclear.

It is also unclear how many Spaniards became bilingual in Nahuatl. In the early colonial period, the religious expected to operate in Nahuatl, even with central Mexican natives who were not Nahuas. But even among the religious, language policies changed and fewer Europeans learned Nahuatl. Doubtless in many work situations where Spaniards supervised natives, Nahuatl continued in usage: obraje regulations, for example, were translated into Nahuatl. But the extent of Spaniards' bilingualism is unknown.

There was an abrupt cessation of documentation in Nahuatl when Mexico gained its political independence from Spain in 1821, but fewer records had been kept in Nahuatl even in the last quarter of the eighteenth century. The lack of acceptance of Nahuatl documentation in legal contexts in an independent Mexico is the most likely explanation for this phenomenon. Colonial New Spain had given natives a separate and unequal legal status, the *república de indios*, but independent Mexico abolished the formal system of racial divisons entirely. Colonial courts accepted Nahuatl oral testimony and written documents with Spanish translation, whereas the new system apparently did not. If this is in fact the explanation for the break in Nahuatl documentation, it suggests that Nahuatl record-keeping did not have an independent existence in native communities, or ceased to have one by the end of the colonial period.

The documentation in Nahuatl is very rich and affords insight into native culture. The different types of documents produced by natives in both form and content are also an index of continuity and change in native life. Prehispanic records largely dealt with dynastic lineages, taxation, and land tenure. In the immediate post-conquest period, taxation and records of landholding were sometimes still kept in pictorial form with written explanations in Nahuatl. In the Cuernavaca region, the earliest surviving full-length documentation in Nahuatl (from the 1530s or 1540s) is a group of house-to-house censuses done to determining the size of the population and its liability for tribute. It has no pictorial content, but follows a form that could easily be shown pictorially. Spanish-style legal documents, such as wills, bills of sale, and receipts for purchase, began to appear by the second half of the sixteenth century. They closely follow in Nahuatl the form and content of similar records in Spanish. This indicates direct introduction from the Spanish world into the native, but natives' widespread acceptance of these legal forms is significant. Prehispanic native society had both a tradition of writing and a strong legal system, which were doubtless key factors in the early adoption of the Spanish legal forms.

Other types of Nahuatl documentation include annals, poetry, primordial titles, and theatrical plays. None of these is self-reflective or literature for its own sake as developed in the Western tradition. Many Nahuatl texts have flowery language, and the Nahua love of language emerges, particularly in the poetry; but the history and glorification of corporate entities, their warriors and culture heroes, and perhaps their relation to the divine, are the common themes.

Annals were year-by-year notations of events in a given altepetl. They were usually anonymous but often kept for many years by the same person, reflecting that person's particular loyalties, especially to his own political subdivision of the altepetl. Annals most often contain political information about given altepetl, such as changes in officeholding. But also noted was news of general interest including such natural phenomena as earthquakes, fires, floods, famines, and such celestial events as eclipses and comets. Local scandals, celebrations, breaches of public order, and the like, as well as the arrival of papal bulls and royal decrees, make reading Nahuatl annals similar to reading a newspaper. The most noteworthy writer of Nahua annals was Chimalpahin, a native of Amecameca living in Mexico City at the turn of the seventeenth century. Other important annals were written at this point, but there are none for the late colonial period.

Nahuatl poetry or song was a high and unified form of expression with particular richly metaphorical language and rigorous forms of presentation. Generally the themes of these songs were the glories of war, pride in one's altepetl and people, and the divine. Metaphors of flowers, birds, and music for the beauty and ephemerality of life are standard features. The poetic form has obvious prehispanic roots, and examples of this form exist for the sixteenth century, but none survives in writing for the subsequent period.

Primordial titles (*títulos*), which supposedly documented an altepetl's right to its territory, are a late colonial phenomenon, none from before 1650 being known. They are highly individualistic, unlike Nahuatl songs, which have a set form and content. The most likely motivation for the creation of the títulos was to establish the legality of an altepetl's claim of territory. The timing of the composition is simultaneous with the growth of native population and increased pressure on native landholding. Culturally, these documents are a mixture of prehispanic history and events of the early colonial, all seen through the prism of a particular altepetl. The accounts of events are often not what modern historians would call historically accurate, but these documents are nevertheless extremely interesting, for they reveal the town's perceptions of its history. Historical personalities like the conqueror Cortés and the first viceroy can be conflated into a single figure, for example. But the documents are highly revealing of a town's perceptions of its history, and are a deliberate attempt to base a town's claims to territory on historical tradition or fact. Probably composed with the Spanish legal system in mind, these titles did not have standing in Spanish courts to prove ownership. Some seem to be deliberately falsified, with mixtures of fact and fiction, and self-serving accounts of colonial history, but this may not have been the intent, at least not in all cases. For indigenous history, these primordial titles represent a distinct and important source. Because the language is so difficult and the documentation scattered, they have not been utilized as extensively as other colonial Nahuatl documentation, but they have great potential for cultural history.

Overall, the corpus of documents in Nahuatl affords a great range of information on native society during the colonial period. Those interested in central Mexico now have available a substantial number of the most important Nahuatl texts in translation. Scholarship on colonial central Mexico has increasingly taken account of the native element in historical processes, and done so in recent years using documents from the native point of view.

The abrupt cessation of record keeping in Nahuatl at independence in 1821 is significant, and is an index of a real shift in the status of natives in the subsequent period. Native towns did not cease to exist; many modern anthropologists have studied important Nahuatl-speaking towns. But indigenous towns were seemingly more marginalized in the national period of Mexican history. The Spanish colonial system was paternalistic toward the natives and did not treat them as equals legally or socially, but the system did protect and to a certain extent promote the vigor of indigenous corporate life. The Spanish colonial system clearly exploited and abused natives through various institutions, including the encomienda, repartimiento, and the Church. Spaniards had legally acquired a substantial amount of land in central Mexico, and the hacienda became a private and informal institution for exploitation of individual natives. Indigenous towns continued to hold a significant though diminished portion of land but were able to hold on to at least some of it through colonial protections for corporate landholdings. Indigenous towns and individual natives pursued lawsuits in Spanish courts, submitting documents in Nahuatl and giving testimony in the language.

These protections ceased with independence. Legal equality of all races was mandated with the abolition of the caste system, which had kept natives at the bottom of the social system. Liberal reforms of the mid-nineteenth century were another assault on native towns, destroying the legal basis for the collective land ownership that had kept some portion of native lands in their hands.

Indigenous communities during the colonial period experienced decline of their populations, their resources, and the integrity of their indigenous culture. A colonial society developed in central Mexico, with a distinct place for natives at the bottom of the hierarchy but clearly within the system. The continued existence of central Mexican towns with significant native populations and distinct cultural traits is evidence of cultural tenacity, but the deleterious impact of colonial rule is also evident.

BIBLIOGRAPHICAL ESSAY

The information in this article on colonial central Mexican natives comes from a rich documentary base in both Spanish and Nahuatl, of which a number of the most important collections have been published, and form the post–World War II historiography. The *Handbook of Middle American Indians* (Austin, TX, 1972–76) is the most comprehensive bibliographical source for Mesoamerican ethnohistory, vols. 12–15 (Austin, TX, 1972–75). *The Handbook of Latin American Studies* since 1960 has published a biennial annotated bibliography on Mesoamerican ethnohistory, both prehispanic and colonial. Peter Gerhard's *A Guide to the* Historical *Geography of New Spain* (Oklahoma, 1993), is a valuable reference work.

The serious scholar as well as the interested student will be rewarded by existing historiography of central Mexican natives. Two works are of utmost importance to Nahua studies: Charles Gibson's *Aztecs Under Spanish Rule* (Stanford, CA, 1964) and James Lockhart's *The Nahuas after the Conquest* (Stanford, CA, 1992). Gibson draws heavily on Spanish-language sources, charting political and religious structures in towns, social and economic organization, and land tenure for the whole colonial period. Lockhart, on the other hand, has written a history of the Nahuas based exclusively on documentation in the native language of Nahuatl, and he particularly stresses cultural change reflected in language. It builds on, modifies, and complements Gibson's work; it incorporates findings of many scholars listed below. Also an important general work is *The Conquest of Mexico* (Cambridge, United Kingdom, 1993) by Serge Gruzinski, which deals with more issues than the title suggests. Studies of specific institutions for governing Indians include Woodrow Borah's *Justice by Insurance* (Berkeley, CA, 1983); Lesley Bird Simpson's *The Encomienda in New Spain* (Berkeley, CA, 1950); and Robert Himmerich y Valencia, *The Encomenderos of New Spain, 1521–1555* (Austin, TX, 1991).

For the Conquest, there are accounts from both Spanish and various native points of view, all of which are available in recent editions. Hernán Cortés's *Letters from Mexico* and Bernal Díaz del Castillo's *True History of the Conquest of Mexico*, both published in numerous editions (with varying titles), give the Spaniards' point of view, with much detail on the initial contact situation with natives. The Franciscan Bernardino de Sahagún's chronicle of the conquest of Mexico from the defeated Tenochcan point of view is volume 12 of his *General History of the Things of New Spain* (Salt Lake City, 1975). The entire twelve volumes have been published in a facsimile edition, and the entire Nahuatl text has been translated to English by Arthur Anderson and Charles Dibble, published as *The Florentine Codex* (Salt Lake City, 1950–82). Sahagún's revision of Conquest history has been published as *The Conquest of New Spain, 1585 Revision* (Salt Lake City, 1989). The Tlaxcalan point of view is presented in Diego Muñoz Camargo's history of Tlaxcala, published as *Relaciones Geográficas del Siglo XVI: Tlaxcala* (Mexico, 1984). Dominican friar Diego Durán's work based on written Nahuatl sources has been translated by Doris Heyden, *History of the Indies of New Spain* (Oklahoma, 1994). And an interesting and suggestive work is Tzvetan Todorov's *The Conquest of America* (New York, 1984), an interpretation of the conquest from more than a military point of view.

A collection of translations by James Lockhart entitled *We People Here: Nahuatl Account of the Conquest of Mexico* (Los Angeles, CA 1994) includes a number of lesser-known but important texts: The Annals of Tlatelolco; a petition to the Crown by the government of Huexotzinco for its participation in the Conquest; a selection of Codex Aubin; and the documents from Cuauhtinchan. Finally, *Codex Chimalpahin*, has fascinating information about colonial-era descendants of the Aztec kings (Salt Lake City, 1997).

Formal texts in classical Nahuatl were recorded in the sixteenth century, the most important of which is Sahagún's *General History*, just cited, but which also includes the *Cantares Mexicanos: Songs of the Aztecs*, translated and edited by John Bierhorst (Stanford, CA, 1985), and *The Bancroft Dialogues: Art of Nahuatl Speech*, translated and edited by Frances Karttunen and James Lockhart (Los Angeles, 1982). The annals of the seventeenth-century Nahua annalist, don Domingo Francisco de San Antón Chimalpahin Quauhtlehuanitzin, more commonly known as Chimalpahin, have been published in two volumes as *Codex Chimalpahin*, translated and edited by Arthur J. O. Anderson and Susan Schroeder (Oklahoma, 1997). Also worthy of interest are the *Anales de Tecamachalco* (Mexico, 1981).

Finally, Toribio de Benavente, better known by his Nahuatl appellation, Motolonía ("poor," "afflicted"), and one of the first Franciscans to arrive in New Spain in 1524, wrote extensively about Nahuas in the early colonial period. His *Memoriales o Libro de las Cosas de la Nueva España y los Naturales de Ella* (Mexico, 1971) is also available in an abridged English translation by Elizabeth Andros Foster, *Motolinia's History of the Indians of New Spain* (Westport, CT, 1973).

A number of full-length studies of important towns or regions also exist in the secondary literature. These include Charles Gibson's pioneering *Tlaxcala in the Sixteenth Century* (New Haven, 1952); S. L. Cline's reconstruction of a late-sixteenth-century Nahua community, *Colonial Culhuacan, 1580–1600: A Social History of an Aztec Town* (Albuquerque, 1986), is based on the largest extant collection of sixteenth-century native wills, *The Testaments of Culhuacan*, translated and edited by Cline and Miguel León-Portilla (Los Angeles, 1984); and Robert Haskett's study of the Morelos region, *Indigenous Rulers: An Ethnohistory of Town Government in Colonial Cuernavaca* (Albuquerque, 1991), which has some useful data on native electoral practices. Susan Schroeder's book, *Chimalpahin and the Kingdoms of Chalco* (Tucson, 1991), analyses important concepts of native sociopolitical organization. Rebecca Horn's *Post Conquest Coyoacan: Nahua-Spanish Relations in Central Mexico, 1519–1650* (Stanford,

CA, 1997) adds detail on an important Nahua town. A very important anthology on the sixteenth century is *Indian Women of Early Mexico*, edited by Susan Schroeder et al., (Oklahoma, 1997). Susan Kellogg's *Law and the Transformation of Aztec Culture, 1500–1700* has some valuable material for the early period, but should be used with caution since she makes generalizations from a very few cases. Finally, an anthology with a number of useful articles on central Mexico is *Dead Giveaways: Indigenous Testaments of Colonial Mesoamerica and the Andes*, edited by Susan Kellogg and Matthew Restall (Salt Lake City, 1998).

The attempt by Christian religious to convert the central Mexican natives was first analyzed by Robert Ricard in *The Spiritual Conquest of Mexico* (Berkeley, CA, 1966). Ricard's work remains important despite new scholarship. Recent scholars have revised Ricard's view, particularly Louise M. Burkhart in her monograph *The Slippery Earth: Nahua-Christian Moral Dialogue in Sixteenth-Century Mexico* (Tucson, 1989). J. Jorge Klor de Alva has published a number of articles on Nahua Christianity, including "Spiritual Conflict and Accommodation in New Spain," in *The Inca and Aztec States* (New York, 1982), "Martin Ocelotl," in *Struggle and Survival* (Berkeley 1981); and "Contar vidas: la autobiografía y la reconstrucción del ser nahua," *Arbor* (1988): 515–16. Both Burkhart's and Klor de Alva's work rely heavily on Nahuatl texts composed by or under the direction of the Spanish religious. Also worthy of notice is Serge Gruzinski's work, *Man Gods of the Mexican Highlands* (Stanford, CA, 1989). Susan Schroeder has published an interesting piece based on a completely Nahua source and point of view, "Chimalpahin's view of Spanish ecclesiastics in colonial Mexico," in *Indian-Religious Relations in Colonial Spanish America* (Syracuse, 1989). A collection of seventeenth-century incantations in Nahuatl, by Hernando Ruiz de Alarcón and published under the title *Treatise on the Heathen Superstitions that Today Live Among the Indians Native to this New Spain, 1629* (Norman, OK, 1984), indicates that many native religious beliefs survived the spiritual conquest.

Local-level Nahuatl documentation is abundant, and consists of formal annals, municipal records, censuses, testaments, bills of sale, and *cacicazgo* records. A useful anthology of the basic types of local-level documents is *Beyond the Codices* (Berkeley, CA, 1976). A number of the most important collections have been published or soon will be. The early-sixteenth-century censuses from Cuernavaca constitute the Nahuatl earliest data on household and family structure, tribute and land tenure, and historical linguistics. Two of these volumes have been published with transcription and translation, one by Eike Hinz et al., *Aztekischer Zensus* (Hanover, 1983), and the other, by S. L. Cline, *The Book of Tributes: Early Sixteenth-Century Nahuatl Censuses from Morelos* (Los Angeles, 1993). Pedro Carrasco has published a series of articles on these censuses, including "The joint family in ancient Mexico: The Case of Molotla," in *Essays on Mexican Kinship* (Pittsburgh, 1974), and "Family structure of 16th century Tepoztlan," in *Process and Pattern in Culture* (Chicago, 1964). The mainly pictorial *Matrícula de Huexotzinco*, published in facsimile edition by Hans J. Prem (Graz, 1974), is an early and rich census. A unique collection of municipal records in Nahuatl is published as *The Tlaxcalan Actas: A Compendium of the Records of the Cabildo of Tlaxcala 1545–1627*, edited by James Lockhart, Arthur J. O. Anderson, and Frances Berdan (Salt Lake City, 1986). Other valuable documents from single towns include *Colección de documentos sobre Coyoacan, I & II* (Mexico, 1976–78), edited by Pedro Carrasco and Jesús Monjarás-Ruiz, and Heinrich Berlin's edition of the *Anales de Tlatelolco* (Mexico, 1948), a portion of which is translated into English in James Lockhart's *We People Here*, mentioned above. A sampling of the records of native elite families who had entailed estates is found in *Cacicazgos y Nobiliario Indígena de la Nueva España* (Mexico, 1963), edited by Guillermo S. Fernández de Recas. Historical linguistics throw considerable light on cultural change in the Nahua sphere. Frances Karttunen and James Lockhart's work on colonial Nahuatl, particularly seen in their study entitled *Nahuatl in the Middle Years* (Berkeley, CA, 1976), is extremely useful. Karttunen's article, "Nahuatl literacy," in *The Inca and Aztec States* (New York, 1982), is a succinct and insightful description. As noted, Lockhart's massive study of colonial Nahua culture based on Nahuatl materials uses to great advantage insights from historical linguistics. Karttunen's *Analytical Dictionary of Nahuatl* (Austin, TX, 1983) and R. Joe Campbell's *A Morphological Dictionary of Classical Nahuatl* (Madison, WI, 1985) are valuable for tracing the appearance of specific terms. The dictionary of the Franciscan Fray Alonso de Molina, *Vocabulario en lengua mexicana* (Mexico, 1970), first published in the sixteenth century and still in print, remains invaluable.

Land tenure is an important topic that has received considerable treatment in the literature. Articles by S. L. Cline, H. R. Harvey, Teresa Rojas Rabiela, and Barbara J. Williams in *Explorations in Ethnohistory* (Albuquerque, 1984) deal with different aspects of central Mexican land tenure and cultivation. Hans J. Prem's study *Milpa y Hacienda: Tenencia de la tierra indígena y española en la cuenca de Alto Atoyac, Puebla, México, 1520–1650* (Wiesbaden, 1978), Bernardo García Martínez's *Los Pueblos de la Sierra* (Mexico, 1987), and Cheryl English Martin's *Rural Society in Colonial Morelos* (Albuquerque, 1985) are valuable monographs specifically dealing with land tenure.

Socioeconomic information on Nahuas in the early post-conquest period can be found in Codex Mendoza, a compilation of pictorial and written data on indigenous towns subject to the Triple Alliance and their tribute obligations. Easily available is the first-rate scholarly analysis by Frances F. Berdan and Patricia Rieff Anawalt, *The Essential Codex Mendoza* (Berkeley, CA, 1997). Alonso de Zorita, a sixteenth-century Spanish judge, wrote a report on the Nahuas that is available in English translation, *Life and Labor in Ancient Mexico: The Brief and Summary Relation of the Lords of New Spain*, translated by Benjamin Keen (New Brunswick, NJ, 1971).

Research on colonial Nahuas continues to draw on new archival sources in Nahuatl, allowing us to reconstruct in great detail many aspects of life for Indians in central Mexico. In addition, the continued publication of major collections of native texts from the colonial period make major sources available to interested readers. A further important trend in the reconstruction of the colonial world of natives are works such as R. Douglas Cope's *The Limits of Racial Domination: Plebeian Society in Colonial Mexico City, 1660–1720* (Madison, WI, 1994), which details the place of Indians in the colonial capital, including their participation in the great riots of 1692. Another type of documentation useful for understanding Indians' place in colonial society are so-called *casta* paintings, which were created in the eighteenth century to show the socioeconomic and racial stratification in the late colonial society. A beautiful collection of reproductions is published in *Las Castas Mexicanas: Un Género Pictórico Americano* by María Concepción García Sáiz (Mexico, 1989). Such pictorial documentation of the shifts in colonial society are important for our understanding of Indians.

17

NATIVE PEOPLES OF CENTRAL MEXICO SINCE INDEPENDENCE

FRANS J. SCHRYER

MEXICO CITY, WINTER 1990

On one side of the national basilica, near one of the entrances to the *zócalo* (central square), stands a miniature replica model of the ancient Aztec city of Tenochtitlan, displaying its temples and canals. This display, separated from the sidewalk by a railing, is in the center of an archaeological excavation recently completed in the heart of the city. A crowd of onlookers gathers around it as a persuasive and articulate young man harangues about its true significance – how the ancient civilization of the Aztecs, based on harmony, order, and a largely vegetarian diet, was destroyed by the gold-lusting, meat-eating barbarians from Europe. He points out how another materialistic European nation to the north (the United States) continues to dominate and oppress the Mexican people. His message is that only a radical change in attitudes can save Mexico from its many trials and tribulations. He pleads for a return to the customs and traditions of the glorious Aztecs. The young man looks and speaks like any of the Mexican working-class people crowding into the central square on a holiday, except that his complexion is somewhat lighter. A young man in the crowd, probably a university student (but with a much darker complexion), interrupts the public speaker and tells him he has no right to act as unofficial guide and spokesman because he knows nothing about Mexican history or social science. The public speaker holds his ground while the rest of the crowd looks on. A shoving match almost breaks out, but the student backs off and walks away, muttering *"pinche indio ignorante"* (stupid Indian) under his breath. A few meters away, a middle-aged woman wearing a traditional Mazahua blouse and skirt, her hair done up in ribbons, sits on the sidewalk beside several neatly piled cones of Mexican peaches. Holding on to the woman's skirts with one hand, a young girl holds out her other upturned hand with a pleading gesture, both oblivious to the commotion going on down the street. Several blocks farther, at the end of another busy avenue that ends in the *zócalo*, stands a modern concrete building housing the national legislature. There a group of native men from the Huasteca region are holding a day-and-night vigil as part of a nationwide protest against the newly (and many feel fraudulently) elected president of the Mexican republic. They are camped out on a separate part of the lawn and have brought along their own placards. They are also protesting the torture of comrades who belong to an independent and indigenously based peasant organization. They speak a mixture of their own regional language and broken Spanish. A spokesman tells me that they need more land and technical assistance, that they have already set up their own cattle cooperative, and that they want their children to be able to eat meat on a regular basis, just like the rich people who live in Mexico City.

This anecdote, witnessed by the author, illustrates the contradictions and complexities of intraethnic relations in central Mexico. It would be misleading to treat all native people in this region as a homogeneous group. While all subject to a single national state, they display as much internal variation in terms of class stratification, social organization, and discourse as any other category of people distributed over a geographically diverse landscape. Even people with the same native language or identity may exhibit different forms of local administration, economic activities, and relations with non-natives. Any attempt to reconstruct their history must include such variation and be sensitive to different perspectives. Regardless of such heterogeneity, we must try to answer the question why some native communities have maintained a distinctive identity and way of life since the time of independence, while others have become completely absorbed into the mainstream (Mexican) culture; we must also examine how different native peoples strategically selected or reinterpreted specific items of the dominant culture and how their actions have shaped the socioeconomic make up of central Mexico as a whole. At the same time, it is crucial to remember that these diverse native peoples have one thing in common – a shared historical experience characterized by dispersion, survival, and renewal.

CENTRAL MEXICO AS A REGION

According to the *Handbook of Middle American Indians,* central Mexico consists of "the southeastern part of the Central Plateau (the Mesa Central) plus its eastern slopes with part of the adjoining coastal plain and parts of the Balsas Basin to the south."[1] This geographically defined area roughly coincides with the boundaries of the two bishoprics of Mexico and Puebla during the colonial era (see Map 17.1). Once the core region of the Aztec empire, central Mexico became the hub of New Spain, a multiethnic state where native peoples still constituted a sizable majority on the eve of independence. The six and a half Mexican states that today roughly correspond to central Mexico comprise several indigenous cultural and linguistic groups as defined by anthropologists. Map 17.2 shows the distribution of these native cultural areas, although one should keep in mind that these cultural areas overlap with those of other regions. For example, small enclaves of Zapotecs or Mixtecs originally from Oaxaca have long been part of the landscape in the southern fringe of central Mexico, especially in the Atoyac river basin in southern Puebla. In the northwest corner, Nahuatl and Nähñu speakers spill over into several neighboring regions, while the northern tip of central Mexico gradually merges into the semitropical Huasteca region. Here lowland Nahuas have coexisted with Huastecs since before the Spanish Conquest.

There has always been a great deal of intermingling among the various native groups of central Mexico, even though they may speak different languages. In Guerrero, as many as four main language groups coexisted in some localities, and by time of independence, Spanish had become the *lingua franca* in the weekly *tianguis,* or regional marketplace. Social contact, especially for commercial transactions, took place over long distances; at the turn of the century, numerous Otomí ambulant traders from the semi-arid Mesquital Valley used to cross the deep gorges and steep slopes of the Sierra Madre Oriental mountain range to sell trinkets to Nahua peasants in the tropical forests of the Huasteca of Hidalgo. Many older Nahuas in this region also remember how, in the last century, Nähñus (whom they referred to as *xingris*) built most of the stone fences (*petriles*) that separated *milpas* (cornfields) and communal pastures in numerous Nahua villages in the *municipio* of Yahualica. Even closer

[1] Pedro Carrasco, "Central Mexican Highlands: Introduction", in *Handbook of Middle American Indians,* ed. Robert Wauchope, (Austin, TX, 1969), vol. 8, part 2, p. 579.

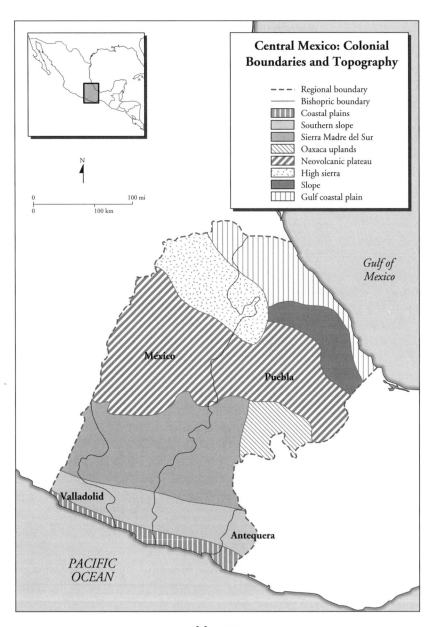

Central Mexico: Colonial Boundaries and Topography

- – – – Regional boundary
- ——— Bishopric boundary
- Coastal plains
- Southern slope
- Sierra Madre del Sur
- Oaxaca uplands
- Neovolcanic plateau
- High sierra
- Slope
- Gulf coastal plain

N

0   100 mi
0   100 km

Gulf of Mexico

México

Puebla

Valladolid

Antequera

PACIFIC OCEAN

Map 17.1

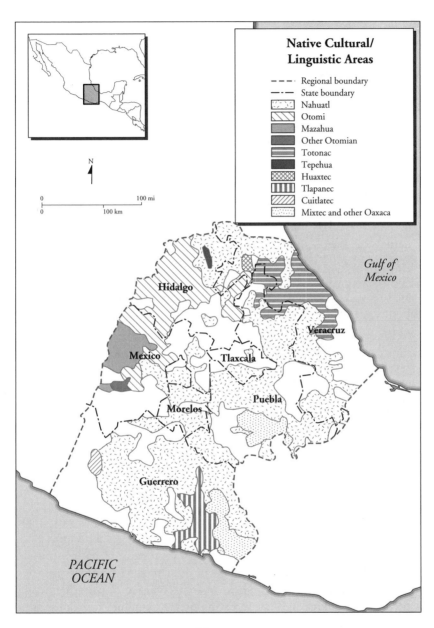

Map 17.2

ties were forged between some of the numerically smaller native groups. Thus, before the introduction of motorized transport (around 1940), the Popolocas (also spelled Popolucas) of San Felipe Otlaltepec (in southern Puebla) felt a close affinity with Mixtecos from the nearby Acatlan region; traders from both ethnic groups traveled together to Tehuacan to sell their respective products, such as *petates* (palm mats) and straw hats.

Such patterns of interaction and interdependency define central Mexico as a socioeconomic region. One element that binds its many subregions and ethnic groups together is their common link with Mexico City as economic or administrative center. No history of native people in the region can ignore their relationship with this and other nearby urban centers located in the highland plateau and nearby intermontane valleys (those of Tlaxcala – Puebla, Toluca, and Morelos). The cities of Pachuca, Cuernavaca, Puebla, and Toluca played a crucial role as central marketplaces and, with the exception of Puebla (originally founded by the Spanish conquerors), have a rich native history going back to precolumbian times. The Indian presence in these cities, including the national capital itself, was still highly visible at the time of independence. Andrés Lira has documented a strong sense of community and a de facto parallel form of native administration for many neighborhoods and villages located inside what is today the federal district, which is practically synonymous with present-day Mexico City. His description of the politics of land tenure and local government throughout the nineteenth and early twentieth centuries, in what were once two separate native administrative units (*parcialidades*), illustrates the continuity of colonial institutions set up for native peoples, a separate ethnic identity and an ongoing struggle against a city government run by non-natives, long after the formal abolition of both native self-government on the local level and the category of *indio* itself.

In purely numerical terms, most of these cities today, with their overwhelmingly non-native populations, are no longer as important a component of native America. However, the presence of native seasonal workers, the fact that the headquarters of numerous native affairs agencies are located there, and their impressive archaeological displays (depicting a prehispanic golden age) all serve important symbolic functions. In a nation where a hegemonic discourse proclaims the importance of a native heritage, yet where the national elites continues to pay lip service to the ideals of cultural and linguistic pluralism, the juxtaposition of these elements epitomizes the contradictions and tensions associated with an ongoing struggle by people of diverse origins over both meaning and power. Larger urban centers also continue to attract natives from rural areas as students, servants, migrants, traders, and political representatives.

KEY ISSUES: DISPERSION VERSUS SURVIVAL

Ironically, in 1821 the political independence of Mexico marked the beginning of a systematic policy of cultural genocide and the increasing loss of native languages, including Nahuatl, or *mexicano*, which once served as an important second *lingua franca* for the region as a whole. Before independence, many legal and historical documents relating to central Mexico were still written in Nahuatl, and native litigants could present their cases in their own languages. Independence gave an Amerindian word (Meshico) to a new country; but the rulers of the new Mexican state did not want to recognize or acknowledge the languages, social fabric, or cultural values of the descendants of ancient Mexico. Yet native people who did not speak Spanish continued to be classified as *naturales* (with a connotation of "commoners"), a separate category from *gente de razón* ("people who can reason"). The term *indio* ("Indian"), officially abolished after independence, was still widely used in daily discourse, although its meaning changed; once a recognized legal status that conferred both rights and obligations on a conquered people subject to the Spanish Crown, by the end of the nineteenth century it was commonly used by upper-class Mexicans to refer to all poor, illiterate country people. It is thus not surprising that so many natives wanted to lose the stigma of being people "without reason" and *indios*.

Between independence and the present, most native peoples were culturally absorbed into a more Europeanized, Spanish-speaking nation. In 1821, native peoples probably still constituted more than 70 percent of the population of central Mexico; around the time of the Revolution, that number had declined to less than a half of the population, if we employ knowledge of a native language as the main criterion. By the time we reach 1980 the percentage of native people (or *indígenas*) for central Mexico was down to approximately 12 percent. However, unlike other parts of North America, Mexico was characterized by considerable continuity in its genetic population, with a high level of miscegenation and a much lower rate of immigration from abroad. Consequently, most

of its inhabitants are considered to be mestizos (offspring of both Europeans and native peoples) rather than "whites" or Euro-Americans.[2]
Nevertheless, despite an official ideology emphasizing racial and cultural
blending, the majority of people in central Mexico are predominantly
European (increasingly North American) in terms of their worldview and
values. The majority of Mexicans also hold a prejudicial or paternalistic
attitude vis-à-vis people whom they classify as "Indians." Native peoples,
who experience discrimination on a daily basis, are likely to be called by
such derogatory terms as *inditos* ("little Indians"), *compadritos*, or *com-
pas.*[3]

Notwithstanding a dramatic decline in numbers (and the corresponding loss of native culture), the native peoples of central Mexico have not
been passive bystanders or victims. Native communities were involved in
broader-based political movements, and some of their native sons (fewer
daughters) rose to prominence on the regional level. The inhabitants of
native villages in such key regions as Morelos and the Sierra Norte de
Puebla played an active part in forging their own regionally based version
of Mexican nationalism and radical liberalism, together with rural mestizos. Their discourse, which incorporated alternative ways of defining
citizenship, land ownership, and political institutions was in turn the
outcome of an uneven but ongoing process of contestation among men
and women, peasants, village notables, schoolteachers, and merchants
within predominantly native rural regions. Moroever, native symbols
have shaped national (mestizo) culture, especially in the twentieth century. Much of the artistic and political development of postrevolutionary
Mexico was nourished by the native traditions that were adopted by the
leaders of the same national state that also tried to modify or destroy a
separate native discourse. Simultaneously, partly acculturated native intellectuals (many of whom ended up in Mexico City) did not always
agree with and sometimes adamantly opposed the interpretation of native
cultures by non-native (or pseudo-native) intellectuals. They in turn
forged their own version of native discourse, which formed the basis of
the creation of a new form of native ethnicity. Such multistranded

---

[2] The term *mestizo* refers more to cultural than phenotypic traits and does not have the same
connotations as the term *metis* in the context of North America.
[3] The Spanish term *compadre* (literally "co-parent"), which refers to a form of fictive kinship, does
not have negative connotation; however, its diminutive form and this contraction is used in
different parts of central Mexico to refer to native people in a very condescending or derogatory
fashion.

interactions form part of a complex dynamic that may yet produce some surprising results.

Whether or not native people will survive as a separate component of Mexican society, especially in the case of central Mexico, is to some degree problematic. Native and non-native rural communities share many cultural traits, including the system of fictive kinship known as *compadrazgo*[4] and most folk customs. Indeed, some scholars have argued that most of these cultural traits have a medieval European rather than a prehispanic origin, although a great deal of the "material" culture (especially ways of preparing food and agricultural technology) is authentically "native," even in the case of rural mestizos. However, according to most ethnic studies specialists today, ethnic boundaries are not dependent on the specific content of culture but, rather, on the interpretation of a wide range of real or imputed differences forming the basis of contrasting identities.

Although an integral part of a single nation-state, a significant minority of native men and women continue to identify themselves as, or are considered to be, different from other Mexicans. The survival of distinct native communities, ethnic conflicts, and periodic cultural revivals have been characteristic of the last 150 years. The basis for such ethnic differentiation is hard to determine. Like much of the rest of Latin America, a separate native identity (as well as objectively defined cultural differences) has in large part been associated with the use of native languages, even if such languages are only spoken at home or on special occasions. However, this relationship between language use and native identity is a complex one; the increasing use of Spanish and the relegation of native languages to very specific and narrow contexts may go hand in hand with growing ethnic pride. Moreover, the existence of unique patterns of social interaction and native identities, distinct from those of "mainstream" Mexico, are by no means intrinsically dependent on linguistic diversity. One cannot exclude the possibility that an increasing number of Spanish-speaking mestizos (especially those associated with formerly native communities) might yet change their identity to that of "Indian." Whether or when they will be accepted as such by the rest of those people who

---

[4] *Compadrazgo*, or "co-parenthood," is a form of ritual kinship established through such religious ceremonies as baptism or matrimony, involving one of the children of the co-parents who thereby become the *padrino*, or godparent, of the child. In central Mexico, as in most of Mesoamerica, the relationship between the godparent and the real parent has greater social significance than that between godparent and godchild.

today consider themselves to be native people, remains to be seen. Regardless of the role of language, the survival of a separate native ethnic component in central Mexico in the future will very much depend on the day-to-day social practices of native people in their ongoing struggle to maintain or regain access to land and other resources and formal recognition of political autonomy on the local or regional level. Control over formal education is another factor, and it will become more crucial in the future. It is thus necessary to examine all facets of the native experience in central Mexico and how each has changed over time.

NATIVE LANGUAGES

If one were to draw a map of central Mexico showing the areas where at least some proportion of the population spoke native languages around 1821, it would be almost completely filled in. Eyewitness accounts indicate a process of rapid linguistic assimilation already occurring throughout the central plateau region between 1840 and 1850. Numerous parish documents referred to the larger number of *castas* (rather than "Indians") in this region and how they were gradually being absorbed by the Spanish-speaking population. By the end of the last century there were several large areas of completely monolingual Spanish speakers: part of the highland plateau, including the northern half of the federal district and the southern tip of Hidalgo; sections of the Tlaxcala–Puebla valley; the southwestern corner of Mexico state; and parts of the lower, southern half of the state of Puebla. By the middle of the twentieth century, the situation had become completely reversed; in most of central Mexico, speakers of native languages had become completely blended into the mestizo, Spanish-speaking rural population, while regions with communities where native languages were still spoken were restricted to islands or clusters. Map 17.3 shows the distribution of such clusters, which have a fairly high proportion of native speakers today, as well as those that still did so until around 1940. In all of these regions, native languages are maintained through daily social intercourse in the context of towns, villages, and neighborhoods where native people live and work together.

Many anthropologists use the term *regions of refuge* to describe the areas where linguistically distinct native communities are still found today. Such regions consist of inaccessible places, with a combination of subsistence cultivation and crafts. Mestizo regions are usually associated with lowlands and fertile valleys, with industry or commercial agriculture.

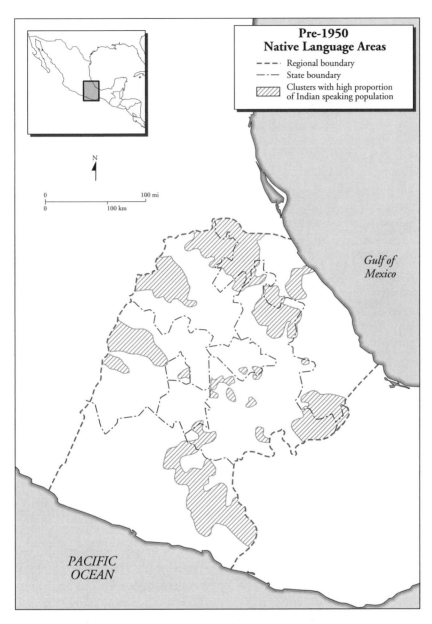

Map 17.3

However, the geographical distribution of native speakers contradicts this simplistic model of native survival. While a large number of native communities are located in more remote, mountainous regions, there is no clear correspondence between the proportion of native people and the type of terrain, climate, or proximity to major urban centers. In Morelos, an area of continuous human habitation long before the Conquest, one might expect the Nahua language to have survived only in the northern highlands and to be fairly evenly distributed in that part of the state. However, *municipios* with Nahuatl speakers are found in only some sections of the highlands and in at least one part of the fertile lowland valley (in Temixco and Cuautla). This geographical distribution of Nahuatl speakers dates back to at least the middle of the 1900s. Nor can one say that native people are found only in villages that have had at least a limited land base going right back to colonial times. For instance, among the Nähñus of Temoayan (on the edge of the Valley of Toluca), peons who lived in settlements within the boundaries of a larger hacienda preserved their speech and their ethnic identity as much as their peasant counterparts from upland barrios with their own communal land. Similarly, the majority of the Mazahuas in the *meseta* of Ixtlahuaca–Toluca (also in the state of Mexico) were once peons of large haciendas. They, too, have continued to preserve their identity and their language even though they live within commuting distance of Mexico City (just like the Nahuas of Morelos and Tlaxcala). Indeed, in some regions, the survival of native languages is even inversely related to altitude and level of land; thus, in the northeastern corner of the state of Hidalgo, Nahuas who live in the low-lying, semitropical foothills of the Sierra Madre still speak their own language and have maintained a separate culture regardless of the prevailing pattern of land tenure, relative prosperity, or when their villages were established. In contrast, the same group of Nahuas in the neighboring Sierra Alta de Hidalgo all but lost their linguistic as well as their ethnic distinctiveness over thirty years ago.

Although native peoples are more likely to be poor peasants, the use of native languages should not be equated with class in a simplistic fashion. Statistical data from the 1970 census for Morelos can be used to demonstrate that the survival of ethnic identity (as measured by linguistic retention) does not correspond to level of alphabetization, economic class structure (as measured by the proportion of peasants versus workers), or the proportion of people with secondary schooling. Put in a nutshell, being "Indian" is not the same thing as being poor. This finding can also be supported by census data on the relationship between ethnicity and literacy (in Spanish). For example, between 1890 and 1910, literacy rates in indigenous communities in the sugar-producing districts of southern Puebla display a wide range of variation; at the turn of the century, only 3 percent of the population was literate in a *municipio* where 83 percent spoke Nahuatl (in Zoquititlan, district of Tehuacán); in contrast, in another *municipio* (Cohueacan, Matamoros), where 93 percent of the population spoke indigenous languages, 29 percent of the men and 15 percent of the women were literate.

The connections between level of ethnic identity retention and the survival of native languages are complex and indeterminate. Social scientists interested in causal explanations could identify many factors operating at the regional level: the outcome of past political struggles for autonomy and access to land, the extent of social interaction with other native people in the economic sphere, and the ability of the owners of large estates to maintain the social isolation of native workers. For example, the impact of rapid industrialization seems to account for the loss of the Nahuatl language that took place between 1870 and 1920 in the area between the cities of Tlaxcala and Puebla. However, this factor cannot explain why native communities on the slopes of the Malinche volcano (to the east of the highway connecting these two cities) have preserved Nahuatl to this day. Moreover, villages in the southern part of this native subregion, which are closer to the city of Puebla, use Nahuatl to a greater extent than those in the northern part. Some linguists explain that this higher level of usage of Nahuatl is because southern communities are more dependent on a traditional agrarian base, even though the men of such communities regularly work as masons, painters, or construction workers in the city of Puebla during the slack season of agriculture. Yet ironically, a greater loss of Nahuatl as the language of daily discourse in the northern zone – with a much higher level of proletarianization (through migrant labor in Mexico City) – has resulted in the adoption of greater ethnic or *indigenista* solidarity. Indeed, throughout Tlaxcala "Indianness" is expressed through the identification with agricultural work and conservative dress rather than through the use of Nahuatl. In my own research I have found that the nature and dynamics of internal class tensions are equally relevant for explaining variations in the level of linguistic and ethnic retention on the village level. A greater understanding of these interrelated phenomena in central Mexico will require more research on the economic and political history of native peoples at both the micro and macro levels, without losing sight of the changing social structure of native society.

THE CHANGING SOCIAL STRUCTURE OF NATIVE COMMUNITIES

At the time of independence, many native people in both central and southern Mexico were members of former "Indian republics" or native *pueblos*, with their own land base and separate administrative structures. These structures, especially religious institutions, were altered as a result of reforms initiated under the Bourbon dynasty in the late eighteenth century and continued under a series of Liberal governments. The setting up of *municipios* (which usually covered an area greater than that under the jurisdiction of the formerly separate native governments), combined with a state policy regarding the dissolution of communal land tenure, were the major factors responsible for the loss of ethnic solidarity. However, native people in many communities resisted or adapted in creative ways. These communities, consisting of peasant farmers, merchants, and artisans, represent the continuation of former "Indian republics" with a unique form of social organization, albeit a reduced land base. Although the new town government (*ayuntamiento*) usually came under the control of Spanish-speaking mestizos, sometimes the leading citizens of former native administrative centers were able to use the new institution of town councils to assert their authority over local non-Indians. Many features of the old colonial system of village administration (including a high level of self-regulation) thus survived in native communities, despite the introduction of a republican form of government on the national level.

The survival of some measure of native autonomy on the local level seemed to depend not only on the relative isolation of native villages but on their level of economic prosperity before the implementation of the Liberal reforms. This principle can be illustrated by comparing the degree of internal cohesion and ethnic survival of different pueblos and barrios that became subject to the municipality of Mexico City after independence. In the more humid southern section of the former *parcialidad* of San Juan Tenochtitlan, native farmers and merchants involved in intensive market gardening (associated with fertile *chinampas*) or in the cutting and selling of fodder, kept their own language and customs well into the twentieth century. By means of strict endogamy and restriction on outsiders, they managed to maintain control over their resources and even developed their own intellectual elite. In contrast, the natives who lived in the northern part of the city, along the two avenues that led to the Villa de Guadalupe (site of the shrine of the Mexican Virgin), for the most part comprised destitute families who made a living from marginal fishing and making salt on the edges of desiccating lakes. Their communal lands were technically still administered on their behalf as a single block of land (associated with the *parcialidad* of Santiago Tlatelolco), but in effect the income (rents) from their communal pastures (which had long been rented out to mestizo businessmen) were appropriated by non-native leaders. This part of what is now the metropolitan center of Mexico City was the first to lose both its ethnic cohesion and its separate culture.

However, the loss of access to land and a lack of self-government did not always lead to a disintegration of social ties based on ethnic solidarity. Although this was true for most native communities that became engulfed by expanding urban centers based on Western models, one cannot say the same for the countryside. Native peoples who were forced to leave their villages, and who settled permanently inside the boundaries of private estates (or haciendas), did not invariably lose their culture or unique patterns of social interaction. The Mazahua hacienda communities in the state of Mexico have already been mentioned. In 1900, in the state of Puebla, in the Tehuacan district – with twenty-three haciendas and an almost completely native rural population – many natives lived within the boundaries of landed estates. Examples from the state of Hidalgo include Chalahuiyapan, Huitzachahual, and Ecuatitla, all settlements of Nahua peons who worked for haciendas in the district of Huejutla. Such landless natives were legally subordinate to the authority (and sometimes the whim) of non-native owners of haciendas or *ranchos*. However, this does not mean that members of such native settlements could not learn to manipulate the paternalistic symbols and complex set of economic ties that bound them to landowners and estate administrators, while forging their own patterns of social interaction.

The Mexican Revolution, a decade of civil war and political upheaval (starting in 1910), further altered patterns of social interaction within native communities. Revisionist historians today see this turbulent period as only an interlude in an ongoing process of industrial capitalist development and gradual state expansion, which had already started in the second half of the nineteenth century. However, the Mexican Revolution did bring about a new legal system for land tenure and a different kind of official state ideology. Starting in the 1920s, a more vigorous expansion of central state power and the implementation of yet another land reform represented new challenges for native communities. Peasant villages that had maintained some form of corporate (usually communal) structure, as well as former hacienda settlements (now turned into *ejidos*)[5], had to respond to new external realities and to cope with new types of mestizo politicians. In this process, the more striking contrasts in the class structure and internal social organization between independent native towns (pueblos) and native hacienda villages were diminished.

The Closed Corporate Community

The social structure of native pueblos, throughout Mesoamerica, is usually depicted as a closed corporate community. This type of community is highly endogamous and usually restricts outsiders from living or owning property within its physical boundaries. One of the most important features of the closed corporate peasant community, according to the classic model of Eric Wolf, is the civil-religious hierarchy (also known as the *cargo* or *mayordomía* system). Adult men take turns occupying a series of alternating civil and religious posts of increasingly higher rank, until one reaches the influential level of elder (also known as *principal*). This institution, which has both political and religious aspects, involves the sponsorship of religious feasts (usually in the honor of a particular patron saint) by individual households. Women play a major role at this level, since they not only do most of the work involved in food preparation and marketing but activate the social networks necessary to prepare large public events. Such women also have informal authority. Most native communities in central Mexico do not seem to have preserved quite as elaborate a form of this system as in other parts of Mesoamerica, but a modified version can still be found in parts of Puebla, Tlaxcala, Hidalgo, and Guerrero. Indeed, at least one full-fledged and elaborate civil-religious hierarchy was still reported as late as 1970s for a Nahua village in the Valley (and state) of Mexico, near Texcoco.

Several historians and anthropologists have argued that the civil-religious hierarchy emerged in the nineteenth century as a consequence

---

[5] The *ejido*, modeled after a form of communal land tenure found in colonial Mexico, is a form of landholding established after the Revolution. The land is officially owned by the groups of peasants who enjoy rights of usufruct in perpetuity, but cannot sell or rent out the land they work.

of changes in the national political and economic system after independence, which put tremendous pressures on native religious brotherhoods (*cofradías*). In the colonial period, one part of the communally owned village land was usually set aside for such *cofradías*. The proceeds from this land (or from community-owned cattle) were used to defray the cost of major public feasts, including communal expenditures on food and drink. Increasing competition over such proceeds among government officials, native elites, the Catholic Church, and the peasantry (who wanted to use this portion of the commons to cover their own daily subsistence in times of increasing economic hardship) led to the disappearance of many *cofradías*. Instead, the sponsorship of feasts became the responsibility of individual households. A proliferation of religious posts on the local level then became intertwined with civil posts in a single "ladder" system, increasingly less dependent on direct control by either state or church.

A great deal of controversy among scholars revolves around the meaning and function of the civil-religious hierarchy. One point of debate is whether this institution was a defensive strategy used by native communities (despite the obviously Western or colonial origin of many of its elements) or a means of further exploitation of native peasants by the larger society. Ethnographic and historical evidence supports both sides of the argument. The issue can only be resolved by taking into account local and regional differences since there is a range of variation in the degree to which this institution acted to redistribute local resources. Another issue of contention is whether or not it operated as an effective mechanism for leveling internal wealth differences, thereby preventing or attenuating the formation of permanent classes within native peasant villages. To answer this question requires the examination of status distinctions and class formation from a broader historical perspective.

As in most other peasant communities in the world, the extent of internal class differentiation and other forms of stratification in American native communities has varied over time and by region, depending on population pressure, the availability of natural resources, and the level of commercialization of the regional economy. The turbulent period associated with the War of Independence and its aftermaths saw the disappearance of status distinctions between native nobles and commoners in larger former "Indian republics," although the elders or *principales* continued to exercise considerable influence. Given the disruptions of the economy caused by war, most members of the village elite, including wealthier families, suffered a decline in both wealth and standards of living. With a greater emphasis on subsistence production and a lack of opportunities for village entrepreneurs, the civil-religious hierarchy probably did act as an effective leveling mechanism at least up until the 1870s, especially in communities that were successful in preventing the encroachment of outsiders. However, there is abundant evidence that the civil-religious hierarchy (and other features of the so-called closed corporate community) did not prevent the re-emergence and further development of internal class differences in indigenous regions during the last two decades of the nineteenth century. The classic form of the civil-religious hierarchy remained intact in both subsistence-oriented villages and those with a higher level of integration into the cash economy.

In most of central Mexico, the civil-religious hierarchy was transformed starting in the late 1920s, with the introduction of a more efficient centralized state bureaucracy (including a host of new local level political posts). In what became a de facto one-party system, the appointment of people to local civil posts came increasingly under government control. State representatives (usually mestizos from larger centers) not only had to approve the nomination or election of municipal officials, but in some cases even intervened in the religious ceremonial system. Increased integration into the national political system greatly reduced local autonomy and often resulted in a separation of civil and religious posts at the local level – which meant that villagers were left to run a predominantly religious hierarchy. This dissolution of a single, integrated civil-religious hierarchy started much sooner in central than it did in southern Mexico, resulting in a much truncated system in all but the fringe regions of central Mexico by the 1950s. Nevertheless, the survival of a form of religious hierarchy represents the continuation of some level of village autonomy. However, this strategy is not unique to native communities since native peoples are not the only ones who can utilize folk religion to strengthen community bonds (and, in some cases, also legitimize a process of internal class differentiation). Religious hierarchies are also found in mestizo communities that were once Indian republics. But we must not forget that mestizos were not the only ones who learned how to fight for greater control over other, purely secular institutions.

Native Ejidos

Ejido committees (with *comisariados*) were introduced after the Revolution as a new form of village administration, with the implementation of land redistribution. Although not specifically designed only for native people, the political posts associated with this new form of government afforded the first opportunity for the inhabitants of native settlements, hitherto subject to a hacienda administration, to manage their own affairs. With rare exceptions, such as the Nahua village of Santa Cruz in Huejutla (Hidalgo), the workers who lived in communities within the boundaries of haciendas had not been allowed to organize their own religious fiestas, and thus did not have the civil-religious hierarchy just described. This explains why the term *mayordomo* had a completely different meaning in native hacienda villages, where it meant a labor supervisor and intermediary between peasants and landowner, instead of the sponsor of a religious celebration. Nahua peasants in hacienda communities in Huejutla also did not use the system of toponyms (to identify family groupings sharing patrilocal residence) so commonly associated with Nahua society, although they did have their own type of personal naming systems.

This situation changed drastically with the expropriation of hacienda land, when former day laborers and sharecroppers were not only given title to the land they cultivated but also the right to practice their religion any way they chose. In some cases the president or some other member of the *ejido* committee might even be put in charge of religious affairs or collaborate closely with a *juez*, the holder of a minor judicial post associated with any small rural community. Although technically in charge of regulating access to newly allocated land, the jurisdiction of *ejido* officials extended to other aspects of village life. This was particularly true for smaller communities of former hacienda workers (*peones acasillados*) and new settlements established by native land recipients after winning a struggle for access to better land. In larger mestizo towns – and also in established native communities that received additional land in the form of an *ejido* grant – the *ejido* administration was but a parallel and minor form of government. In contrast, for former Indian peons who did not belong to an independent village, *ejido* status provided an opportunity to create new forms of autonomy and cultural expression. For example, in the Huasteca of Hidalgo, the inhabitants of Chalahuiyapan first built their own chapel and subsequently became participants in an annual pilgrimage to the cathedral in Huejutla.

THE STRUGGLE FOR CONTROL OVER LAND

Going back even before Mexican independence, the struggle of native peoples for land has been intrinsically related to legal battles in the courts, ideological debates, and – whenever conditions were favorable – armed rebellion. The implementation of the Ley Lerdo (part of the liberal legislation of 1856, which tried to abolish all forms of collective-owned rural property) threatened the very existence of native communities, giving rise to confrontations as well as alliances among members of various social strata. The inhabitants of former Indian republics also reacted in different ways. Many found creative solutions to stave off, delay, or even prevent the complete breakup of village lands; others had no choice but to rebel when deprived of part or all of their village lands. Even then, wealthy village notables sometimes did not act in the same way as poor villagers did. Reactions depended in part on the type of relationships established between native communities and various types of haciendas or smaller estates known as ranchos.

The Encroachment of Haciendas

Increasing encroachment of haciendas on native landholding communities started before the implementation of the Liberal reform. Such encroachment was particularly severe in the fertile, sugar-producing lowlands of Morelos and Puebla, and in the grain-growing regions of the valleys of the central plateau (parts of Mexico, Tlaxcala, and Puebla). One method used by hacienda owners was to appropriate surplus communal (village) land they had already been renting for nominal fees in periods of declining population growth. Villagers also had to give up communally owned land used as collateral to *hacendados* who had provided cattle or financial "assistance" to village governments to cover the costs of community ceremonies. The expansion of haciendas in all of these regions, as well as on the coastal plains, was temporarily slowed down with the weakening of centralized state power and intraelite conflict in the first half of the nineteenth century. Such internecine fighting afforded peasants and day laborers the opportunity to revolt. During the War of Independence, natives communities in both the Valley of Mesquital and the plains of Apan attacked local estates after they joined the insurrection of Fathers Miguel Hidalgo and José María Morelos. This semi-arid region, used primarily for the production of small livestock and pulque,[6] was characterized by rising social tensions resulting from increasing competition between native peasant communities and absentee landowners. According to John Tutino, native communities in grain-producing parts of the central plateau region did not revolt or attack local haciendas at that time because greater economic interdependency and a kind of symbiosis between estate and village in those regions made up for their declining autonomy.

This delicate equilibrium between estate and village in much of central Mexico did not last long; hacienda owners continued to take over the lands of their native neighbors both in areas of rapid economic expansion, such as Morelos (which was becoming an important sugar-producing regions), and in parts of the central plateau where large estates experienced rapid decline because of shrinking markets and competition from other regions. In the wheat-producing valleys of Puebla, landowners whose estates were already becoming economically marginal faced shortages of field laborers at a time when native producers, as a way to meet their subsistence needs, were starting to rely more on cultivating village lands than working on hacienda lands. As a result, landowners resorted to coercion and blatantly illegal labor recruitment methods. In both of these cases, members of native communities fought against landowners both in the courts and by means of land invasions. However, in periods of political stability, the national government restored to the usurpers most of the land that had been won by native peasants.

The implementation of the Ley Lerdo allowed these same hacienda owners and other entrepreneurs to accelerate their takeover of community lands under the protection of the law. Further encroachment led to more litigation and further revolts by native communities, especially during the turbulent period of civil war (1855–61), foreign intervention (1855–67), and the restoration of a still weak and divided republic (1867–76). The appropriation of additional communal lands was done in various ways, often in stages. Initially it was more common for outsiders to claim (by means of a *denuncia*) those sections of community land that they were already renting. This usually meant a dramatic loss of income from rents that native pueblos had hitherto used to defray ceremonial

---

[6] Pulque is an alcoholic beverage made from the juice of the *maguey* cactus plant.

expenses, finance schools or hospitals, or as a kind of charitable fund for those most in need. Next, local officials would distribute the rest of the communally owned village land to groups of native occupants (for exorbitant fees). These new, now private, native landowners often ended up selling this land to richer members of their community or to outsiders.

The partitioning of communal lands initially took place only in peasant communities with more efficient means of communication and that were near larger towns. Mexico City is somewhat of an exception since the lands of the two former native *parcialidades* continued to be administered as a single corporate entity. In this case (and others, as we shall see) the preservation of communal land benefited members of both a mestizo and a native elite, who were able to siphon off the income from such collectively owned land for their personal benefits or to provide income for municipal governments run by non-natives. Under such circumstances, it was usually the poor native peasants who petitioned for a distribution of communal land so that they could have more effective control over local resources. Whatever may have been the underlying motives, the authorities of both mestizo and native towns and villages in most of the central Mexican countryside managed to delay this process for a few decades. Not only was there vehement opposition from native pueblos, but logistical problems and the cost of measuring small plots of land for distribution to their users made the implementation of the Liberal land reform legislation unfeasible. Even regional administrators (*jefes políticos*) paid lip service to edicts coming from state capitals. The full implementation of the law did not occur until after 1880 (in many places not until the 1890s), a period of stronger state control and greater scope for capitalistic expansion under the regime of Porfirio Díaz. By that time, litigations through the courts no longer offered a viable means of reducing the damages done by dubious or unlawful takeovers of village land, and it became too risky to attempt open rebellion.

The Liberal legislation on land tenure in the first half of the nineteenth century provided the legal framework that allowed an already existing process of land concentration to proceed more smoothly once economic conditions were ripe. That was certainly the case in Mexico City, where rapid population growth and urban expansion did not really start until after 1860. Only then did massive encroachment on both native land and town centers begin in earnest. The same could be said for the countryside. In the last quarter of the nineteenth century, the already densely populated highland plateau of central Mexico witnessed an economic boom for hacienda owners and foreign investors. Not only was the process of internal class differentiation accentuated in both native and non-native communities, but large estate owners were able to entice increasing numbers of sharecroppers and seasonal laborers from land-poor native villages. Haciendas in the flatter, fertile regions of the central plateau and valleys of Mexico also became more diversified; their owners were modern businessmen who got involved in food processing, helped finance the building of railroads, and mechanized many of their operations. However, these commercial landowners were not adverse to using labor-intensive techniques if they could profit from employing cheap native laborers; indeed, they revived the same paternalistic system and used the same type of discourse as their more "feudal" predecessors.

The modern hacienda system subsequently spread to new parts of central Mexico. For example, what were once smaller haciendas and ranchos in the eastern section of the state of Mexico grew at the expense of both privately owned farms and Mazahua communities. Their new owners not only became involved in lumbering (to supply railroad ties) in addition to cultivating grain and raising animals, but started cultivating zacaton (a type of grass that can be turned into fibers) on land previously of marginal economic value. The growing of zacatón is a native tradition going back to prehispanic days, and had long provided the raw material for native artisans to produce brooms. Under the modern hacienda system, the cultivation of zacaton expanded greatly when a home craft was transformed into a capitalistic, semimechanized operation to produce brushes then used to groom horses all over Europe and North America. Unlike what happened in the henequen (sisal) zone of the Yucatan Peninsula – where capitalistic landowners resorted to forced Mayan labor, bordering on slavery – the hacienda owners of the northwestern part of the state of Mexico utilized a more deceptive combination of paternalistic discourse and patron–client bonds to gain access to an abundant supply of Mazahua or Otomí labor.

The Formation of a Ranchero Economy

The growth of large landed estates at the expense of native communities (and the absorption of surplus native labor) was not the only pattern of land tenure that developed. At the same time that commercial haciendas were taking hold in the highland plateau, a more complex class structure and land tenure system (involving a combination of communal land tenure, tiny privately owned plots, and medium-sized estates known as ranchos) emerged in the mountainous regions and the rolling foothills that divide the highland plateau from the Gulf Coast in the east and the Pacific Coast in the west. Not all of these parts of central Mexico had a large native population around the middle of the nineteenth century. For instance, in the Sierra de Jacala region (which includes Pisaflores) the original Pame inhabitants had long ago been driven out or disappeared. Except for a few Nahuatl-speaking peasants who had entered this area from the neighboring *municipio* of Tamazunchale (in the state of San Luis Potosi), most of the population was mestizo. In contrast, the Huasteca of Hidalgo and the Sierra Norte de Puebla had a predominantly native population, and with the exception of a few small cattle haciendas, land still belonged to native communities. Map 17.4 indicates where these developing *ranchero* regions were located. All of these areas received an influx of mestizos who descended from the highlands; some European immigrants also settled in these regions.

For the most part, haciendas in intermontane valleys did not encroach on native villages in ranchero or *montaña* regions. The dynamics of class and ethnic relations were quite distinct from that of the highland plateau since wealthy natives (who continued to be active members of native communities) and mestizo rancheros alike benefited from the Liberal reforms. Newcomers also established more complex ties of interdependency with native villages. There were conflicts and frictions, but on the whole, mestizo migrants learned to accommodate themselves to existing native institutions. They even learned the local languages. In northern Puebla, mestizo farmers or cattle breeders did encroach on some community land on the northern and southern margins of the Sierra Norte; but on the whole, newcomers limited their demand for land to very small pastures and sites for liquor stills (to make *aguardiente*) or *trapiches* (animal-powered sugar mills). Likewise, in Guerrero, the expansion of colonial haciendas or mestizo ranchos at the expense of communal land took place only in the region around Chilapa. The original Spanish settlers of these largely mountainous regions, as well as mestizo newcomers, became commercial middlemen (as well as rancheros) who engaged in long-distance trade, while simultaneously developing ties of reciprocity with their native customers. Thus, rather than destroying the native village economy in the mountainous regions, such outsiders accommodated themselves to its existence.

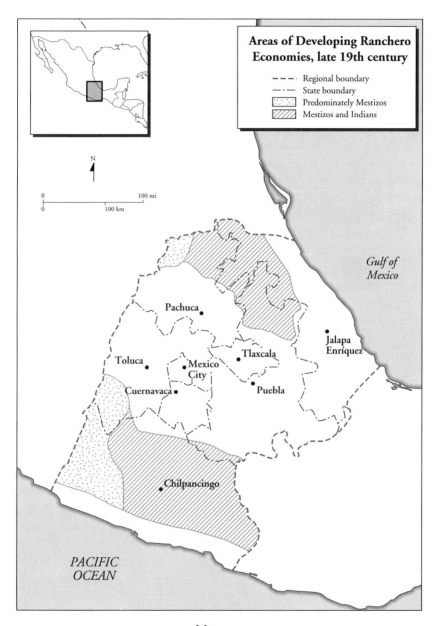

Map 17.4

A slightly different pattern of accommodation emerged in the region of Huejutla in northwestern Hidalgo, where members of Nahua communities also became "rancheros."[7] While not as actively involved in regional politics as their mestizo counterparts, wealthier Nahua peasants became traders and money lenders and set up small commercial ranchos. Mestizos sometimes moved into Nahua villages (even if these villages were not administrative centers) while at the same time maintaining strong ethnic distinctions between themselves and their native neighbors. Nahua communities in the district of Huejutla were able to keep much of their communal land intact through manipulation of the national legal system. One way of doing so was though a procedure that enabled large groups of villagers to register their land as the property of an agricultural society (*sociedad agrícola*), a form of private co-ownership (*condueñazgo*) recognized under Mexican law. Native communities in other parts of central Mexico also used this legal option as a way to defend their communal lands. For example, in the Popoloca town of San Felipe (referred to earlier), a *sociedad*, set up as early as the 1830s, still controlled most of the towns's communal land until well into the 1960s. In the case of the Huasteca of Hidalgo, mestizo newcomers sometimes joined such agricultural societies together with the representatives of Nahua pueblos. This also happened among the Totonacos in the Papantla region of Veracruz. Such native *sociedades* were dominated by a village elite of wealthier natives who set aside section of land for the poor. In other cases, individual land titles were also held in trust by a single village representative. In villages that did this, such as Tecacahuaco (now part of the municipio of Atlapexco), land taxes continued to be paid as a single unit up to the 1960s, even though there were significant differences in the amount of land cultivated by its inhabitants.

In the mountainous ranchero regions, with their lush vegetation, plentiful rainfall, and (up to around 1940) relatively low population densities, sections of formerly communal land did end up in the hands of outsiders. However, in Huejutla, mestizo politicians continued to recognize the original communal land boundaries of all Nahua pueblos, even if portions of village land became private property or were sold to outsiders. Mestizo rancheros, some of whom owned land inside these communal boundaries, learned how to manipulate the cultural values and social

---

[7] For ambiguity inherent in using the term "Indian ranchero," see Schryer, *Ethnicity and Class Conflict*, 317–18.

institutions of Nahua pueblos, just as native leaders took advantage of the national legal system. Each side realized that communal boundaries had as much to do with judicial authority as with rights of access to land. Nahua authorities were able to continue recruiting communal labor (*faena*), sometimes for their own benefit and at other times for their more powerful mestizo counterparts, just as the *caciques* or *principales* of Indian republics had done in the colonial era. Such communal labor was also used for the upkeep or building of mule trails and for the construction and maintenance of the town squares and school buildings, even if these were also used by mestizos.

In the middle of the twentieth century, with the widespread land reform of Lázaro Cárdenas, small landowners in most of the *montaña* regions (in both Guerrero and Puebla) were affected only to a limited degree since most rural properties were smaller than the legal limits for expropriation. Moreover, a large percentage of the inhabitants of native communities owned small private plots of land. Again, the Huasteca of Hidalgo is the exception; both Nahua and mestizo *caciques* conspired to prevent even limited land reform by creating huge fictitious *ejidos*. The boundaries of these *"ejidos"* and their administrative structures coincided with those of original corporate villages. In fact, many people (mestizo and Nahua) continued to buy and sell plots of land, and wealthy Nahua cattle ranchers monopolized more than their share of communal pastures. Many aspects of the land tenure and administrative structures of Nahua pueblos, dating back to the colonial era, thus remained intact because they coincided with the class interests of both wealthy Nahua families and mestizo rancheros. This does not mean that the passive resistance and actions of other native peasants did not play a role; the survival of such communities guaranteed at least some access to land needed for subsistence and became the legal basis for future land claims. But not until recently did poor native peasants become pitted against small property-owners now legally classified as *pequeños propietarios* (small proprietors).

The Struggle Against Pequeños Propietarios

Over the last hundred years, the economic relationships of native employers, merchants, and landowners with their economic subordinates were not that different from those of mestizo rancheros. However, these relationships were legitimized and expressed in culturally distinct ways.

Cultural and ethnic differences also came to the fore during the violent protests by peasants in northwestern Hidalgo in the 1970s and 1980s. The land invasions and political violence associated with this recent struggle over land afford some insights into the complex dynamics of native insurrections in other parts of central Mexico in the nineteenth century or during the Mexican Revolution. As in earlier agrarian revolts, both poor Nahua and poor mestizo peasants and day laborers were involved. However, radical peasants from the two groups, although sometimes acting in concert, did not behave in the same way or use the same tactics, nor did their respective struggles lead to the same outcomes.

Like earlier struggles over land, peasant movements in the 1970s were caused by a breakdown of a modus vivendi between native peasants and mestizo landowners resulting from rapid and lopsided economic development. In the Huasteca of Hidalgo, this took the form of a combination of the expansion of new forms of cattle production, rapid demographic growth, the erosion of the subsistence economy, and the loss of part-time employment opportunities outside Nahua communities. Moreover, many native communities (like their mestizo counterparts) had become increasingly divided into different economic strata during the boom years of the 1950s and 1960s. Wealthy Nahua villagers did not want to join the peasant movement, and in some cases open class conflict even erupted between day laborers and commercial landowning farmers or ranchers within large Nahua communities. In fact, sometimes poor mestizo peasants took part in land invasions directed against Nahua ranchers who lived in traditional Nahua communities. Such internal class conflicts took place alongside a more general peasant movement directed against absentee landowners. However, unlike their mestizo counterparts, poor Nahua peasants were not willing to divorce rights to land from eligibility to live in a particular village. They insisted that village landowners or people who had not supported land invasions leave their communities. Where such radicals won, their communities were transformed into something approximating the closed corporate community as first described by Eric Wolf. Even in villages where class structures remained intact, ongoing and less overt internal conflict had as much to do with definitions of communal boundaries and the meaning of village institutions as with land and control of local government. In contrast, radical mestizo peasants in the Huasteca of Hidalgo preferred to set up their own *ejido* administration, separate from other aspects of local government.

Agrarian conflicts in areas that had once been "Indian republics" also took a different form from those occurring in parts of the Huasteca where haciendas date back to the colonial era. Groups of Nahua peasants in lower-lying parts of the *municipios* of Huejutla and San Felipe Orizatlán, who had once been *peones acasillados* of cattle haciendas, joined the struggle for land after waiting for years to obtain extension of *ejidos* set up in the 1940s; but their legal claims were not as strong as those of Nahua peasants in the formerly communal zone who inhabited purely fictitious *ejidos*. The contrasts in the political behavior of neighboring Nahua and mestizo peasant agrarians were also not as great as in formerly independent communal villages. However, even in old *ejidos* (dating from the 1940s) one finds closer supervision of outsiders (including school-teachers) in Nahua communities, and a greater emphasis on community (and ethnic) solidarity. Many Nahua *ejidos* (both old and new) gave members without officially designated parcels access to a special section of "communal land," set aside as a kind of reserve for subsistence activities (contrary to standard *ejido* procedure as regulated by the Mexican Land Reform office).

THE INDIAN PRESENCE IN NATIONAL POLITICS

Although closely intertwined, the participation of native people in the broader political arena is not always synonymous with the defense of community land. In the first two decades after independence, members of a small elite of educated natives who lived in Mexico City voiced their protest against a government policy that would abolish all native corporate rights or special institutions designed for native ethnic minorities. These educated natives, some of whom were prominent in city politics, not only fought for the preservation of corporate landholding associated with former *parcialidades*, but also wanted to preserve the Colegio de San Gregorio, a school especially set up for the education of native students. However, native involvement in national politics did not always involve struggling for the preservation of native culture and a separate identity. For many natives, politics was a mechanism for individual upward mobility in a mestizo-dominated society, and sometimes politicians of native descent acted against the best interests of their own ethnic group.

The best-known case is that of Benito Juárez, a "full-blooded Zapotec" Indian from Oaxaca who became Mexico's first liberal national president and who led republican forces against the French invasion of 1861. Benito Juárez has become one of the heroes in the official mythology of mestizo Mexico, which accords native people an equal place in national history. In fact, Juárez, although brought up in a native community, not only became highly acculturated but also identified himself as a Europeanized Mexican. Juárez's political program (especially the law of *desamortización* to privatize land ownership) set up the legal mechanisms that eventually brought about the disintegration or destruction of a great number of native communities in central Mexico and elsewhere. No matter how good his intentions, his actions were consistent with the combination of disdain and paternalism he exhibited in writing about his own people.

The abolition of Indian republics after independence left no room for official native representation, and national politicians rarely understood and never acknowledged the existence of native cultures. They saw native peoples as either "uncivilized" or "poor, exploited Indians." This situation explains the reported lack of interest of most native people in national politics in times of peace, especially in the nineteenth century. However, when it came to issues that really mattered to them, native peasants, merchants, and small-town elites were just as actively involved in national politics as non-natives. The reality of a strong sense of ethnic cohesion by many native communities, and their constant struggle to maintain some level of autonomy, created the need for brokers or intermediaries between native communities and the state (or those who sought to take over state control). This role was often played by local and regional native leaders who kept in close contact with their constituencies. Their abilities to defend native community interests became especially critical when such communities faced external threats. Just as large groups of Mexicans from different classes sometimes united when they shared a common political goal, so, too, did various native peoples (both village elites and commoners) join together, but often for reasons quite different from those of their mestizo counterparts. For example, the participation of the Totonacos of Papantla in a violent rebellion, starting in 1836, had as much to do with a Church edict prohibiting native religious celebrations as with economic grievances concerning the encroachment of landowners and attempts to cut off traditional trading patterns considered to be contraband. The social and cultural importance of these celebrations, involving a syncretic religion quite distinct from that of the Spanish-speaking population, was something non-natives would have found difficult to understand.

Indigenous People and Military Service

Native communities frequently made strategic gains during periods of civil war or revolution. Military as well as political involvement in such turbulent times reflected their strategic importance from a national perspective, when rival national political factions often wooed native leaders to join broader political movements and military battles. In the nineteenth century, both Liberals and Conservatives learned that forced recruitment or conscription were not effective ways to gain loyal soldiers, particularly among native peasants. They therefore had to win the support of native people, especially in the *montaña* regions, by promising protection, reduced taxes, or help in defending community land. In the predominantly native region of northern Puebla, Juan Francisco Lucas, a Nahua military leader who became the "patriarch of the Sierra," built a regional power base through his control over an indigenous citizen-army composed of peasant volunteers, especially in Nahua regions with a long tradition of resistance and autonomy. His success in organizing Indian fighting units for the National Guard, and in obtaining supplies from native communities, was in large part because Liberal reforms had not adversely affected native communities in such communities. However, the level of voluntary participation of native people in the National Guard, and patterns of rebellion, did not take the same form even within such regions as the Sierra de Puebla. For instance, the Totonacos, who had retained control of land in the warmer and more humid northern part of the sierra, preferred to provide supplies and pay a military tax to the same political faction supported by highly militarized Nahuas in the less hospitable northern zone. The latter also suffered from severe land shortages. Moreover, in the case of Totonacos, we cannot dismiss the reluctance of powerful local mestizos to arm the same people who had recently killed outsiders encroaching on their land. Forms of participation in armed conflicts also reflected traditions of warfare going back to prehispanic times; one historian has argued that the behavior of armed Nahuas (referred to as *cuatecomacos*) recruited by Lucas resembled those described for Aztec warriors.[8]

Native communities in Guerrero also managed to obtain a reduction

---

[8] See Guy P. C. Thompson's "Los indios y el servicio militar en el México decimonónico," in Antonio Escobar O., compiler, *Indio, Nación y Comunidad* (Mexico, CIESAS, 1993).

in taxes and a greater say in running local government by frequent
rebellions during the 1840s and by allying themselves with the federalist
faction in national politics. The successful political career of Juan Alvarez,
who played an important role in national politics in the first half of the
nineteenth century, can be largely attributed to his ability to act as a
broker between peasant (at that time largely native) communities and the
newly independent Mexican state. Indeed, the support Alvarez received
from native communities was a principal reason why he and other mestizo politicians won their bid to set up the state of Guerrero itself in
1849. Although a Liberal (and for a short period in 1856, president of
Mexico), Alvarez was also a political ally of Juan de Dios Rodríguez
Puebla, a radical native leader in Mexico City who advocated the preservation of the lands and schools in the possession of the capital city's
native communities. Even the most bitter enemies of the Liberals, the
French invaders and Maximilian of Austria, similarly depended on native
support in strategic areas. They even publicly proclaimed a pronative
policy, and some writers have suggested they might have won if they had
gone much further in implementing it.

The discrepancy between the reality of a strong native presence and
the invisibility of native people in national public life can acount for the
seemingly fickle nature of native politicians who became prominent on
the national level. Juan Galicia Chimalpopoca, originally linked to a
conservative, proclerical faction, was appointed administrator of the formerly native communal lands in Mexico City in 1856, after the revolution
of Ayutla (initiated by the liberal *caudillo* Juan Alvarez, in opposition to
General Antonio López de Santa Anna). This same native intellectual
(who sometimes changed the order of his surnames to emphasize his
Nahua affiliation) became president of the Junta Protectora de Clases
Menesteras, a judicial body in charge of defending the interest of native
communities, under the Austrian emperor Maximilian during the French
intervention (1863–67). A similar pattern of changing affiliation is associated with other native politicians who became prominent on the national level, such as José Calixto Vidal and Juan Rodríguez Acatlan.
Rather than indicating a lack of loyalty to a specific cause, the political
behavior of such political leaders can be seen as evidence of a consistent
commitment to a different vision of Mexico – one with a place for
"Indians." Their loyalty to their own native constituencies in turn ensured the local support these leaders needed to weather the political
storms of the nineteenth century. Thus, Juan Francisco Lucas not only

managed to maintain control over the Sierra de Puebla during a succession of different governments and political parties, but he was also able to make the transition from being an ally of Porfirio Díaz, to being a supporter of the revolutionary Francisco Madero in 1910 and subsequently a representative of Venustiano Carranza.

Despite the presence of a handful of native leaders in the national arena, non-native political leaders were for the most part able to take advantage of native clients and rarely furthered the long-term interests of Mexico's aboriginal population. The situation during the Mexican Revolution, primarily fought between rival mestizo factions, was not that different. The revolutionary leader most closely identified with "fighting for the Indians" was Emiliano Zapata in Morelos. Zapata was himself a mestizo, but at least part of his army, and even a few officers, must have been people from native communities since a large number of Morelos's population still spoke Nahuatl. The Zapatistas gained further native adherents when they expanded their operations into Puebla and especially Tlaxcala, with its heavy concentrations of communities that had remained native and a long-standing tradition of pride in a Tlaxcalan Nahua heritage. In all these areas the largely mestizo leaders of the Zapatista movement had close contact with native peasants who still spoke Nahuatl, or identified themselves as such. However, only during the last stages of the Revolution, when they were losing, did these leaders broaden their vision to include a greater respect for and recognition of native culture. In a last-ditch attempt to woo the agrarian supporters of Cirilo Arenas in Tlaxcala (who had switched their support to a rival revolutionary leader), the Zapatistas circulated several letters written in the Nahuatl language of the region. They were handwritten and meant to be read aloud. Only at that point did Zapata and his followers make a deliberate effort to translate national symbols and concepts into categories appropriate to native culture. So far, no evidence of any other official circular like the one sent by Zapata to Nahua villagers in Puebla and Tlaxcala has been found.

Ironically, native revolutionary leaders in other parts of central Mexico did not necessarily belong to the Zapata or Villa factions associated with the more radical wing of the revolution. For instance, in the Huasteca of Hidalgo, a minor revolutionary leader called Nicolás Portes (also known as "El Indio Portes") and the Lara family of Yahualica (both Nahuatl-speaking) were affiliated with the more conservative Carranza faction. Their forays against a rival (and at one point Villista) faction was perceived by some local Spanish-speaking ranchero families from the mestizo town of Atlapexco as an "Indian uprising" because of a long-standing enmity between Atlapexco and Yahualica, a more established administrative center with a large Nahua population. However, the "Indian" faction associated with Yahualica included the descendants of several Spanish families who had been colonial administrators; that same faction was also affiliated with powerful mestizo politicians in the neighboring *municipio* of Huejutla. Such external politicians, who tapped into the discontent and grievances of native communities, were also able to profit from long-standing disputes among rival native villages. With the possible exception of Zapata, revolutionary leaders in Mexico rarely took into account the broader, long-term concerns and alternative worldviews of native peoples.

Factionalism

The logic of native political participation takes on a different form during times of relative political stability on the national level. Native communities still depend on leaders capable of representing them in dealing with external power structures, especially to maintain control over village lands won in earlier struggles of resistance. However, the potential for in-fighting among rival leaders persists, as illustrated by the period following the Mexican Revolution. While initially providing the land base needed to raise standards of living and to maintain ethnic solidarity, government-controlled *ejidos* were prone to internal conflicts. Such disputes, in turn, were an excuse for outside politicians to intervene, and in many cases conflicts were created or exacerbated by non-natives. Factional in-fighting over control of *ejido* committees, as well as over local peasant leagues, went hand in hand with the emergence of native strongmen or *caciques*.[9] Just as in colonial times, native power holders, acting as brokers between native communities and the national state, occupied an ambivalent place. Although members of a stratum of economically and politically more powerful native people, they still had to represent and defend their broader ethnic constituency vis-à-vis mestizo politicians and middlemen.

The Mazahuas illustrate the dynamics of postrevolutionary native in-

[9] The use of the term *cacique* in twentieth-century Mexico, which can refer to both natives and non-natives who combined economic and political power (including the use of armed force), has pejorative connotations. The corresponding system of *caciquismo*, however, has elements of paternalistic control, which give it some degree of legitimacy. See Paul Friedrich, "A Mexican Caci-cazgo," *Ethnology* 4 (1965): 190–209.

volvement in politics in central Mexico and its long-term implications. On the surface, the operation of *ejido* committees for Mazahua peasants in the Valley of Toluca, and their attendant factionalism (in the 1920s and 1930s), did not differ radically from those for mestizo peasants. Members of both rural groups were able to take advantage of the declining power of the hacienda owners to strengthen their own subsistence activities, especially traditional *milpa* cultivation. Native and mestizo peasants alike became more directly involved in craft activities and in the cultivation and processing of zacaton. However, when demographic growth resulted in new land shortages (at a time when market demand for zacaton products was low), mestizo peasants had a competitive advantage in switching over to other economic activities. Mestizos had not only a greater familiarity with the national language and political system, but also a wider and better set of contacts with relatives or former employees in the urban sector. That more Mazahua than mestizo peasants remained poor twenty or thirty years later further reinforced the existing system of ethnic discrimination based on a stereotype of the "poor Indian" as opposed to the "progressive mestizo." Continued discrimination and economic vulnerability (and hence the need for protection) was the basis for the relatively greater, but at the same time unstable, power of native *cacique*-type middlemen. Throughout rural Mexico such agrarian *caciques* have helped native peasants to become economically more self-sufficient (at least for a while) and also to maintain a separate culture (and local autonomy). But the renewed expansion of a more industrialized and bureaucratic system again put native peoples at a disadvantage and caused the rapid downfall of many traditional native *caciques*.

Political unrest caused by regional underdevelopment in native regions motivated the Mexican government to found special institutions for native peoples. Drawing on the ideals and theories of Mexican anthropologists, this program, called *indigenismo*, was controlled by mestizo urban intellectuals. For the most part, it paid lip-service to the importance of respecting cultural differences, while introducing forced acculturation in the cause of eliminating exploitation and marginality. An important component of this program was the employment of bilingual teachers as a more efficient means of eventually replacing native languages with Spanish. A combination of education programs and community development projects under the auspices of this new institution also created a new brand of native broker. The impact of these *indigenista* programs in central Mexico came late, however. Originally conceived during the Cárdenas era, large coordinating centers were not established until the early 1950s, and the first one in central Mexico was not started until 1963 in a remote region of Guerrero. The Mazahuas in the state of Mexico and both Nähñus and Nahuas in Hidalgo were not exposed to this institution until a decade later, in the 1970s. The long-term impact is only being felt today, as we shall see.

Another development on the national level is the government-sponsored National Councils of Indian Nations (Consejos Supremos), introduced in 1970 by Luis Echeverría. These councils gave formal representation to native peoples on the national level. However, the government party (PRI) carefully selects these native representatives. In the Huejutla region of Hidalgo, local representatives initially included radical Nahua agrarian leaders (some of whom were subsequently assassinated during the agrarian struggles of the 1970s). After 1980, the government appointed increasingly less radical people, such as conservative Nahua professionals and small businessmen.

THE STRUGGLE FOR A SEPARATE IDENTITY

The 1970s Nahua revolt in Huejutla, which received extensive press coverage, is the most recent example of a bitter conflict involving native communities in central Mexico. Although many Nahua peasants successfully wrested back control over their communities and gained access to ancestral lands, the struggle still continues in a less dramatic fashion. The issues today are not so much access to land (although this is still important) but economic exploitation by commercial middlemen (almost invariable former mestizo rancheros) and the failure of the mestizo-dominated state bureaucracy to provide more favorable terms of credit or to create new sources of employment in the region. At the same time, a more clearly ethnic struggle is also being waged on the local level within the educational system, where radical bilingual teachers are leading a fight against the ideological hegemony of the mestizo state. These teachers want to introduce a more meaningful set of values and symbols needed to promote a greater sense of self-worth and ethnic pride. This ideological struggle is happening at the same time that broader economic and political forces at the national level are simultaneously eroding earlier forms of ethnic solidarity and facilitating the emergence of new form of native ethnic identity.

Up until twenty years ago, almost all educated natives left to go to Mexico City or to state capitals and quickly lost both their language and their identity. However, starting in the early 1980s – with improved communication to hitherto isolated regions, greater competition for jobs and customers in the capital, and increasing amenities in most small towns in the countryside – younger native lawyers, doctors, engineers, and government employees started moving back to small towns in their home regions. Here they joined the ranks of an already large number of native (bilingual) teachers who have become an integral part of predominantly rural native regions in central Mexico. Today's native professionals (in towns like Huejutla and Orizatlán, in Hidalgo), frequently utilize native languages and maintain patron–client relationships with poor (often monolingual) natives while simultaneously living in a larger Spanish-speaking mestizo world. Numerous native lawyers have also become brokers in a new system of economic exploitation and political control. Nevertheless, these intermediaries, who form part of a new educated native village elite, are increasingly identifying and portraying themselves as native people (*indígenas*). From a more cynical (and functionalist) perspective, one could argue that this revival of native identity by better-off or educated native peoples is the outcome of a deliberate policy of cooptation by the national state in times of increasing social unrest. Additional resources for officially designated native regions provide a temporary pay-off for emphasizing one's native heritage and at the same time channel dissent into acceptable directions. However, one cannot ignore the unexpected or unplanned development of more radical forms of ethnic consciousness by native professionals, even though they became what they are thanks to state programs.

The Revival of Native Cultures

Many native intellectuals who have set up their own independent organizations are today criticizing the official and largely mestizo *indigenista* institutions for not doing enough to defend native culture and for not appointing real natives to run the programs, which are supposed to help integrate the native population into national society. Their political pressures forced the government under José López Portillo to develop a new program of pluriculturalism. Although created largely on paper, this program has provided the basis for a new form of discourse open to different interpretations. This new discourse is now becoming a tool in the struggle for greater cultural as well as political autonomy by native peoples from all across Mexico. In central Mexico, Nahua intellectuals from the Huasteca region (both Hidalgo and Veracruz) are playing a leading role in the ongoing struggle for a new identity, although they also cooperate with other native groups. In Pachuca, the capital of Hidalgo, Nahua and Nähñu teachers who belong to a dissenting association of teachers, are engaged in a process of mutual dialogue, although they have different perspectives. Some natives in central Mexico are also identifying with a new pan-Indian movement across Latin America, including members of radical political movements that operate outside the rules of the Mexican political system.

The ideological and political struggle led by indigenous intellectuals is not the only expression of native peoples, reasserting a new identity. Eight thousand Nahua and Totonaco natives in the state of Puebla have organized themselves into a rural cooperative movement called Tosépan Titataniské ("we will overcome together"). In Mexico City, migrant native women of largely low socioeconomic status are becoming increasingly more open about identifying themselves as members of native minorities. In turn, they are becoming accepted by other urban Mexicans and no longer need to change their attire when they enter the city or be ashamed about speaking their own languages. Most of these women (as well as their male relatives) have been commuting back and forth between the national capital and their home regions for several decades. While the men tend to work as part-time bricklayers, the women specialize in selling small retail items of fresh fruit and nuts. These "Marías," as they have come to be known by mainstream Mexicans, have managed to carve out ethnic niches in the informal urban sector: Mazahua fruit vendors in the Merced market; Nähñus from Hidalgo and Querétaro who sell *pepitas* (edible fruit seeds) in the northern part of the city; and gum vendors and beggars from the Nähñu town of Amealco (Querétaro) usually seen in downtown Mexico. Unlike their rural mestizo neighbors, they tend not to emigrate in a permanent fashion, although some are now setting up second homes in the capital city. Mexico City is thus becoming more "Indian," just as it was a hundred years ago. A similar pattern of temporary urban migration, resulting in native neighborhoods (albeit in marginal suburban sections) is exemplified by the unskilled Nahua miners in the city of Pachuca, most of whom returned to live in the village of Tetla (*municipio* of Yahualica) in the state of Hidalgo in the late 1980s.

The survival of unique forms of social organization and identities in the face of acculturative pressures from the national society should not be seen solely as the outcome of a policy on the part of landowners or governments who want to keep native peoples apart and separate to exploit them or control them. Ethnic survival among both bilingual and monolingual natives – in some cases even the presence of a separate identity in corporate-type communities that have become completely Spanish-speaking – is the outcome of creative responses to the hardships and challenges of living in a third-world setting characterized by uneven development and increasing impoverishment. However, with a combination of universal education as the main agent of socialization, and ever-accelerating penetration of the national economic and political system into the most remote corners of rural Mexico, the pressures to assimilate will likewise increase. In the future, native control over land and village government will no longer suffice for the survival of a separate identity and the further development of native culture. With each new crisis or period of adjustment, a few more native communities will lose their distinct heritage and identity – unless educated natives can win the battle to run their own institutions, especially their own schools (regardless of which language is used).

Some native teachers involved in this battle for a more permanent revival of native culture are again writing in their own mother tongues. For example, Jesús Salinas Pedraza has produced a 250,000-word account of his people's culture (that of the Nähñu Indians in the state of Hidalgo), using a microcomputer introduced to this native group by an anthropologist.[10] These native writers do not presently have the resources to do a general synopsis of their own history. Even if they could, they would discover that few serious scholars have specifically focused on native peoples in the nineteenth and early twentieth centuries. My task in writing this chapter was likewise hampered by a scarcity of publications, and I drew heavily on a few key books and articles plus my own work on Nahuas in the state of Hidalgo. This beginning only provides a glimpse of the native experience in central Mexico since independence, a glimpse that I hope native people will use to write their own history or counterhistory. I leave the last word to one of them:

> Take heart, take heart, my native brethren
> Let us not allow the coyotes to devour us

[10] See John Noble Wilford, "In a Publishing Coup, Books in Unwritten Languages," *The New York Times*, 31 December 1991, pp. B5, 6.

Let us strengthen our resolve with only our words
Thus we will defend our language, our wisdom
from a Nahua poem by
Tirso Bautista Cárdenas[11]

BIBLIOGRAPHICAL ESSAY

Apart from some problems of precisely defining central Mexico as a region, in writing this chapter I was hampered by a scarcity of publications specifically focusing on the history of native peoples in central Mexico after independence. One problem researchers will encounter is that scholars specializing in this time period often fail to distinguish between mestizos and native peoples, especially when dealing with the peasantry. Specific references to native peoples in central Mexico are most commonly found in works that are written from interdisciplinary studies but that usually focus on other topics. I thus had to draw heavily on a few key books and articles, plus my own more recent work on Nahuas in the state of Hidalgo: Frans J. Schryer, *Ethnicity and Class Conflict in Rural Mexico* (Princeton, NJ, 1990). Another important source is the recent work of Florencia Mallon, who has brought some new perspectives to bear on gender dynamics, the role of ethnic divisions, racist ideology, and native discourse in the process of nation building in nineteenth-century Mexico.

Many of the more ethnographically oriented studies conducted in central Mexico in the 1930s, 1940s, and 1950s, such as those carried out by both Robert Redfield and Oscar Lewis in Tepoztlán, Morelos, focus on the usually predominantly mestizo or highly acculturated municipal administrative centers (or *cabeceras*). See Robert Redfield, *Tepotztlán: A Mexican Village* (Chicago, 1973). Much less attention is paid to smaller outlying hamlets, which are more likely to have a greater proportion of native peoples. Consequently, one often has to interpret and read between the lines. This also holds for more recent studies, such as Hugo Nutini's two-part *Ritual Kinship* (Princeton, NJ, 1984). Even the first volume, co-authored with Betty Bell and entitled "The Structure and Historical Development of the Compadrazgo System of Rural Tlaxcala," emphasizes uniformity and cultural homogeneity resulting from a gradual process of acculturation, going back about eighty years, to the point

---

[11] My translation of the last four lines of a contemporary Nahuatl poem, in *Xochitlajtolkoskatl* (Poesía nauatl contemporánea), ed. Joel Martínez Hernández, (Tlaxcala, 1987), 79–80.

where it is almost impossible to distinguish clearly Indian from mestizo communities (p. 234). Moreover, there are almost no references or ethnographic details pertaining to hamlets (or ranchos).

Some historians pay much more attention to outlying hamlets but do not explicitly deal with ethnic differentiation, as in a study of the application of the laws of *desamortización* in a remote region of the state of Mexico. See Frank Schenk, "Dorpen uit de doden hand (de privatizering van het grondbezit van agrarische gemeenschappen in het district Sultepec, Mexico (1856–1893)" (doctoral dissertation, Leiden, 1986). Moreover, even seemingly completely Spanish mestizo municipalities might have recently had one or two isolated native communities that have since become completely assimilated or disappeared. See Frans Schryer, *The Rancheros of Pisaflores* (Toronto, 1980) for scattered references to Nahuas, Otomís, and Pames.

Historical accounts that specifically deal with native issues in the nineteenth and twentieth centuries tend to focus on peripheral areas, as opposed to the highland plateau part of central Mexico. Some of these are not yet published or appear in sources that are not well known. However, they frequently touch on other topics and issues that are relevant for all regions. In the case of Guerrero, Peter Guardino's "Peasants, Politics and State Formation in Early 19th Century Mexico: Guerrero, 1800–1855," (doctoral dissertation, University of Chicago, 1990), chap. 5, makes the point that native peoples were sometimes capable of establishing authority over non-Indians even after the formal abolition of "Indian republics" and the introduction of new *ayuntamientos* so often thought to be automatically dominated by mestizos and Spaniards. His dissertation also mentions interdependencies and frequent interactions among native peoples from different linguistic groups who use Spanish as a *lingua franca* in the marketplace. For Puebla, see Guy Thompson, "Montaña and Llanura in the Politics of Central Mexico: The Case of Puebla, 1820–1920," in *Region, State and Capitalism in Mexico*, ed. Wil Pansters and Arij Ouweneel (Amsterdam, 1989), and David LaFrance and G. P. C. Thompson, "Juan Francisco Lucas: Patriarch of the Sierra Norte de Puebla," in William Beezley and Judith Ewell, *The Human Tradition in Latin America* (Wilmington, DE, 1987), 1–13.

For the Huasteca of Hidalgo, I relied on the 1994 doctoral thesis of Antonio Escobar Ohmstede of CIESAS, "Los Pueblos Indios en las Huastecas, 1750–1853 (cambios y continuidades)"; and Antonio Escobar and Frans J. Schryer, "Las sociedades agrarias en el Norte de Hidalgo," *Mexican Studies/Estudios Mexicanos* 8, no. 1 (1992). The last reference debunks earlier interpretations of the process of land reform implemented by the Liberals, by demonstrating how native communities were able to consolidate their control over land using the same legal mechanisms once thought to be associated only with the usurpation of native land. That native people in other parts of central Mexico also set up their own landholding partnerships and shareholder corporations (*sociedades*) is also mentioned in Chenaut's chapter and Jäcklein's book cited later in this section. Additional case studies dealing with the history of native people in central Mexico also appear in *Indio, nación y comunidad en el México del Siglo XIX* (Mexico, 1993) compiled by Antonio Escobar Ohmstede and Patricia Lagos Preisser. That volume, which deals with the relationships between native communities and the Mexican state, includes a study of ethnic resistance and defense of native territory in the region of Cuetzalán (in Puebla) by Pablo Valderrama Rouy and Carolina Ramírez Suárez. One of the contributors, Rina Ortiz Peralta, in a chapter entitled "Inexistentes por decreto," which deals with the present state of Hidalgo, covers part of the highland plateau region in an analysis of legislation that abolished a separate legal status for native communities in that jurisdiction.

An excellent comparative study focusing mainly on the middle of the nineteenth century, and including an analysis of discourse and communal hegemony, is Florencia Mallon's *Peasant and Nation: The Making of Postcolonial Mexico and Peru* (Berkeley, CA, 1995). That book deals with the political part that native peoples in both Morelos and the Sierra Norte de Puebla played in forging the Mexican nation. Some treatment of native workers and peasant farmers living in the highland plateau region, including the revival of "feudal" methods of labor recruitment during the Porfiriato, can be found in Ricardo Rendón Garcini, "Paternalism and Moral Economy on Two Tlaxcala Haciendas in the Llanos de Apan," in *Region, State and Capitalism in Mexico* (Amsterdam, 1989), 37–46. The only book that discusses the history of native communities in the vicinity of Mexico City is the historical monograph of Andrés Lira, *Comunidades Indígenas frente a la Ciudad de México: Tenochtitlan y Tlatelolco, sus pueblos y barrios, 1812–1919* (Mexico, 1983). That book also provides background information and references to several native politicians who became prominent on the national level.

Books dealing with political life and policy in general during the nineteenth century invariably include some sections on the role of natives. Some good examples are T. G. Powell, *El liberalismo y el campesinado en el centro de México* (Mexico 1974), 44–45; Charles Hale, *Mexican Liberalism in the Age of Mora, 1821–1853* (New Haven, CT, 1968), 218, and Jack Autrey Dabbs, *The French Army in Mexico* (The Hague, 1963), 70. The political role of native peoples comes more to the forefront in works specifically focusing on peasant rebellions. Eric Van Young emphasizes the millenarian aspects of native uprisings at the time of the War of Independence. See his chapter, "The Raw and the Cooked: Elite and Popular Ideology in Mexico, 1800–1821," in *The Indian Community of Colonial Mexico* ed. Arij Ouweneel and Simon Miller (Amsterdam, 1990), 295–321. Other works dealing with the role of native peoples in uprisings and rebellions include John Tutino, *From Insurrection to Revolution in Mexico* (Princeton, NJ, 1986); Leticia Reina, *Las rebeliones campesinas en México (1819–1906)* (Mexico, 1980); Victoria Chenaut, "Comunidad y ley en Papantla a fines del siglo XIX," in Luís María Gatti and Victoria Chenaut, *La costa totonaca: cuestiones regionales II* (Tlalpan, 1987); Margarita Carbo, "La Reforma y la intervención: el campo en llamas," in *Historia de la cuestión agraria*, 82–74; Antonio Escobar Ohmstede, "Movimientos campesinos: manipulación de la élite?" unpublished manuscript (1989), 15; Elio Masferrer Kan, "Las condiciones históricas de la etnicidad entre los totonacos," *América Indígena* 46 (1986): 745; and Antonio Ibarra, "Tierra, sociedad e independencia," in *Historia de la Cuestión Agraria Mexicana*, ed. Enrique Semo, (Mexico, 1988), 14.

Some of the historical literature can also provide useful insights into how native peoples were portrayed by non-natives, nor can the topic of representation of natives be avoided in discussions of Mexico's only "full-blooded Indian" president, Benito Juárez. See Charles A. Weeks, "Uses of a Juárez Myth in Mexican Politics," *Politico* 39 (1974): 210–33. For a brief summary of his life, see W. Wendell Blancké, *Juárez of Mexico* (New York, 1971), 23–32. One Mexican social thinker, writing at the turn of the century, who provided a more sophisticated early account of the complex relationships between class and ethnicity is Andrés Molina Enríquez. See his *Los grandes problemas nacionales* (Mexico City 1978; first published 1909). However, even he could not avoid racial stereotypes in writing about native peasants. For a useful commentary on Molina's analysis of class and ethnicity in general (including his subcategory of

"Indian-mestizos"), see Richard Roman, "Ethnicity, Class, and Nation-ality in Mexico," *Canadian Review of Studies in Nationalism* 12 (1985): 65–80. Molina's book also provides some figures on the proportion of the Mexican population speaking native languages, although I had to rely on many other sources in order to extrapolate statistical figures on lan-guage use for central Mexico during different time periods. My main source for the beginning of the nineteenth century was B. H. Slicher van Bath, *Bevolking en Economie in Nieuw Spanje* (Amsterdam, 1981), 55, 228–30. For more recent figures I relied on tables or charts from various books and articles, especially Pierre Beaucage, "La condición indígena en Méx-ico," *Revista Mexicana de Sociología* 1 (1988): 197; and a map showing the distribution of Indian languages around 1940 in Pedro Carrasco, "Central Mexican Highlands: Introduction," in Robert Wauchope, ed., *Handbook of Middle American Indians* (Austin, TX, 1969), vol. 8, part 2, p. 580.

For much of the information on the recent history of native peoples in central Mexico, especially on the level of local communities, we must turn to social anthropology and other disciplines. Until just a few years ago, anthropologists dealing with contemporary native peoples in Meso-america tended to use the ethnographic present and dealt primarily with social organization on the village level, with rituals, and with such aspects of daily life as how people make a living. However, sometimes even classic ethnographic accounts may contain passages that afford useful glimpses of local history, sometimes going back to the end of the nine-teenth century. These include Oscar Lewis, *Life in a Mexican Village: Tepoztlan Restudied* (Urbana, IL, 1963), xxiv–xxv, 127; Hugo G. Nutini and Barry L. Isaac, *Los pueblos de Habla Nahuatl de la Región de Tlaxcala y Puebla* (Mexico, 1974); Barbara L. Margolies, *Princes of the Earth* (Washington, DC, 1975); Klaus Jäcklein, *Un Pueblo Popoloca* (Mexico, 1974), 73, who also included a key reference to interethnic relations among different native groups; and Alicja Iwanska, *Purgatory and Utopia* (Cambridge, 1971).

After 1970, an increasing number of anthropological studies became much more historically oriented. For central Mexico, and particularly the state of Morelos, I recommend Arturo Warman, . . . *Y venimos a contra-decir* (Mexico, 1976), 43, and Guillermo de la Peña, *A Legacy of Promises* (Austin, TX, 1981), chap. 7. Unfortunately, in both of these books, which are based on research in regions that have become predominantly mes-tizo, the issue of a separate native identity is mentioned only in passing. Other more general works, or those dealing with neighboring regions, that I found useful in writing about the history of native communities in central Mexico include Ronald Spores, "Multi-Level Government in Nineteenth Century Oaxaca," in *Five Centuries of Law and Politics in Central Mexico*, ed. Ronald Spores and Ross Hassig, (Nashville, 1984), 154; Laura Nader, *Harmony Ideology* (Stanford, CA, 1990), 2–3; and Lynn Stephen, "The Politics of Ritual: The Mexican State and Zapotec Autonomy, 1926–1989," in *Class, Politics and Popular Religion in Mexico and Central America*, ed. Lynn Stephen and James Dow (Washington, DC, 1990). Specific mention of *caciques* in indigenous communities is made in Paula L. W. Sabloff, "El caciquismo en el ejido postrevolucionario," *América Indígena* 37 (1977): 851–81; and Paul Friedrich, *The Princes of Naranja* (Austin, TX, 1986). Several more historically oriented works, especially those of Spores and Hassig, demonstrate the survival of old (colonial) forms of administration in native communities, a phenomenon already identified for other parts of Mexico and Guatemala.

Going back as early as the 1950s, a few anthropologists with a strong historical slant started develop systematic models that have influenced the way historians have interpreted native communities in the past. The best-known and most commonly cited are Gonzalo Aguirre Beltrán's *Regiones de refugio* (Mexico, 1967), and Eric Wolf's key article, "Closed Corporate Peasant Communities in Mesoamerica and Central Java," *Southwest Journal of Anthropology* 13 (1957): 1–18. These models of the traditional native community, and particularly various interpretations of the Mesoamerican civil-religious hierarchy, have since become the subject of a great deal of debate and controversy about their origins, contemporary functions, and survival. For examples from central Mexico, see Henry Torres Trueba, "Nahuat Factionalism," *Ethnology* 12 (1973): 463–74; Billie R. De Walt, "Changes in the Cargo System of Mesoamerica," *Anthropological Quarterly* 48 (1975): 101; Pierre Durand, *Nanacatlán (Société paysanne et lutte de classes au Mexique)* (Montreal, 1975); Lourdes Arizpe S., *Parentesco y Economía en una Sociedad Nahua* (Mexico, 1973), 126–33; and Danièle Dehouve, *El tequío de los santos y la competencia entre los mercaderes* (Mexico, 1976). For a description of one of the few surviving full-fledged civil-religious hierarchies in the highland plateau region, see Jay Sokolovsky, "Local Roots of Community Transformation in a Nahuatl Indian Village," *Anthropological Quarterly* 51 (1978): 1–26, which deals with a small village near Texcoco, not too far from Mexico City. For a comprehensive overview of much of this and other anthropological and sociological literature before 1980, see Cynthia Hewitt de

Alcántara, *Boundaries and Paradigms* (Leiden, 1982). Recently Eric Wolf has rethought his original model in his article "The Vicissitudes of the Closed Corporate Peasant Community," *American Ethnologist* 13 (1986): 325–29.

After 1980, the debates became more nuanced and there was more cross-fertilization among historians and anthropologists. For example, James Greenberg was the first to point out that there is a range of variation in the way the cargo system is used to redistribute resources. See his *Santiago's Sword: Chatino Peasant Religion and Economics* (Berkeley, CA, 1981), 21. In a similar vein, Schryer's *Ethnicity and Class Conflict* provides historical and ethnographic evidence that the classic form of the civil-religious hierarchy remained intact in both subsistence-oriented villages and those with a higher level of integration into the cash economy, an argument made earlier in Marie Noëlle Chamoux, *Indiens de la Sierra* (Paris, 1981), 193–96. Of particular interest to historians is the seminal article by John K. Chance and William B. Taylor, "Cofradias and cargos: an historical perspective on the Mesoamerican civil-religious hierarchy," *Journal of the American Ethnological Society* 12 (1985): 1–26. That article argues that this institution did not develop into its classic form until the first half of the nineteenth century, as opposed to the early colonial, as previously thought. In his subsequent work, focusing on the postrevolutionary period, Chance relies on much of the evidence provided by anthropological accounts to demonstrate that in native communities, the civil-religious hierarchy gradually became transformed into religious hierarchies. See his "Changes in Twentieth-Century Mesoamerican Cargo Systems," in *Class, Politics, and Popular Religion in Mexico and Central America*, ed. Lynn Stephen and James Dow (Washington, DC, 1990). Accounts of how this transformation resulted from the increasing interference of state officials in local community affairs, following the Mexican Revolution, appear in Danièle Dehouve, "L'Influence de l'état dans la transformation du système des charges d'une communauté indienne mexicaine," *L'Homme* 14 (1974): 87–108; and in Kate Young's doctoral dissertation at London University (1976). Lynn Stephen reinforces the argument in her "Mexican State and Zapotec Autonomy," in Stephen and Dow, *Class, Politics, and Popular Religion*, 46–49.

For a detailed analysis of the connections between participation in the civil-religious hierarchy and peasant militancy, see F. J. Schryer, John Fox, and Sally Humphries, "Variation in Peasant Militancy and the Civil-Religious Hierarchy in Tlalchiyahualica, Mexico," *European Review*

of Latin American and Caribbean Studies 47 (1989): 21–41. Other researchers are also addressing the long-neglected gender issue in relationship to
this topic, although not necessarily in the context of central Mexico. See
Lynn Stephen, "Mexican State and Zapotec Economy," and Holly H.
Matthews, "We are Mayordomos: a Reinterpretation of Women's roles
in the Mexican Cargo System," *American Ethnologist* 17 (1985): 285–301.
The interdisciplinary nature of much of the current research touching
on native issues, including such topics as civil rituals and other aspects of
popular culture, as well as music, can be gleaned from works dealing
with much broader issues and geographical areas. A good example is a
reader, *Rituals of Rule, Rituals of Rebellion* (Wilmington, DE, 1994), ed.
William H. Beezley, Cheryl English Martin, and William French, which
includes chapters on more specialized topics by some of the authors
already mentioned who have done work in central Mexico. A volume
entitled *Pilgrimage in Latin America*, ed. Ross Crumrine and Alan Mor-
inis (Westport, CT, 1991), likewise refers to both the historical and the
contemporary aspects of pilgrimages in central Mexico organized by
native people. That book includes a chapter by H. R. Harvey (pp. 91–
107) dealing with the Otomí of Huixquilucan and a conclusion by
Schryer (pp. 357–68), "Agrarian Conflict and Pilgrimage."
   Another research topic that has always had a direct bearing on the
history of native peoples in central Mexico is the survival and transformation of ethnic identities. Two quite different interpretations are represented by Judith Friedlander, *Being Indian in Hueyapan* (New York,
1975), chap. 4, and Rodolfo Stavenhagen, "Problemas étnicos y campesinos" (Mexico, 1980). Whereas the latter acknowledges assertive forms of
native identity, the former argues that any mention of a separate ethnic
group only plays into the hands of those who naively see "Indian" people
as poor and passive. She also makes a strong case for the artificial nature
of a separate ethnic identity among native peoples by arguing that most
of the "typical" Indian traits identified by anthropologists are of medieval
Spanish origin, quoting the earlier work done by scholars like Ralph
Beal; see Beal's "Notes on Acculturation," in *Heritage of Conquest*, ed.
Sol Tax (New York, 1968), 226–27. A number of anthropological case
studies also focus on specific variables that may have a bearing on ethnic
identity, such as Louis C. Faron, "Micro-Ecological Adaptations and
Ethnicity in an Otomi Municipio," *Ethnology* 19 (1980): 279–96; Lourdes
Arizpe, *Migración, etnicismo y cambio económico* (1978); and Chamoux's
Indiens. The latter work, dealing with a Nahua community in the Sierra

Norte de Puebla, traces the evolution of complex ethnic relations back
to the end of the nineteenth century (pp. 40–44). Likewise, Arizpe's
monograph, as well as those of Margolies and Iwanska mentioned earlier,
include valuable information on the salience of a separate ethnic identity
and cultural traits (including languages) among native peoples living
inside the boundaries of haciendas.

Anthropologists are also turning their attention to the emergence of
new forms of native identity among professionals of native background
and mestizo intellectuals who want to restore a "purer" form of Nahua
culture. See Alicja Iwanska, *The Truth of Others* (Cambridge, 1977), 6–7,
where she contrasts the attitudes and goals of such a new, indigenous
"elite" of professionals, mainly in the field of education, with a group of
nonindigenous Mexicans, sometimes labeled as "pseudo native intellectuals," who want to restore Mexico to its glorious Aztec past. In examining the creation of new forms of native identity by native intellectuals,
we cannot avoid examining the politics of education and the emergence
of a school of thought known as *indigenismo*. For a good summary of
earlier antecedents of native education policies of and how they developed in the nineteenth century, see Antonio Escobar Ohmstede, "La
educación para el indígena en la Colonia y el siglo XIX," in Carlos
García Mora, ed., *La Antropología en México, Panorama histórico*, vol. 3
(Mexico, 1990). Escobar shows how a special school for native education
in Mexico City, originally established for the sons of what remained of
the native nobility, was later transformed into an institution of both
elementary and higher education for native students from different
regions.

However, most of the literature on *indigenismo*, especially as it relates
to both rural development and more general educational policy, focuses
on developments in the twentieth century. See Christian Deverre and
Raul Reissner, "Les Figures de L'Indien-Problème: L'Evolution de
L'Indigénisme Mexicain," *Cahiers Internationaux de Sociologie* 68 (1980):
149–69; Miguel León-Portilla, "Etnías indígenas y cultura nacional mes-
tiza," *América Indígena* 39 (1979): 601–21; Rodolfo Stavenhagen, "El
Indigenismo en México: Ideológica y Política," *L'Etat et les Autochtones
en Amérique latine/au Canada* (Quebec, 1988); Henri Favre,
"L'Indigénisme mexicain," *Notes et études documentaires* (1976), 67–84.
For the official government view, see Nahmad Salomon, "Mexican Colonialism?" *Society* 19 (1981): 51–58. A more critical perspective, and one
representing the development of the polemics of ethnic opposition by

native professionals, can be found in Natalio Hernández and Francisco Gabriel Hernández, "La ANPIBAC y su política de participación," Documentos de la Segunda Reunión de Barbados *Indianidad y Descolonización en América Latina* (Mexico, 1979), 357–72. In the 1980s a host of other publications written by native professionals started appearing in Mexico. Although most deal with more general and national themes, some focus on the role of education in specific regions in central Mexico. One example is Claro Moreno G. and Botro Gazpar A.'s *Qué somos los maestros bilingües en el Valle de Mesquital?* (Mexico, 1982), the first of a series called *Etnolingüística* put out by INI/SEP.

Some scholars have paid paid more attention to the ambivalent position occupied by native intellectuals, including native schoolteachers, in the process of mediation between rural native communities and national state. See Marie Odile Marion Singer, *El movimiento campesino en Chiapas* (Mexico, 1983), 62; Robert Wasserstrom, *Class and Society in Central Chiapas* (Berkeley, CA, 1983), 176–77; Ulrich Köhler, "Ciclos de poder en una comunidad indígena de México: Política local y sus vínculos con la vida nacional," *América Indígena* 46 (1986): 435–51. For an analysis of the process whereby native scribes, trained by INI, became *caciques* in the 1950s and 1960s in another region of Mexico, namely Chiapas, see Jan Rus, "The 'Comunidad Revolucionaria Institucional': The Subversion of Native Government in Highland Chiapas, 1936–1968," in Gilbert Joseph and Daniel Nugent, eds., *Everyday Forms of State Formation: Revolution and the Negotiation of Rule in Modern Mexico* (Durham, NC, 1994), 284–98. For an example of the classroom itself, and village schools in central Mexico, as an arena of contestation as well as the building of hegemony before the introduction of the policy of *indigenismo*, see Elsie Rockwell, "Schools of the Revolution: Enacting and Contesting State Forms in Tlaxcala, 1910–1930," in Joseph and Nugent, *Everyday Forms of State Formation*, 170–208. Although Rockwell's study does not focus on ethnicity per se, her work provides insights into the tensions between non-native schoolteachers and Nahua students and elders (see especially pp. 195–96).

Historical linguists have added new insights into the dynamic of the relationship between ethnic identity retention and the survival of native languages. Claudio Lomnitz-Adler has shown how language retention and class factors are not as strongly linked as previously thought, despite the tendency for mainstream Mexicans to label all poor peasants as *Indios*.

See his "Clase y etnicidad en Morelos: Una nueva interpretación," in *América Indígena* 39 (1979): 460–65. Two articles by Jane Hill and Kenneth Hill focus on the disappearance of the Nahuatl language in Tlaxcala but also show how, despite a high level of linguistic assimilation, a separate "Indian" identity continues to be associated with the use of traditional dress and participation in *milpa* agriculture. See their jointly authored works "Mixed grammar, purist grammar, and language attitudes in modern Nahuatl," in *Language and Society* 9 (1980), 321–48, and "Language Death and Relexification in Tlaxcalan Nahuatl," *International Journal of Sociology and Language* 12 (1977): 67. The political dimensions of language and native identity during the Mexican Revolution have also been addressed by a well-known Mexican author more familiar for his work on the ancient Aztecs: Miguel León-Portilla, *Los Manifiestos en Nahuatl de Emiliano Zapata* (Mexico, 1978), 41–47. León-Portilla also criticizes the treatment of this topic in John Womack, *Zapata and the Mexican Revolution* (New York, 1969), 70–71.

Many other researchers, from a variety of disciplines, have also touched on the theme of native identity or language in central Mexico. I gained valuable insights from one scholar whose primary research interest was the role of women schoolteachers: Mary Kay Vaughan, "Economic Growth, Schooling and Literacy in Late Nineteenth Century Mexico," a paper presented at the International Symposium on Education and Economic Development held in Valencia, Spain (September 1989), 26. We cannot dismiss the historical implications of anthropological studies focusing on the migration of native men, and particularly women, to Mexico City. See Lourdes Arizpe, *Indígenas en la ciudad de México: el caso de las "Marías"* (Mexico, 1975); Carlos García Mora, "La migración indígena a la ciudad de México," *América Indígena* 37 (1977): 657–69; and Centro de Estudios de Población, *Caminantes de la Tierra Ocupada* (Pachuca, 1986).

Finally, readers should be aware that not everyone agrees on which of several regions discussed in this chapter should be subsumed under the label "central Mexico," especially in its northeastern quadrant. Some authors argue that it makes more sense to treat the Huasteca (with parts of Hidalgo and Veracruz, and even small sections of Puebla and Querétaro) as a separate cultural, socioeconomic, and geographical region, deserving its own history. See Angel Bassols Batalla, *Las Huastecas en el desarrollo regional de México* (Mexico, 1977), chap. 3. Much of that semitropical region, including the foothills of the Sierra Madre Oriental range, gradually merges into the higher mountains and meseta that constitute the heartland of central Mexico. A narrow band of Nahua communities going back to prehispanic times connects the Meztitlán region of Hidalgo with both northern Veracruz and southern San Luis Potosi, thus making it difficult to demarcate clearly the highland portion of central Mexico from its tropical lowland coastal hinterland. However, toward the west, the rest of the highland plateau of central Mexico has been more clearly separated from the Tarascan region, since well before independence, by a broad band of non-native communities. Similarly, the southern half of Veracruz is completely mestizo, while the Balsas Basin divides the native population of central Mexico from the much higher concentration of native peoples in Oaxaca and eastern Guerrero. See Pedro Carrasco, "Central Mexican Highlands," 579.

18

NATIVE PEOPLES OF THE GULF COAST FROM THE COLONIAL PERIOD TO THE PRESENT

SUSAN DEANS-SMITH

Since this chapter was written, several new studies have recently appeared, which include: Antonio Escobar Ohmstede, *De cabeceras á pueblos-sujetos. Las continuidades y transformaciones de los pueblos indios de las Huastecas hidalguense y veracruzana, 1750–1853* (Ph.D. diss., El Colegio de México, 1994), and "Del gobierno indígena al Ayuntamiento constitucional en las Huastecas hidalguense y veracruzana, 1780–1853"; *Mexican Studies–Estudios Mexicanos*, vol. 12, no. 1 (1996); David Skerrit, "Tres culturas: un nuevo espacio regional (el caso de la colonia francesa de Jicaltepec, San Rafael)," in Odile Hoffman and Emilia Velázquez eds., *Las llanuras costeras de Veracruz: la lenta construcción de regiones* (Jalapa: ORSTOM-Universidad Veracruzana, 1994); David Buckles and Jacques Chevalier, *A Land Without Gods: Process Theory, Maldevelopment and the Mexican Nahuas* (London: Zed Books, 1995); and Victoria Chenaut, *Aquellos que Vuelan: Los Totonacas en el Siglo XIX* (Mexico, 1995). I wish to thank Heather Fowler-Salamini for her valuable suggestions and comments on this chapter.

Perhaps one of the most memorable figures to emerge from Bernal Díaz del Castillo's *History of the Conquest of New Spain* (London, 1972) is the so-called Fat Chief from Cempoala, one of the first indigenous lords to meet with Hernando Cortez. One might be forgiven for assuming that such an encounter and its impact on the native peoples who inhabited and inhabit the region of the Gulf Coast of Mexico have stimulated considerable historical research. Unfortunately this has not been the case, and the rich literature on the pre-conquest societies of the Gulf Coast has yet to be matched by that for the post-conquest period. Although the region has long attracted archaeologists and anthropologists, we lack, for the most part, a substantial corpus of monographic ethnohistorical studies especially for the colonial period comparable to those, for example, of Nancy Farriss and Matthew Restall on the Maya or James Lockhart and his students on the Nahua. Historical studies of the region have tended to focus on its political and economic development particularly during the nineteenth and twentieth centuries and have ignored the very rich potential this area offers for our understanding of the cultural resilience of the indigenous peoples in the face of the dramatic, often catastrophic changes from the early sixteenth century up until the present day. Recent studies suggest, however, that the focus is shifting and that the indigenous communities are beginning to receive the attention they deserve. Nevertheless, although a few suggestive studies have recently examined central issues such as indigenous responses to political change (especially liberalism) in postindependence Mexico, patron–client relationships, agrarian relations, and rural rebellion, other equally important questions that concern land tenure and labor practices, tribute and taxation, the fate of the indigenous nobility, social organization, the shifting meanings of "Indian" identity and ethnicity, cultural change, family and domestic relationships, ritual and religion, gender roles, and the impact of environmental changes over the past four and a half centuries, have yet to receive systematic and substantial attention. The lack of substantial colonial ethnohistories for the region creates an immediate hindrance to tracing out changes and continuities across time and the differing experiences of the indigenous peoples within the region, and from a variety of perspectives, social and cultural as well as economic and political. This is compounded by the tendency for analyses of the indigenous communities in the nineteenth century to privilege class over ethnicity, with the unfortunate consequence that "Indians" disappear into "peasants." Simply put, what we lack is the ability to construct a narrative representing the voices and experiences of the indigenous peoples in a more substantive manner than is currently the case. Given the current status of the historiography of the indigenous peoples of the Gulf Coast region, therefore, it seemed premature to attempt a meaningful synthesis. Indeed, a review of the literature suggested that any synthesis as such would have yielded an eccentric blend of the general studies on the region, which tend to base their historical reconstructions on extrapolations from studies of the prehispanic cultures, agrarian histories of the Gulf Coast (as distinct from histories of the indigenous communities per se), and contemporary ethnography. I have chosen, therefore, to provide a bibliographical survey designed to orient the reader to a variety of "starting points" for thinking about the history of the indigenous peoples of the Gulf Coast and future research directions.

The Gulf Coast is defined as roughly coterminous with the modern day state of Veracruz, much of which formed part of the territory known as Totonacápan (Maps 18.1 and 18.2). This is defined by Isabel Kelly and Angel Palerm in *The Tajín Totonac, History, Subsistence, Shelter and Technology* (Washington DC, 1950) as follows: "This area lies along the Gulf Coast, roughtly from the Río Cazones, in the north, to the Río de la Antigua, in the south. Inland, it includes a large section of the eastern slopes of the Sierra Madre, as well as parts of the highlands of Puebla. The westernmost limits are represented by Pahuatlán . . . ; by several settlements in the vicinity of Acaxochitlán, on the present Hidalgo–Puebla frontier; and by Zacatlán, in modern Puebla. From Zacatlán, the boundary runs almost due east to Jalacingo . . . and Atzalan . . . , thence southeast to the Gulf, at the mouth of the Antigua" (p. 3). The major ethnic groups include the Huastec communities from the frontier with Tamaulipas to the Cazones River, Totonac communities from the Cazones River to the Nautla River; the eastern fringes of the Sierra Madre Oriental, that is, along the modern Puebla–Veracruz border, form the boundary of the highland Totonac communities, and Nahuas in the central area of Veracruz, primarily Zongólica. Finally, the southern zone, inhabited by the Zoque–Popoluca and Gulf Nahuas, includes the Papaloapan and Coatzacoalcos river valleys and the Santa Marta sierra, almost all of whom were paying tribute to the Triple Alliance when the Spaniards conquered Mexico. The Huasteca (derived from Cuextlan) is a zone of ecological complexity which includes portions of northern Veracruz, southern Tamaulipas, Hidalgo, Puebla, and San Luis Potosi. For the purposes of the review of the literature that follows, the main emphasis is on the modern-day geographical territory of Veracruz, although some references will be made to the adjacent zones in Puebla, Hidalgo, and San Luis Potosi that have bearing on the historical development of the indigenous peoples in the region.

Linguistically, Totonac was spoken in the sixteenth century across a wide area that stretched from the Sierra de Puebla to the coast, where it extended from the Río Cazones on the north to the Río de la Antigua on the south. The jurisdiction of Misantla seems to be the most extensive area of Totonac speech. The distribution of sixteenth-century Totonac and its Nahua bilingualism is discussed by Palerm and Kelly in *The Tajín*

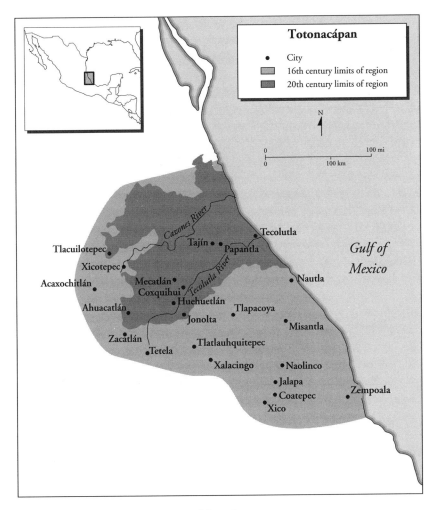

Totonacápan

• City

16th century limits of region

20th century limits of region

N

0   100 mi

0   100 km

Cazones River

Tecolutla

Tlacuilotepec

Tajín • • Papantla

Xicotepec

Gulf of Mexico

Acaxochitlán

Mecatlán •   • Nautla

Coxquihui   *Tecolutla River*

Ahuacatlán •   • Huehuetlán

Jonolta •   Tlapacoya

Zacatlán •   • Misantla

• Tetela   • Tlatlauhquitepec

• Xalacingo   • Naolinco

• Jalapa   Zempoala

• Coatepec

Xico

Map 18.1

Totonac. The Huastecs speak a form of Maya that according to lexico-statistics may have split from the rest of the Maya languages about 1500 B.C. The Huastecs, like the Totonacs, once occupied much more territory than they held in the sixteenth century. The major reason for territorial contraction appears to be the advance of Nahua groups including the later Aztec, which pushed the Huastecs northward. A good introduction to the pre-conquest period in this area is Richard E. W. Adams, *Prehis-*

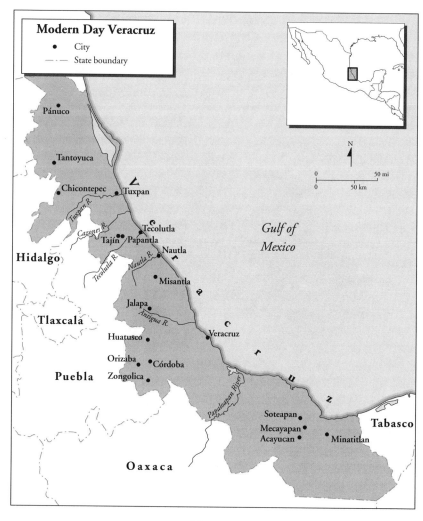

Map 18.2

toric Mesoamerica (Norman, OK, 1991), and José García Payón, "Evolución histórica del Totonacapán." In *Miscelánea Paul Rivet. Octagenario Dicata*, vol. 1 (Mexico, 1958), 443–53. Indispensable as reference guides to this region are the volumes on "Guide to Ethnohistorical Sources," vols. 12–16, *Handbook of Middle American Indians* (hereafter HMAI) (Austin, TX, 1973–75), and Peter Gerhard, *A Guide to the Historical Geography of*

New Spain (Cambridge, 1972). Although now somewhat dated, the following secondary studies remain invaluable as a starting point for anyone interested in the indigenous peoples of the Gulf Coast. On the Totonacs, the classic study by Isabel Kelly and Angel Palerm, *The Tajín Totonac, History, Subsistence, Shelter and Technology* (Washington DC, 1950), is indispensable. A shortened version of this discussion may be found in Isabel Kelly, "The Modern Totonac," in *Huastecos, Totonacos y Sus Vecinos,* ed. Ignacio Bernal and Eusebio Dávalos Hurtado (Mexico, 1953): 175–86, and H. R. Harvey and Isabel Kelly, "The Totonac," in *HMAI,* vol. 8, part 2, (Austin, TX, 1969). Also useful are Roberto Williams García, *Los Totonacos* (Mexico, 1962), Walter Krickeberg, *Los Totonacas: contribución a la etnografía histórica de la América Central* (Mexico, 1933), Luis Arturo González Bonilla, "Los totonacos," *Revista Mexicana de Sociología* 4, no. 3 (1942), and José Luis Melgarejo Vivanco, *Totonacapán* (Xalapa, Veracruz, 1943). Kelly and Palerm examine the Tajín Totonac from the pre-conquest period up until the late 1940s. Of particular interest is their discussion on the marked differences between highland and lowland cultures and on some of the cultural elements of the Totonacs, which they argue derive, possibly, more from the circum-Caribbean region than from Mesoamerica. A good introduction to the Huastec peoples is provided by Robert M. Laughlin, "The Huastecs," in *HMAI, Ethnology,* vol. 7, part 1, ed. Evon Z. Vogt (Austin, TX, 1969), Joaquín Meade, *La Huasteca Veracruzana,* 2 vols. (Mexico, 1962), *Huastecos, Totonacos y Sus Vecinos,* Roberto Williams-García, *Los Huaxtecos* (Mexico, 1961), Guy Stresser-Péan, "Les Indiens huasteques," in *Huastecos, Totonacos y sus Vecinos.* The Popoluca of southern Veracruz are discussed in George M. Foster, "The Mixe, Zoque, Popoluca," *HMAI,* vol. 7 (Austin, TX, 1969), "The Geographical, Linguistic, and Cultural Position of the Popoluca of Veracruz," *American Anthropologist* 45 (1943): 531–46, and his classic study, *A Primitive Mexican Economy* (1942; repr. Westport, CT, 1982), a case study of the Zoque-Popoluca of Soteapán. Also useful is Ralph L. Beals, "Southern Mexican Highlands and Adjacent Coastal Regions," in *HMAI,* vol. 7, and Howard Law, "Mecayapán, Veracruz: An Ethnographical Sketch" (unpublished M.A. thesis, University of Texas at Austin, 1960), who focuses on the Nahua or Nahuats of the Gulf Coast (so distinguished because they speak the "t" dialect as opposed to the "tl" dialect spoken in other areas such as the Central Valley of Mexico).

More recent studies on the region that also provide quite good overviews of the native peoples of the Gulf Coast include S. J. K. Wilkerson, "Ethnogenesis of the Huastecs and Totonacs" (Ph.D. diss., Tulane University, 1973), and "Huastec Presence and Cultural Continuity in North-Central Veracruz, Mexico," *Actes du XLII Congrès International des Américanistes* (1979), 41–55; Lorenzo Ochoa, ed., *Huastecos y Totonacos, una antología histórico cultural* (México, 1989); and Bernardo García Martínez, *Los pueblos de la Sierra. El poder y el espacio entre los indios del norte de Puebla hasta 1700* (Mexico, 1987). An outstanding study of the Huastec or Teenek is by Janice B. Alcorn, *Huastec Mayan Ethnobotany* (Austin, TX, 1984), which contains a wealth of information on the historical and contemporary social, economic, and cultural conditions of the Teenek Tsabaal in Veracruz and San Luis Potosi. On the Zoque-Popoluca see Guido Münch, *Etnología del istmo Veracruzano* (Mexico, 1982), *Medio ambiente y economía de los zoque-popolucas*, Dirección General de Culturas Populares (Mexico, 1983), and Richard Bradley, "Processes of Sociocultural Change and Ethnicity in Southern Veracruz, Mexico" (Ph.D. diss. University of Oklahoma, 1988). Bradley's study also examines the interaction between the Gulf Nahuat and the Sierra Popoluca.

It was during the Late Postclassic period in central Veracruz that the area known as El Totonacapán emerged. The major centers included Quauhtochco, which was conquered by the Aztec between A.D. 1450 and 1472, located in the Orizaba–Córdoba district. The most densely inhabited regions included Cempoala, the first Mesoamerican city to be seen by the Spaniards, near the coast with a regional population estimated at 250,000 and between 80,000 and 120,000 in the city itself. The center of Jalapa, farther inland, had about 120,000 inhabitants, while smaller centers such as Colipa had 24,000 and Papantla, 60,000. Descriptions of the pre-conquest relationships between the Totonacs and the Mexica, and the subjugation of the former by the Mexica may be found in Diego Durán, *Historia de las Indias de Nueva España e Islas de la Tierra Firme*, ed. Angel M. Garibay K., (Mexico, 1967); Jerónimo de Mendieta, *Historia eclesiástica Indiana*, ed. Joaquín García Icazbalceta, facsimile of the 1870 edition (Mexico, 1971); and Fray Alonso de Mota y Escobar, "Memorias del Obispado de Tlaxcala" [1609–21], in *Anales del Institutio Nacional de Antropología e Historia*, vol. 1 (1945). The accounts of Bernal Díaz del Castillo, *The Conquest of New Spain*, and to a lesser degree, Hernando Cortez, *Letters from Mexico*, trans. and ed. Anthony Pagden (New Haven and London, 1986) provide important insights into Totonac culture and society at the time of the Spanish invasion, despite their

Eurocentric biases. Scattered descriptions of the indigenous peoples of this region may be found in the works of the most important chroniclers of the colonial period. Of particular interest is Fray Bernardino de Sahagún, *Historia general de las cosas de Nueva España* (Mexico, 1956), especially Book 10. Also useful is Miguel León-Portilla, "Los huaxtecos según los informantes de Sahagún," *Estudios de Cultura Nahuatl* 5 (1966): 15–29. Bartolomé de Las Casas, *Apologética historia sumaria*, ed. (Mexico, 1967), ed. Edmundo O'Gorman (Mexico, 1967), contains descriptions of the Totonacs based on information provided by one of Hernando Cortez's pages who lived with them for four years. One of the most important descriptions of the Totonacs is to be found in Fray Juan de Torquemada, *Los veinte y un libros rituales y Monarquía indiana*, ed. Miguel León-Portilla, 7 vols. (Mexico, 1975–83). During his time as guardian of the Convent of Zacatlán in 1600, Torquemada began to learn Totonaca working with Don Luis, a Totonac *cacique*, as one of his major informants. For an introduction to codices that relate to the Veracruz region, see José Luis Melgarejo Vivanco, "Códices Veracruzanos," in *Huastecos, Totonacos y sus vecinos*. Two of the most important codices from the Borgia group have been identified as being from central-eastern Veracruz: the Codex Fejervary-Mayer and the Codex Laud are guides to ritual and ceremony as discussed by P. Anawalt, "Costume Analysis and the Provenience of the Borgia Group Codices," *American Antiquity* 46 (1981): 837–52. Elio Masferrer Kan, "Relaciones geográficas y memorias del Totonacapán. Siglos XVI y XVII," *Cuadernos del Norte de Veracruz*, nos. 15 and 16 (Mexico, 1982–83), and José Velasco Toro, *Fuentes para la historia del Totonacapán*, Cuadernos del IIESES, no. 6 (Xalapa, 1987), provide a good introduction to the *relaciones geográficas* related to this region. Particularly interesting is Diego Pérez de Arteaga, *Relación de Misantla* [1579], with "Foreword and Notes" to the *Relación* by David Ramírez Lavoignet (Mexico, 1962), who describes the subjugation of the Totonacs by the Aztecs in the Misantla region by 1194, and Totonac reactions to Cortez's arrival, as does Mota y Escobar "Memorias del Obispado de Tlaxcala," [1609–21]. Also of interest is the *Descripción del pueblo Gueytlalpa (Zacatlán, Xuxupango, Matlatlán, y Chila, Papantla) por el alcalde mayor Juan de Carrión, 30 de Mayo 1581*, Notas de José García Payón (Xalapa, 1965), which contains information on Papantla before the Spanish invasion, and the impact of Spanish conquest on the region. Additional primary sources for general descriptions of the area and its inhabitants during the colonial period include José Antonio de Villaseñor y

Sánchez, *Theatro americano: descripción de los reinos de la Nueva España y sus jurisdicciones* (Mexico, 1746); Francisco del Paso y Troncoso, *Papeles de la Nueva España* (Madrid, 1905), vols. 3 and 4, and *Epistolario de la Nueva España 1508–1818*, vol. 14 (Mexico, 1940); and Alexander von Humboldt, *Ensayo político sobre el reyno de la Nueva España* (Mexico, 1973).

The Gulf Coast populations were devastated by the Spanish presence, a combination of disease, Spanish atrocities, and enslavement and deportation to the Antilles, although the impact was by no means homogeneous throughout the region. The earliest accounts of the demographic decline of the Totonacs may be found in Díaz del Castillo, *The Conquest of New Spain*, and Mota y Escobar, "Memorias del Obispado de Tlaxcala," in *Anales del Instituto Nacional de Antropología e Historia*, vol. 1 (1945). Mota y Escobar estimates that at the time of Cortez's arrival there were 30,000 tributaries in Cempoala. By the mid-seventeenth century this tributary population had declined to 8. Laughlin, "The Huastecs," in *HMAL*, vol. 7 (Austin, TX, 1969), describes the drastic reduction of the Indian population in the area between 1526 to 1533 under the vicious governorship of Nuño de Guzmán. Alcorn provides a brief overview of the Spanish treatment of the Huastecs in *Huastec Mayan Ethnobotany*. Indigenous communities farther inland and away from the coast suffered less spectacular demographic changes, but population decline and dislocation occurred nevertheless. S. J. K. Wilkerson suggests that the area population around Papantla in 1610 was 2 percent of that immediately before the Conquest, in "Eastern MesoAmerica from Prehispanic to Colonial Times," *Actes de XLII Congrès International des Américanistes* (1979), 131–33. Good summaries of the demographic conditions of Totonacapán at the time of conquest and the sources for their reconstruction may be found in Kelly and Palerm, *The Tajín Totonac*, and Sherburne F. Cook and Lesley Byrd Simpson, *The Population of Central Mexico in the Sixteenth Century* (Berkeley, CA, 1948). See also Angel Palerm, "The Agricultural Basis of Urban Civilization in Mesoamerica," in *Ancient Mesoamerica: Selected Readings*, ed. John A. Graham (Berkeley, CA, 1970), 60–74, and José de Solís, "Congregación de los pueblos de los Agualulcos y provincia de Guazaqualco – 1599," *Boletín del Archivo General de la Nación* 16 (1945): 215–46, 429–79.

The impact of the Spanish invasion and conquest differed throughout the region, with the lowland coastal and central areas experiencing the most disastrous consequences of Spanish settlement and economic reorganization. Major *encomienda* grants included Cempoala, originally held by Cortez then passed on to Alvaro de Saavedra, and finally to Rodrigo de Albornoz. Díaz del Castillo describes the abuses of the inhabitants of Cempoala by Rodrigo de Albornoz in *The Conquest of New Spain*. Andrés de Tapia received Papantla in *encomienda*, which was inherited by his son and grandson. Misantla was originally granted to Luis de Saavedra. Zongólica was divided between two *encomenderos*, one of whom was Pedro de Sepúlveda. Most of the surviving Indian communities were under Crown control by the 1560s.

Spanish concentration on livestock and cattle raising was especially destructive since it destroyed the Indians' *milpas*. A good case study is Misantla, descriptions of which may be found in Mota y Escobar, "Memorias del Obispado de Tlaxcala"; Leonardo Pasquel, "Cronología de Misantla," *Revista Jarocha* 17 (1967): 3–15; David Ramírez Lavoignet, *Misantla* (Mexico, 1959); and "Notas históricas de Misantla," in *Huastecos, Totonacos y sus vecinos*. The Nahua communities of the Zongólica Sierra and in the temperate lands around Córdoba and Orizaba suffered from land expropriations since many of the lands were given in *mercedes* to Spanish settlers. For descriptions of land tenure and usage, and Spanish–Indian relations in this area see Gonzalo Aguirre Beltrán, *El Señorío de Cuauhtochco–Luchas agrarias en México durante el Virreinato* (Mexico, 1940; 3rd ed., 1991), and "Zongólica: Los marqueses de Sierra Nevada y las luchas agrarias durante la colonia," *La Palabra y el Hombre* (1987), 5–30. Manuel B. Trens, *Historia de Veracruz*, 6 vols. (Jalapa, 1947), provides a good overview of conflicts between indigenous communities and Spanish landowners. Odile Hoffman discusses land disputes between Spaniards and indigenous communities in the Coatepec region in the late eighteenth century in *Tierras y territorio en Xico, Veracruz* (Xalapa: Gobierno del Estado de Veracruz, 1992). Also useful is Renée González de la Lama, "Rebels and Bandits: Popular Discontent and Liberal Modernization in Nineteenth-Century Veracruz, Mexico," chap. 1 (Ph.D. diss., University of Chicago, 1990). Historians tend to agree that land was not the major source of conflict among indigenous communities and between Spaniard and Indian in the northern and southern parts of the region until the nineteenth century. See González de la Lama, "Rebels and Bandits," Michael Ducey, "From Village Riot to Regional Rebellion: Social Protest in the Huasteca, Mexico, 1760–1870" (Ph.D. diss., University of Chicago, 1993); Antonio Escobar Ohmstede, "Las Comunidades Indígenas en la Huasteca, 1750–1856. Cohesión y resistencia" (forthcoming); and Bradley, "Processes of Sociocultural Change and Ethnicity in Southern Veracruz, Mexico."

The Totonacs' experience seems comparable to that of the Maya and Mixtecs in that Spanish presence was less intrusive and transformative in the early post-conquest period, with significant changes in social and political organization occurring in the eighteenth century, although the Conquest clearly had a divergent impact on the Totonacs. The lowland communities saw their lands distributed in *mercedes* and used as cattle *estancias*, whereas the Totonacs of the sierra remained untouched because of difficulties of communication in their habitat regions and partly because the area did not have minerals or other products attractive to Spaniards. See Kelly and Palerm, *The Tajín Totonac*. The only products of importance were vanilla concentrated in and around Papantla, which the Spanish financed for export to Spain, and later tobacco, which resulted in the gradual commercialization of the local indigenous economies. A good overview of Papantla may be found in Adriana Chávez-Hita, *Papantla, Veracruz: imágenes de su historia* (Archivo General del Estado de Veracruz, 1990). Alexander von Humboldt describes the Totonacs' exploitation in the production of vanilla in the Intendancy of Veracruz, in his *Ensayo Político*. Susan Deans-Smith, *Bureaucrats, Planters, and Workers – the Making of the Tobacco Monopoly in Bourbon Mexico* (Austin, TX, 1992), examines the incorporation of the indigenous communities around Córdoba, Orizaba, Huatusco, and Zongólica into the operations of the Royal Tobacco Monopoly as small planters and field-workers for Spanish and mestizo planters. A good complement is Michael Ducey's analysis of the consequences of the *exclusion* of indigenous communities from monopoly operations, particularly around Papantla, in "From Village Riot to Regional Rebellion: Social Protest in the Huasteca, Mexico, 1760–1870." Both studies show the ability of the indigenous communities affected either to benefit from, or to mobilize against, state intrusion in the region by means of petitions and use of the Spanish judicial system, flight, and riot. George Foster "The Mixe-Zoque Popoluca," in *HMAI*, vol. 7 (Austin, TX, 1969), Münch, *Etnología del Istmo Veracruzano*, and Bradley, "Processes of Sociocultural Change and Ethnicity in Southern Veracruz," argue that it was not until after the Mexican Revolution that significant contact between the Sierra Popoluca and surrounding non-Popoluca peoples occurred. For the northern and southern regions of Veracruz, the Liberal reforms of the nineteenth century, the Mexican Revolution, and rapid incursions of the capitalist development in the region appear to have had more serious consequences for the indigenous communities and their autonomy than did the Spanish Conquest.

The process of evangelization in the Gulf Coast region and indigenous responses to Catholicism during the colonial period are poorly studied. Robert Ricard in his now classic but much critiqued study, *The Spiritual Conquest of Mexico* (Berkeley, CA, 1966), conceded that Catholicism remained weak in certain regions of Mexico, the Gulf Coast being one of them. The idolatry trial of Don Juan, the *cacique* of Matlatlán in 1540, who conducted traditional native religious ceremonies in which the entire village participated, provides evidence of the early resilience of native religion. See "Proceso seguido por Fray Andrés de Olmos en contra del cacique de Matatlán," in *Procesos de indios idólotras y hechiceros*, Publicaciones del Archivo General de la Nación, vol. 3 (Mexico, 1912), 205–15. Torquemada also tells of the destruction of an idol worshiped by the Totonacs close to Zacatlán, *Monarquía indiana*, and Bartolomé de Las Casas, in *Apologética historia sumaria*, discusses the persistence of Totonac religious rites and customs despite the destruction of their idols by Cortés. Kelly and Palerm in *The Tajín Totonac* argue that conversion to Catholicism was limited compared to other regions and cite the case of Misantla, which was abandoned by missionaries as early as 1579. Mota y Escobar's "Memorias del Obispado de Tlaxcala" provides fascinating insights into the erratic process of Catholic conversion and the retention of traditional beliefs by the indigenous communities. As the Bishop of Tlaxcala, he traveled to Papantla in 1610 and commented on the "nonconformity" of the Totonacs, who complained of the exhorbitant quantity of provisions they were expected to provide to the priests daily. Tajín continued to be used as a place of worship. As further evidence of the resilience of native practices, a bilingual confessional was published in 1752 (republished in 1837) and allegedly distributed throughout the region of Totonacapán in order to stamp out idolatry. See Francisco Domínguez, "Doctrina de la lengua de Naolingo (Confesionario Bilingue)," in *Arte de Lengua Totonaca*, ed. Joseph Zambrano Bonilla (Puebla, 1752), and *Autor Desconocido – Arte de la lengua Totonaca*, facsimile edition, with an Introduction by Norman A. McQuown (Mexico, 1990). Humboldt refers to the "idolatrous" practices among the Totonacs, in *Ensayo político* and in *Papeles de la Nueva España*, ed. Francisco del Paso y

Troncoso, 2nd series, vol. 5 (1905), 168. Gonzalo Aguirre Beltrán provides an intriguing discussion of religious syncretism in his study of *Zongólica. Encuentro de dioses y santos patronos* (Mexico, 1962).

Although the notarial archives of Orizaba contain scattered documents written in Nahuatl (mainly for the eighteenth century), one of the obstacles to deepening our understanding of indigenous responses to Spanish colonialism and to changes and continuities in land tenure, family and social organization, ritual, and cultural practices in the Gulf Coast region may be the paucity of documents available in the native languages. Even so, scholars are beginning to analyze in creative and imaginative ways issues such as constructions of cultural and ethnic identity and how they shape indigenous responses and strategies to defend their communities. One of the few studies that specifically examines the question of ethnicity and the changing constructions of ethnic boundaries among the indigenous communities during the colonial period is Elio Masferrer Kan, "Las condiciones históricas de la etnicidad entre los totonacas," *América Indígena* 46, no. 4 (1986). He examines the "Nahuatlization" of the Totonacs and the ethnic strategies used by them in their interaction and confrontation with the Spanish and mestizos in the colonial and republican periods. Masferrer's study examines how the indigenous communities used the local political and judicial bodies to their advantage and to protect their communities and lands.

The eighteenth century witnessed considerable economic growth in Mexico, a characteristic of which was the incorporation of peripheral regions into a wider market economy, and an increase in the power of the colonial state. Such growth resulted in increased conflict between Spanish and indigenous communities, and the Gulf Coast is no exception, although the conflict was confined to particular zones. Indigenous communities defended themselves against an increasingly interventionist state, abusive local officials, and increased taxation, through negotiation, political alliances, and popular resistance. Some of the best research we have for this period focuses on resistance and rebellion of the indigenous peoples of the region. For a discussion of the increase in indigenous protest in the eighteenth century, particularly the Papantla revolt of 1767, see Ducey's dissertation on the Veracruz Huastec, "From Village Riot to Regional Rebellion," González de la Lama, "Rebels and Bandits," and Joaquín Meade, *La Huasteca Veracruzana.* Escobar Ohmstede, "Las Comunidades Indígenas en la Huasteca, 1750–1856. Cohesión y resistencia," documents fifteen indian rebellions in the jurisdictions of Papantla, Chicontepec, and Huejutla, all of which would remain centers of rebellion in the nineteenth century. Ducey, Escobar Ohmstede, and González de la Lama argue that although external influences such as fiscal reforms (the establishment of the tobacco monopoly and more efficient tax collection) placed greater pressure on the indigenous peasantry, local exploitation by merchants, the *repartimientos de comercio*, power conflicts between local personalities (Indian and Spanish), and manipulation of local elections contributed significantly to the volatility of some communities, particularly Papantla, which experienced rebellion in 1764, 1767, and 1787. Ducey argues that another distinctive feature of the Huastec indigenous communities is the incorporation of outsiders into indigenous village struggles by villagers who actively recruited Spanish allies to further their own factional interests. This differs from indigenous strategies in the Guadalajara region, for example, which attempted to counteract internal divisions in the face of external pressure or agency. Ducey suggests that an important topic of future research is the intensification of internal stratification within the villages and its consequences for rural rebellion and retention of cultural identity. For discussion of why it was the most prosperous pueblos that revolted rather than those undergoing the greatest stress, see González de la Lama, "Rebels and Bandits." On rebellions in the center and south of the region, primarily Misantla and Acayucán, see González de la Lama, "Rebels and Bandits," Leonardo Pasquel, "Cronología de Misantla" in *Revista Jarocha* 17 (1967), and Angel Miguel Cuevas y Pérez, *Mizantla, Historia y Leyenda* (Jalapa, 1984). The 1787 uprising in Acayucán is also discussed by Brian R. Hamnett in *Roots of Insurgency. Mexican Regions, 1750–1824* (Cambridge, 1986), 79–80, who stresses the onerous demands of the *repartimiento*, imposed by the *alcaldes mayores* in partnership with merchants from Puebla, as a major cause of the rebellion. What these case studies suggest is that the Indian revolts of the Gulf Coast region are typical of late colonial indigenous rebellion in general in that they focused on local grievances not Spanish rule, yet are distinguished by the fact that many of the rebellions did not focus on land as a central issue.

Acayucán, Misantla, and Papantla became important bases for insurgency activity during the Mexican War of Independence from Spain and remained centers of rural discontent in the nineteenth century. In Papantla, Serafín Olarte supported independence in 1813 in the sierra of Coxquihui, commanded a rebel army of 400 Totonac Indians and resisted at least seven royalist attacks during a four-year period. See Margarita Olivo

Lara, "Serafín Olarte," in *Revista Jarocha* 34–35 (1964–65): 42–43, Juan Zilli, "Tres Jefes insurgentes," in Carmen Blázquez, *Veracruz, textos para su historia*, 145, as well as discussions in Ducey, "From Village Riot to Regional Rebellion," Escobar Ohmstede, "Las Comunidades Indígenas en la Huasteca," and González de la Lama, "Rebels and Bandits." Papantla is a good example of the dominance of particular families in local indigenous politics, in this case the Olarte family. Serafín fought against the royalists and his son Mariano continued the conflict that culminated in the rebellion of 1836–38.

The Gulf Coast continued to be a volatile region in the nineteenth century as Indian communities responded aggressively to economic and political reform, politically divided elites, and a weak state. By 1800, 91 percent of Veracruz's population were tribute-paying Indians (see John Tutino, *From Insurrection to Revolution* [Princeton, NJ, 1986], 393). As in other regions, the difference between the colonial period and the postindependence period lies in the scope and scale of the rebellions, some of which developed into regional rather than local movements. The specific responses in the Gulf Coast depended on the regional differences that continued to be quite marked by the beginning of the nineteenth century, distinguished by the pace of agrarian commercialization in the region, land tenure, and degree of incorporation in, or marginalization from, the local and regional economies. González de la Lama, "Rebels and Bandits," gives a good description of the ecological and economic zonation of the region.

Although they do not deal specifically with the indigenous communities of the regions and as individual actors, the following descriptions by nineteenth-century writers provide useful information on demographics and social and economic conditions: Joaquín Arroniz, "La costa de Sotavento (1869)," *Boletín de la Sociedad de Geografía y Estadística de la República Mexicana* 1, no. 7 (1869): 534–32; José María Bauza, "Bosquejo geográfico y estadístico del partido de Papantla" (1845), in *Boletín de la Sociedad Mexicana de Geografía y Estadística* 5 (1857); Guillermo Prieto, *Excursión a Jalapa en 1875 – Cartas al nigromante* (Mexico, 1968); Manuel de Segura, "Apuntes estadísticos del distrito de Orizaba formados en el año de 1839," *Boletín de la Sociedad Mexicana de Geografía y Estadística* 4 (1854): 3–71; Mariano Ramírez, "Estadística del partido de Córdoba formada en 1840," *Boletín de la Sociedad Mexicana de Geografía y Estadística* 4 (1854): 73–112; Carl Sartorius, "Memoria sobre el estado de la agricultura en el partido de Huatusco (1865)," *Boletín de la Sociedad Mexicana de Geografía y Estadística* (February 1870): 141–56, (March 1870): 157–97; Andrés Iglesias, *Soteapán en 1856* (Mexico, 1973); José María Iglesias, *Acayucán in 1831* (Mexico, 1966); *Noticias estadísticas de la Huasteca y de una parte de la Sierra Alta en el año de 1853* (Mexico, 1869). Alfred H. Siemens, *Between the Summit and the Sea: Central Veracruz in the nineteenth Century* (Vancouver, 1990), examines foreign travelers' accounts of Veracruz in the nineteenth century from their disembarkation at the port of Veracruz and their journey along the Veracruz–Jalapa road and on to Mexico City. Useful references and synopses are included of less well known European observers of Mexico in the nineteenth century, such as Carl Wilhem Koppe, for example, who discusses the Totonacs of Misantla in his *Mexikanische Zustände aus den Jahren 1830 bis 1832* (Stuttgart and Augsburg, 1837). Their "roadside ethnography" provides insights into the perceptions, largely negative, of the indigenous peoples in general (particularly vituperative is Carl Sartorius in his *Mexico About 1850* [Stuttgart: Brockhaus, 1961]. Also helpful for official reports is Carmen Blázquez, ed., *Gobierno del Estado de Veracruz: Informes de sus gobernadores, 1826–1986,* 22 vols. (Mexico, 1986).

For secondary sources that provide a broader context for understanding the political and economic shifts and pressures faced by indigenous communities in the nineteenth century, see Arthur Schmidt, "The Social and Economic Effect of the Railroad in Puebla and Veracruz, Mexico, 1867–1911" (Ph.D. diss., Indiana University, 1974); Eugene Wiemers, "Agriculture and Enterprise in Nineteenth-Century Mexico: Córdoba and Orizaba at Mid-Century" (Ph.D. diss., University of Chicago, 1988); Ricardo Corzo Ramírez y Carmen Blázquez Domínguez, "La iglesia en Veracruz: inicios de la restauración republicana, 1867–1869," *La palabra y el hombre* 72 (1989): 205–51; and Carmen Blázquez Domínguez, *Veracruz liberal, 1858–1860* (Mexico, 1986).

Intensely affected by state-directed modernization in the nineteenth century, the inhabitants of Veracruz in general and the indigenous population in particular were subjected to division of communal lands, compulsory public education, centralization of political power, anticlerical policies, prohibition of public processions, secularization of marriage, and fiscal reforms. The volatile intermingling of liberalism and Catholic conservatism, ethnicity and nationalism, in combination with agrarian commercialization and state centralization, not surprisingly found their manifestations in an increasingly rebellious indigenous peasantry in various parts of the Gulf Coast. Popular mobilization and resistance ex-

pressed by indigenous leaders and communities frequently became associated with wider, national movements and multiclass coalitions as
Mexican elites drew on Indian support in the civil wars that racked
Mexico in the nineteenth century. Local grievances focused on taxation,
conscription, clerical interference with popular religion, the liberal project of disentailment, and imposition of unwanted officials. A good
introduction to some of the most important issues is Guy P. C. Thomson, "Agrarian Conflict in the Municipality of Cuetzalán: The Rise and
Fall of 'Pala' Agustín Dieguillo, 1861–1894," *Hispanic American Historical
Review* 71, no. 2 (1991), who explores the significance of the Nahua leader
Francisco Agustín Dieguillo from Cuetzalán in the Sierra de Puebla, and
his attempts (largely successful) to prevent encroachment by non-Indians
on the common lands of the municipality of Cuetzalán, originally part
of Totonacápan. Thomson points out that although the Cuetzaltecos are
Nahua linguistically, "they resemble their Totonac neighbors to the
north in many aspects of family organization (a strong patriarchal and
patrilocal pattern), dress . . . and ceremonial life (the dance of the *vola-
dores*). In spite of the cultural receptiveness of Nahua Cuetzaltecos, and
of continuous commercial exchange and agricultural cooperation, there
is still very little intermarriage between mountain Nahua and lowland
Totonacs" (p. 210). This particularly nuanced discussion examines how
Pala Agustín followed a dual strategy that reflected the two political
worlds in which Indians moved in nineteenth-century Mexico and that
represented his support of the Liberal cause in the Sierra as well as for
the preservation of local Indian autonomy. It highlights several research
questions that need to be systematically pursued, especially for the Gulf
Coast region in the nineteenth century. Among these are the extent to
which indigenous peoples were able to shape the process of community
land privatization through a mixture of clientelism and collective action,
the local repercussions of the replacement of the *pueblos de indios* by new
political institutions established in the late eighteenth century at the
district and provincial level (*jefe político*, intendant, subdelegate, *ayuntamientos constitucionales*), and the broader significance of indigenous
movements as reflecting a particular type of Liberal clientelism. As
Thomson suggests, "The attraction of Indians to certain aspects of Mexican Liberalism, and their willingness to 'pay tribute' to the Liberal cause,
suggest that a revision is needed for the still prevalent view that mid-
nineteenth-century liberalism was an urban-based, middle-class, minority
movement, which was anathema to rural, community-based, and (espe-

cially) Indian Mexico" (p. 209). A good complementary study to Thomson is by Pablo Valderrama Rouy y Carolina Ramírez Suárez, "Resistencia étnica y defensa del territorio en el Totonacapan serrano: Cuetzalan en el siglo XIX," in Antonio Escobar O., ed., *Indio, nación y comunidad en el México del siglo XIX* (Mexico, 1993). Antonio Escobar Ohmstede analyzes the ways in which indigenous communities in the Veracruz and Hidalgo Huasteca used *condueñazgo* (an intermediate form of division of land and an alternative to individual partition) to conserve their communal space and how they were able to achieve relative autonomy in their dealings with local *ayuntamientos*. He also emphasizes the differences between the composition of the *condueñazgos* in Papantla, which was composed mainly of Indians, and those in the Huasteca (both Hidalgo and Veracruz), many of which had a multiracial and multiethnic population. See "Los condueñazgos indígenas en las Huastecas Hidalguense y Veracruzana: ¿Defensa del espacio comunal?" in Antonio Escobar O., ed., *Indio, nación y comunidad en el México del siglo XIX* (Mexico, 1993).

González de la Lama, "Rebels and Bandits: Popular Discontent and Liberal Modernization in Nineteenth-Century Veracruz, Mexico," and Michael Ducey, "From Village Riot to Regional Rebellion," which focuses on the Veracruz Huasteca, examine indigenous peasant rebellions in nineteenth-century Veracruz. González de la Lama is particularly sensitive to the ethnic dimensions of these rebellions, especially with regard to the Totonac and Popoluca struggles and the relationship among culture, ritual, and rebellion, and argues that the cause of the majority of the revolts was not the distribution of land but was the combination of liberal reforms, primarily secularization, subdivision of communal lands, imposition of political chiefs, and compulsory primary education. Also useful is his "Revueltas populares y gavillas en Veracruz: 1867–1905," *La Palabra y el Hombre*, 69 (1989); Ducey, "Tierras comunales y rebeliones en el norte de Veracruz antes del porfiriato, 1821–1880: El proyecto liberal frustrado," *Anuario*, vol. 6 (Jalapa, 1989); Chávez-Hita, *Papantla*; and José Velasco Toro, "Indigenismo y rebelión Totonaca en Papantla 1885–1886," *América Indígena* 39 (1979).

One of the largest insurrections that began in Papantla, led by Mariano Olarte, a protégé of Antonio López de Santa Anna, lasted for two years between 1836 and 1838 and spread throughout the geographical limits of the Papanteca region and to those areas of Puebla and Hidalgo where Totonac ethnicity remained strong. The causes of the insurrection included expansion of livestock raising at the expense of the lands on which vanilla and maize were produced, frequent abuses by the local Spaniards who monopolized vanilla production, electoral irregularities of 1834–35, and the prohibition of religious fiestas. Olarte declared the *Plan de Papantla*, the text of which demonstrates how a local movement may be linked to national politics given the federalist character of the plan and its emphasis on electoral and fiscal matters. For discussion of this movement, see Jorge Flores D., *La revolución de Olarte en Papantla, 1836–1838* (Mexico, 1938), 73–81, David Ramírez Lavoignet, *Papantla de Olarte* (Xalapa, 1981), Ducey, "Tierras comunales y rebeliones," José Luis Blanco Rosas, "Territorio y política," in *Coxquihui, Chumatlán y Zozocalco: tres municipios totonacas del estado de Veracruz (Historia y Realidad Actual: 1821–1857)* (Xalapa, 1987), and Trens, *Historia de Veracruz*. The importance of ethnic identity in the Olarte rebellion is also discussed by Chávez-Hita, *Papantla*, and González de la Lama, "Rebels and Bandits," both of whom examine the importance of the religious syncretism of the Totonacs and the relationship between ritual and revolt. Also useful is Elio Masferrer, "Los factores étnicos en la rebelión Totonaca de Olarte en Papantla (1836–1838)," *Cuicuilco* 14–15 (July–December 1984): 24–32, and "Movimientos sociales en el Totonacapan (siglo XIX)," in *México Indígena* 16 (1987): 24–31.

Leticia Reina, *Las rebeliones campesinas en México, 1819–1906* (Mexico, 1984), is a good overview of the nineteenth-century rebellions in the region, including the Olarte rebellion, as well as the uprisings among the Totonac and Nahua communities in the Huasteca Veracruzana between 1845 and 1849 led by Luciano Velázquez, Juan Nepomuceno Llorente, and Manuel Herrera. She also reprints the texts of the various "plans" that emerged from many of the movements, notably the *Plan de Papantla*, 1836, the *Plan de Tantoyuca*, 1846, and the *Plan de Amatlán* of 1847. The *"guerra de castas"* that erupted in the Huasteca between 1845 and 1849 focused on the pueblo of Amatlán and its conflict with the local hacienda, a conflict that resulted in the granting of lands to the Indian peasantry of Amatlán. See Escobar Ohmstede, "Las Comunidades Indígenas en la Huasteca, 1750–1856," and Moisés González Navarro, "Las guerras de castas," *Historia Mexicana* 26 no. 1 (1976): 70–126.

The second half of the nineteenth century saw indigenous resistance increase in the face of aggressive agrarian commercialization, acquisition of communal property, tax increases, and impositions by the authorities. Rebellions erupted in Misantla, Orizaba, and Minatitlán in the 1850s and

1860s provoked by the Ley de Sorteo, abusive local authorities, and high prices for flour and meat. Organized indigenous resistance produced the *Nuevo Plan de Tantoyuca*, (1856) authored by Rafael Díaz, the text of which is also reprinted in Reina, *Las rebeliones campesinas en México*. González de la Lama, "Rebels and Bandits," notes the radical nature of the *Nuevo Plan de Tantoyuca*, which called for a war on private property. The Ley de Sorteo of 1853, an aggressive version of the draft, and a cholera epidemic in 1857 contributed further to social dislocation and disorganization, which in 1853 generated considerable resistance from the Totonacs in Misantla, who sought alliances with other Totonac communities. See González de la Lama, "Rebels and Bandits," and Reina, *Las rebeliones campesinas en México*, for discussion of the significance of these movements and their consequences for the indigenous communities.

The last quarter of the nineteenth century proved particularly volatile as the region underwent major economic transformation and reorientations as a result of three major developments: exploration for oil, the expansion of commercial agriculture, especially coffee, and development of the railroads. Governors of Veracruz turned their attention to the fundamental problem of privatizing Indian lands, no longer occupied with the North American invasions of 1847 and the French invasion of 1862. Land distribution within the state of Veracruz did not begin until the 1880s and 1890s, except in the central parts of the region. In the 1880s a series of revolts occurred that were directly related to the issue of land distribution, especially in the case of Papantla, which represented the climax of indigenous resistance among the Totonacs. Repeated petitions to prevent division of their lands by the Totonacs to the state congress were denied, and in 1885 a process of land division known as *condueñazgo* began. The arbitrariness with which the division of lands was carried out, an unusual drought that resulted in a scarcity of grain, increases in taxes, and renewed attempts to impose the anticlerical law of 1874 calling for the repression of religious and ceremonial celebrations (especially the prohibition of public processions) provoked general discontent. The leader of the 1885 rebellion, Antonio Díaz Manfort, also known as the "holy doctor," and about whom very little is known, wielded considerable influence among the indigenous peoples of Jalacingo, Misantla, and Papantla. The rebellion did not last long and was quickly repressed. Among Díaz Manfort's demands were abolition of civil marriage, recognition of Catholic ritual and procession, and the defense of *fueros*. For a discussion of the significance of these demands in relation to the ethnic dimensions of this rebellion, see González de la Lama, "Rebels and Bandits," and his "Los papeles de Díaz Manfort: una revuelta popular en Misantla (Veracruz), 1885–1886," *Historia Mexicana* 39, no. 2 (1989): 475–521. Attempts to centralize political power provoked several revolts that focused on political (compulsory education as well as taxation) rather than agrarian issues, and that were directed at the local *jefes políticos* and against abuses in local elections. For the Papantla region, see José Velasco Toro, "La política desamortizadora y sus afectos en la región de Papantla, Ver.," *La Palabra y el Hombre* 72 (1989): 137–62, and "Indigenismo y rebelión totonaca en Papantla 1885–1886," *América Indígena*, vol. 39 (1979). Also useful is Sergio Florescano Mayet, "El proceso de destrucción de la propiedad comunal de la tierra y la rebelión indígena en Veracruz, 1826–1910," *La Palabra y el Hombre* 52 (1984).

Assessments of the Zoque–Popoluca and Nahuat communities in southern Veracruz can be found in Bradley, "Processes of Sociocultural Change and Ethnicity in Southern Veracruz, Mexico," who argues that despite expansion in agrarian commercialization it was not until after the French invasion that land disputes became common and led to numerous rebellions by the Sierra Popoluca. See also Félix Báez-Jorge, *Los Zoques–Popolucas* (1973), and González de la Lama, "Rebels and Bandits." Reina, *Las rebeliones campesinas en México, 1819–1906*, discusses the rebellions in the canton of Acayucán between 1881 and 1884, which focused on the dispossession of lands and attempts to regain them by the indigenous peasantry and on the demand for the abolition of personal tribute. Also useful for the Acayucán and Minatitlán region is Elena Azaola Garrido, *Rebelión y derrota del magonismo agrario* (Mexico: SEP, 1982).

Good starting points for discussions of indigenous concepts of community and ethnic identity during the nineteenth century can be found in Victoria Chenaut, "Comunidad y Ley en Papantla a fines del siglo XIX," in *La costa totonaca: cuestiones regionales II* (Mexico, 1987), "Costumbre y resistencia étnica. Modalidades entre totonacas," in *Entre la ley y la costumbre. El derecho consuetudinario* (Mexico, 1990), and "Delito y ley en la huasteca veracruzana (segunda mitad del siglo XIX)," in *La Palabra y el Hombre*, no. 69 (Xalapa, 1989), a particularly interesting analysis in which she compares the Nahuatl community of Chicontepec and Totonac community of Papantla, their forms of ethnic resistance, and their relationship to the state between the 1870s and 1890s. See also Pablo Valderrama Rouy and Carolina Ramírez Suárez, "Resistencia étnica y defensa del territorio en el Totonacápan serrano: Cuetzalán en el siglo XIX," in Antonio Escobar O., ed., *Indio, nación y comunidad en el México del siglo XIX.* Gender studies are virtually nonexistent for this period, as are analyses of kinship and domestic relations. One suggestive study containing data relevant to family relations, marriage, and divorce in Papantla between 1869 and 1927 is Victoria Chenaut, "La costa totonaca: divorcio y sociedad en el Porfiriato," in Jesús Ruvalcaba and Graciela Alcalá, eds., *Huasteca I. Espacio y tiempo, mujer y trabajo* (Mexico: CIE-SAS, 1993). Chenaut argues that of thirty-eight cases of divorce in the judicial district of Papantla, 47.36 percent involved petitions from indigenous women against their husbands for reasons of ill-treatment or infidelity. Furthermore, these cases often involved the family group as a whole in that recently married women in accordance with patrilocal patterns moved in with their husbands' families, only to experience tensions and conflicts with family members.

Between 1910 and 1918 many Totonac villages were caught up in the Mexican Revolution, and between 1920 and 1930 many of them participated in the agrarian movement, which had particularly vicious repercussions in the southern part of Totonacapán, where more than 50,000 peasants in the region were assassinated. See González de la Lama, "Rebels and Bandits," and Leonardo Pasquel, "Cronología de Misantla," *Revista Jarocha* 17 (1967): 3–15. One of most significant results of Sierra Popoluca reactions to revolutionary activity in southern Veracruz was the breakup of the Sierra Popoluca nucleus and the establishment of two quite distinct Sierra Popoluca locales, to the west and the east of Soteapán. Nahuat reaction to the Mexican Revolution is characterized as passive resistance partly, or so Bradley argues, so as not to provoke the Sierra Popoluca. See Bradley's discussion in "Processes of Sociocultural Change and Ethnicity in Southern Veracruz, Mexico," and George Foster, *A Primitive Economy.* González de la Lama in "Rebels and Bandits" argues that since the revolution the Sierra Popoluca have continued to form satellite communities throughout the eastern Tuxtlas. Useful for a wider context of the regional responses to the Mexican Revolution and popular mobilization is Alan Knight, *The Mexican Revolution,* 2 vols. (Cambridge, 1986). Knight's concept of "ecology of popular revolt," which, he argues, needs to be combined with a consideration of the cultural and ethnic constructions present in the communities, is a particularly helpful model to follow for future research on indigenous communities' diverse responses to revolutionary upheaval in this region. Also useful for broad discussions of agrarian radicalism in the region during and after the Mexican Revolution are Romana Falcón, and Soledad García Morales, *La semilla en el surco, Adalberto Tejeda y el radicalismo en Veracruz, 1883–1960* (Mexico, 1987); Leonardo Pasquel, *La rebelión agraria de Acayucán en 1906* (Mexico, 1976); Romana Falcón, *El agrarismo en Veracuz. La etapa radical, 1928–1935* (Mexico, 1977); Heather Fowler Salamini, *Agrarian Radicalism in Veracruz, 1920–1938* (Lincoln, NE, 1978); Ivonne Carrillo Dewar, "La lucha por la tierra de las comunidades indígenas en el norte de Veracruz," in Olivia Domínguez Pérez ed., *Agraristas y agrarismo.* (Xalapa: Gobierno del Estado, 1992), and David Skerrit, *Una historia agraria en el centro de Veracruz, 1850–1940* (Xalapa: Universidad Veracruzana, 1989).

In the late twentieth century an estimated 117,533 Totonac speakers live in Veracruz, approximately 60,000 Teenek speakers live among five Veracruz *municipios* and eight San Luis Potosi *municipios*, and an estimated 16,500 Popolucas and 13,500 Nahuas continue to adapt to changing circumstances, often at the expense of and erosion of their own cultural identity. Particularly striking in studies of contemporary indigenous communities is the focus on internal strains within the communities in combination with external pressures. The economic development of the Gulf Coast in the twentieth century and its consequences for indigenous culture and survival is an area requiring extensive research. As with the historical studies on the nineteenth century and the revolutionary period, the main tendency has been to privilege class over ethnicity, thus ignoring or minimizing the ethnic dimensions of indigenous action and the relationship between culture and power. Although Frans J. Schryer's study focuses on Huejutla and the Nahua communities in Puebla, his discussion has bearing on current debates surrounding the Huastec region. See his *Ethnicity and Class Conflict in Rural Mexico* (Princeton, NJ, 1990).

One of the most thorough accounts of the impact of economic development on the Popolucas and Nahuas in the twentieth century is Guido Münch, *Etnología del istmo Veracruzano* (Mexico, 1982), who examines communities in the municipalities of Soteapán, Acayucán, Hueyapán de Ocampo, Oluta, Sayula, Texistepec, Cosoleacaque, Mecayapán and Pajapán in southern Veracruz. See also the articles in Domínguez Pérez, ed., *Agraristas y agrarismo*; David Buckles and Jacques Chevalier, "Ejido versus bien comunales: Historia política de Pajapán"; Emilia Velázquez H., "Reforma agraria y cambio social entre los nahuas de Mecayapán";

and José Luis Blanco, "Tierra ritual y resistencia entre los populucas de Soteapán." Bradley, "Processes of Sociocultural Change and Ethnicity in Southern Veracruz, Mexico," also examines the economic strategies of, and impact of, capitalist development on the Sierra Popolucas and the Nahuats. A major influence within the region was the introduction of coffee in 1880s, which contributed to a breakdown of the semi-isolation and self-sufficiency of many indigenous communities. Bradley argues that coffee plantations created socioeconomic differentiation within communities, new forms of internal and external relations among the participants, and the rise of local level *caciquismo*. Coffee production continues to be a major source of cash income in addition to their subsistence agriculture, as well as a cause of major schisms among the Sierra Popoluca themselves. George Foster, *A Primitive Mexican Economy*, is an interesting discussion of Popoluca land ownership and the distinction between collective ownership of land but individual ownership of coffee trees. See also Foster's "The Mixe, Zoque, Popoluca," *HMAI*, vol. 7 (Austin, TX, 1969). Assessments of the impact of the coffee economy on the Nahua communities in the Zongólica area can be found in Daniel K. Early, *Café: Dependencia y Efectos. Comunidades Nahuas de Zongólica. Ver., en el Mercado de Nueva York* (Mexico, 1982), and Daniel Early and Julia Capistrán, "Condiciones de los cafecultores nahuas en la Sierra de Zongólica,' *Boletín Técnico Cafetalero* 1, no. 2 (Mexico, 1976), 3–27. Howard Law, "Mecayapán, Veracruz. An Ethnographic Sketch" provides an overview of a Nahua community in the late 1940s and 1950s. Kelly and Palerm, *El Tajín Totonac*, and Isabel Kelly, "The Modern Totonacs," in *Huastecos, Totonacos y Sus Vecinos*, 175–86, provide a good assessment of the local Totonac economy up until the 1950s. This is well complemented by Victoria Chenaut's "Primeras notas de campo, ejidos, vainilla, y campesinos," in *La costa totonaca: cuestiones regionales II*, ed., Luis María Gatti (Mexico, Cuadernos de la Casa Chata, no. 158, 1987), which explores the economic rationality of the Totonac peasantry, and the gradual replacement of vanilla cultivation since the late 1950s by citriculture (oranges) and livestock, supplemented by subsistence agriculture of maize, beans, and chile. Also useful is Luis María Gatti, "La Huasteca Totonaca (u otra vez la Cuestión regional)," in *La costa totonaca: cuestiones regionales II*. Chávez-Hita, *Papantla*, discusses the postrevolutionary economy of Papantla, the rise and fall of vanilla cultivation, and the consequences of the oil industry as Poza Rica emerged as the political and commercial center of the zone at the expense of Papantla. Traditional agriculture in the lowlands is threatened by the oil industry, increased cattle ranching by mestizos, and extensive deforestation. For consideration of ecological issues and policies of the region in general, see Jean Revel-Mouroz, "Mexican Colonization Experience in the Humid Tropics," in *Environment, Society, and Rural Change in Latin America*, ed., D. A. Preston (London, 1980), 83–102, and Carmen Viqueira, "Análisis e interpretación de los resultados obtenidos en una comunidad de agricultores de selva tropical: Tajín," in *Percepción y Culturas, Un Enfoque Ecológico* (Mexico, 1977). Robert M. Laughlin, "The Huastecs," in *HMAI*, vol. 7 (Austin, TX, 1969), provides an overview of the local economies of the Huastec region based on a variety of crops and animal husbandry in the 1960s. A good update may be found in Alcorn, *Huastec Mayan Ethnobotany*, who stresses the combination of subsistence agriculture, cash cropping, and wage labor.

For analyses of contemporary Totonac society and culture (at least up until the 1940s and 1950s), see Kelly and Palerm, *The Tajín Totonac*, and Carmen Viqueira and Angel Palerm, "Alcoholismo, brujería, y homocidio en dos comunidades rurales de México," *América Indígena* III, vol. 14 (1954). The latter study examines the social stresses in two Totonac pueblos, Tajín and Eloxochitlán. More recent studies include Salvador Francisco, "Concepción cultural del ciclo de vida de los totonacos," *La Palabra y el Hombre* 57 (1986) and Elio Masferrer Kan, "El compadrazgo entre los totonacos de la sierra," *América Indígena* 44, no. 2 (1984). Assessments of persistence and change in present-day Popoluca communities can be found in Bradley, "Processes of Sociocultural Change and Ethnicity in Southern Veracruz, Mexico," who argues that the increasing integration of the area and capitalist development, rather then resulting in homogenization of the local Sierra Popoluca population, can actually strengthen ethnicity and ethnic identification. He traces changes in the ethnic identities and boundaries among the Sierra Popoluca and Nahuats, and the intra- and interethnic rivalry that has characterized the communities up until the present day. Also useful are Foster, "The Mixe–Zoque Popoluca," in *HMAI*, vol. 7 (Austin, TX, 1969); Félix Báez-Jorge, *Los zoque-popolucas. Estructura Social* (Mexico, 1973); Emilio Pascual Reyes, *Etnohistoria de los zoque-popolucas* (Mexico, 1982), María Fernanda Tovar, *Los Popolucas* (Mexico, 1982). Münch, *Etnología del istmo Veracruzano*, provides a thorough description of the social organization, changes in dress, and cultural practices of the Popolucas and Nahuas of southern Veracruz. Also useful on the Nahuas – in addition to Bradley, "Processes of Sociocultural Change and Ethnicity in Southern Veracruz, Mexico," Münch, *Etnología del istmo Veracruzano*, and Law, "Mecayapán" – is Luis Reyes García and Dieter Christensen, *El añillo de Tlalócan. Mitos, oraciones, cantos y cuentos de los Nawas actuales de los Estados de Veracruz y Puebla* (Mexico, 1989), which contains transcripts of tales, myths, and songs from Nahua communities in Amatlán de los Reyes and the sierra de Zongólica. On the Huasteca region, see Alicia González Cerecedo, "Antropología y medicina: el Mirador Chicontepec, Veracruz," *La Palabra y el Hombre* 63 (1987): 31–46, Lorenzo Ochoa Salas, "Atavío, hechicería y religión de los Huaxtecos," *Actes du XLII Congrès International des Américanistes* (1979), 67–76, Manuel Alvarez Boada, *La música popular en la Huasteca Veracruzana* (Mexico, 1985), and "La música indígena en Chicontepec, Veracruz," *La Palabra y el Hombre* 63 (1987): 49–56. Alcorn, *Huastec Mayan Ethnobotany*, is a superb introduction into what she terms the "cognized environment" of the Teenek Tsabaal. Particularly interesting is her analysis of *brujería*, curers, and ethnomedicine.

Catholicism, even in its syncretic form, remains a powerful force in the region but is subject to competition from evangelical sects. This topic is examined in Carlos Garma, "Las lágrimas de la virgen ya no caen aquí: Ritual y cosmología entre católicos y protestantes totonacas," *Cuicuilo* 14–15 (December 1984): 3–24. Protestant sects have been a major influence on various Zoque–Popoluca towns. See Münch, *Etnología del Istmo Veracruzano*; Félix Báez-Jorge, "La semana santa entre los Zoques–Popolucas de Soteapán: aspectos sincréticos," *Anuario Antropólogico* (1971), 241–63; Benjamin Elson, "The Homshuck: A Sierra Popoluca Text," *Tlalócan* 2 (1947): 193–214, Foster, *Sierra Popoluca Folklore and Beliefs* (Berkeley, CA, 1945), and his "Mixe, Zoque, Popoluca," vol. 7, *HMAI*. Bradley, "Processes of Sociocultural Change and Ethnicity in Southern Veracruz, Mexico," discusses the impact of the Summer Institute of Linguistics and the conversion of the eastern Popoluca to Protestanism – which, he argues, enabled them to lessen their isolation and to forge contacts with Protestants outside their immediate region. Alain Ichon, *La religión de los Totonacs de la Sierra* (Mexico, 1973; reprint 1982), examines Totonac communities in the sierra of northern Puebla on the border of modern-day Veracruz. He provides one of the few comprehensive descriptions of Totonac religion and cosmology in the twentieth century, and ranges across Totonac myths, deities, ceremonial rites surrounding birth and death, sacred landscapes, both indigenous and Catholic, and sacred and secular dances. Elizabeth Carmichael and Chloë Sayer, *The Skeleton at the Feast – the Day of the Dead in Mexico* (Austin, TX, 1991) include Totonac accounts of Nínín (the Day of the Dead) gathered from informants who live close to El Tajín, acquired with the help of Totonac anthropologists, founding members of the Colegio del Idioma Totonaca, and such accounts are also in Domingo García García and Crescencio García Ramos, *Nínín* (Papantla, 1983), and Crescencio García Ramos, "Puchaw: la ofrenda totonaca," *Boletín informativo del Instituto de Antropología* 2 (1983).

A good introduction to the current state of indigenous languages in the region is Carolyn Joyce MacKay, "A Grammar of Misantla Totonac" (Ph.D. diss., University of Texas at Austin, 1991). MacKay argues that Misantla Totonac is rapidly being replaced by Spanish as Totonac is no longer acquired by children as a first language and the existing speakers are elderly. See also Celestino Patiño, *Vocabulario totonaco* (Xalapa, 1907), and Paulette Levy, *Fonología del Totonaco de Papantla, Veracruz* (Mexico, 1987). For a discussion of active indigenous support for bilingual, bicultural education to Totonac children in the Tajín region, see Carmichael and Sayer, *The Skeleton at the Feast*. Robert M. Laughlin, "The Huastec," in *HMAI*, vol. 7, discusses the process of rapid dissolution of Huastec culture based on the decline of Huastec monolingualism, although Alcorn's study, *Huastec Mayan Ethnobotany* does not necessarily bear this out as of the 1980s. On the Nahuat dialect, see Howard Law, "Greeting Forms of the Gulf Aztecs," *Southwestern Journal of Anthropology* 4 (1948): 43–48, and "Tamakasti: A Gulf Nahuat Text," *Tlalócan* 3 (1952): 344–60.

Studies that explore the ongoing political struggles and resistance of indigenous groups within the region include González de la Lama, "Rebels and Bandits," who briefly discusses contemporary ethnic conflict among the Sierra Popoluca and Totonac communities. As recently as the early 1960s, Totonacs from the Papantla area organized an armed insurrection in protest against the government and agrarian policy. The pueblos involved were heavily repressed and an army batallion was stationed there until 1970. The Olarte family of Tenixtepec headed a movement to reclaim lands in the area of Tecolutla in 1980. See Gatti, "La Huasteca Totonaca (u otra vez la Cuestión regional)," in *La costa Totonaca: cuestiones regionales II*. Landowners around Soteapán have joined in the Organización de Pueblos Popolucas Independientes (OPPI) to prevent local powerful livestock owners from transforming their *milpas* into pasture grounds. Also active in the Huasteca region is the Organización

Independiente de los Pueblos Unidos de las Huastecas (OIPUH), which denounces the repression, violence, and injustice inflicted upon the indigenous peoples through the centuries. See González de la Lama, "Rebels and Bandits," and Rodolfo Stavenhagen, *Derecho indígena y derechos humanos en América Latina* (Mexico, 1988).

While much research still needs to be carried out, the literature surveyed suggests that like many other indigenous populations in Mexico, indigenous communities of the Gulf Coast have proven to be resilient to intrusion, adaptive to change, and active participants in shaping their lives, despite centuries of violence and marginalization engineered by both Spanish and Mexican dominance. Survival strategies include legal (use of courts and the law) and extralegal forms of resistance (rebellion), yet the more subtle forms of survival and how "Indian" identities change remain to be explored. What is also striking is that some recent case studies suggest that we may have to revise our interpretations of the impact and significance of liberalism for the indigenous communities. Although general interpretations tend to stress the destructive forces unleashed by Mexican Liberalism on the indigenous communities, the basic tenets of which were anathema to them, some recent studies argue that some indigenous communities were able not only to forge alliances with local elites to defend their own interests but to do so as part of a broader movement in support of liberal agendas. Why and how such differing responses emerged demand much more archival research. What also emerges from the extant literature is the central importance of the question of ethnicity in local politics and the need to explore relationships among class, gender, and ethnicity, among the indigenous communities, local and regional elites, and the state, and how they change over time. Finally, two major themes – gender (especially the impact of economic development on the division of labor, gender roles, employment opportunities and how they in turn affect the integrity of communities and ethnic and cultural practices), and the impact of the Catholic Church on popular religous practices of the native peoples of the Gulf Coast – remain virtually unexplored.

19

THE INDIGENOUS POPULATION OF OAXACA FROM THE SIXTEENTH CENTURY TO THE PRESENT

MARÍA DE LOS ANGELES ROMERO FRIZZI

The present-day state of Oaxaca is located in the south of Mexico where the Eastern Sierra Madre and the Southern Sierra Madre come together (Map 19.1). Covering an area of slightly more than 95,000 square kilometers, Oaxaca is a mountainous land, and the sierras form an essential part of its landscape. Because of its mountain ranges Oaxaca is host to a diversity of climates and a wide variety of flora. There are dry, arid hills where nothing grows but pipe organ cactus and other xerophytes; warm, humid slopes facing the sea where tropical forests flourish; and pine and oak woods at an altitude of about 3,000 meters (Map 19.2). The mountains have forced the inhabitants to develop an economy adapted to the hilly terrain, the scarcity of fertile soil and the utilization of different ecological environments. Only 9 percent of the area of the present-day state is arable land; the rest is covered with forest or shrubs or else is unsuitable for agriculture. The flatlands are located predominantly along the Pacific Coast, especially in the Mixtec region, in the Isthmus of Tehuantepec, and in the central valleys, but not all of it is agriculturally productive. In the rest of Oaxaca flat land is limited to narrow strips along riverbanks or in small valleys between the mountain ridges.

The human aspect of Oaxaca is as complex as its orography. Traditionally it is said that there are sixteen indigenous or ethnolinguistic groups in Oaxaca. They are the Amuzgo, Chatino, Chinantec, Chocho, Chontal, Cuicatec, Huave, Ixcatec, Mazatec, Mixe, Mixtec, Nahuatl, Popoloca (or Popoluca), Trique, Zapotec and Zoque. More recent studies mention only fourteen groups, taking into account that the Popoloca are

I would like to thank the following persons for their help: Anselmo Arellanes, Jutta Blauert, Manuel Esparza, Nancy M. Farriss, Hans-Ruedi Frei, Sergio Perelló, Leticia Reina, and Francisco José Ruiz Cervantes.

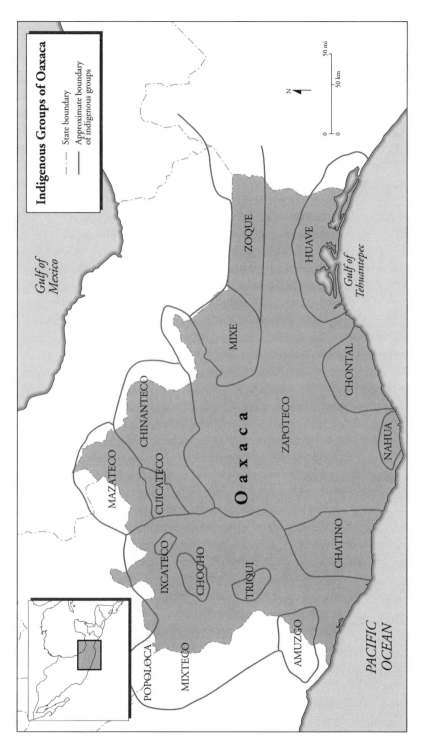

Indigenous Groups of Oaxaca

--- State boundary
--- Approximate boundary
of indigenous groups

Gulf of Mexico

ZOQUE

HUAVE

Gulf of Tehuantepec

MIXE

CHINANTECO

MAZATECO

CUICATECO

CHONTAL

Oaxaca

ZAPOTECO

NAHUA

IXCATECO

CHOCHO

TRIQUI

CHATINO

POPOLOCA

MIXTECO

AMUZGO

PACIFIC OCEAN

N

0   50 mi
0   50 km

Map 19.1

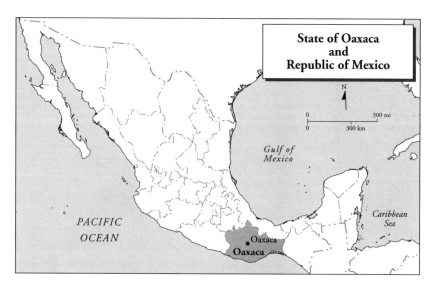

Map 19.2

reduced to a few migrant families and the Ixcatec group is made up of a very few old people who barely maintain a limited knowledge of their language.

The linguistic categorization is somewhat misleading for several reasons. The majority of indigenous peoples in Oaxaca identify more closely with their village or community than with their ethnolinguistic group. Furthermore, many of the language families, such as Zapotec, Mixtec, and Mazatec, encompass a variety of regional languages, making for a more diverse picture than the number sixteen would suggest.

Oaxaca is the state reputed to have the highest percentage of indigenous population in Mexico. According to the 1990 census, 19.3 percent of the national total of Indian-language speakers lived in Oaxaca; in 1993, 39.1 percent of the state's population over five years of age spoke an Indian language. Two of the state's native groups, the Zapotecs and the Mixtecs, are among the largest in all of Mexico, with 342,000 and 239,000 speakers respectively. At the other end of the spectrum, the very few native speakers of Ixcatec and Chocho are on the verge of disappearing (Map 19.3). It should also be noted that not all of the groups mentioned are confined solely within the political boundaries of Oaxaca. For example, although the Mixtec population extends into Puebla and

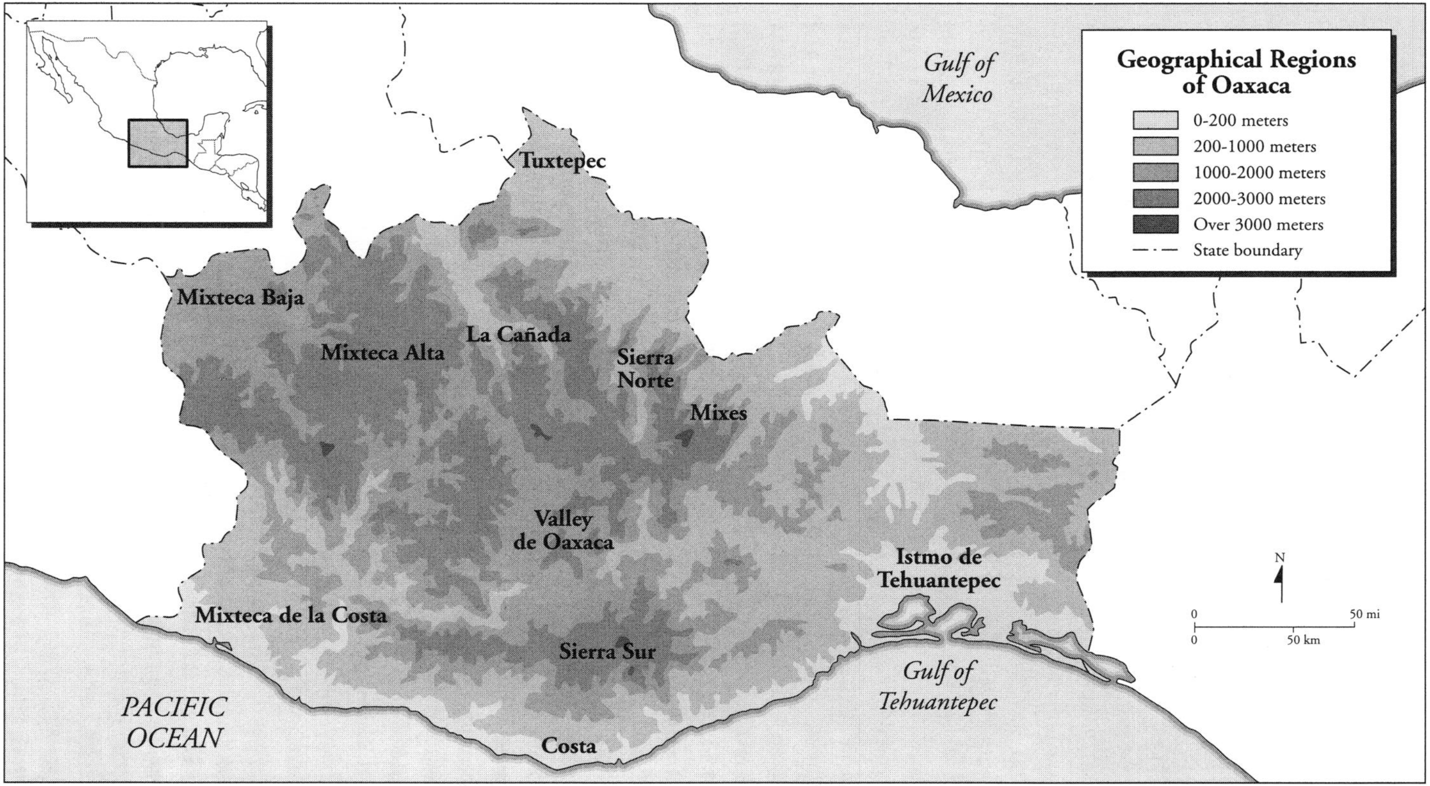

Map 19.3

Guerrero, the large majority lives in Oaxaca; yet only a few Zoque villages are found in Oaxaca outside their main area of concentration in Chiapas. Despite their great variety and geographical dispersion, Oaxaca's indigenous groups have many common historical features that permit us to discuss them as a unit.

Oaxaca has been the site of human settlement since very ancient times. In approximately 1500 B.C. sedentary settlements already existed in the central valleys and in the Mixteca and there are sites where human occupation has been continuous from approximately 1150 B.C. until the present day.[1] At the beginning of the sixteenth century, Oaxaca supported a population of nearly 1.5 million. According to the 1980 census, the number has increased to 3,228,895. This prolonged use of the soil in an extremely fragile environment has given rise to problems of erosion, which have reached alarming proportions in some areas of the state, such as the Mixteca.

During the prehispanic epoch, Oaxaca occupied a position in the heart of Mesoamerica that permitted it to enrich itself through contact with Mayas and Nahuas, and to establish an exquisitely refined culture of its own. Mixtec and Zapotec writing and calendars are the oldest in Mesoamerica, and they used some phonetic signs. Just before the Spanish Conquest they wrote their history in books, using a script based on ideographic elements that permitted communication between speakers of different languages. The contrast between this glorious past and the poverty of today could not be more dramatic. Present-day Oaxaca presents a sad spectacle: a large part of its population suffers from malnutrition, illness, illiteracy, and isolation. The state has one of the highest mortality rates in Mexico, and its contribution to the gross national product is less than 2 percent. Half a millennium of history, from the arrival of the Spaniards in 1519 to the end of the twentieth century, has produced the most pathetic of changes. These changes are the subject of this study.

CONQUEST AND THE INDIGENOUS RESPONSE

On the eve of the Spanish arrival, the territory of Oaxaca was by no means a single political entity. The peoples who inhabited it practiced

---

[1] Kent V. Flannery and Joyce Marcus, *The Cloud People: Divergent Evolution of the Zapotec and Mixtec Civilizations* (New York, 1983).

various forms of social and political organization. While the Mixes, the Chontales and other groups had a relatively egalitarian social structure and great political fragmentation, the Mixtecs and the Zapotecs of the isthmus and the valleys lived in a highly stratified society with a minor level of political fragmentation. At the top of the social ladder in these last two groups, the ruling hereditary lords, later called *caciques* by the Spaniards, possessed a nearly divine status. Their power sprang from their capacity to influence the forces of nature, like the rain and the earth's fertility, and from the control they were able to exercise over men and territory. The lower rungs held a range of ranks from the nobles closest to the governor down to the humblest of serfs.

The spatial distribution of the indigenous states was adapted to Oaxaca's mountainous geography. It consisted of a central settlement surrounded by a series of dependent villages located in different ecological niches. The dependent villages were separated by mountains and gorges but united in their recognition of the ruling lords. Wars between these chieftains for control of the few irrigated parcels or because of their many rivalries were a feature of daily life. These conflicts produced constant changes in the regional political structure, creating complex multiethnic domains. In 1519, when the Castilians arrived, the reactions of the indigenous peoples of Oaxaca varied from the creation of political alliances with the intruders to extreme hostility. The Zapotec lord of Tehuantepec sought an alliance with Hernán Cortés (also spelled Hernando Cortez) before his captains set foot on land. The Mixes and Zapotecs of the mountains, on the other hand, shut themselves off in the hills and for decades resisted any contact. From the outset, the Mixtecs and the Zapotecs of the valleys showed an interest in taking advantage of these strangers. The Spanish penetration into Oaxaca was very complex. In some areas the attitude of the indigenous lords paved the way for them; in others, the conquest was brutal and was characterized by the use of dogs and the insatiable Spanish thirst for gold and slaves. But even in the most hospitable areas, Spanish rule was not consolidated until the 1530s; in other areas this was not possible until thirty years later.

Spanish rule began to take shape as soon as the conquerors were able to establish the city of Antequera in the center of the valleys. Although at first it was nothing more than a tiny island with eighty citizens (*vecinos*) in the midst of thousands of indigenous inhabitants, the city was the most obvious sign of the inevitable Spanish presence. It was also in the 1530s that most of the indigenous kingdoms of the Mixteca and the valleys gave recognition to the Spaniards by means of tribute. For the natives, this was a continuation of the tribute they had formerly paid the Mexicas; for the Spaniards, it was the economic base that made their continued presence in the territory possible. From 1530 until the beginning of the 1560s, tribute was the main source of sustenance for the economy of New Spain. Thanks to tribute, the Spaniards had food, labor, and the means to initiate other economic activities. But the dependent economy of tribute was a part of the past. The sixteenth century had begun under the auspices of a mercantile economy that soon made its presence felt in Oaxaca. The city was the place where the first activities that were not dependent on native tribute began. From 1529 on, the city's inhabitants used Indian bearers – whom they had acquired in war or through agreement with noble natives – to transport wine, cloth, and other European merchandise from the port of Veracruz. They then traded these goods to natives or sent them to Guatemala along prehispanic trade routes.[2] Commerce emerged as the economic activity that unified Oaxaca with the rest of the world. Spaniards and natives alike took part in it. Mixtec nobles, who had been traders since antiquity, profited from the improvements introduced by the Spaniards, the beasts of burden and ships that left the Pacific Coast for Soconusco to get cacao. The indigenous nobles became the principal merchants of Oaxaca in the sixteenth century, more important than the Spaniards themselves.

Hernán Cortés, who had reserved for himself several villages in the valleys of Oaxaca and the Isthmus of Tehuantepec, shared these mercantile interests. On the land of Cortés's estate near the city of Antequera, his administrators introduced wheat cultivation, raised silkworms, and built hydraulic mills. Other Spaniards – soldiers, settlers, and monks – introduced wheat, barley, citrus fruit, sheep, cows, metal tools, and a variety of other things. The natives began to participate in these changes. At first it was the nobility who was most interested in utilizing the innovations, but soon the changes reached the rest of the society.

The Mixtecs and the Zapotecs of the valleys assimilated innumerable elements of their conquerors' culture. By 1540, they were growing wheat in the Mixteca Alta and the Valley of Etla, cultivating with plows and putting metal tips on their old wooden tools. The Mixtec kingdoms became famous for their silk, cultivating silkworms and their thread, which was sold in the city of Puebla. From there they brought Castilian

---

[2] Unpublished manuscript, Justicia, leg. 231, Archivo General de Indias, Sevilla.

wine, linens, and religious articles for their new Catholic churches. The livestock industry was also important, so much so that in certain regions the herds of the natives, both noble and commoners, were bigger than the Spaniards'. Nor was that the total extent of economic exchange: the natives supplied the Spaniards with various products and used money and credit in their transactions. Frequently the Spaniards complained that the Indians charged them high prices.

These changes may seem very radical to us, but they nevertheless took place within the structures of the indigenous society. The natives continued to take care of their basic needs with their crops of corn, beans, peppers, and squash. The new activities nourished a commerce in luxury items – in a way a continuation of prehispanic commerce. Up to then, the natives had carried cacao, cotton, and feathers; now they brought wine, iron, and linen cloth. The new commerce arose as activities of the nobility or as collective enterprises of neighborhoods around the church. The nobility and the barrios were an essential part of the prehispanic social structure. The monks and settlers were responsible for introducing innovations, but their success was due to indigenous interest. Between about 1540 and 1570, silk, livestock breeding, and red cochineal dye brought wealth to the villages, so much so that in some cases they paid their tribute with ease and retained considerable sums for the important expenses of their indigenous culture: the consumption of the nobility and that of their new Catholic church, its saints and the religious festivals that recalled those of the old prehispanic calendar. The nobles dressed in Flanders linen and the churches were adorned with golden goblets, Castilian candles, and linen altar cloths.[3] Far from behaving like defeated natives, these Mixtecs and Zapotecs prolonged the splendor of their past into the sixteenth century. The difference was that they now did it in the context of a mercantile economy that linked them with the most highly developed economic centers of New Spain and Europe.

These economic changes formed part of an intensive process of acculturation that permeated every area of native life, a process that cannot be explained solely by reference to the Spanish presence. Recent studies show that the change took place because of the interests of the natives themselves, although again their response was varied and complex. Counter to this welcoming of things Spanish demonstrated by the Mix-

---

[3] Nicolás León, ed., *Códice Sierra* (Mexico, 1933); and unpublished manuscript, Civil, leg. 516, Archivo de la Nación, Mexico.

tecs and Zapotecs, the natives of the southern sierra resented the changes and rose up against the Spaniards. In 1546 a messianic-style rebellion demanded the expulsion of the Spaniards and a return to the prehispanic situation.

FROM THE DESTRUCTURING OF THE INDIGENOUS KINGDOMS TO THE CONSOLIDATION OF COLONIAL SOCIETY

As the end of the sixteenth century approached, the scales tipped in favor of the Spaniards. The very mercantile economy developed by the indigenous peoples had created new channels of social mobility that eroded the hierarchical structure of the native domains. Around 1590 the natives of the valleys and the Mixteca refused to obey their lords: they refused to build houses for them, work for them, or render them tribute. The weakening of the nobility meant the disappearance of the regionally based indigenous societies and favored the consolidation of colonial power. A little before the arrival of the Spaniards, several native lords – those of Tututepec, Tehuantepec, Zaachila, and others – had wielded their power over broad regions. As these leaders attempted to identify themselves with the Spanish – even then only in external ways, by dressing like them and riding horseback – they weakened their own traditional power and contributed to the consolidation of Spanish power. Increasingly the natives appealed to Spanish courts, seeking reductions in tribute or using the courts to arbitrate old rivalries. The power of the indigenous nobility slowly shrank to a single settlement and no longer reached all the people. By the end of the sixteenth century, peasant villages existed in place of indigenous kingdoms.

The Spaniards brought with them not only their innovations but also, unfortunately, smallpox, measles, and other diseases against which the local population had no defenses. In a little more than one century (from 1520 to 1650), the native population of Oaxaca declined from 1.5 million to about 150,000. Epidemics were the worst enemy of the indigenous efforts to preserve their cultural vigor. At the same time, they were the principal ally of the Spanish in consolidating their rule, weakening the power of the lords even more by killing off the men and women in their domains. Even the indigenous lords of the Oaxaca valleys who had taken advantage of the confusion caused by the Spanish presence to extend their influence to new territories, becoming great landowners in the process, watched as the lands occupied by their tenant farmers (or serfs) became depopulated. In the last third of the century of the Conquest, we encounter an indigenous society with serious problems. From then on we may speak of Oaxaca as being under a consolidated Spanish power.

During these years, from the Conquest until about 1580, Oaxaca, like other indigenous regions, had been a key element in the colonial and even the worldwide economy. This was not only because it had paid the tribute that gave a start to the new Hispanic economy, but also, and above all, because its new economic activities had nourished both internal and external commerce with the selling of raw materials that were in demand in the colonial economy, and with the consumption of imported articles such as wine, cloth, paper, metal tools, and other objects. By the end of the sixteenth century, the indigenous economy had lost its initial vigor. In Oaxaca the communal enterprises were undergoing difficulties as silk production declined for want of labor and because of competition with Chinese silk, which began to be imported around 1565. Dye production also declined, and cultivation was concentrated on the most fertile land. The native responses to these losses had complicated consequences. Lords and villages changed the direction of their economy by emphasizing the raising of small livestock. As before, they continued to depend on their corn and bean crops for food; for sale, or for times when there were crop failures, they raised sheep and goats. The livestock increased after each epidemic and began to occupy lands left vacant. Thousands of hectares were used for grazing large and small livestock. The result is difficult to evaluate: on the one hand, the livestock brought income to the villages, income they needed to maintain their community life and invigorate their culture; on the other hand, where flocks were introduced in areas with a fragile ecological equilibrium, like the Mixteca Alta, erosion was accelerated.

In the center and north of New Spain, the Spanish had taken over the key elements of the economy: mining, commerce, and manufacturing. In Oaxaca, however, the Spanish economy did not have the same impact. The indigenous lords, in spite of everything, continued to own large amounts of land and the Indian herds were larger than those of the Spaniards. Even so, it is possible to discern growth in Spanish activity by the end of the sixteenth century. The city of Antequera was already an important settlement, and its inhabitants had received royal grants of land (*mercedes*) on which to practice agriculture or raise livestock. Not all of these grants, however, became important productive units. In the valleys, Spanish property during the sixteenth century lacked importance. Of these grants, only a few prospered, and by the middle of the next century they became the basis of the first haciendas, although most of them were still small and unimportant. The lords and the indigenous peoples continued to hold most of the land, and for supplies, the Spanish city depended primarily on native production. The importance of the city of Antequera lay in mercantile exchange with other indigenous regions. Its income came from traffic in cacao, indigo and other raw materials which the Spanish traders brought from Central America and sent to the cities of Puebla and Mexico. In exchange, they sent Indian clothing and imported articles to Guatemala. When all is said and done, this commerce continued to be indigenous in large part, even though the Spanish traders participated in it.

Slowly the Spaniards penetrated other regions of Oaxaca. In the coastal Mixteca, haciendas appeared that raised large livestock, and Spanish traders monopolized the cotton grown by the natives. On the Isthmus of Tehuantepec, Spanish cattle farms grew in number. In spite of this, throughout most of Oaxaca the natives practiced an economy of their own, which had a dual aspect: basic crops, and trade in whatever they could not obtain in their own region. The Zapotecs of the Isthmus of Tehuantepec brought salt and fish up to the mountain-dwelling Mixes and Zapotecs.[4] The Chinantecs sold fish, and other groups traded in cotton. The corn trade was extremely important since many villages were not self-sufficient. The different regions maintained contact with the Spanish, but this did not seem to alter the indigenous world radically.

In the Mixteca, the situation was different. From very early on, this region had established close relations with the colonial economy. From the end of the sixteenth century on there had been a group of Spanish traders established in the principal regional villages who, thanks to the support of dealers in Puebla and Mexico, operated as intermediaries between village production and colonial demand. By the middle of the seventeenth century, this commerce was affected by very severe problems in the colonial economy, including a drop in the price of silver, the principal export product. The Puebla dealers, who had until then extended easy credit, began to restrict it only to large traders, particularly members of their own families. Interregional commerce began to operate

---

[4] Unpublished manuscript, Tierras, leg. 226, exp. 5, AGN.

only on the basis of restricted credit and ended in the displacement of poor Spaniards and Mixtec traders. The former became ranchers, and since they had no land they had to rent it from the lords and the villagers. For the indigenous traders, this loss was irreparable: their activities were reduced to internal trafficking in the Indian zone itself.[5]

In the middle of the seventeenth century, the indigenous economy suffered from a lack of workers and lower prices for its products. In the Mixteca the main sources of income for the lords and the villages were the sale of small livestock and rents collected by leasing land they did not need to Spanish ranchers. In order to obtain articles they had become accustomed to having in the preceding century, they became dependent on the Spanish traders, who extended credit to them, to be paid later in tallow, hides, wool, and cochineal. In these dealing, known as *repartimientos de mercancías*, an important role was also played by the *alcaldes mayores*, Spanish officials appointed to administer justice and collect tribute in the indigenous regions. These administrators distributed merchandise and cash to the natives, and after a few months went back to collect in local products. The distribution networks of the *alcaldes mayores* extended throughout Oaxaca, but in the mountains they became the principal nexus of the Indian economy. Although they used their power to force the natives to buy more merchandise than they needed, their business in fact depended more on the times and the changes suffered by the indigenous culture. The natives needed candles for their new religion; the mules and machetes sold by the magistrates were indispensable for their exchanges and transportation in the mountains. In addition, the article the natives bought did not usually amount to much, and they delayed paying for them for months and even years. The real problem was the low prices they received for their own products.

The natives tolerated the *alcaldes mayores* because in remote areas they were practically the only means of obtaining the articles they wanted in exchange for their cochineal and blankets. Only when abuses in allotments or in prices reached intolerable levels did they rise up in arms, and stone, imprison, or even kill the official. This is what happened in 1660 in Tehuantepec, when the Zapotecs rebelled against their *alcalde mayor* because he allotted them more cotton than they could weave. This date marks the worst point in the chain of problems that had been accumu-

[5] María de los Angeles Romero Frizzi, *Economía y vida de los españoles en la Mixteca Alta: 1519–1720* (Mexico, 1990).

lating in the villages. The uprising extended beyond Tehuantepec to the sierra of the Mixes and the Chontales, in the Mixteca Baja, the northern Zapotec sierra, and among the Chinantecs. The rebellion of 1660 was the last great colonial revolt in Oaxaca, marking the end of the vigorous response that had been given by the natives in the sixteenth century.

INDIGENOUS COLONIAL SOCIETY: NEW ADAPTATIONS

Around 1660 a new census showed that the native population had stopped declining and had begun to recover slowly. With the threat of total extinction overcome, the days to follow promised the possibility of rebuilding native culture. By this time a Catholic church had been built in practically every village; in the mountains, the old prehispanic temples were covered with dust and overgrown with weeds. But in the indigenous mind, the saints, archangels, and virgins were combined with prehispanic concepts. The very characteristics of the Oaxaca economy – that is, the haciendas of relatively little importance, villages that had retained ownership of all or most of their land – made it possible for the natives to keep a certain amount of autonomy and to treat the colonial world as an external sector.

The most radical change in the villages had been the loss in importance of the indigenous lords. By now many chiefs had neither the large tracts of land nor the men to work them. Their profits had shrunk and also their sacred power. Of course, the change was very complex: in the valleys there were lords at the beginning of the seventeenth century who, just like the Spaniards, had to resort to employing indebted laborers to work their fields; others had sold their land to the haciendas or had transferred them to village ownership. As the political influence of the lords declined, a process of democratization accelerated with the passage of time. But in the valleys of the mid-eighteenth century, there were still lords like those of Etla and Cuilapan who owned vast amounts of land, with whole villages of tenant farmers at their service.[6] In the Mixteca other *caciques*, related to those of the valleys, retained land in the mountains or on the coast. Yet in spite of their economic power, their authority was in question. Whole villages declared that they had never recognized any lords. In attempts to prove this, they brought long and costly suits before the *audiencia*; while these actions enabled them to avoid recogniz-

---

[6] William B. Taylor, *Landlord and Peasant in Oaxaca* (Stanford, CA, 1972).

ing their *caciques*, they also strengthened Spanish power. The position left vacant by the high nobility was filled by a revitalization of communal structures, organizations that must have gone back to very ancient times in Indian history, before the consolidation of native elites.[7] These communitarian practices, moreover, meshed well with the Spanish ideas of communal ownership of land and the political organization of the local governments and of religious brotherhoods. Such institutions, with their Spanish appearance, allowed indigenous culture to survive. Their importance during the entire colonial era depended on their responding well to the most intimate needs of the colonial villages, even though they reflected the problems and divisions created by contact with the Spanish.

From the middle years of the sixteenth century, in some cases at the request of the natives themselves, the Spaniards had transferred the institution of the town council (*cabildo*) to the villages. For a number of years the *caciques* occupied the central post of governor within this political organization. The offices in the second echelon, such as *alcaldes* and *regidores*, were held by nobles who used them to reserve political control for themselves even as the power of the *cacique* declined. After 1725 in the Mixteca and the valleys there were no longer any *caciques* acting as rulers. In these areas, the Spanish type of economy filtered down into even the lowest sectors of Indian society, conferring higher incomes and accompanying political influence on some of the more entrepreneurial commoners (*macehuales*). This movement toward democratization was most evident in areas of greatest economic activity, such as the Mixteca and the valleys, but even in the mountains the indigenous structure, which was egalitarian and based on strong family ties, was transformed to open up new channels of upward mobility.

In spite of the changes that implied the adoption of Hispanic political organization, the local government incorporated the indigenous ideas of a society structured through hierarchies. The nobles and rich *macehuales* continued to occupy different positions in the government. They were also ultimately responsible for the administration of communal property, which consisted of the livestock and land that belonged to the saints and to the whole village, and whose exploitation covered the cost of collective needs: crop losses, taxes imposed by the colonial government, and church expenses including the festivals of the religious calendar. The position of

---

[7] Marcello Carmagnani, *El regreso de los dioses: el proceso de reconstitución de la identidad étnica en Oaxaca, siglos XVII y XVIII* (Mexico, 1988), 109.

mayordomo, the administrator of the property of *cofradías* (confraternities), also fell to the same circle of nobles. The *cofradías* that focused around the worship of a saint had been introduced by Spaniards, but in the villages they functioned as a religious mantle for ancestral communal properties.

The *cofradías* and other communal organizations were the common denominator of indigenous life. Formerly, the men of the lords' domains collectively sowed the fields meant for the support of their rulers and their religion; this was how they kept order in this world and in the supernatural one. During the colonial period, these properties had diversified and, above all, become commercial. Most of the *cofradías* in Oaxaca depended on the sale of their products in order to earn income. In the Mixteca, there were brotherhoods that owned very large flocks and had so many head of livestock that they had to rent pastureland from other villages. On the coast in the area of Huatulco, the villages had herds of large animals. The brotherhoods of the Mixteca earned income by renting their land to livestock ranchers, planting corn and selling it, or making cash loans at low interest to inhabitants of their villages. In the northern sierra, a region of important indigenous markets, the *cofradías* owned teams of oxen or mules and also capital, which they lent at low interest rates. The *cofradías* not only supported the supernatural world of the saints; they also nourished a large part of the Oaxacan economy. *Cofradías* were one of the most commercially oriented sectors of society and one of the most monetized, since they could count as much on the labor of their members as on the sale of their products for the cash income they received.

The revitalization of native culture in the eighteenth century was accompanied by the proliferation of internal tensions within indigenous society. Some of the problems resulted from contact with the Spanish, while others were completely Indian in nature. During the course of the century, the indigenous population multiplied, renewing pressure on the few parcels of irrigated land. The question of the control of these fields had played a substantial part – although not the only one – in the rivalries between the prehispanic kingdoms. In the last colonial century the need to retain these fields arose again, not only because of demographic pressure, since the population was still lower than sixteenth century levels, but also because in some regions the Spanish had bought the best land. Nevertheless, lawsuits over land, among villages and between village and *caciques,* were an indigenous problem. With the recovery of their population, villages regained the vigor they had lost, and with it their ancestral rivalries. The history of the eighteenth century is saturated with suits among villages for control of fields. Fights among themselves tended to be more dramatic than those they waged against Spaniards. In the Mixteca, for every suit brought against a Spaniard there were three between indigenous parties. In the valleys, where Spanish property was becoming more and more important, the villages fought against each other. This spectacle was echoed in the mountains and on the coast, where Spanish property was practically nonexistent and the Spanish population minimal. The only exceptions were in the isthmus and La Cañada, where there were more suits brought against property belonging to Spaniards.

The natives cannot be blamed for all these suits, since most of them took place in the Mixteca and the valleys, regions with a more commercialized economy, a higher degree of acculturation, and considerable advances in Spanish interests. Part of the problem was due precisely to the destructuring of the old indigenous kingdoms. In these two regions it was very common for villagers to bring suit against their *cacique*. Although the *caciques* had lost their political influence, they had held on to large tracts of land that they claimed to own. The villages claimed that they were the owners. The problem emanated from a change in the concept of land use and *caciques*' loss of prestige. The larger issue was the introduction of the Spanish concept of private property. In order to finance the litigations that lasted for years, even centuries, both *caciques* and villages needed cash income, which they obtained by renting out their land. This situation aggravated the lawsuits and linked them more closely to the mercantile economy. Those who gained from these struggles were the Spanish small livestock ranchers in the Mixteca and the farming and ranching haciendas of the valleys.

The history of the eighteenth century clearly shows the connections between the advance of both the economy and Spanish power, and the internal conflicts of the villages.[8] The development of Hispanic property in the Mixteca is the most obvious case. It is true that the Spaniards who arrived in the region in the sixteenth century had received *mercedes*: land from the Spanish Crown. But these land grants had reverted very quickly to the natives when the Spaniards decided to sell their land and devote themselves to commerce. Beginning in the second half of the seventeenth

---

[8] Rodolfo Pastor, *Campesinos y reformas: La Mixteca, 1700–1856* (Mexico, 1987), 223–30.

century, Spanish economic activity was focused around the breeding and fattening of livestock, and around the cultivation of sugarcane and its processing into syrup and liquor at the end of the same century. All this took place on lands rented from the villages and the *caciques*. In the valleys, the situation was different. There, on the haciendas or ranches, the Spanish did indeed become owners of the land, which they bought during the worst of the demographic crisis. The haciendas expanded by buying small parcels of land, but some of their land was also rented, mainly from the *caciques*, who in the eighteenth century preferred to rent out their land rather than try to exploit it directly. Even in the valleys the land belonging to the *caciques* was scattered. This system had made sense in the prehispanic era because it permitted the best use of different types of soil and different ecological niches. In the eighteenth century, the *caciques* lacked men to sow their fields, so it was more convenient to rent fields out. By the end of that century, half of the commercial agricultural produce of the bishopric of Oaxaca came from these Spanish properties.

Gains in Spanish landholding notwithstanding, the really important activity in Oaxaca was commerce. Spanish livestock production in the Mixteca, on the isthmus, and on the coast depended in large part on the demand from the mining centers and the urban nuclei of central and northern New Spain. Village production of blankets, tallow, wool, cochineal, and other products was also linked to this same demand. The trading allowed even the most isolated villages in the mountains to have contact with the new Hispanic economy and even with international trade. It also permitted villagers to earn the money they needed in their colonial culture. From the Hispanic trading centers, the cities of Puebla and Mexico, the networks spread out and tied these distant worlds together. From Puebla the mule trains set out loaded with products destined for Spanish traders based in regional centers such as Teposcolula, Tehuantepec, and others. There the merchandise was deposited in the warehouses, soon to be picked up by small dealers who functioned as intermediaries between these provincial capitals and mountain villages.

In the eighteenth century the Mixteca received linens from Flanders, cloth from Puebla and Holland, and many other items. The composition of these imported products was approximately as follows: 47 percent were European products, especially textiles; 38 percent were from New Spain, mostly textiles; 5 percent came from other colonies; and 6 percent were

from the Far East.[9] The intermediaries and the *alcaldes mayores* distributed these products throughout the Mixteca and other regions. Merchandise from Europe and New Spain was exchanged for the village products
of cochineal, cotton, wool, tallow, and salted meat, which little by little
paid for the imports. In Oaxaca, trade functioned on time and credit. A
product delivered today might not be paid for until several months or
even several years later.

In spite of all the problems – slow transportation, low money supply,
the marginal solvency of the buyers – trade forged the links that united
Oaxaca with the world. This commerce did not depend only on the use
of force to require the natives to accept products they did not want, as
has sometimes been claimed; rather, it flourished because of the changes
that had taken place in indigenous culture and society – including
changes in their religion, agricultural methods, commerce, and style of
dressing. The problem was that for their raw materials, they received low
prices, and this led to a gradual drain of local resources. Wealth accumulated elsewhere, in the hands of the middlemen and the more enterprising individuals of the villages themselves. By the second half of the
eighteenth century, even though a large portion of the population had a
low standard of living, there were wealthy natives in Oaxaca who viewed
the communitarian structures as ballast for their ambitions.

LIBERAL WINDS: END OF THE COLONIAL WORLD, START OF A NATION

In the second half of the eighteenth century important transformations
took place in Europe. England's revolution in technology and production
led to its textiles flooding the world. Liberal ideas spread from France to
Spain, where its monarchs, influenced by these ideas and driven by
economic necessity, undertook an ambitious reform of the empire. From
then on, the bases of the old colonial order would be questioned and
transformed.

The Spanish monarchs had their sights on the communal properties
of the villages. By the late 1700s the property of the Indian *cofradías* had
been expropriated to finance the creation of the Banco de San Carlos
and to support the urgent economic needs of the Spanish Crown. Al-

[9] Romero Frizzi, *Economía y vida*, 274.

though many villages managed to conceal their holdings through crafti-
ness and their remote locations, others were deprived of the communal
property that was fundamental to the functioning of their economy. The
assault on the confraternities in regions where about 90 percent of the
population was indigenous must have been devastating. In fact, the
revolts against the colonial order intensified at the end of the that century.

The War of Independence only worsened these problems and the
years that followed were not better: anarchy, civil war, popular uprisings,
and foreign invasions. During the first decades of Mexico's independence, in spite of serious political fluctuations, liberal ideas gained a
foothold. Mexican Liberals were opposed to corporate structures including the Indian villages, their communal lands, and their *cofradías*. They
thought these organizations, in regarding the collective good above that
of the individual, inhibited personal initiative, limited competition, and
hampered economic growth. The Liberals wanted to build a modern
nation, to introduce new technology and put an end to a type of agricultural production oriented principally toward subsistence and small markets. In its place they wanted to establish an agriculture that leaned
toward a well-integrated market. To accomplish this, they would have to
modernize the roads and put idle land into production. It would be
necessary to transfer land to the private sector and do away with the
barriers erected by the villages and their collectivist ideas.

Mexico began its life as an independent country facing severe problems. Mineral production fell by a third in value, demand lessened, and
the internal market was affected. The lack of safety on the roads created
by political instability exacerbated the problems that slowed down commercial traffic. Various governments raised taxes, and to make matters
worse, local production of dyes and textiles had to compete with English
products. These problems tore apart Oaxaca's economy: the period between 1820 and the middle of the century was one of crisis and depression. In 1832, agricultural and livestock production fell to half of its 1780
levels. Obviously the zones most severely affected were those that had
been the most fully integrated into the colonial market: the Mixteca and
the valleys. But the mountain and isthmus villages also had to face radical
changes in the nineteenth century.

The changes were profound in the Mixteca. During the first half of
the century its general economy and the communal organization of its
villages were adversely affected. There was an increase in private owner-

ship of the land and the transfer of other resources to private hands. Some haciendas that bred small livestock disappeared because of the stagnant economy. Very few hacienda owners prospered; those who did took advantage of the instability to acquire property at low prices. The haciendas became concentrated in the hands of a few and eventually accounted for a third of the region's livestock. The ranchers, mestizos, and rich Indians channeled anticorporate liberal ideas to their own advantage and bought land belonging to poor Mixtec smallholders or took over vacant land. The agricultural and livestock haciendas increased in number, signifying the emergence of a middle-class sector that benefited from privatization.[10] The villages, on the other hand, were the big losers of the nineteenth century.

Many villages were deprived of the resources of their corporate organizations, and at the same time, owing to a series of political reforms, they lost their capacity to defend their collective rights. Only the isolated villages with mostly indigenous populations were, in spite of everything, able to keep relative control over their communal organizations. But in general, there was a disarticulation of the corporate properties and the local governments, and a corresponding increment in the fragmentation of the villages, lawsuits over land, and a new social structure. Incredibly, the indigenous society was even less linked to the marketplace than before.

In the middle of the eighteenth century, about three-fourths of the Mixteca had not regularly produced for the New Spain market. Nevertheless, these same natives, as members of their communities, had been the owners of the ranches and flocks of small livestock belonging to the indigenous *cofradías*. These organizations had produced one-fourth of the products destined for the market in the Mixteca Alta. The *cofradías'* earnings had been an important source of support for the precarious subsistence economies of this majority of poor Mixtecs. Around 1832, during the first decade of Mexican independence, the number of Mixtecs who produced for the market had decreased by 75 percent, and they were no longer able to rely on the aid of their *cofradías*. The majority of Mixtecs underwent a process of pauperization during the nineteenth century, whereas the affluent and middle-class groups profited from the changes of those times.[11]

Our knowledge about other indigenous groups of Oaxaca is not as

---

[10] Pastor, *Campesinos y reformas*, 453 ff.   [11] Ibid.

detailed as it is for the Mixtecs. Nevertheless, we know that the changes of the nineteenth century penetrated other groups, including those that, like the Zapotecs in the Sierra Norte and the Isthmus of Tehuantepec, had preserved a relative autonomy. The Zapotec, Mixe, and Chinantec villages had been connected to the New Spain trade through their own traders and by merchants and *alcaldes mayores* who carried cochineal and especially blankets out of the region. In addition to this trade, the villages maintained an active indigenous commerce that may have been of pre-hispanic origin. I_n exchange for their blankets and dyes, the natives obtained, among other things, cotton fiber, mules, and money. The mules were indispensable to the indigenous market system that linked the Zapotecs of the isthmus with the those of the sierra, the Mixes, the Chinantecs and other natives. Products from high altitudes were traded for fish and salt from the coast. Above all, this market allowed zones with corn shortages to acquire corn through purchase or barter.

In the isthmus, the situation was not very different. Although in this region there were large livestock haciendas, the natives had retained communal control of most of the land and of the salt deposits on the coast. Salt was important in their diet because it allowed them, in spite of the hot climate, to preserve fish and meat. It was also an important article of trade. The Zapotecs of the isthmus took part in an active interchange with other natives of Oaxaca and with the Mayas of Guatemala, to whom they brought cloth and salt.[12] Although the *alcaldes mayores* had also penetrated local traffic, the Zapotecs of the isthmus, because of their location far from New Spain's centers of commerce, were able to keep control of their commerce when other indigenous groups like the Mixtecs had lost theirs long before. The isthmus Zapotecs also produced cochineal and indigo for the international market and sold these articles to the traders on the coast of the Gulf of Mexico.

This economy changed in the nineteenth century. Although we lack studies of this topic, it is probable that the most isolated villages were less affected by the trend toward privatization than they were by changes in national and international commerce. There is evidence, though only partial, that some mountain villages continued to manage their communal property until the middle of the nineteenth century without major changes. This was not true of commerce. The blankets from the Sierra Norte not only lost part of their old centers of consumption, they also

---

[12] John Tutino, "Rebelión indígena de Tehuantepec," *Cuadernos Políticos* 24 (1980): 89–100.

had to compete with English cotton cloth. Their dyes, cochineal and indigo, lost their international markets owing to the production of English aniline dyes.

The decline of the dyes and blanket weaving had other consequences for the sierra. These products had brought income into the villages that was used to acquire, among other things, corn from other native areas. Both the culture of the cochineal insect and the weaving of cotton had been labor-intensive activities, but neither required large quantities of land. The cochineal insect was bred in prickly pear thickets that grew in native families' backyards, and the cotton was brought from the lowlands of Veracruz. Thus the industry had contributed to a decrease in pressure on the land. When these activities failed, two problems arose: new litigation over land, and the beginning of emigration.[13] In the isthmus, trade in indigo, cochineal, and textiles survived the new situation; these activities were supplemented by control of the salt deposits. In 1825, the government had ordered that a monopoly over the salt deposits of Tehuantepec be granted to a private party so they could be exploited in a more productive manner than they were by the natives. The measure provoked extreme discontent, not only among the Zapotecs but also among all the natives who had participated in this commerce: Zoques, Mixes, Zapotecs of the sierra, and Chontales. In addition, the new owners of the livestock haciendas in the isthmus tried to spread out into the villages' land. The struggle against the privatization of salt and land lasted, with fluctuations, until the second half of the nineteenth century, the villages repeatedly maintained that these communal properties belonged to them and their saints.

The nineteenth century ruined the equilibrium that the natives had achieved during the colonial era. The response was not long in coming: the natives rose up in arms. Whereas during the preceding century indigenous revolts had been generally of short duration and seldom involved several villages together, in the 1800s the rebellions continued throughout the century and covered vast regions, including groups like the Triquis, which had until then remained peaceful. Triquis and Mixtecs were in rebellion from 1832 to 1857, allying themselves with national political groups in trying to defend the property belonging to their *cofradías* and the communal lands of their villages. On the isthmus, in

---

[13] Hans-Ruedi Frey, *Development and Tradition in Indian Oaxaca* (Ph.D. diss., University of Zurich, 1990).

1827, a village burned the property of some private owners; years later, in 1834, the communities rose up in arms for control of the salt deposits and the land. The conflict was also directed against the merchants of the city of Oaxaca for control over commerce. The waves of violence extended to many villages, and the problems lasted two or three decades.[14]

In 1857, after years of political convulsion throughout Mexico, liberal ideas were incorporated into a new constitution. This fact, far from calming the situation, provoked civil war and French intervention. In spite of the uncertain political climate, the laws mandating the distribution of communal property to private owners began to be implemented. In Oaxaca, the reaction of villages varied from region to region. In the valleys, where a tendency toward the privatization of arable lands already existed among the Indians, disentailment proceeded against less opposition. This did not mean there were no problems, however. The law established that once the distribution took place, new owners could buy the remaining land, especially land they were already renting at the time. This process made it easier for the large hacienda owners of the valleys and the Mixteca, who had been renting communal land from the villages, to become the owners of that land. Many communities, rather than risk losing their land, decided to divide up among their members the land belonging to the *cofradías*. The process especially affected the villages of the valleys, where in 1867 alone there were 604 disentailments. But it also reached some settlements on the isthmus and in the coastal Mixteca. Only the civil war and the foreign intervention of 1857–68 delayed this process of privatization in Oaxaca for a few years. By 1870 most of the land in Oaxaca still had not been converted to private property.

PEACE AT THE END OF THE CENTURY: CONSOLIDATION AND CRISIS OF THE LIBERAL REFORM

That year, 1870, was also when the Liberals finally regained power. In spite of the struggles between factions of the Liberal wing, the years that followed were comparatively peaceful, politically, on the state and national level. The villages of Oaxaca tried to rebuild their battered economy. Since the middle of the century the liberal governments themselves had tried to find a substitute for cochineal, promoting new products for

---

[14] Leticia Reina and Francisco Abardía, "Cien años de rebelión en Oaxaca," in *Lecturas históricas de Oaxaca*, ed. María Angeles Romero (Mexico, 1990), III.

export, such as coffee, tobacco, cotton, and other items. Coffee was especially successful, and although it never became as important as cochineal had been, it was the new crop that allowed the natives to complement their basic ones. Coffee was introduced into the Chinantec sierra, the southern sierra of Pochutla among the Mixes, in Choapan, Cuicatlán, and in all the areas where the climate was suitable. The Mixteca and the valleys, whose land was not suited to coffee growing, remained outside the process.

Coffee was brought to the villages by Oaxaca traders who had regional influence. In the northern sierra, the new officials – political bosses – required every family to plant twenty-five coffee trees annually.[15] The trader, indigenous and mestizo, came to the sierra and, as in colonial times, traded corn, bread, cloth, and liquor in advance exchange for the coffee harvest to come. The problem, as before, was low prices. The producers received scarcely a third of the price of the coffee. Those responsible for introducing coffee into remote areas of the sierra continued to increase their regional power. Some of them were connected to state power groups and were in control of the regional trade networks. These were the new *caciques*, individuals who established client relationships with the indigenous producers: they paid them little and demanded loyalty in exchange for their support and protection.

Coffee spread throughout the villages. In some areas – for example, among the Chinantecs – a class of small entrepreneurs arose and social stratification was accentuated. The coffee business encouraged a more individualistic spirit among the natives themselves. Those who planted the trees and spent years tending them before the first harvest began to consider the land, the communal forest of old, as their own private property. This aggravated internal tensions in the villages, and boundary disputes among villages flared up again.[16] In spite of the difficulties, the decade of the 1870s was one of agricultural growth in Oaxaca, in terms both of basic crops and commercial crops such as sugarcane, indigo, and coffee. Statewide production of corn, which had remained at about 29,000 tons a year from 1861 to 1869, increased to an annual average of about 80,000 tons in the decade of the 1870s. Coffee production, which had been 73,000 tons in 1861, increased to an annual average of 228,000

[15] C. M. Young, *The Social Setting of Migration: Factors Affecting Migration from a Sierra Zapotec Village in Oaxaca, Mexico* (Ph.D. diss., University of London, 1978), chap. 7.
[16] Hans Ruedi Frey, *Development and Tradition*.

tons during the five-year period from 1874 to 1879. The increase in agricultural production was due to the natives. In spite of the commercial middlemen, indigenous markets recovered and the birthrate went up. The population of Oaxaca increased by more than 1 percent a year in demographic growth, a figure that had not been achieved since the end of the eighteenth century.

The economy of Oaxaca was experiencing a period of growth when Porfirio Díaz came to power in 1877. The Porfiriato has generally been considered an era of economic growth. In the north of the country a manufacturing industry was developed, the mining of industrial metals began to be more important than that of precious metals, and communications and finance networks were modernized. It is often said that the economic advances in the south took place thanks to a renewed push to privatize the land, which opened up hitherto idle land to cultivation. Other factors were the introduction of foreign capital and the construction of the railroad. A closer look at the situation of Oaxaca, however, shows a different picture of those years.

In 1877, 77 percent of the population of Oaxaca was indigenous, and there was a high rate of monolingualism. Even the majority of the nonindigenous population lived in small settlements scattered throughout the countryside (90% of the total population was rural). In spite of a relatively strong movement to privatize village land (in 1878, 1,097,000 hectares of communal land remained), and even though in some areas coffee, tobacco, or sugarcane plantations had been established, most of the land was worked by natives using native methods. The economic growth that occurred in Oaxaca from 1869 to 1885 was due to the efforts of the natives, and not to foreign capital or even to the railroad. Although foreign capital was introduced into Oaxaca after these years, it did not become important until much later, from 1900 to 1911. The railroad reached the city of Oaxaca in 1892 although it had difficulty operating for two years, and the Tehuantepec railroad, which crossed the isthmus, was inaugurated in 1907. Contrary to common perception, the introduction of national and foreign capital destructured and weakened indigenous production and trade systems.

National and state interests in tobacco had been a factor since about 1770. In coffee, investment did not begin until 1885. Coffee prospered mainly in the southern sierra and in all the rest of the tropical zones, where plantations were established on disentailed village lands. Throughout the state, tropical crops for export began to gain in importance: tobacco, rubber, bananas, and others. In accordance with the push to modernize, new laws passed in the 1890s accelerated the privatization process. The laws established that, first of all, communal land had to be divided up into private property among the inhabitants of the villages, with each to receive a parcel worth 200 pesos. The remaining land would be sold to those able to make it produce most efficiently. Sometimes, in accordance with what the government had intended, land that had never been cultivated was sold in this manner, but in other cases the government sold land that had been forest land or reserves held by the villages to accommodate population growth, or simply areas that allowed for crop rotation. Such lands were adjudicated to members of the state and national bourgeoisie and to foreign companies. Many tropical produce companies emerged during the first decade of the twentieth century: the Cerro Mojarra Plantation Company, the Palmer and Pinkan Company, Mexican Land and Coffee Company, and many more. The old colonial haciendas, located mainly in the valleys, were also able to expand thanks to the new legislation.[17]

The change in landholding patterns took place in an extremely uneven manner. Generally speaking, half of the land distributed went to only one-quarter of the total number of heads of peasant families. Some peasants received barely three-quarters of a hectare, others a little more – 2 hectares. Still others received much less. In one village, ninety-one individuals had only 10 hectares, while other natives who had more money were able to acquire considerable acreage. What happened with the majority of peasant landless? We don't know for sure. Probably some continued to plant their communal fields, which, in spite of everything, survived. Others became day laborers on the new haciendas and plantations established during the Porfiriato, or else had to emigrate to work in the textile factors of Veracruz. Looking at the other side of the new land tenure system, the five largest haciendas in the state had an average of 50,000 hectares each. If the situation is examined region by region, some differences can be noted. The most heavily affected zones were the regions of Tuxtepec and La Cañada, followed by the Mixteca and the valleys, and finally the isthmus and the coast. But while in the Mixteca

---

[17] Francie R. Chassen, *Del Porfiriato a la Revolución, Oaxaca, 1902–1911* (Ph.D. diss., Universidad Nacional Autónoma de México, 1987).

small parcels of land were distributed (30 hectares on average), on the coast and the isthmus the average was 1,000 hectares.[18]

How was this change in land tenure in Oaxaca reflected in the region's production? The production of corn, although it went through severe oscillations, possibly owing to climatic changes, continued to grow from 1870 until the early 1880s, after which it remained relatively stable until 1900, when it fell off. Thanks to the new laws introduced during the Porfiriato, the indigenous villages began the twentieth century with more inhabitants, less food, and less land. The situation must have been extremely complex since some villages participated in coffee production and other commercial crops, but the general impression is that the Porfiriato managed to ruin the indigenous economy. It broke the logic of a dual economy that combined the production of basic foodstuffs with the cultivation of crops for sale, allowing villages to buy corn when it was needed, to purchase what was not produced in their own region, and to carry on their ceremonial life and their culture. The capitalist-style production system that was introduced in an effort to supplant the indigenous economy did not yield the desired results.

Modern capital investment reached Oaxaca just before the world economy fell into depression. Although the crisis did not occur until 1907, prices of export products had begun to decline at the end of the nineteenth century. The indigenous economy was hardly booming. Corn production, in spite of reaching higher volumes than anticipated, was destined for a shrunken market and constantly threatened by either drought or excessive rains. There were years of excellent harvests with very low prices, followed by years with high prices and hunger. Also, the natives' manner of producing counter to price trends (they increased production while prices were going down) was anachronistic. Inequalities persisted within Indian society, and some natives capitalized on the adjudication laws to their own benefit.

In all, the legacy of the Porfiriato was devastating for Oaxaca. A few statistics will help us to understand this phenomenon. In 1877, at the beginning of the Díaz regime, Oaxaca, along with the states of Puebla, Mexico, and Michoacán, occupied second place in the national production of corn. It was the third largest producer of sugarcane and the leader

---

[18] Manuel Esparza, "Los proyectos de los liberales en Oaxaca," in Leticia Reina, ed., *Historia de la cuestión agraria mexicana: Oaxaca* (Mexico City, 1988), II, 280–96.

in indigo production. In 1888, it was third in corn production, and its sugar and indigo production had lost their importance.[19] The capital investment that had such unfortunate results in Oaxaca was more successful in other states. The sugar produced in Oaxaca could not compete with sugar from the states of Morelos and Veracruz; the indigo business, formerly conducted by indigenous traders from Tehuantepec, had been pushed aside by dyes produced on the state plantations in Chiapas. Clearly the mountains presented a difficult obstacle to surmount. The small, hilly parcels, where fertile soil alternated every few meters with marginal or useless soil, worked better in the indigenous economy.

THE REVOLUTION OF 1910 AND THE DISTRIBUTION OF LAND

The brusque changes produced in all of Mexico by the Porfiriato, together with the tensions caused by the crisis in the world economy, culminated in the outbreak of a violent revolution. The struggle began in northern Mexico in 1910 and spread throughout the country, taking on a different character in each region. In Oaxaca, the revolution was the culmination of the discontent accumulated over many years, which had been manifested in regional revolts like the one on the isthmus (1879) and the Chatino revolt (1881). Revolutionary violence spread through the regions like the Mixteca, where the land had remained principally in the hands of the natives, and also in places like Tuxtepec, La Cañada, and the isthmus, where land had been handed over to foreign companies and to national and state capitalists.[20]

Agrarian problems, however, were not the only source of discontent. The reasons for the conflict were many and complex: the worsening of tensions within the indigenous society, the deterioration of its economy, the natives' resentment of state interference in their community life, and more. To this we may add the political discontent that existed in the nonindigenous sectors of society and the new fiscal policy. On the isthmus, the Zapotec villages fought to preserve political control in the

---

[19] Margarita Nettel, *Geografía estatal de Mexico*, Workbook 23, Departamento de Investigaciones Históricas, INAH (Mexico City), n.d.
[20] Francisco José Ruiz Cervantes, "De la bola a los primeros repartos: 1910–1924," in Reina, ed., *Historia de la cuestión agraria*, II, 331–423.

local government and to recover control of their lost salt deposit. In Tuxtepec, where the largest number of hectares in the whole state had been adjudicated (the hectares handed over in this zone exceeded 2 million; in other areas, such as the coast, the coffee-growing southern sierra, and Tehuantepec, the average was 380,000 hectares), the revolt was started by small landowning farmers and was mainly political in nature. In the Mixteca, where there were few haciendas, Zapata's movement was very diffuse.

Some villages, in fact, fought because they had lost their land to a few larger owners in the middle of the nineteenth century. Others did so in order to acquire new land – not hacienda or ranch land, but land belonging to a neighboring village that was an ancestral rival. During the revolution in Oaxaca, it was common for neighboring villages involved in ancient quarrels over land to take opposite sides in the war. One village would be Zapatista if the other was Maderista. They were motivated more by their local problems than by a clear understanding of the national conflict. In the Zapotec sierra of Ixtlán, a key region in the history of Oaxaca during the turbulent years from 1912 to 1920, the regional leaders – who in turn had strong ties with the bourgeoisie of the city of Oaxaca as well as interests in national politics – struggled to get rid of the changes imposed by the new centralism of Venustiano Carranza. When the mountain *caudillos* rose in arms and went so far as to declare Oaxaca a sovereign state with respect to the rest of the federation, their base of support lay with the village natives. The latter entered the fray in order to fight against their neighboring villages. Perhaps they were quite unaware of the way in which their old rivalries from prehispanic times were now interwoven with the interests of the national bourgeoisie. But that was the situation. Amid this welter of arguments and rationales, there were some regions whose elders would claim years later that they had never known what they were fighting for, nor whether the men who had crossed their land sacking crops and robbing livestock were really Zapata supporters, Madero supporters, or Carranza supporters. They remembered only that they had been saved from greater devastation by the miraculous intervention of their saints.

The most violent years of the revolution lasted until 1917. Later, the fury of the struggle cooled off, but it continued until a little after 1920. Those highly uncertain years gave the coup de grâce to the little that had survived of the indigenous economy. Trade in blankets and other cotton textiles that had gone from Oaxaca to Guatemala nearly disappeared.

The manufacture of these textiles in the valleys and the Sierra Norte, which in 1900 occupied nearly 10,000 indigenous weavers (whereas the factories of the Porfiriato had 600 salaried weavers), was reduced to the local consumption level.[21] Coffee was also affected. When the interregional coffee trade declined, the indigenous economy became oriented around a highly precarious subsistence. To make matters worse in Oaxaca, several of the Porfirian capital investors fled the province. The estates and plantations were destroyed, and the port structures constructed on the isthmus were abandoned. By the time the most violent stage of the revolution was over, Oaxaca's economy was in ruins.

In the postrevolutionary period of the early 1920s, Mexican agriculture, stock raising, manufacturing, and mining – only petroleum was an exception – faced a deteriorating situation even though world demand was high following World War I. A slow push toward recovery began in 1925, only to be halted by the Great Depression of 1929. In this uncertain economic climate, the new governments fixed their sights on the need to modernize the country by increasing production and shaping a capitalist-style economy. But such goals were not compatible, at least in the short run, with one of the principle achievements of the revolution: the return of the land to the peasants. Under such circumstances, the agrarian reform underwent tensions, compromises and declining production. National and state governments distributed only a minimum of land and argued that agrarian reform was complete by 1928, despite the large numbers who remained landless.

The national situation was reflected in Oaxaca. In 1920, part of the old Porfirian structure was still in existence. Large properties had been affected by instability and national economic crisis, but not by agrarian policy. Even foreign companies like United Fruit and the Giorgio Company began to make new investments in the Tuxtepec area. Few natives in Oaxaca were aware that they could regain the land they had lost during the Porfiriato.[22] Thus, from 1917 to 1920, only about 3,000 hectares were redistributed in Oaxaca. In the years that followed, obstacles continued to limit redistribution. Opposition existed within the government itself, and even day laborers and cattle ranchers in the countryside feared losing their livelihood if the haciendas were broken up. In spite of

[21] Hellen P. Clements, "Historia de una comunidad artesana," in Romero, ed., *Lecturas históricas*, IV.

[22] Anselmo Arellanes, personal communication (1990).

these difficulties, government land commissioners appeared in the state to organize the peasants to channel their concerns. An organizational form typical of modern Mexico began to emerge during those years: popular demands were co-opted by government organizations, enhancing the power of the state.

The large landholders took action against the new awareness of peasants. In the valleys of Oaxaca, on the coast, and in the sierra of Miahuatlán, landlords formed their own armed units, stringing up and murdering agrarian reformers and burning their villages. But thanks to constant pressure from agrarian groups, the breakup of the large haciendas went forward. By 1933, 128,000 hectares had been apportioned, an average of 8,000 hectares per year. But 80 percent of these lands were not arable or could be cultivated only with great difficulty.

In 1934 national policy took an abrupt turn when General Lázaro Cárdenas stepped into the presidency. He proposed new directions: agriculture would become the base of the country's economic development. This goal would be achieved by the implementation of agrarian reform, the extension of credit to peasants for increasing production, the formation of peasant organizations, the establishment of rural technical schools, and other programs. This plan aimed, first, to satisfy the needs of national consumption, and then to progress to agricultural export. In addition to implementing these programs, Cárdenas nationalized the oil industry, fomented industry in general, and started a socialist-style education program that reached the farthest corners of the country through rural teachers. The changes came to Oaxaca, which in 1934 was immersed in a subsistence agricultural economy. Eighty-six percent of its population was rural, and the population was rising while in other parts of the country it was declining. Eighty-six percent of the fields were sown with beans and corn. Barely 10 percent of the state's land was sown with crops for the market, such as coffee, bananas, or sugarcane.

Between 1935 and 1940, the amount of land apportioned to the peasants tripled from the 128,000 hectares granted between 1915 and 1933 to more than 396,000 hectares. Irrigation systems were built, and there was talk of opening new roads, establishing health programs, and bringing in electricity. Programs of agricultural and livestock development were implemented: mulberry trees and grapevines were brought to the Mixteca. An attempt was made to foment silk production again. More than two hundred credit unions were formed, and the Banco de Crédito Agrícola began to operate as an intermediary between villages and consumption centers with the goal of paying producers better prices for their crops. Nevertheless, good intentions collided with a reality that was too complex.

Cárdenas's programs have been praised on the national level for helping the most defenseless sectors of society. Although these programs may have been a tonic in other parts of the country, in Oaxaca it seems to have been different. The little information we have indicates that some problems, instead of disappearing, got worse. Agrarian reform, in fact, did redistribute land from the largest properties. Of 121 properties with more than 5,000 hectares in 1930, only 19 remained in 1940, and their total area was reduced from 2 million to 170,000 hectares. This was clearly an enormous achievement, but the division of land was far from equitable and was altered over time by economic problems.

The exchange of land acquired a frantic pace, affecting medium-sized properties (of 50 to 5,000 hectares) and even smaller parcels of 5 to 50 hectares. All these properties declined in number between 1930 and 1940, with medium-sized holdings dropping from 1,500 to 500, and smaller parcels from 8,400 to 3,700. We do not know for sure why such small properties were affected, but perhaps in this case the breakup of parcels was due less to agrarian reform than to economic problems afflicting owners and forcing them to sell. What we do know is that the medium-sized properties that survived the Cárdenas era were fewer in number but on average larger than before. On the other hand, many of the small parcels were divided into even tinier plots, creating a large class of penurious peasants whose only assets were parcels of less than 5 hectares, and in some cases, less than 1 hectare. By the end of Cárdenas's regime, about 90 percent of the rural properties had less than 5 hectares, and together they constituted scarcely 4.5 percent of the total land area. At the opposite extreme, the enormous haciendas of the Porfiriato had disappeared, but others (0.2% of the number of properties) that were in the medium-size range of about 1,000 hectares accounted for 84 percent of the land. Only the *ejidos*, a new form of collective land tenancy, had grown in number and acreage.

The result of these years was the consolidation of an unequal social structure within the indigenous regions themselves, a situation that was reflected in deteriorating living conditions. Between 1930 and 1940, while the infant mortality rate for all of Mexico decreased from 131.6 to 125.7 (per 1,000 live births), in Oaxaca the number increased from 111.8 to 131.6. The overall death rate (thousands per year) also declined in the country as a whole – from 26.7 in 1930 to 22.8 in 1940 – but in Oaxaca it rose from 27.6 to 31.2 in the same time period. Emigration in search of better living conditions rose dramatically in the 1930s. Oaxaca had the highest number of emigrants – a total of 55,000 men and women – of any other Mexican state but Guanajuato.

CONTEMPORARY OAXACA: 1940 TO THE 1980S

The high incidence of very small farms in Oaxaca during the postrevolutionary period in Mexico would be, in years to come, a determining factor in its history and its problems. There still exist villages in which three-quarters of the heads of families do not have enough land to sustain themselves for the whole year. Other difficulties compound the problems of small farm size: the isolation of Oaxaca from the principal centers of Mexican economic development, and the lack of a diversified economy adapted to Oaxaca's human and ecological characteristics and capable of absorbing the labor available in the state.

During the 1940s and 1950s, Oaxaca went backward with respect to other regions, a situation that was largely the result of the economic policy of the Mexican state. First of all, the national government focused all its efforts on regions with greater agricultural potential in the northern part of the country, ignoring the indigenous south. The subsequent goal of industrialization was supported by a policy that kept salaries low by controlling the prices of basic foods, especially corn but also wheat and beans. The price control policy, which functioned as a subsidy to the city from the country, had devastating effects in agricultural states like Oaxaca, where, for example, in 1950 about 85 percent of the land was sown in basic crops. The *ejidos* and numerous tiny farms grew mostly corn, beans, and wheat, whereas medium-sized owners could place greater emphasis on commercial crops without having to abandon the basic ones.

All the agricultural producers in Oaxaca – *ejidatarios*, small farmers, and medium-sized owners – were adversely affected by the price control policy. Although it is true that many peasants produced for their own consumption, this did not mean, and does not mean today, that corn was never sent to market. On the contrary, part of it was sold when cash income was needed for some expense, but it had to be sold at low prices. If a peasant wanted to buy clothing or medicine, it was prohibitively expensive. Indians had to make up for short corn supplies and unfair prices by seeking employment outside Oaxaca, either in Mexican cities or abroad. In the 1960s, 290,000 people left Oaxaca, or about 15 percent of the state's 1970 population.

After this, in spite of a few years when the prices of basic crops rose, the general and logical tendency has been to abandon the basic crops. Peasants who can do so prefer to dedicate their land to the cultivation of crops for sale or other activities such as livestock. Commercial crops have grown in volume and variety, but even so, in 1985, 68 percent of the land continued to be sown in basic crops. This is partly because of the cultural importance of corn in indigenous culture, but also because commercial crops do not prosper in the poor, unirrigated soil of much of Oaxaca.

Even crops destined for the marketplace present problems. Some of them, especially coffee, are cultivated using methods that hardly differ from those of colonial times. Others, such as sesame seeds, citrus, and other fruits, are better integrated into the market, to the benefit of the villagers who cultivate them. Activities like forestry have had little regional impact on the creation of employment or the generation of an internal market. The crops destined for the market exhibit wide variety and complexity, but since coffee has been the most important commercial crop in this century, let us focus on it.

Although the production of crops for sale has a long history in Oaxaca, control over the coffee crop has been accompanied by indescribable violence in the twentieth century. This violence has its roots in how the producing regions are related to the international market. Demand has risen in the twentieth century and requires increasing quantities from every crop. This fact runs counter to the characteristics of production in most of Oaxaca, where small parcels produce smaller volumes. On the other hand, the poor indigenous farmer takes his product to market not when prices are high but, rather, when he needs money – when his daughter is getting married or his wife is sick, or when he needs to cover expenses pertaining to the civil or religious administration of his village. This permits traders to acquire crops in advance without extending loans to the producers. It is the trader who hoards or sells the crop depending on prices. The relations of middlemen with the producers go even further than commercial transactions. They may be godfathers or distant relatives. They lend money when money is needed and corn when the crop fails. Thus the traders are assured of the natives' loyalty because anyone who opposes their control becomes an enemy to their supporters.[23] The

[23] James B. Greenberg, *Blood Ties: Life and Violence in Rural Mexico* (Tucson: University of Arizona Press, 1989).

hoarding of coffee has aggravated internal problems in the villages and problems among them as well. The Triquis live in a state of continuous warfare, fighting among themselves, and the traders sell them arms in exchange for coffee. Among the Chatinos, violence is a part of daily life. Official institutions like INMECAFE (Mexican Coffee Institute) do little to end this situation. They operate as intermediaries and offer a better price, but they do not manage to do so in an efficient manner, first because they do not reach the most remote corners of the sierra, and second because they do not give money in advance for the crop as the *caciques* had.

In spite of these problems, Oaxaca has been among the three principal coffee-producing states in Mexico since 1950. Nevertheless, in the 1960s Oaxaca's gross product declined from 1.9 percent of the gross national product to 1.5 percent. This prompted the national government, once again, to implement dozens of development plans to modernize Oaxaca. New roads had already been tried, as had programs to improve commercial crops. A large dam was built in the northern part of the state, but it turned out to benefit the lowlands of Veracruz while creating enormous problems for the Mazatecs in northern Oaxaca.

Development plans multiplied especially after the 1960s. Projects were initiated by SARH (Secretariat of Agriculture and Hydraulic Resources), INI (National Indigenous Institute), and many other agencies. Programs and commissions proliferated, and many have persisted until the present day with programs focusing on the construction of infrastructure programs: electrification, roads, irrigation, health clinics, schools, ports, refrigeration plants, and so forth. Other projects aimed more directly to increase productivity.

These different programs had at least one shared characteristic: they were all guided by the idea that Oaxaca was backward because its natives were conservative, lacked initiative, and continued to use rudimentary technology. From this perspective, solutions were linked to the introduction of modern technology: tractors in the valley, pumps for irrigation, chemical fertilizers, and improved seed. Yet after years of work and millions of pesos invested, Oaxaca still lagged far behind the rest of the country. Why? Incredibly, very few studies have evaluated the achievements and failures of these initiatives. Although onchocercosis and malaria were controlled in tropical zones, the infant mortality rate decreased, and life expectancy at birth increased, some of these indicators still fell below the national average.

Bureaucratic delays, inefficiency, and corruption explain part of the problem, but structural factors also presented obstacles. In the sierras of Oaxaca, the modernizing experts tried to apply knowledge that was inappropriate for the very steep terrain and that did not take into account the huge variability in soil types within a single village. These experts were uninformed about and even disdained the ancestral wisdom of the peasant and its logic. They recommended only one type of chemical fertilizer for all areas – despite their diversity. The massive use of improved seed, in addition to requiring a dependable water supply and good soil – factors pretty scarce in Oaxaca – could mean the loss of a genetic arsenal of corn varieties adapted to each corner of the sierra. Oaxaca is one of the Mexican states with the most varieties of corn. In spite of its deficiencies, new land has been opened to cultivation and the use of fertilizer has been diffused in Oaxaca. The spread of chemical fertilizers may be a response to problems felt by the peasants in the face of the deterioration of their land. Another problem is the difficulty of continuing to use traditional techniques for clearing land, which have not worked in the face of heavy demographic pressure because they retard recuperation of forests and facilitate erosion. Currently, chemical fertilizers are used on half of the cultivated land in Oaxaca, but the results are uneven. Only in years of good rain – a factor beyond peasants' control – does the use of fertilizer on second- or third-rate land increase the yield.

Those who benefited from these plans and increased the productivity of their lands were middle-sized producers who had better-quality land; there the use of fertilizer boosted harvest by 50 percent. Poor peasants – most of the natives of Oaxaca – who applied these techniques ended up indebted to the bank, which made it even more necessary for them to leave their villages in search of resources.[24]

In spite of the long history of problems, the indigenous groups of Oaxaca continue to demonstrate great vitality at the end of the twentieth century. The range of responses they have given and continue to provide is limitless. In the last two decades, from 1980 to 1996, Mixtec, Zapotec, Mixe, Chinantec, and other Indian leaders have formed an impressive number of organizations, whose goals include the following: revitalization and respect for their languages, their culture, and their lifestyle; training programs; support for productive activities like forest management and

---

[24] Jutta Blauert, "Rural Development Projects Compared: The Mixteca Oaxaqueña," paper presented at the SLAS Meeting, Bradford, England, 1989.

commercialization of coffee. Among the groups that have been formed are the Coalición Obrero Campesino Estudiantil del Istmo (COCEI), Movimiento Unificado de Lucha Triqui (MULT), Servicios del Pueblo Mixe (SER), and others, like MICHIZA, which are dedicated to the commercialization of coffee, corn, and other products in Mixtec, Chinantec, Chatino, Cuicatec, and Zapotec communities.

In 1994, some of these organizations succeeded in introducing a bill in the Oaxaca state legislature that would require the constitution to recognize their traditional practice of electing their own authorities. Today, at the close of the century, Oaxaca, like other parts of the world, is experiencing contradictory tendencies. On one hand, there is a growing impulse in the world market to liberalize the rules of the game; on the other, Indian peoples (who do not want to be called "ethnic groups") are putting up a tenacious fight to have their rights recognized and also to become integrated into a national and world economy in an equitable and dignified manner.

The future looks uncertain. There is no doubt that indigenous peoples deserve a more prosperous future, one that cannot be achieved without changes to their economy and links to the outside; but we also know that intensifying the relationship between Indians and world economic development will generate new tensions in their society and culture. Some Indians, like the isthmus Zapotecs who live near an oil refinery and an important Pacific port, will succeed in adapting. But there are other instances in which Indians are already experiencing grave problems as a result of tensions between traditionalists and those who believe that communal organization itself is an impediment to their individual development. It is possible that in the first decades of the twenty-first century Oaxaca will be converted into a truly pluricultural state (understood as a situation of equality and respect), and that Mexico will have to modify its constitution to accommodate the demands of its peoples of Mesoamerican origin. It is equally probable that the tensions of modernization will end up creating new problems in the Indian communities.

BIBLIOGRAPHICAL ESSAY

There are two basic bibliographies of Oaxaca: María de los Angeles Romero Frizzi, *Bibliografía antropológica de Oaxaca* (Oaxaca, 1974); and María de la Luz Topete, *Bibliografía antropológica de Oaxaca, 1974–1979* (Oaxaca, 1980). Each lists works in anthropology, archaeology, history, and linguistics. They include *La bibliografía antropológica y sociológica*, compiled earlier by Jorge Martínez Ríos (Mexico City, 1961), and works on Oaxaca listed in *Bibliografía de Mesoamérica* by Ignacio Bernal (Mexico City, 1962). Among the important general introductions to the study of Oaxaca's indigenous populations are vol. 7 of the *Handbook of Middle American Indians*, ed. Robert Wauchope (Austin, TX, 1969). Also useful is the shorter work by John Chance, "Colonial Ethnohistory of Oaxaca," in vol. 4 of the *Supplement to the Handbook of Middle American Indians* (Austin, TX, 1986).

One of several general histories of Oaxaca, the classic text by José Antonio Gay, *Historia de Oaxaca*, 2 vols. [1881] (Oaxaca, 1978), treats the period from the prehispanic era to the War of Independence. Jorge Fernando Iturribarría covers the prehispanic period to 1955 in *Oaxaca en la historia* (Mexico City, 1955); see also his *Breve historia de Oaxaca* (Mexico City, 1944) and other studies. For a more recent treatment, which includes selections from the most important works published between 1943 and 1985, see the collection edited by María de los Angeles Romero and Marcus C. Winter, *Lecturas históricas de Oaxaca*, prehispanic to 1930, in 4 vols. (Mexico City, 1990). Leticia Reina, *Historia de la cuestión agraria, Oaxaca*, 2 vols. (Mexico City, 1988), surveys the prehispanic period to 1980 with an emphasis on changes in land tenure.

There are no rich collections – like those on central Mexico – for the colonial period in Oaxaca. The only chronicler was Fray Francisco de Burgoa, who wrote in the mid-seventeenth century. His *Geográfica descripción* . . . (the richest in information on the indigenous society) and *Palestra historial*, both published recently by Porrúa (Mexico City, 1989), are indispensable reference works. For a study of Mixtec and Zapotec language and culture, see Fr. Juan de Córdova, *Arte en lengua zapoteca y vocabulario en lengua zapoteca* [1593] (Mexico City, 1953). Other general sources on New Spain contain important references to Oaxaca: Francisco Cervantes de Salazar, *Crónica de la Nueva España, papeles de la Nueva España*, vols. 2 and 3, third series (Mexico City, 1936); Antonio de Herrera, *Historia general de los hechos de los castellanos* . . . , vol. 1, chaps. 10 and 11 (Madrid, 1934); Fr. Toribio de Motolonía, *Memoriales* (Mexico City, 1903); *Relación de los obispados de Tlaxcala, Michoacán, Oaxaca y otros lugares* (Mexico City, 1903). Collections of documents include: *Papeles de la Nueva España*, compiled by Francisco del Paso y Troncoso, which includes *La suma de visitas de pueblos* [1541] and *Las relaciones geográficas* [1580], both recently published by the Universidad Nacional

Autónoma de México. See also *El libro de las tasaciones de los pueblos de la Nueva España* [1530 to 1560] (Mexico City, 1952). For the eighteenth century, José Antonio de Villaseñor y Sánchez, *Teatro americano* [1742–48], 2 vols. (Mexico City, 1952), provides a global view of the bishopric of Oaxaca.

Finding aids for documents on Oaxaca include the many guides available in the Archivo de la Nación in Mexico City and those prepared by Miguel Saldaña and Ronald Spores, *Documentos para la ethnohistoria del estado de Oaxaca* (Nashville, 1973, 1975). The Archivo General del Estado de Oaxaca has also published catalogues of its documents (1650 to the 1800s) [Oaxaca, 1983, 1985]. Indexes to two of the richest colonial judicial archives are: María Angeles Romero and Ronald Spores, *Indice del Archivo del Juzgado de Teposcolula* (Oaxaca 1976), and John Chance, *Indice del Archivo Judicial de Villa Alta* (Nashville, 1978). A complete guide to the colonial codices of Oaxaca can be found in the *Handbook of Middle American Indians*, vol. 14 (Austin, TX, 1975); also very useful is the catalogue by Joaquín Galarza, *Códices y pinturas tradicionales indígenas del AGN* (Mexico City, 1997). These codices have been little studied in relation to the moment in which they were produced, and they constitute a very rich source for understanding the process of cultural change in Oaxaca.

Among the major works of the well-studied colonial period are those by Woodrow Borah on a variety of topics. Some of the most important are: "El origen de la sericultura en la Mixteca Alta," *Historia Mexicana*, 13 (1963); "The Collection of Tithes in the Bishopric of Oaxaca during the Sixteenth Century" and "Tithe Collection in the Bishopric of Oaxaca, 1601–1867," both in *Hispanic American Historical Review* 21 (1941) and 29 (1949), respectively. See *The Population of the Mixteca Alta, 1520–1960* (Berkeley, CA, 1968) and other works by Sherburne F. Cook and Woodrow Borah. Spanish landowning and the capacity of indigenous *caciques* to retain their property has been studied by William B. Taylor, *Landlord and Peasant in Colonial Oaxaca* (Stanford, CA, 1972). John K. Chance has written on the colonial city of Antequera in *Race and Class in Colonial Oaxaca* (Stanford, CA, 1978) and on the northern sierra in *Conquest of the Sierra: Spaniards and Indians in Colonial Oaxaca* (Norman, OK, 1989). An interesting analysis of indigenous culture and recomposition during the colonial period is Marcello Carmagnani, *El regreso de los dioses: El proceso de reconstitución de la identidad étnica en Oaxaca, siglos XVII y XVIII* (Mexico City, 1988). Serge Gruzinksi's *La colonización de lo imaginario: Sociedades indígenas y occidentalización en el México español, siglos XVI–XVII* (Mexico City, 1991) contains some interesting references to Oaxaca. On the control of raw materials by *alcaldes mayores*, see Brian R. Hamnett, *Politics and Trade in Southern Mexico, 1750–1821* (Cambridge, 1971).

The Mixteca is one of the best-known regions thanks to the anthropological work of Ronald Spores: *The Mixtec Kings and Their People* (Norman, OK, 1967) and *The Mixtecs in Ancient and Colonial Times* (Norman, OK, 1984). On the development of the colonial economy in the Mixteca and the creative indigenous response from 1540 to 1570, see María de los Angeles Romero, *Economía y vida de los españoles en la Mixteca Alta, 1510–1720* (Mexico City, 1990). Rodolfo Pastor, *Campesinos y reformas: La mixteca, 1700–1856* (Mexico City, 1987), provides an excellent view of the changes to Mixtec society wrought by the Bourbon reforms and by Liberal politics. Indispensable for a study of fluctuations in the colonial economy of Oaxaca in general and of the Mixteca in particular is Rodolfo Pastor et al., *Fluctuaciones económicas en Oaxaca durante el siglo XVIII* (Mexico City, 1979). In general, there are fewer studies on the Zapotecs than on the Mixtecs, an exception being Joseph Whitecotton, *The Zapotecs: Princes, Priests and Peasants* (Norman, OK, 1977). The history of the Isthmus of Tehuantepec has been little studied in spite of the vigor of its indigenous culture. The work of Judith F. Zeitlin is one exception; see, for example, her "Ranchers and Indians on the Southern Isthmus of Tehuantepec: Economic Change and Indigenous Survival in Colonial Mexico," *Hispanic American Historical Review* 69, no. 1 (1989). Another study that spans the colonial period and the first half of the nineteenth century is John Tutino, "Rebelión indígena en Tehuantepec," *Cuadernos Políticos* 24 (1980). On the rebellion of 1660, see Basilio Rojas, *La rebelión de Tehuantepec* (Mexico City, 1964), and Hector Díaz Polanco, *El fuego de la inobediencia* (Mexico City, 1992). María de los Angeles Romero Frizzi, *El sol y la cruz: Historia de los pueblos indios de Oaxaca* (Mexico City, 1996), summarizes Oaxacan colonial history with an emphasis on the Mixtecs and the Zapotecs of the Sierra Norte.

There are good studies for each period of the nineteenth century, including: Carlos María de Bustamante, *Memoria estadística de Oaxaca y descripción del valle del mismo nombre (1774–1848)* (Mexico City, 1963); José María Murguía y Galardi, *Apuntamientos estadísticos de la provincia de Oaxaca en esta Nueva España* (Oaxaca, 1861), and his manuscript of

1827 at the University of Texas, *Extracto general que abraza la estadística toda en su primera y segunda parte del estado Oaxaca y ha reunido del orden del Supremo Gobierno e Intendente de Provincia*; Matías Romero, *El estado de Oaxaca* (Barcelona, 1866). A complete set of the *Memorias de los gobernadores* can be found in the Oaxacan state archives; these reports are unequaled as a source of quantitative data and as reflecting the political beliefs of the ruling class. Principal secondary sources on the nineteenth century are: Fernando Iturribarría, *Historia de Oaxaca, 1821–1867*, IV (Mexico City, 1935–55), on political and other facets of history; Charles R. Berry, *The Reform in Oaxaca, 1855–1876: A Microhistory of the Liberal Revolution* (Lincoln, NE, 1981); Rodolfo Pastor, *Campesinos y reformas* (Mexico City, 1987), which has an excellent analysis of the changes produced in the Mixteca by Liberal ideas; and John K. Chance and William Taylor, "Cofradías and Cargos: An Historical Perspective on the Mesoamerican Civil Religious Hierarchy," *American Ethnologist* 12, no. 1 (1985). Hans-Ruedi Frey, "Development and Tradition in Indian Oaxaca" (Ph.D. diss., University of Zurich, 1990), compares the Zapotecs and Chinantecs of the Sierra Norte with the Huave zone from the nineteenth century to the present.

Principal works on the Porfiriato and the early Revolution include: Francisco Belmar, *Breve reseña histórica y geográfica del estado de Oaxaca* (Oaxaca, 1901); Cayetano Esteva, *Nociones elementales de geografía histórica del estado de Oaxaca* (Mexico City, 1913); Cassiano Conzatti, *El estado de Oaxaca y sus recursos naturales* (Oaxaca, 1920); and Manuel Martínez Gracida, *Colección de cuadros sinópticos de los pueblos, haciendas y ranchos del estado libre y soberano de Oaxaca* (Oaxaca, 1883). Much of Martínez Gracida's work has never been published and can be found in the Biblioteca Pública de Oaxaca. Andrés Portillo, *Oaxaca en el centenario de la independencia nacional* (Oaxaca, 1910) and other authors like Basilio Rojas (on coffee production), Rosas Solaegui, Francisco Salazar, and Angel Taracena should also be consulted. Recent work on the Porfiriato includes: Francie R. Chassen, "Oaxaca: del Porfiriato a la Revolución," (Ph.D. diss., Universidad Nacional Autónoma de México, 1986); Chassen and Hector Martínez, "El desarrollo económico de Oaxaca a finales del Porfiriato," *Revista Mexicana de Sociología* 48 (1986). The main works on the Revolution in Oaxaca are: Francisco Ruiz Cervantes, *La revolución en Oaxaca: El movimiento de soberanía* (Mexico City, 1986); Paul Garner, "The Rise and Fall of State Sovereignty: Oaxaca, 1910–1925," in Mark Wasserman and Thomas Benjamin, eds., *Provinces of the Revolution:*

Essays on Regional Mexican History, 1910–1929 (Albuquerque, 1990); and
Garner, *La revolución en provincia: Soberanía estatal y caudillismo en las
montañas de Oaxaca, 1910–1920* (Mexico City, 1988).
The interested researcher should consult bibliographies on Oaxaca in
the twentieth century. Many studies exist on a wide variety of topics
including community, indigenous economy, indigenous religion, development plans, effects of agrarian reform, and political problems. The
Instituto Nacional de Estadística, Geografía e Información has published
a great deal of valuable statistical material covering 1900 to the present
on land tenure, production, living conditions, and so on; especially useful
is *Estadísticas históricas de México*, vol. 2 (Mexico City, 1985). In its series
on social anthropology, the Instituto Nacional Indigenista has published
various books on Oaxaca, ranging from the classic works of the 1930s
through the monographs of the 1980s. Volumes 5, 6, and 7 of its series
(published since 1995) entitled Etnografía Contemporánea en los Pueblos
Indígenas de México are on Oaxacan groups.

Principal works on the twentieth century can be categorized according
both to Indian groups and to topic. For a general overview of indigenous
groups, see Miguel Bartolomé and Alicia Barabas, *Dinámica étnica en
Oaxaca* (Mexico City, 1986, 1990). For the Amuzgos, Chochos, Chontales, Nahuas, and Popolocas of Oaxaca, there are only short works on
very specific topics, but general, though brief, descriptions may be found
in Carlos Basauri, *La población indígena de México* (Mexico City, 1940),
and Lucio Mendieta y Núñez, *Etnografía de México* (Mexico City, 1857).
Oaxaca's minority Indian groups have been touched upon in Miguel
Bartolomé and Alicia Barabas, *La pluralidad en peligro* (Mexico City,
1996). On the Cuicatecs, the work of Eva Hunt is important. See also
the work of Roberto J. Weitlaner on Cuicatecs and other groups in the
north of Oaxaca, some of which is in *Papeles de la Chinantla*, 7 vols.
(Mexico City, 1960–73). On the Mazatecs of northern Oaxaca, see Eckart
Boege, *Los mazatecos ante la nación: Contradicciones de la identidad étnica
en el México actual* (Mexico City, 1988). Recent studies on the Mixes
emphasize their religion; see, for example, Frank J. Lipp, *The Mixe of
Oaxaca: Religion, Ritual and Healing* (Austin, TX, 1991), and Etzuko
Kuroda, *Bajo el Zempoaltepetl: La sociedad mixe de las tierras altas y sus
rituales* (Oaxaca, 1993).

The Chatinos have received considerable recent attention. From the
historical perspective, the best work is James B. Greenberg, *Blood Ties:
Life and Violence in Rural Mexico* (Tucson, 1989). Also important are

Miguel Bartolomé and Alicia Barabas, *Tierra de la palabra: Historia y etnografía de los chatinos* (Mexico City, 1982), and Jorge Hernández Díaz, *Café amargo: Diferenciación y cambio social entre los chatinos* (Oaxaca, 1987). On the problem of the Triquis, see Agustín García Alcaraz, *Tinujei: Los triquis de Copala* (Mexico City, 1973), and León Javier Parra y Jorge Hernández Díaz, *Violencia y cambio social en la región triqui* (Mexico City, 1994). The Mixtecs have been better studied in a large number of books and articles, although there is no overall study of Mixtec problems for this century. Alejandro Marroquí, *Tlaxiaco, la ciudad mercado* (Mexico City, 1978), is important. On the Mixtec migrations, see Douglas Butterworth, *Tilantongo, comunidad mixteca en transición* (Mexico City, 1975); on coastal violence related to *caciques*, see Veronique Falnet, *Viveré si Dios quiere* (Mexico City, 1977); on social organization, see Robert Ravicz, *Organización social de los mixtecos* (Mexico City, 1965); and on Mixtec views of social relations, see John Monaghan, *The Covenants with Earth and Rain: Exchange, Sacrifice, and Revelation in Mixtec Society* (Norman, OK, 1995).

On the sierra Zapotecs, see Julio de la Fuente, *Yalalaq: Una villa zapoteca serrana* (Mexico City, 1977); Richard L. Berg, *El impacto de la economía moderna sobre la economía tradicional* (Mexico City, 1974); and Michael Kearney, *The Winds of Ixtepeji* (New York, 1972). The complicated linguistic panorama of the Zapotecs is treated in Juan José Rendón, *Diversificación de las lenguas zapotecas* (Oaxaca, 1995). Isthmus Zapotecs themselves have produced the best work on their culture: for example, the magazine *Neza* published in the 1930s, the magazine *Guchachi' Reza*, and other publications of the Casa de Cultura and the city government of Juchitán in the 1980s and 1990s. Also important are the works of Beverly Chiñas and Leticia Reina on development projects in the isthmus.

There are other important works for understanding Oaxaca in recent times. Arthur D. Murphy and Alex Stepik, *Social Inequality in Oaxaca: A History of Resistance and Change* (Philadelphia, 1991), studies the city of Oaxaca. On the market system, see Ralph Beals, *The Peasant Marketing System of Oaxaca* (Berkeley, CA, 1975). On the role of artisanry in Oaxacan valley economies, see Scott Cook, *Zapotec Stoneworkers* (Washington, DC, 1982), *Peasant Capitalist Industry* (Washington, DC, 1984), and Cook and Leigh Binford, *Obliging Needs: Rural Petty Industry in Mexican Capitalism* (Austin, TX, 1990). On unemployment in the valleys, see María Luisa Acevedo, *Desempleo y subempleo en los valles centrales de Oaxaca* (Mexico City, 1982); on modernization in agriculture, see Carol Turkenik, "Agricultural Production Strategies in a Mexican Peasant Community" (Ph.D. diss., UCLA, 1975). There is no single study on the effects of development plans for the whole state. Jutta Blauert's doctoral thesis entitled "Autochthonous Approaches to Rural Environmental Problems in Mexico" (London, 1990) offers a detailed study with a historical perspective. An overall view of the varied problems in Oaxaca is provided in Raúl Benítez Zenteno, ed., *Sociedad y política en Oaxaca, 1980* (Oaxaca, 1980). Enrique Marroquí treats the complex theme of religion in Oaxaca in *La cruz mesiánica: Una aproximación al sincretismo católico indígena* (Oaxaca, 1989), and in *El conflicto religioso en Oaxaca, 1976–1993* (Mexico City, 1996).

20

THE LOWLAND MAYAS, FROM THE CONQUEST TO THE PRESENT

GRANT D. JONES

At the time of the Spanish conquest, lowland Maya-speaking peoples occupied a vast region that today encompasses the three Mexican states of the Yucatan Peninsula (Yucatan, Campeche, and Quintana Roo), eastern Tabasco, the lowland tropical forests of eastern Chiapas, the department of Peten, Guatemala, and parts of Alta Verapaz, Guatemala, and northwestern Honduras. At the time of first Spanish contact the native peoples of this territory, which extends more than 650 kilometers north-south and about 450 kilometers east-west at its widest point, spoke primarily variants of Yucatecan Maya. A smaller number of speakers of several related Cholan Maya languages occupied the southern and western portions of the lowlands.

The Maya lowlands demonstrated less linguistic diversity than other regions of Mesoamerica, but historical and geographic factors fostered the development of distinctive regional traditions in pre-conquest times. These traditions found their expression in localized and often opposed political territories of varying degrees of centralization, in a variety of regional economies and interregional trade relationships, and, of course, in localized cultural differences. Such differences required the European conquerors and their colonial and national period descendants to impose alternative methods in the conquest and administration of the subregions of the lowlands, and the Mayas in turn responded in various ways to these challenges to their autonomy. The lowland Maya world of today is thus a product of complex cultural and historical forces.

Only in the past few decades have modern scholars begun to examine these forces in detail. Twentieth-century research has produced many more archaeological studies of prehispanic lowland Maya civilization than of document-based examinations of the colonial and national period Mayas. Cultural and social historical research, whether pursued by historians or anthropologists, continues to lag far behind archaeological study, despite the accessibility of a relatively rich documentary base. Ethnographic field studies of the Maya peoples continue to be published, although many remain relatively inaccessible in the form of unpublished doctoral dissertations. Much research remains to be done, and the outline presented here may well be substantially revised in the coming years.

The North American diplomat John Lloyd Stephens's vivid early-nineteenth-century travelogues first exposed the modern North American and European community to spectacular ancient Maya monuments in Yucatan and Honduras.[1] These were illustrated by the British artist Frederick Catherwood and were originally published only a few years before the 1848 outbreak of the Caste War of Yucatan. Stephens recognized that the living Mayas themselves were the descendants of the inhabitants of these ruined cities and, in contrast to contemporary opinion, that these had not been built by the architects of ancient Egypt. His thoughtful speculations on the factors that might have led to the transformation of such a great native civilization into a peasantry, reduced to laboring for Spanish-speaking masters, represent the beginnings of modern historical scholarship on the lowland Maya.

THE PRESENT DISTRIBUTION OF THE LOWLAND MAYAS IN HISTORICAL PERSPECTIVE

Today the vast majority of speakers of Yucatec, the largest of the Yucatecan language groups, occupy the rural areas of the Mexican states of Yucatan, Campeche, and Quintana Roo. These make up about half of a total population of more than a million. Yucatec and linguistically related Mopan speakers total only about 10,000 in Belize, less than 7 percent of this former British colony's total population. The Yucatec Mayas, who migrated to Belize during the Caste War, occupy communities in the two northern districts of the country (Corozal and Orange Walk) and the Cayo district in the west. The Mopans are located in the southern Toledo district and in nearby San Luis, Peten, but once occupied a much larger area of eastern Peten and southern Belize. K'ekchi (or Kekchi)-Maya speakers who have migrated to Belize from Baja and Alta Verapaz

---

[1] John L. Stephens, *Incidents of Travel in Central America, Chiapas and Yucatan* (New York, 1969), and *Incidents of Travel in Yucatan* (New York, 1963), originally published in 1841 and 1843, respectively.

over a period of more than a century, today total about 4,000 in that country; others have migrated to Peten as well. The linguist Otto Schumann estimated that in 1971 there were only about 500 speakers of Itza, a Yucatecan language, in San José and San Andrés on Lake Petén Itzá and in Succotz in the Cayo district of Belize. A repressive language policy during the 1930s had disallowed children from speaking Itza Maya in the schools, all but eliminating it from use by the younger generation. The linguist Charles Andrew Hofling estimates that today only several dozen individuals still speak Itza Maya.[2] Speakers of Cholan languages in Chiapas, including Chontal Maya, have nearly disappeared, and the language is extinct in Tabasco, southern Belize and Peten, Baja and Alta Verapaz (except for Ch'orti' (or Chorti) speakers of non-lowland origin), and Honduras. The formerly isolated Yucatec-speaking Lakandons of eastern Chiapas today number only about 500 individuals, and even these are threatened by the takeover of most of their lands by loggers and colonists.

Such numbers, based on actual speakers of the language rather than their general cultural characteristics or their ethnic self-perception, can, of course, be misleading. Nonetheless, they serve to demonstrate the point that Maya speakers today are few in number in much of the southern lowlands, whereas they maintain the language in large numbers in Yucatan. Most of the population declines in the south occurred during the sixteenth century, although substantial numbers remained in the south at the end of the seventeenth century. Conquest, periodic reconquest, epidemics, and forced relocation were among the principal factors that caused their decline as distinct linguistic-ethnic populations (Map 20.1).

CHANGE AND CONTINUITY IN MAYA CULTURAL HISTORY

The lowland Maya people had long been accustomed to outside influences due to interaction with other Mesoamerican peoples from beyond their borders and to the dislocations that resulted from their own expanding and contracting spheres of political influence. Spanish conquest and colonization, although probably more devastating in their impact than any of these earlier events, must therefore be seen as yet another major

---

[2] Otto Schumann G., *Descripción Estructural del Maya Itza del Petén, Guatemala C. A.* (Mexico, 1971), 9–10; Charles Andrew Hofling, *Itza Maya Texts with a Grammatical Overview* (Salt Lake City, 1991).

Distribution of Spanish Colonial-period Lowland Maya Languages

Yucatec Language
— · — · — Present-day state boundary

Map 20.1

stage of Maya history. Descendants of Caste War rebels still speak about the tragedies of their own history and consider a time when they will again be the sole inhabitants of their lands.[3] We are only beginning to appreciate the significance of this strong ideology of historical autonomy and cultural preservation for the survival of Maya culture during the nearly five centuries since the Spanish Conquest. Despite efforts by outsiders to appropriate Maya history into the mainstream of the Western world, the Mayas have retained their own vision of their place in history and have struggled, against formidable odds, in order to act out that vision.

The three fundamental processes of accommodation, avoidance, and resistance have characterized lowland Maya history since the Conquest. Although each of these processes was certainly an adaptive response to colonial and postcolonial rule, it is best to think of them as active strategies for the preservation and continuity of Maya history itself. Selective accommodation to Western culture and society, although forced upon the Mayas by governments, missionaries, and economic forces, became in Maya hands a tool for retaining autonomy with a modicum of external conformity. Avoidance, which for the Mayas meant privacy and the minimization of external contact, enabled them to maintain a way of life that remained relatively unfamiliar to many outsiders. Resistance on occasion broke out into open and intense anti-European rebellion but in most cases was used by the native population as a subtle means of turning avoidance into noncooperation.

In the sections that follow this perspective is interwoven with a discussion of major events and institutions that resulted from European conquest and colonization and from the impact of modern political and economic forces. Following a brief overview of lowland Maya culture at the time of the Conquest, I review European conquest activities in the region, the Mayas' demographic responses to conquest, the changing circumstances of Maya life during the Spanish colonial and national periods, the long-term changes experienced by the Mayas in their cultural life, the central importance of rebellion and resistance as Maya responses to external authority, and, finally, the present situation of the Maya peoples of the lowlands.

---

[3] Paul Sullivan, *Unfinished Conversations: Mayas and Foreigners Between Two Wars* (New York, 1989), xvi–xvii.

THE LOWLAND MAYAS AT THE TIME OF THE SPANISH
CONQUEST

The best-known contact-period lowland Maya region is the northern half
of the Yucatan Peninsula, the only area that the Spanish colonial province
governed effectively. This area, administered by the three Spanish *villas*
of Mérida in the northwestern corner of the peninsula, the port town of
Campeche on the Gulf Coast, and Valladolid in the eastern interior, was
undoubtedly the most densely settled lowland native region at that time
of the Conquest. Rainfall in the northernmost sections of the limestone
shelf that underlies the peninsula is relatively low, and vegetation is thin.
Although both natives and Spaniards were dependent primarily upon
natural wells (*cenotes*) for water and found agriculture to be marginally
productive in some areas, certain geographical features compensated for
these inconveniences. The climate was reasonably healthy. Foot transportation was easily accomplished across the flat, dry land. Salt flats along
the northern coast provided income for elites as a result of the demand
for salt in other regions. Finally, the physical situation of the northern
region was advantageous as a location near the major coastal trade routes
that connected central Mexico to eastern Central America, following the
Gulf Coast from the Veracruz region along the Isthmus of Tehuantepec
and Tabasco, around the peninsula, and toward the south all the way to
Honduras.

The contact-period population of the peninsula proper, most of it
concentrated in the north, has been estimated to have been as low as
300,000 and as high as 8 million. Little firm evidence exists to support
any figure between these extremes, although there were surely at least a
million persons throughout the region. Reconstructing the contact-
period population of the vast southern lowlands is even more difficult
given the paucity of data. Some early Spanish reports indicate sizable
communities in these areas, especially along the riverine systems that
drain Peten toward coastal Tabasco, Belize, and Guatemala and around
the lakes of the central Peten. A conservative extension of these scattered
reports to the region as a whole would suggest a total population of no
fewer than 500,000 and probably considerably more.

In the dry, riverless northern portion of Yucatan, sizable towns of up
to several thousand individuals were located along the coast and in the
interior adjacent to available underground water sources. Natural rainfall,

sizable lakes, ponds, and large rivers occur with increasing frequency toward the south. The Mayas of the south chose to locate their communities near permanent sources of water, just as they had done in Postclassic times. Riverine locations were particularly desired for reasons of ease of canoe transportation and thus for the advantages they offered in trading goods to points along the coasts. Coastal settlements in the south, however, were apparently few in number, with most of the larger riverine settlements being located some distance upstream on major rivers.

The Mayas of the northern lowlands – a region defined roughly by of a line drawn from Champotón (formerly Chanputun) on the Gulf Coast to the Bahía de la Ascención on the Caribbean – constituted a single ethnic group of Yucatec speakers. These were divided into between fourteen and eighteen politically distinct territories or provinces of varying degrees of centralization, their capitals known as *kuchkab'alob'*. Some of these provinces had earlier formed a confederation with its capital at Mayapan, but by the mid-fifteenth century this alliance had collapsed. The provinces were in a state of uneasy semi-alliance when the Spaniards first arrived, with the Xiws of the Mani province to the west and the Kokoms of the Sotuta province to the east remaining the principal antagonists. This east-west division was to influence many native events from the Conquest itself through the nineteenth century.

To the southeast, between the Bahía de la Ascención and the New River in Belize, were the predominantly coastal provinces of Waymil and Chetumal (or Chaktemal). The capital towns of these two provinces, B'ak'jalal (later Salamanca de Bacalar) and Chetumal, commanded positions near the mouths of the Hondo and New rivers and played a central role in trade with the interior peoples to their south and southwest. South of Chetumal was the cacao-producing Tz'ul Winikob' province, reached from there via the New River (then also known as the Tz'ul Winikob' River) and the Belize River. The capital town of Tz'ul Winikob' was Tipuj, strategically adjacent to Itza territory on the Macal branch of the upper Belize River.

All of these provinces were Yucatec-speaking, although characterized by dialectical differences and, in some coastal towns, by linguistic influences from Chontal traders of Akalan origins. Of the southern Yucatecan-speaking populations the most important was found along the lakes of the central Peten. These were said to ruled by a group known as Itzas, who, according to their own histories, had migrated to Peten from Chich'en Itza (or Chichén Itzá) in the north, probably during the fifteenth century A.D. The Itzas, whose military prowess impressed Spaniards and other native groups alike, remained fully independent from Spanish rule until their conquest in 1697, a century and a half after the establishment of Mérida in the north.

The Itza capital was on the island in Lake Petén Itzá that is today Ciudad Flores, the capital of the department of Peten. The Itzas called their capital Nojpeten, "Large Island," and modern writers often refer to it as Tayasal. Until 1697 the Itzas exerted political and military influence over much of Peten and, on occasion, even parts of Belize. Directly north of the Itza heartland, toward Campeche, were a number of communities in a region known in colonial times as Kejach. These constituted a separate southern province at the time of contact, but they were later joined by refugees fleeing Spanish-controlled Yucatan. West of the Kejach was the Chontal-speaking province of Akalan, with its capital, the trade center Itzam K'anak (probably the archaeological site known as El Tigre), located on the upper Candelaria River. Chontal speakers also occupied the Tabasco coastal lowlands to the west.

Southwest of Itza territory, along the upper tributaries of the Usumacinta River in Peten and eastern Chiapas, were several communities of speakers of Cholan languages known in colonial times as Lakandons, some of whom remained unconquered until the 1690s. The contemporary Lakandons to their north speak Yucatec and are probably descendants of people from the Kejach region. Other Cholan speakers, including the Xokmos, occupied the forests to the east of these Chols; these groups are very poorly known. Toward the southeast and east of the Itzas lived Yucatecan-speaking people known as Mopans, the ancestors of the present-day Mopans of San Luis, Peten, and of San Antonio, Toledo, in Belize. Some seventeenth-century communities in southern Belize contained both Mopan and Cholan speakers. The so-called Manche Chols, named for their principal town of Manche in southernmost Peten, appear to have been the last of the eastern Cholan-speaking groups to remain ethnically distinct and autonomous. The Manche Chols were forcibly relocated to Alta Verapaz by Spanish forces on several occasions, with their final removal occurring shortly after the 1697 Spanish conquest of the Itzas.

J. Eric S. Thompson proposed in 1977 that the Kejaches, Yucatec-speaking Lakandon, Itzas, Mopans, and those that we now know inhabited the Tz'ul Winikob' province, constituted a common ethnic group that he labeled the Chan Mayas. Some researchers have doubted this

assumption of ethnic unity and his further claim that these people were
the descendants of the inhabitants of the great Classic period sites of
central Peten. They have considered it more likely that most of the
ancestors of these southern speakers of Yucatecan Maya languages had
migrated from the north in a series of small population movements
during Postclassic times (A.D. 1000–c. 1525), displacing Cholan speakers
whose own ancestors were probably the original inhabitants of most of
Peten in Classic times. Others, including this author, believe, on the
basis of further epigraphic and ethnohistorical research, that the dominant presence of Yucatecan speakers in much of the southern lowlands is
of great antiquity.

The high degree of linguistic continuity throughout the lowlands in
historic times was very important. Yucatecan-speaking Mayas could travel
almost anywhere throughout the lowlands and be understood, as in fact
this highly mobile population often did. Maya-speaking Spaniards (or
those supplied with only a single Yucatec-speaking interpreter) from
Yucatan – missionaries, soldiers, and traders – could likewise understand
and be understood over a vast territory. The lowland linguistic situation
had profound implications for the development of long-distance Maya
communication, the survival of native autonomy movements, the foster-
ing of freedom of movement, and the long-term expansion of Yucatecan
Spanish political and economic interests in the larger lowland region.

The contact-period lowland Mayas practiced, as they still do, the
swidden and long-term cultivation of a wide variety of crops. Of these,
maize, beans, squash, chiles, and various orchard-grown fruits were the
most important subsistence crops. Cotton was widely grown for clothing,
especially in northeastern Yucatan. The people of lowland Tabasco and
the river valleys of Belize and southeastern Quintana Roo produced fine
quality cacao, which in the form of chocolate beans served as a major
export item to northern Yucatan, owing both to demand for the beverage
and to the bean's value as currency. Local environmental variations
resulted in considerable regional economic specialization in the production of other crops such as annatto, calabashes, and allspice; in the
manufacture of canoes and paddles; in the extraction of vast quantities
of sea salt along the northern coast, in the culture of bees for their honey
and wax; and in the crafting of stone tools, shell jewelry, ceramic religious
vessels, and elaborately woven and embroidered cotton cloth and clothing. The trade of many of these items within the lowland region was
brisk, as was the export of various products to other regions of Meso-

america, especially salt, cotton cloth, honey, and slaves from northern Yucatan. In return, from areas often far distant to the north and south, the lowland Maya received obsidian, chert, jade, copper artifacts, and even turquoise (from the present-day U.S. Southwest, via central Mexico) and gold (from lower Central America). Native nobles, ruling families, and other leaders sought to control both coastal and riverine trade as well as production, and thereby to maintain a standard of living well above that of the average commoner.

The Maya social system in Yucatan was hierarchical, with classes of hereditary nobles, commoners, and slaves. The nobility held all political offices within defined multi-town territories as well as in the towns themselves, and they monopolized military offices, the priesthood, and courts of justice; some of them also controlled trade networks as long-distance merchants. They also enjoyed preferential access to certain productive lands, to the agricultural labor of commoners, and to the productive coastal salt flats. Inheritance to office and property was apparently traced primarily in the male line, with several localized lineage groups dominating most political and many economic affairs. Recent research suggests, however, that matrilineal relationships may also have been important in the social construction of the nobility. Exogamous groups crosscut both location and social class but had local governance structures within town wards. Territorially defined political groups varied from those that were highly centralized, sometimes with a primary ruler and his kin dominating a substantial number of towns, to those that were little more than a group of locally governed allied communities. Even the more centralized polities, however, were probably characterized by joint decision-making through the actions of councils made up of the confederated heads of local towns.

Households occupied extended-family stone or wood dwellings, often in the midst of household orchards, subsistence gardens, and the ubiquitous beehives. The size, location, quality of dwellings reflected class status and wealth. The principal ceremonial buildings were normally situated in the central areas of towns, as were the residences of the wealthy elite. Well-maintained roads connected towns, and other roads and paths connected places great distances apart. Stone, and in some areas wood or henequen, fortifications were constructed to protect against raids by military and political rivals.

Like all Mesoamericans, the lowland Mayas believed in a complex, hierarchical supernatural world of gods and other spiritual forces. Religious symbolism was rich, and the knowledge required to understand the astrological, calendrical, and natural significance of the Maya cosmos required specialized knowledge controlled fully only by the priesthood. Books written in hieroglyphic characters were in active use by the nobility in some areas for decades after the Spanish Conquest; in the unusual case of the Itzas, these were still being consulted at the end of the seventeenth century. Human sacrifice, while emphasized by the Spaniards, was probably far less frequent than commonly asserted.

Most lowland Maya societies and cultures resembled in outline many of the features brought to the New World by the Spaniards themselves, for instance, centralized organization into a highly stratified agrarian society; traditions of warfare; an urban mode of life; male-dominated systems of governance; a priestly hierarchy; an emphasis on public ritual, ceremony, and religious architecture; and the use of literacy as a tool of elite control. Spaniards, of course, were deeply impressed by the differences they perceived between themselves and the Mayas, especially those involving religious beliefs and ritual. In fact, many military men overtly conceived of the Mayas as New World Moors: "infidels" who, no matter how civilized they might be, required conversion and pacification under the heavy arm of military authority (Map 20.2).

THE SPANISH CONQUEST OF THE LOWLAND MAYAS

Yucatan was first contacted by Spaniards no later than 1511, when a ship sailing from Panama to Santo Domingo was blown off course, foundering off the eastern coast of the peninsula. The Mayas spared the lives of two of the survivors, Gerónimo de Aguilar and a nobleman named Gonzalo Guerrero, who were living among the native population when Hernán Cortés (also spelled Hernando Cortez) stopped at Cozumel on his way to the Veracruz coast. The next two expeditions to reach Yucatan apparently sought to capture slaves to work in the Antilles, where massive declines in the native populations had caused labor shortages for Spanish enterprises. In 1517 Francisco Hernández de Córdoba reached Yucatan during a voyage from Havana, forced ashore at Ekab' on Cabo Catoche as the result of a storm. The Maya inhabitants attacked his party, which then sailed along the northern and western coast until reaching Chanputun, where further attacks forced them to return to Cuba. The next year Juan de Grijalva set out to explore Yucatan with 250 to 300 men in four ships, claiming Cozumel island in the name of the crown. This

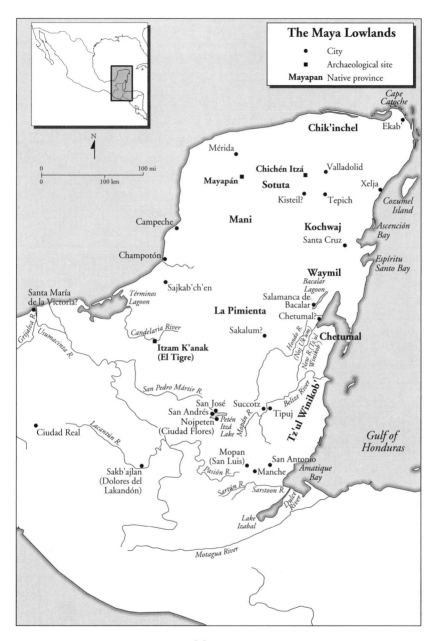

The Maya Lowlands

- • City
- ■ Archaeological site
- **Mayapan** Native province

Cape
Catoche

Chik'inchel Ekab'

Mérida

Chichén Itzá ■ Valladolid

Mayapán ■ **Sotuta** Xelja

Kisteil? Tepich

Cozumel
Island

Campeche **Mani** **Kochwaj** Ascención
Bay

Santa Cruz

Champotón Espíritu
Santo Bay

Waymil
Bacalar
Sajkab'ch'en Lagoon

Santa María Términos Salamanca de
de la Victoria? Lagoon **La Pimienta** Bacalar

Chetumal?

Candelaria River Sakalum? **Chetumal**

Grijalva R. **Itzam K'anak**
Usumacinta R. **(El Tigre)**

San Pedro Mártir R.

San José Succotz Belize River

San Andrés Tipuj

Ciudad Real Nojpeten Petén
(Ciudad Flores) Itzá
Lake Mopán R.

Lacantún R.

Mopan
(San Luis) San Antonio **Gulf of**
Honduras

Sakb'ajlan Pasión R. Manche Amatique
(Dolores del Bay
Lakandón) Sartún R. Sarstoon R.

Lake
Izabal

Motagua River

N

0   100 mi
0   100 km

Map 20.2

party then sailed to Campeche, where they defeated an attack by Mayas, voyaging from there to the Laguna de Términos and on to the Pánuco River. They returned to Campeche and were again attacked there before returning to Cuba.

Cortés himself stopped at Cozumel in 1519 on his way to the Veracruz coast, where he organized his eventual conquest of Tenochtitlan, the Aztec capital. There the *conquistador* ransomed the shipwrecked sailor Gerónimo de Aguilar, who had learned the Maya language well. Aguilar's language teachers unwittingly facilitated the conquest of central Mexico by enabling him to serve as a translator. Aguilar could apparently speak Yucatec with the famous Doña Marina, Cortés's probably trilingual (Chontal-, Yucatec-, and Nahua-speaking) mistress, whom the conqueror met in Tabasco and took with him on his conquest of Tenochtitlan.

Following the successful conquest of Tenochtitlan, in 1525 Cortés led a large exploratory party of Spanish troops and native retainers from Coatzacoalcos across Chontal Akalan, Kejach, and Itza territory on his way to Honduras. He met AjKan Ek', the Itza ruler, at Nojpeten, where he left a cross and a lame horse. He provided the first descriptions of the broad territorial and economic influence of the Itzas, who were not officially recontacted – this time by Franciscan priests – for nearly a century; in 1618 Cortés's cross, it was said, was still standing at the Itza capital.

Francisco de Montejo, also a participant in the Mexican conquest, was the first to receive the Spanish Crown's patent to conquer Yucatan, beginning his project in 1527. Although they were probably already devastated by epidemic diseases introduced by earlier European visitors to a population without natural resistance, the Mayas put up a vicious resistance to Montejo's efforts to conquer the northeastern and south-eastern parts of the peninsula. On Montejo's first voyage to Yucatan he was, however, received peacefully at Cozumel by the island's ruler, Naum Pat, who assisted him in the establishment of a short-lived Spanish villa on the peninsula near Xelja opposite the southern end of the island, which he named Salamanca.

Over a six-month period Montejo's troops easily "pacified" some of the interior, but met strong fortifications and armed opposition in the Chik'inchel province, where ten or twelve Spaniards and many more Mayas lost their lives. Soon thereafter he set out southward to the rich coastal town of Chetumal, where he hoped at last to find gold and a better location for his villa. Montejo learned that Gonzalo Guerrero was living there and had reportedly married a Maya woman and adopted Maya dress and customs. Guerrero, however, refused to join the Spanish explorers and was accused by contemporary European writers of fomenting a vicious Maya attack against Montejo. Native messengers falsely informed Montejo that his lieutenant Alonso Dávila, who had taken troops by land to support Montejo at Chetumal, had been killed with all his men. By the time Montejo returned to Salamanca following further explorations toward Honduras, Dávila had abandoned Xelja, having moved the villa northward to Xamanha (Zamanca).

Montejo thereupon returned to New Spain, leaving Dávila and a few troops at Xamanha, where they apparently carried out slaving missions against the interior Mayas, who were then sent off to the West Indies. Montejo returned in 1529 with a broader mandate to stabilize the small Spanish colony of Santa María de la Victoria in Tabasco and to use this location as a new base from which to mount a new campaign in adjoining Yucatan. Dávila abandoned Xamanha in order to assist Montejo and his son, Francisco Montejo the Younger, in the continuing conquest of Tabasco.

Dávila was appointed in 1530 to establish a base on the west coast of Yucatan, which he reached via the Akalan province. He found a friendly welcome at the large fortified town of Chanputum which had already received peace emissaries from Montejo. Montejo soon joined Dávila, and together they decided to establish the villa of Salamanca at the nearby coastal settlement of Campeche, where Montejo issued the first *encomiendas* in Yucatan to his soldiers. Dávila set out across the peninsula in 1531 to conquer the southeastern part of Yucatan, with the aim of establishing another Spanish town at the trading post of Chetumal near the mouth of the Rio Hondo. Dávila found Chetumal abandoned and established a town for the soldiers nearby, which they called Villa Real. Before long, however, the Mayas of the region rose up against the conquerors and laid siege to Villa Real, forcing Dávila to retreat to Honduras.

Despite better success in the northern part of the peninsula, Montejo's men began to abandon him by 1534, choosing to opt for Peru, where tales of gold rendered the mineral poverty of Yucatan and its hostile population an unappealing venture. During that year the Spanish evacuated their forces from Yucatan a second time. By then, however, Montejo had already seriously disrupted Maya life, turning prisoners of war into slaves – as many as 50,000, according to one source – for export to New Spain.[4] Epidemics had already taken a major toll, and the surviving population braced itself for the Spaniards' return.

Six years later, in 1540, Montejo's son and nephew began once more to move against the Mayas of Yucatan. This time they were better prepared, and the Mayas were probably too exhausted and decimated by disease to mount an effective resistance. The Montejos founded Mérida in 1542, although the town was soon thereafter attacked by hostile groups from the eastern part of the peninsula. The Spanish *villas* of Campeche, Valladolid, and Salamanca de Bacalar, in the remote southeast near Chetumal, were established by 1544. By this time the northernmost part of the peninsula was firmly in Spanish hands, with little resistance offered in the west but much in the east. The southeastern the provinces of Chetumal, Waymil, and Tz'ul Winikob' experienced especially harsh treatment by Melchor and Alonso Pacheco before the inhabitants finally succumbed. According to the Franciscan father Lorenzo de Bienvenida, who established the first mission at Bacalar in about 1546,

Nero was not more cruel than [Alonso Pacheco]. . . . Even though the natives did not make war, he robbed the province and consumed the foodstuffs of the natives, who fled into the bush in fear of the Spaniards, since as soon as [this captain] captured any of them, he set the dogs on them. And the Indians fled from all this and did not sow their crops, and all died of hunger. I say all, because there were pueblos of five hundred and one thousand houses, and now one which has one hundred is large. . . . Tying them to stakes, he cut the breasts off many women, and hands, noses, and ears off the men, and he tied squashes to the feet of women and threw them in the lakes to drown merely to amuse himself.[5]

These genocidal conquest methods, combined with the early imposition of slavery and tribute, led the Mayas to react in 1546 with widespread offensives against the Spaniards around the towns of Bacalar and Valladolid. The Spaniards spend months in crushing the revolt of 1546, which left the eastern and southeastern Maya territories in a state of confusion. Many native inhabitants fled to the unconquered and unexplored interior

[4] William L. Sherman, *Forced Labor in Sixteenth-Century Central America* (Lincoln: University of Nebraska Press, 1979), 52. Although the practice of exporting slaves captured in war predated the Conquest, the numbers must have been far fewer than those involved in Montejo's operation.

[5] Robert S. Chamberlain, *The Conquest and Colonization of Yucatan, 1517–1550* (Washington, DC, 1948), 235. The original letter from Bienvenida to Felipe II, dated 10 February 1548, is published in *Cartas de Indias* (Madrid, 1877), 70–82.

regions of the peninsula. From then on, throughout most of the colonial period, the principal source of Maya resistance came from these interior regions, where a constantly restocked mix of runaways and the hardened attempted to retain an autonomous way of life. At the moral, if not the geographical, center of this interior land of avoidance and anticolonial resistance were the Itza Mayas on Lake Petén Itzá. Well aware of this fact, Spanish policy was consciously designed over a period of nearly two centuries to encircle Itza territory and to isolate it from external trade ties. This policy was only partially successful, however, as the Itzas frequently managed to recruit their frontier neighbors as allied participants in a war of attrition against slow but steady Spanish encroachments on their frontiers.

The colonial province of Yucatan was born in violence and prolonged armed resistance for which the Spaniards had been ill prepared. The Maya battles waged against Spaniards, although localized, were fierce, characterized by sophisticated strategy, the use of guerrilla tactics, and the application of remarkable skills in defensive and offensive warfare. The Mayas were ultimately no match, however, for mounted Spaniards who used firearms – at least not in the more open, drier, and less densely forested areas of the north. There, rebellion was forced to go underground in the form of more subtle methods of resistance, or its population opted to relocate in the unconquered jungles. In southern uprisings, however, armed Spaniards found their weapons and horses to be of little value, and it was many more years before they learned how best to confront the enemy in these thick tropical forests. Dominican missionaries working in Verapaz during the late sixteenth century and the seventeenth century attempted to Christianize the southern Peten Chols without arms, but even they were unsuccessful in achieving permanent converts. Conversion in the north was also a complex process, and supposed resistance to early missionary efforts there was met in 1562 by a harsh *auto de fé* into Maya "idolatry" by the famous Franciscan, later bishop of Yucatan, Fray Diego de Landa.

During the early 1600s, Franciscan missionaries became convinced that until the Itza stronghold on Lake Petén Itzá converted to Christianity and accepted the legitimacy of the Spanish crown, the complete Christianization and pacification of the rest of the peninsula would be impossible. According to this view, the Itzas were the principal cause of the draining away of human resources caused by runaways who abandoned the *encomiendas*. Using Maya millennial prophecy as their major weapon, hardy Franciscans visited the Itza capital of Nojpeten in 1618 and 1619, when they thought that the Itza king, AjKan Ek', would accept their interpretation of the *k'atun* (or *Katun*) prophecies as discussed in a later section that the time had come to embrace the Christian faith. AjKan Ek' and his priests, however, had a different interpretation of these prophecies and made it clear to the friars that the time for their capitulation was not yet at hand. In fact, the friars were lucky to get away with their lives.

In 1695 another Franciscan friar, Andrés de Avendaño, masterminded a second effort to use prophecy in order to effect Itza capitulation. This time the Itza ruler, another member of the Kan Ek' dynasty, accepted Avendaño with open arms, agreeing that K'atun 8 Ajaw, which was to begin in 1696 or 1697, was the time for him to bring his people into the Christian fold and to recognize the king of Spain. AjKan Ek', however, had enemies in his midst who had other ideas, and on his 1696 visit to Nojpeten, Avendaño also barely escaped with his life. By now the Itza problem had become a major colonial embarrassment, and troops were sent from Campeche to destroy the Itza capital. The Spanish captured Nojpeten in a bloody battle on 13 March 1697, during which many Maya defenders lost their lives. Then, just as Mayas everywhere had done for nearly two centuries, the surviving defenders sought refuge in the forests, leaving the Spanish militia in charge of an abandoned Maya town without a supporting population. The Itza conquest, despite efforts to repopulate the Itzas in towns on the shores of Lake Petén Itzá, was a dismal failure.

Actually, this conquest was only an afterthought to a less ambitious plan to connect the province of Guatemala with that of Yucatan. This plan resulted in the 1695 "conquest" by Guatemalan troops of several Chol-speaking Maya communities, the most important of which was Sakb'ajlan (thereafter known as Nuestra Señora de los Dolores or Dolores del Lakandon) on the Lacantún River in eastern Chiapas. Only after Fray Andrés de Avendaño had convinced the governor of Yucatan of his belief that the Itzas would accept conversion and lay down their arms at the beginning of K'atun 8 Ajaw did plans to ensure their pacification with arms proceed.

DEMOGRAPHIC RESPONSES TO CONQUEST AND COLONIZATION

Although most scholars believe that contact-period population declines in the Maya lowlands were less severe than in the more densely populated highland areas of Mesoamerica, there is little evidence to support this assumption. Estimates of the contact-period population of the Maya lowlands vary widely owing to two principal factors that prevent an accurate reconstruction. The first of these is the nearly forty-year period between the initial Spanish arrival and the first colonial population counts, by which time European diseases had severely affected the native population. The second is that only the northern Yucatan peninsula was sufficiently "pacified" to allow an accurate count even at later dates, leaving the bulk of the lowland territories uncounted. As noted earlier, the total population of the Maya lowlands probably exceeded a million persons at the time of initial European contact.

The European-introduced diseases probably took their major demographic toll well before the first count taken in northern Yucatan in 1549–50, which indicated a population of about 240,000. Estimates for the southern lowlands are unavailable until 1582. These, which incorporate only those Mayas in Belize and southeastern Quintana Roo who were under the direct control of the *encomenderos* at Salamanca de Bacalar, indicate only between 850 and 1,500 persons between 1582 and 1643 – clearly a small percentage of the largely unconquered southern populations. That these population figures are far too small is indicated by a reconstruction of the central Peten population at approximately 60,000 on the eve of the 1697 conquest.

The diseases unwittingly introduced by Europeans included smallpox, measles, and influenza. These, along with typhus, yellow fever, and, by the eighteenth century, malaria, interacted with other natural disasters that in combination had major effects on Maya populations and on their strategies for survival. Epidemic diseases reduced the subsistence and tribute-paying labor pool, resulting in periodic famines and flight from centers of colonial control to the outlying forests in search of food. Cycles of drought and locust infestations further exacerbated these factors, all of which combined to keep the permanent native population of the northern lowlands at a relatively small level.

Population recovery in Yucatan was therefore slow. The Maya population of the peninsula had fallen to about 165,000 by the first decade of the seventeenth century, rose to about 210,000 by the 1640s, then plunged to about 100,000 by 1688.[6] This late demographic disaster was the combined result of a virulent yellow fever epidemic in 1648 and harsh

[6] Nancy M. Farriss, *Maya Society Under Colonial Rule: The Collective Enterprise of Survival* (Princeton, NJ, 1984), 59.

Spanish labor policies that caused many Mayas to flee to the forests during the 1650s and 1660s. Gradual population growth, punctuated by smaller famine-induced losses and characterized by a growing ratio of non-Mayas to Mayas, continued through the eighteenth century. By 1794 the total population of the colonial province of Yucatan had reached 357,000, of whom 254,000, or 71 percent, were classified as Mayas.[7] These trends continued through the nineteenth century until the eve of the Caste War, when the total population had reached about 580,000. By 1869 the enumerated population had dropped to approximately 363,000, reflecting a loss of more than 100,000 lives during the war and the survival of as many as 100,000 refugees in the southeastern forests.[8] Ever since then, however, population has grown enormously in Yucatan, surpassing one million persons in 1970, of whom about half speak the Maya language.

Although colonial records indicate the flight of tens of thousands of Yucatec Mayas from the northern *encomiendas* to the territories across the base of the peninsula during the late sixteenth and seventeenth centuries, no accurate estimate of the numbers of these refugees exists for any single point in time. They clustered primarily in the Kejach region south of Sajkab'ch'en, in the territory of southern Quintana Roo (the old Kochwaj province) known as La Pimienta, and in the cacao-producing upper Belize river valley. Others may have been incorporated in the populations in the vicinity of Lake Petén Itzá, which, as already noted, may have reached a total of 60,000 by the time of the Itza conquest. Of these refugees only the tiny population of Yucatec-speaking Lakandon, who are probably the direct descendants of the seventeenth-century Kejach, survived as autonomous groups into the late twentieth century. An estimated 88 percent of the Itza-area populations died during the first decade of colonial rule (1697–1706), largely because of epidemic diseases and warfare.

The fate of the Yucatecan-speaking refugee populations has yet to be carefully documented, although a host of factors are known to have reduced the number of forest dwellers during the seventeenth and eighteenth centuries, including English-sponsored slaving raids by Miskitosj, forced removal of populations back to Yucatan; disease; loss of territory

[7] Sherburne F. Cook and Woodrow Borah, *Essays in Population History: Mexico and the Caribbean,* vol. 2 (Berkeley, CA, 1974), 114.
[8] Cook and Borah, *Essays in Population History,* 128.

to English logwood cutters; and their incorporation into a Spanish-speaking mestizo (biologically mixed European-native) lower class. A forest population, known as *"huites"* (from *huidos,* or runaways), still inhabited eastern and southeastern Yucatan during the first half of the nineteenth century, and the southern Caste War independent groups known as the *pacíficos del sur* probably had direct ties to earlier refugee populations. The Yucatec-speaking Mayas in northern Belize today are primarily descendants of Caste War refugees from towns in Yucatan and from these older southern independent populations.

The small population of Chols in southern Belize and Peten were forcibly removed to Alta Verapaz during the late seventeenth century, where they gradually merged with speakers of K'ekchi Maya. Most of the Chol-speaking Lakandons were resettled around Huehuetenango during the early 1700s. These were incorporated with other populations at this location and gradually ceased to be identified by their former ethnic and linguistic labels. Of the southernmost lowland Mayas, only the Mopan Mayas of Belize and Peten, whose numbers are small, continue to form a strong linguistic and cultural entity. The K'ekchi Mayas, some of whom are descendants of K'ekchi – Chol ancestors, have, however, become a significant presence in Belize over the past century.

MAYA RESPONSES TO COLONIAL POLICY AND PRACTICE

As in all areas of Spanish America the colonial system imposed upon the lowland Mayas systems of tribute, forced labor, and Christianization. The particular conditions of Yucatan and the areas to the south resulted in cultural changes that were more subtle than in many areas, although by the end of the colonial period much of Yucatec Maya culture had been significantly altered.

Of the Spanish methods used to exploit the Maya population the *encomiendas* were perhaps the most significant forms of native reorganization. These grants to the tribute of the native populations to Spanish conquerors and their descendants, or to the Crown itself, despite laws outlawing them elsewhere in the Spanish New World, were retained in Yucatan until the late 1700s. The *encomiendas* extracted coinage, cacao, cotton cloth, maize, and other native products that were consumed in the colony or sold by Spaniards on the open market. Although the required tribute payments were at first relatively small, the policy of *encomienda* sought to concentrate the Mayas in stable, centrally administered towns. This policy directly contradicted their traditional patterns of dispersed settlement and individual physical movement.

As in colonial situations throughout history, the Spanish governed the Maya by means of "indirect rule," appointing local native leaders to keep the peace in individual towns, to assure conformity with Spanish civil and religious law, to collect tributes and other forced payments, to organize labor for public works and private service, to provide services for religious and secular visitors, and even to provide instruction in Christianity and other ritual services to inhabitants of the towns. In contrast to the hierarchical territorial political organization of precolumbian times, the principal towns were all of equivalent political status in relation to the Spanish *villas*. During much of the colonial period the principal Spanish-approved native leaders were descendants of the precolumbian nobility, but eventually, some studies suggest, the old distinction between nobility and commoner became less pronounced, and the native population took on the qualities of a common underclass in relation to those of Spanish descent. Other studies, however, indicate that these social distinctions within the Maya population remained important through at least the mid-nineteenth century and that they played a major role in the development of the Caste War of Yucatan.

The principal secular governing body of the colonial native towns was the *cabildo*, or town council (also known as *república de indios*), consisting of one or two *alcaldes*, and four *regidores*; these were often assisted by other minor officials. Many towns had, in addition, a "governor" or *cacique* (sometimes known by the old Maya title, *b'atab'* or *batab*), who wielded considerable influence over the *cabildo*. Governors and councils of towns of sufficient importance were assisted by a scribe or clerk who kept records and prepared official correspondence. Although the council and governor normally dealt with routine day-to-day legal, financial, and labor matters, some town officers were occasionally called on to recruit and even lead temporary militias to help round up runaways in neighboring and distant forests. Community members sometimes brought legal charges against their governors and other officials, usually accusing them of extraordinary behavior or physical mistreatment. Although these men did engage in corruption and misuse of office, their behavior was undoubtedly reinforced by excessive labor or monetary demands by their Spanish overlords. Some native officers were strong defenders of native legal rights and took complaints against Spaniards directly to responsible government officials.

In addition to the secular *cabildos*, town leaders (known collectively as *principales*) also belonged to the *cofradías*, or religious brotherhoods, that were responsible for care and rituals of the saints associated with particular towns. The most important religious figure in the town was known as the *maestro* – usually identified as a *maestro cantor* (choirmaster or singing teacher) or *maestro de capilla* (chapel master or teacher). These individuals, who, like the governor or *b'atab'*, served for extended periods of time under an ostensible lifetime appointment, exercised a host of religious and educational duties that were all the more important in light of the frequent absence of a Spanish priest for weeks or months at a time. As representatives of an educated, literate sector of colonial Maya society, the *maestros* enjoyed high prestige and wielded considerable political and moral influence. Not surprisingly, they were sometimes accused of "idolatrous" practices, and some of them undoubtedly were the principal community repositories of traditional "non-Christian" religious and historical knowledge. Even today, village *maestros* in some areas enjoy religious prestige that may overshadow that of the clergy.

Encomienda towns, despite Spanish efforts to govern them, were demographically unstable. As Farriss and others have demonstrated, their members shifted their residence by process of intercommunity marriage and migration, moved off to newly formed agricultural hamlets, and ran away from Spanish control to the forest zones. Despite intense efforts to force the Mayas to stay in central locations, the native population moved about constantly, changing town affiliations, establishing new villages, and sometimes even moving far into the forests beyond to avoid colonial control. Such residential mobility was probably an ancient pattern, and its continuity under Spanish rule made it difficult to maintain control over individuals, to say nothing of maintaining a dependable tribute-paying population. Spanish responses to this physical fluidity of the population took the form of periodic roundups known as reductions or congregations. The Maya population, however, was like a leaking dam, which *encomenderos* were unable to plug effectively throughout the entire course of the colonial period.

Far more onerous as a system of labor than the *encomiendas* was the complex and varied system known generically as *repartimiento*, which in Yucatan frequently took the form of distribution of cash payments or, less frequently, of European products (cloth from Flanders, European jewelry, and European finished clothing) to Mayas in return for fixed demands for payment in the form of native goods. Cotton cloth was the dominant product demanded, and in some cases unspun cotton was extorted from cotton-growing regions and distributed elsewhere for *repartimiento* conversion into the final woven product. The *repartimiento* in its various forms was nominally illegal, but colonial administrators, their bureaucratic appointees, and even church officials applied the system knowing that their punishment for doing so would be nothing more than a small fine – a tax, in effect, applied to hefty incomes derived from selling these goods to New Spain and elsewhere. During the late seventeenth century, when *repartimiento* demands were at their peak, the *encomienda* populations, unable to meet the Spanish demand for such forest products as honey and wax, purchased these goods from runaways in the forest in exchange for such needed items as metal tools made by Maya blacksmiths.

The net effect of the *encomienda* and *repartimiento* in the Yucatan peninsula was, therefore, to increase the attractiveness of the choice to flee southward to the forests. The refugees not only escaped colonial economic pressures but also became entrepreneurs in an intra-Maya trading system that, ironically, was fueled by the colonial system itself.

The Spanish Franciscan and secular priests also applied charges for their services, and a host of additional taxes in support of the colonial bureaucracy further drained the already strained rural economy. Although outright slavery was outlawed soon after the Conquest, forms of "personal service" for public works and private Spanish dwellings, in return for negligible payment, separated Maya families as their members were forced to work in Spanish households for part of the year. These forms of exploitation were recorded in words of bitterness by a Maya chronicler:

> The beginning of forcible separation,
> > The beginning of forced labor for the Spaniards
> And the sun priests,
> > Forced labor for the town chiefs,
> Forced labor for the teachers,
> > Forced labor for the public prosecutors,
> By the boys,
> > By the youths of the towns,
> While the force of great suffering
> > Afflicted the suffering people.
> These were the very poor,
> > These were the very poor who did not rebel

At the oppression
That was inflicted on them.
This was the Antichrist
Here on earth,
The Earth Lions of the towns,
The foxes of the towns,
The Bedbugs of the towns
Are the bloodsuckers of the poor peasants here.[9]

Such direct economic exploitation in a society whose commoner population had never been wealthy was serious enough, but other requirements also fostered resentment. Mayas were themselves used to round up
runaways from *encomienda* towns, often under the military command of
their own nobility who had succumbed to Spanish interests. They were
thus forced to participate in the punishment of rebels and resisters whose
cause they must have admired. Others, confounded by Spanish demands
for theological purity in religion, were punished for participating in even
the most benign of rituals that Spaniards considered to be partially pagan
in nature. Those who were most open in their use of native censers, for
example, were assumed by Spaniards to be "idolaters" and were punished
harshly by whippings and imprisonment.

Maya society itself exhibited certain characteristics that made their
governance by colonial officials, *encomenderos*, and missionaries particularly difficult and thus "prone" to the chance for the spread of anti-
Spanish strategies. In addition to the pattern of ungovernable population
movement, the Spaniards or their Creole descendants faced, first of all,
the problem of sheer numbers. While Spaniards were largely confined to
a few rather small urban and rural settlements, the Mayas were everywhere: in the towns, in the *encomienda* villages, and in the bush. They
outnumbered the Spaniards many times over. They had excellent communication with other Mayas all across the peninsula owing to extended
ties of kinship and long-distance trade networks that continued to flourish throughout the colonial period. These personal and economic networks were fostered by the literacy of some Mayas, who had learned how
to write at the sides of Franciscan priests but who later chose to use their
knowledge for purposes of resistance. Some of these literate Mayas became underground leaders with strong religious, charismatic characteris-

---

[9] Munro S. Edmonson, *Heaven Born Mérida and Its Destiny: The Book of Chilam Balam of Chumayel* (Austin, Texas, 1986), 110.

tics. Some took on the role of prophets and set up rebel headquarters in the southern forests, donning bishop's garb and presiding over well-controlled economies that, ironically, received income from Maya peasants in the north who needed these forest products in order to pay excessive tributes that their own labor alone could not fulfill.

The Mayas were exceedingly adept at keeping secrets from Spaniards – not an impossible task given their superior numbers and their collective dislike of the oppressor. They adapted culturally to Europeans' efforts to wring information from them by honing the ability to remain silent even under the use of torture. Their answers to leading questions about their activities posed by Spanish investigators were brief, spare, and noncommittal.

Even the Maya literature of the colonial period was designed to confuse Spanish readers who might see it. The Books of Chilam Balam, written in Maya in the Spanish script taught by Spanish priests, contain a great deal of esoteric information concerning history, prophecy, divination, religious ritual, and ritual language. The poetic language of these books is notoriously difficult to translate and may well have been intentionally obfuscated to keep Spaniards from discovering their real meaning. Modern linguists, unfortunately, have great difficulty as well in understanding these important texts.

One element of the Books of Chilam Balam, however, is fairly well understood for its historical significance: that is, the importance of the sections addressing the repetitive cycles of time known as *k'atuns*. The *k'atun* cycle was only one element of many in the complex, interlocking system of Maya calendars, but we now know that it was a critical means by which the Maya could communicate to one another about the importance of timing of events in the past and in the future. Each *k'atun* lasted a little less than twenty years and was associated with a particular set of characteristic events or qualities that were recorded for the previous times the *k'atun* occurred. These events and qualities would, the Mayas believed, characterize the next twenty year period when the same *k'atun* occurred. Thirteen different *k'atuns* followed one after the other in a precise order, and at the end of a cycle of thirteen they repeated one another all over again. Thus, what happened in K'atun 8 Ajaw between 1441 and 1461 had significance for what might happen in the same *k'atun* 256 years later, between 1697 and 1717. This use of history to put the future in the foreground and interpret it was a powerful political and ideological tool of resistance against colonialism, since it was understood by Mayas throughout the peninsula but was, for the most part, kept entirely secret from the Spaniards.

Maya rebel priests who tried to attract followings used such prophecies to foreshadow or even control events. For example, when Spaniards at Bacalar learned about the impending uprising in 1638, they reported that villagers told them that local Maya leaders at Tipuj insisted that

they were to give obedience to their king and wished them to abandon their town, saying that if they did not do so all would die and be finished, because at such a time the Itzas would come to kill them and there would be many deaths, and hurricanes would flood the land.[10]

The year 1638 was the beginning of K'atun 1 Ajaw, when, according to similar language in the Book of Chilam Balam of Tizimin, there "will be the ending of words: the great war. . . . Fires and hurricane rains are the burden of the k'atun."[11] Such prophecies provided flexibility to Maya leaders, who took advantage of their general vagueness and openness to interpretation and manipulation. They appealed to many Mayas, who bought readily into any ideology that even suggested the possibility that someday the foreigners might leave and that justice might be restored.

Spanish-speaking people understood many of these qualities of Maya culture and reacted with characteristic and understandable paranoia. Spanish correspondence is filled with statements of fears of attack, even though very few of these fears actually materialized. An annual moment of panic occurred, for example, during the processions for Holy Week in the Spanish towns, when rumors of Maya attack would surface. Eventually, those who marched in these processions took to carrying their weapons. Even in normal times any Maya stranger in town was viewed with suspicion, and the slightest rumor quickly ballooned out of proportion and sent tremors all the way to Mérida.

During the colonial period, when these fears were nearly constant, certain regular activities on the part of Spaniards were designed to prevent such dangers of attack from occurring. Every few years the headquarters of runaway Mayas in the southern forests were attacked, their charismatic leaders executed, their ritual objects confiscated and destroyed, and the runaways brought back to be redistributed on the *encomiendas* where they "belonged." Bishops, governors, and lesser offi-

---

[10] Unpublished manuscript, 20 September 1638, Legajo 360 in Audiencia de México section, Archivo General de Indias, Seville.

[11] Edmonson, *Heaven Born Mérida*, 213.

cials frequently carried out tours of the *encomienda* towns to root out anti-Spanish criminal activity and idolatry. Although in the early days such *visitas* produced many "idols" and even hieroglyphic books, in later years the subtle techniques of hiding information allowed for little in the way of direct evidence for anti-Spanish activity. Even a century after the Conquest, however, missionaries and soldiers were able to turn up caches of "idols" in such out-of-the-way places as Cozumel, where they were ready to be shipped throughout the peninsula.

Late colonial period resistance in Yucatan was primarily a process of intentional avoidance and subtle, nonviolent terrorism, not open rebellion. The Mayas were slippery physical objects, moving about and running away right under the Spaniards' noses. They were hard to catch, and the cost of military ventures into the dense jungle was so high that most runaways were never caught. Besides, the small colonial budget of Yucatan was strained by the costs of defending the coasts from pirates and English logwood cutters around Tabasco and the eastern coasts – leaving little for those who sought runaways in the bush. Native guerrilla tactics frightened every type of soldier – Spanish, mulatto, or Maya – who was called to serve on these expeditions. By the time most of these ragged militia units reached their destinations deep in the forests, the native guides, scouts, carriers, and foot soldiers had run away in fear, leaving only a few hardy soldiers to fend for themselves against ambushes and a hostile natural environment.

Most of the time, then, the Mayas simply terrorized their European rulers by acting in ways that made them difficult to govern. They talked among themselves in prophetic terms about the inevitabile end of Spanish rule. They changed their residence in unpredictable fashion. They ran away, sometimes abandoning entire communities. They maintained underground religious movements under the very noses of the Spaniards and established cult centers in isolated areas. They kept secret and seditious books of history and prophecy. Rebel leaders in the forests used these prophecies to attract followers, spreading an ideology of native resistance and even branding their members to make certain that they would not return to their *encomienda* towns.

Sometimes their methods were more hostile. The forest rebel leaders sometimes kidnaped *encomienda* Mayas against their will. They attacked towns on the southern frontiers of northern Yucatan. They threatened and even on occasion murdered visitors – priests, Maya retainers, and soldiers – who dared to visit their isolated centers in the forests. On other occasions, however, their strategies fostered only the abandonment of *encomienda* towns through recruitment to remote locations under rebel control.

A major flare-up occurred in 1624 at the town of Sakalum deep in the southeastern forests of what is today the Mexican state of Quintana Roo. In this case a massacre of Spaniards and Mayas attending church, by forest rebels, was in direct response to their mistreatment by a Spanish officer who intended to open a road all the way to Lake Petén Itzá and to conquer the Peten Mayas. Well aware of these intentions, the Itzas had only a few weeks earlier massacred a party of Mayas from Tipuj, and the Franciscan priest who accompanied them. But the Sakalum massacre was only a prelude to an Itza-fostered rebellion throughout Belize in 1638, when the people of Tipuj, citing Itza interpretations of the *k'atun* prophecies, declared their independence from Spanish control and engineered the abandonment of nearly every colonial Maya town south of Bacalar. Little violence characterized this show of resistance, however. Later, in the forests south of Campeche in 1668 and 1678, when prophecies of rebellion were circulating widely in response to the *repartimiento* activities of a particularly rapacious Spanish governor and his cronies, thousands of Mayas from the northern *encomienda* towns deserted their homes to join the forest rebels and runaways.

On only one occasion during the colonial period, in 1761, did an uprising of sorts actually go so far as to threaten to overthrow the colonial regime. In that year, in the Sotuta province where the 1546 rebellion had broken out, a Maya leader reportedly incited a widespread revolt centered at the town of Kisteil, with the ultimate aim of ridding the peninsula for once and for all of the Spanish Creoles. Supposedly taking his name from the last Itza ruler, Jacinto Kan Ek' was crowned and dressed with the mantle of the town's patron saint, Our Lady of the Conception – calling himself King Jacinto Uk Kan Ek', Chichan Montezuma. His goal, he was quoted as saying in a sermon to those gathered around during a fiesta at Kisteil, was to organize a rebellion that would free the Mayas from Spanish subjugation and allow them to "throw off their yoke of servitude."[12]

Drunken Spanish militiamen apparently stirred up the crowd even more by attacking the multitude indiscriminantly, and a few days later

[12] Victoria Reifler Bricker, *The Indian Christ, the Indian King: The Historical Substrate of Maya Myth and Ritual* (Austin, TX, 1981), 73.

new, sober troops invaded Kisteil and forced the inciters to flee to the bush. Kan Ek' was eventually captured, tortured mercilessly, and executed with a blow to the head; eight other leaders were hanged and drawn and quartered, and their bodies displayed publicly. Kisteil's fields were sown with salt, its buildings destroyed, and its population dispersed. Whether the Kisteil rebellion was the result of a well-organized conspiracy, as some contemporary writers maintained, or whether it was simply the outcome of one leader's momentary delusions of grandeur, blown out of proportion by observers of the time, is not yet clear. Further research may provide some of the answers.

AGRARIAN TRANSFORMATIONS AND THE CASTE WAR OF YUCATAN

The gradual deterioration of Creole income from *encomiendas* during the seventeenth century, owing to demographic declines in the native population, resulted, primarily in northwestern Yucatan, in the expansion of *estancias* (cattle ranches) owned a growing landed class of Creoles. By the mid-eighteenth century these individuals had already transformed these estates into haciendas with resident Maya laborers, producing, in addition to cattle, significant amounts of maize for local sale and consumption. Following Mexican independence in 1821, liberal land-ownership policies facilitated the extension of agrarian estates into the richer agricultural zones of the central peninsula. Sugarcane was the principal crop produced by these plantations, which rapidly appropriated supposedly "vacant" and communal lands that had been the principal areas on which the Mayas had grown their subsistence crops. Many Mayas were forced to become resident *peones* in a system of production that directly conflicted with the spatial and temporal requirements of their traditional swidden methods of food production.

Recent studies argue that these transformations of Yucatan's colonial precapitalist tribute economy into a full-blown capitalist agrarian economy during the decades following independence were the primary causes of the outbreak of the Caste War in Yucatan, which occurred in the areas most affected by sugarcane production. In contrast to nineteenth-century Creole writers, who regarded the Caste War as an ethnic or racial expression of centuries of pent-up anti-Spanish hatred on the part of the Maya, current scholarship sees this event as an agrarian, peasant uprising against the conditions wrought by plantation agriculture. A long history of colonial period Maya resistance and rebellion would, in fact, seem to support the Creole perspective, but there can be no doubt that agrarian conditions were the immediate factor that sparked this most important episode in modern Maya history. Terry Rugeley, in a recent study, has argued that the "causes" of the Caste War were multiple and complex, involving not only Maya responses to land shortages but also such additional factors as breakdowns in control over the peasantry by national period political leaders, growing peasant discontent with the excess charges by the Catholic clergy and others, threats to the prestige of the surviving Maya nobility, and increasing unwillingness to grant local elite Creole leadership the powers they sought.[13]

The prelude to the Caste War opened in January 1847, when Maya troops serving one faction of a civil war between white Yucatecan political leaders bolted from their officers in Valladolid and violently attacked the town's Spanish-speaking inhabitants. After a week of fighting the Mayas trickled back home, and the Creoles waited in fear of a renewed attack – too afraid to have the mass of perpetrators arrested. A few months later, however, a purported Maya plot was discovered, and one implicated rebel, Manuel Antonio Ay, was arrested and shot before a firing squad on 26 July. Before he died he offered the following statement indicating his deeply rooted rationale for revolt:

We poor Indians are aware of what the whites are doing to injure us, of how many evils they commit against us, even to our children and harmless women. So much injury without basis seem to us a crime. Indeed, therefore, if the Indians revolt, it is because the whites gave them reason . . . if we die at the hands of the whites, patience. The whites think that these things are all ended, but never. It is so written in the book of Chilam Balam, and so even has said Jesus Christ, our Lord on earth and beyond, that if the whites will become peaceful, so shall we become peaceful.[14]

Only four days later, the first massive rebellion in the history of Yucatan broke out in earnest with the massacre by armed Mayas of twenty or thirty Spanish-speaking families at the northeastern town of Tepich. That year, 1848, was, in fact, to be the first of a new *k'atun* and may have been chosen for this reason as the opportune moment to strike.

Over the succeeding months many thousands died, both Mayas and whites. What had begun as a class conflict over issues of land, tax, and

[13] Terry Rugeley, *Yucatan's Maya Peasantry and the Origins of the Caste War* (Austin, TX, 1996).
[14] Nelson Reed, *The Caste War of Yucatan* (Stanford, CA, 1964), 48–49.

labor reform soon turned into a predominantly ethnic struggle between Mayas and Creoles. Peace negotiations were attempted but failed, and by mid-1848 Maya rebels had overcome most of the Yucatecans' forces and were holding a hostage population under siege at Mérida. At this moment, to the rebel leaders' dismay, the Maya foot soldiers began to drift away as the need to plant their crops reportedly took precedence over their determination to reclaim the peninsula. The tide quickly turned against the rebel forces, and within a few months some of the remaining Maya forces had fled to the southeastern, sparsely inhabited forests of Quintana Roo. The estate-dwelling Mayas of the northeast had not sided with the rebels and remained there as an important source of labor.

The Caste War was over in one sense, but in another it had just begun. Over the next fifty-three years the 10,000 or more rebels who now occupied these remote forests established a new society under their own hierarchical military, civil, and religious leadership. In many ways this revitalized and restructured society superficially resembled pre-conquest Maya forms, but the fundamental institutions were of colonial and nineteenth-century Maya origins: a priesthood associated with the church, and a civil-military hierarchy derived from Yucatecan militia organizations and preexisting community political structures. Despite increasing political factionalism, the refugee rebels continued for years to strike against the frontier towns and dreamed of eventually retaking the entire peninsula with the help of a succession of miraculous wooden crosses through which they heard the word of God. The so-called Cult of the Talking Cross gave them a symbol of unity and strength appropriate to their conviction that they – and not the Yucatecans of Spanish descent – were the true Christians in a moral as well as a military struggle. The refugees survived economically, aided by British shipments of arms from Belize, by rents collected from British woodcutters, and by loot recovered in attacks on Yucatecan towns, which in turn paid for arms and everyday supplies purchased from merchants in Belize.

In 1901 the Cruzob' rebels (named for their reverence for the Cross) were routed by Yucatecans from their headquarters at Santa Cruz, where they had constructed a massive church during the 1850s. Santa Cruz was later returned to Maya control, although factionalism related to the pressures of chicle extraction and hostility toward outside economic interest groups continued to divide the dispersed groups of rebels descendants for many years. Today the original town of Santa Cruz is a Mexicanized urban center (Felipe Carrillo Puerto), and a major highway passes directly through the original rebel territories. Externally introduced political, economic, and ideological changes are rapidly transforming this rebel Maya society.

The Caste War nearly destroyed the peninsula's sugarcane economy and left many former southern agricultural zones totally abandoned. During the last decades of the nineteenth century the haciendas of the northwest, however, had largely recovered with the rapid expansion of the production of henequen, a plant from which sisal fiber is derived. By the early twentieth century more diversified agricultural estates had spread beyond the henequen zone as well, further decreasing the number of free Maya peasant communities. The effects of the Mexican Revolution were delayed in Yucatan, and it was not until the 1930s that the Mayas began to benefit from massive programs of land reform. Sugarcane estates, owned by Creole Yucatecan refugees and Englishmen and worked by Caste War Maya refugees, operated in northern Belize during the late nineteenth and early twentieth centuries. Land redistributions there during the 1950s resulted in the rapid growth of Maya smallholder participation in sugarcane production and the simultaneous decline of subsistence production.

CULTURAL ACCOMMODATION IN MAYA HISTORY

Most scholars of the Maya have been more impressed by the accommodation of Maya culture to externally induced change than by the resistance that has been stressed in the foregoing pages. This is not surprising given the external "Westernized" characteristics of so many modern Maya communities, where one discovers, for example, that children attend Spanish- or English-language schools, that local politics are integrated into regional and national systems, that Catholic priests and evangelical missionaries have strong followings, and that North American–style baseball is an important symbol of community pride. Such superficial indicators of "acculturation," however, often belie deeper expressions of ethnic identity, just as throughout post-conquest history the Maya have donned external trappings of Western culture even while regarding themselves completely different from those of European or mixed ancestry.

Lowland Maya society and culture has changed markedly, however, since the Spanish Conquest. Except in Peten, and in other remote frontier zones, much had already been lost by the end of the sixteenth

century: the nobility, for example, had lost most of its leadership influence; lineages had ceased to function except as exogamous name groups;
multifamily dwellings had been replaced by smaller family units in accordance with Spanish practice; native control over long-distance coastal
trade and salt production had been ceded to the colonists; some groups
were moved wholesale to new locations far from their places of birth;
and people under colonial control could no longer participate openly in
traditional rituals or use the old public temples. These were matters over
which the Mayas had little choice, as such changes were forced upon
them.

To dwell upon such negative losses, however, would be to overlook
the subtle and creative techniques by which the native population
adapted to the overwhelming changes in their social environment. They
adapted by continually reinventing Maya culture with new as well as old
materials at hand, a process that continues even today. This mingling of
cultural traditions must be seen not as simply a juxtaposition of ideas
and external symbols but, rather, as the result of constant readjustments
in the face of external change that redefine what it is "to be Maya."

A simple example must suffice. On entering the most traditional Maya
villages in rural Yucatan and Quintana Roo, one is still greeted by a
open, roofed-over altar upon which rests a wooden cross clothed in an
embroidered dress of the style worn by Maya women. Such altars mark
each of the road entrances to the village. They indicate the four cardinal
points, denote the boundaries between the settlement and the outside
world, and point the way to the sacred plaza, where traditionally a
cottonwood tree was planted near the church. Crosses may also mark the
cardinal points of the plaza, delineating the community's sacred precinct.
Inside the church, which is aligned with the cardinal directions, its altar
toward the east, one will find images of Catholic saints and, possibly,
several more wooden crosses. The Maya theme of directionality has
strong pre-conquest roots. The cross symbol, essential to both Christians
and pre-conquest Mayas, represents not only accommodation to Christianity but also, along with the ceiba tree, the eternal tree of life. The
village saints in the Christian church once replaced Maya deities and
today are the personal patrons and spiritual caretakers of the village's
welfare. Such physical entities are combined through a variety of historical experiences and from several origins to create something that is at
once new and ancient – and quintessentially Maya. The unmistakable
"Mayaness" that strikes outside observers in some traditional lowland

Maya communities reflects a strong historical sense of cultural identity and self-worth, maintained despite centuries of attitudes and behaviors that have marked them as the lowest rural and urban social class.

Today, as in the past, many Maya communities still have shaman/ priest leaders who assist the townspeople in celebrating rituals associated with the agricultural cycle and with illness and health. Such ritual activities went on even in the face of intense missionization in earlier centuries, as they posed little threat to the priests' insistence on theological purity in matters associated with Christian dogma. In many communities there are also still religious leaders whose duties are more closely related to the Christian ritual cycle. These are likely the direct descendants of the *maestros* (or religious teachers) recruited by colonial priests to teach the doctrine to children and to serve the community's religious needs in the priests' absence. In the Maya religious system these are also ideally part of a larger cosmological and ritual entity, just as mixed cosmological physical symbols combine to serve a greater conceptual whole.

THE PRESENT SITUATION OF THE LOWLAND MAYA

No area of the lowland Mayas has been immune to the immense transformations wrought during the mid- and late twentieth century. Foremost of these have had their origins in the economic sector, such as the introduction of new sources of agricultural income to the rural areas (e.g., large-scale henequen production in northwestern Yucatan, smallholder sugarcane farms in northern Belize, various levels of rice production in southern Belize, and cattle ranching in many areas), increases in the rate of rural-urban and rural-rural migration, the stimulation of new forms of employment related to tourism, the introduction of new and improved roads and electric power, and the growth of craft industries such as hammock making. In some areas where the rural subsistence economy has been replaced by cash crop production, whether in the hands of larger capitalist producer-employers or in the hands of rural "peasants" themselves, the resulting cultural changes have been deep and irreversible. As more subsistence farmers among the lowland Maya populations shift to alternative sources of income, observers sometimes witness losses in the use of Maya languages and in the practice of traditional ceremonies, the recognition of traditional religious and secular community offices, participation in noneconomic community ritual obligations, and the commitment to remain loyal to rural community roots.

Despite the great staying power of lowland Maya culture during the colonial period through the first half of this century, changes that are now occurring pose far more of a threat to the integrity of this way of life than any events that occurred during previous centuries. Efforts by government and private agencies and by grass-roots cultural organizations to stimulate ethnic survival face severe challenges in the face of other more powerful factors, including loss of traditionally available lands and the lack of sufficient rural employment opportunities. Even the formerly most remote areas are subject to external sources that may challenge local value systems through the introduction of standardized compulsory primary-level education, the increasing influence of evangelical churches, the ready availability of television programming, and exposure to new and culturally different migrant populations that have been attracted from densely populated regions to new colonization schemes in the lightly inhabited lowlands. On the other hand, some Maya groups and individuals have found that such new sources of knowledge and experience can help empower younger generations to rediscover and reinforce their own identities in practical ways.

The impact of migration and resultant population growth in tropical forest regions, along with rapidly increasing cattle production and logging operations, not only threatens the survival of indigenous societies but also has a disastrous impact on the stability of fragile ecozones, especially in Peten, Belize, Chiapas, Campeche, and Quintana Roo. The January 1994 outbreak of armed rebellion in Chiapas reflected not only the poverty of the already densely populated highland indigenous regions of that state but also growing alarm over ecosystem destruction in the lowlands, over the desperate economic situation of indigenous highland migrants who have colonized lowland zones, over severe inequities in land distribution that now extend across lowland and highland zones alike, and over the potential impact of the North American Free Trade Agreement (NAFTA) upon indigenous peoples in all regions. As overcrowding and economic pressures in highland Guatemala, other Central American republics, and elsewhere in Mexico force even more people to abandon their communities and move onto lands once occupied by southern lowland Maya populations, both social unrest and patterns of environmental destruction are likely to take center stage in the future history of this region.

It would certainly be a mistake to anticipate the rapid decline of lowland Maya culture. The very poverty and slow development pace that afflict most of the rural region inhabited by the lowland Mayas may have tempered in past decades the rate of cultural change and reduced the attractiveness of choosing to give up a relative security rooted in tradition for one that holds doubtful promise for the future. Nonetheless, what was once perhaps the greatest adaptive strength of lowland Maya society – its ability to adapt flexibly to external pressures by individual and group population movement to new agricultural zones – is no longer an attractive option in the face of new economic realities. The promise of new economic opportunities for future generations appears now to lie not in the formerly open, now rapidly filling, frontier but, rather, in a handful of rapidly modernizing cities and towns where the Mayas' traditionally rural-based culture finds little positive reinforcement.

Maya cultures have successfully reinvented themselves before, however, and the recent appearance of indigenous cultural organizations representing themselves in the press and on the Internet, and lobbying for recognition and respect at national and international levels suggests they will continue to practice cultural innovation and reinvention on a scale never before contemplated. The future of the lowland Maya clearly bears watching as their representatives employ increasingly available electronic and print technologies for interregional and cross-continental communication, and as they seek new strategies through political representation, educational reform, active roles in tourism, and other social means both to preserve and to adapt their ethnic identities to a rapidly changing world.

BIBLIOGRAPHICAL ESSAY

Background sources for lowland Maya prehistory are contained in several useful archaeological surveys, including *The World of the Ancient Maya*, by John S. Henderson (Ithaca, NY, 1978); *Ancient Maya Civilization*, by Norman Hammond (New York and Cambridge, 1982); *The Ancient Maya*, by Sylvanus Morley and Robert W. Sharer (Stanford, CA, 1994); and *The Maya*, by Michael D. Coe (New York, 1993). Two popular and stimulating works on Maya civilization, the second of which relates contemporary Maya culture to the ancient past, are Linda Schele and David Freidel, *A Forest of Kings: The Untold Story of the Ancient Maya* (New York, 1992), and David Freidel and Linda Schele, *Maya Cosmos: Three Thousand Years on the Shaman's Path* (New York, 1995). For the Postclassic period in particular, so important for understanding lowland society and culture at the time of European contact, see *The Lowland*

Maya Postclassic, ed. Arlen F. Chase and Prudence M. Rice (Austin, TX, 1985), and *Los mayas de los tiempos tardíos*, ed. Miguel Rivera and Andrés Ciudad (Madrid, 1986). Anthony P. Andrews provides a useful overview and extensive bibliography in his "Late Postclassic Lowland Maya Archaeology," *Journal of World Prehistory* 7 (1993): 35–69.

An extensive general bibliography for colonial period Yucatecan ethnohistory is contained in *Maya Society under Colonial Rule: The Collective Enterprise of Survival*, by Nancy M. Farriss (Princeton, NJ, 1984). Gilbert Joseph's essay, "From Caste War to Class War: The Historiography of Modern Yucatan," *Hispanic American Historical Review* 65 (1985): 111–34, and his book *Rediscovering the Past at Mexico's Periphery: Essays on the History of Modern Yucatan* (Tuscaloosa, AL, 1986) provide thorough guides to the modern historical and some of the ethnographic literature on the region. *Bibliografía antropológica de Yucatán*, by Juan Ramón Bastarrachea (Mexico, 1984), provides an extensive topical guide to published anthropological and historical sources, located in libraries in Mérida, Yucatan, for the entire span of Yucatan's history. Sergio Quezada's *Relación documental para la historia de la provincia de Yucatán, 1540–1844* (Mérida, 1992), contains an extensive, well-indexed listing of primary sources on Yucatan in archives in Spain and Mexico. Edward H. Moseley and Edward D. Terry's edited survey, *Yucatan: A World Apart* (Tuscaloosa, AL, 1980), is a good general introduction to sources and historical topics. Sources for the colonial period in the less-well-known southern lowlands are included in *La paz de Dios y del rey: La conquista de la selva lacandona, 1525–1821*, by Jan de Vos (Mexico, 1980), and in *Maya Resistance to Spanish Rule: Time and History on a Maya Frontier*, by Grant D. Jones (Albuquerque, NM, 1989).

Published Spanish colonial sources on the Maya lowlands are less extensive than for other regions of Mesoamerica. Alfred M. Tozzer's translated edition, with extensive commentary, of Diego de Landa's *Relación de las cosas de Yucatán* (Cambridge, MA, 1941), remains the best English edition of this important work. Mercedes de la Garza and her associates published a definitive edition of the late-sixteenth-century *Relaciones histórico-geográficas de la gobernación de Yucatán* Mexico, 1983. Documents pertaining to the notorious sixteenth-century Franciscan investigation of native "idolatry" in Yucatán constitute the bulk of France V. Scholes and Eleanor B. Adams's *Don Diego Quijada, Alcalde Mayor de Yucatán, 1561–1565*, 2 vols. (Mexico, 1938). Scholes and others compiled *Documentos para la historia de Yucatán, 1561–1565*, 3 vols. (Mérida, 1936–

38), a major collection of Spanish documents on colonial Yucatan and Campeche, including the Church and Spanish–native relations.

Apart from Landa's *Relación*, the most important single-authored colonial history of Yucatan is the Franciscan Diego López de Cogolludo's 1688 *Historia de Yucatán*, published in a facsimile edition (2 vols., Mexico, 1957) and as a reprint of a nineteenth-century edition (2 vols., Graz, 1971). This important book was the primary source for many later historical works and presents much firsthand and documented information about Maya–Spanish interactions.

For a guide to post-conquest native-produced literature, see Munro S. Edmonson and Victoria Reifler Bricker, "Yucatecan Maya Literature," in *Supplement to the Handbook of Middle American Indians*, vol. 3 (Austin, TX, 1985), 44–63. Edmonson's translations of two of the Yucatec-language Books of Chilam Balam, while controversial, are good introductions to this genre of historical-religious writing and contain references to earlier translations and editions (including those of Alfredo Barrera Vásquez and Ralph L. Roys) of these and other such works: *The Ancient Future of the Itza: The Book of Chilam Balam of Tizimin* (Austin, TX, 1982) and *Heaven Born Merida and Its Destiny: The Book of Chilam Balam of Chumayel* (Austin, TX, 1986). The linguist William F. Hanks has initiated innovative approaches to the study of Maya colonial texts in his "Authenticity and Ambivalence in the Text: A Colonial Maya Case," *American Ethnologist* 13 (1986): 721–44, and in his chapter in William F. Hanks and Don S. Rice's *Word and Image in Mayan Culture: Explorations in Language, History and Representation* (Salt Lake City, 1989).

We are indebted to the path-breaking and prolific ethnohistorian Ralph L. Roys for two major syntheses of lowland Maya culture and society at the time of Spanish contact: *The Indian Background of Colonial Yucatan* (Washington, DC, 1943; reprint edition, Norman, OK, 1972), and *The Political Geography of the Yucatan Maya* (Washington, DC, 1957); see also his "Lowland Maya Native Society at Spanish Contact," in *Handbook of Middle American Indians*, vol. 3 (Austin, TX, 1965), 659–76. Peter Gerhard, a historical geographer, has provided a useful supplement to Roys' *Political Geography* with his *The Southeast Frontier of New Spain* (Princeton, NJ, 1979), covering in addition Tabasco, Laguna de Términos, Chiapas, and Soconusco. Robert Chamberlain's *The Conquest and Colonization of Yucatan* (Washington, DC, 1948) remains the most thorough study of the earliest years of the Maya – Spanish encounter in Yucatan. In his *Maya Conquistador* (Boston, 1998), Mathew Restall offers a revised view of the Conquest, emphasizing the Maya perspective on conquest and colonization as told in Maya-language writings. Inga Clendinnen's *Ambivalent Conquests: Maya and Spaniards in Yucatan, 1517–1570* (Cambridge, 1978) presents a more interpretive account of the mid-sixteenth century, examining in detail the Franciscan inquisition of the early 1560s into Spanish accusations of Maya idolatry. Her analysis of early Franciscan activities among the Mayas should be read in conjunction with Stella María González Cicero's *Perspectiva religiosa en Yucatán, 1517–1571: Yucatán, los franciscanos y el primer obispo fray Francisco de Toral* (Mexico, 1978). Sergio Quezada's *Pueblos y caciques yucatecos, 1550–1580* (Colegio de México, Mexico, D. F., 1993) offers an important revision of Roys' model of Maya society in Yucatan at the time of contact in light of new research on the early colonial period.

Victoria Reifler Bricker's chapters on Spanish conquests in the Maya lowlands in her *Indian Christ, Indian King: The Historical Substrate of Maya Myth and Ritual* (Austin, TX, 1981) provide well-documented introductions to the interactions of Spaniards and Mayas as the boundaries of colonial control gradually extended into the tropical forest interiors. The long-delayed late-seventeenth-century Spanish conquest of the Itza Mayas of Peten, Guatemala, was first described in a precolonial apology by the Spanish chronicler Juan de Villagutierre Soto-Mayor, in a work first published in 1701; this work is available in English translation as *History of the Conquest of the Province of the Itzá* (Culver City, CA, 1983). The report by the Franciscan missionary Andrés de Avendaño y Loyola of his encounters with the Itzas in 1696, on the eve of this conquest, has been published in transcription as Fray Andrés de Avendaño y Loyola, *Relación de las dos entradas que hice a la conversión de los gentiles ytzáex, y cehaches* (Möchmüll, 1997), edited by Temis Vayhinger-Scheer, and in translation as *Relation of Two Trips to Peten Made for the Conversion of the Heathen Ytzaex and Cehaches* (Culver City, CA., 1987), edited with commentary by Frank E. Comparato. *Nicolás de Valenzuela: conquista del lacandón y conquista del Chol*, edited with commentary by Götz Freiherr von Houwald, 2 vols. (Berlin, 1979), contains extensive documentation of the Guatemalan conquest of the Chol-speaking Lakandons during the mid-1690s, an event closely related to the Itza conquest. Grant D. Jones's examination of the Itza conquest provides new interpretations of Itza history and social organization, as well as a narrative analysis of the 1697 conquest and its impact on the native populations of Peten and Belize (*The Conquest of the Last Maya Kingdom* [Stanford, CA, 1998]).

Any student of the lowland Maya should be familiar with Nancy M. Farriss's sweeping study of the entire colonial period in Yucatan, *Maya Society under Spanish Rule: The Colonial Enterprise of Survival* (Princeton, NJ, 1984). Of no less importance is Robert W. Patch's masterful analysis of Maya – Spanish economic and social relations during the second and third centuries of the colonial period, *Maya and Spaniard in Yucatan, 1648–1812* (Stanford, CA, 1993). Manuel Christina García Borneol's *Yucatán: pública y encomienda bajo los Austria* (Seville, 1978) focuses on the long-lived tribute system and on evidence for Yucatan's demographic history. Isabel Fernández Tejedo's *La comunidad indígena maya de Yucatán, siglos xvi y xvii* (Mexico, 1990) is a well-documented synthesis of the economic foundations of Maya colonial communities and systems of Spanish exploitation; its coverage of the less-studied Tabasco region helps fill an important void. France V. Scholes and Ralph L. Roys' older but superbly researched *The Maya Chontal Indians of Acalan-Tixchel: A Contribution to the History and Ethnography of the Yucatán Peninsula* (Washington, DC, 1948; reprinted Norman, OK, 1968) contains a wealth of data on the frontier regions of the southwestern peninsula, especially concerning the formation of Spanish missions and semi-independent Maya life in the Kejach region. Several of the various colonial period Maya groups of the southern frontier areas, including lowland Chiapas, Baja Verapaz, the Guatemalan Peten, and Belize, have been the subject of two aforementioned studies: *La paz de Dios y del rey*, by Jan de Vos, and *Maya Resistance to Spanish Rule*, by Grant D. Jones.

Documentary investigations of single Maya communities, such as Philip C. Thompson's *Tekanto: A Case Study of a Mayan Town in Colonial Yucatan* (New Orleans, forthcoming) utilize Maya-language community records, provide highly controlled multiyear evidence, and can shed important new light on the local operation of Maya society in a colonial context. Matthew Restall also focuses on Maya-language sources and the structure of community and society in his recent *The Maya World: Yucatec Culture and Society, 1550–1850* (Stanford, CA, 1997). For focused discussions of this approach, see Restall's "Torture in the Archives: Mayans Meet Europeans," *American Anthropologist* 95 (1993): 139–52, and " 'He Wished it in Vain': Subordination and Resistance Among Maya Women in Post-Conquest Yucatan," *Ethnohistory* 42, no. 4 (1995): 577–94.

Detailed historical demographic studies of the lowland Maya were initiated with Sherburne F. Cook and Woodrow Borah's longitudinal study, "The Population of Yucatan," in their *Essays in Population History: Mexico and the Caribbean* (Berkeley, CA, 1979), 1–179. More recently, García Borneol has reinterpreted some of the conclusions in her *Yucatán: pública y encomienda bajo las Austria,* and David J. Robinson has carried out a case study of native migration demographics in eighteenth-century Yucatan, reported in his edited volume *Studies in Spanish American Population History* (Boulder, CO, 1981), 149–73. Robert W. Patch's *Maya and Spaniard in Yucatan, 1648–1812* also contains important discussions of demographic isьues in colonial Yucatan, and Grant D. Jones's *The Conquest of the Last Maya Kingdom* analyzes the demographic impact of seventeenth- and eighteenth-century epidemics on the Maya populations of the southern lowlands.

The rapprochement of historical archaeology and ethnohistorical research is a recent phenomenon in the Maya lowlands, but several studies have recently begun to fill this void. Anthony P. Andrews's "Historical Archaeology in Yucatan: A Preliminary Framework," *Historical Archaeology* (1981): 1–18, provides a useful overview for Yucatan. *Ecab: Poblado y provincia del siglo XVI en Yucatán* (Mexico, 1979), by Andrews and Antonio Benavides C., and Arthur G. Miller and Nancy M. Farriss's "Religious Syncretism in Colonial Yucatan: The Archaeological and Ethnohistorical Evidence from Tancah, Quintana Roo," in *Maya Archaeology and Ethnohistory,* ed. Norman Hammond and Gordon R. Willey (Austin, TX, 1979), offer examples of the potential for such interdisciplinary cooperation. These approaches have been particularly fruitful at the colonial Maya towns of Lamanay (also written "Lamanai") and Tipuj in Belize. For introductions to this work and further bibliography, see Elizabeth Graham, David M. Pendergast, and Grant D. Jones, "On the Fringes of Conquest: Maya–Spanish Contact in Colonial Belize," *Science,* 246 (1989): 1254–59, and David M. Pendergast, Grant D. Jones, and Elizabeth Graham, "Locating Maya Lowlands Spanish Colonial Towns: A Case Study from Belize," *Latin American Antiquity* 4 (1993): 59–73. Background to another such interdisciplinary project, in this case focusing on the seventeenth-century Itzas of central Peten, is presented in "La geografía política del Petén central, Guatemala, en el siglo xvii: la arqueología de las capitales mayas," by Don S. Rice, Prudence M. Rice, and Grant D. Jones, *Mesoamérica* 14, no. 26 (1993): 281–318.

While early archaeological studies of the lowland Maya were dominated by Europeans and North Americans, much late-nineteenth-century and early-twentieth-century historical research was written primarily by ladino Yucatecan intellectuals. Some of this "elite" work responded to the need for new understandings of the history of Maya – ladino relations following the violent years of the Caste War of Yucatán, which devastated the peninsula's economy from 1848 throughout the rest of the century. Most important of these were Eligio Ancona's *Historia de Yucatán desde la época más remota hasta nuestros días,* 3 vols. (Mérida, 1878–79); Serapio Baqueiro's study of the Caste War, *Ensayo histórico sobre las revoluciones de Yucatán desde el año 1840 hasta 1864,* 2 vols. (Mérida, 1878–79); and Juan Francisco Molina Solís's study of the colonial period, *Historia de Yucatán durante la dominación española,* 3 vols. (Mérida, 1904–13).

Archaeological, historical/ethnohistorical, and even ethnographic research in Yucatan was dominated from the early 1930s through the late 1950s by an ambitious, highly structured program sponsored and organized by the Carnegie Institution of Washington. From this research emerged not only the richly detailed studies of the early colonial period by Roys, Scholes, Adams, and other ethnohistorians, but also pioneering ethnographic research in rural Yucatan and Quintana Roo. The best known of these ethnographic works were carried out by the American anthropologist Robert Redfield and the Yucatecan anthropologist Alfonso Villa Rojas: *Chan Kom: A Maya Village,* by Redfield and Villa Rojas (Washington, DC, 1934); *A Village that Chose Progress: Chan Kom Revisited,* by Redfield (Chicago, 1950); *The Folk Culture of Yucatan,* by Redfield (Chicago, 1941); and *The Maya of East Central Quintana Roo,* by Villa Rojas (Washington, DC, 1945; New York, 1997). Although of great value for their ethnographic details, these studies lacked adequate historical grounding in the modern political economy of Yucatan.

The historian Howard F. Cline initiated a revisionist approach to Yucatecan history with the largely unpublished studies of pre- and post–Caste War political economic transformations; those that were published included "The Sugar Episode in Yucatan, 1815–1850," *Journal of Inter-American Economic Affairs* 1 (1947–48): 79–100, and "The Henequen Episode in Yucatan, 1830–1890," *Journal of Inter-American Economic Affairs* 2 (1948): 30–51. Arnold Strickon built upon Cline's findings, in order to demonstrate the weakness of Redfield's more synchronic approach to modern Maya rural life, in his "Hacienda and Plantation in Yucatan: An Historical-Ecological Consideration of the Folk-Urban Continuum in Yucatan," *América Indígena* 25 (1965): 25–63. Since then, studies of the development of capitalist agrarian systems in Yucatan, their impact on the outbreak of the Caste War, and their unique mode of recovery during the post–Caste War era have burgeoned.

For literature pertaining to the origins of haciendas in Yucatan during the late colonial period, see Robert W. Patch, "Agrarian Change in Eighteenth-Century Yucatan," *Hispanic American Historical Review* 65 (1985): 21–49; Patch's *Maya and Spaniard in Yucatan, 1648–1812*; Farriss, *Maya Society Under Colonial Rule*, 366ff.; and Joseph, chap. 3 of his *Rediscovering the Past at Mexico's Periphery*. Terry Rugeley's *Yucatan's Maya Peasantry and the Origins of the Caste War* (Austin, TX, 1996) provides a stimulating new analysis, utilizing many primary sources not consulted by previous writers, of the multiple social, political, and economic circumstances that resulted in the Caste War. His work is of particular interest for its focus on the role of Maya elites in the origins of the war (see also Rugeley's "The Maya Elites of Nineteenth-Century Yucatan," *Ethnohistory* 42, no. 3 (1995): 477–93).

For the Caste War itself, see Howard F. Cline, "The War of the Castes and Its Consequences," in his microfilmed *Related Studies in Early Nineteenth Century Yucatecan Social History* (Chicago, 1950); Nelson Reed's popular book, *The Caste War of Yucatan* (Stanford, CA, 1964); *Guerra social en Yucatán*, by Ramón Berzunza Pinto (Mexico, 1965); chapters by Bricker, Dumond, and Jones in *Anthropology and History in Yucatan*, ed. Grant D. Jones (Austin, TX, 1977); chap. 8 in Bricker, *The Indian Christ, the Indian King*; Moisés González Navarro, *Raza y tierra: La guerra de castas y el henequén* (Mexico, 1970); Marie Lapointe, *Los mayas rebeldes de Yucatán* (Zamora, Michoacan, 1983), and a detailed bibliography on the topic prepared by Sergio Quezada et al., *Bibliografía comentada sobre la cuestión étnica y la guerra de castas de Yucatán, 1821–1910* (Mérida, 1986). Don E. Dumond's new study of the Caste War, *The Machete and the Cross: Campesino Rebellion in Yucatan* (Lincoln, NE, 1997) is a major synthesis of the topic.

The aftermath of the Caste War, later political developments, and the impact of the henequen age on the population of Yucatan are treated in various recent works, including Luis Millet Cámara et al., *Hacienda y cambio social en Yucatán* (Mérida, 1984); Allen Wells, *Yucatan's Gilded Age: Haciendas, Henequen, and International Harvester, 1860–1915* (Albuquerque, NM, 1985); Gilbert M. Joseph, *Revolution from Without: Yucatan, Mexico, and the United States, 1880–1924* (Cambridge, 1982), *Rediscovering the Past at Mexico's Periphery* (University, AL, 1986); and Joseph and Gilbert's *Summer of Discontent, Seasons of Upheaval: Elite*

Politics and Rural Insurgency in Yucatan, 1876–1915 (Stanford, CA, 1997). Paul Sullivan's *Unfinished Conversations: Mayas and Foreigners Between Two Wars* (New York, 1989) uses ethnohistorical, ethnographic, and linguistic approaches in a stimulating analysis of interactions between twentieth-century descendants of the rebel Mayas of Quintana Roo and various outsiders, including other ethnographers and archaeologists. The nineteenth- and twentieth-century political economy of the Yucatan Peninsula is also treated in Jeffrey T. Brannon and Gilbert M. Joseph, eds., *Land, Labor, and Capital in Modern Yucatan: Essays in Regional History and Political Economy* (Tuscaloosa, AL, 1991).

The impact of chicle production on the long-ignored Guatemalan Peten, along with other nineteenth- and twentieth-century socioeconomic forces, are treated in Norman B. Schwartz, *Forest Society: A Social History of Peten, Guatemala* (Philadelphia, 1990). Several articles in a special issue of *América Indígena* 47, no. 1 (1987), contain useful information about modern Maya history in Belize, as do the chapters by O. Nigel Bolland and Grant D. Jones, *Anthropology and History in Yucatan*; see also Bolland, *Colonialism and Resistance in Belize: Essays in Historical Sociology* (Benque Viejo, Belize, 1988), 91–150. For the impact of modern sugarcane production on the Yucatec Maya of northern Belize, see Grant D. Jones, *The Politics of Agricultural Development in Northern British Honduras* (Winston-Salem, NC, 1971), and the Harvard University doctoral dissertation by Ira R. Abrams, "Cash Crop Farming and Social and Economic Change in a Yucatec Maya Community in Northern British Honduras" (Cambridge, MA, 1973). Yucatecan Maya settlement and community formation in western Belize are discussed from the Maya perspective in Ambrosio Tsul's *After One Hundred Years: The Oral History and Traditions of San Antonio, Cayo District, Belize* (Belize, 1993). *Maya Atlas, the Struggle to Preserve Maya Land in Southern Belize* (Berkeley, CA, 1997), compiled by the Toledo Maya Cultural Council and the Toledo Alcaldes Association, represents in detail, with rich ethnographic and geographical detail and visual illustration, efforts by the Mayas of southern Belize to establish a Maya homeland and to preserve the region's fragile ecosystem in the face of threats by logging and road construction.

Ethnographic studies published since those of Redfield and Villa Rojas afford important insights into recent and contemporary forces of change in lowland Maya communities. For Yucatan and Campeche, see Irwin Press, *Tradition and Adaptation: Life in a Modern Yucatan Maya Village* (Westport, CT, 1975); Richard Thompson, *The Winds of Tomorrow:*

Social Change in a Maya Town (Chicago, 1974); Alice Littlefield, *La industria de las hamacas en Yucatán, México* (Mexico, 1976); and Betty B. Faust, *Mexican Rural Development and the Plumed Serpent: Technology and Maya Cosmology in the Tropical Forest of Campeche Mexico* (Westport, CT, 1997). Also consult Rhoda Halperin, "Redistribution in Chan Kom: A Case for Mexican Political Economy," in Halperin and James Dow, eds., *Peasant Livelihood: Studies in Economic Anthropology* (New York, 1973), for a review of earlier studies of Chan Kom, and Mary Elmendorf, *Nine Mayan Women* (New York, 1976), for a restudy of Chan Kom. The most recent reexamination of this famous community is Alicia Re Cruz's, *The Two Milpas of Chan Kom: Scenarios of a Maya Village Life* (Albany, NY, 1996). Macduff Everton's *The Modern Maya: A Culture in Transition* (Albuquerque, NM, 1991) is a sensitive and historically informed semi-popular work, illustrated with marvelous black-and-white photographs.

In addition to Sullivan's *Unfinished Conversations*, Allan F. Burns's *An Epoch of Miracles: Oral Literature of the Yucatec Maya* (Austin, TX, 1983) focuses mainly on the Mayas of Quintana Roo and also contains examples of oral history (see also Burns's chapter in Jones, *Anthropology and History in Yucatán*). Other recent historically informed ethnographic studies of the Santa Cruz Maya of Quintana Roo include *La resistencia maya*, by Miguel Alberto Bartolomé and Alicia Mabel Barabas (Mexico, 1981). For the Mopan and K'ekchi Mayas of southern lowland Belize, see James R. Gregory, *The Mopan: Culture and Ethnicity in a Changing Belizean Community* (Columbia, MO, 1984) and Richard R. Wilk, *Household Ecology: Economic Change and Domestic Life among the K'ekchi Maya in Belize* (Tucson, AZ, 1991). For the Yucatec-speaking Lakandon, see the ethnographic study by R. Jon McGee, *Life, Ritual, and Religion among the Lacandon Maya* (New York, 1990), and a valuable account by a gifted journalist, *The Last Lords of Palenque: The Lacandon Mayas of the Mexican Rain Forest*, by Víctor Perera (New York, 1982). Jan de Vos has compiled historical and modern writings on the threatened Lakandon rain forest and its inhabitants in *Viajes al desierto de la soledad: cuando la selva Lacandona aún era selva* (Mexico, 1988). Other studies of this small and endangered population are reviewed in Robert B. Taylor, *Indians of Middle America* (Manhattan, KS, 1989), 188–206.

Norman B. Schwartz has published an autobiography of a ladinoized Maya from Peten: *A Milpero of Peten, Guatemala: Autobiography and Cultural Analysis* (Newark, DE, 1977). Scott Atran's "Itza Maya Tropical Agro-Forestry," *Current Anthropology* 14 (1993): 633–99, provides a bibliography of the Peten Itzas and examines the modern Itza agroeconomic system in Peten in light of both pre-conquest systems and issues concerning tropical forest destruction and threats to Itza cultural survival. On recent efforts to preserve and revitalize the Itza Maya language, see Charles A. Hofling, "Indigenous Linguistic Revitalization and Outsider Interaction: The Itzaj Maya Case," *Human Organization* 55, no. 1 (1996): 1–9.

21

THE HIGHLAND MAYA

W. GEORGE LOVELL

Little by little heavy shadows and black night enveloped our fathers and grandfathers and us also, oh, my sons!. . . . All of us were there thus. We were born
to die!

Annals of the Cakchiquels

Despite the lament of a sixteenth-century Kaqchikel chronicler, the highland Maya sustain a vibrant, living presence, one that no student of
Mesoamerica can fail to notice. Even modern government censuses,
which tend to enumerate fewer Indians than there actually are, record
significant highland Maya populations, today in excess of 1 million in the
Mexican state of Chiapas and between 5 and 6 million in the case of
Guatemala. If, in the national context of Mexico, the Maya of Chiapas
exist as one of dozens of Indian minorities among a mass of mestizos or
mixed bloods, their counterparts across the border constitute a more
palpable demographic force, for Maya-speaking peoples make up about
half of Guatemala's total population (Tables 21.1–21.4 and Maps 21.1–
21.4). Numbers are important but, by themselves, merely scratch the
surface of the story. Only by viewing the highland Maya in historical
perspective can their conspicuous presence be more fully appreciated.

Who are these native peoples? How, through the centuries, have they
managed to survive? What sorts of lives have they lived? Why should

This chapter reflects a personal interest in the subject matter dating back to my first visit to Chiapas
and Guatemala in 1974. Since then I have had the opportunity not only to travel regularly to
highland Maya country but also to conduct historical research on it and its inhabitants elsewhere,
especially in the Archivo General de Indias in Seville. Over the years my work on the highland
Maya has been generously supported by the Advisory Research Committee at Queen's University,
the Killam Program of Canada Council, and the Social Sciences and Humanities Research Council
of Canada. I owe a tremendous debt, intellectually speaking, to scores of fellow *mayistas*, whose
published work I bring to the reader's attention in the Bibliographical Essay and without which this
chapter could not have been written.

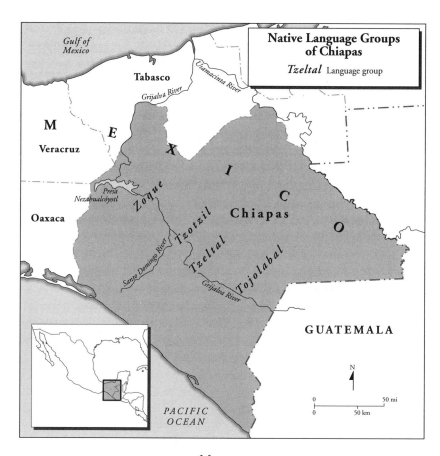

Map 21.1

their lot concern us? Such questions have ignited debate for some time, from the brave stand made by enlightened Europeans like Bartolomé de Las Casas, a Dominican friar who championed native rights in the sixteenth century, to the passionate voice of Rigoberta Menchú, a Maya woman whose award of the Nobel Peace prize in 1992, like the communiqués of Subcomandante Marcos following the Zapatista uprising in 1994, focused international attention on more recent burdens, more recent iniquities, more recent threats to Maya survival.

Survival itself is the key issue, but one we should contemplate carefully. Caution must especially be exercised so as not to romanticize or oversimplify what happened in history. The pages of *National Geographic*

Table 21.1. *The Highland Maya of Chiapas, 1950–90*

Year	Estimated Maya population	Percentage of total Mexican population
1950	160,000	0.62
1980	390,000	–
1990	617,250	0.61

Sources: For 1950, see Anselmo Marino Flores, "Indian Population and Its Identification," in *Handbook of Middle American Indians,* vol. 6 (Austin: University of Texas Press, 1967), 20, and Evon Z. Vogt, "The Maya," in *Handbook of Middle American Indians,* vol. 7 (Austin: University of Texas Press, 1969), 23; for 1980, see Francesc Ligorred, *Lenguas indígenas de México y Centroamérica* (Madrid: Editorial MAPFRE, 1992), 223; and for 1990, see *La Jornada* (15 December 1991). Jan Rus, "Local Adaptation to Global Change: The Reordering of Native Society in Highland Chiapas, Mexico, 1974–1994," in *European Review of Latin American and Caribbean Studies* 58 (1995): 75, furnishes a figure of 847,751 for the "indigenous population" of Chiapas in 1990. This figure would include a number of non-Maya Indians.

Table 21.2. *The Highland Maya of Guatemala, 1950–94*

Year	National census count of Maya population	Percentage of total Guatemalan population
1950	1,495,905	53.6
1964	1,809,535	42.2
1973	2,260,024	43.8
1980	2,536,523	41.9
1994	4,037,449	42.8

Source: W. George Lovell and Christopher H. Lutz, " 'A Dark Obverse': Maya Survival in Guatemala, 1520–1994," in *Geographical Review* 86, 3 (1996): 400.

are filled with glossy portrayals of Maya peoples as anachronistic relics, timeless throwbacks to a golden age before the Spanish Conquest. Marxist texts cultivate another image, one in which Maya peoples emerge as inert victims forged and preserved by colonial or neocolonial exploitation. Neither depiction fits satisfactorily what we now know to have been variable experiences, for the confrontation between natives and newcomers was something that differed quite markedly from region to region, if not from place to place within a region. If we view Mayas as subjects and not as objects, if we look beyond antiquated myths and clichéd stereotypes, then perhaps we can see them instead as social actors, as human agents who respond to invasion and domination in order to mold, at least in part, important elements of their culture.

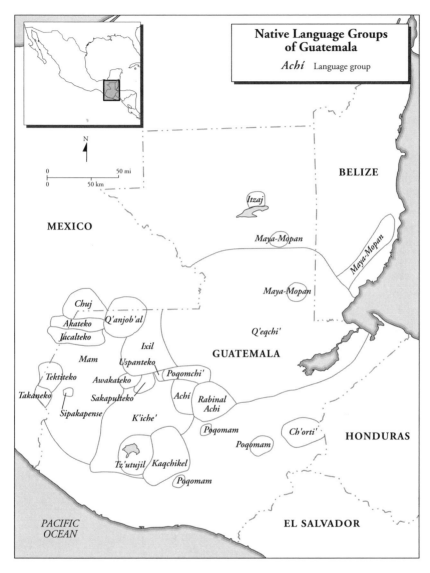

Map 21.2

This chapter delineates some of the ways in which the highland Maya have reacted and responded in order to survive almost five centuries of conquest. In constructing a narrative, evidence is laid down in the form of a pyramid, the base of time past narrowing toward the peak of time

Table 21.3. *Maya speakers in Chiapas, 1950–90*

Language group	Estimated number of speakers		
	(1950)	(1980)	(1990)
Tzeltal	75,000	200,000	306,000
Tzotzil	48,250	150,000	268,500
Tojolabal	37,000	40,000	42,500

Sources: For 1950, see Anselmo Marino Flores, "Indian Population and its Identification," in *Handbook of Middle American Indians*, vol. 6 (Austin: University of Texas Press, 1967), 22, and Evon Z. Vogt, "The Maya," in *Handbook of Middle American Indians*, vol. 7 (Austin: University of Texas Press, 1969), 23; for 1980, see Francesc Ligorred, *Lenguas indígenas de México y Centroamérica*, (Madrid: Editorial MAPFRE, 1992), 223; and for 1990, see *La Jornada* (15 December 1991). Jan de Vos, *Vivir en frontera: La experiencia de los indios de Chiapas* (Mexico City: Instituto Nacional Indigenísta, 1994), 35, furnishes a figure of 716,012 people in Chiapas being able to speak a natvie language. This figure would include a number of non-Maya native speakers.

present. Such a structure is designed to emphasize the historical forces that shape, and the cultural context that frames, current predicaments. The colonial experience, which spans the years between 1524 and 1821, receives particular attention, for it was during this period that the inequality that pervades later times was irreducibly cast. The vicissitudes of highland Maya life in the nineteenth and twentieth centuries are dealt with more summarily in two periods, one of reform and revolution from 1821 to 1954, and one of marginalization and neglect from 1954 on. The portrayal of broad patterns and general trends is punctuated throughout by the inclusion of case specifics, a device whereby some balance may be struck between the rendering of essence and the provision of detail.

THE COLONIAL EXPERIENCE

Following their remarkable victory at Tenochtitlan, the consequences of which placed much of central Mexico under acknowledged Spanish control, Hernán Cortés (also known as Hernando Cortez) and his men turned their attention to lands and peoples informants told them lay to the south and east, in far-off regions where Aztec influence reached but where Aztec authority did not generally prevail. Chiapas and Guatemala were two such regions, perhaps best known at Tenochtitlan for the

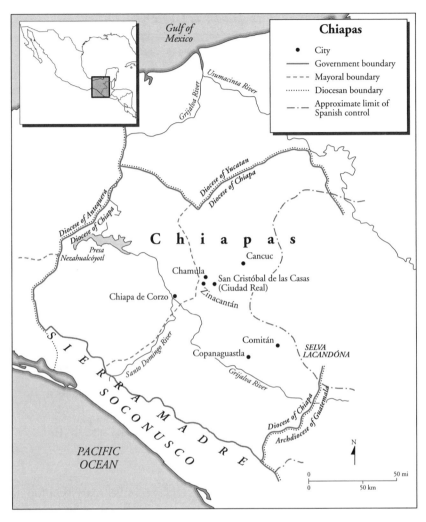

Map 21.3

quality of the cacao, cochineal, and quetzal feathers they produced. When Spaniards ventured to these parts, they encountered difficult situations in which wars of conquest would have to be waged not against a cohesive, well-integrated state but against quarrelsome, disparate polities long accustomed to harboring grudge and grievance amongst themselves. Under these circumstances, conquest would neither be sudden nor sure.

Table 21.4. *Maya speakers in Guatemala, 1973–93*

	Estimated number of speakers		
Language group	(1973)	(1980)	(1992)
Achí	58,000	50,000	–
Akateko	–	20,000	39,826
Awakateko	16,000	15,000	34,476
Ch'orti'	52,000	25,000	74,600
Chuj	29,000	30,000	85,002
Ixil	71,000	50,000	130,773
Jakalteko (Popti')	32,000	25,000	83,814
K'iche' (Kichee')	967,000	1,000,000	1,842,115
Kaqchikel	405,000	500,000	1,002,790
Mam	644,000	500,000	1,094,926
Poqomam	32,000	30,000	127,206
Poqomchi'	50,000	50,000	259,168
Q'anjob'al	112,000	100,000	205,670
Q'eqchi'	361,000	400,000	711,523
Sakapulteko	21,000	20,000	42,204
Sipakapense	3,000	3,000	5,944
Tektiteko (Teko)	2,500	3,000	4,755
Tz'utujil	80,000	80,000	156,333
Uspanteko	2,000	2,000	21,399

Sources: For 1973, see Pamela Sheetz de Echerd, ed., *Bibliografía del Instituto Lingüístico de Verano de Centroamérica* (Guatemala City: Instituto Lingüístico de Verano, 1983), 4–7; for 1980, see Francesc Ligorred, *Lenguas indígenas de México y Centroamérica* (Madrid: Editorial MAPFRE, 1922), 220–23; and for 1992, see Leopoldo Tzian, *Mayas y Ladinos en cifras: El caso de Guatemala* (Guatemala City: Editorial Cholsamaj, 1994), 20–25. Tzian considers Achí a variant of K'iche'. He provides a figure of 13,077 for speakers of Mopan and 1,783 for speakers of Itzaj. The Mopan and the Itzaj are both lowland Maya groups.

The expedition that Luis Marín led to Chiapas in February 1524 found there several well-organized societies, none of them especially powerful but all able to draw upon resolute local loyalties. Marín's small party made its way through Zoque country, the westernmost part of Chiapas, with no apparent difficulty. The Zoques, whose language links them more with Mixe than with Maya, then occupied land in the middle Grijalva Basin. Farther upriver, at the site of present-day Chiapa de Corzo, Marín fought with the Chiapanecos, a group of undetermined origin. After their surrender, Marín marched his men into the heart of the central highlands, where Maya peoples more properly defined awaited him. He passed through Zinacantán before taking on Tzotzil forces at

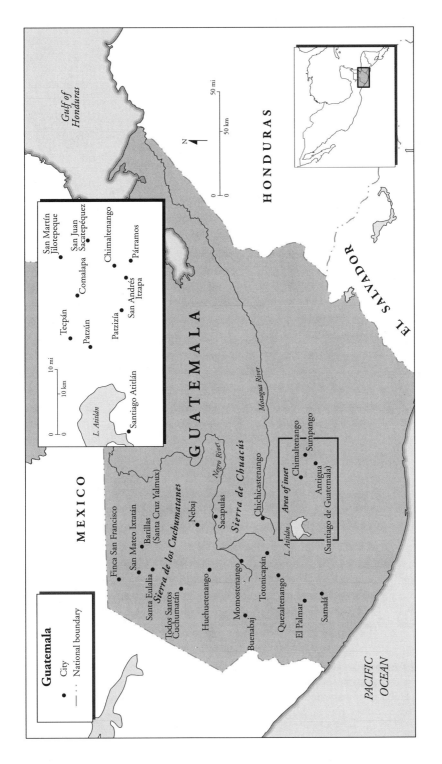

Map 21.4

Chamula. Rather than continue east and south through the highlands toward Guatemala, which would have resulted in skirmishes with Tzeltal communities and their Coxoh-speaking (possibly Tojolabal) neighbors, Marín headed back toward Tabasco. His expedition, on the whole, had more to do with strategic reconnaissance than with the formal establishment of Spanish rule. It was not until almost four years later, by which time Pedro Portocarrero and Diego de Mazariegos had reentered Chiapas from different directions and with larger troops of men, that Maya peoples in the central highlands came under more effective Spanish domination. Their mountain territory was initially administered as part of New Spain, thereafter (1530–1821) as part of Guatemala, save for a brief, four-year period (1540–44) when Chiapa (as Spaniards called the inland province) governed itself. The center of Spanish settlement in colonial Chiapas was Cuidad Real, the present-day San Cristóbal de las Casas.

Shortly before Marín penetrated from the north, forces led by Pedro de Alvarado trekked through the Soconusco littoral, which lies below Spanish Chiapa to the south of the Sierra Madre, en route to Guatemala. No appreciable native resistance was encountered along the Pacific Coast. Following an ascent into the Guatemalan highlands, however, a number of battles ensued. Alvarado's main opponents were the K'iche's, after whose defeat other Maya peoples had to be dealt with, one by one by one, the Mam, the Ixil, and the Ch'orti' only three among many. On several occasions Kaqchikel warriors fought alongside the Spaniards, as in the conquest of the Tz'utujiles of Atitlán. Kaqchikel allegiance withered after barely six months, when excessive demands for tribute caused them to stage a rebellion that lasted almost four years. The Kaqchikeles tell us:

Then Alvarado asked the kings for money. He wished them to give him piles of metal, their vessels and crowns. And as they did not bring them to him immediately, Alvarado became angry with the kings and said to them: "Why have you not brought me the metal? If you do not bring with you all of the money of the tribes, I will burn you and I will hang you," he said to the lords.

Next Alvarado ordered them to pay twelve hundred *pesos* of gold. The kings tried to have the amount reduced and they began to weep, but Alvarado did not consent, and he said to them: "Get the metal and bring it within five days. Woe to you if you do not bring it! I know my heart!" Thus he spoke to the lords.

Half the money had already been delivered when we escaped. . . . We scattered ourselves under the trees, under the vines, oh, my sons! All our tribes joined in the fight against Alvarado. . . . Hostilities began against the Spaniards.

They dug holes and pits for the horses and scattered sharp stakes so that they should be killed. . . . The People fought them, and they continued to fight a prolonged war.[1]

Some Maya groups, the Q'eqchi's and the Uspantekos among them, actually inflicted temporary defeat on the invaders before succumbing to later, better-organized acts of aggression. In one meandering foray, Portocarrero, responsible for Spanish gains against the Kaqchikeles in 1527, pushed north and west across Guatemala and on into Chiapas, where he met up with Mazariegos in Comitán. This meeting most likely occurred in 1528; by that time, Maya peoples in central Chiapas may have been subdued, but the followers of Alvarado were still hard-pressed in Guatemala. Not until some ten years later, in certain areas considerably longer, did Spaniards in Guatemala bring the natives to heel. Maya resistance, then, made the task of military subjugation a bloody, protracted affair.

The ability of Maya peoples to raise armies large enough to impede Spanish intrusion is an important indication that the highlands of Chiapas and Guatemala supported sizable populations during the early conquest period. If disagreement persists as to, precisely, how many Indians were alive when Spaniards first arrived, less contested is the fact that conquest was more or less contemporaneous with a process of native depopulation that lasted well into the seventeenth century and, in the case of Chiapas, far beyond. Table 21.5 indicates the varying size of the contact estimates proposed by several scholars who focus attention on Guatemala. Of the estimates represented, those advanced by Denevan and by Lovell and Lutz (2 million in each case) relate to all or a substantial portion of present-day national territory. Sanders and Murdy (500,000 to 800,000) cover only highland Guatemala, while Zamora (315,000) deals exclusively with the western half of the country. Solano (300,000) never defines his spatial orbit clearly, but his calculations incorporate a huge area. Differences in territorial extent, therefore, should be borne in mind when comparisons are being made between the estimates.

Crossing the border into Chiapas finds us working with fewer studies of colonial Maya demography, which limits discussion to stark essentials. Fortunately, these are provided by the solid research of Peter Gerhard, who estimates a native population of some 275,000 at contact to have

---

[1] Adrían Recinos and Delia Goetz, trans., *The Annals of the Cakchiquels* (Norman, OK: University of Oklahoma Press, 1953), 123–27.

Table 21.5. *Native depopulation in sixteenth-century Guatemala*

Year (approximate)	Denevan	Lovell and Lutz	Sanders and Murdy	Zamora	Solano
1520	2,000,000	2,000,000	500–800,000	315,000	300,000
1550	–	427,850	–	121,000	157,000
1575	–	236,540	–	75,000	148,000
1600	–	133,280	–	64,000	195,000

Sources: William M. Denevan, ed., *The Native Population of the Americas in 1942*, 2nd ed. (Madison: University of Wisconsin Press, 1992); W. George Lovell and Christopher H. Lutz, "Conquest and Population: Maya Demography in Historical Perspective," in *Latin American Research Review* 29, no. 2 (1994): 133–40; William T. Sanders and Carson Murdy, "Population and Agricultural Adaptation in Highland Guatemala," in *The Historical Demography of Highland Guatemala*, ed. Robert M. Carmack, John D. Early, and Christopher H. Lutz (Albany, NY: Institute for Mesoamerican Studies, 1982), 32; Francisco de Solano, *Los mayas del siglo XVIII* (Madrid: Ediciones Cultura Hispánica, 1974), 62–96; and Elías Zamora Acosta, "Conquista y crisis demográfica: la población indígena del occidente de Guatemala en el siglo XVI," *Mesoamérica* 6 (1983): 291–328.

fallen to 70,000 by 1650, risen to 72,000 by 1700, dropped again by 1800 to 53,000, to number approximately 58,000 at the time of independence (Table 21.6).

Just as, no matter the numbers involved, there is now general agreement that native depopulation was drastic if not catastrophic, so also is it increasingly recognized that of the combination of factors responsible for Indian demise, the part played by epidemic disease was most crucial. The highland Maya, like native peoples from Alaska to Tierra del Fuego, had no natural immunity to a horrific array of Old World infections. Consequently, they found themselves in a vulnerable position when maladies such as smallpox, measles, mumps, and plague, transferred inadvertently by Spanish conquerors and African slaves, entered their virgin-soil environments.

As with studies in population history, our knowledge of disease incidence during the sixteenth century tends to be better developed for Guatemala. Much of the widespread illness reported there, however, must also have affected Chiapas. As many as eight pandemics swept through Guatemala in the century or so between 1519 and 1632, with more localized episodes occurring over the same period. Bouts of sickness often triggered other crisis scenarios, for poor health resulted in failure to plant fields, which in turn led to food scarcity and the onset of famine. Throughout the *Annals of the Cakchiquels* are scattered numerous refer-

Table 21.6. *The Indian population of Chiapas and Soconusco, 1511–1821*

Province	1511	1550	1600	1650	1700	1750	1800	1821
Chiapas	275,000	125,000	85,000	70,000	72,000	65,000	53,000	58,000
Soconusco	80,000	7,000	6,600	4,000	2,700	4,650	4,200	4,000

Source: Peter Gerhard, *The Southeast Frontier of New Spain* (Princeton, NJ: Princeton University Press, 1979), 25.

ences to disease outbreaks, none more graphic than the description of an undetermined pestilence that actually reached Guatemala before the Spaniards themselves did:

It happened during the twenty-fifth year [1519–20] the plague began, oh, my sons! First they became ill of a cough, they suffered from nosebleeds and illness of the bladder. It was truly terrible, the number of dead there were in that period. . . . It was in truth terrible, the number of dead among the people. The people could not in any way control the sickness.

Great was the stench of the dead. After our fathers and grandfathers succumbed, half of the people fled to the fields. The dogs and the vultures devoured the bodies. The mortality was terrible. Your grandfathers died, and with them died the son of the king and his brothers and kinsmen. So it was that we became orphans, oh, my sons! So we became when we were young. All of us were thus.[2]

The immediate results of Spanish intrusion, then, were warfare, disease outbreaks, and demographic collapse. After the trauma of these disruptions came the onerous responsibility of being subject to the rule of Spain, a colonial status that demanded expressions of loyalty and terms of commitment far different than those adhered to before. Various institutions were introduced by which means imperial designs and expectations were to be implemented. Two key institutions that featured in the apparatus of conquest were *encomienda* and *congregación*.

The history of *encomienda* is complex, but it remained throughout the sixteenth and seventeenth centuries a device whereby privileged Spaniards or their Creole descendants received tribute in labor, goods, or cash from Indians entrusted to their charge. *Encomiendas* were not grants of land but, rather, awards to enjoy the fruits of what the land and its people could provide, whether prized items such as gold, silver, salt, and cacao or less spectacular produce like corn, beans, cloth, and chickens. The

[2] Recinos and Goetz, *Annals of the Cakchiquels*, 115–16.

entitlement carried with it certain obligations, among them arranging that Indians held in *encomienda* received instruction in the tenets and practice of the "Holy Catholic Faith," an obligation with which few lay Spaniards saw fit to comply.

Early grants of *encomienda*, assigned by a dizzying array of governors to Spaniards who had served the Crown with distinction, often entailed the allocation of substantial amounts of tribute. *Encomenderos*, individuals who held and shared *encomiendas*, wielded considerable power early on as recipients of Indian tribute, but the Crown's role with respect to *encomienda* was one of strategic curtailment. It eventually took measures to dismantle privileges – placing restrictions on labor provisions, for example, and limiting inheritance beyond one or two generations – so that even the most enterprising of *encomenderos* would be stopped from becoming the equivalent of a feudal lord. Of particular importance in this regard were reforms carried out between 1548 and 1555, when Alonso López de Cerrato served as president of the Audiencia de Guatemala, a court whose members were appointed by the Crown and charged with the day-to-day government of a far-flung jurisdiction that stretched from Chiapas to Costa Rica. When abolished by the Bourbon regime in the eighteenth century, *encomienda* represented little more than a modest type of pension.

Discussions of *encomienda* in the area administered by (and as) the Audiencia de Guatemala usually take the Cerrato years as their point of departure. This tendency is understandable, best explained by the fact that our earliest extant list of *encomiendas* – who held them, what kinds of tribute they received, which communities were involved – was compiled during the Cerrato presidency. Cerrato's actions, especially his freeing of Indian slaves and his pioneering role in attempting to put the New Laws of 1542 into effect, certainly warrant recognition. Focusing on Cerrato, however, has served to deflect our interest from looking at *encomienda* when the institution operated (from a Spanish viewpoint) at its most remunerative and (from a Maya perspective) at its most exploitative – the first twenty years or so after conquest, when *encomenderos* themselves set the tribute quotas, when the moderating hand of royal government was nonexistent. A much-needed corrective to understanding the pre-Cerrato history of *encomienda* is provided by Wendy Kramer, who concludes that "far from being the starting point of the Guatemalan *encomienda*, or reflecting recent innovations wrought by the new President, Cerrato's [assessment] reflects the circumstances and allegiances of six different men, influenced by and responding to the vicissitudes of eleven different governments."[3] These six different men and their eleven different governments (Table 21.7) often assigned or exchanged, confirmed, or removed *encomienda* privileges each worth thousands of pesos annually.

Some idea of the reward or burden at stake, and a concrete measure of the difference between pre-Cerrato and Cerrato times, may be gained by examining the particulars of one *encomienda*. Huehuetenango, in the early sixteenth century a Mam community in western Guatemala close to the border with Chiapas, provides useful data on *encomienda* obligations and illuminates the process of change over time.

A doughty Spaniard named Juan de Espinar held Huehuetenango in *encomienda* from 1525 until his death in the 1560s, with one ten- to twelve-month hiatus (1530–31) when the privilege went to Francisco de Zurrilla. For more than thirty-five years, a mix of cleverness, persistence, and political savvy, coupled with a toughness that drifted, at times, into outright cruelty, made Espinar the master of Huehuetenango. He also had keen entrepreneurial instincts, controlling the sale of Indian tribute and developing an elaborate infrastructure of mining and agricultural activities in and around Huehuentenango. He began mining operations after realizing that, about 10 kilometers to the south of Huehuetenango, along the course of the Rio Malacatán, gold placer deposits could be worked. Good fortune for Espinar proved a curse for the Indians he controlled as *encomendero*. In papers later prepared for litigation, Espinar claimed that when Huehuetenango was in its heyday, he earned approximately 9,000 pesos each year from his involvement in mining and another 3,000 pesos from his agricultural transactions.

Espinar lived long enough to feel the effects of the population base of Huehuetenango shrink to a fraction of what it had been when he was initially awarded the *encomienda* (Table 21.8). One nondisease factor that affected the population size of his *encomienda* was that during the first five years of his tenure (until 1530) Espinar held not just Huehuetenango itself but also a handful of surrounding towns he lost the right to later on, when they were assigned to other Spaniards. Espinar's forfeiting Huehuetenango for one year to Zurrilla led to a lawsuit in which he recorded the bounty that he had been deprived of. His desire to retain

[3] Wendy Kramer, *Encomienda Politics in Early Colonial Guatemala, 1524–1544: Dividing the Spoils* (Boulder, CO: Westview Press, 1994), 236.

Table 21.7. *Awards of* encomienda *in early colonial Guatemala, 1524–48*

Governors, lieutenant governors and interim governors	Tenure in office	Number of awards	Number of *encomenderos*
Pedro de Alvarado	1524–26	25	21
Jorge de Alvarado	1527–29	86	56
Francisco de Orduña	1529–30	12	11
Pedro de Alvarado	1530–33	77	45
Jorge de Alvarado	1534–35	7	6
Pedro de Alvarado	1535–36	18	10
Alonso de Maldonado	1536–39	12	8
Pedro de Alvarado	1539–40	7	3
Francisco de la Cueva	1540–41	13	5
Bishop Marroquín and Francisco de la Cueva	1541–42	18	16
Alonso de Maldonado	1542–48	30	20

Source: Wendy Kramer, *Encomienda Politics in Early Colonial Guatemala, 1524–1544: Dividing the Spoils* (Boulder, CO: Westview Press, 1994), 245.

Table 21.8. *The tributary population of Huehue-tenango and subject towns, 1530–31 and 1549*

Head/subject town	1530–31	1549
Huehuetenango (includes Chiantla)	3,000–3,500	500
Santiago Chimaltenango (Chimbal, Chinbal)	500	35
San Juan Atitán (Atitán)	–	–
San Pedro Necta (Niquitlán, Niquetla)	200	20

Source: Wendy Kramer, W. George Lovell, and Christopher H. Lutz, "Fire in the Mountains: Juan de Espinar and the Indians of Huehuetenango, 1525–1560," in David Hurst Thomas, ed. *Columbian Consequences*, vol. 3 (Washington, DC: Smithsonian Institution, 1991), 272.

Huehuetenango makes perfect sense, for the loss was substantial: the commodities listed in the middle column of Table 21.9 would have fetched a handsome return when sold off at market. Furthermore, service provisions at the gold mines alone represent between 43,200 and 72,000

Table 21.9. Ecomienda *obligations in Huehuetenango in 1530–31 and 1549*

Commodity or service	1530–31	1549
Clothing	800 lengths of cotton cloth 400 loinclothes 400 jackets 400 blouses 400 skirts 400 sandals	300 lengths of cotton cloth
Foodstuffs	Unspecified amounts of corn, beans, chile, and salt 108–26 large jugs of honey	Harvest from planting 22.5 bushels of corn Harvest from planting 7.5 bushels of black beans 100 loads of chile 100 cakes of salt
Fowl	2,268 turkeys	12-dozen chickens
Other Items	400 reed mats	Harvest from planting 6 bushels of cotton
Labor	40 Indian men sent to work in and around Santiago de Guatemala in twenty-day shifts all year 120–200 Indian men sent to work in the gold mines in twenty-day shifts all year 30 Indian women sent to the gold mines each day in order to make tortillas and prepare food	6 Indian men to act as general servants
Slaves	80 male and 40 female workers who worked in the gold mines	

Source: Wendy Kramer, W. George Lovell, and Christopher H. Lutz, "Fire in the Mountains: Juan de Espinar and the Indians of Huehuetenango, 1525–1560," in David Hurst Thomas, ed. *Columbian Consequences,* vol. 3 (Washington, DC: Smithsonian Institution, 1991), 274–75.

work-days per year on the part of Indian men, and 10,800 work-days per year on the part of Indian women. The right-hand column of Table 21.9 reflects the shrunken, tamed *encomienda* of Huehuetenango after Cerrato had wrestled with the beast. Even though the prize at midcentury was noticeably less, Espinar could still console himself with the knowledge that he held the eleventh-largest entrustment of Indians in all Guatemala, not including those *encomiendas* in which tribute was paid to the Crown.

Encomiendas encompassed, in varying spatial degree, one or more communities that Spaniards referred to as *pueblos de indios,* Indian towns in the municipal sense of central place and surrounding countryside, segregated areas where non-Indians in theory were not supposed to settle. Upon arrival, Spaniards observed that, morphologically, highland Maya settlements were decidedly more dispersed than nucleated, with what little urbanization as had developed to be restricted to defensive hilltop sites not in the least conducive to efficient administration. The policy of *congregación* was designed to deal with this anarchy, and *pueblos de indios* were the result of its zealous implementation.

As promulgated by Spanish law, *congregación* was a means whereby Indians found dwelling in scattered rural groups would be brought together, converted to Christianity, and forged into harmonious, resourceful communities that reflected imperial notions of orderly, civilized life. To the Church, especially to members of the Dominican and Franciscan orders, fell the difficult job of getting Indian families down from the mountains and resettled in towns built around a Catholic place of worship. The mandate to missionize, and the rationale behind it, is spelled out clearly in a royal order issued on 21 March 1551:

With great care and particular attention we have always attempted to impose the most convenient means of instructing the Indians in the Holy Catholic Faith and the evangelical law, causing them to forget their ancient erroneous rites and ceremonies and to live in concert and order; and, so that this might be brought about, those of our Council of the Indies have met together several times with other religious persons . . . and they, with the desire of promoting the service of God, and ours, resolved that the Indians should be reduced to villages and not be allowed to live divided and separated in the mountains and wildernesses, where they are deprived of all spiritual and temporal comforts, the aid of our ministers, and those other things which human necessities oblige men to give one to another; therefore . . . the viceroys, presidents, and governors [are] charged and ordered to execute the reduction, settlement, and indoctrination of the Indians.[4]

From the *Annals of the Cakchiquels* we also have a record of how conversion and "congregation" appeared to native eyes:

Fray Pedro de Angulo and Fray Juan de Torres . . . arrived from Mexico. The Fathers of Santo Domingo began our instruction. The Doctrine appeared in our language. . . . Up to that time we did not know the word or the commandments of God; we had lived in utter darkness. No one had preached the word of God to us.

---

[4] As rendered by Lesley B. Simpson, *Studies in the Administration of the Indians in New Spain* (Berkeley: University of California Press, 1934), 43.

In the fifth month of the sixth year after the beginning of our instruction in the word of Our Lord God, the houses were grouped together. . . . Then the people came from the caves and the ravines. On the day 7 Coak [October 30, 1547] this city [Sololá] was founded and all the tribes were here.[5]

The rhetoric of *congregación* belongs very much to what Carlos Fuentes calls the "legal country," a colonial fiction distinctly at odds with the "real country" that came into being. In the overall vision of empire, few single endeavors differed in outcome so dramatically from original intent as did *congregación*, prompting contemporary observers to express outrage, astonishment, and despair that such a grand scheme could amount to so little. *Congregación* made its mark on the landscape at an early date. In fact, *pueblos de indios* created by regular and secular clergy in the course of the sixteenth century (Table 21.10) persist today as *municipios*, or townships, that anthropologists have considered the key units in defining Maya community life. But no sooner had Spaniards resettled Indians where the former deemed suitable than numbers of the latter drifted back to the mountains they and their families had been moved from. Why did this happen? What caused the grip of *congregación* to become undone?

For one thing, *congregación* was carried out not by persuasion but by force. Entire families shifted against their will from one location to another made it unlikely that members who found the experience disagreeable, if not hateful, would stay put. Indians repeatedly fled to outlying rural areas to escape the exploitation they suffered while resident in a town or nearby. There they could be free of compulsory demands to furnish tribute, provide labor, work on local roads or the parish church, and serve as human carriers. The refuge of the mountains was also sought when disease struck, its occurrence in (and impact on) *pueblos de indios* often causing greater loss of life because of human crowding than arm's-length subsistence in the hills. Furthermore, how the Maya farmed the highlands was usually best undertaken by living not in large, agglomerated centers but in small, dispersed groups.

There is next the issue of interdenominational friction and the deployment of spiritual resources. Along with the Mercedarians, a less-dominant third party in the missionary enterprise, Dominicans and Franciscans waged what Adriaan van Oss calls a "territorial dispute" while simultaneously driven by the higher calling of *congregación*. The two largest,

---

[5] Recinos and Goetz, *Annals of the Cakchiquels*, 134–36.

Table 21.10. Pueblos de Indios *founded in the sixteenth century*
by regular and secular clergy

Type of clergy	*Pueblos* founded by 1555	*Pueblos* founded by 1600
Dominicans	47	82
Franciscans	37	108
Mercedarians	6	42
Secular Clergy	5(?)	104
TOTAL	95	336

Source: Adriaan C. van Oss, *Catholic Colonialism: A Parish History of Guatemala, 1524–1821* (Cambridge: Cambridge University Press, 1986, 43).

most powerful orders each carved out a sphere of influence relative to the colonial capital of Santiago de Guatemala, the present-day Antigua Guatemala. Dominicans moved into the far north and west, responsible for a vast, daunting expanse that stretched from Verapaz across the Chuacús and Cuchumatanes mountains to Chiapas. Franciscans opted for a more manageable central beat within a 50-kilometer radius of Lake Atitlán. The *pueblos de indios* established in the confines of their jurisdictions both orders guarded jealously against rival encroachment. Bickering between them diverted energy from the pressing concern of native conversion and became so tiresome that a royal order was issued on 22 January 1556 commanding the friars, accused of "petty ambition" and "name calling," to resolve their differences and conduct themselves in a more seemly, Christian fashion.[6]

Such behavior, in the eyes of the Crown, set a bad example and made little practical sense, for friars were few and their responsibilities many. Indeed, throughout the colonial period, less than a thousand missionaries arrived to propagate the faith among the Mayas of Guatemala. Civil authorities well recognized the uphill battle their religious associates faced daily: two Crown officers, Antonio Rodríguez de Quesada and Pedro Ramírez de Quiñones, openly acknowledged that "in these parts there is a great lack of missionaries."[7] By the mid-sixteenth century the Dominicans were so overextended that they ceded the area from Huehuetenango

[6] Adriaan C. Van Oss, *Catholic Colonialism: A Parish History of Guatemala, 1524–1821* (Cambridge: Cambridge University Press, 1986), 35–36.
[7] Archivo General de Indias (hereafter AGI), Audiencia de Guatemala (hereafter AG) 9A (Antonio Rodríguez de Quesada and Pedro Ramírez de Quiñones to the Crown, 25 May 1555).

south to the border with Soconusco to the Mercedarians, a more acceptable choice to the Dominicans than their Franciscan adversaries. For their part, as early as 1552 the Franciscans requested permission from the Crown to assume responsibility for establishing missions in Dominican territory, "because the fathers of Santo Domingo are just not up to it."[8] Dominican hegemony, however, prevailed in Chiapas. At the other end of the Maya realm, to the south and east of Santiago, none of the three orders established a significant presence, leaving the Guatemalan "Oriente" in the proselytizing hands of the less experienced secular clergy.

The divide, in terms of missionary jurisdiction, between a "secular" east and a "regular" west is an important one to recognize. Ecclesiastical divisions, however, serve only to underscore another more profound process of regionalization, one best articulated by Murdo MacLeod in his landmark work on colonial Central America.

MacLeod argues that exploitation of the Guatemalan resource base operated differentially in such a way that Spanish attention focused on the cacao-rich Pacific Coast and on the rolling, temperate lands to the south and east of the capital, where indigo could be grown, cattle grazed, and two or even three corn crops harvested each year. Spaniards viewed the highlands of the *tierra fría*, or cold land, to the north and west of Santiago – more difficult of access and with fewer entrepreneurial options – as far less attractive. Their interest in the north and west, therefore, was never as intense as in the south and east. When Spanish attitudes concerning the worth of the land were translated into thousands of individual actions, they resulted in a notably different colonial experience.

South and east of Santiago de Guatemala, where native communities were encroached upon more, cultural and biological assimilation proceeded at a brisker pace. In the Oriente, as also in neighboring El Salvador, Spaniards and Africans mixed with Indians to create a predominantly mestizo or ladino milieu. Pockets of native inhabitants in these parts, whether displaced highland Maya or autochthonous Nahua-speaking Pipil, could always be found. Cheap Indian labor, after all, was the basis of economic prosperity, which fluctuated in cycles of boom and bust as the search for a successful cash crop saw cacao and indigo give way to cochineal and sarsaparilla and, eventually, to coffee and bananas in our day. To the north and west of the capital, however, where

---

[8] AGI, AG 168 (Fray Juan de Mansilla to the Crown, 30 January 1552).

opportunities for enrichment were less and where fewer Spaniards were inclined to settle, Maya peoples withstood the onslaught of acculturation more resiliently, holding on to much of their land, retaining Maya principles of community organization, and guarding a sense of identity that was resolutely their own. Maya languages were kept alive, as were Maya ways of worshiping the gods. Daily chores and the seasonal round followed a Maya, not a Spanish, rhythm. Even time itself, the days and months that make up a year, ticked on with a Maya pulse. When, existentially, *congregación* is situated within this larger cultural panorama, Maya reaction to it takes on a vital, formative dynamic.

Condemned by geography to inhabit a backwater region in the Spanish scheme of empire, the highland Maya shaped for themselves a culture of refuge in which Hispanic traits and institutions were absorbed and mixed with native ones, often in elaborate ways that baffled, mocked, and in the end eroded imperial authority. Periodization is somewhat difficult. Certainly by the seventeenth century, patterns of hybrid mores were much in evidence, but the trend had set in much earlier. Recognition that all was far from well, that *congregación* was not unfolding according to plan, prompted the following remarks of Pedro Ramírez de Quiñones, penned in frustration on 20, May 1556:

There is great disorder among the Indians in matters that relate to their government and administration. Things are chaotic, lacking direction. Grave public sins abound. What is most of concern is that their actions go unpunished, without redress, because they are not brought to the attention of the *audiencia*. In most *pueblos de indios* people live much as they wish to, or can, and since the *audiencia* cannot arrange for visitations to be made, we, its officers, cannot vouch for one-tenth of the territory we are in charge of.[9]

Even when Indians displaced by *congregación* chose to remain within its spatial embrace, they frequently regrouped in town or close by along pre-conquest domestic lines Spaniards called *parcialidades*. These were social units of great antiquity, organized as patrilineal clans or localized kin affiliates, and usually associated with particular tracts of land. Unfamiliarity on the part of missionaries as to the discrete nature of *parcialidades* often resulted in several of them being thrown together to form, in theory, a single Indian community. Once gathered around a new center, however, *parcialidades* would preserve their aboriginal identity by contin-

---

[9] AGI, AG 94 (Pedro Ramírez de Quiñones to the Council of the Indies, 20 May 1556).

uing to operate socially and economically as separate components rather than merging to form a corporate body. Far from being the placid, homogeneous entities that colonial legislation conjures up, many *pueblos de indios* turned out to be a mosaic of *parcialidades* that touched but did not interpenetrate, that coexisted but did not always cooperate. In the Guatemalan province of Totonicapán, for instance, nine *pueblos de indios* alone comprised over thirty *parcialidades*, each of them assessed individually for tribute-paying purposes (Table 21.11) in the late seventeenth century. One of these towns, Sacapulas, even managed to arrange that land be held and farmed by *parcialidad*, as did other *pueblos de indios*. *Parcialidades* might also be correlated with specific *cofradías*, religious sodalities originally introduced for the worship of a favored saint but which, over time, came to serve as useful Christian cover for more suspect forms of worship.

If residential commitment to *congregación* resulted in a certain degree of improvisation, town abandonment led to manifest aberrations. The rot, once again, set in early. Sacapulas, for example, may not have crystallized quite as its Dominican founders first imagined, but once their convent had been established on the south bank of the Rio Negro, a well-defined community did form around it. Another matter entirely was the outlying countryside, as an eyewitness account by two dedicated friars vividly reveals.

Writing to the Crown from the convent at Sacapulas on 6, December 1555, Tomás de Cárdenas and Juan de Torres spoke their minds about the tremendous obstacles working against effective *congregación*. They mention, first, the difficulties imposed by the physical environment, stating not unreasonably that "this part of the sierra is the most rugged and broken to be found in these lands." Making their way across it, Cárdenas and Torres had stumbled upon groups "of eight, six, and even four houses or huts, tucked and hidden away in gullies where, until the arrival of one of us, no other Spaniard had reached." The friars lament that during their trek they discovered "idols in abundance, not just concealed but placed in people's houses more or less as they had them before they were baptized." Indians, they contend, populate such desolate, faraway places so that "no-one could reach there who might disturb or destroy their evil living." The people they had found living that way, the Dominicans state with some relief, "now that they are housed together will have less opportunity to practice idolatry and, ourselves, more opportunity to watch over them." Thus resettled, Indians "can more

Table 21.11. Pueblos *and* parcialidades *in Totonicapán, c. 1683*

Pueblo de indios	Parcialidades	Tributaries
Aguacatán	Aguacatán	64
	Chalchitán	91
	Comitán	4
Chajul	Box	3
	Ilom	30
	San Gaspar	64
	Uncavav	9
Chiquimula	San Marcos	24
	Santa María	120–29*
Cotzal	Chil	10
	Cul	28
	San Juan	20–29*
Cunén	Magdalena	6
	San Francisco	114
Momostenango	Santa Catalina	50
	Santa Ana	40
	Santa Isabel	38
	Santiago	224
Nebaj	Cuchil	26
	Osolotén	16
	Salquil	10–19*
	Santa María	76
Sacapulas	Acunil	48
	Bechauazar	42
	Cuatlán	84
	Magdalena	8
	Tulteca	45
Totonicapán	Pal	–
	San Gerónimo	–
	San Marcos	–
	San Francisco	320–29*

*This manuscript was badly burned in a fire in the archive earlier this century. Those figures marked with an asterisk indicate that the last numeral was so charred as to be illegible, or has completely disintegrated. In four instances, therefore, only an estimate can be made of the tribute-paying population of the *parcialidad.*

Source: Archivo General de Indias, Contaduria 815.

readily be instructed not only in matters that concern Our Holy Faith but also in proper human conduct." To those who might bemoan that *congregación* is carried out involuntarily, that it shifts families from one place to another against their will, Cárdenas and Torres declare "there is no sick person who does not find the taste of medicine unpleasant." Indians in this sense are "like children," and so "one must do not what most pleases them but what is best for them." If, at times, the tone of the friars is sober and paternalistic, so also is it poignant and valedictory. Nowhere do the two Dominicans capture more perceptively why native families might resist and resent resettlement than when they remark: "Among all these Indians there is not one who wishes to leave behind the hut passed on to him by his father, nor to abandon a pestilential ravine or desert some inaccessible crags, for that is where the bones of his forefathers rest."[10]

Solemn words, but voiced with a sense of foreboding that soon proved well-founded. Five years after Cárdenas and Torres addressed the Crown, the native leaders of Santiago Atitlán also wrote to complain that, in outlying settlements for which they were held accountable, lived "rebellious Indians who wish to remain outside our authority and who disobey our orders concerning what tribute should be paid."[11] Even near the capital city desertion was rife; the years between 1575 and 1578 witnessed "many Indians" in the environs of Santiago "move about, in hiding, from one place to another" rather than be forced to furnish their own tribute as well as pay that part deemed still to be owed by deceased relatives.[12] Around this same time, farther north in the Verapaz, it was reported that "*parcialidades* and entire families leave to live idolatrously in the mountains." Two large *pueblos de indios*, Santa Catalina and Zulbén, had been abandoned almost completely by 1579, only five years after the Bishop of Verapaz himself had supervised the process of *congregación*. At Santa María Cahabón, baptized Mayas allegedly gave up civilized life to join unconquered Lacandones and so-called Manche Chols in pre-Christian barbarism on the other side of the frontier.[13]

A century or so later, after the Bishop of Guatemala, Andrés de las Navas, had twice toured his jursidction and heard disturbing reports

---

[10] AGI, AG 168 (Tomás de Cárdenas and Juan de Torres to the Crown, 6 December 1555).
[11] AGI, AG 53 (*Principales* and *Caciques* of [Santiago] Atitlán to the Crown, 1 February 1561).
[12] AGI, AG 10 (President Pedro de Villalobos to the King, October 5, 1575 and Eugenio de Salazar to the King, 15 March 1578).
[13] AGI, AG 10 (Bishop of Verapaz to the King, 1581?).

from parish priests about fugitivism, lawlessness, idolatry, and tax evasion, he prepared a dossier that leaves little doubt about how widespread
native disobedience had become. Outside San Juan Sacatepéquez, at a
place called Pajuiú, Indians "who neither hear mass nor confess their
sins" had lived "for upwards of twenty years, dwelling there under the
pretext of growing corn." Other centrally located *pueblos de indios* –
Chimaltenango, Párramos, Patzicía, Patzún, San Andrés Itzapa, San Martín Jilotepeque, Sumpango, and Tecpán among them – also drew the
bishop's wrath. Religious backsliding was but one example of wayward-
ness that concerned him. At Comalapa, the parish priest told of "day-
keepers and witchdoctors," informing Las Navas: "After we preach to
them, warning them that they must cease their ancient superstitions, they
leave church and are heard to ask: 'Why should we abandon the ways of
our grandfathers and ancestors?'"

Such attitudes among Indians living reasonably close to Santiago were,
if anything, magnified farther away from the capital, nowhere more
blatantly than at San Mateo Ixtatán. There, in the upper reaches of the
Sierra de los Cuchumatanes, Fray Alonso de León recorded that he had
recently been informed "that some eighty families do not figure on the
tribute list," which meant not only that "His Majesty is losing revenue"
but also that "all these fugitives do not attend mass or go to confession."
The relationship between father and son, De León declared, was one in
which "nothing is passed on save for how to take care of the cornfields
and how to live all day long like savages in the hills." He feared that
proper codes of behavior would never take root, for the people of San
Mateo "are at each other's throats, all year long." What distressed Fray
Alonso most was that Indians had decided "to build a shrine, on no
authority but their own, up in the hills some distance from town, at
precisely the same spot where the sacrificial altar of pagan times used to
be." The shrine was located "on a hill top, between the remains of
ancient temples, which they call *cues,* where on any given day may be
found charcoal and incense and other signs of burnt offerings." De León
disclosed that "further transgressions against Holy Church include the
sacrifice of turkeys, taken up to the hills to be dispatched with the blood
of other animals." Each March, at a place two leagues distant from town,
wood was piled at the foot of crosses that were later set on fire. The
"indios diabólicos" of San Mateo, it was alleged, "with their nasty habits
and evil ways have contaminated the entire town in such a way that it

remains Christian in name only."[14] Fray Alonso ended up having to run for his life, chased out of San Mateo by the villainy of Indians he believed were possessed by the devil and who were plotting to kill him.

Life in the "real country," then, jarred dramatically with the blueprint legislated in the "legal country." It would be a mistake to imagine, however, that even though the highland Maya made unworthy converts, nothing could be gained from exploiting them, that Spaniards somehow were disposed to shrugging off their quest for power and enrichment that easily. Officials of both the Church and the Crown from time to time did very well at native expense, legally or otherwise.

In terms of illegality, one the most obnoxious demands placed on native communities came in the form of *repartimientos*. Under this practice, *corregidores* and *alcaldes mayores,* district governors who actually bought public office with a view to making money from it, supplied Indians with various commodities, insisting that they be purchased at prices favorable to the seller, regardless of whether or not the merchandise was desired by the recipients in the first place. A reverse strategy was to force a sale at rock-bottom prices in one area, then resell at higher prices in another. *Repartimientos* appear on the scene in the sixteenth century, and feature in the seventeenth also. They were rampant, however, in the eighteenth century, especially in Chiapas, where they were thrust upon Tzeltal and Tzotzil as well as Zoque communities with willful insistence (Table 21.12). A popular item in these dealings was cotton, which district governors distributed in raw, bulk form among native women, compelling them to spin it into thread and then to weave it into lengths of cloth, or *mantas*. The finished article yielded a tidy profit – for the *corregidor* or *alcalde mayor*, not the worker.

Just as Indians were vulnerable to exploitation by government officials, so also did they fall prey to exactions by the clergy. An order issued as early as 1561 stipulated what goods and services priests could legitimately request from their parishioners. Theoretical limits, however, were not always adhered to, and so while some selfless individuals found God's calling among the Maya, others concerned themselves more with personal gain than with native salvation. Records indicate that abuses were once again rampant in the eighteenth century, with priests and friars accused

---

[14] AGI, AG 159 (Andrés de las Navas et al.), *Testimonio de los autos hechos sobre la perdición general de los indios de estas provincias y frangentes continuous que amenazan su libertad,* 1689).

Table 21.12. *Profits earned on* repartimientos *by the* alcalde mayor *of Ciudad Real (San Cristóbal de las Casas) in Chiapas, 1760–65*

Activity	Windfall (in pesos)
Spinning 500,000 pounds of raw cotton into 100,000 pounds of thread	27,500
Forced production of 100,000 pounds of cochineal	16,000
Forced production of 150,000 pounds of cacao	10,000
Forced production of 12,000 bunches of tobacco	3,750
Miscellaneous forced sales	13,475

Source: Robert Wasserstrom, *Class and Society in Central Chiapas* (Berkeley, Los Angeles, and London: University of California Press, 1983), 47.

of various excesses, including failure to reimburse for personal services, selling livestock without the owner's consent, overzealous collection of funds to celebrate mass or to hear confession, and embezzlement of *cofradía* assets.

It was in fact – or so the Dominican chronicler Francisco Ximénez tells us – the announcement that Bishop Juan Bautista Alvarez y Toledo intended to conduct yet another *visita*, a pastoral tour of inspection, that sparked the only full-scale native uprising during the colonial period, the so-called Tzeltal Revolt of 1712–13. In Chiapas, the *visitas* of Alvarez y Toledo were legendary, for they seldom left the *cajas de comunidad*, community trust funds set up by missionaries but invested in by Indians to lessen the impact of all sorts of calamity, with much in reserve. His impending arrival, it should be noted, came barely ten years after serious disturbances elsewhere in Chiapas, as well as in neighboring parts of Guatemala, had marked the inquiry into acts of corruption perpetrated by Francisco Gómez de Lamadriz. The bishop's intended swoop must also be seen in the context of tribute demands and *repartimiento* obligations, not to mention the swirl of Maya religiosity, a heady mix in which many a turn was unpredictable. Concerning the latter, from the Tzeltal community of Cancuc hailed a figure around whom Maya protest would in vain be mounted, a young woman who took the name María de la Candelaria or María de la Cruz, whom followers believed communicated in this life with the Virgin Mary in the next. Rise up, declared the Tzeltal visionary to her wretched kin, and put an end to Spanish tyranny, for that King and his God are dead, replaced by a Maya Redeemer who will put right all Maya woes:

I, the Virgin who has descended to this Sinful World, call upon you in the name of Our Lady of the Rosary and command you to come to this town of Cancuc, bringing with you all the silver from your churches, their ornaments and bells, together with [the contents of] the *cajas* [*de comunidad*], drums, and the books of the *cofradías*, for now neither God nor King exist. For this reason you must come immediately, because if you do not you will be punished for not coming when I and God beckoned you.[15]

Following María's startling pronouncements, in which the influence of the Tzotzil prophet Sebastián Gómez de la Gloria must also be mentioned, more than twenty towns rose in rebellion, furnishing armies of 3,000 to 6,000 men. The revolt, however, failed to spread far beyond its Tzeltal–Tzotzil heartland. Maya insurgency eventually crumpled in the face of concerted Spanish response from an alarmed viceroy in Mexico City; well-equipped militia were sent to Chiapas from Tabasco and Guatemala. Rebel communities, whose ringleaders were garrotted or shot by firing squad, suffered terribly for years thereafter. The old order was restored, if anything with more brutality than before, for colonial Spaniards were not the sort of people who failed to grasp the importance of teaching a lesson. The exercise in authority was certainly not lost on the highland Maya, who afterward understood better the fine line between resistance and revolt. A century later, in Totonicapán, even when Indians confronted an ailing regime on the verge of collapse, they knew better than allow riots over the payment of tribute to trigger full-fledged rebellion.

As independence drew near, it was apparent that little had changed, or was about to, in the fundamental way that Spaniards from all walks of life treated and related to Indians. For them, as for Creoles and ladinos, Maya subordination was not an issue of polemic or debate: it was simply taken for granted, something that was regarded as a natural right, an unqueried fixture in the imperial enterprise. Coexistence under these terms fostered neither compassion nor respect. What it did breed were mutual feelings of suspicion, distrust, hatred, and fear. "The colo-

---

[15] As rendered by Francisco Ximénez, *Historia de la provincia de San Vicente de Chiapa y Guatemala de la orden de predicadores,* 3 vols. (Guatemala: Sociedad de Geografía e Historia de Guatemala, 1929–31), III, 271.

nial regime," writes the Guatemalan historian Severo Martínez Peláez, "was a regime of terror."[16] Michael Taussig concurs, and offers some trenchant remarks of his own. Terror, he asserts, is not just "a physiological state" but "a social fact and a cultural construction whose baroque dimensions allow it to serve as the mediator *par excellence* of colonial hegemony." Like many features created by Spanish conquest, the specter of terror – pervading "spaces of death" where "Indian, African, and White gave birth to the New World" – haunted Maya life to scar and disfigure succeeding centuries.[17]

REFORM AND REVOLUTION

The shared reality of being Maya links highland communities in Chiapas and Guatemala after independence, but it was inevitable that forming part (if only by historical accident) of two distinct national agendas would result eventually in varying postcolonial experiences. For much of the nineteenth century, however, the highland Maya on both sides of what at first was a very artificial border struggled against similar problems. Only in the twentieth century did it mean something different to be highland Maya in Mexico as opposed to highland Maya in Guatemala.

After Agustín de Iturbide reached an independence accord in 1821 with the last Spanish viceroy, those Creoles from Central America who had supported him chose initially to identify themselves with Mexico. This arrangement lasted only two years, for the imperially minded Iturbide proved unresponsive to Central American concerns, thus fomenting a move to secede and form the United Provinces of Central America, itself doomed to early dismemberment into the present-day republics of Guatemala, Honduras, El Salvador, Nicaragua, and Costa Rica. Chiapas stayed within the Mexican fold, the only unit of what (since 1561) had been governed as the Audiencia de Guatemala to do so.

In both Chiapas and Guatemala the battle to overthrow Spain was followed by prolonged internal conflict between Conservatives and Liberals for control of government office. Differences between the two political factions were many, but centered around a Conservative prefer-

---

[16] Severo Martínez Peláez, *La patria del criollo: Ensayo de interpretación de la realidad colonial guatemalteca* (San José: Editorial Universitaria, 1971), 518.
[17] Michael Taussig, "Culture of Terror, Space of Death: Roger Casement's Putomayo Report and the Explanation of Torture," *Comparative Studies in Society and History* 26, no. 3 (1984): 468.

ence for maintaining Hispanic-derived institutions that sought to preserve the colonial status quo, in contrast to a Liberal preference for creating an entirely new social and economic order that viewed progress as attainable by promoting capitalist ties with the outside world. In terms of the impact of ideology on highland Maya ways, conservatism represented more a continuation of the culture of refuge shaped during colonial times. Liberalism, on the other hand, signified Maya assimilation into a modern, outward-looking ladino state. Conservative practices often resulted in minimal cultural change at the community level, whereas Liberal policies promoted changes that would alter irrevocably long-established ways of living with the land. Neither side could claim undisputed hegemony until the 1860s and 1870s, when Liberal authority eventually prevailed.

In Chiapas, interparty feuding resulted in more than twenty-five transfers of government before 1850. What remained constant among the ebb and flow of politicians was the steady deterioration of native welfare, especially loss of land. Maya communities forfeited land that was declared "vacant" or "unused" to enterprising non-Indians, who announced their intention to put it to "good use," particularly more temperate tracts that were suitable for export crops. Many lowland Maya communities in Soconusco disappeared completely during the process, with highland settlements, save for land in the immediate vicinity of town centers, severely affected also.

Jan Rus writes that "of twenty-five intact Tzotzil and Tzeltal townships that existed at independence, all suffered this fate to one degree or another." His research shows that one ambitious family, the Larraínzars, took possession of three-quarters of the community land of Chamula, 476 *caballerías* (about 20,000 hectares) of a total of 636. Along with adjacent land expropriated from two other townships, the Larraínzars created Nuevo Edén, a vast estate measuring some 874 *caballerías*. Rather than physically abandon land they considered theirs, Indians stayed on as hired hands, working on tobacco and sugar plantations at lower elevations. Rus reckons that, by midcentury, more than seven hundred families found themselves in this predicament, their male heads of household furnishing three days of labor each month in order to retain a plot for subsistence. Nuevo Edén, while certainly "one of the more spectacular depredations of its kind," was nonetheless "hardly unique," for in a little over two decades "more than a quarter of Chiapas's Indians" saw themselves transformed from "free villagers into permanently and legally-obligated peons and laborers."[18] Ladino encroachment accelerated under the Reform Laws passed by Liberal president Benito Juárez, who put the laws into effect in 1863. George Collier informs us that ladinos then acquired "several formerly communal tracts" in Zinacantán, where, between 1838 and 1875, Robert Wasserstrom calculates "approximately half of the town's residents became tenants."[19] On the eve of the Mexican Revolution, after the modernization initiatives of Liberal dictator Porfiro Díaz (1876–1910), more than 10 million pesos of foreign capital had been invested in Chiapas, much of it in coffee production in Soconusco and in logging operations in the far east of the state, in the tropical rain forests along the banks of the Usumacinta River. To indentured Maya labor from the highlands fell the task of harvesting Soconusco coffee and downing prize stands of primary-growth mahogany and cedar.

Liberals in Guatemala dominated political life between 1823 and 1839, but their plans for radical reform were stalled if not reversed for three decades thereafter, when Rafael Carrera led the Conservatives to power following a popular uprising. A shrewd, astute individual who came to be known as "protector of the people," Carrera undid the work of his Liberal predecessor, Mariano Gálvez, and created a stable paternalist state founded on restored Hispanic institutions. The extent to which Indians in Guatemala actually benefited from Carrera's political agenda is unclear. Although Lee Woodward maintains that "Carrera's pro-Indian policy did indeed protect the Indians from further encroachment on their land and labour during the 1840s," he concedes that "after 1850 that protection began to lessen as Carrera became more clearly attached to the Guatemalan elite."[20] Whatever interpretation is favored, compared to what was then happening to the highland Maya in Chiapas, Carrera served their counterparts in Guatemala as a useful if temporary shield.

The Liberals regained political office in Guatemala in 1871, six years after Carrera's death, and under the stewardship of Justo Rufino Barrios

---

[18] Jan Rus, "Whose Caste War? Indians, Ladinos, and the Chiapas 'Caste War' of 1869," in Murdo J. MacLeod and Robert Wasserstrom, eds., *Spaniards and Indians in Southeastern Mesoamerica* (Lincoln and London: University of Nebraska Press, 1983), 132–33.

[19] George A. Collier, *Fields of the Tzotzil: The Ecological Bases of Tradition in Highland Chiapas* (Austin and London: University of Texas Press, 1975), 144, and Robert Wasserstrom, *Class and Society in Central Chiapas* (Berkeley, Los Angeles, and London: University of California Press, 1983), 134–35.

[20] Ralph Lee Woodward, Jr., "Changes in the Nineteenth-Century Guatemalan State and Its Indian Policies," in Carol A. Smith, ed. *Guatemalan Indians and the State, 1540–1988* (Austin: University of Texas Press, 1990), 68.

began to implement with fervor what they had been frustrated from doing four decades earlier. Attacks on Indian land and assaults on Indian labor were inevitable consequences of the Liberal vision of progress. Liberal legislation demanded that land be formally declared and, if possible, registered not by collective but by individual title. Government proclamations, however, did not always reach Maya ears, nor were they completely understood when they did. As in Chiapas, extensive tracts of land considered "unclaimed" by the Liberal administration fell into the hands of Creoles and ladinos far more conversant than Indian farmers with the details of reform legislation. Case studies of this unprecedented encroachment are still appallingly scarce. Given the political sensitivity of the issue, the magnitude of the appropriation and the impact that it wrought may never precisely be ascertained. Scholarly opinion ranges from Robert Naylor's rather vague impression of there being "little discernible change" in highland Maya life, of its continuing "much the same as before," to Carol Smith's more realistic but undocumented assertion that native communities "lost about half of the lands they traditionally claimed during the colonial period."[21] More systematic research on the topic is clearly in order.

Land acquisition was fueled by the realization that several regions of Guatemala, especially the Verapaz highlands and the Pacific piedmont, offered ideal growing conditions for the cultivation of coffee. Zones that had been relatively untouched by the cacao boom and indigo fever of colonial times, Verapaz and the Pacific *boca costa* became the focus of considerable land speculation. Investment by domestic and foreign capital resulted in coffee's emerging during the second half of the nineteenth century as Guatemala's principal export crop, a position it has maintained in the national economy from the time of Barrios until today.

When organized on a plantation or *finca* basis, as for the most part it is in Guatemala, coffee production demands intensive labor inputs only at harvest time. What suits the requirements of coffee planters best, therefore, is a seasonal workforce, one that provides labor when needed and that can be dispensed with when not. As in Chiapas, for more than a century now, migrant Mayas from the highlands have met this requirement.

---

[21] Robert A. Naylor, "Guatemala: Indian Attitudes Toward Land Tenure," *Journal of Inter-American Studies* 9, no. 4 (1967): 629, and Carol A. Smith, "Local History in Global Context: Social and Economic Transitions in Western Guatemala," *Comparative Studies in Society and History* 26, no. 2 (1984): 204.

The methods adopted to procure an adequate flow of labor have varied over the years. Outright coercion in the form of a draft known as *mandamiento,* authorized by President Barrios in November 1876, reinforced the long-standing practice of legalized debt peonage, which endured in Guatemala well into the twentieth century, when it was eventually replaced by a vagrancy law requiring individuals holding less than a stipulated amount of land to work part of each year as wage laborers for others: anyone farming ten or more *cuerdas,* but less than the three or four *manzanas* that qualified him for an exemption, was expected to work one hundred days; anyone farming less than ten *cuerdas* was expected to work one hundred and fifty days.[22] A *libreta,* or identification book, had to be carried at all times, and was best inspected with the requisite number of days fulfilled. The effects of these demands, David McCreery argues, was "to aggravate social differentiation within communities and contribute to the breakdown of corporate self-protective structures." McCreery asserts also that such demands "underwrote the profitability of the chief export, impoverished the rural population, and contributed to the preconditions for present-day violence."[23]

Two case studies furnish a wealth of local detail to support McCreery's assertion, one by Shelton Davis concerning what took place in and around Santa Eulalia, another by Robert Carmack concerning events at Momostenango. Davis reckons that, between 1880 and 1920, roughly 70 percent of Santa Eulalia's communal holdings fell into ladino hands, including highly prized tracts in the *tierra caliente* of the Ixcán region, "zones of greatest ecological and economic potential." Of fifty-five lots titled in these parts, Indians received only nine; of the 1,520 *caballerías* involved in the titling process, Indians were awarded 183.[24] Ladinos titled land, as the government wished, individually, not as a corporate body, the customary Maya way of laying claim. Titles issued to ladinos were frequently in excess of thirty *caballerías.* As ladinos carved up outlying areas in the *tierra caliente,* Indians concentrated on acquiring legal hold of the *tierra fría* in the vicinity of the town center. A classic Latin American dichotomy emerged of large, ladino-owned estates in the lowlands and a patchwork of small, Indian-tilled fields in the highlands.

---

[22] A *cuerda* is a variable unit of land, measuring either 0.11 acres or 0.27 acres. A *manzana* equals approximately 1.7 acres.

[23] David J. McCreery, "Debt Servitude in Rural Guatemala, 1876–1936," *Hispanic American Historical Review* 63, no. 4 (1983): 758–59.

[24] A *caballería* of land measures about 112 acres or 45.4 hectares.

Davis records that the first land to be lost lay near Santa Cruz Yalmux, where a group of ladinos from Huehuetenango claimed some two hundred *caballerías*. The claimants, members of the local militia, made their case on 22, May 1888, appearing in person before General Manuel Lisandro Barillas, then president of Guatemala. They laid claim on the grounds that: (1) the holdings of Santa Eulalia in *tierra fría* "were large and sufficient" for the Indians who lived there; (2) the petitioners would deploy the lands to which they sought title "for the development of capitalistic agriculture"; (3) during "the rise to power of Justo Rufino Barrios," Huehuetenango played a "military role" that the government was obliged to recognize; and (4) issuing title to land would allow for the creation of a new *municipio*, which would function "as a military outpost for the protection of the frontier between Mexico and Guatemala" along the Rio Usumacinta. Despite protests that the claimants "only wished to gain title to this land so as later to resell it to Indian residents," the Barillas government awarded two hundred *caballerías* of Yalmux land to the ladinos of Huehuetenango in July 1888. On October 17 of that same year the *municipio* of Barillas came into being. The choice of place name directly linked government action with the erosion of the Maya estate.[25]

Indians at Momostenango, Carmack records, "lost their best agricultural lands under Liberal rule, forty-six *caballerías* of rich, flat lands in Buenabaj, and several hundred *caballerías* of piedmont lands in El Palmar and Samalá." Although the amount of land lost in absolute terms was smaller than at Santa Eulalia, the seizure of native property was such that, with population doubling in size during the nineteenth century, the average family holding fell to less than half a hectare, meaning that "land shortage reached crisis proportions." Carmack considers the Liberal reforms to have been "disastrous" and "objectionable" to the extent that, in 1876, they spawned "full-scale guerrilla warfare," which the Barrios regime brutally suppressed. Adopting strategies resorted to by the Guatemalan armed forces a century later, Barrios ordered his militia "to burn houses and crops in all rebel zones of Momostenango" and to resettle forcibly in town "many families suspected of aiding the rebels."

Government troops soon emerged victorious, capturing and imprisoning rebel soldiers, many of whom were executed. Carmack concludes

[25] Shelton H. Davis, *La tierra de nuestros antepasados* (Antigua Guatemala: Centro de Investigaciones Regionales de Mesoamérica, and South Woodstock, VT: Plumsock Mesoamerican Studies 1997), 40–44.

that "the final fifty years of Liberal rule in Momostenango were a time of intense political and economic repression for the Indians," with local ladinos building "close personal links with national dictators." Ladinos took advantage of these ties "to establish an authoritarian system of government within the community." Some 1,000 to 2,000 Momostecos, Carmack reckons, were channeled to the coffee-growing piedmont each year, as well as being pressed into public service within the township itself. In this fashion, Indians contributed more than 336,000 days per year (16 percent of the total available) in coerced labor. They were overseen in their efforts by ladinos who ruled by means of "an elaborate mix of terror and paternalism." In another strategy resorted to by later oppressors, Indian males, in order to prove their allegiance to "a virtual fascist state," were forced to participate "in almost constant militia and active duty service," which meant that community "security" took precedence over personal or family affairs.[26]

We also have at hand some descriptive material that provides a glimpse of other human costs involved in modernizing Guatemala. Consider, for example, the observations made at Nebaj in 1913 by the Irish-Canadian archaeologist Robert Burkitt, who recorded throughout Ixil country "an unceasing coming and going of labour contractors and plantation agents getting out gangs of Indians for the Pacific Coast." Burkitt pulled no punches and spoke frankly about what he saw:

Years ago when I first visited Nebaj, it was a different place from now. I had struck the place at an especially bad moment. The plantation agents were at the height of their activity, scattering money, advance pay for work, and every Indian was able to buy rum. The rum business and the coffee business work together in this country, automatically. The plantation advances money to the Indian and the rum seller takes it away from him and the Indian has to go to work again. Work leads to rum and rum leads to work. I used to think that Chichicastenango was the drunkenest town in the country, but now I think it is Nebaj. My plans at Nebaj were upset by rum. There are two ruin places that I know of that are to be got at from Nebaj and I did nothing at either of them, and one of them I never even saw. The Indians I was going to take were never sober.[27]

Burkitt's plans for archaeological exploration had to be abandoned because native guides and helpers were, as he worded it, "drunk from

---

[26] Robert M. Carmack, "Spanish-Indian Relations in Highland Guatemala, 1800–1944," in Mac-Leod and Wasserstrom, *Spaniards and Indians in Southeastern Mesoamerica*, 242–44.

[27] Robert Burkitt, "Explorations in the Highlands of Western Guatemala," *The Museum Journal of the University of Pennsylvania* 21, no. 1 (1930): 58.

morning till night." However, while we acknowledge Burkitt's frustrations, let us not overlook what all this might have meant for the people he was living among. The "advance pay for work" that Burkitt refers to was the *habilitación*, a loan impoverished Indians must have found hard to turn down, especially if proffered with a bottle of *aguardiente* in July or August, when corn prices are usually high and a family meal difficult to come by. Not only was the age-old culture of refuge gradually broken down: for some, a short-term contract with a plantation signaled the beginning of a process that led, in the end, to their staying on as resident workers or *colonos*. Alain Dessaint reckons that, between 1894 and 1930, the Nebaj area Burkitt was surveying sent 6,000 Indian laborers to work each year on piedmont *fincas*, not all of whom made it back home to Ixil country.[28]

Maud Oakes, engaged in anthropological fieldwork at Todos Santos, recorded an incident during her stay there that highlights the migrant labor problem quite dramatically. Oakes writes:

One morning early in January, 1946, Petrona, the wife of my neighbour Domingo, came to see me. Her eyes were swollen from crying. In very incoherent Spanish she told me that Domingo had signed a contract for himself and his son, Andrés, with Señor López, who owned the *tienda* [store] in the village, to work on a coffee *finca* beyond Quezaltenango. She went on to say that she expected her baby in a month and a half, and how could she look after three children get wood, and plant corn if neither Domingo nor Andrés was there to help her?

Domingo then entered the house and told me the whole story. The year before, he and Andrés were both sick for two months, so sick that they nearly died. In consequence, he was not able to plant his corn. When he was better he could not work for he still had no strength. He had only a little corn. He therefore signed a contract with Señor López for money. He was to receive sixteen dollars and for this he and Andrés, aged fourteen, would both have to work sixty-four days picking coffee on the *finca*. They would have to walk there and back, which would take four to five days each way. At the *finca* they would be given huts, too poor to keep out the mosquitoes, and unground corn, nothing else. If they got sick they would get no medical care; and all this for less than one dollar a week apiece.[29]

Since the time of Burkitt and Oakes, important changes have occurred in the way that plantation labor is recruited in Guatemala. The necessity

[28] Alain Dessaint, "Effects of the Hacienda and Plantation Systems on Guatemala's Indians," *América Indígena* 22 (1964): 340–41.
[29] Maud Oakes, *The Two Crosses of Todos Santos: Survivals of Mayan Religious Ritual* (Princeton, NJ: Princeton University Press, 1951), 241.

of coercing labor, however, has diminished over the years, as explosive population growth in Guatemala, and the need to earn more money to feed more mouths, usually ensure a plentiful workforce. This has especially been the case among Indian *minifundistas*, peasant smallholders an estimated 90 percent of whom live with their families on plots of land too tiny to provide year-round employment and subsistence. If enforcement in the guise of labor drafts or vagrancy laws has vanished, the structural inequality and ethnic manipulation that propel seasonal migration have not. In Guatemala, 2 percent of the total number of farms occupy 65 percent of total farm area, while 90 percent of the total number of farms account for 16 percent of total farm area. The best land continues to be used to grow coffee, along with cotton, bananas, and sugarcane, for export, not to feed malnourished local populations, 70 percent of whom live in a state of poverty U.N. statisticians describe as "extreme."

The only serious attempt to confront, if not redress, these and other socioeconomic injustices occurred during a "revolutionary" ten-year period (1944–54) from which, as a modern nation, Guatemala has yet to recover. How foreign interests and domestic opposition joined forces to obstruct and then overthrow the democratically elected government of Jacobo Arbenz Guzmán is sufficiently well known to warrant no reiteration here. If one accepts the reasoning of Robert Wasserstrom over that of Jim Handy and Piero Gleijeses, then Arbenz "sought mitigation, not metamorphosis," and the reforms he implemented in essence constituted "a modest program, not a daring one." As Wasserstrom sees it, Arbenz operated under the misapprehension that "Guatemala's internal difficulties stemmed chiefly from the ignorance and isolation of its Indian population." What Arbenz and his supporters failed to understand was that "commercial agriculture in Guatemala represented a special form of capitalism which had itself promoted the spread of subsistence farming and *minifundia* land tenure." Enacted in the belief that "old antagonisms between Indians and Ladinos would disappear as in time Indian serfs were integrated into national life," the Arbenz platform challenged and was defeated by a more powerful and insidious variant of capitalism that had long since adapted itself to the ethnic and geographical peculiarities of Guatemala. What Arbenz never understood, Wasserstrom argues, was that capitalism had evolved symbiotically in Guatemala to create a situation wherein highland Maya communities and piedmont *fincas* existed in varying degrees of interdependence, one to another. In this specific setting, capitalist logic dictated that "if the former endure, the latter are ensured the labor they need."[30] It was not the first mutation of capitalist modes of production that the highland Maya were subjected to, nor would it be the last.

Whatever benefits accrued to Indians under Arbenz, they were decidedly short-lived. In the wake of the Mexican Revolution, the highland Maya in Chiapas may be said to have fared a little better, for despite the persistence of glaring inequalities and serious loopholes in landholding legislation, native communities there at least had some of their grievances addressed, if by no means resolved.

The first fifteen years or so after civil war had abated saw the coffee economy of Chiapas continue to grow, albeit sporadically, with Indian labor (as in Guatemala) one of the cornerstones of prosperity. Reform came first in relation to employment conditions, specifically the establishment in the late 1930s of the Oficina de Contrataciones and the Sindicato de Trabajadores Indígenas. These agencies, respectively, required Indians who worked on plantations to negotiate a contract and to join a union, thus in theory affording them government guarantees that (1) they would receive the legal minimum wage and (2) they would be treated in accordance with labor codes advocated by the Cárdenas administration in Mexico City. Much of the credit in organizing Indian labor belongs to Erasto Urbina, a popular figure who modeled himself after his presidential mentor. Urbina's success on the labor front gave him the confidence, after Cárdenas appointed him director of the Department of Indian Protection, to organize land restitution, which involved returning to native communities as *ejidos* many of the holdings they had been deprived of during the nineteenth century.

While Urbina's record is impressive, Wasserstrom again champions caution, for estate owners "were generally permitted to retain their buildings and other capital improvements as well as their choicest lands and irrigated parcels." Wasserstrom estimates that "of the 62,000 families which had benefited from agrarian reform, fully one-third possessed insufficient resources to sustain themselves." His appraisal of land reform at Zinacantán, furthermore, indicates that "nearly half of those families eligible to receive allotments" were excluded from the process, with most estate owners retaining "both their best fields and their control over local

---

[30] Robert Wasserstrom, "Revolution in Guatemala: Peasants and Politics under the Arbenz Government," *Comparative Studies in Society and History* 17, no. 4 (1975): 478.

water supplies." Consequently, "60 percent of the town's final grant consisted of forests and hillsides, while only 40 percent contained seasonably arable farmlands."[31] Shortcomings such as these, together with the near total absence of government initiatives in remote and deprived eastern areas of Chiapas, tempered considerably the impact of reform. The fact remains, however, as Collier succinctly puts it, that legislation governing land and landholding, in the central highlands at any rate, "transformed Indian communities from a patchwork of small Indian hamlets interspersed between ladino properties into an area of consolidated and continuous Indian control."[32] No reparation akin to this has ever been dreamed of by any government in Guatemala.

MARGINALIZATION AND NEGLECT

The second half of the twentieth century marks the bifurcation of highland Maya destiny into two more clearly defined trajectories, even though decades of marginalization and neglect ensure that poverty prevails as the common native lot in both Chiapas and Guatemala. Politically, Chiapas is perhaps the more complex of the two cases to come to terms with. While Indians there have had to contend with all sorts of discrimination, as the stories of Rosario Castellanos and B. Traven undeniably attest, even as wary an observer as Wasserstrom admits that, by 1950, "agrarian reform and similar measures had profoundly altered the entire fabric of social relations in central Chiapas."[33] What, then, in subsequent decades put such tremendous strain on the social fabric and eventually caused it to be torn asunder, resulting in the Zapatista uprising of 1, January 1994?

As with Guatemala, mention can first be made of the accelerated rate of population increase from 1950 on. Viewed in a long, retrospective sweep, the population history of both Chiapas and Guatemala (see Tables 21.1–21.6) may be interpreted as one in which, following demographic collapse in the wake of conquest, it took more than four centuries for native peoples to regain their numbers at contact, only for a doubling in size to occur over the space of a generation. Such unprecedented recent growth would tax the political resolve and place a material burden on the resources of most countries, but in two such fundamentally divided

---

[31] Wasserstrom, *Class and Society*, 167, 171.   [32] Collier, *Fields of the Tzotzil*, 150.
[33] Wasserstrom, *Class and Society*, 214, 251.

nations as Mexico and Guatemala, where the gap between a few rich and many poor assumes an ethnic as well as a class dimension, the implications for social stability have been profound.

For decades, the Mexican government maintained peace in the countryside by adhering to the rhetoric, if not always the reality, of land reform, enshrined in Article 27 of the Mexican constitution. By extending at least the promise of land reform to impoverished rural communities, as well as providing access to credit and subsidizing basic provisions such as corn and milk, the Partido Revolucionario Institucional (PRI) could count on widespread peasant support, election after election. Chiapas has been a loyal PRI supporter, voting 89.9 percent in favor of the PRI candidate, Carlos Salinas de Gortari, in the 1988 presidential elections. Salinas's predecessor, Miguel de la Madrid (1982–88), had earlier presided over an austerity program designed by the international banking community to reduce Mexico's staggering foreign debt, which the country had accumulated during a short-lived but disastrous oil boom between 1972 and 1982. Salinas was prepared to squeeze PRI's peasant base even more, in order to satisfy external pressures demanding a "structural adjustment" of the Mexican economy and to usher the country into a new era marked by Mexico's partnership with the United States and Canada in the North American Free Trade Agreement (NAFTA). Coupled with a vision of modernization similar to that of Liberal dictator Porfirio Díaz a century ago, in which land, labor, and natural resources would be opened up to investment from abroad in an effort to stimulate economic development, the politics of NAFTA spelled increased hardship for poor people in regions like Chiapas, especially in eastern frontier parts of the state, where living conditions are particularly difficult.

Matters lurched toward breaking point in 1992, when the Salinas government, in a dramatic reversal of the PRI's raison d'être, redrafted Article 27 of the Mexican constitution, thereby ending a commitment to land reform that, in effect, had defined the state's relationship to its peasant constituency for half a century. "In Chiapas," insist George Collier and Elizabeth Lowery Quaratiello, "where many land claims have yet to be resolved after languishing in the state bureaucracy for years, the repeal of land reform legislation robbed many peasants not just of the possibility of gaining a piece of land, but, quite simply, of hope." The Zapatista uprising, which Collier and Quaratiello believe to be "primarily a peasant rebellion, not an exclusively Indian rebellion," is perhaps best understood as a popular protest against government violation of a long-standing social contract.[34] Although it began in Chiapas, most certainly involves Maya Indians, and addresses an array of native rights and issues, the Zapatista challenge transcends local and regional borders and reverberates with symbolic significance throughout Mexico, forcing an ongoing reappraisal of national politics, economics, ideology, and identity.

In Guatemala, the Cold War politics that had much to do with the demise of the Arbenz government in 1954 have been as entrenched and all-pervasive as PRI posturing in Mexico. Six years after the overthrow of Arbenz, junior officers in the national armed forces staged an abortive coup against the government of General Ydígoras Fuentes, the aftermath of which signaled the beginning of a brutal civil war that raged, off and on, for thirty-six years. Fighting in the 1960s took place mostly in the Oriente, that part of Guatemala where ladinos outnumber Indian inhabitants, but when guerrilla insurgents shifted the focus of their activities farther west and north in the 1970s, the stage was set for a bloody confrontation in highland Maya country.

The front presented by a series of military governments to the outside world was that their troops were engaged in a counterinsurgency war to rid Guatemala of "communist subversion." Between 1978 and 1983, violence claimed the lives of tens of thousands of Maya Indians, most of whom in all likelihood never knew who Karl Marx was, let alone understood or agreed with the ideals he upheld. Military governments headed by three generals, Romeo Lucas García, Efraín Ríos Montt, and Oscar Mejía Víctores, bear most responsibility for the atrocities. Guerrilla insurgents, however, are by no means blameless. Especially in Huehuetenango and El Quiché, Indians suffered dreadfully when the Army of the Poor retreated in the face of sustained government offensives, leaving behind unarmed villagers to bear horrific reprisal for having provided food, shelter, or moral support for the rebels. Caught in the crossfire, hundreds of Maya communities paid dearly for their proximity to insurrection, whether direct or indirect, real or perceived. The carnage visited upon the residents of Finca San Francisco, a remote settlement in the department of Huehuetenango near the border with Chiapas, is no more barbarous than scores of other such incidents. One eyewitness, whose

---

[34] George A. Collier and Elizabeth Lowery Quaratiello, *Basta! Land and the Zapatista Rebellion in Chiapas* (Oakland, CA: Institute for Food and Development Policy, 1994), 7 and 45.

testimony has been corroborated by fellow survivors, furnishes the following account of events at Finca San Francisco on 17, July 1982:

The soldiers took our wives out of the church in groups of ten or twenty. Then twelve or thirteen soldiers went into our houses to rape our wives. After they were finished raping them, they shot our wives and burned the houses down. . . . All of our children had been left locked up in the church. They were crying, our poor children were screaming. They were calling us. Some of the bigger ones were aware that their mothers were being killed and were shouting and calling out to us. . . . They took the children outside. The soldiers killed them with knife stabs. We could see them. They killed them in a house in front of the church. They yanked them by the hair and stabbed them in their bellies; then they disembowelled our poor little children. Still they cried. When they finished disembowelling them, they threw them into the house, and then brought out more. Then they started with the old people. "What fault is it of ours?," the old people asked. "Outside!" a soldier said. They took the poor old people out and stabbed them as if they were animals. It made the soldiers laugh. Poor old people, they were crying and suffering. They killed them with dull machetes. They took them outside and put them on top of a board; then they started to hack at them with a rusty machete. It was pitiful how they broke the poor old people's necks. . . . They began to take out the adults, the grown men of working age. They took us out by groups of ten. Soldiers were standing there waiting to throw the prisoners down in the patio of the courthouse. Then they shot them. When they finished shooting, they piled them up and other soldiers came and carried the bodies into the church.[35]

Any popular rural base enjoyed by guerrilla insurgents in the early 1980s was eroded, bit by bit, not only by vile deeds such as those recorded for Finca San Francisco but also by aerial bombardment, the destruction of personal property and belongings, the burning of crops and supplies, the killing of livestock, and the regrouping of suspect native communities into "model villages" and "development poles" watched over by government troops and army-organized civil defense patrols. The magnitude of any future repair, in highland Maya country most of all, will be immense.

In 1986, a civilian government presided over by Vinicio Cerezo Arévalo took office in Guatemala. Cerezo was succeeded, five years later, by another civilian president, Jorge Serrano Elías. Serrano abolished constitutional guarantees on 25 May 1993 in an attempt to rule by decree, a

---

[35] Cultural Survival and Anthropology Resource Center Research Report, *Voices of the Survivors: The Massacre at Finca San Francisco, Guatemala* (Peterborough, NH: Transcript Printing, 1983), 36–37.

measure that met with popular resistance and ultimately led to his removal. A former human rights ombudsman, Ramiro de León Carpio,
assumed the presidency on 6 June 1993. He, in turn, handed over office
in January 1996 to Alvaro Arzú, whose government signed a "firm and
lasting" peace accord with guerrilla insurgents on 29 December 1996.

Land reform, however, does not figure in the terms of the peace accord
nor does it appear to be a priority issue on Arzú's presidential agenda. It
is difficult to imagine how a peace that is supposed to be "firm and
lasting" can be attained without a fundamental reappraisal of the way
land in Guatemala is owned and operated. Guatemala is not a poor
country. It is rich in resources, natural and human. Guatemala has been
made a poor country because access to its resources, especially its land
resources, is characterized by crippling structures of inequality. Until the
land question is confronted, and the dignity of Maya peoples with it, the
root cause of civil unrest goes unaddressed.

Meanwhile, as did their forefathers centuries ago, the highland Mayas
continue to adapt and survive, responding to adversity or a lack of
opportunity in ways that force us, again and again, to reappraise our
conventional, at times erroneous, representations of them in the literature. No longer, for instance, can we consider the mountain retreats of
Chiapas and Guatemala to be their exclusive or predominant spatial
domain, for the highland Maya now live and work far from their places
of origin in Mesoamerica. They are especially numerous across the southern United States, in California, Texas, and Florida, three of the many
states to which Mayas from Guatemala fled during the violent years of
the early 1980s. Concentrations of Guatemala Mayas, however, may also
be found much farther north, in the cities of Chicago, Boston, and
Providence, Rhode Island, even in parts of Canada. Static portrayals of
the highland Maya as rural, village-bound "men of corn," to use the
term of the Guatemalan writer Miguel Angel Asturias, must be reconciled
with myriad ongoing improvisations, for survival hinges, as ever, on
doing whatever it takes to make ends meet, including living and working
in an unfamiliar North American urban setting thousands of miles from
home.

While the highland Maya diaspora began as a response to violence
and repression in Guatemala, political refugees have since been joined by
a flood of people seeking economic and social improvement. As many as
a million Guatemalans are presently believed to reside, some legally, most
not, in the United States and Canada, a significant number of them

Mayas. An estimated $500 million are sent or taken back to Guatemala each year in the form of family remittances, the impact of which, at the level of individual communities, can be considerable. For example, the Guatemalan newspaper *Prensa Libre* on 13 November 1996 reported that, in 1995, the Q'anjob'al community of Santa Eulalia alone received $3 million in family remittances, dispatched by the more than 6,000 Mayas from Santa Eulalia who live and work in the United States, most of them in California. Coming to grips with migration networks in a transnational realm that encompasses the United States and Canada, as well as Mexico and Guatemala, is today as much a reality of highland Maya life as confronting the demands of *encomienda* and *mandamiento* in bygone eras. No matter the challenge, the highland Maya are culturally equipped to endure.

BIBLIOGRAPHICAL ESSAY

In terms of English-language historiography, the highland Maya make their first appearance in the seventeenth century through the eyes of Thomas Gage, whose experiences in Chiapas and Guatemala make fascinating reading. Gage's portrayal of Maya life under Spanish rule, like the cleric himself, is not without its blemishes and idiosyncrasies, but his firsthand observations of conquest in action are striking, if not entirely trustworthy. A. P. Newton's *The English-American: A New Survey of the West Indies, 1648* (London, 1928) tampers with Gage's original text far less than does J. Eric S. Thompson's *Thomas Gage's Travels in the New World* (Norman, OK, 1958). Two centuries after Gage was on the scene, the American traveler John Lloyd Stephens opened up the Maya world as never before, pioneering a literary genre with his *Incidents of Travel in Central America, Chiapas, and Yucatan* [1841] (New York, 1949). Good travel writing is as venerable a forum as any to begin studying the Maya. Our age, unfortunately, has tended to promote quantity rather than quality, but Ronald Wright's *Time Among the Maya* (London, 1989) is a notable exception. The Maya tracts of the same author's *Stolen Continents: The Americas Through Indian Eyes Since 1492* (Boston, 1992) also engage the reader provocatively, telling the centuries-old story of invasion, resistance, and rebirth by resorting, as much as possible, to native testimony and points of view. Walter F. Morris's *Living Maya* (New York, 1987), the text of which is illuminated by the haunting photographs of Jeffrey J. Foxx, is a useful general introduction to Indian life in

Chiapas, as is Victor Perera's *Unfinished Conquest* (Berkeley, CA, 1993) for Guatemala.

More specialized scholarly contributions are perhaps best assessed by consulting the *Handbook of Middle American Indians*, 16 vols. (Austin, TX, 1964–76), especially vol. 6 (1967), vol. 7 (1969), vol. 12 (1972), and vol. 13 (1973). Many of the *Handbook* entries are now a bit dated, but lots can be learned from searching out a classic essay that has helped shape the way we think. Such is the case with Oliver La Farge's "Maya Ethnology: The Sequence of Cultures," in *The Maya and their Neighbor*, ed. C. L. Hill et al. (New York, 1940), 281–91, a pioneering exploration of processes of historical change. The Columbus Quincentenary unleashed a flood of print reassessing the impact of European intrusion on Native American ways. Two ambitious works of synthesis in which several contributions deal with issues of Maya survival are the six-volume *Historia General de Centroamérica* (San José, 1994), a project coordinated by Edelberto Torres-Rivas, and the six-volume *Historia General de Guatemala* (Guatemala City, 1993–99), a project coordinated by Jorge Luján Muñoz.

Studies that situate the highland Maya in the Spanish scheme of empire tend to be overshadowed by the literature available on central Mexico and the Yucatán, as a number of scholars observe in a roundtable discussion published in *Mesoamérica* 14 (1987). Murdo J. MacLeod's *Spanish Central America: A Socioeconomic History, 1520–1720* (Berkeley, CA, 1973) has served as the landmark work for the past quarter-century and will likely serve a similar purpose for years to come. With Robert Wasserstrom, MacLeod edited a valuable collection of essays, *Spaniards and Indians in Southeastern Mesoamerica* (Lincoln, NE, 1983), in which the central theme of ethnic relations is developed beyond the colonial period into the nineteenth and twentieth centuries, for both Chiapas and Guatemala. For readers of English, Wasserstrom furnishes an impressive survey of the former region, *Class and Society in Central Chiapas* (Berkeley, CA, 1983), as does Jan de Vos, *Vivir en frontera: La experiencia de los indios de Chiapas* (Mexico, 1994), for readers of Spanish. Neither title has a direct counterpart in the literature on Guatemala. Their closest equivalent might be Severo Martínez Peláez's *La patria del criollo: Ensayo de interpretación de la realidad colonial guatemalteca* (San José, 1971), but this Marxist extravaganza concentrates on the colonial period, whereas Wasserstrom and De Vos surge on into modern times.

Other publications that focus attention on colonial Chiapas include

Peter Gerhard's elegant historical geography, *The Southeast Frontier of New Spain* (Princeton, NJ, 1979; Norman, OK, 1993), and the doctoral dissertation of Janine Gasco, *Cacao and the Economic Integration of Native Society in Colonial Soconusco, New Spain* (Santa Barbara, CA, 1987). An essay by Rodney C. Watson, "Informal Settlement and Fugitive Migration amongst the Indians of Late-Colonial Chiapas," in *Migration in Colonial Spanish America*, ed. David J. Robinson, (Cambridge, 1990), 238–70, is most informative, as is the magnum opus of Antonio García Leon, *Resistencia y utopia: Memorial de agravias y crónica de revueltas y profecías acaecidas en la Provincia de Chiapas*, 2 vols. (Mexico City, 1985). Sidney David Markman's *Architecture and Urbanization in Colonial Chiapas, Mexico* (Philadelphia, 1984) offers considerably more than its title suggests, for it also addresses such issues as control of labor, native population decline, and the incidence of epidemic disease. Markman's macro approach contrasts with the more microlevel sensitivities of Mario Humberto Ruz, best represented by *Copanaguastla en un espejo: Un pueblo tzeltal en el Virreinato* (San Cristóbal de las Casas, 1985) and *Savia india, floración ladina: Apuntes para una historia de las fincas comitecas, siglos XVIII y XIX* (Mexico City, 1992). A volume edited by Ruz, *Los hombres legítimos* (Mexico City, 1981) focuses attention on the still little-known Tojolabal Maya. Both macro-and microlevels of analysis are deployed by Kevin Gosner in his ornately crafted *Soldiers of the Virgin* (Tucson, AZ, 1992), which interprets the Tzeltal Revolt of 1712 in terms of the "moral economy" thesis perhaps best associated with the work of E. P. Thompson and James C. Scott in non-Mesoamerican parts of the world. Another insightful analysis of the Tzeltal Revolt is Juan Pedro Viqueira, *Indios rebeldes e idólatras: Dos ensayos históricos sobre la rebelión india de Concuc, Chiapas, acaecido en el año de 1712* (Mexico City, 1997). The colonial experience of the Lacandón Maya of eastern Chiapas is given intense scrutiny by Jan de Vos in *La paz de Dios y del Rey: La conquista de la Selva Lacandona por los españoles* (Mexico City, 1980). A superb piece of archival sleuthing by Gudrun Lenkersdorf, *Génesis histórica de Chiapas, 1522–1532: El conflicto entre Portocarrero y Mazariegos* (Mexico City, 1993), reconfigures the formative circumstances of the early conquest period, in the light of which certain subsequent events in the history of Chiapas are more plausibly explained.

Compared to Chiapas, work on the colonial period in Guatemala is more advanced, with some important contributions stressing aspects of Indian resistance as much as the undeniable reality of the Spanish Conquest. The best introduction to the literature is Robert M. Carmack's *Quichean Civilization: The Ethnohistoric, Ethnographic, and Archaeological Sources* (Berkeley, CA, 1973), a meticulous appraisal of the strengths and weaknesses of all sorts of recorded information. Carmack evaluates celebrated Maya texts like the *Popol Vuh* and *The Annals of the Cakchiquels*, as well as scores of lesser-known but invaluable native testimony. A recent addition to this absorbing literature is Karen Dakin and Christopher H. Lutz, *Nuestro pesar, nuestra aflicción: Memorias en lengua náhuatl enviadas a Felipe II por indígenas del Valle de Guatemala hacia 1572* (Mexico City, 1996). Working mostly with difficult Spanish documents, William L. Sherman's *Forced Native Labor in Sixteenth-Century Central America* (Lincoln, NE, 1979) fills a large gap in our knowledge of how Spaniards controlled and exploited the native population. The role played by the church in forging an Indian "west" and a ladino "east" in Guatemala is explored by Adriaan C. Van Oss in *Catholic Colonialism: A Parish History of Guatemala, 1524–1821* (Cambridge, 1986), which in fact is far less a "parish history" than a history of parish formation. Lawrence Feldman's *A Tumpline Economy* (Culver City CA, 1985) analyzes systems of production and patterns of distribution in the much-neglected Oriente. A similar concern with economic geography pervades Jorge Luján Muñoz's *Agricultura, mercado y sociedad en el Corregimento del Valle de Guatemala, 1670–80* (Guatemala City, 1988). Luján Muñoz focuses on the capital city and environs of Santiago de Guatemala, also the spatial centrepiece of Christopher H. Lutz's sociodemographic history *Santiago de Guatemala, 1541–1773: City, Caste, and the Colonial Experience* (Norman, OK, 1994). Ralph H. Vigil, in *Alonso de Zorita: Royal Judge and Christian Humanist, 1512–1585* (Norman, OK, 1987), charts the life and times of a Crown official who, like President Alonso López de Cerrato, at least tried to impose government authority by enforcing laws aimed at improving Indian welfare around the middle of the sixteenth century. The turbulent first years of conquest and colonization are adroitly handled by Wendy Kramer, whose *Encomienda Politics in Early Colonial Guatemala, 1524–1544: Dividing the Spoils* (Boulder, CO, 1994), much like the work of Lenkersdorf on Chiapas, breaks new scholarly ground.

Due, in large measure, to the efforts of Robert M. Carmack, we tend to have a better understanding of Quichean cultural experiences than those of other highland Maya groups. Two of Carmack's best works are *The Quiché Mayas of Utatlán: The Evolution of a Highland Guatemalan Kingdom* (Norman, OK, 1981) and *Rebels of Highland Guatemala: The*

Quiché-Mayas of Momostenango (Norman, OK, 1995). Increasingly, however, Maya neighbors of the K'iche' are attracting attention. The Kaqchikel, for example, are the subject of Barbara E. Borg's doctoral dissertation, *Ethnohistory of the Sacatepéquez Cakchiquel Maya, ca. 1450–1690 AD* (Columbia, MO, 1986), and inspired Robert M. Hill II to synthesize years of work in *Colonial Cakchiquels: Highland Maya Adaptations to Spanish Rule, 1600–1700* (Forth Worth, TX, 1991). Likewise, with Sandra L. Orellana's *The Tzutujil Mayas: Continuity and Change, 1250–1630* (Norman, OK, 1984), our awareness of that people's experience is improved considerably. For non-Maya peoples whose proximity to Guatemala exposed them to similar historical processes, especially in neighboring El Salvador, William R. Fowler's *The Cultural Evolution of Ancient Nahua Civilizations: The Pipil–Nicarao of Central America* (Norman, OK, 1989) is a key contribution. Also important for comparative purposes are two works by Linda A. Newson, *The Cost of Conquest: Indian Survival in Honduras Under Spanish Rule* (Boulder, CO, 1986) and *Indian Survival in Colonial Nicaragua* (Norman, OK, 1987).

Discontent erupting into localized rebellion is explored by María del Carmen León Cázares in *Un levantamiento en nombre del Rey Nuestro Señor* (Mexico City, 1988) and by Severo Martínez Peláez in *Motines de indios: La violencia colonial en Centroamérica y Chiapas* (Puebla, 1985). Native resistance in one form or another permeates the doctoral dissertation of Juan Pedro Viqueira, *Cronotopología de una región rebelde* (Paris, 1998), which focuses on Indian life in Chiapas in the seventeenth and eighteenth centuries. Issues of cultural continuity and change surface throughout Elías Zamora Acosta's *Los mayas de las tierras altas en el siglo XVI: Tradición y cambio en Guatemala* (Seville, 1985). Zamora's regional perspective – his area of study is the Province of Suchitepéquez and Zapotitlán – is mirrored by Michel Bertrand's *Terre et societé coloniale* (Mexico City, 1987), which deals with Rabinal and the Baja Verapaz, and by W. George Lovell's *Conquest and Survival in Colonial Guatemala* (Kingston and Montreal, 1985, 1992), which is a historical geography of the Sierra de los Cuchumatanes. Lovell is particularly interested in the dynamics of *congregación*, which he confronts in terms of Carlos Fuentes's vision of the "real country" and the "legal country" in "Mayans, Missionaries, Evidence, and Truth: The Polemics of Native Resettlement in Sixteenth-Century Guatemala," *Journal of Historical Geography* 16, no. 3 (1990): 277–94, and in "Spanish Ideals and Mayan Realities in Colonial Guatemala," *Geo Journal* 26, no. 2 (1992): 181–85. With Christopher H.

Lutz, Lovell has also sustained an interest in Maya population history, summarized in "Conquest and Population: Maya Demography in Historical Perspective," *Latin American Research Review* 29, no. 2 (1994): 133–40, and examined at length in *Demography and Empire: A Guide to the Population History of Spanish Central America, 1500–1821* (Boulder, CO, 1995). The link between native population decline and outbreaks of sickness is explored by Lovell in "Disease and Depopulation in Early Colonial Guatemala," in *"Secret Judgments of God": Old World Disease in Colonial Spanish America*, ed. Noble David Cook and W. George Lovell (Norman, OK, 1992), 49–83. The disease factor remains the least understood in terms of nuanced, sophisticated appreciation of the variables that shaped the native colonial experience throughout Spanish America.

Ironically, we often know more about the events and circumstances of life in Central America under Spanish rule than we do about postcolonial times, as Ralph Lee Woodward, Jr., observes in "The Historiography of Modern Central America since 1960," *Hispanic American Historical Review* 67, no. 3 (1987): 461–96. Woodward himself has devoted a lifetime's work to redressing the imbalance, culminating in his painstaking study of *Rafael Carrera and the Emergence of the Republic of Guatemala, 1821–1871* (Athens, GA, 1993). One of Woodward's former students, David J. McCreery, has invested years coming to terms with the nineteenth and early twentieth centuries, from which commitment *Rural Guatemala, 1760–1940* (Stanford, CA, 1994) adds considerably to our knowledge of land, labor, and native experiences. W. George Lovell reviews the work of Woodward and McCreery, and other relevant contributions, in "The Century After Independence: Land and Life in Guatemala, 1821–1920," *Canadian Journal of Latin American and Caribbean Studies* 19, no. 37–38 (1996): 243–60. Woodward and McCreery are two of the ten contributors to Carol A. Smith's edited volume, *Guatemalan Indians and the State, 1540–1988* (Austin, TX, 1990), which examines power relationships between the rulers and the ruled from the time of the Spanish conquest on. The same theme, played out in the nineteenth and early twentieth centuries, receives insightful treatment by Robert M. Carmack in "Spanish-Indian Relations in Highland Guatemala, 1800–1944," in *Spaniards and Indians in Southeastern Mesoamerica*, ed. MacLeod and Wasserstrom, eds. (Lincoln, NE, 1983), 215–52. The current balance of scholarship, once again, is tilted in favor of Guatemala, but noteworthy contributions concerning Chiapas include Thomas Benjamin, *A Rich Land, A Poor People: Politics and Society in Modern Chiapas* (Albuquerque, 1989);

George A. Collier, *Fields of the Tzotzil: The Ecological Bases of Tradition in Highland Chiapas* (Austin, TX, 1975); Jan Rus, "Whose Caste War? Indians, Ladinos, and the Chiapas 'Caste War' of 1869," in *Spaniards and Indians in Southeastern Mesoamerica*, ed. MacLeod and Wasserstrom, 127–68; and Jan de Vos, *Oro verde: La conquista de la Selva Lacandona por los madereros tabasqueños* (Mexico City, 1988).

If Chiapas lags behind Guatemala somewhat in terms of scholarly output, the same cannot be said of the region's rich literary tradition, perhaps best articulated to the outside world by the enigmatic B. Traven. While Traven's six "Jungle Novels" (*Government; The Carreta; March to the Montería; Trozas; The Rebellion of the Hanged*; and *General from the Jungle*) are for the most part cast in a social realist vein, his short stories (some of those in *The Night Visitor*, for example) often resonate with more spiritual or mystical concerns. The same is also true of two novels by Rosario Castellanos, available in English translation as *The Nine Guardians* (London, 1959) and *The Book of Lamentations* (New York, 1996). Guatemala's preeminent writer is the Nobel prize-winning Miguel Angel Asturias, many of whose best works are inspired by Maya folklore and mythology.

The so-called Guatemalan Revolution of 1944–54, especially what it represented for Indian communities, is open to several interpretations. In terms of Maya gains, Robert Wasserstrom, in "Revolution in Guatemala: Peasants and Politics under the Arbenz Government," *Comparative Studies in Society and History* 17, no. 4 (1975): 443–78, believes it amounted to very little. The opposite view is argued by Jim Handy in *Revolution in the Countryside: Rural Conflict and Agrarian Reform in Guatemala, 1944–1954* (Chapel Hill, NC, 1994). In explaining the downfall of Arbenz, Handy stresses an array of internal factors as much if not more than the part played by external agents. The foul play of the CIA has been discussed by a number of writers, among them Richard Immerman, *The CIA in Guatemala: The Foreign Policy of Intervention* (Austin, TX, 1982) and Piero Gleijeses, *Shattered Hope: The United States and the Guatemalan Revolution, 1944–1954* (Princeton, NJ, 1991). Questions of land and land ownership that were central to the reforms called for by Arbenz, questions that remain to this day the bedrock of any meaningful political agenda, are addressed in the two-volume study edited by J. C. Cambranes, *500 años de lucha por la tierra: Estudios sobre propiedad rural y reforma agraria en Guatemala*, 2 vols. (Guatemala City, 1992).

Modern anthropological research on the highland Maya has produced several distinguished contributions, often set in the specific context of one particular *municipio* or township. The best "community studies" show an awareness of the importance of history, even if far too many float ungrounded in an ethereal, ethnographic present not in any way connected to a concrete, ethnographic past; for a critique of the latter tendency, see W. George Lovell and William R. Swezey, "Indian Migration and Community Formation: An Analysis of *Congregación* in Colonial Guatemala," in *Migration in Colonial Spanish America*, ed. David J. Robinson (Cambridge, 1990), 18–40. Four edited collections, spanning the half-century between 1940 and 1990, allow an appraisal to be made of how the "state-of-the-art" has evolved. These are (1) Clarence L. Hay, Ralph L. Linton, Samuel K. Lothrop, Harry L. Shapiro, and George C. Vaillant, eds., *The Maya and Their Neighbors* (New York, 1940); (2) Sol Tax, ed., *Heritage of Conquest: The Ethnology of Middle America* (New York, 1952); (3) Carl Kendall, John Hawkins, and Laurel Bossen, eds., *Heritage of Conquest: Thirty Years Later* (Albuquerque, NM, 1983); and (4) Victoria R. Bricker and Gary H. Gossen, eds., *Ethnographic Encounters in Southern Mesoamerica: Essays in Honor of Evon Z. Vogt, Jr.* (Albany, NY, 1989). Among the classics, Maud Oakes, *The Two Crosses of Todos Santos* (Princeton, NJ, 1951) and Oliver La Farge and Douglas Byers', *The Year Bearer's People* (New Orleans, 1931), live on as literary as well as anthropological narratives. Historically informed ethnographies have more recently been constructed by Shelton H. Davis, *La tierra de nuestros antepasados* (Antigua Guatemala, and South Woodstock, VT, 1997), which deals with the Q'anjob'al of Santa Eulalia, and by John M. Watanabe, *Maya Saints and Souls in a Changing World* (Austin, TX, 1992), which focuses on the Mam of Santiago Chimaltenango. Two other valuable contributions are Victoria R. Bricker, *The Indian Christ, the Indian King: The Historical Substrate of Maya Myth and Ritual* (Austin, TX, 1981), and Robert M. Hill II and John Monaghan, *Continuities in Highland Maya Social Organization: Ethnohistory in Sacapulas, Guatemala* (Philadelphia, 1987).

In Guatemala, studies of contemporary Maya culture inevitably have to deal with the violence unleashed on their communities especially between 1978 and 1983. The horror of these tragic years has already been confronted in several titles, among them Victor Montejo, *Testimony: Death of a Guatemalan Village* (Willimantic, CT, 1987); Robert M. Carmack, ed., *Harvest of Violence: The Maya Indians and the Guatemalan Crisis* (Norman, OK, 1988); Beatriz Manz, *Refugees of a Hidden War: The*

Aftermath of Counterinsurgency in Guatemala (Albany, NY, 1988); David Stoll, *Between Two Armies in the Ixil Towns of Guatemala* (New York, 1993); Ricardo Falla, *Massacres in the Jungle: Ixcán, Guatemala, 1975–1982* (Boulder, CO, 1994); W. George Lovell, *A Beauty That Hurts: Life and Death in Guatemala* (Toronto, 1995); Yvon Le Bot, *La guerra en tierras mayas: Comunidad, Violencia y modernidad, 1970–1992* (Mexico City, 1995). Angela Delli Sante, *Nightmare or Reality: Guatemala in the 1980s* (Amsterdam, 1996); Robert S. Carlsen, *The War for the Heart and Soul of a Highland Maya Town* (Austin, TX, 1997); César Castañeda, *Lucha por la tierra, retornados y medio ambiente en Huehuetenango* (Guatemala City, 1998); Jennifer Schirmer, *The Guatemalan Military Project: A Violence Called Democracy* (Philadelphia, 1998); and Clark Taylor, *Return of Guatemala's Refugees: Reweaving the Torn* (Philadelphia, 1998). Nowhere are the events and circumstances of the war years more monumentally rendered than in the four-volume *Guatemala: Nunca Más* (Guatemala City, 1998), a human rights milestone that cost the man who orchestrated its painful but necessary compilation, Bishop Juan José Gerardi, his life. Gerardi's mission was to have a team of researchers recover historical memory, which it has done in a way that allows not only survivors but also their persecutors an opportunity to be heard. The war wounds of Guatemala will take a long time to heal.

Very importantly, Maya Indians have begun to speak for themselves. One voice that has reached millions is that of Rigoberta Menchú, whose collaboration with Elizabeth Burgos-Debray resulted in the publication of *I, Rigoberta Menchú: An Indian Woman in Guatemala* (London, 1984) some of the details of Menchú's testimony have been disputed by David Stoll in *Rigoberto Menchú and the Story of All Poor Guatemalans* (Boulder, Co, 1998). The Nobel laureate's *Crossing Borders* (London, 1998) charts the later stages of her eventful life. Menchú may be considered one of the forerunners of a genuine Maya renaissance in Guatemala, a cultural awakening in which Indians address their reality as painters, poets, novelists, teachers, and university professors as well as engaged political activists; for a predominantly non-Maya discussion of the phenomenon, see Carol A. Smith, "Maya Nationalism," *NACLA Report on the Americas: The First Nations, 1492–1992*, 25, no. 3 (1991): 29–33; Kay B. Warren "Language and the Politics of Self-Expression: Mayan Revitalization in Guatemala," *Cultural Survival Quarterly* 18, nos. 2 and 3 (1994): 81–86; Richard Wilson, *Maya Resurgence in Guatemala: Q'eqchi Experiences* (Norman, OK, 1995); and Edward F. Fisher and R. McKenna Brown, eds., *Maya Cultural Activism in Guatemala* (Austin, TX, 1996). Maya views of the "Maya Movement" are also available, including Demetrio Cojtí Cuxil, *Configuración del pensamiento político del pueblo maya* (Quetzaltenango, 1991), and Víctor Gálvez Borrell, ed., *Que sociedad queremos? Una mirada desde el movimiento y las organizaciones mayas* (Guatemala City, 1997). With thirty-six years of war now at an end, Mayas in Guatemala are taking advantage of political opportunities as never before. Mayas outside Guatemala also have their part to play, as revealed by Norita Vlach in *The Quetzal in Flight: Guatemalan Refugee Families in United States* (Westport, CT, 1992); Allen Burns in *Maya in Exile: Guatemalans in Florida* (Philadelphia, 1993); Jacqueline Hagan in *Deciding to Be Legal: A Maya Community in Houston* (Philadelphia, 1994); and Susanne Jonas in "Transnational Realities and Anti-Immigrant State Policies: Issues Raised by the Experiences of Central American Immigrants and Refugees in a Trinational Region," *Estudios Internacionales* 6, no. 11 (1995): 17–29.

In Chiapas, the fallout of the Zapatista uprising on 1 January, 1994 continues to shake Mexico. Several contributions provide helpful orientation, including George Collier and Elizabeth Lowery Quaratiello, *Basta! Land and the Zapatista Rebellion in Chiapas* (Oakland, CA, 1994); John Ross, *Rebellion from the Roots: Indian Uprising in Chiapas* (Monroe, ME, 1995); Frank Bardacke and John Ross, eds., *Shadows of Tender Fury: The Letters and Communiqués of Subcomandante Marcos and the Zapatista Army of National Liberation* (New York, 1995); Yvon Le Bot and Maurice Najman, *El sueño Zapatista* (Mexico City, 1997); and Carlos Montemayor, *Chiapas: La rebelión indígena de México* (Mexico City, 1997). Two edited collections that concentrate on historical background are Juan Pedro Viqueira and Mario Humberto Ruz, eds., *Chiapas: Los rumbos de otra historia* (Mexico City, 1995), and Kevin Gosner and Arij Ouweneel, eds., *Indigenous Revolts in Chiapas and the Andean Highlands* (Amsterdam, 1996). Among a plethora of recent titles, Neil Harvey's *The Chiapas Rebellion: The Struggle for Land and Democracy* (Durham, NC, 1998) and John Womack's *The Zapatista Revolt in Chiapas* (New York, 1999) may prove to be definitive studies of the historic insurrection.

INDEX